Microsoft® PUBLISHER 2013

INTRODUCTORY

Joy L. Starks

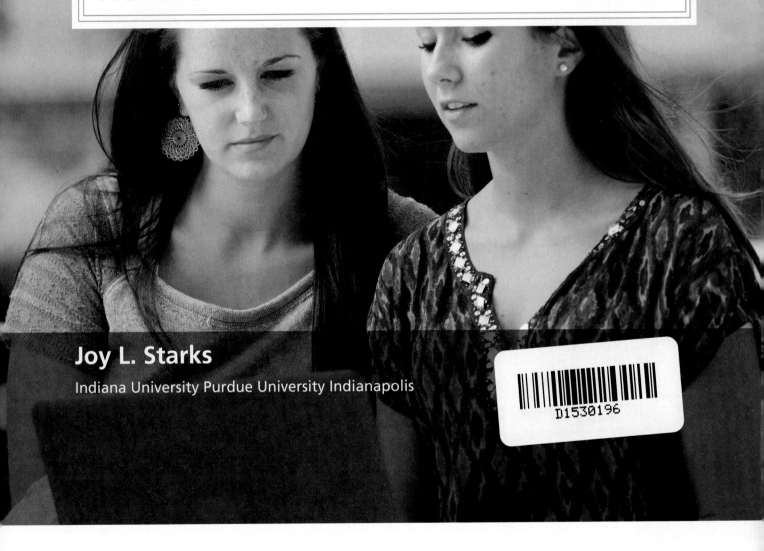

Indiana University Purdue University Indianapolis

D1530196

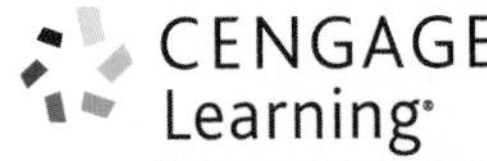

Australia • Brazil • Japan • Korea • Mexico • Singapore • Spain • United Kingdom • United States

Microsoft® Publisher 2013: Introductory
Joy L. Starks

Executive Editor: Kathleen McMahon

Product Manager: Caitlin Womersley

Associate Product Manager: Crystal Parenteau

Editorial Assistant: Sarah Ryan

Print Buyer: Julio Esperas

Director of Production: Patty Stephan

Content Project Manager: Divya Divakaran, PreMediaGlobal

Development Editor: Ashlee Welz Smith

Senior Brand Manager: Elinor Gregory

Market Development Manager: Kristie Clark

Market Development Manager: Gretchen Swann

Marketing Coordinator: Amy McGregor

QA Manuscript Reviewers: Jeffrey Schwartz, John Freitas, Serge Palladino, Susan Pedicini, Danielle Shaw, Susan Whalen

Art Director: GEX Publishing Services, Inc.

Text Design: Joel Sadagursky

Cover Design: Lisa Kuhn, Curio Press, LLC

Cover Photo: Tom Kates Photography

Product Management, Indexer, Proofreader, Photo Researcher, and Composition: PreMediaGlobal

© 2014 Cengage Learning

ALL RIGHTS RESERVED. No part of this work covered by the copyright herein may be reproduced, transmitted, stored or used in any form or by any means graphic, electronic, or mechanical, including but not limited to photocopying, recording, scanning, digitizing, taping, Web distribution, information networks, or information storage and retrieval systems, except as permitted under Section 107 or 108 of the 1976 United States Copyright Act, without the prior written permission of the publisher.

For product information and technology assistance, contact us at
Cengage Learning Customer & Sales Support, 1-800-354-9706

For permission to use material from this text or product,
submit all requests online at **cengage.com/permissions**
Further permissions questions can be emailed to
permissionrequest@cengage.com

Microsoft and the Office logo are either registered trademarks or trademarks of Microsoft Corporation in the United States and/or other countries. Cengage Learning is an independent entity from the Microsoft Corporation, and not affiliated with Microsoft in any manner.

Library of Congress Control Number: 2013937520

ISBN-13: 978-1-285-16729-9
ISBN-10: 1-285-16729-5

Cengage Learning
20 Channel Center Street
Boston, MA 02210
USA

Cengage Learning is a leading provider of customized learning solutions with office locations around the globe, including Singapore, the United Kingdom, Australia, Mexico, Brazil, and Japan. Locate your local office at: **international.cengage.com/region**

Cengage Learning products are represented in Canada by Nelson Education, Ltd.

To learn more about Cengage Learning, visit **www.cengage.com**

Purchase any of our products at your local college bookstore or at our preferred online store at **www.cengagebrain.com**

Printed in the United States of America
1 2 3 4 5 6 7 17 16 15 14 13

Microsoft® PUBLISHER 2013

INTRODUCTORY

Contents

Microsoft Office 365

Office 365 Essentials

Microsoft Publisher 2013

CHAPTER ONE

Creating a Flyer

CHAPTER TWO
Publishing a Trifold Brochure

CHAPTER THREE
Designing a Newsletter

Preface

The Shelly Cashman Series® offers the finest textbooks in computer education. We are proud that, since Microsoft® Office 4.3, our series of Microsoft® Office textbooks has been the most widely used in education. With each new edition of our Office books, we make significant improvements based on the software and comments made by instructors and students. For this Microsoft® Publisher 2013 text, the Shelly Cashman Series development team carefully reviewed our pedagogy and analyzed its effectiveness in teaching today's Office student. Students today read less but need to retain more. They need not only to be able to perform skills, but also to retain those skills and know how to apply them to different settings. Today's students need to be continually engaged and challenged to retain what they're learning.

With this Microsoft® Publisher 2013 text, we continue our commitment to focusing on the users and how they learn best.

Objectives of This Textbook

Microsoft® Publisher 2013: Introductory is intended for a first course on Publisher 2013. No experience with a computer is assumed, and no mathematics beyond the high school freshman level is required. The objectives of this book are:

- To offer an introduction to Microsoft® Publisher 2013
- To expose students to practical examples of the computer as a useful tool
- To acquaint students with the proper procedures to create publications suitable for coursework, professional purposes, and personal use
- To help students discover the underlying functionality of Publisher 2013 so they can become more productive
- To develop an exercise-oriented approach that allows learning by doing

The Shelly Cashman Approach

A Proven Pedagogy with an Emphasis on Project Planning

Each chapter presents a practical problem to be solved within a project planning framework. The project orientation is strengthened by the use of the Roadmap, which provides a visual framework for the project. Step-by-step instructions with supporting screens guide students through the steps. Instructional steps are supported by the Q&A, Experimental Step, and BTW features.

A Visually Engaging Book That Maintains Student Interest

The step-by-step tasks, with supporting figures, provide a rich visual experience for the student. Callouts on the screens that present both explanatory and navigational information provide students with information they need when they need to know it.

Supporting Reference Materials (Quick Reference)

With the Quick Reference, students can quickly look up information about a single task, such as keyboard shortcuts, and find page references to where in the book the task is illustrated.

Integration of the World Wide Web

The World Wide Web is integrated into the Publisher 2013 learning experience with (1) BTW annotations; (2) BTW, Q&A, and Quick Reference Summary webpages; and (3) the Learn Online resources for each chapter.

End-of-Chapter Student Activities

Extensive end-of-chapter activities provide a variety of reinforcement opportunities for students to apply and expand their skills through individual and group work. To complete some of these assignments, you will be required to use the Data Files for Students. Visit www.cengage.com/ct/studentdownload for detailed access instructions, or contact your instructor for information about accessing the required files.

New to this Edition

Enhanced Coverage of Critical Thinking Skills

A New Consider This element poses thought-provoking questions throughout each chapter, providing an increased emphasis on critical thinking and problem-solving skills. Also, every task in the project now includes a reason *why* the students are performing the task and *why* the task is necessary.

Enhanced Retention and Transference

A new Roadmap element provides a visual framework for each project, showing students where they are in the process of creating each project, and reinforcing the context of smaller tasks by showing how they fit into the larger project.

Integration of Office with Cloud and Web Technologies

A new Lab focuses entirely on integrating cloud and web technologies with Publisher 2013, using technologies like blogs, social networks, and SkyDrive.

More Personalization

Each chapter project includes an optional instruction for the student to personalize his or her solution, if required by an instructor, making each student's solution unique.

More Collaboration

A new Research and Collaboration project has been added to the Consider This: Your Turn assignment at the end of each chapter.

Instructor Resources

The Instructor Resources include both teaching and testing aids, and are available for download by logging in at login.cengage.com. The Instructor Resources include:

INSTRUCTOR'S MANUAL Includes lecture notes summarizing the chapter sections, figures, and boxed elements found in every chapter; teacher tips; classroom activities; lab activities; and quick quizzes in Microsoft® Word files.

SYLLABUS Easily customizable sample syllabi, which cover policies, assignments, exams, and other course information.

FIGURE FILES Illustrations for every figure in the textbook in electronic form.

POWERPOINT PRESENTATIONS A multimedia lecture presentation system that provides slides for each chapter. Presentations are based on chapter objectives.

SOLUTIONS TO EXERCISES Includes solutions for all end-of-chapter and chapter reinforcement exercises.

TEST BANK Test banks include 112 questions for every chapter, featuring objective-based and critical thinking question types, including page number references and figure references, when appropriate.

DATA FILES FOR STUDENTS Include all the files that are required by students to complete the exercises.

ADDITIONAL ACTIVITIES FOR STUDENTS Consist of Chapter Reinforcement Exercises, which are true/false, multiple-choice, and short answer questions that help students gain confidence in the material learned.

Learn Online

CengageBrain.com is the premier destination for purchasing or renting Cengage Learning textbooks, eBooks, eChapters, and study tools at a significant discount (eBooks up to 50% off Print). In addition, CengageBrain.com provides direct access to all digital products, including eBooks, eChapters, and digital solutions, such as CourseMate and SAM, regardless of where purchased. The following are some examples of what is available for this product on www.cengagebrain.com.

Student Companion Site The Student Companion Site reinforces chapter terms and concepts using true/false questions, multiple-choice questions, short answer questions, flash cards, practice tests, and learning games, all available for no additional cost at www.cengagebrain.com.

SAM: Skills Assessment Manager Get your students workplace-ready with SAM, the market-leading proficiency-based assessment and training solution for Microsoft® Office! SAM's active, hands-on environment helps students master Microsoft® Office skills and computer concepts that are essential to academic and career success, delivering the most comprehensive online learning solution for your course! Through skill-based assessments, interactive trainings, business-centric projects, and comprehensive remediation, SAM engages students in mastering the latest Microsoft® Office programs on their own, giving instructors more time to focus on teaching. Computer concepts labs supplement instruction of important technology-related topics and issues through engaging simulations and interactive, auto-graded assessments. With enhancements including streamlined course setup, more robust grading and reporting features, and the integration of fully interactive MindTap Readers containing Cengage Learning's premier textbook content, SAM provides the best teaching and learning solution for your course.

MindLinks MindLinks is a new Cengage Learning Service designed to provide the best possible user experience and facilitate the highest levels of learning retention and outcomes, enabled through a deep integration of Cengage Learning's digital suite into an instructor's Learning Management System (LMS). MindLinks works on any LMS that supports the IMS Basic LTI open standard. Advanced features, including gradebook exchange, are the result of active, enhanced LTI collaborations with industry-leading LMS partners to drive the evolving technology standards forward.

CourseNotes

course|notes™
quick reference guide

Cengage Learning's CourseNotes are six-panel quick reference cards that reinforce the most important and widely used features of a software application in a visual and user-friendly format. CourseNotes serve as a great reference tool during and after the course. CourseNotes are available for software applications, such as Microsoft® Office 2013. There are also topic-based CourseNotes available for Best Practices in Social Networking, Hot Topics in Technology, and Web 2.0. Visit www.cengagebrain.com to learn more!

About Our Covers

The Shelly Cashman Series is continually updating our approach and content to reflect the way today's students learn and experience new technology. This focus on student success is reflected on our covers, which feature real students from The University of Rhode Island using the Shelly Cashman Series in their courses, and reflect the varied ages and backgrounds of the students learning with our books. When you use the Shelly Cashman Series, you can be assured that you are learning computer skills using the most effective courseware available.

Textbook Walk-Through

The Shelly Cashman Series Pedagogy: Project-Based — Step-by-Step — Variety of Assessments

Roadmaps provide a visual framework for each project, showing the students where they are in the process of creating each project.

Step-by-step instructions provide a context beyond the point-and-click. Each step provides information on why students are performing each task and what will occur as a result.

PUB 4 **Publisher Chapter 1** Creating a Flyer

Roadmap

In this chapter, you will learn how to create the flyer shown in Figure 1–1 on the previous page. The following roadmap identifies general activities you will perform as you progress through this chapter:

1. CUSTOMIZE the TEMPLATE options such as choice, color scheme, and font scheme.
2. NAVIGATE the interface and SELECT objects.
3. REPLACE placeholder TEXT.
4. DELETE OBJECTS you do not plan to use in the publication, if any.
5. FORMAT the TEXT in the flyer.
6. INSERT GRAPHICS in placeholders and in other locations, as necessary.
7. FORMAT PICTURES by adding borders and styles.
8. ENHANCE the PAGE by repositioning and aligning objects.
9. PRINT and EXIT the publication.
10. OPEN and REVISE the publication.

At the beginning of step instructions throughout the chapter, you will see an abbreviated form of this roadmap. The abbreviated roadmap uses colors to indicate chapter progress: gray means the chapter is beyond that activity, blue means the task being shown is covered in that activity, and black means that activity is yet to be covered. For example, the following abbreviated roadmap indicates the chapter would be showing a task in the Format Text activity.

1 CUSTOMIZE TEMPLATES | 2 NAVIGATE & SELECT | 3 REPLACE TEXT | 4 DELETE OBJECTS | 5 FORMAT TEXT
6 INSERT GRAPHICS | 7 FORMAT PICTURE | 8 ENHANCE PAGE | 9 PRINT & EXIT | 10 OPEN & REVISE

Use the abbreviated roadmap as a progress guide while you read or step through the instructions in this chapter.

...blisher

...e using a computer to step through the project in this chapter and you ...ns to match the figures in this book, you should change your screen's ...366 × 768. For information about how to change a computer's resolution, ...fice and Windows chapter at the beginning of this book.

...owing steps, which assume Windows 8 is running, use the Start screen ...ox to run Publisher based on a typical installation. You may need to ask ... how to run Publisher on your computer. For a detailed example of the ...marized below, refer to the Office and Windows chapter.

...Start screen and search for a Publisher 2013 tile. If your Start screen contains ...r 2013 tile, tap or click it to run Publisher and then proceed to Step 5. If ...creen does not contain the Publisher 2013 tile, proceed to the next step to ...the Publisher app.

...rom the right edge of the screen or point to the upper-right corner of the ...display the Charms bar and then tap or click the Search charm on the Charms ...lay the Search menu.

...**blisher** as the search text in the Search box and watch the search results ...the Apps list.

...k Publisher 2013 in the search results to run Publisher.

...lisher window is not maximized, tap or click the Maximize button on its title ...ximize the window (Figure 1–2).

PUB 6 **Publisher Chapter 1** Creating a Flyer

To Select a Template

1 CUSTOMIZE TEMPLATES | 2 NAVIGATE & SELECT | 3 REPLACE TEXT | 4 DELETE OBJECTS | 5 FORMAT TEXT
6 INSERT GRAPHICS | 7 FORMAT PICTURE | 8 ENHANCE PAGE | 9 PRINT & EXIT | 10 OPEN & REVISE

Templates are displayed as **thumbnails,** or small images of the template, in the template gallery. The thumbnails are organized by publication type (for example, Flyers); within publication type, they are organized by purpose or category (for example, Marketing) and then alphabetically by design type. Publisher groups additional templates into folders. The following steps select an event flyer template. ***Why?** An event flyer template contains many of the objects needed to create the desired concert flyer.*

1

- In the Publisher start screen, tap or click BUILT-IN to display the built-in templates.
- Scroll down to display the desired publication type (in this case, Flyers) (Figure 1–3).

Q&A Why does my list look different?
It may be that someone has downloaded additional folders of templates on your system. Or, the resolution on your screen may be different. Thus, the size and number of displayed folders may vary.

Figure 1–3

2

- Tap or click the Flyers thumbnail to display the Flyer templates and folders of additional templates (Figure 1–4).

Q&A Can I go back and choose a different category of templates?
Yes, you can tap or click the Back button in the upper-left corner of the template gallery, or you can tap or click Home or Flyers in the breadcrumb trail to move back to those previous locations.

Experiment

- Scroll through the available templates and tap or click various flyers in the list. Watch the preview change in the template information pane.

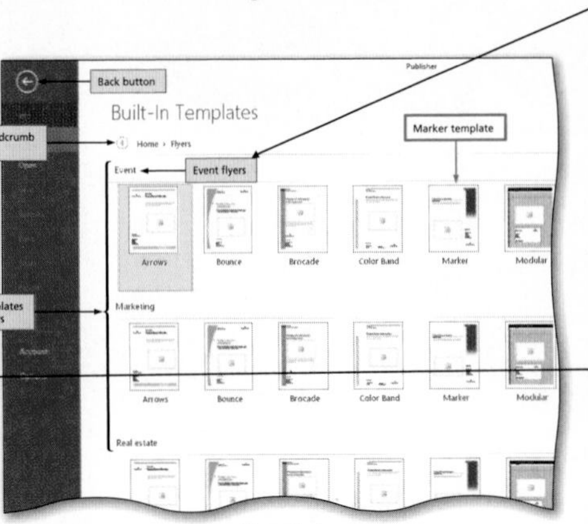

Figure 1–4

Navigational callouts in red show students where to click.

Explanatory callouts summarize what is happening on screen.

Experiment Steps within the step-by-step instructions encourage students to explore, experiment, and take advantage of the features of the Office 2013 user interface. These steps are not necessary to complete the projects, but are designed to increase confidence with the software and build problem-solving skills.

Q&A boxes anticipate questions students may have when working through the steps and provide additional information about what they are doing right where they need it.

Publisher Chapter 1

3

- Tap or click the Marker thumbnail in the Event category (Figure 1–5).

Q&A Could I use a different template? You could, but it does not have the same features as the template used in this chapter.

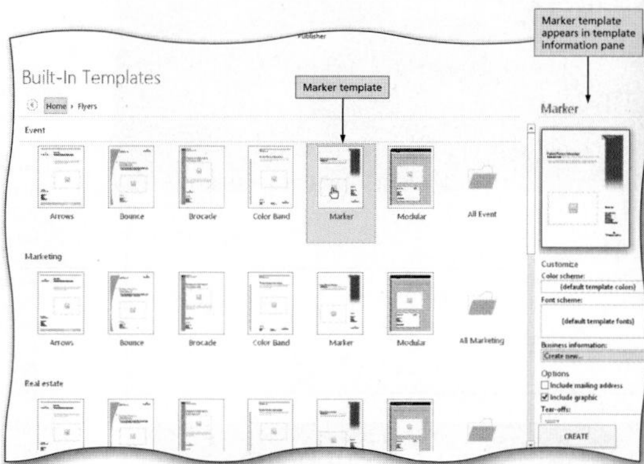

Figure 1–5

CONSIDER THIS

Does it make any difference which color scheme and font scheme you use?
Yes. The choice of an appropriate template, font, and color scheme is determined by the flyer's purpose and intended audience. For example, in this concert flyer about a blues band, the Navy color scheme helps connect the audience with the name of the band. The Flow font scheme uses a Calibri rounded font for the heading. Calibri is a sans serif font, meaning it has no flourishes on individual letters, and is suitable for print publications.

Customizing Templates

Once you choose a template, you should make choices about the color scheme, font scheme, and other components of the publication. A **color scheme** is a defined set of colors that complement each other when used in the same publication. Each Publisher color scheme provides four complementary colors. A **font scheme** is a defined set of fonts associated with a publication. A **font**, or typeface, defines the appearance and shape of the letters, numbers, and special characters. A font scheme contains one font for headings and another font for body text and captions. Font schemes make it easy to change all the fonts in a publication to give it a new look. Other customization options allow you to choose to include business information, a mailing address, a graphic, or tear-offs.

BTW
Font Schemes
Choose a font scheme that gives your flyer a consistent, professional appearance and characterizes your subject. Make intentional decisions about the font style and type. Avoid common reading fonts such as Arial, Times New Roman, and Helvetica that are used in other kinds of print publications. Flyers are more effective with stronger or unusual font schemes.

Consider This boxes pose thought-provoking questions with answers throughout each chapter, promoting critical thought along with immediate feedback.

Chapter Summary

In this chapter, you learned to choose a publication template, se publication, delete objects in a publication, insert a picture with a print publication as a web publication. The items listed below learned in this chapter, with the tasks grouped by activity.

Enter and Format Text
Autofit Text (PUB 28)
Bold Text (PUB 27)
Change Text Direction (PUB 32)
Check Spelling as You Type (PUB 21)
Enter Tear-Off Text (PUB 23)
Increase the Font Size (PUB 31)
Italicize Text (PUB 28)
Replace Other Text (PUB 19)
Replace Placeholder Text (PUB 17)
Underline Text (PUB 31)

Graphics
Apply a Picture Style (PUB 36)
Change the Border Color (PUB 38)
Insert a Picture from a Storage Device (PUB 39)
Set the Weight of a Border (PUB 37)
Use the Picture Placeholder (PUB 34)

Prepare a Web Publication
Change Document Properties (PUB 43)
Change the Background (PUB 50)
Insert a Hyperlink (PUB 48)

Pr

Sa

Print
Pri

Select
Ali
Co

De
Deselect an Object (PUB 18)
Hide the Page Navigation Pane (PUB 13)
Move an Object (PUB 41)
Resize an Object (PUB 42)
Select an Object (PUB 14)
View Whole Page (PUB 15)
Zoom (PUB 15)

Templates
Choose Publication Options (PUB 8)
Select a Template (PUB 6)

CONSIDER THIS

What decisions will you need to make when creating your next publication?
Use these guidelines as you complete the assignments in this chapter and create your own publications outside of this class.

1. Select template options.
   a) Select a template that matches your need.
   b) Choose font and color schemes determined by the flyer's purpose and audience.
2. Choose words for the text.
   a) Replace all placeholder and default text.
   b) Add other text boxes as necessary; delete unused items.
3. Identify how to format various objects in the flyer.
   a) Use bold, underline, and italics for emphasis.
   b) Autofit the text to make the flyer easy to read.
4. Find the appropriate graphic(s).
5. Determine whether the flyer will be more effective as a print publication, web publication, or both.
   a) Insert any necessary hyperlinks.
   b) Consider creating a background for web publication.

Consider This: Plan Ahead box presents a single master planning guide that students can use as they create documents on their own.

Textbook Walk-Through

Chapter Summary A listing of the tasks completed within the chapter, grouped into major task categories in an outline format.

Publisher Chapter 1

Chapter Summary

In this chapter, you learned to choose a publication template, set font and color schemes, enter text in a publication, delete objects in a publication, insert a picture with a style and border, print a publication, and save a print publication as a web publication. The items listed below include all the new Publisher skills you have learned in this chapter, with the tasks grouped by activity.

CONSIDER THIS

What decisions will you need to make when creating your next publication?

...apter and create your own publications outside of this class.

...flyer's purpose and audience.

...ems.

...int publication, web publication, or both.

...n.

Apply Your Knowledge This exercise usually requires students to open and manipulate a file that parallels the activities learned in the chapter.

STUDENT ASSIGNMENTS

CONSIDER THIS

How should you submit solutions to questions in the assignments identified with a ✻ symbol?

Every assignment in this book contains one or more questions identified with a ✻ symbol. These questions require you to think beyond the assigned publication. Present your solutions to the questions in the format required by your instructor. Possible formats may include one or more of these options: write the answer; create a document that contains the answer; present your answer to the class; discuss your answer in a group; record the answer as audio or video using a webcam, smartphone, or portable media player; or post answers on a blog, wiki, or website.

Apply Your Knowledge

Reinforce the skills and apply the concepts you learned in this chapter.

Editing a Flyer with Text, Graphic, and Tear-Offs

Note: To complete this assignment, you will be required to use the Data Files for Students. Visit www.cengage.com/ct/studentdownload for detailed instructions or contact your instructor for information about accessing the required files.

Instructions: Your brother is in charge of advertising his 10-year class reunion. He has asked you to help him with editing the text, graphic, and tear-offs. You produce the flyer shown in Figure 1–76.

Perform the following tasks:

1. Run Publisher and open the file Apply 1-1 Class Reunion Flyer from the Data Files for Students.
2. Tap or click the Major Heading default text and drag to select it. Type **`10-Year Reunion Gym Party!`** to replace the text.
3. Tap or click the Subheading default text box and then drag the text to select it. Type **`05/21/15`** to replace the text.
4. Tap or click the default bulleted text and then press CTRL+A to select all of the text. Type the following text, pressing the ENTER key at the end of each line.

   `Wear your letter jacket!`

   `Show your school spirit!`

   `High School Gym!`

   `7:00 p.m.!`

   `RSVP to Jesse by 05/07/15!`
5. Tap or click one of the tear-offs, type **`Jesse`** and then press the ENTER key. Type **`402-555-1306`** to finish entering the text. Tap or click outside the tear-offs to synchronize them. If requested by your instructor, use your name in the tear-offs.
6. Select the text in the attention getter sunburst shape and replace it with the text shown in Figure 1–76.
7. Select the attention getter and change the border weight to 6 point, using the Shape Outline button (DRAWING TOOLS FORMAT tab | ShapeStyles group).
8. At the top of the flyer, select the picture placeholder. Tap or click the picture placeholder icon to display the Insert Pictures dialog box. Use Office.com Clip Art to search for a picture related to academics, similar to the one shown in Figure 1–76.

Extend Your Knowledge

Extend the skills you learned in this chapter and experiment with new skills. You may need to use Help to complete the assignment.

Creating a Flyer from Scratch

Instructions: You have been asked to create a flyer to remind students to vote. You decide to start from scratch to create the flyer shown in Figure 1–77.

Perform the following tasks:

1. Run Publisher and select the Blank 8.5 × 11" template.
2. Tap or click the More button (PAGE DESIGN tab | Schemes group) and then select the Bluebird color scheme.
3. Tap or click the Scheme Fonts button (PAGE DESIGN tab | Schemes group) and then select the Office Classic 1 font scheme.
4. Tap or click the Pictures button (INSERT tab | Illustrations group) and then navigate to the Data Files for Students. Insert the graphic named, Extend 1-1 Decorative Rectangle. Move it as necessary to approximately the center of the page.
5. Insert a second picture from the Data Files for Students named, Extend 1-1 Blue Rectangle. Move it to the upper-center as shown in Figure 1–77.
6. Tap or click the Online Pictures button (INSERT tab | Illustrations group) and then search Office.com Clip Art for a graphic of an American flag. Move the graphic to the upper

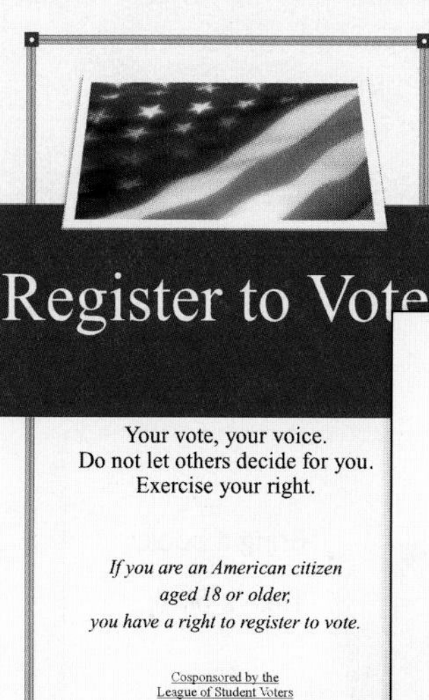

Figure 1–77

Extend Your Knowledge projects at the end of each chapter allow students to extend and expand on the skills learned within the chapter. Students use critical thinking to experiment with new skills to complete each project.

b. Before typing the text, click the Font Color arrow (HOME tab | Font group) and then choose a white color. Type the text, `Register to Vote!` and then autofit it.

c. Draw another text box below the first one. Tap or click the Font Color arrow (HOME tab | Font group) and then choose a black color. Tap or click the Bold button (HOME tab | Font group). Tap or click the Center button (HOME tab | Paragraph group) and then type the text shown in Figure 1–77.

d. Repeat Step 7c for the next text box and format the text italic.

e. Repeat Step 7c for the last text box and format the text underlined.

f. If requested to do so by your instructor, add the name of your voting location to the flyer.

8. Save the file with the file name, Extend 1-1 Vote Flyer Complete.
9. Submit the file in the format specified by your instructor.
10. When would you use a template instead of creating a flyer from scratch that contains only the fields you need? Was formatting the font before you typed easier than selecting text and formatting it afterward?

Analyze, Correct, Improve

Analyze a publication, correct all errors, and improve the design.

Making Changes to a Web Flyer

Note: To complete this assignment, you will be required to use the Data Files for Students. Visit www.cengage.com/ct/studentdownload for detailed instructions or contact your instructor for information about accessing the required files.

Instructions: Your community is trying to promote its community garden. A former gardener created the website shown in Figure 1–78 using Publisher, but it has several issues. You decide to improve the flyer. Run Publisher and open the file, Analyze 1-1 Community Garden Web Flyer.

Analyze, Correct, Improve projects call on the students to analyze a file, discover errors in it, fix the errors, and then improve upon the file using the skills they learned in the chapter.

Figure 1–78

Continued >

Textbook Walk-Through

PUB 60 Publisher Chapter 1 Creating a Flyer

STUDENT ASSIGNMENTS

Analyze, Correct, Improve *continued*

1. Correct Correct the date on the flyer. This year's event is March 25. The flyer still has default text in the lower-left corner. If requested to do so by your instructor, insert your community and your phone number. The website listed in the lower-right corner should be a hyperlink. Resize any text boxes whose text wraps awkwardly.

2. Improve Each of the text boxes seems to be a different font size. Choose a large size for the main heading. Change the description text to best fit and then increase or decrease the fonts in the lower text boxes so that they all match. Choose to make them all bold. Align objects horizontally with each other and with the margins. Correct the misspelled word. Change the color scheme to an all green color scheme such as Green or Floral. Experiment with different font schemes. Save the document using the file name, Analyze 1-1 Community Garden Flyer Complete. Submit the revised document in the format specified by your instructor.

3. What errors existed in the starting file? How did creating consistency in font sizes enhance the publication? Did changing the color scheme improve the effectiveness of the flyer? What other improvements would you make?

In the Labs

Design, create, modify, and/or use a publication following the guidelines, concepts, and skills presented in this chapter. Labs 1 and 2, which increase in difficulty, require you to create solutions based on what you learned in the chapter; Lab 3 requires you to create a solution, which uses cloud and web technologies, by learning and investigating on your own from general guidance.

Lab 1: Creating a Sign-Up Sheet

Problem: The Self-Defense Club on campus would like you to create a sign-up sheet for students who want to take classes in the Fall semester. You decide to look through Publisher's templates for an appropriate flyer to use as a starting point. You create the flyer shown in Figure 1–79.

Perform the following tasks:

1. Run Publisher. In the template gallery, click BU
2. In the Event group, click the All Event folder to the end of the list and select the Company Sign
3. Customize the template with the Alpine color sc publication.
4. Tap or click the Event Title placeholder text to s the ENTER key. Type `Classes` to finish replac
5. Tap or click the description placeholder text to s ENTER key at the end of each line. The last line
   `Learn the techniques you need to pr`
   `Prepare now, for the event you hope`
   `Classes will be held on Thursdays th`
   `Easy to learn. Gain confidfence. Be`
6. Press and hold or right-click the misspelled wor
7. Press and hold or right-click the text box and th
8. Change the Date text, Date: 00/00/00, to `Fall`
9. Change the Time text, Time: 00:00, to `7:00-8`

In the Lab Three in-depth assignments in each chapter that require students to apply the chapter concepts and techniques to solve problems. One Lab is devoted entirely to Cloud and Web 2.0 integration.

Consider This: Your Turn exercises call on students to apply creative thinking and problem solving skills to design and implement a solution.

Creating a Flyer Publisher Chapter 1 PUB 63

STUDENT ASSIGNMENTS Publisher Chapter 1

Date: Nov. 4th
Book Swap
Time: 10:00 a.m.
Bring a book.
Take a book.
Located in the Library Courtyard
State University
918.555.8642
mrs.jones@mrsj.edu

Figure 1–81

Instructions:

1. Open the file named, Lab 1-3 Book Swap Flyer, from the Data Files for Students.
2. Insert a picture and format it as shown in Figure 1–81.
3. If requested to do so by your instructor, change the email address to your email address.
4. Save the presentation on SkyDrive in the Publisher folder using the file name, Lab 1–3 Book Swap Flyer Complete.
5. Submit the assignment in the format specified by your instructor.
6. When would you save one of your files for school or your job on SkyDrive? Do you think using SkyDrive enhances collaboration efforts? Why?

Consider This: Your Turn

Apply your creative thinking and problem solving skills to design and implement a solution.

1: Creating an Advertisement

Personal/Academic

Part 1: You attend a college that is famous for its Department of Dance. Students who major in dance are required to complete internships as dance instructors. Because you are a computer

Continued >

Office 2013 and Windows 8: Essential Concepts and Skills

Microsoft product screen shots used with permission from Microsoft Corporation.

Objectives

You will have mastered the material in this chapter when you can:

- Use a touch screen
- Perform basic mouse operations
- Start Windows and sign in to an account
- Identify the objects in the Windows 8 desktop
- Identify the apps in and versions of Microsoft Office 2013
- Run an app
- Identify the components of the Microsoft Office ribbon
- Create folders
- Save files
- Change screen resolution
- Perform basic tasks in Microsoft Office apps
- Manage files
- Use Microsoft Office Help and Windows Help

Office 2013 and Windows 8: Essential Concepts and Skills

This introductory chapter uses Publisher 2013 to cover features and functions common to Office 2013 apps, as well as the basics of Windows 8.

Roadmap

In this chapter, you will learn how to perform basic tasks in Windows and Publisher. The following roadmap identifies general activities you will perform as you progress through this chapter:

1. SIGN IN to an account
2. USE WINDOWS
3. USE features in Publisher that are common across Office APPS
4. FILE and folder MANAGEMENT
5. SWITCH between APPS
6. SAVE and manage FILES
7. CHANGE SCREEN RESOLUTION
8. EXIT APPS
9. USE ADDITIONAL Office APP FEATURES
10. USE Office and Windows HELP

At the beginning of the step instructions throughout the chapter, you will see an abbreviated form of this roadmap. The abbreviated roadmap uses colors to indicate chapter progress: gray means the chapter is beyond that activity, blue means the task being shown is covered in that activity, and black means that activity is yet to be covered. For example, the following abbreviated roadmap indicates the chapter would be showing a task in the Use Apps activity.

1 SIGN IN | 2 USE WINDOWS | 3 USE APPS | 4 FILE MANAGEMENT | 5 SWITCH APPS | 6 SAVE FILES
7 CHANGE SCREEN RESOLUTION | 8 EXIT APPS | 9 USE ADDITIONAL APP FEATURES | 10 USE HELP

Use the abbreviated roadmap as a progress guide while you read or step through the instructions in this chapter.

Introduction to the Windows 8 Operating System

Windows 8 is the newest version of Microsoft Windows, which is a popular and widely used operating system. An **operating system** is a computer program (set of computer instructions) that coordinates all the activities of computer hardware, such as memory, storage devices, and printers, and provides the capability for you to communicate with the computer.

The Windows operating system simplifies the process of working with publications and apps by organizing the manner in which you interact with the computer. Windows is used to run apps. An **app** (short for application) consists of programs designed to make users more productive and/or assist them with personal tasks, such as desktop publishing or browsing the web.

The Windows 8 interface begins with the **Start screen**, which shows tiles (Figure 1). A **tile** is a shortcut to an app or other content. The tiles on the Start screen include installed apps that you use regularly. From the Start screen, you can choose which apps to run using a touch screen, mouse, or other input device.

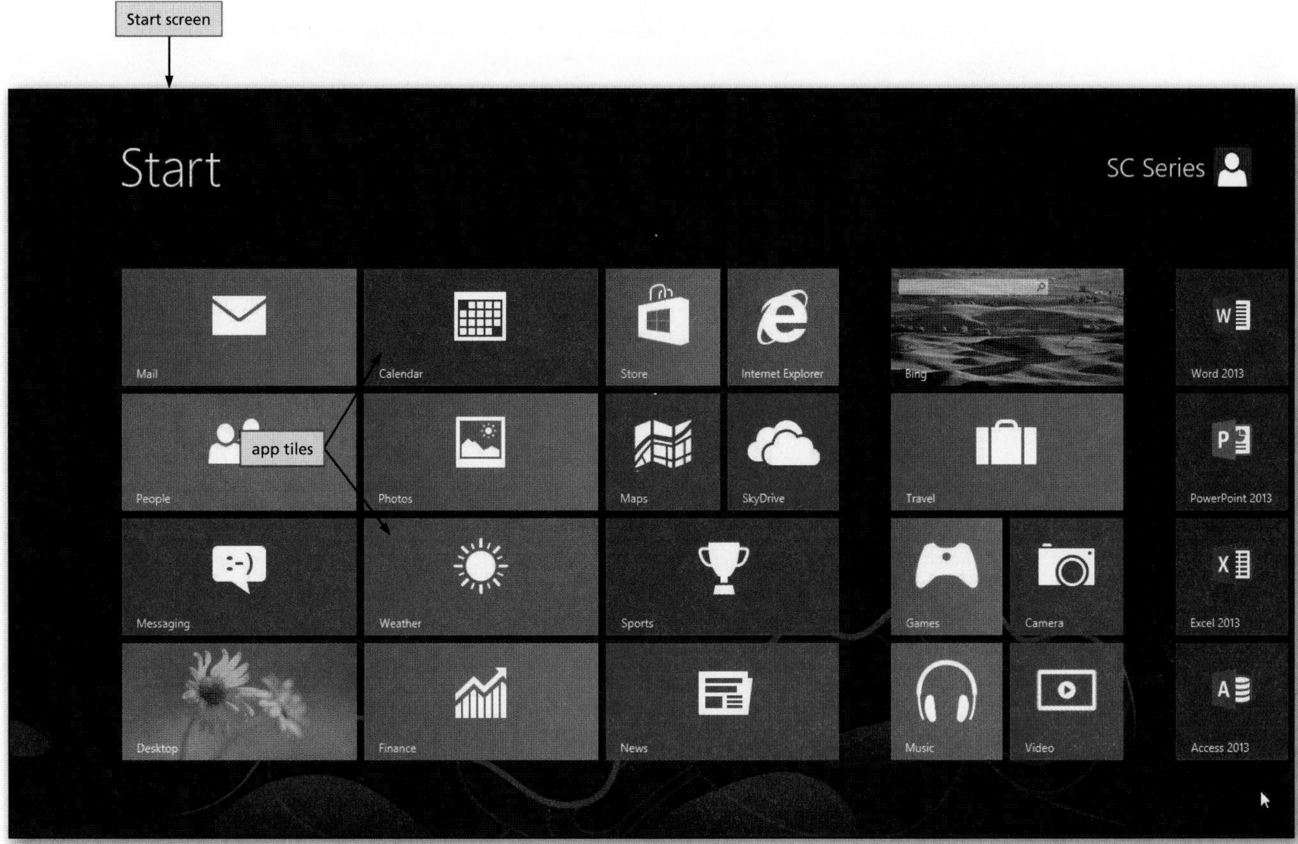

Figure 1

Using a Touch Screen and a Mouse

Windows users who have computers or devices with touch screen capability can interact with the screen using gestures. A **gesture** is a motion you make on a touch screen with the tip of one or more fingers or your hand. Touch screens are convenient because they do not require a separate device for input. Table 1 on the next page presents common ways to interact with a touch screen.

If you are using your finger on a touch screen and are having difficulty completing the steps in this chapter, consider using a stylus. Many people find it easier to be precise with a stylus than with a finger. In addition, with a stylus you see the pointer. If you still are having trouble completing the steps with a stylus, try using a mouse.

Table 1 Touch Screen Gestures

Motion	Description	Common Uses
Tap	Quickly touch and release one finger one time.	Activate a link (built-in connection) Press a button Run a program or an app
Double-tap	Quickly touch and release one finger two times.	Run a program or an app Zoom in (show a smaller area on the screen, so that contents appear larger) at the location of the double-tap
Press and hold	Press and hold one finger to cause an action to occur, or until an action occurs.	Display a shortcut menu (immediate access to allowable actions) Activate a mode enabling you to move an item with one finger to a new location
Drag, or slide	Press and hold one finger on an object and then move the finger to the new location.	Move an item around the screen Scroll
Swipe	Press and hold one finger and then move the finger horizontally or vertically on the screen.	Select an object Swipe from edge to display a bar such as the Charms bar, Apps bar, and Navigation bar (all discussed later)
Stretch	Move two fingers apart.	Zoom in (show a smaller area on the screen, so that contents appear larger)
Pinch	Move two fingers together.	Zoom out (show a larger area on the screen, so that contents appear smaller)

© 2014 Cengage Learning

BTW

BTWs

For a complete list of the BTWs found in the margins of this book, visit the BTW resource on the Student Companion Site located on www.cengagebrain.com. For detailed instructions about accessing available resources, visit www.cengage.com/ct/studentdownload or contact your instructor for information about accessing the required files.

BTW

Touch Screen Differences

The Office and Windows interfaces may vary if you are using a touch screen. For this reason, you might notice that the function or appearance of your touch screen differs slightly from this chapter's presentation.

CONSIDER THIS

Will your screen look different if you are using a touch screen?

The Windows and Microsoft Office interface varies slightly if you are using a touch screen. For this reason, you might notice that your Windows or Publisher screens look slightly different from the screens in this book.

Windows users who do not have touch screen capabilities typically work with a mouse that has at least two buttons. For a right-handed user, the left button usually is the primary mouse button, and the right mouse button is the secondary mouse button. Left-handed people, however, can reverse the function of these buttons.

Table 2 explains how to perform a variety of mouse operations. Some apps also use keys in combination with the mouse to perform certain actions. For example, when you hold down the CTRL key while rolling the mouse wheel, text on the screen may become larger or smaller based on the direction you roll the wheel. The function of the mouse buttons and the wheel varies depending on the app.

Table 2 Mouse Operations

Operation	Mouse Action	Example*
Point	Move the mouse until the pointer on the desktop is positioned on the item of choice.	Position the pointer on the screen.
Click	Press and release the primary mouse button, which usually is the left mouse button.	Select or deselect items on the screen or run an app or app feature.
Right-click	Press and release the secondary mouse button, which usually is the right mouse button.	Display a shortcut menu.
Double-click	Quickly press and release the primary mouse button twice without moving the mouse.	Run an app or app feature.
Triple-click	Quickly press and release the primary mouse button three times without moving the mouse.	Select a paragraph.
Drag	Point to an item, hold down the primary mouse button, move the item to the desired location on the screen, and then release the mouse button.	Move an object from one location to another or draw pictures.
Right-drag	Point to an item, hold down the right mouse button, move the item to the desired location on the screen, and then release the right mouse button.	Display a shortcut menu after moving an object from one location to another.
Rotate wheel	Roll the wheel forward or backward.	Scroll vertically (up and down).
Free-spin wheel	Whirl the wheel forward or backward so that it spins freely on its own.	Scroll through many pages in seconds.
Press wheel	Press the wheel button while moving the mouse.	Scroll continuously.
Tilt wheel	Press the wheel toward the right or left.	Scroll horizontally (left and right).
Press thumb button	Press the button on the side of the mouse with your thumb.	Move forward or backward through webpages and/or control media, games, etc.

© 2014 Cengage Learning

*Note: The examples presented in this column are discussed as they are demonstrated in this chapter.

Scrolling

A **scroll bar** is a horizontal or vertical bar that appears when the contents of an area may not be visible completely on the screen (Figure 2). A scroll bar contains **scroll arrows** and a **scroll box** that enable you to view areas that currently cannot be seen on the screen. Tapping or clicking the up and down scroll arrows moves the screen content up or down one line. You also can tap or click above or below the scroll box to move up or down a section, or drag the scroll box up or down to move to a specific location.

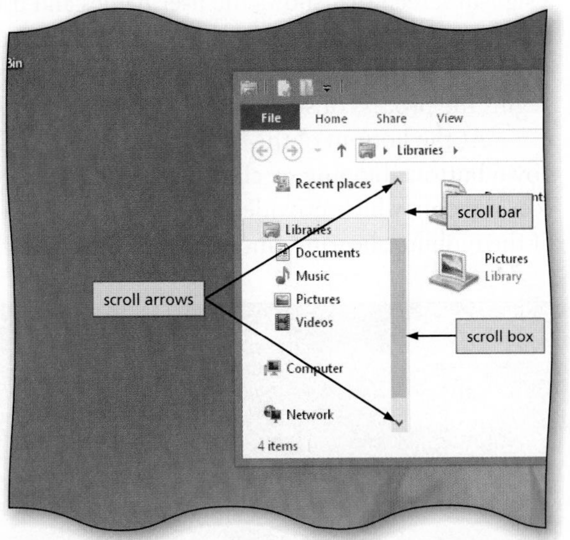

Figure 2

BTW

Pointer

If you are using a touch screen, the pointer may not appear on the screen as you perform touch gestures. The pointer will reappear when you begin using the mouse.

BTW

Minimize Wrist Injury

Computer users frequently switch between the keyboard and the mouse while using Publisher; such switching strains the wrist. To help prevent wrist injury, minimize switching. For instance, if your fingers already are on the keyboard, use keyboard keys to scroll. If your hand already is on the mouse, use the mouse to scroll. If your hand is on the touch screen, use touch gestures to scroll.

CONSIDER THIS

What should you do if you are running Windows 7 instead of Windows 8?

Although Windows 8 includes several user interface and feature enhancements, many of the steps in this book work in both Windows 7 and Windows 8. If you have any questions about differences between the two operating systems or how to perform tasks in an earlier version of Windows, contact your instructor.

Keyboard Shortcuts

In many cases, you can use the keyboard instead of the mouse to accomplish a task. To perform tasks using the keyboard, you press one or more keyboard keys, sometimes identified as a **keyboard shortcut**. Some keyboard shortcuts consist of a single key, such as the F1 key. For example, to obtain help in many apps, you can press the F1 key. Other keyboard shortcuts consist of multiple keys, in which case a plus sign separates the key names, such as CTRL+ESC. This notation means to press and hold down the first key listed, press one or more additional keys, and then release all keys. For example, to display the Start screen, press CTRL+ESC, that is, hold down the CTRL key, press the ESC key, and then release both keys.

Starting Windows

It is not unusual for multiple people to use the same computer in a work, educational, recreational, or home setting. Windows enables each user to establish a **user account**, which identifies to Windows the resources, such as apps and storage locations, a user can access when working with the computer.

Each user account has a user name and may have a password and an icon, as well. A **user name** is a unique combination of letters or numbers that identifies a specific user to Windows. A **password** is a private combination of letters, numbers, and special characters associated with the user name that allows access to a user's account resources. An icon is a small image that represents an object, thus a **user icon** is a picture associated with a user name.

When you turn on a computer, Windows starts and displays a **lock screen** consisting of the time and date (Figure 3a). To unlock the screen, swipe up or click the lock screen. Depending on your computer's settings, Windows may or may not display a sign-in screen that shows the user names and user icons for users who have accounts on the computer (Figure 3b). This **sign-in screen** enables you to sign in to your user account and makes the computer available for use. Tapping or clicking the user icon begins the process of signing in, also called logging on, to your user account.

At the bottom of the sign-in screen is the 'Ease of access' button and a Shut down button. Tapping or clicking the 'Ease of access' button displays the Ease of access menu, which provides tools to optimize a computer to accommodate the needs of the mobility, hearing, and vision impaired users. Tapping or clicking the Shut down

Figure 3a

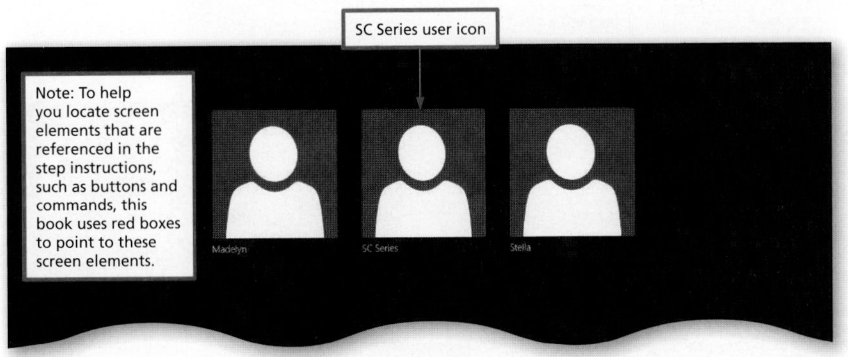
SC Series user icon
Note: To help you locate screen elements that are referenced in the step instructions, such as buttons and commands, this book uses red boxes to point to these screen elements.
Madelyn
SC Series
Stella

Figure 3b

button displays a menu containing commands related to restarting the computer, putting it in a low-power state, and shutting it down. The commands available on your computer may differ.

- The Sleep command saves your work, turns off the computer fans and hard disk, and places the computer in a lower-power state. To wake the computer from sleep mode, press the power button or lift a laptop's cover, and sign in to your account.
- The Shut down command exits running apps, shuts down Windows, and then turns off the computer.
- The Restart command exits running apps, shuts down Windows, and then restarts Windows.

BTW

Q&As

For a complete list of the Q&As found in many of the step-by-step sequences in this book, visit the Q&A resource on the Student Companion Site located on www.cengagebrain.com. For detailed instructions about accessing available resources, visit www.cengage.com/ct/studentdownload or contact your instructor for information about accessing the required files.

To Sign In to an Account

1 SIGN IN | 2 USE WINDOWS | 3 USE APPS | 4 FILE MANAGEMENT | 5 SWITCH APPS | 6 SAVE FILES
7 CHANGE SCREEN RESOLUTION | 8 EXIT APPS | 9 USE ADDITIONAL APP FEATURES | 10 USE HELP

The following steps, which use SC Series as the user name, sign in to an account based on a typical Windows installation. ***Why?*** *After starting Windows, you might be required to sign in to an account to access the computer's resources.* You may need to ask your instructor how to sign in to your account. If you are using Windows 7, skip these steps and instead perform the steps in the yellow box that immediately follows these Windows 8 steps.

- Swipe up or click the lock screen (shown in Figure 3a) to display a sign-in screen (shown in Figure 3b).
- Tap or click the user icon (for SC Series, in this case) on the sign-in screen, which depending on settings, either will display a second sign-in screen that contains a Password text box (Figure 4) or will display the Windows Start screen (shown in Figure 5 on the next page).

password text box
SC Series
Password
Submit button
'Ease of access' button
Shut down button

Figure 4

Q&A

Why do I not see a user icon?
Your computer may require you to type a user name instead of tapping or clicking an icon.

What is a text box?
A text box is a rectangular box in which you type text.

Why does my screen not show a password text box?
Your account does not require a password.

- If Windows displays a sign-in screen with a password text box, type your password in the text box.

- Tap or click the Submit button (shown in Figure 4 on the previous page) to sign in to your account and display the Windows Start screen (Figure 5).

Q&A

Why does my Start screen look different from the one in Figure 5?
The Windows Start screen is customizable, and your school or employer may have modified the screen to meet its needs. Also, your screen resolution, which affects the size of the elements on the screen, may differ from the screen resolution used in this book. Later in this chapter, you learn how to change screen resolution.

How do I type if my tablet has no keyboard?
You can use your fingers to press keys on a keyboard that appears on the screen, called an on-screen keyboard, or you can purchase a separate physical keyboard that attaches to or wirelessly communicates with the tablet.

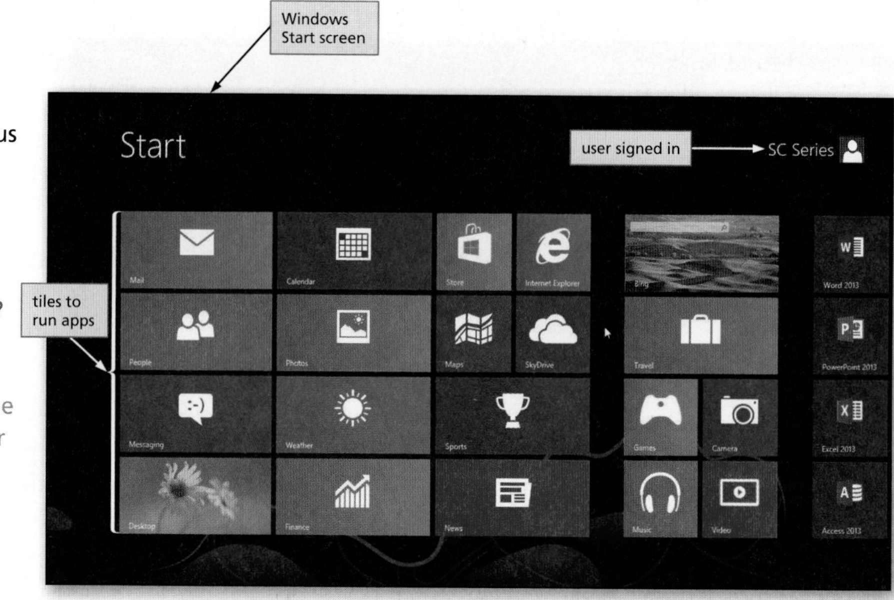

Figure 5

To Sign In to an Account Using Windows 7

If you are using Windows 7, perform these steps to sign in to an account instead of the previous steps that use Windows 8.

1. Click the user icon on the Welcome screen; depending on settings, this either will display a password text box or will sign in to the account and display the Windows 7 desktop.
2. If Windows 7 displays a password text box, type your password in the text box and then click the arrow button to sign in to the account and display the Windows 7 desktop.

The Windows Start Screen

BTW
Modern UI
The new Windows 8 user interface also is referred to as the Modern UI (user interface).

The Windows Start screen provides a scrollable space for you to access apps that have been pinned to the Start screen (shown in Figure 5). Pinned apps appear as tiles on the Start screen. In addition to running apps, you can perform tasks such as pinning apps (placing tiles) on the Start screen, moving the tiles around the Start screen, and unpinning apps (removing tiles) from the Start screen.

If you swipe up from the bottom of or right-click an open space on the Start screen, the App bar will appear. The **App bar** includes a button that enables you to display all of your apps. When working with tiles, the App bar also provides options for manipulating the tiles, such as resizing them.

CONSIDER THIS

How do you pin apps, move tiles, and unpin apps?

- To pin an app, swipe up from the bottom of the Start screen or right-click an open space on the Start screen to display the App bar, tap or click the All apps button on the App bar to display the Apps list, swipe down on or right-click the app you want to pin, and then tap or click the 'Pin to Start' button on the App bar. One way to return to the Start screen is to swipe up from the bottom or right-click an open space in the Apps list and then tap or click the All apps button again.
- To move a tile, drag the tile to the desired location.
- To unpin an app, swipe down on or right-click the app to display the App bar and then tap or click the 'Unpin from Start' button on the App bar.

Introduction to Microsoft Office 2013

Microsoft Office 2013 is the newest version of Microsoft Office, offering features that provide users with better functionality and easier ways to work with the various files they create. These features include enhanced design tools, such as improved picture formatting tools and new themes, shared notebooks for working in groups, mobile versions of Office apps, broadcast presentations for the web, and a digital notebook for managing and sharing multimedia information.

Microsoft Office 2013 Apps

Microsoft Office 2013 includes a wide variety of apps such as Word, PowerPoint, Excel, Access, Outlook, Publisher, OneNote, InfoPath, SharePoint Workspace, and Lync:

- **Microsoft Word 2013**, or Word, is a full-featured word processing app that allows you to create professional-looking documents and revise them easily.
- **Microsoft PowerPoint 2013**, or PowerPoint, is a complete presentation app that enables you to produce professional-looking presentations and then deliver them to an audience.
- **Microsoft Excel 2013**, or Excel, is a powerful spreadsheet app that allows you to organize data, complete calculations, make decisions, graph data, develop professional-looking reports, publish organized data to the web, and access real-time data from websites.
- **Microsoft Access 2013**, or Access, is a database management system that enables you to create a database; add, change, and delete data in the database; ask questions concerning the data in the database; and create forms and reports using the data in the database.
- **Microsoft Outlook 2013**, or Outlook, is a communications and scheduling app that allows you to manage email accounts, calendars, contacts, and access to other Internet content.
- **Microsoft Publisher 2013**, or Publisher, is a desktop publishing app that helps you create professional-quality publications and marketing materials that can be shared easily.
- **Microsoft OneNote 2013**, or OneNote, is a note taking app that allows you to store and share information in notebooks with other people.
- **Microsoft InfoPath Designer 2013**, or InfoPath, is a form development app that helps you create forms for use on the web and gather data from these forms.
- **Microsoft SharePoint Workspace 2013**, or SharePoint, is a collaboration app that allows you to access and revise files stored on your computer from other locations.
- **Microsoft Lync 2013** is a communications app that allows you to use various modes of communications such as instant messaging, videoconferencing, and sharing files and apps.

Microsoft Office 2013 Suites

A **suite** is a collection of individual apps available together as a unit. Microsoft offers a variety of Office suites, including a stand-alone desktop app (boxed software), Microsoft Office 365, and Microsoft Office Web Apps. **Microsoft Office 365**, or Office 365, provides plans that allow organizations to use Office in a mobile setting while also being able to communicate and share files, depending upon the type of plan selected by the organization. **Microsoft Office Web Apps**, or Web Apps, are apps that allow you to edit and share files on the web using the familiar Office interface. Table 3 on the next page outlines the differences among these Office suites.

Table 3 Office Suites

Apps/ Licenses	Office 365 Home Premium	Office 365 Small Business Premium	Office Home & Student	Office Home & Business	Office Professional
Word	✔	✔	✔	✔	✔
PowerPoint	✔	✔	✔	✔	✔
Excel	✔	✔	✔	✔	✔
Access	✔	✔			✔
Outlook	✔	✔		✔	✔
Publisher	✔	✔			✔
Lync		✔			
OneNote			✔	✔	✔
InfoPath		✔			
Licenses	5	5	1	1	1

© 2014 Cengage Learning

During the Office 365 installation, you select a plan, and depending on your plan, you receive different apps and services. Office Web Apps do not require a local installation and are accessed through SkyDrive and your browser. **SkyDrive** is a cloud storage service that provides storage and other services, such as Office Web Apps, to computer users.

CONSIDER THIS

How do you sign up for a SkyDrive account?

- Use your browser to navigate to skydrive.live.com.
- Create a Microsoft account by tapping or clicking the 'Sign up now' link (or a similar link) and then entering your information to create the account.
- Sign in to SkyDrive using your new account or use it in Publisher to save your files on SkyDrive.

Apps in a suite, such as Microsoft Office, typically use a similar interface and share features. Once you are comfortable working with the elements and the interface and performing tasks in one app, the similarity can help you apply the knowledge and skills you have learned to another app(s) in the suite. For example, the process for saving a file in Publisher is the same in PowerPoint, Excel, and the other Office apps. While briefly showing how to use Publisher, this chapter illustrates some of the common functions across the Office apps and Office identifies the characteristics unique to Publisher.

Running and Using an App

To use an app, such as Publisher, you must instruct the operating system to run the app. Windows provides many different ways to run an app, one of which is presented in this section (other ways to run an app are presented throughout this chapter). After an app is running, you can use it to perform a variety of tasks. The following pages use Publisher to discuss some elements of the Office interface and to perform tasks that are common to other Office apps.

Publisher

Publisher is a powerful desktop publishing (DTP) app that assists you in designing and producing professional-quality publications such as newsletters, brochures, flyers, logos, signs, catalogs, cards, and business forms. Using Publisher, you easily can change the shape, size, and color of text and graphics. You can include many kinds of graphical objects, including mastheads, borders, tables, images, pictures, charts, and web objects in publications, as well as integrate spreadsheets and databases.

To Run an App from the Start Screen

The Start screen contains tiles that allow you to run apps, some of which may be stored on your computer. ***Why?*** *When you install an app, for example, tiles are added to the Start screen for the various Office apps included in the suite.*

The following steps, which assume Windows is running, use the Start screen to run Publisher based on a typical installation. You may need to ask your instructor how to run Publisher on your computer. Although the steps illustrate running the Publisher app, the steps to run any Office app are similar. If you are using Windows 7, skip these steps and instead perform the steps in the yellow box that immediately follows these Windows 8 steps.

1

- If necessary, scroll to display the Publisher tile on the Start screen (Figure 6).

Q&A Why does my Start screen look different?
It may look different because of your computer's configuration. The Start screen may be customized for several reasons, such as usage requirements or security restrictions.

What if the app I want to run is not on the Start screen?
You can display all installed apps by swiping up from the bottom of the Start screen or right-clicking an open space on the Start screen and then tapping or clicking the All apps button on the App bar.

How do I scroll on a touch screen?
Use the slide gesture; that is, press and hold your finger on the screen and then move your finger in the direction you wish to scroll.

Figure 6

2

- Tap or click the Publisher 2013 tile to run the Publisher app and display the Publisher start screen (Figure 7).

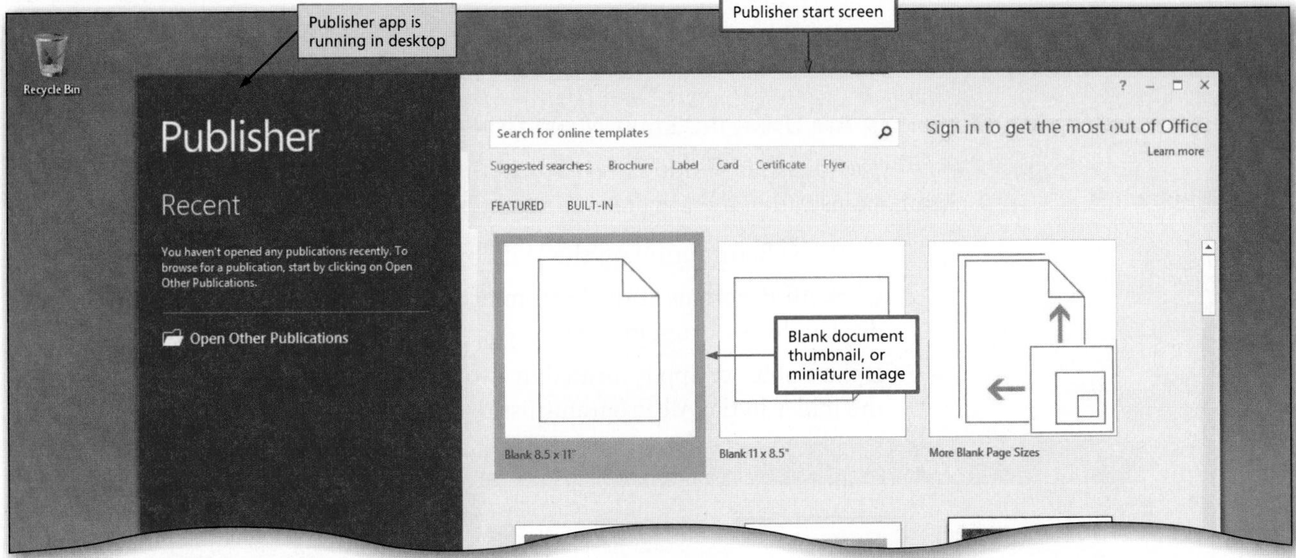

Figure 7

- Tap or click the Blank 8.5 × 11" thumbnail on the Publisher start screen to create a blank Publisher publication in the Publisher window (Figure 8).

Q&A What happens when you run an app?
Some apps provide a means for you to create a blank publication, as shown in Figure 7 on the previous page; others immediately display a blank publication in an app window, such as the Publisher window shown in Figure 8. A **window** is a rectangular area that displays data and information. The top of a window has a **title bar**, which is a horizontal space that contains the window's name.

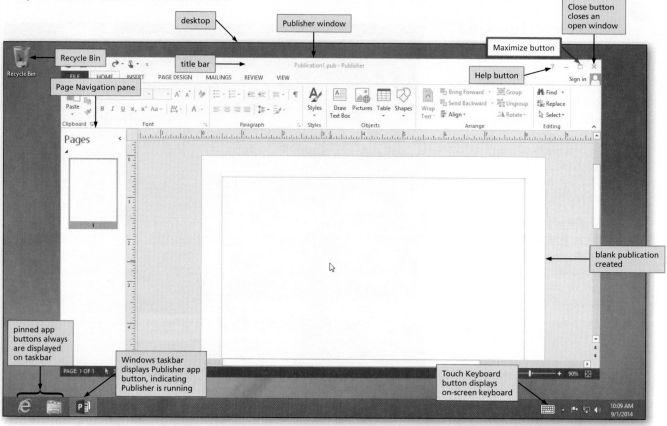

desktop
Publisher window
Close button closes an open window
Maximize button
Recycle Bin
title bar
Help button
Page Navigation pane
blank publication created
pinned app buttons always are displayed on taskbar
Windows taskbar displays Publisher app button, indicating Publisher is running
Touch Keyboard button displays on-screen keyboard

Figure 8

Other Ways

1. Tap or click Search charm on Charms bar, type app name in search box, tap or click app name in results list
2. Double-tap or double-click file created in app you want to run

BTW
Touch Keyboard
To display the on-screen touch keyboard, tap the Touch Keyboard button on the Windows taskbar. When finished using the touch keyboard, tap the X button on the touch keyboard to close the keyboard.

To Run an App Using the Start Menu Using Windows 7

If you are using Windows 7, perform these steps to run Publisher using the Start menu instead of the previous steps that use Windows 8.

1. Click the Start button on the Windows 7 taskbar to display the Start menu.
2. Click All Programs at the bottom of the left pane on the Start menu to display the All Programs list.
3. If the Publisher app is located in a folder, click, or scroll to and then click, the folder in the All Programs list to display a list of the folder's contents.
4. Click, or scroll to and then click, the app name (Publisher, in this case) in the list to run the selected app.

Windows Desktop

When you run an app in Windows, it may appear in an on-screen work area app, called the **desktop** (shown in Figure 8). You can perform tasks such as placing objects in the desktop, moving the objects around the desktop, and removing items from the desktop.

Some icons also may be displayed in the desktop. For instance, the icon for the **Recycle Bin**, the location of files that have been deleted, appears in the desktop by default. A **file** is a named unit of storage. Files can contain text, images, audio, and video. You can customize your desktop so that icons representing apps and files you use often appear in the desktop.

To Switch between an App and the Start Screen

1 SIGN IN | 2 USE WINDOWS | 3 USE APPS | 4 FILE MANAGEMENT | 5 SWITCH APPS | 6 SAVE FILES
7 CHANGE SCREEN RESOLUTION | 8 EXIT APPS | 9 USE ADDITIONAL APP FEATURES | 10 USE HELP

While working with an app, such as Publisher, or in the desktop, you easily can return to the Start screen. The following steps switch from the Publisher app to the Start screen. ***Why?*** *Returning to the Start screen allows you to run any of your other apps.* If you are using Windows 7, read these steps without performing them because Windows 7 does not have a Start screen.

- Swipe in from the left edge of the screen, and then back to the left, or point to the lower-left corner of the desktop to display a thumbnail of the Start screen (Figure 9).

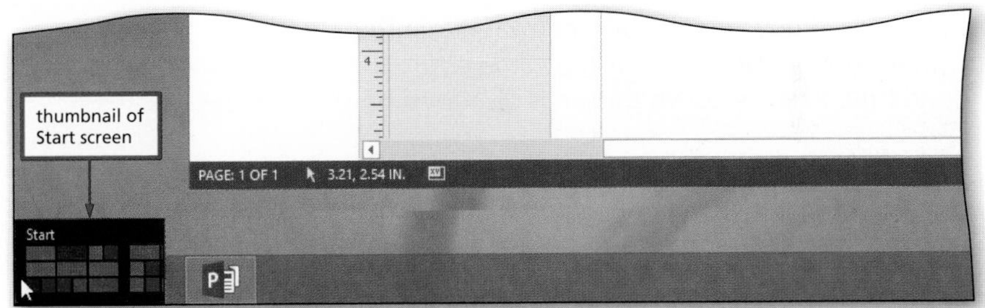

Figure 9

- Tap or click the thumbnail of the Start screen to display the Start screen (Figure 10).

- Tap or click the Desktop tile to redisplay the Publisher app in the desktop (shown in Figure 8).

Figure 10

Other Ways

1. Press WINDOWS key to display Start screen
2. Swipe in from right edge, tap or click Start charm

To Maximize a Window

Sometimes content is not visible completely in a window. One method of displaying the entire contents of a window is to **maximize** it, or enlarge the window so that it fills the entire screen. The following step maximizes the Publisher window; however, any Office app's window can be maximized using this step. ***Why?*** *A maximized window provides the most space available for using the app.*

1

- If the Publisher window is not maximized already, tap or click the Maximize button (shown in Figure 8 on page OFF 12) next to the Close button on the window's title bar to maximize the window (Figure 11).

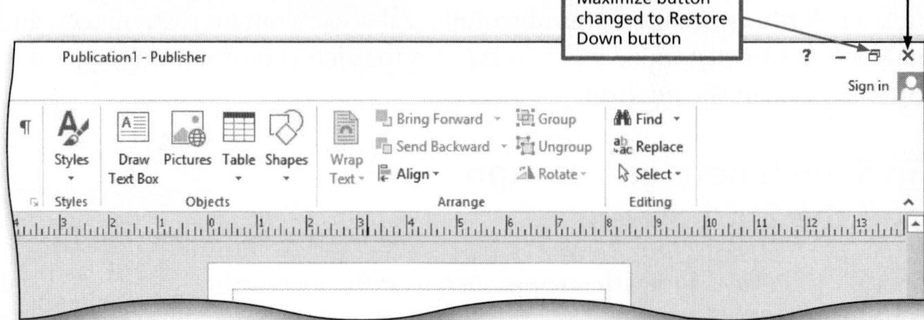

Figure 11

Q&A

What happened to the Maximize button?
It changed to a Restore Down button, which you can use to return a window to its size and location before you maximized it.

How do I know whether a window is maximized?
A window is maximized if it fills the entire display area and the Restore Down button is displayed on the title bar.

Other Ways

1. Double-tap or double-click title bar
2. Drag title bar to top of screen

Publisher Window, Ribbon, and Elements Common to Office Apps

The Publisher window consists of a variety of components to make your work more efficient and publications more professional. These include the workspace, page layout, scratch area, Page Navigation pane, ribbon, mini toolbar, shortcut menus, Quick Access Toolbar, and Microsoft Account area. Most of these components are common to other Microsoft Office apps; others are unique to Publisher.

The **page layout** contains a view of the publication page, all the objects contained therein, plus the guides and boundaries for the page and its objects (Figure 12). The default (preset) view is **Single Page view**, which shows the publication on a mock sheet of paper in the Publisher workspace.

Scroll Bars You use a scroll bar to display different portions of a publication in the publication workspace. At the right edge of the workspace is a vertical scroll bar. A horizontal scroll bar appears at the bottom. On a scroll bar, the position of the scroll box reflects the location of the portion of the publication that is displayed in the workspace.

Status Bar The **status bar**, located at the bottom of the publication window above the Windows taskbar, presents information about the publication, the progress of current tasks, and the status of certain commands and keys; it also provides controls for viewing the publication. As you type text or perform certain tasks, various indicators may appear on the status bar.

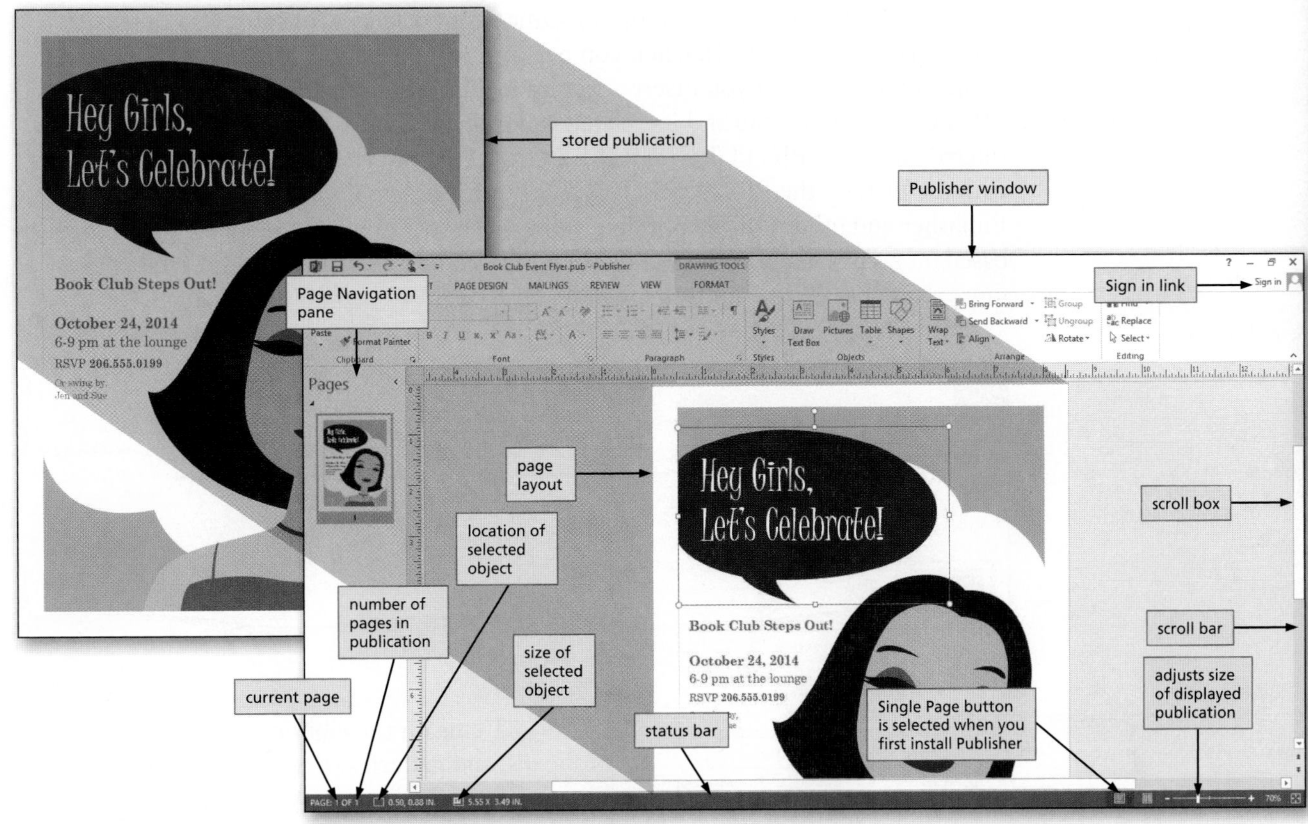

Figure 12

The left side of the status bar in Figure 12 shows the current page followed by the total number of pages in the publication, the location of the selected object, and the size of the selected object. The right side of the status bar includes buttons and controls you can use to change the view of a publication and adjust the size of the displayed publication.

Ribbon The ribbon, located near the top of the window below the title bar, is the control center in Publisher and other Office apps (Figure 13). The ribbon provides easy, central access to the tasks you perform while creating a publication. The ribbon consists of tabs, groups, and commands. Each **tab** contains a collection of groups, and each **group** contains related commands. When you run an Office app, such as Publisher, it initially displays several main tabs, also called default or top-level tabs. All Office apps have a HOME tab, which contains the more frequently used commands.

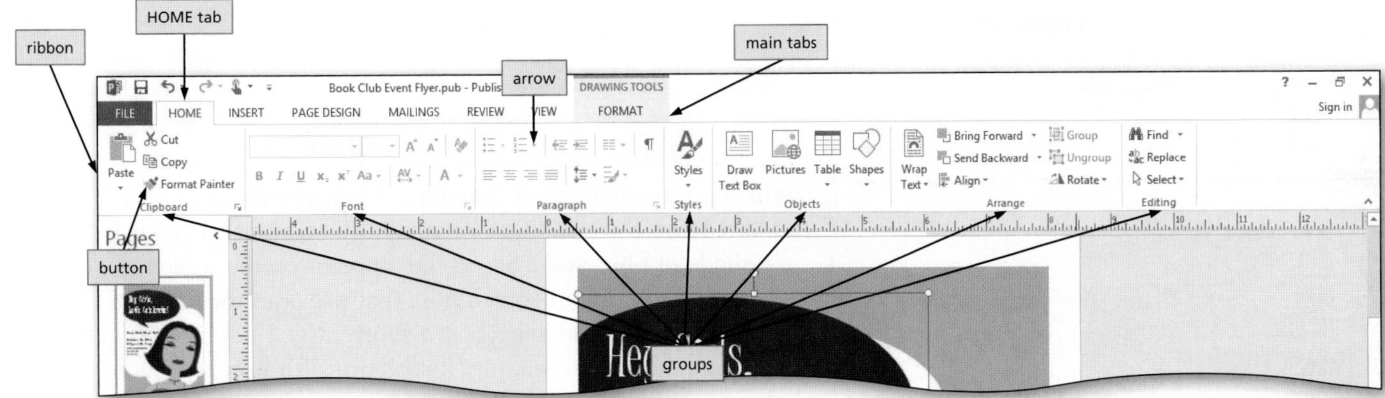

Figure 13

In addition to the main tabs, the Office apps display **tool tabs**, also called contextual tabs (Figure 14), when you perform certain tasks or work with objects such as pictures or tables. If you insert a picture in a Publisher publication, for example, the PICTURE TOOLS tab and its related subordinate FORMAT tab appear, collectively referred to as the PICTURE TOOLS FORMAT tab. When you are finished working with the picture, the PICTURE TOOLS FORMAT tab disappears from the ribbon. Publisher and other Office apps determine when tool tabs should appear and disappear based on tasks you perform. Some tool tabs, such as the TABLE TOOLS tab, have more than one related subordinate tab.

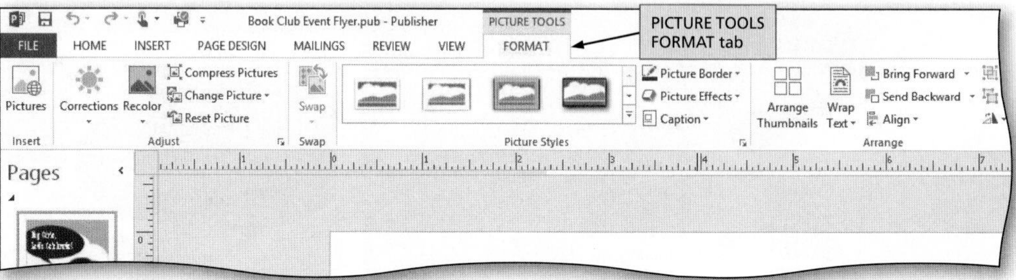

Figure 14

PICTURE TOOLS FORMAT tab is one of many tool tabs that appear automatically depending on the task you perform

as you move pointer from one gallery option to next, Publisher shows live preview of style in publication, so that you can see effect of option in publication before selecting it

picture changes to Bevel Perspective Left, White as you point to that style in gallery

Figure 15

Items on the ribbon include buttons, boxes, and galleries (shown in Figure 13 on the previous page). A **gallery** is a set of choices, often graphical, arranged in a grid or in a list. You can scroll through choices in an in-ribbon gallery by tapping or clicking the gallery's scroll arrows. Or, you can tap or click a gallery's More button to view more gallery options on the screen at a time.

Some buttons and boxes have arrows that, when tapped or clicked, also display a gallery; others always cause a gallery to be displayed when tapped or clicked. Most galleries support **live preview**, which is a feature that allows you to point to a gallery choice and see its effect in the publication — without actually selecting the choice (Figure 15). Live preview works only if you are using a mouse; if you are using a touch screen, you will not be able to view live previews.

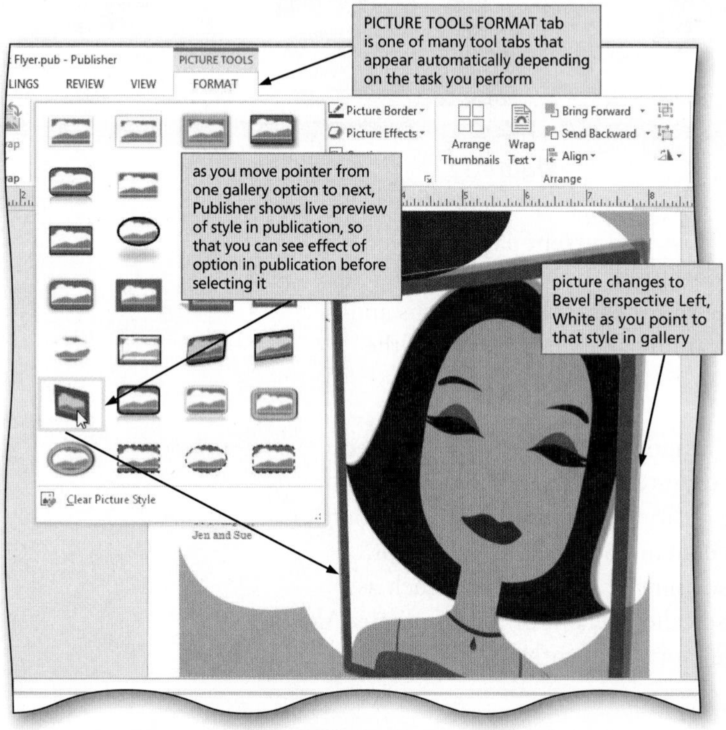

Quick Access Toolbar

Touch/Mouse Mode button

ScreenTip for Paste arrow

pointer on Paste arrow

Figure 16

Some commands on the ribbon display an image to help you remember their function. When you point to a command on the ribbon, all or part of the command glows in a shade of blue, and a ScreenTip appears on the screen. A **ScreenTip** is an on-screen note that provides the name of the command, available keyboard shortcut(s), a description of the command, and sometimes instructions for how to obtain help about the command (Figure 16).

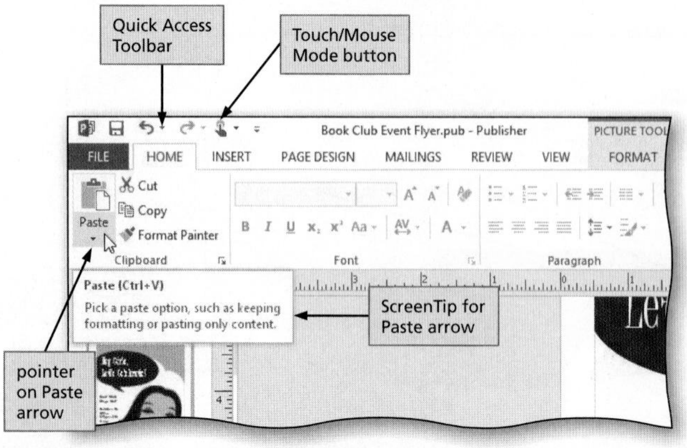

Some groups on the ribbon have a small arrow in the lower-right corner, called a **Dialog Box Launcher**, that when tapped or clicked, displays a dialog box or a task pane with additional options for the group (Figure 17). When presented with a dialog box, you make selections and must close the dialog box before returning to the publication. A **task pane**, in contrast to a dialog box, is a window that can remain open and visible while you work in the publication.

BTW
Touch Mode
The Office and Windows interfaces may vary if you are using Touch mode. For this reason, you might notice that the function or appearance of your touch screen in Publisher differs slightly from this book's presentation.

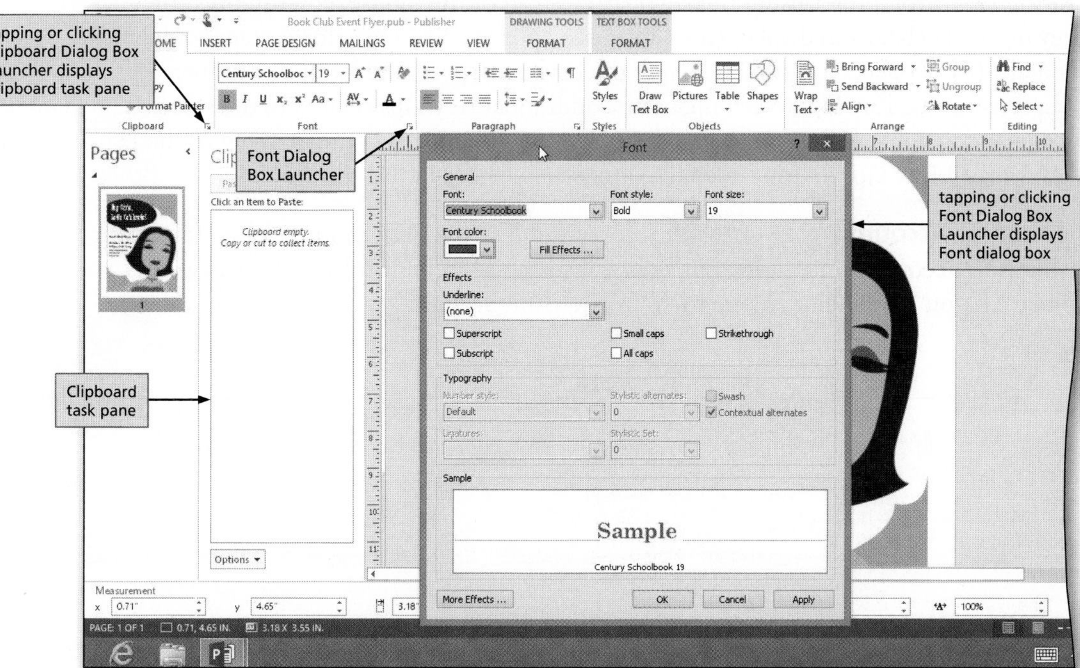

Figure 17

Mini Toolbar The **mini toolbar**, which appears automatically based on tasks you perform, contains commands related to changing the appearance of text in a publication (Figure 18). If you do not use the mini toolbar, it disappears from the screen. The buttons, arrows, and boxes on the mini toolbar vary, depending on whether you are using Touch mode versus Mouse mode. If you press and hold or right-click an item in the publication window, Publisher displays both the mini toolbar and a shortcut menu, which is discussed in a later section in this chapter.

All commands on the mini toolbar also exist on the ribbon. The purpose of the mini toolbar is to minimize hand or mouse movement.

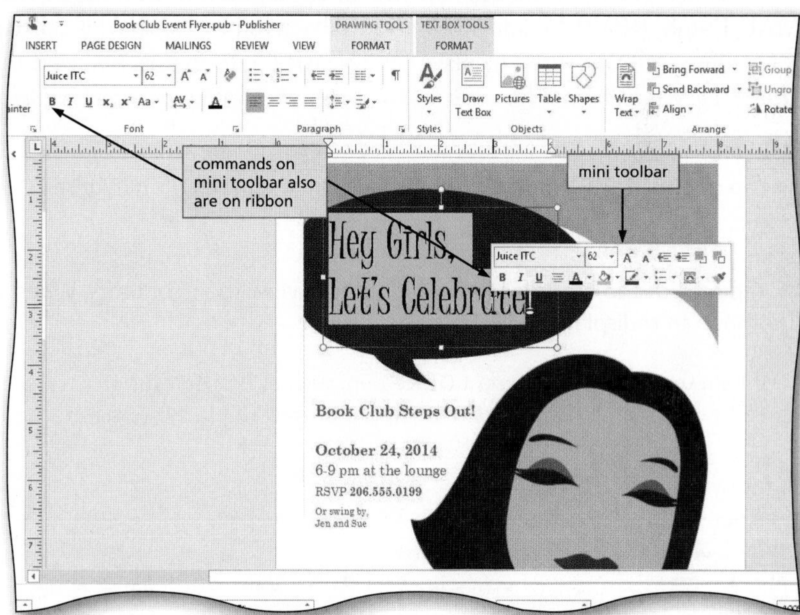

Figure 18

Quick Access Toolbar The **Quick Access Toolbar**, located initially (by default) above the ribbon at the left edge of the title bar, provides convenient, one-tap or one-click access to frequently used commands (shown in Figure 16). The commands on the Quick Access Toolbar always are available, regardless of the task you are performing. The Touch/Mouse Mode button on the Quick Access Toolbar allows you to switch between Touch mode and Mouse mode. If you primarily are using touch gestures, Touch mode will add more space between commands on menus and on the ribbon so that they are easier to tap. While touch gestures are convenient ways to interact with Office apps, not all features are supported when you are using Touch mode. If you are using a mouse, Mouse mode will not add the extra space between buttons and commands. The Quick Access Toolbar is discussed in more depth later in the chapter.

> BTW
> **Turning Off the Mini Toolbar**
> If you do not want the mini toolbar to appear, tap or click FILE on the ribbon to open the Backstage view, tap or click Options in the Backstage view, tap or click General (Publisher Options dialog box), remove the check mark from the 'Show Mini Toolbar on selection' check box, and then tap or click the OK button.

KeyTips If you prefer using the keyboard instead of the mouse, you can press the ALT key on the keyboard to display **KeyTips**, or keyboard code icons, for certain commands (Figure 19). To select a command using the keyboard, press the letter or number displayed in the KeyTip, which may cause additional KeyTips related to the selected command to appear. To remove KeyTips from the screen, press the ALT key or the ESC key until all KeyTips disappear, or tap or click anywhere in the app window.

Microsoft Account Area In this area, you can use the Sign in link to sign in to your Microsoft account. Once signed in, you will see your account information as well as a picture if you have included one in your Microsoft account.

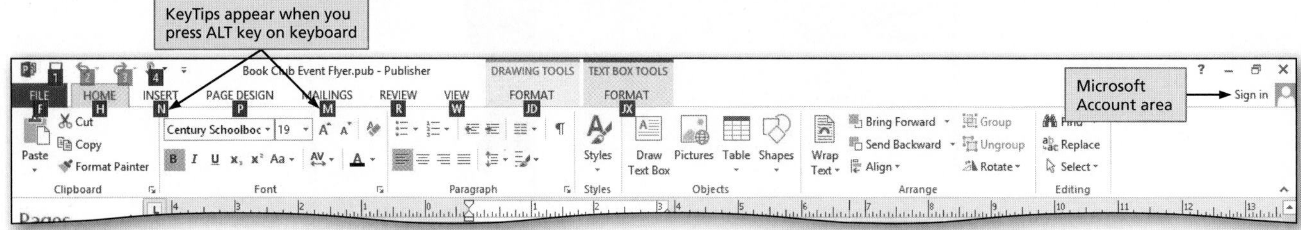

Figure 19

To Display a Different Tab on the Ribbon

1 SIGN IN | 2 USE WINDOWS | 3 USE APPS | 4 FILE MANAGEMENT | 5 SWITCH APPS | 6 SAVE FILES | 7 CHANGE SCREEN RESOLUTION | 8 EXIT APPS | 9 USE ADDITIONAL APP FEATURES | 10 USE HELP

When you run Publisher, the ribbon displays seven main tabs: FILE, HOME, INSERT, PAGE DESIGN, MAILINGS, REVIEW, and VIEW. The tab currently displayed is called the **active tab**.

The following step displays the INSERT tab, that is, makes it the active tab. ***Why?*** *When working with an Office app, you may need to switch tabs to access other options for working with a publication.*

- Tap or click INSERT on the ribbon to display the INSERT tab (Figure 20).

Experiment

- Tap or click the other tabs on the ribbon to view their contents. When you are finished, tap or click INSERT on the ribbon to redisplay the INSERT tab.

Q&A If I am working in a different Office app, such as PowerPoint or Access, how do I display a different tab on the ribbon?
Follow this same procedure; that is, tap or click the desired tab on the ribbon.

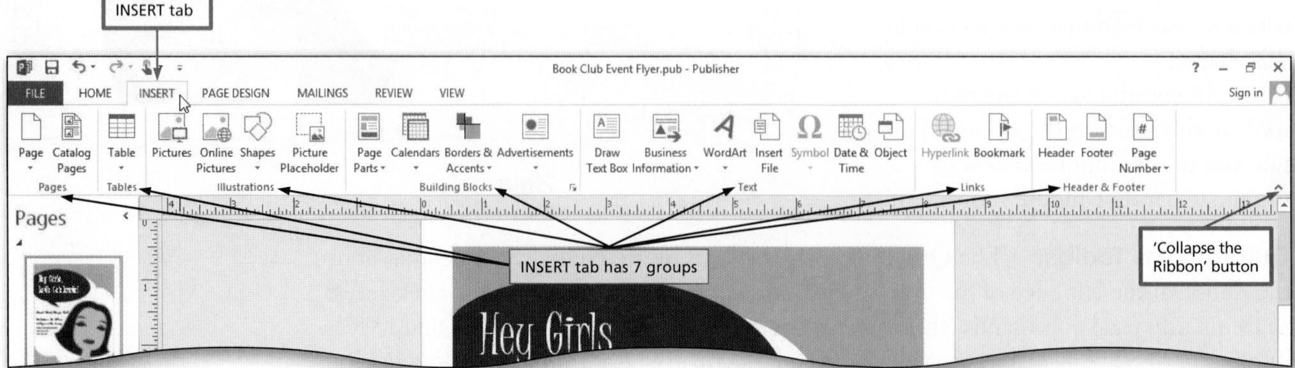

Figure 20

To Collapse and Expand the Ribbon and Use Full Screen Mode

To display more of a publication or other item in the window of an Office app, some users prefer to collapse the ribbon, which hides the groups on the ribbon and displays only the main tabs, or to use **Full Screen mode**, which hides all the commands and just displays the publication. Each time you run an Office app, such as Publisher, the ribbon appears the same way it did the last time you used that Office app. The chapters in this book, however, begin with the ribbon appearing as it did at the initial installation of Office or Publisher.

The following steps collapse, expand, and restore the ribbon in Publisher and then switch to Full Screen mode. ***Why?*** *If you need more space on the screen to work with your publication, you may consider collapsing the ribbon or switching to Full Screen mode to gain additional workspace.*

- Tap or click the 'Collapse the Ribbon' button on the ribbon (shown in Figure 20) to collapse the ribbon (Figure 21).

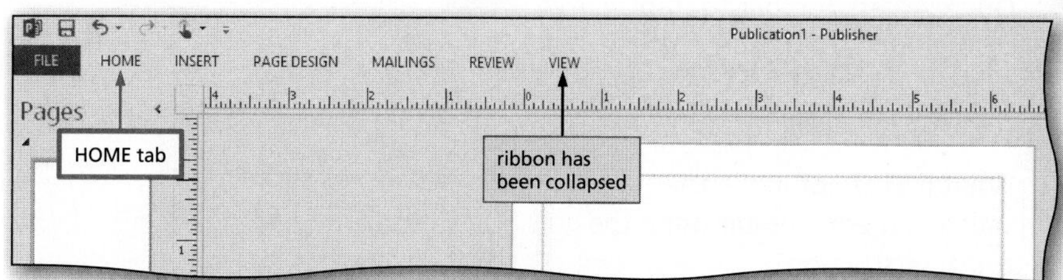

Figure 21

Q&A What happened to the groups on the ribbon?
When you collapse the ribbon, the groups disappear so that the ribbon does not take up as much space on the screen.

What happened to the 'Collapse the Ribbon' button?
The 'Pin the ribbon' button replaces the 'Collapse the Ribbon' button when the ribbon is collapsed. You will see the 'Pin the ribbon' button only when you expand a ribbon by tapping or clicking a tab.

- Tap or click HOME on the ribbon to expand the HOME tab (Figure 22).

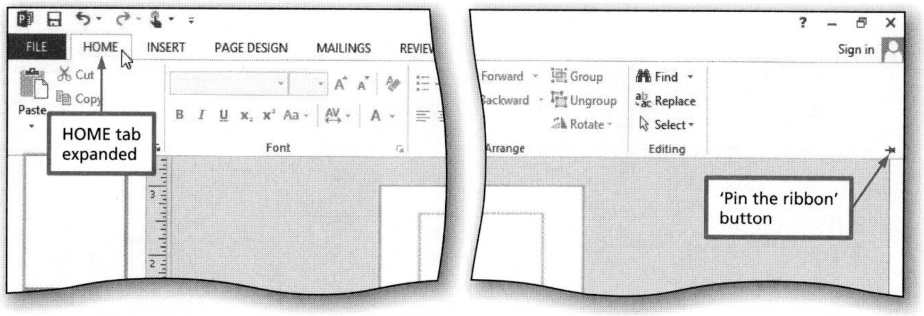

Figure 22

Q&A Why would I click the HOME tab?
If you want to use a command on a collapsed ribbon, tap or click the main tab to display the groups for that tab. After you select a command on the ribbon, the groups will be collapsed once again. If you decide not to use a command on the ribbon, you can collapse the groups by tapping or clicking the same main tab or tapping or clicking in the app window.

Experiment

- Tap or click HOME on the ribbon to collapse the groups again. Tap or click HOME on the ribbon to expand the HOME tab.

- Tap or click the 'Pin the ribbon' button on the expanded HOME tab to restore the ribbon.

Other Ways

1. Double-tap or double-click a main tab on the ribbon
2. Press CTRL+F1

To Use a Shortcut Menu to Relocate the Quick Access Toolbar

When you press and hold or right-click certain areas of the Publisher and other Office app windows, a shortcut menu will appear. A **shortcut menu** is a list of frequently used commands that relate to an object. ***Why?*** *You can use shortcut menus to access common commands quickly.* When you press and hold or right-click the status bar, for example, a shortcut menu appears with commands related to the status bar. When you press and hold or right-click the Quick Access Toolbar, a shortcut menu appears with commands related to the Quick Access Toolbar. The following steps use a shortcut menu to move the Quick Access Toolbar, which by default is located on the title bar.

1

- Press and hold or right-click the Quick Access Toolbar to display a shortcut menu that presents a list of commands related to the Quick Access Toolbar (Figure 23).

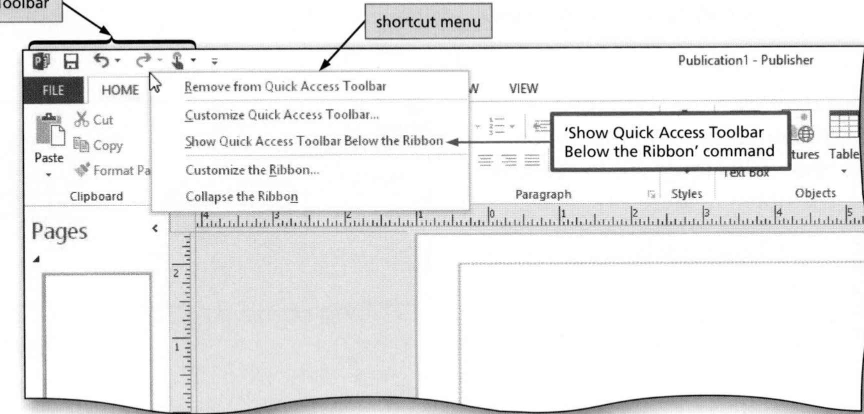

Figure 23

Q&A What if I cannot make the shortcut menu appear using the touch instruction?
When you use the press and hold technique, be sure to release your finger when the square appears on the screen to display the shortcut menu. If the technique still does not work, you might need to add more space around objects on the screen, making it easier for you to press or tap them. Click the 'Customize Quick Access Toolbar' button and then click Touch/Mouse Mode on the menu. Another option is to use the stylus.

2

- Tap or click 'Show Quick Access Toolbar Below the Ribbon' on the shortcut menu to display the Quick Access Toolbar below the ribbon (Figure 24).

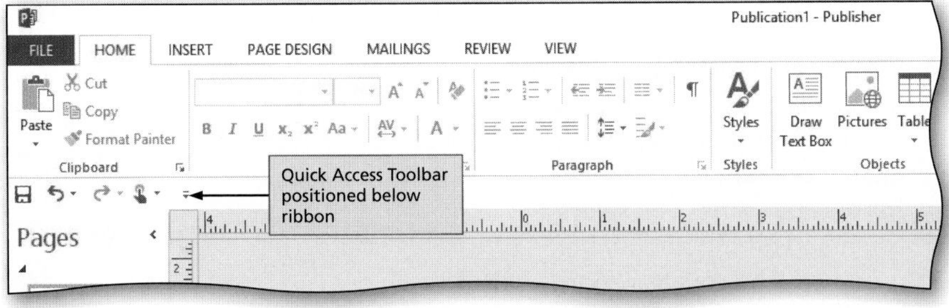
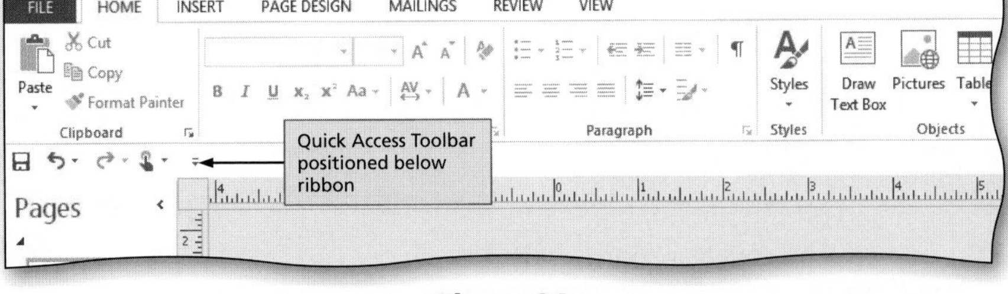

Figure 24

3

- Press and hold or right-click the Quick Access Toolbar to display a shortcut menu (Figure 25).

4

- Tap or click 'Show Quick Access Toolbar Above the Ribbon' on the shortcut menu to return the Quick Access Toolbar to its original position (shown in Figure 23).

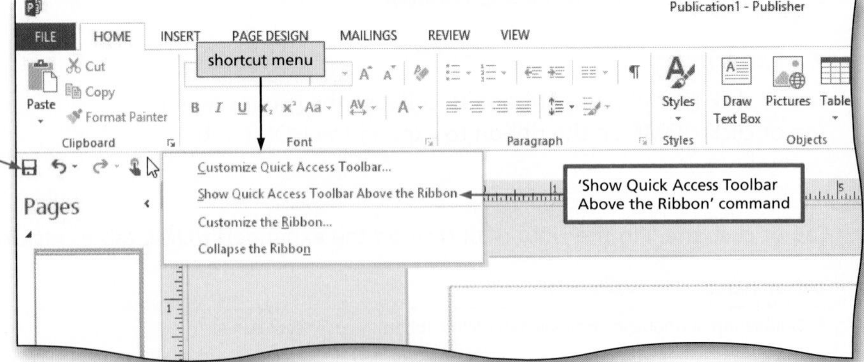

Figure 25

Other Ways

1. Tap or click 'Customize Quick Access Toolbar' button on Quick Access Toolbar, tap or click 'Show Below the Ribbon' or 'Show Above the Ribbon'

To Customize the Quick Access Toolbar

The Quick Access Toolbar provides easy access to some of the more frequently used commands in the Office apps. By default, the Quick Access Toolbar contains buttons for the Save, Undo, and Redo commands. You can customize the Quick Access Toolbar by changing its location in the window, as shown in the previous steps, and by adding more buttons to reflect commands you would like to access easily. The following steps add the Quick Print button to the Quick Access Toolbar in the Publisher window. ***Why?*** *Adding the Quick Print button to the Quick Access Toolbar speeds up the process of printing.*

1

- Tap or click the 'Customize Quick Access Toolbar' button to display the Customize Quick Access Toolbar menu (Figure 26).

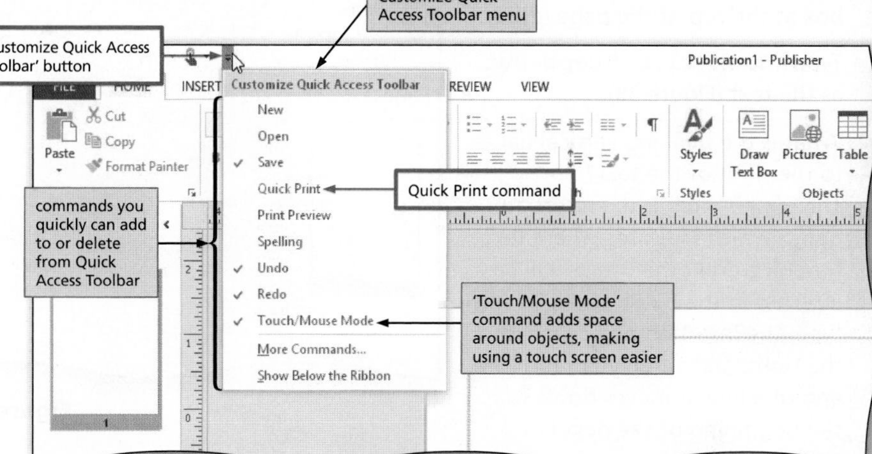

Figure 26

Q&A Which commands are listed on the Customize Quick Access Toolbar menu?
It lists commands that commonly are added to the Quick Access Toolbar.

What do the check marks next to some commands signify?
Check marks appear next to commands that already are on the Quick Access Toolbar. When you add a button to the Quick Access Toolbar, a check mark will be displayed next to its command name.

2

- Tap or click Quick Print on the Customize Quick Access Toolbar menu to add the Quick Print button to the Quick Access Toolbar (Figure 27).

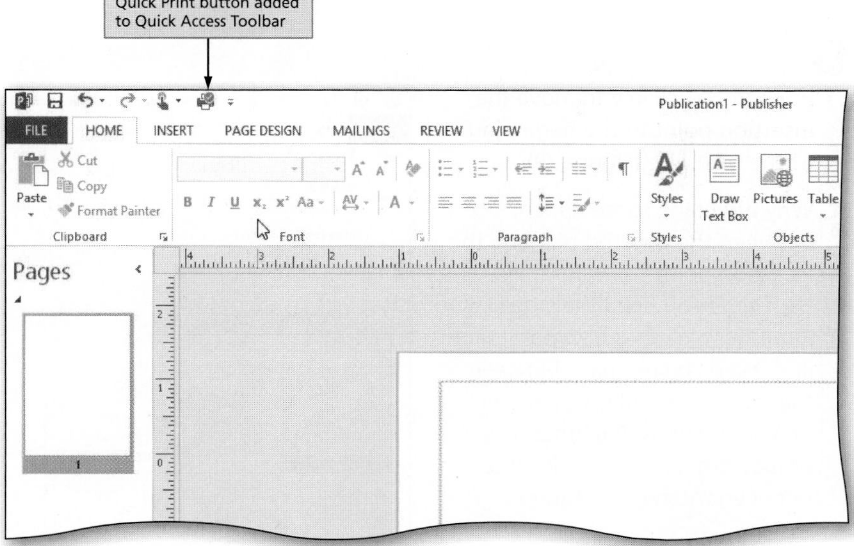

Figure 27

Q&A How would I remove a button from the Quick Access Toolbar?
You would press and hold or right-click the button you wish to remove and then tap or click 'Remove from Quick Access Toolbar' on the shortcut menu or tap or click the 'Customize Quick Access Toolbar' button on the Quick Access Toolbar and then click the button name in the Customize Quick Access Toolbar menu to remove the check mark.

Other Ways

1. Tap or click File on ribbon, tap or click Options button, tap or click 'Quick Access Toolbar' button (Publisher Options dialog box), choose settings, tap or click OK button

To Enter Text in a Publication

1 SIGN IN | 2 USE WINDOWS | 3 USE APPS | 4 FILE MANAGEMENT | 5 SWITCH APPS | 6 SAVE FILES
7 CHANGE SCREEN RESOLUTION | 8 EXIT APPS | 9 USE ADDITIONAL APP FEATURES | 10 USE HELP

A typical task to do in Publisher is to enter text by typing on the keyboard. The following steps create a text box and enter text. ***Why?*** *In Publisher, you must enter text into a text box on the page layout.*

1

- Tap or click the Draw a Text Box button (HOME tab | Objects group), and then drag a small text box at the top of the page layout.
- Type **Book Club Steps Out** as the text (Figure 28).

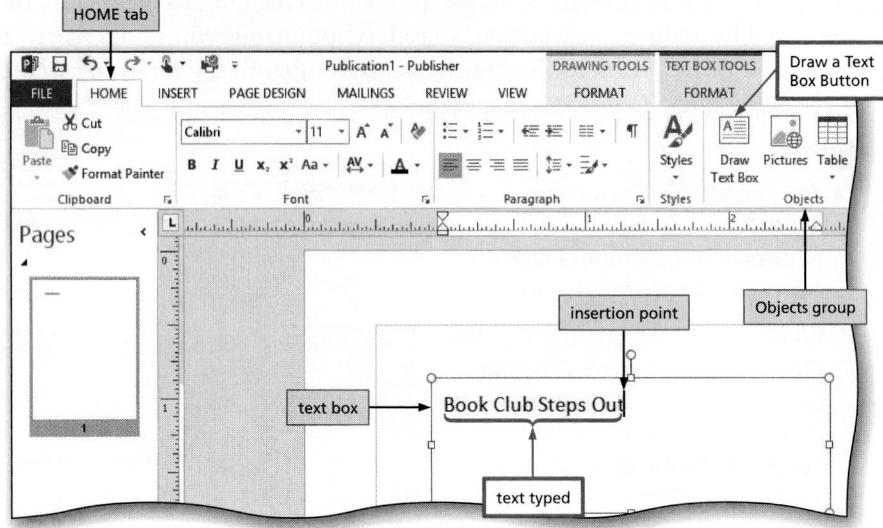

Figure 28

Q&A What is the blinking vertical bar to the right of the text?
The blinking bar is the insertion point, which indicates where text, graphics, and other items will be inserted in the publication. As you type, the insertion point moves to the right, and when you reach the end of a line, it moves down to the beginning of the next line.

What if I make an error while typing?
You can press the BACKSPACE key until you have deleted the text in error and then retype the text correctly.

Why does a circle appear below the insertion point?
If you are using a touch screen, a selection handle (small circle) appears below the text so that you can format the text easily.

2

- Press the ENTER key to move the insertion point to the beginning of the next line (Figure 29).

Q&A Why did blank space appear between the entered text and the insertion point?
Each time you press the ENTER key, Publisher creates a new paragraph and inserts blank space between the two paragraphs. Depending on your settings, Publisher may or may not insert a blank space between the two paragraphs.

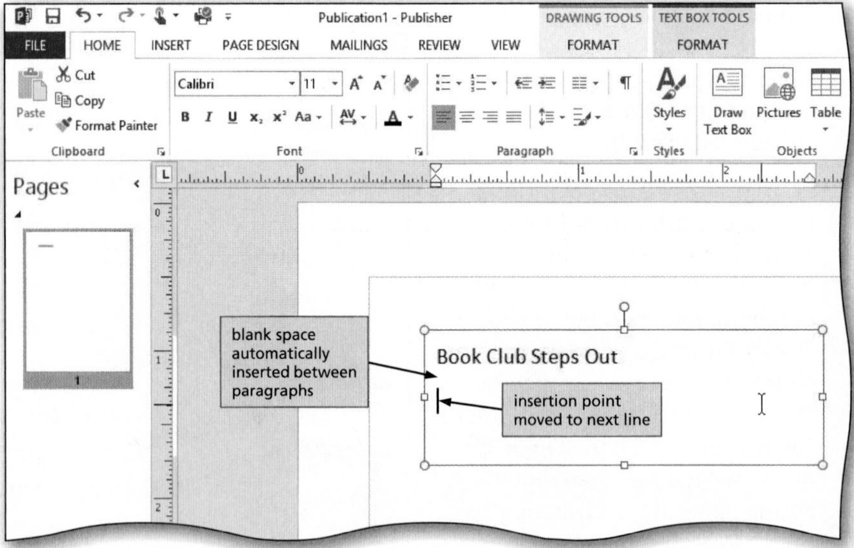

Figure 29

Saving and Organizing Files

While you are creating a publication, the computer stores it in memory. When you save a publication, the computer places it on a storage medium such as a hard disk, solid state drive (SSD), USB flash drive, or optical disc. The storage medium can be permanent in your computer, may be portable where you remove it from your computer, or may be on a web server you access through a network or the Internet.

A saved publication is referred to as a file. A **file name** is the name assigned to a file when it is saved. When saving files, you should organize them so that you easily can find them later. Windows provides tools to help you organize files.

BTW

File Type

Depending on your Windows settings, the file type .pub may be displayed immediately to the right of the file name after you save the file. The file type .pub is a Publisher 2013 publication.

CONSIDER THIS

How often should you save a publication?

It is important to save a publication frequently for the following reasons:

- The publication in memory might be lost if the computer is turned off or you lose electrical power while an app is running.
- If you run out of time before completing a project, you may finish it at a future time without starting over.

Organizing Files and Folders

A file contains data. This data can range from a research paper to an accounting spreadsheet to an electronic math quiz. You should organize and store files in folders to avoid misplacing a file and to help you find a file quickly.

If you are taking an introductory computer class (CIS 101, for example), you may want to design a series of folders for the different subjects covered in the class. To accomplish this, you can arrange the folders in a hierarchy for the class, as shown in Figure 30.

The hierarchy contains three levels. The first level contains the storage medium, such as a hard disk. The second level contains the class folder (CIS 101, in this case), and the third level contains seven folders, one each for a different Office app that will be covered in the class (Word, PowerPoint, Excel, Access, Outlook, Publisher, and OneNote).

When the hierarchy in Figure 30 is created, the storage medium is said to contain the CIS 101 folder, and the CIS 101 folder is said to contain the separate Office folders (i.e., Word, PowerPoint, Excel, etc.). In addition, this hierarchy easily can be expanded to include folders from other classes taken during additional semesters.

The vertical and horizontal lines in Figure 30 form a pathway that allows you to navigate to a drive or folder on a computer or network. A **path** consists of a drive letter (preceded by a drive name when necessary) and colon, to identify the storage device, and one or more folder names. A hard disk typically has a drive letter of C. Each drive or folder in the hierarchy has a corresponding path.

By default, Windows saves publications in the Documents library, music in the Music library, pictures in the Pictures library, and videos in the Videos library.

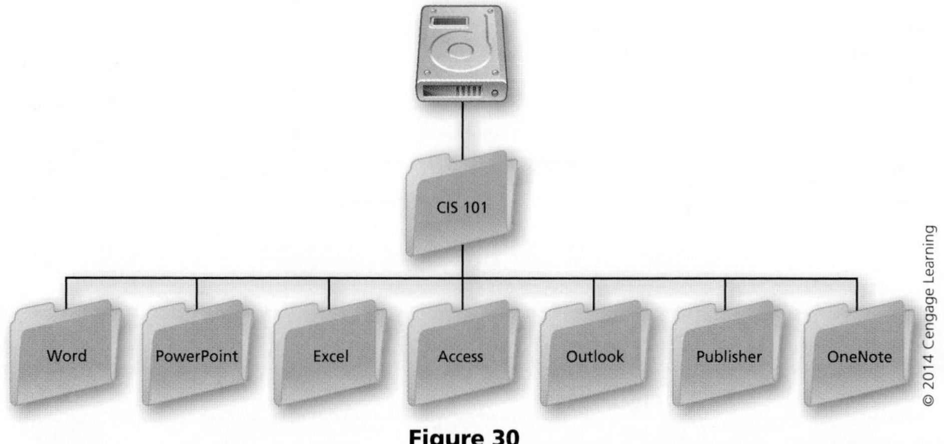

© 2014 Cengage Learning

Figure 30

A **library** helps you manage multiple folders stored in various locations on a computer and devices. It does not store the folder contents; rather, it keeps track of their locations so that you can access the folders and their contents quickly. For example, you can save pictures from a digital camera in any folder on any storage location on a computer. Normally, this would make organizing the different folders difficult. If you add the folders to a library, however, you can access all the pictures from one location regardless of where they are stored.

The following pages illustrate the steps to organize the folders for this class and save a file in a folder:

1. Create the folder identifying your class.
2. Create the Publisher folder in the folder identifying your class.
3. Save a file in the Publisher folder.
4. Verify the location of the saved file.

To Create a Folder

When you create a folder, such as the CIS 101 folder shown in Figure 30 on the previous page, you must name the folder. A folder name should describe the folder and its contents. A folder name can contain spaces and any uppercase or lowercase characters, except a backslash (\), slash (/), colon (:), asterisk (*), question mark (?), quotation marks ("), less than symbol (<), greater than symbol (>), or vertical bar (|). Folder names cannot be CON, AUX, COM1, COM2, COM3, COM4, LPT1, LPT2, LPT3, PRN, or NUL. The same rules for naming folders also apply to naming files.

The following steps create a class folder (CIS 101, in this case) in the Documents library. ***Why? When storing files, you should organize the files so that it will be easier to find them later.*** If you are using Windows 7, skip these steps and instead perform the steps in the yellow box that immediately follows these Windows 8 steps.

- Tap or click the File Explorer app button on the taskbar to run the File Explorer app (Figure 31).

Q&A Why does the title bar say Libraries?
File Explorer, by default, displays the name of the selected library or folder on the title bar.

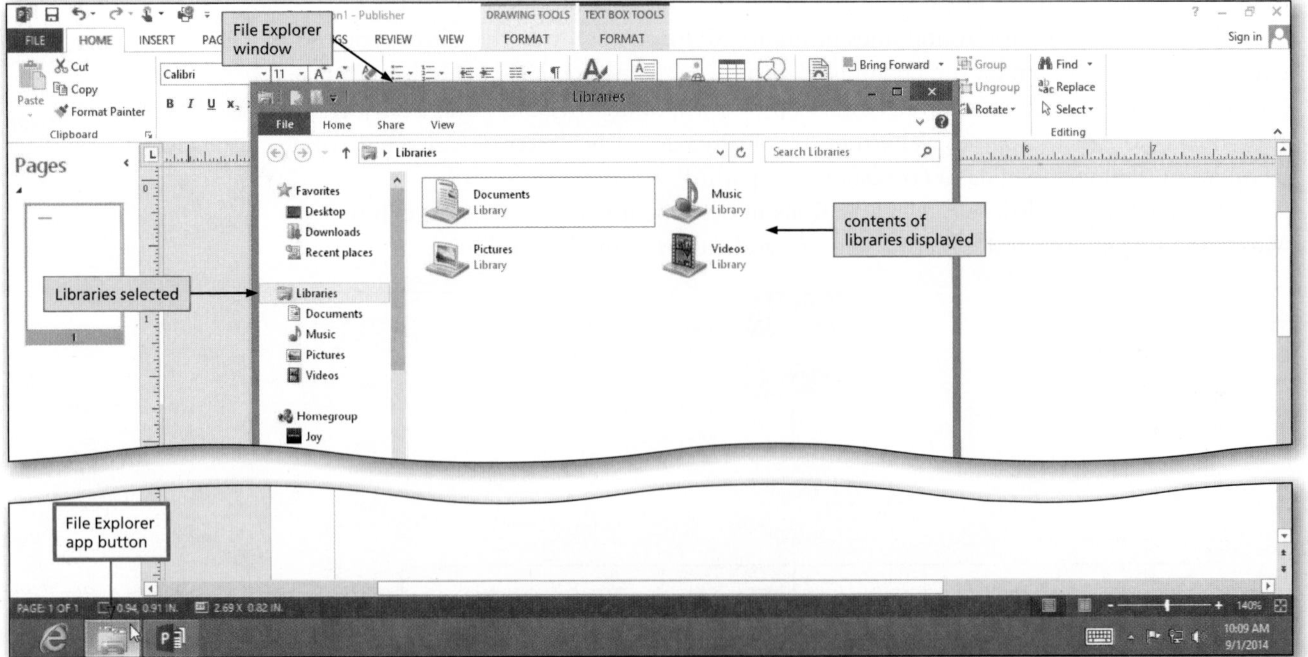

Figure 31

2

- Tap or click the Documents library in the navigation pane to display the contents of the Documents library in the file list (Figure 32).

Q&A What if my screen does not show the Documents, Music, Pictures, and Videos libraries?
Double-tap or double-click Libraries in the navigation pane to expand the list.

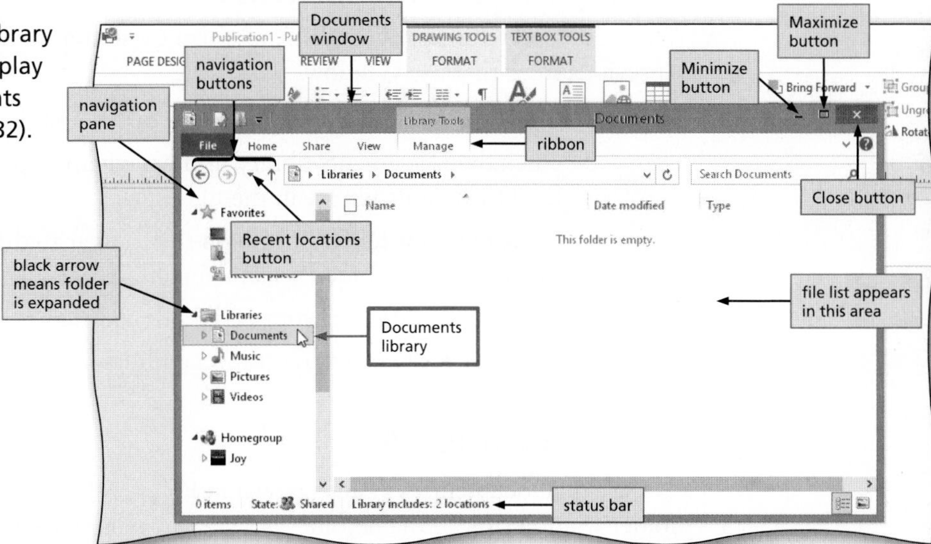

Figure 32

3

- Tap or click the New folder button on the Quick Access Toolbar to create a new folder with the name, New folder, selected in a text box (Figure 33).

Q&A Why is the folder icon displayed differently on my computer?
Windows might be configured to display contents differently on your computer.

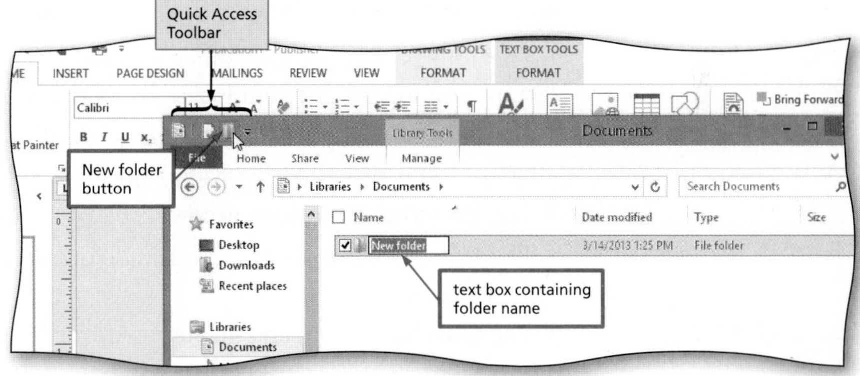

Figure 33

4

- Type `CIS 101` (or your class code) in the text box as the new folder name.
  If requested by your instructor, add your last name to the end of the folder name.
- Press the ENTER key to change the folder name from New folder to a folder name identifying your class (Figure 34).

Q&A What happens when I press the ENTER key?
The class folder (CIS 101, in this case) is displayed in the file list, which contains the folder name, date modified, type, and size.

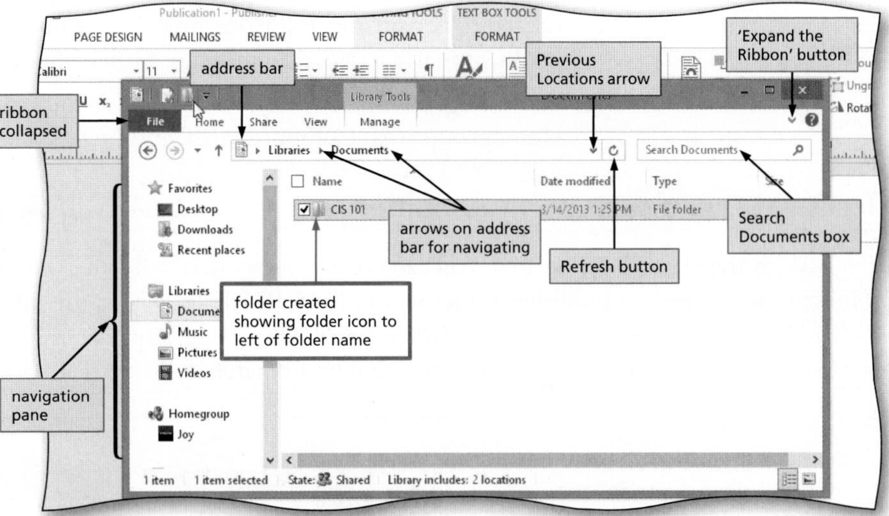

Figure 34

Other Ways

1. Press CTRL+SHIFT+N 2. Tap or click the New folder button (Home tab | New group)

To Create a Folder Using Windows 7

If you are using Windows 7, perform these steps to create a folder instead of the previous steps that use Windows 8.

1. Click the Windows Explorer button on the taskbar to run Windows Explorer.
2. Click the Documents library in the navigation pane to display the contents of the Documents library in the file list.
3. Click the New folder button on the toolbar to display a new folder icon with the name, New folder, selected in a text box.
4. Type `CIS 101` (or your class code) in the text box to name the folder.
5. Press the ENTER key to create the folder.

Folder Windows

The Documents window (shown in Figure 34 on the previous page) is called a folder window. Recall that a folder is a specific named location on a storage medium that contains related files. Most users rely on **folder windows** for finding, viewing, and managing information on their computers. Folder windows have common design elements, including the following (shown in Figure 34).

BTW
The Favorites Area
In the navigation pane, the **Favorites area** shows your favorite locations. By default, this list contains only links to your Desktop, Downloads, and Recent places.

BTW
The Libraries Area
In the navigation pane, the **Libraries area** shows all of the folders included in the library.

- The **address bar** provides quick navigation options. The arrows on the address bar allow you to visit different locations on the computer.
- The buttons to the left of the address bar allow you to navigate the contents of the navigation pane and view recent pages.
- The **Previous Locations arrow** displays the locations you have visited.
- The **Refresh button** on the right side of the address bar refreshes the contents of the folder list.
- The **search box** contains the dimmed words, Search Documents. You can type a term in the search box for a list of files, folders, shortcuts, and elements containing that term within the location you are searching. A **shortcut** is an icon on the desktop that provides a user with immediate access to an app or file.
- The **ribbon** contains five tabs used to accomplish various tasks on the computer related to organizing and managing the contents of the open window. This ribbon works similarly to the ribbon in the Office apps.
- The **navigation pane** on the left contains the Favorites area, Libraries area, Homegroup area, Computer area, and Network area.

To Create a Folder within a Folder

1 SIGN IN | 2 USE WINDOWS | 3 USE APPS | 4 FILE MANAGEMENT | 5 SWITCH APPS | 6 SAVE FILES
7 CHANGE SCREEN RESOLUTION | 8 EXIT APPS | 9 USE ADDITIONAL APP FEATURES | 10 USE HELP

With the class folder created, you can create folders that will store the files you create using Publisher. The following steps create a Publisher folder within the CIS 101 folder (or the folder identifying your class). ***Why?*** *To be able to organize your files, you should create a folder structure.* If you are using Windows 7, skip these steps and instead perform the steps in the yellow box that immediately follows these Windows 8 steps.

- Double-tap or double-click the icon or folder name for the CIS 101 folder (or the folder identifying your class) in the file list to open the folder (Figure 35).

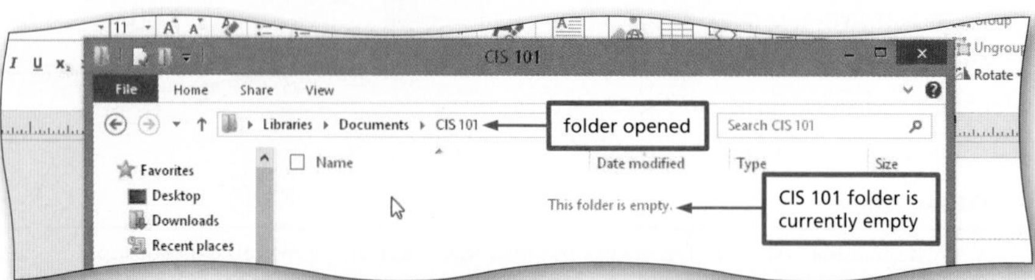

Figure 35

- Tap or click the New folder button on the Quick Access Toolbar to create a new folder within the current folder.
- Type `Publisher` in the text box as the new folder name.
- Press the ENTER key to rename the folder (Figure 36).

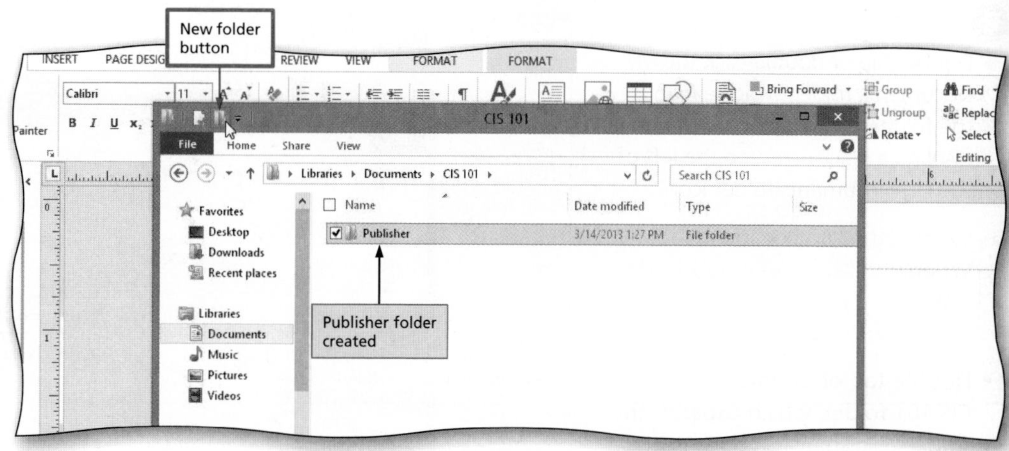

Figure 36

Other Ways

1. Press CTRL+SHIFT+N
2. Tap or click the New folder button (Home tab | New group)

To Create a Folder within a Folder Using Windows 7

If you are using Windows 7, perform these steps to create a folder within a folder instead of the previous steps that use Windows 8.

1. Double-click the icon or folder name for the CIS 101 folder (or the folder identifying your class) in the file list to open the folder.
2. Click the New folder button on the toolbar to display a new folder icon and text box for the folder.
3. Type `Publisher` in the text box to name the folder.
4. Press the ENTER key to create the folder.

To Expand a Folder, Scroll through Folder Contents, and Collapse a Folder

1 SIGN IN | 2 USE WINDOWS | 3 USE APPS | 4 FILE MANAGEMENT | 5 SWITCH APPS | 6 SAVE FILES | 7 CHANGE SCREEN RESOLUTION | 8 EXIT APPS | 9 USE ADDITIONAL APP FEATURES | 10 USE HELP

Folder windows display the hierarchy of items and the contents of drives and folders in the file list. You might want to expand a library or folder in the navigation pane to view its contents, slide or scroll through its contents, and collapse it when you are finished viewing its contents. ***Why?*** *When a folder is expanded, you can see all the folders it contains. By contrast, a collapsed folder hides the folders it contains.* The following steps expand, slide or scroll through, and then collapse the folder identifying your class (CIS 101, in this case).

- Double-tap or double-click the Documents library in the navigation pane, which expands the library to display its contents and displays a black arrow to the left of the Documents library icon (Figure 37).

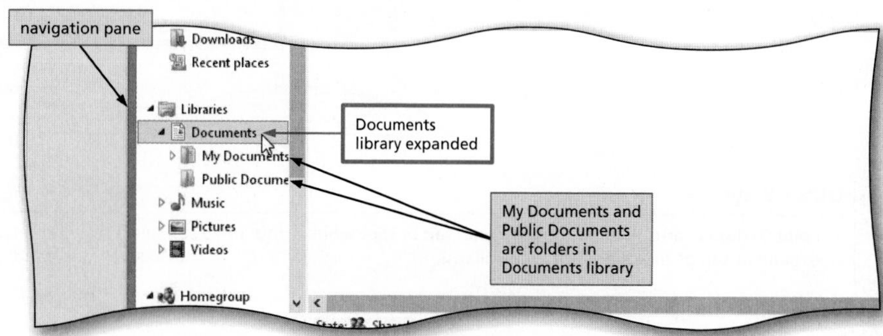

Figure 37

- Double-tap or double-click the My Documents folder, which expands the folder to display its contents and displays a black arrow to the left of the My Documents folder icon.

Q&A What is the My Documents folder?
When you save files on your hard disk, the My Documents folder is the default save location.

- Double-tap or double-click the CIS 101 folder, which expands the folder to display its contents and displays a black arrow to the left of the folder icon (Figure 38).

Experiment

- Slide the scroll bar down or click the down scroll arrow on the vertical scroll bar to display additional folders at the bottom of the navigation pane. Slide the scroll bar up or click the scroll bar above the scroll box to move the scroll box to the top of the navigation pane. Drag the scroll box down the scroll bar until the scroll box is halfway down the scroll bar.

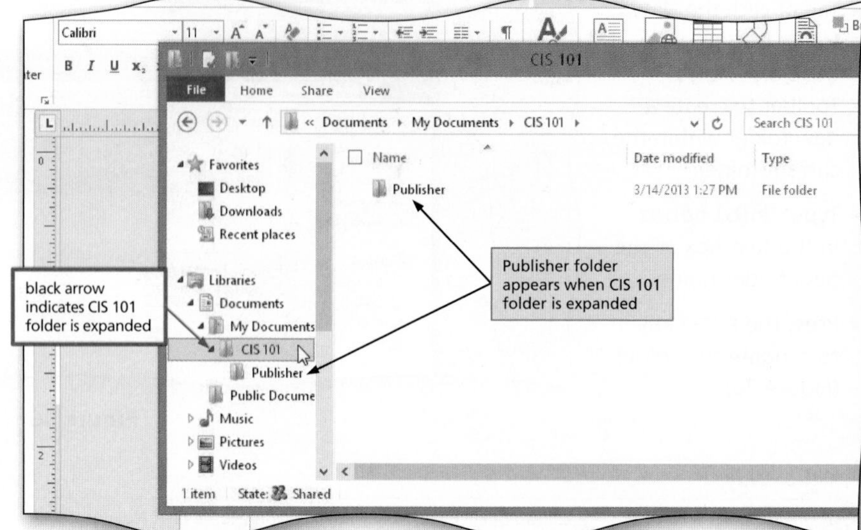

Figure 38

- Double-tap or double-click the folder identifying your class (CIS 101, in this case) to collapse the folder (Figure 39).

Q&A Why are some folders indented below others?
A folder contains the indented folders below it.

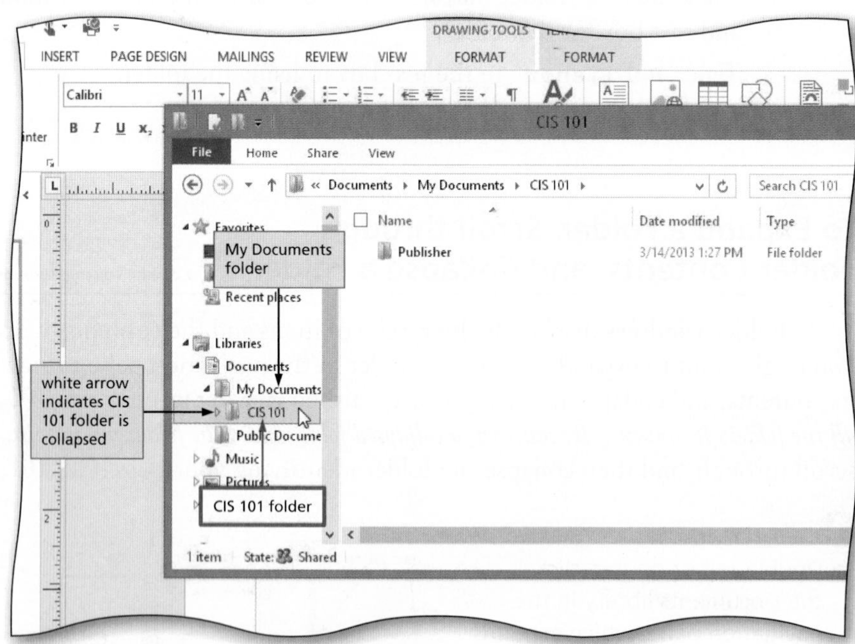

Figure 39

Other Ways

1. Point to display arrows in navigation pane, tap or click white arrow to expand or tap or click black arrow to collapse
2. Select folder to expand or collapse using arrow keys, press RIGHT ARROW to expand; press LEFT ARROW to collapse.

To Switch from One App to Another

You want to save the Publisher file containing the text you typed earlier. Publisher, however, currently is not the active window. You can use the app button on the taskbar and live preview to switch to Publisher.

Why? *By clicking the appropriate app button on the taskbar, you can switch to the open app you want to use.* The steps below switch to the Publisher window; however, the steps are the same for any active Office app currently displayed as an app button on the taskbar.

- If you are using a mouse, point to the Publisher app button on the taskbar to see a live preview of the open publication(s) or to see the window title(s) of the open publication(s), depending on your computer's configuration (Figure 40).

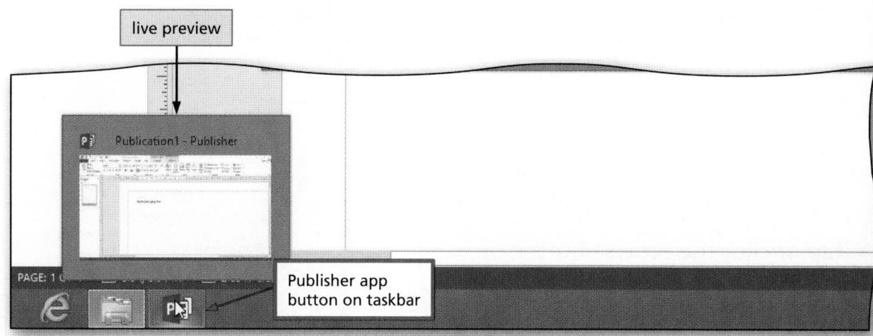

Figure 40

- Tap or click the Publisher app button or the live preview to make the app associated with the app button the active window (Figure 41).

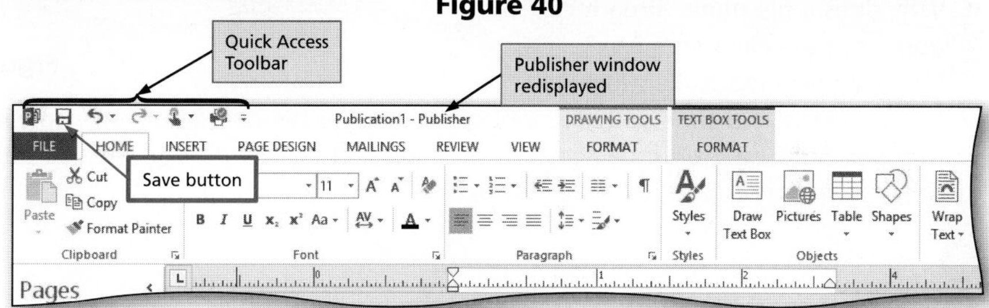

Figure 41

Q&A What if multiple documents are open in an app?
Tap or click the desired live preview to switch to the window you want to use.

To Save a File in a Folder

The following steps save a file in the Publisher folder contained in your class folder (CIS 101, in this case) using the file name, Book Club Event Flyer. ***Why?*** *Without saving a file, you may lose all the work you have completed and will be unable to reuse or share it with others later.*

- Tap or click the Save button (shown in Figure 41) on the Quick Access Toolbar, which depending on settings, will display either the Save As gallery in the Backstage view (Figure 42) or the Save As dialog box (Figure 43 on the next page).

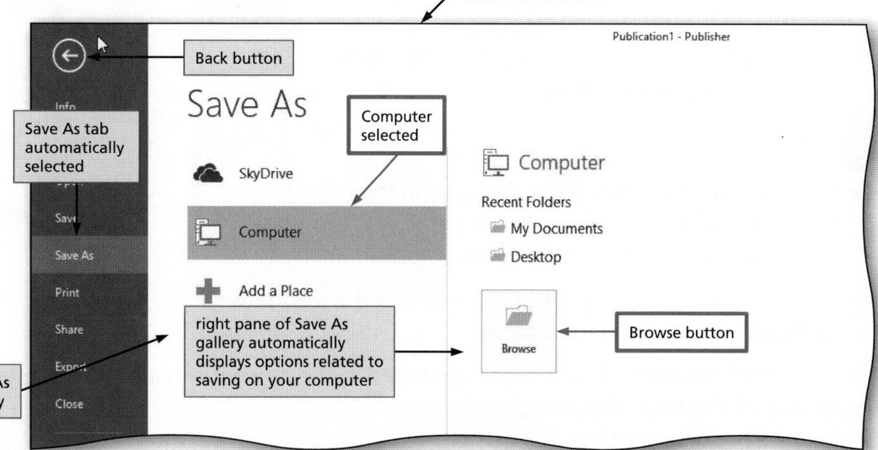

Figure 42

Q&A What is the Backstage view?
The **Backstage view** contains a set of commands that enable you to manage documents and data about the documents.

What if the Save As gallery is not displayed in the Backstage view?
Tap or click the Save As tab to display the Save As gallery.

How do I close the Backstage view?
Tap or click the Back button in the upper-left corner of the Backstage view to return to the Publisher window.

2

- If your screen displays the Backstage view, tap or click Computer, if necessary, to display options in the right pane related to saving on your computer; if your screen already displays the Save As dialog box, proceed to Step 3.

Q&A What if I wanted to save on SkyDrive instead?
You would tap or click SkyDrive. Saving on SkyDrive is discussed in a later section in this chapter.

- Tap or click the Browse button in the right pane to display the Save As dialog box (Figure 43).

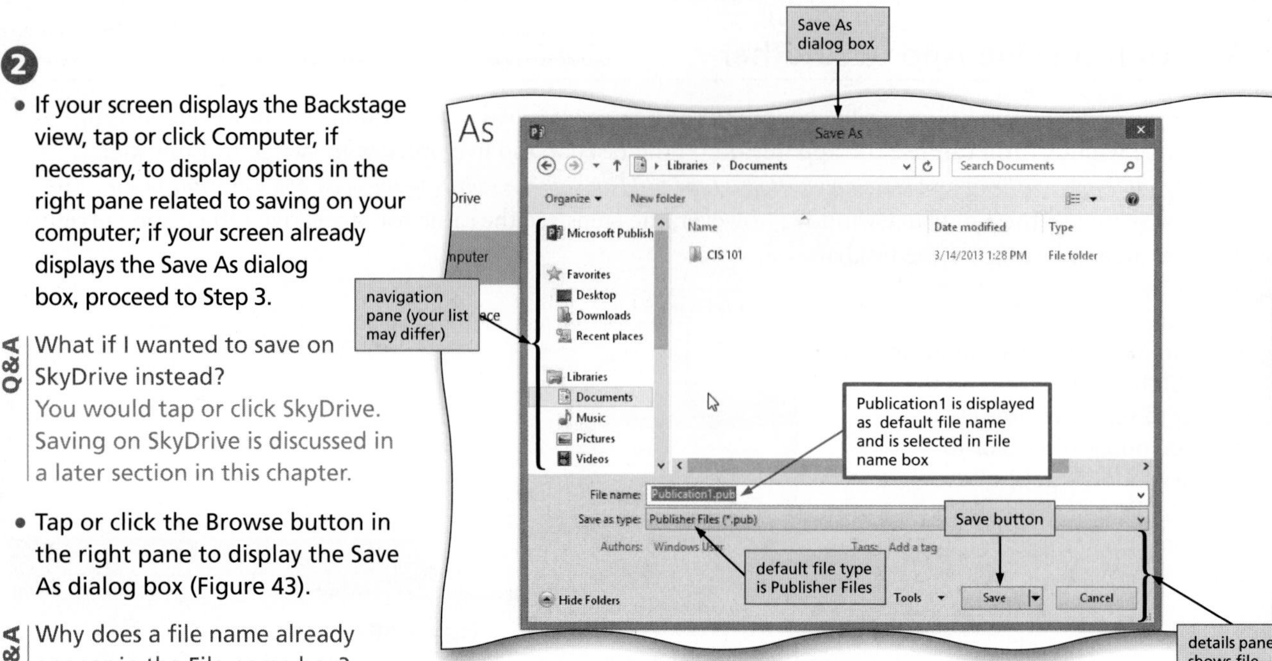

Figure 43

Q&A Why does a file name already appear in the File name box?
Publisher automatically suggests a file name the first time you save a publication. The file name normally consists of the word, Publisher, followed by a number. Because the suggested file name is selected, you do not need to delete it; as soon as you begin typing, the new file name replaces the selected text.

- Type `Book Club Event Flyer` in the File name box (Save As dialog box) to change the file name. Do not press the ENTER key after typing the file name because you do not want to close the dialog box at this time (Figure 44).

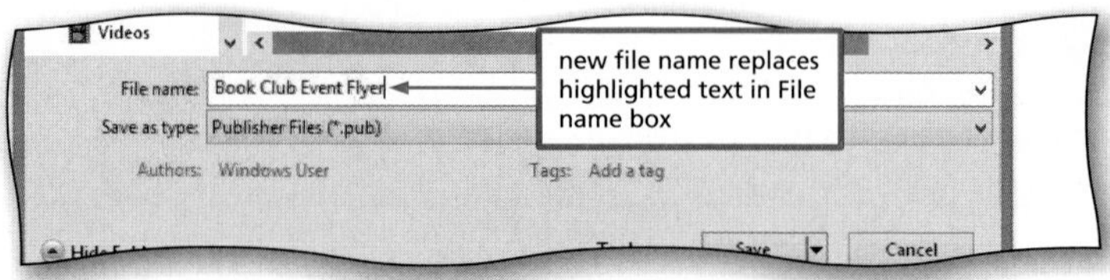

Figure 44

Q&A What characters can I use in a file name?
The only invalid characters are the backslash (\), slash (/), colon (:), asterisk (*), question mark (?), quotation mark ("), less than symbol (<), greater than symbol (>), and vertical bar (|).

4

- Navigate to the desired save location (in this case, the Publisher folder in the CIS 101 folder [or your class folder] in the My Documents folder in the Documents library) by performing the tasks in Steps 4a and 4b.

- If the Documents library is not displayed in the navigation pane, slide to scroll or drag the scroll bar in the navigation pane until Documents appears.

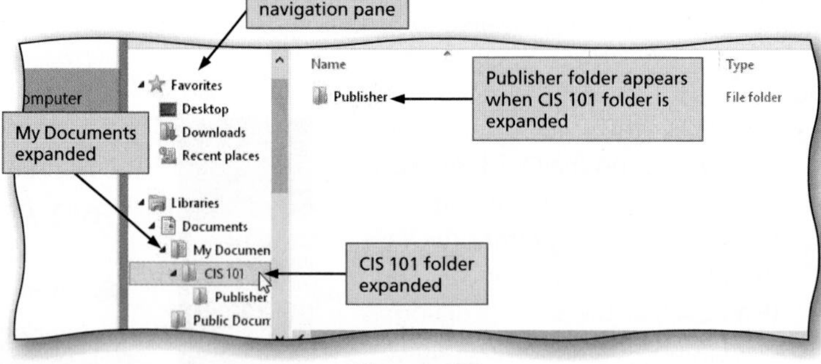

Figure 45

- If the Documents library is not expanded in the navigation pane, double-tap or double-click Documents to display its folders in the navigation pane.
- If the My Documents folder is not expanded in the navigation pane, double-tap or double-click My Documents to display its folders in the navigation pane.
- If your class folder (CIS 101, in this case) is not expanded, double-tap or double-click the CIS 101 folder to select the folder and display its contents in the navigation pane (Figure 45).

Q&A What if I do not want to save in a folder?
Although storing files in folders is an effective technique for organizing files, some users prefer not to store files in folders. If you prefer not to save this file in a folder, select the storage device on which you wish to save the file and then proceed to Step 5.

- Tap or click the Publisher folder in the navigation pane to select it as the new save location and display its contents in the file list (Figure 46).

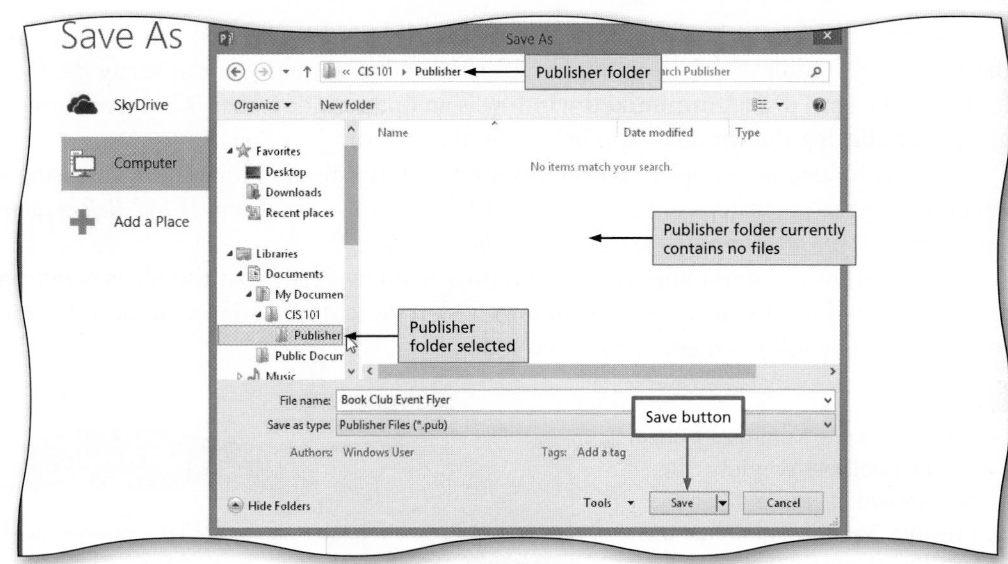

Figure 46

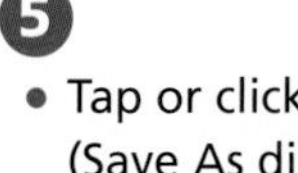

- Tap or click the Save button (Save As dialog box) to save the publication in the selected folder in the selected location with the entered file name (Figure 47).

Q&A How do I know that the file is saved?

While an Office app such as Publisher is saving a file, it briefly displays a message on the status bar indicating the amount of the file saved. In addition, the file name appears on the title bar.

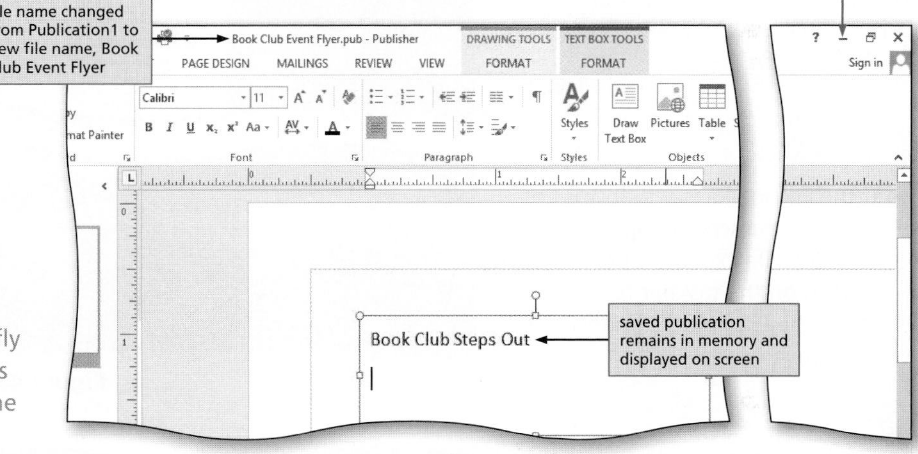

Figure 47

Other Ways

1. Tap or click FILE on ribbon, tap or click Save As in Backstage view, tap or click Computer, tap or click Browse button, type file name (Save As dialog box), navigate to desired save location, tap or click Save button
2. Press F12, type file name (Save As dialog box), navigate to desired save location, tap or click Save button

Navigating in Dialog Boxes

Navigating is the process of finding a location on a storage device. While saving the Book Club Event Flyer file, for example, Steps 4a and 4b in the previous set of steps navigated to the Publisher folder located in the CIS 101 folder in the My Documents folder in the Documents library. When performing certain functions in Windows apps, such as saving a file, opening a file, or inserting a picture in an existing document, you most likely will have to navigate to the location where you want to save the file or to the folder containing the file you want to open or insert. Most dialog boxes in Windows apps requiring navigation follow a similar procedure; that is, the way you navigate to a folder in one dialog box, such as the Save As dialog box, is similar to how you might navigate in another dialog box, such as the Open dialog box. If you chose to navigate to a specific location in a dialog box, you would follow the instructions in Steps 4a and 4b.

To Minimize and Restore a Window

Before continuing, you can verify that the Publisher file was saved properly. To do this, you will minimize the Publisher window and then open the CIS 101 window so that you can verify the file is stored in the CIS 101 folder on the hard disk. A **minimized window** is an open window that is hidden from view but can be displayed quickly by clicking the window's app button on the taskbar.

In the following example, Publisher is used to illustrate minimizing and restoring windows; however, you would follow the same steps regardless of the Office app you are using. ***Why?*** *Before closing an app, you should make sure your file saved correctly so that you can find it later.*

The following steps minimize the Publisher window, verify that the file is saved, and then restore the minimized window. If you are using Windows 7, skip these steps and instead perform the steps in the yellow box that immediately follows these Windows 8 steps.

- Tap or click the Minimize button on the Publisher window title bar (shown in Figure 47 on the previous page) to minimize the window (Figure 48).

Q&A Is the minimized window still available?
The minimized window, Publisher in this case, remains available but no longer is the active window. It is minimized as an app button on the taskbar.

- If the File Explorer window is not open on the screen, tap or click the File Explorer app button on the taskbar to make the File folder window the active window.

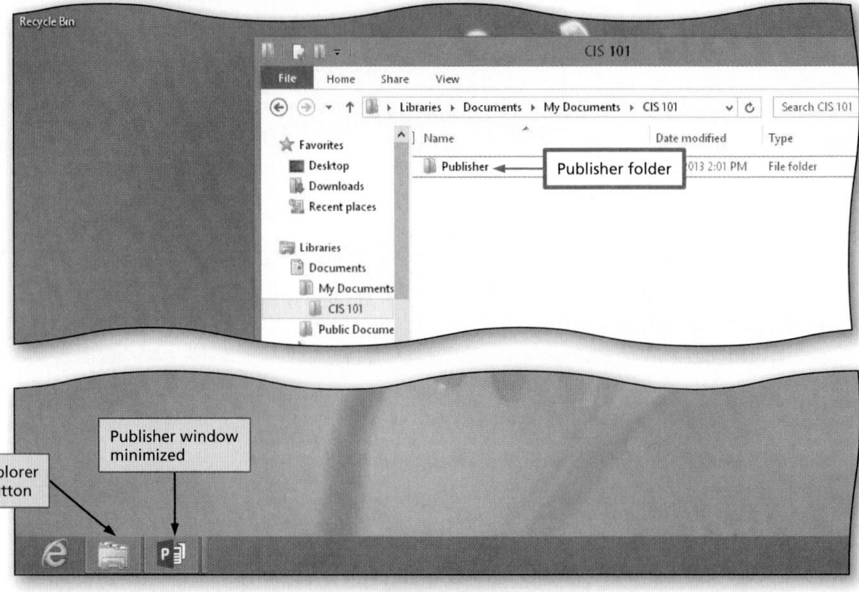

Figure 48

- Double-tap or double-click the Publisher folder in the file list to select the folder and display its contents (Figure 49).

Q&A Why does the File Explorer app button on the taskbar change?
A selected app button indicates that the app is active on the screen. When the button is not selected, the app is running but not active.

- After viewing the contents of the selected folder, tap or click the Publisher app button on the taskbar to restore the minimized window.

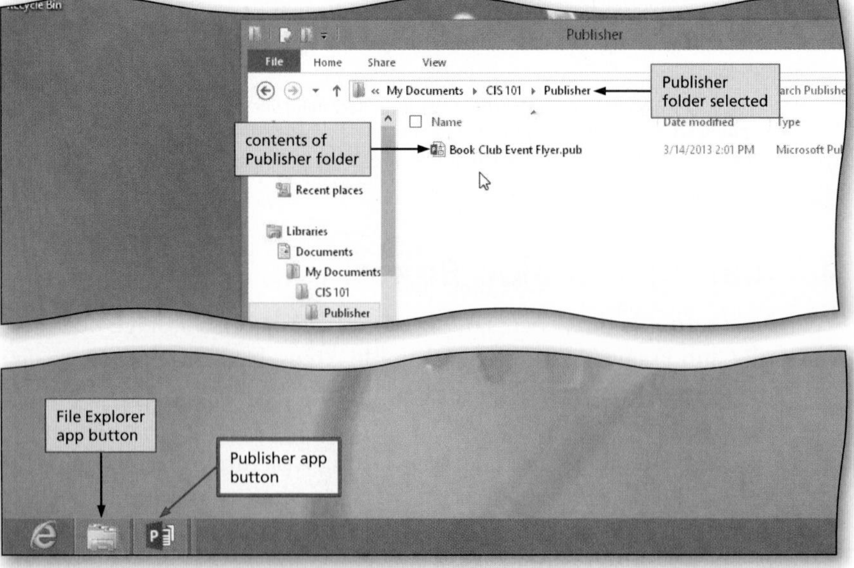

Figure 49

Other Ways

1. Press and hold or right-click title bar, tap or click Minimize on shortcut menu, tap or click taskbar button in taskbar button area
2. Press WINDOWS+M, press WINDOWS+SHIFT+M

To Minimize and Restore a Window Using Windows 7

If you are using Windows 7, perform these steps to minimize and restore a window instead of the previous steps that use Windows 8.

1. Click the Minimize button on the app's title bar to minimize the window.
2. If the Windows Explorer window is not open on the screen, click the Windows Explorer button on the taskbar to make the Windows Explorer window the active window.
3. Double-click the Publisher folder in the file list to select the folder and display its contents.
4. After viewing the contents of the selected folder, click the Publisher button on the taskbar to restore the minimized window.

To Save a File on SkyDrive

One of the features of Office is the capability to save files on SkyDrive so that you can use the files on multiple computers without having to use external storage devices such as a USB flash drive. Storing files on SkyDrive also enables you to share files more efficiently with others, such as when using Office Web Apps and Office 365.

In the following example, Publisher is used to save a file to SkyDrive. ***Why?*** *Storing files on SkyDrive provides more portability options than are available from storing files in the Documents library.*

You can save files directly to SkyDrive from within Word, PowerPoint, Publisher, and Excel. The following steps save the current Publisher file to the SkyDrive. These steps require you have a Microsoft account and an Internet connection.

1

- With the Publisher window active, tap or click FILE on the ribbon to open the Backstage view (Figure 50).

Q&A What is the purpose of the FILE tab?
The FILE tab opens the Backstage view for each Office app, including Publisher.

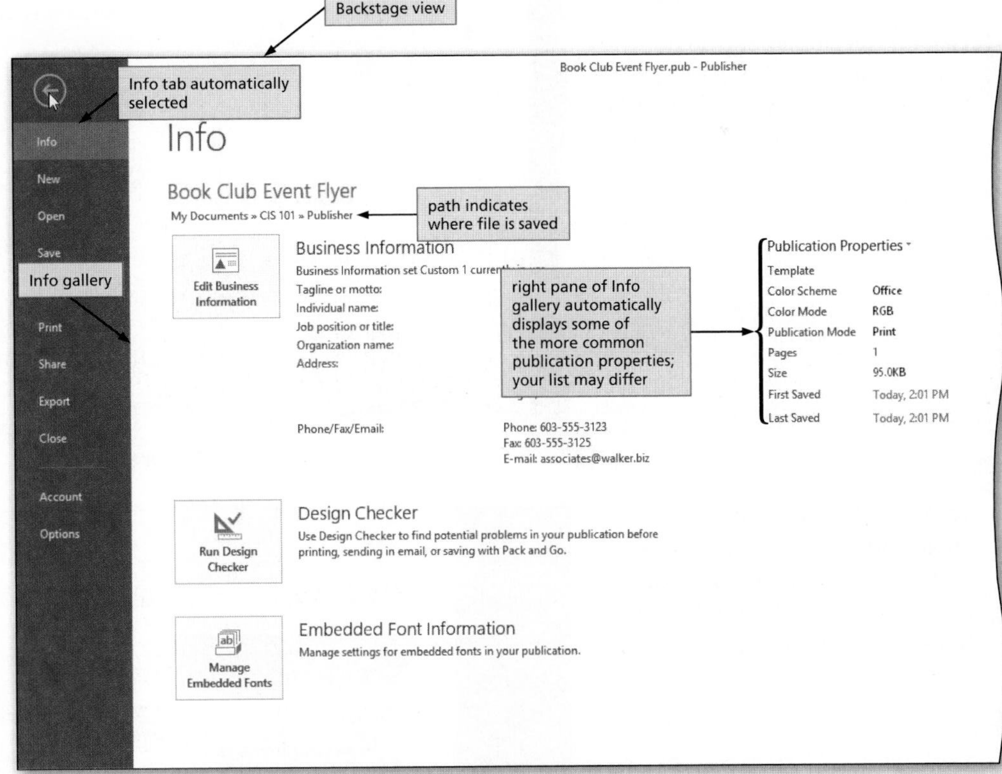

Figure 50

2

- Tap or click the Save As tab in the Backstage view to display the Save As gallery.
- Tap or click SkyDrive to display SkyDrive saving options or a Sign in button, if you are not signed in already to your Microsoft account (Figure 51).

Q&A What if my Save As gallery does not display SkyDrive as a save location?

Tap or click 'Add a Place' and proceed to Step 3.

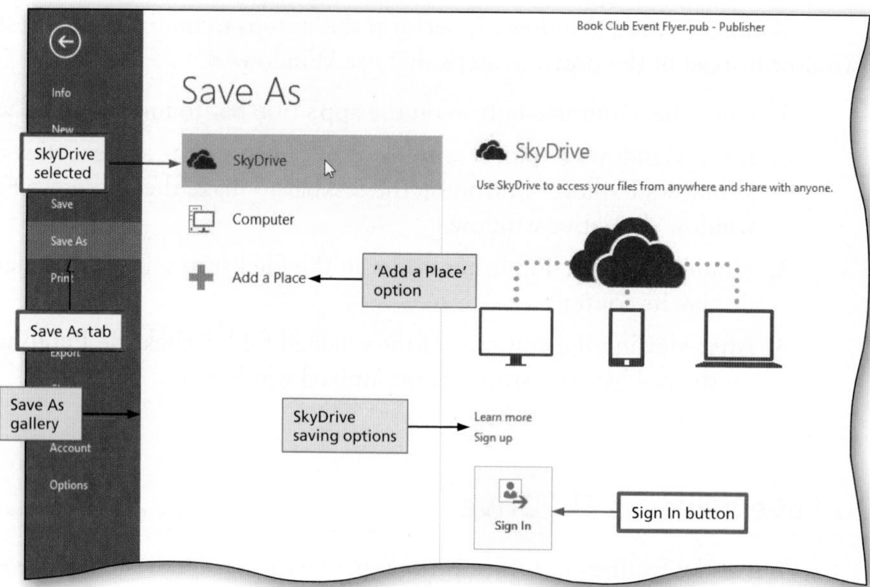

Figure 51

- If your screen displays a Next button, enter your email address and then click the Next button.
- If your screen displays a Sign in button, tap or click it to display the Sign in dialog box (Figure 52).

Q&A What if the Sign in button does not appear?

If you already are signed into your Microsoft account, the Sign in button will not be displayed. In this case, proceed to Step 5.

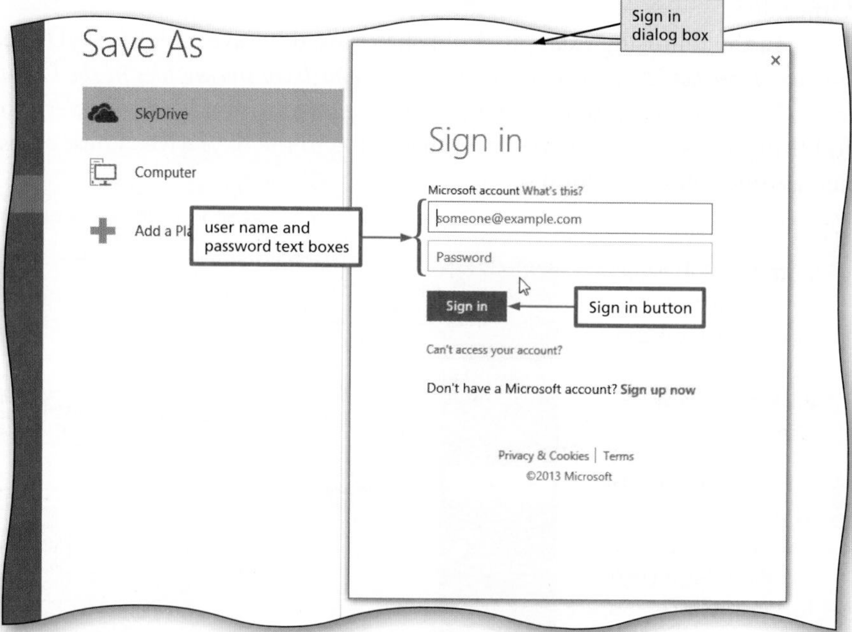

Figure 52

- Type your Microsoft account email address (or user name and password) in the text boxes and then tap or click the Sign in button (Sign in dialog box) to sign in to SkyDrive.

- Tap or click your SkyDrive to select your SkyDrive as the storage location (Figure 53).

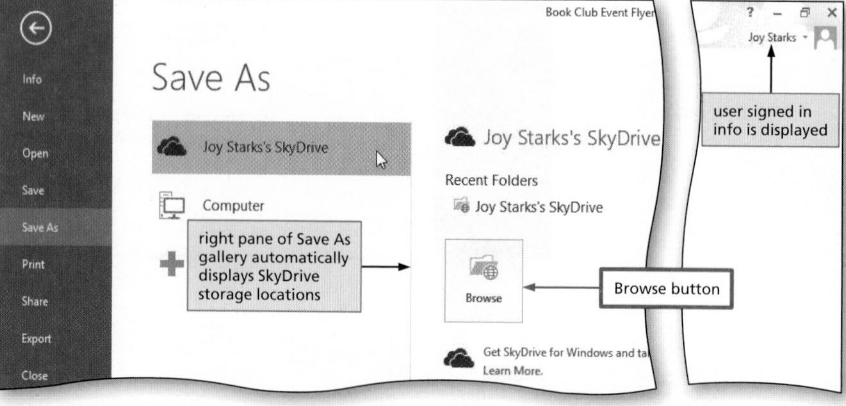

Figure 53

6

- Tap or click the Browse button to contact the SkyDrive server (which may take some time, depending on the speed of your Internet connection). The Save As dialog box will display (Figure 54).

Why does the path in the address bar contain various letters and numbers?
The letters and numbers in the address bar uniquely identify the location of your SkyDrive files and folders.

7

- Tap or click the Save button (Save As dialog box) to save the file on SkyDrive.

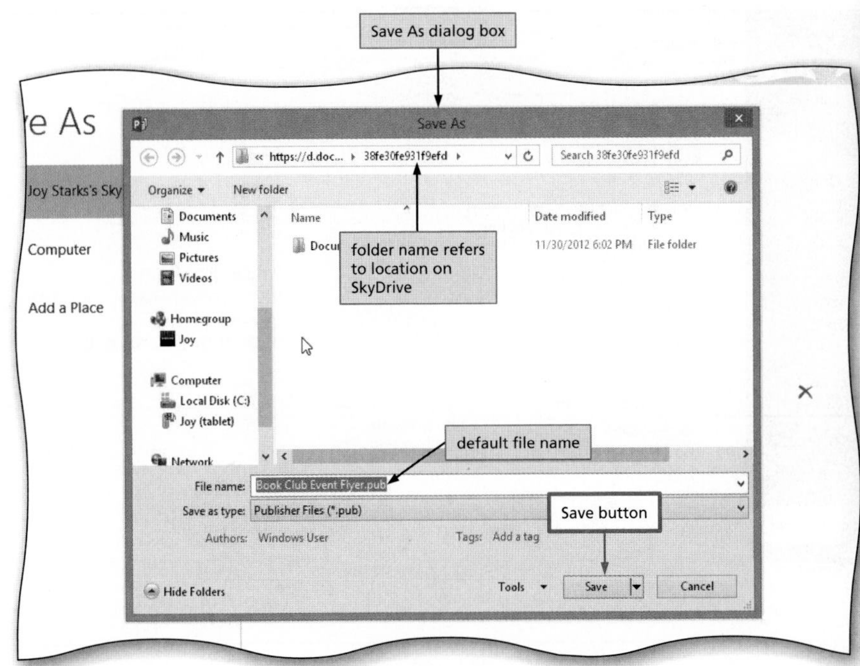

Figure 54

To Sign Out of a Microsoft Account

If you are using a public computer or otherwise wish to sign out of your Microsoft account, you should sign out of the account from the Accounts gallery in the Backstage view. Signing out of the account is the safest way to make sure that nobody else can access online files or settings stored in your Microsoft account. ***Why?*** *For security reasons, you should sign out of your Microsoft account when you are finished using a public or shared computer. Staying signed in to your Microsoft account might enable others to access your files.*

The following steps sign out of a Microsoft account from Publisher. You would use the same steps in any Office app. If you do not wish to sign out of your Microsoft account, read these steps without performing them.

1. Tap or click FILE on the ribbon to open the Backstage view.
2. Tap or click the Account tab to display the Account gallery (Figure 55).
3. Tap or click the Sign out link, which displays the Remove Account dialog box. If a Can't remove Windows accounts dialog box appears instead of the Remove Account dialog box, click the OK button and skip the remaining steps.

   Q&A: Why does a Can't remove Windows accounts dialog box appear?
   If you signed in to Windows using your Microsoft account, then you also must sign out from Windows, rather than signing out from within Publisher. When you are finished using Windows, be sure to sign out at that time.

4. Tap or click the Yes button (Remove Account dialog box) to sign out of your Microsoft account on this computer.

   Q&A: Should I sign out of Windows after removing my Microsoft account?
   When you are finished using the computer, you should sign out of Windows for maximum security.

5. Tap or click the Back button in the upper-left corner of the Backstage view to return to the publication.

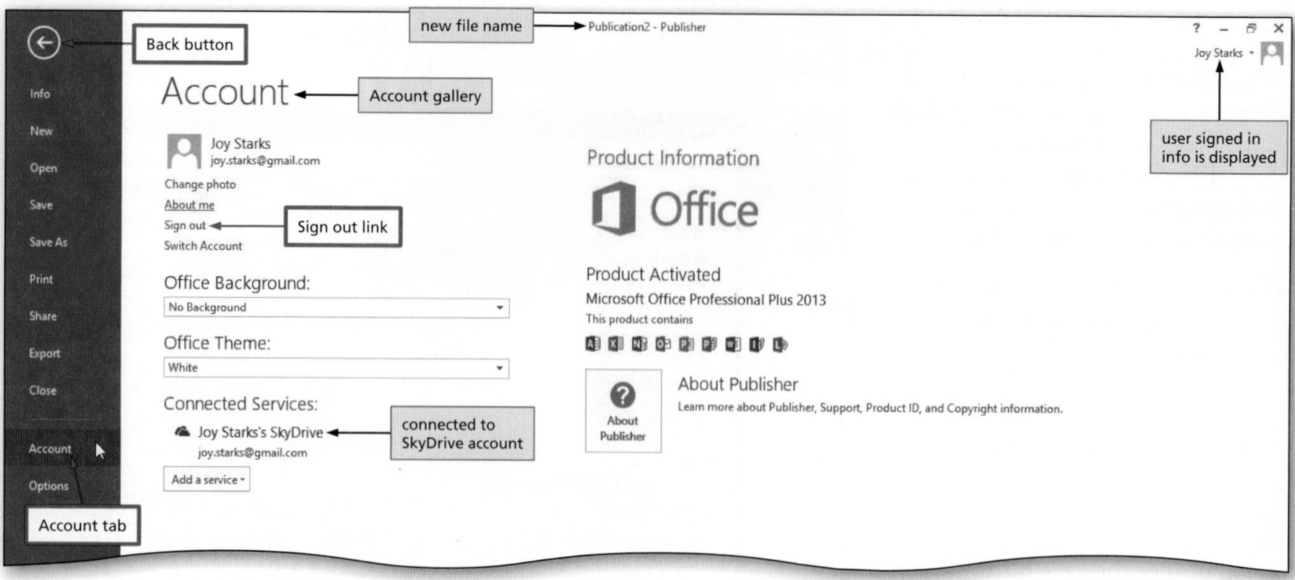

Figure 55

Screen Resolution

Screen resolution indicates the number of pixels (dots) that the computer uses to display the letters, numbers, graphics, and background you see on the screen. When you increase the screen resolution, Windows displays more information on the screen, but the information decreases in size. The reverse also is true: as you decrease the screen resolution, Windows displays less information on the screen, but the information increases in size.

Screen resolution usually is stated as the product of two numbers, such as 1366 × 768 (pronounced "thirteen sixty-six by seven sixty-eight"). A 1366 × 768 screen resolution results in a display of 1366 distinct pixels on each of 768 lines, or about 1,050,624 pixels. Changing the screen resolution affects how the ribbon appears in Office apps and some Windows dialog boxes. Figure 56, for example, shows the Publisher ribbon at screen resolutions of 1366 × 768 and 1024 × 768. All of the same commands are available regardless of screen resolution. The app (Publisher, in this case), however, makes changes to the groups and the buttons within the groups to accommodate the various screen resolutions. The result is that certain commands may need to be accessed differently depending on the resolution chosen. A command that is visible on the ribbon and available by tapping or clicking a button at one resolution may not be visible and may need to be accessed using its Dialog Box Launcher at a different resolution.

Comparing the two ribbons in Figure 56, notice the changes in content and layout of the groups and galleries. In some cases, the content of a group is the same in each resolution, but the layout of the group differs. For example, the same gallery and buttons appear in the Styles groups in the two resolutions, but the layouts differ. In other cases, the content and layout are the same across the resolution, but the level of detail differs with the resolution.

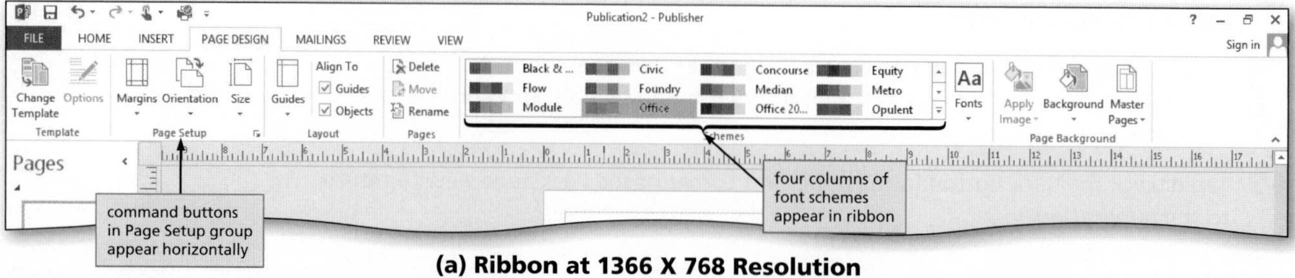

(a) Ribbon at 1366 X 768 Resolution

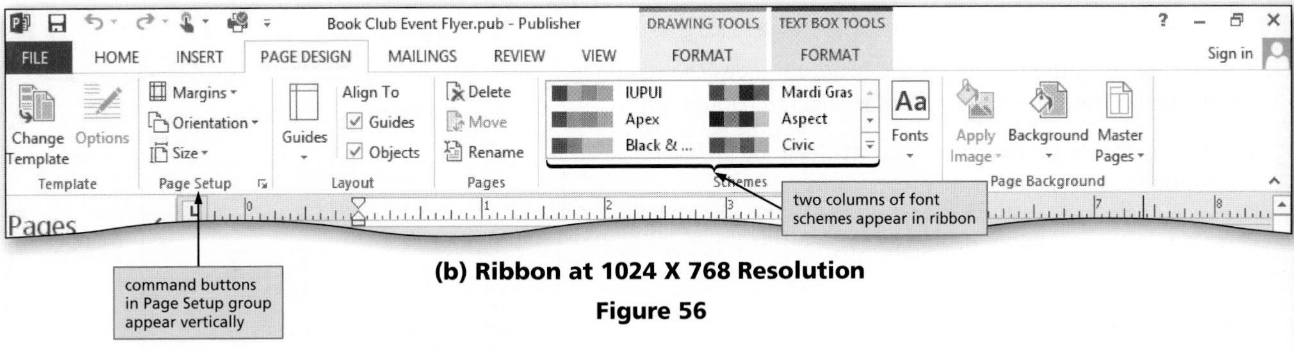

(b) Ribbon at 1024 X 768 Resolution

Figure 56

To Change the Screen Resolution

1 SIGN IN | 2 USE WINDOWS | 3 USE APPS | 4 FILE MANAGEMENT | 5 SWITCH APPS | 6 SAVE FILES
7 CHANGE SCREEN RESOLUTION | 8 EXIT APPS | 9 USE ADDITIONAL APP FEATURES | 10 USE HELP

If you are using a computer to step through the chapters in this book and you want your screen to match the figures, you may need to change your screen's resolution. ***Why?*** *The figures in this book use a screen resolution of 1366 × 768.* The following steps change the screen resolution to 1366 × 768. Your computer already may be set to 1366 × 768. Keep in mind that many computer labs prevent users from changing the screen resolution; in that case, read the following steps for illustration purposes.

1

- Tap or click the Show desktop button, which is located at the far-right edge of the taskbar, to display the Windows desktop.

Q&A I cannot see the Show desktop button. Why not?
When you point to the far-right edge of the taskbar, a small outline appears to mark the Show desktop button.

- Press and hold or right-click an empty area on the Windows desktop to display a shortcut menu that contains a list of commands related to the desktop (Figure 57).

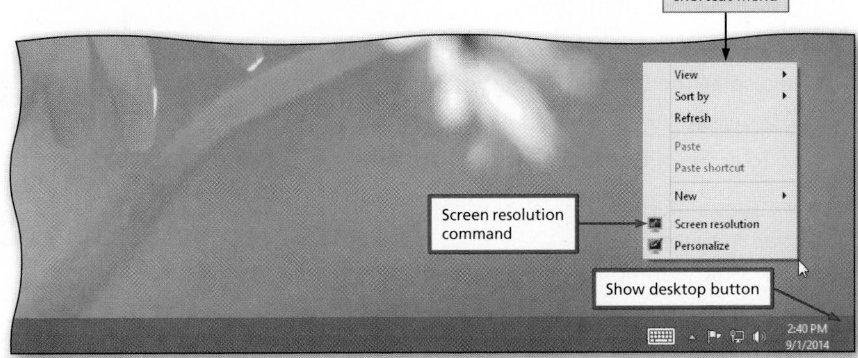

Figure 57

Q&A Why does my shortcut menu display different commands?
Depending on your computer's hardware and configuration, different commands might appear on the shortcut menu.

2

- Tap or click Screen resolution on the shortcut menu to open the Screen Resolution window (Figure 58).

3

- Tap or click the Resolution button in the Screen Resolution window to display the resolution slider.

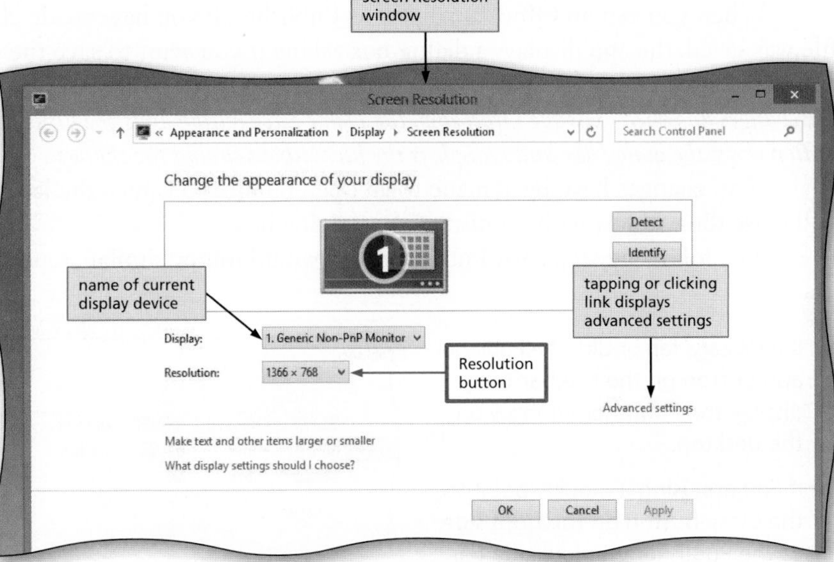

Figure 58

- If necessary, drag the resolution slider until the desired screen resolution (in this case, 1366 × 768) is selected (Figure 59).

Q&A What if my computer does not support the 1366 × 768 resolution?
Some computers do not support the 1366 ×768 resolution. In this case, select a resolution that is close to the 1366 × 768 resolution.

What is a slider?
A **slider** is an object that allows users to choose from multiple predetermined options. In most cases, these options represent some type of numeric value. In most cases, one end of the slider (usually the left or bottom) represents the lowest of available values, and the opposite end (usually the right or top) represents the highest available value.

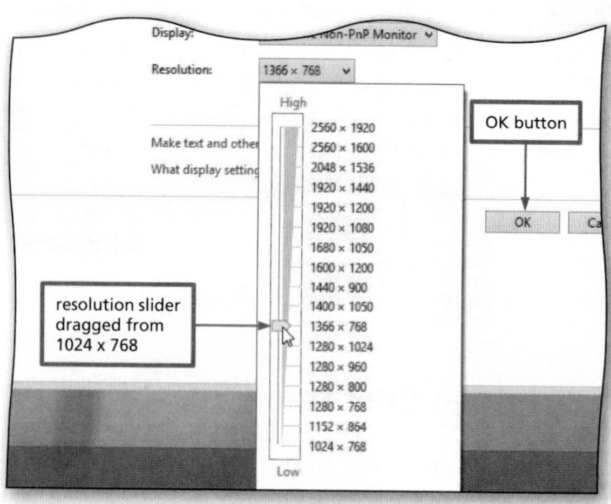

Figure 59

- Tap or click an empty area of the Screen Resolution window to close the resolution slider.
- Tap or click the OK button to change the screen resolution and display the Display Settings dialog box (Figure 60).
- Tap or click the Keep changes button (Display Settings dialog box) to accept the new screen resolution.

Q&A Why does a message display stating that the image quality can be improved?
Some computer monitors or screens are designed to display contents better at a certain screen resolution, sometimes referred to as an optimal resolution.

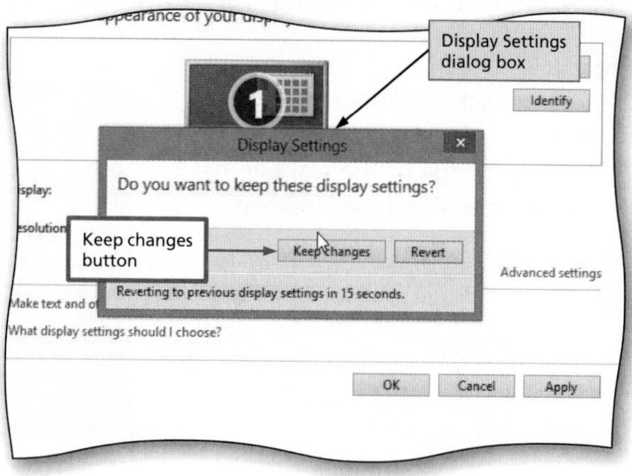

Figure 60

To Exit an App with One Document Open

1 SIGN IN | 2 USE WINDOWS | 3 USE APPS | 4 FILE MANAGEMENT | 5 SWITCH APPS | 6 SAVE FILES
7 CHANGE SCREEN RESOLUTION | **8 EXIT APPS** | **9 USE ADDITIONAL APP FEATURES** | **10 USE HELP**

When you exit an Office app, such as Publisher, if you have made changes to a file since the last time the file was saved, the app displays a dialog box asking if you want to save the changes you made to the file before it closes the app window. ***Why?*** *The dialog box contains three buttons with these resulting actions: the Save button saves the changes and then exits the Office app, the Don't Save button exits the Office app without saving changes, and the Cancel button closes the dialog box and redisplays the file without saving the changes.*

If no changes have been made to an open publication since the last time the file was saved, the Office app will close the window without displaying a dialog box.

The following steps exit Publisher. You would follow similar steps in other Office apps.

- If necessary, tap or click the Publisher app button on the taskbar to display the Publisher window on the desktop.
- If you are using a mouse, point to the Close button on the right side of the Publisher window title bar (Figure 61).

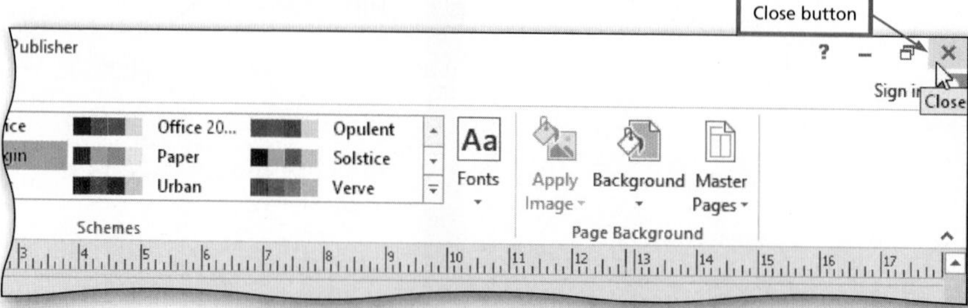

Figure 61

2

- Tap or click the Close button to close the publication and exit Publisher.

Q&A What if I have more than one publication open in Publisher?
You could click the Close button for each open publication. When you click the last open publication Close button, you also exit Publisher. As an alternative that is more efficient, you could press and hold or right-click the Publisher app button on the taskbar and then tap or click 'Close all windows' on the shortcut menu to close all open publications and exit Publisher.

3

- If a Microsoft Publisher dialog box appears, tap or click the Save button to save any changes made to the publication since the last save.

Other Ways

1. Press and hold or right-click the Publisher app button on Windows taskbar, click 'Close all windows' on shortcut menu
2. Press ALT+F4

To Copy a Folder to a USB Flash Drive

1 SIGN IN | 2 USE WINDOWS | 3 USE APPS | **4 FILE MANAGEMENT** | 5 SWITCH APPS | 6 SAVE FILES
7 CHANGE SCREEN RESOLUTION | 8 EXIT APPS | **9 USE ADDITIONAL APP FEATURES** | **10 USE HELP**

To store files and folders on a USB flash drive, you must connect the USB flash drive to an available USB port on a computer. The following steps copy your CIS 101 folder to a USB flash drive. ***Why?*** *It often is good practice to have a backup of your files. Besides SkyDrive, you can save files to a portable storage device, such as a USB flash drive.* If you are using Windows 7, skip these steps and instead perform the steps in the yellow box that immediately follows these Windows 8 steps.

- Insert a USB flash drive in an available USB port on the computer to connect the USB flash drive.

Q&A How can I ensure the USB flash drive is connected?
In File Explorer, you can use the navigation bar to find the USB flash drive. If it is not showing, then it is not connected properly.

- Tap or click the File Explorer app button on the taskbar to make the folder window the active window.

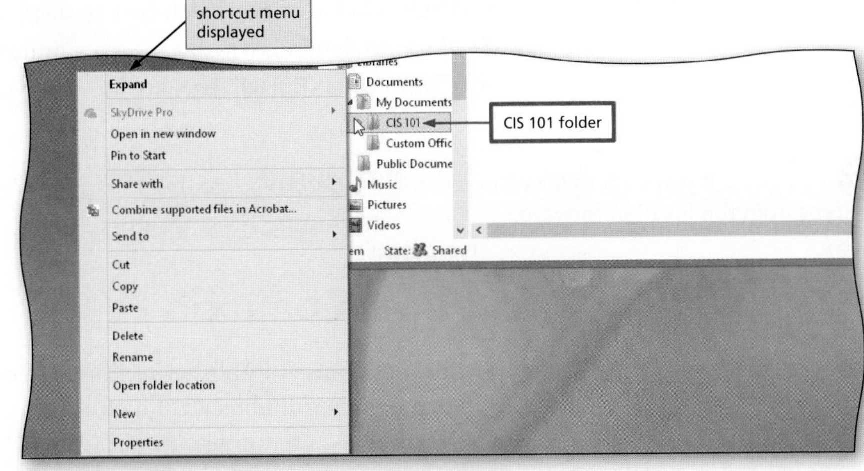

Figure 62

- If necessary, navigate to the CIS 101 folder in the File Explorer window (see Step 4a on page OFF 30 for instructions about navigating to a folder location).
- Press and hold or right-click the CIS 101 folder to display a shortcut menu (Figure 62).

3

- Tap or click Send to, which causes a submenu to appear (Figure 63).

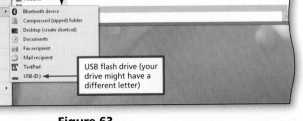

Figure 63

- Tap or click the USB flash drive to copy the folder to the USB flash drive (Figure 64).

Q&A Why does the drive letter of my USB flash drive differ?
Windows assigns the next available drive letter to your USB flash drive when you connect it. The next available drive letter may vary by computer, depending on the number of storage devices that currently are connected.

Figure 64

To Copy a Folder to a USB Flash Drive Using Windows 7

If you are using Windows 7, perform these steps to copy a folder to a USB flash drive instead of the previous steps that use Windows 8.

1. Insert a USB flash drive in an available USB port on the computer to open the AutoPlay window.
2. Click the 'Open folder to view files' link in the AutoPlay window to open the Windows Explorer window.
3. Navigate to the Documents library.
4. Right-click the CIS 101 folder to display a shortcut menu.
5. Point to Send to, which causes a submenu to appear.
6. Click the USB flash drive to copy the folder to the USB flash drive.

Break Point: If you wish to take a break, this is a good place to do so. To resume at a later time, continue to follow the steps from this location forward.

BTW
The Charms Bar
When you swipe in from the right edge of the screen or point to the upper-right edge of your screen, Windows displays the **Charms bar** with commands to help you use and manage the operating system. The Charms bar contains five buttons: Search, Share, Start, Devices, and Settings.

Additional Common Features of Office Apps

The previous section used Publisher to illustrate common features of Office and some basic elements unique to Publisher. The following sections continue to use Publisher to present additional common features of Office.

In the following pages, you will learn how to do the following:

1. Use the Charms bar.
2. Run Publisher using the search box.
3. Open a publication in Publisher.
4. Close the publication.
5. Reopen the publication just closed.
6. Create a blank Publisher publication from Windows Explorer and then open the file.
7. Save a publication with a new file name.

To Run an App Using the Search Box

1 SIGN IN | 2 USE WINDOWS | 3 USE APPS | 4 FILE MANAGEMENT | 5 SWITCH APPS | 6 SAVE FILES | 7 CHANGE SCREEN RESOLUTION | 8 EXIT APPS | **9 USE ADDITIONAL APP FEATURES** | **10 USE HELP**

The following steps, which assume Windows is running, use the search box to run Publisher based on a typical installation; however, you would follow similar steps to run any app. ***Why?*** *Sometimes an app does not appear on the Start screen, so you can find it quickly by searching.* You may need to ask your instructor how to run apps for your computer. If you are using Windows 7, skip these steps and instead perform the steps in the yellow box that immediately follows these Windows 8 steps.

1

- Swipe in from the right edge of the screen or point to the upper-right corner of the screen to display the Charms bar (Figure 65).

Q&A My Charms bar looks different. Did I do something wrong?
If you swipe in from the right edge of the screen, the Charms bar displays buttons on a black background with white labels.

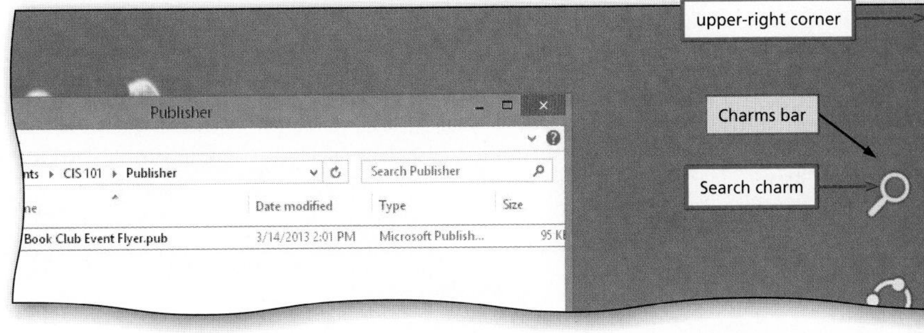

Figure 65

2

- Tap or click the Search charm on the Charms bar to display the Search menu (Figure 66).

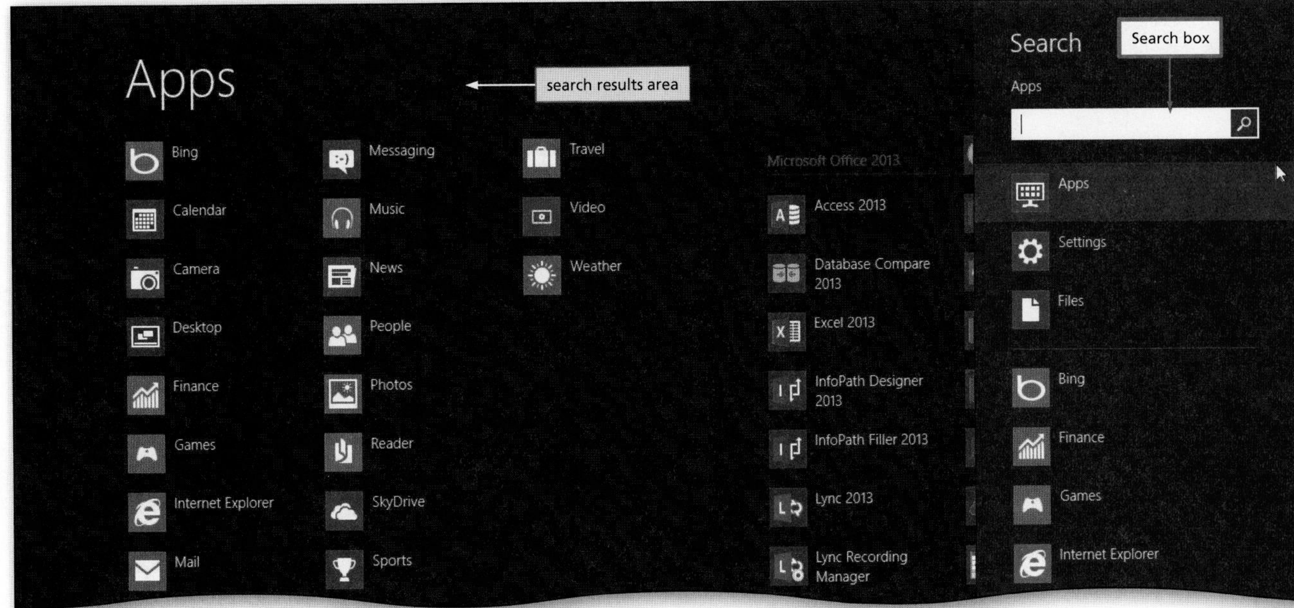

Figure 66

3

- Type `Publisher 2013` as the search text in the Search box and watch the search results appear in the Apps list (Figure 67).

Q&A Do I need to type the complete app name or use correct capitalization?
No, you need to type just enough characters of the app name for it to appear in the Apps list. For example, you may be able to type Publisher or publisher, instead of Publisher 2013.

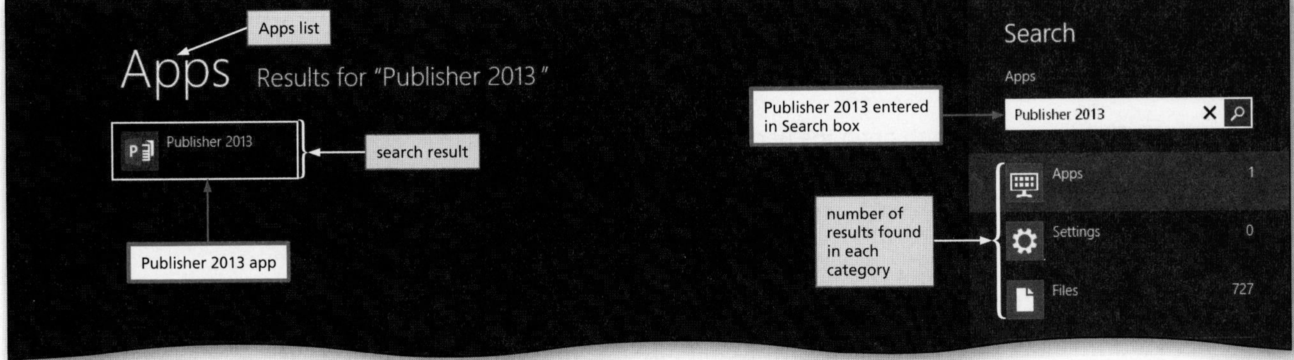

Figure 67

- Tap or click Publisher 2013 in the search results to run Publisher.
- Tap or click the Blank 8.5 × 11" thumbnail to create a blank publication and display it in the Publisher window.
- If the Publisher window is not maximized, tap or click the Maximize button on its title bar to maximize the window (Figure 68).

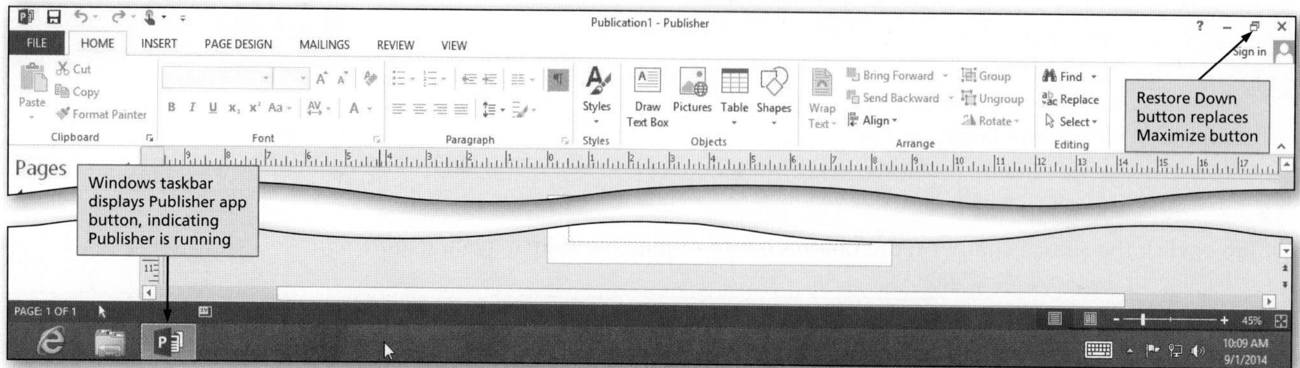

Figure 68

To Run an App Using the Search Box Using Windows 7

If you are using Windows 7, perform these steps to run an app using the search box instead of the previous steps that use Windows 8.

1. Click the Start button on the Windows 7 taskbar to display the Start menu.
2. Type **Publisher 2013** as the search text in the 'Search programs and files' text box and watch the search results appear on the Start menu.
3. Click Publisher 2013 in the search results on the Start menu to run Publisher.
4. Click the Blank 8.5 × 11" thumbnail to create a blank publication and display it in the Publisher window.
5. If the Publisher window is not maximized, click the Maximize button on its title bar to maximize the window.

To Open an Existing File

As discussed earlier, the Backstage view contains a set of commands that enable you to manage publication and data about the publication. ***Why?*** *From the Backstage view in Publisher, for example, you can create, open, print, and save publication. You also can share publication, manage versions, set permissions, and modify publication properties. In other Office 2013 apps, the Backstage view may contain features specific to those apps.* The following steps open a saved file, specifically the Book Club Event Flyer file, that recently was saved.

- Tap or click FILE on the ribbon to open the Backstage view and then tap or click Open in the Backstage view to display the Open gallery in the Backstage view.
- Tap or click Computer to display recent folders accessed on your computer.
- Tap or click the Browse button to display the Open Publication dialog box.
- If necessary, navigate to the location of the file to open as described in Steps 4a and 4b on page OFF 30.
- Tap or click the file to open, Book Club Event Flyer in this case, to select the file (Figure 69).

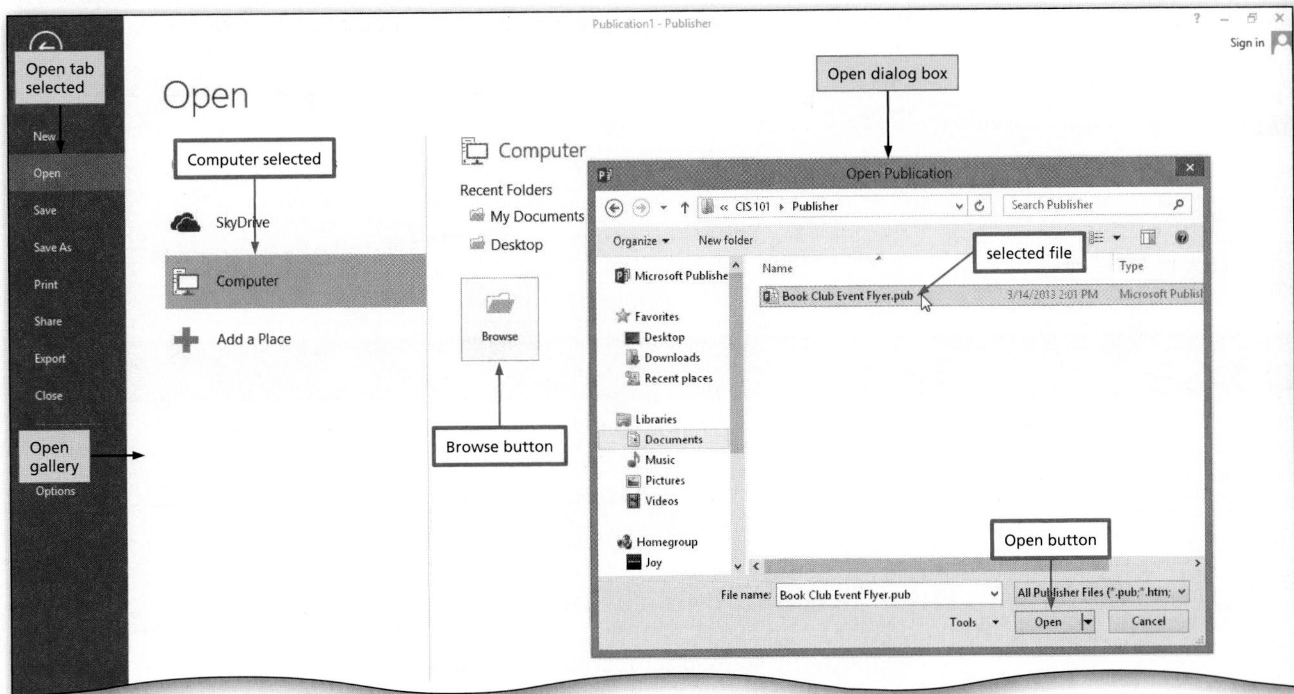

Figure 69

- Tap or click the Open button (Open dialog box) to open the file (shown in Figure 47 on page OFF 30).

Other Ways

1. Press CTRL+O
2. Navigate to file in File Explorer window, double-tap or double-click file

To Create a New Publication from the Backstage View

1 SIGN IN | 2 USE WINDOWS | 3 USE APPS | 4 FILE MANAGEMENT | 5 SWITCH APPS | 6 SAVE FILES
7 CHANGE SCREEN RESOLUTION | 8 EXIT APPS | 9 USE ADDITIONAL APP FEATURES | **10 USE HELP**

You can open multiple documents in an Office program, such as Publisher, so that you can work on the documents at the same time. The following steps create a file, a blank publication in this case, from the Backstage view. ***Why?*** *You want to create a new publication while keeping the current publication open.*

1

- Tap or click FILE on the ribbon to open the Backstage view.
- Tap or click the New tab in the Backstage view to display the New gallery (Figure 70).

Q&A Can I create documents through the Backstage view in other Office apps?
Yes. If the Office app has a New tab in the Backstage view, the New gallery displays various options for creating a new file.

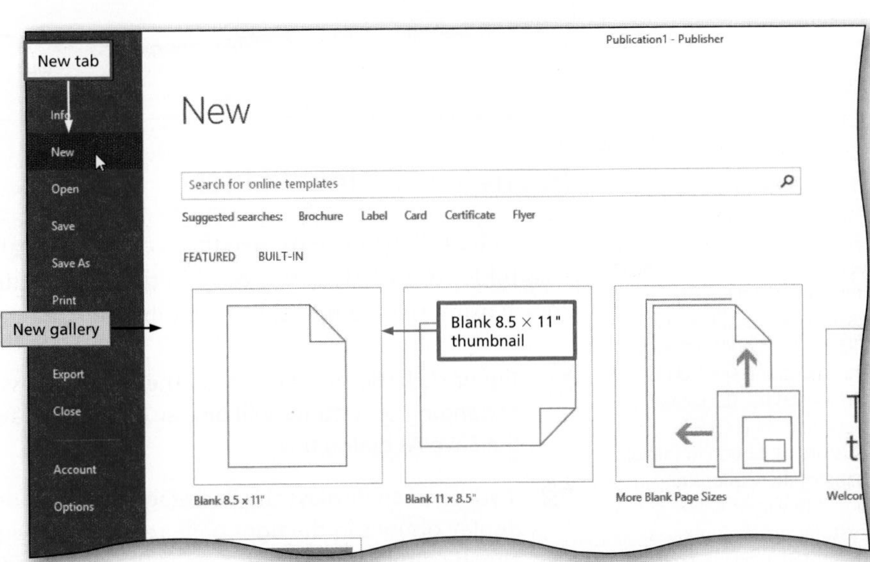

Figure 70

- Tap or click the Blank 8.5 × 11" thumbnail in the New gallery to create a new publication (Figure 71).

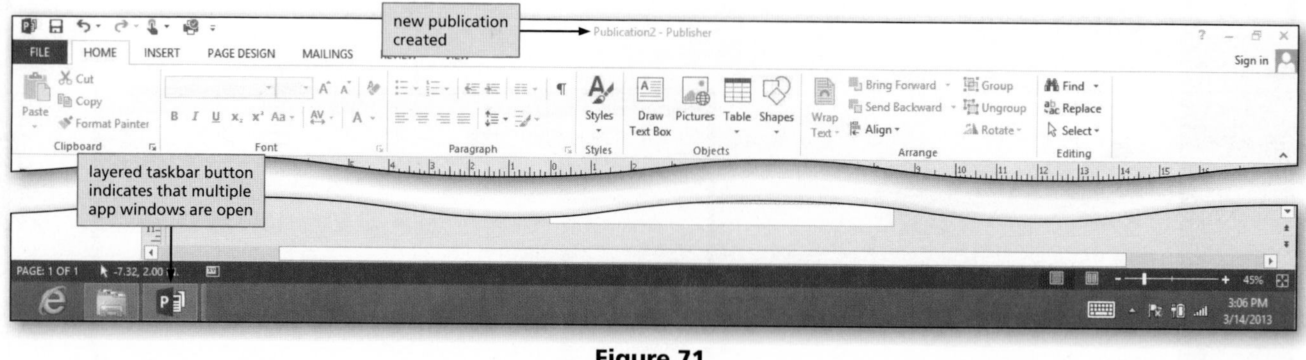

Figure 71

Other Ways

1. Press CTRL+N

To Enter Text in a Publication

The following steps enter text in a publication.

1. Tap or click the Draw a Text Box button (HOME tab | Objects group), and then drag a small text box at the top of the page layout.
2. Type **`Hey girls! Let's celebrate!`** and then press the ENTER key to move the insertion point to the beginning of the next line (Figure 72).

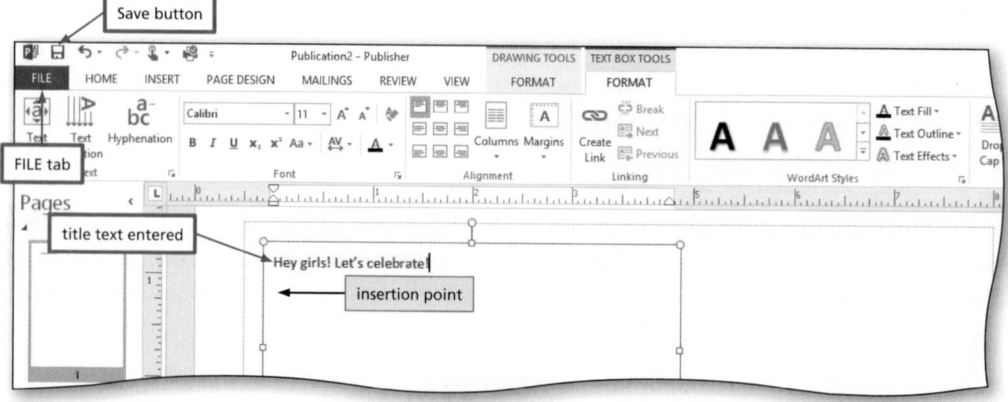

Figure 72

BTW
Customizing the Ribbon
In addition to customizing the Quick Access Toolbar, you can add items to and remove items from the ribbon. To customize the ribbon, click FILE on the ribbon to open the Backstage view, click Options in the Backstage view, and then click Customize Ribbon in the left pane of the Options dialog box. More information about customizing the ribbon is presented in a later chapter.

To Save a File in a Folder

The following steps save the second publication in the Publisher folder in the class folder (CIS 101, in this case) in the My Documents folder in the Documents library using the file name, Book Club Event Flyer 2.

1. Tap or click the Save button on the Quick Access Toolbar (shown in Figure 72), which depending on settings will display either the Save As gallery in the Backstage view or the Save As dialog box.
2. If your screen displays the Backstage view, tap or click Computer, if necessary, to display options in the right pane related to saving on your computer; if your screen already displays the Save As dialog box, proceed to Step 4.

3. Tap or click the Browse button in the right pane to display the Save As dialog box.

4. If necessary, type `Book Club Event Flyer 2` in the File name box (Save As dialog box) to change the file name. Do not press the ENTER key after typing the file name because you do not want to close the dialog box at this time.

5. If necessary, navigate to the desired save location (in this case, the Publisher folder in the CIS 101 folder [or your class folder] in the My Documents folder in the Documents library). For specific instructions, perform the tasks in Steps 4a and 4b on page OFF 30.

6. Tap or click the Save button (Save As dialog box) to save the publication in the selected folder on the selected drive with the entered file name.

To Close a File Using the Backstage View

1 SIGN IN | 2 USE WINDOWS | 3 USE APPS | 4 FILE MANAGEMENT | 5 SWITCH APPS | 6 SAVE FILES
7 CHANGE SCREEN RESOLUTION | 8 EXIT APPS | 9 USE ADDITIONAL APP FEATURES | **10 USE HELP**

Sometimes, you may want to close an Office file, such as a Publisher publication, entirely and start over with a new file. ***Why else would I close a file?*** *You also may want to close a file when you are finished working with it so that you can begin a new file.* The following steps close the current active Publisher file, without exiting Publisher.

- Tap or click FILE on the ribbon (shown in Figure 72) to open the Backstage view (Figure 73).

- Tap or click Close in the Backstage view to close the open file (Book Club Event Flyer 2, in this case) without exiting the active app.

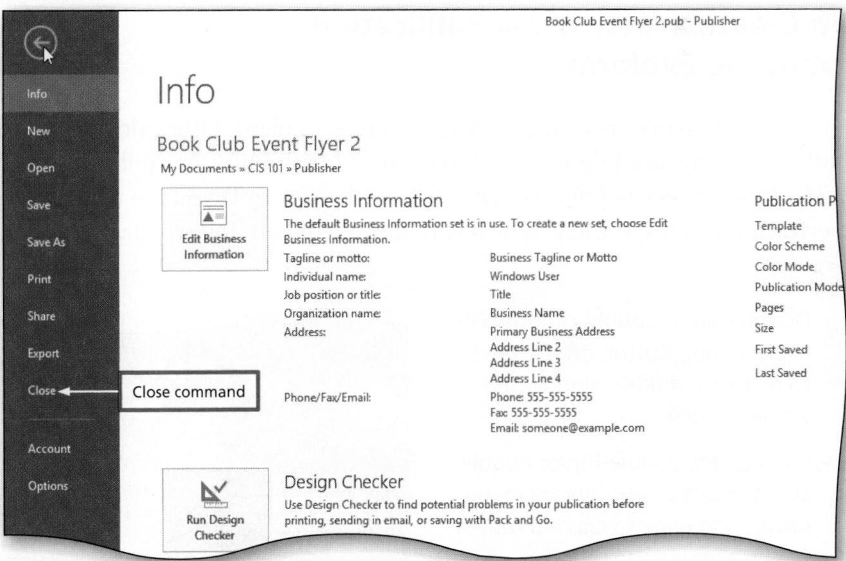

Figure 73

Q&A

What if Publisher displays a dialog box about saving?
Tap or click the Save button if you want to save the changes, tap or click the Don't Save button if you want to ignore the changes since the last time you saved, and tap or click the Cancel button if you do not want to close the publication.

Can I use the Backstage view to close an open file in other Office apps, such as PowerPoint and Excel?
Yes.

Other Ways

1. Press CTRL+F4

To Open a Recent File Using the Backstage View

1 SIGN IN | 2 USE WINDOWS | 3 USE APPS | 4 FILE MANAGEMENT | 5 SWITCH APPS | 6 SAVE FILES
7 CHANGE SCREEN RESOLUTION | 8 EXIT APPS | 9 USE ADDITIONAL APP FEATURES | **10 USE HELP**

You sometimes need to open a file that you recently modified. ***Why?*** *You may have more changes to make, such as adding more content or correcting errors.* The Backstage view allows you to access recent files easily. The following steps reopen the Book Club Event Flyer 2 file just closed.

- Tap or click FILE on the ribbon to open the Backstage view.
- Tap or click the Open tab in the Backstage view to display the Open gallery (Figure 74).

- Tap or click the desired file name in the Recent Publication list, Book Club Event Flyer 2 in this case, to open the file (shown in Figure 72).

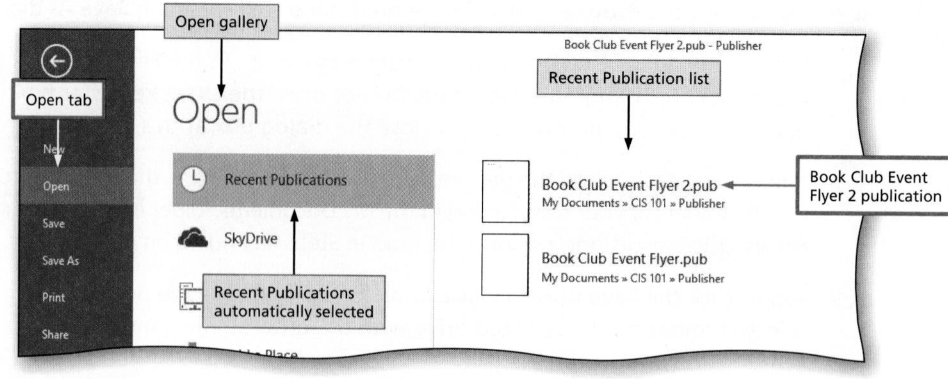

Figure 74

Q&A Can I use the Backstage view to open a recent file in other Office apps, such as PowerPoint and Excel?
Yes, as long as the file name appears in the list of recent files.

Other Ways

1. Tap or click FILE on ribbon, tap or click Open in Backstage view, tap or click Computer, tap or click Browse, navigate to file (Open dialog box), tap or click Open button

To Create a New Blank Publication from File Explorer

1 SIGN IN | 2 USE WINDOWS | 3 USE APPS | 4 FILE MANAGEMENT | 5 SWITCH APPS | 6 SAVE FILES
7 CHANGE SCREEN RESOLUTION | 8 EXIT APPS | 9 USE ADDITIONAL APP FEATURES | 10 USE HELP

File Explorer provides a means to create a blank Office document without running an Office app. The following steps use File Explorer to create a blank Publisher publication. ***Why?*** *Sometimes you might need to create a blank publication and then return to it later for editing.* If you are using Windows 7, skip these steps and instead perform the steps in the yellow box that immediately follows these Windows 8 steps.

- Double-tap or double-click the File Explorer app button on the taskbar to make the folder window the active window.
- If necessary, double-tap or double-click the Documents library in the navigation pane to expand the Documents library.
- If necessary, double-tap or double-click the My Documents folder in the navigation pane to expand the My Documents folder.
- If necessary, double-tap or double-click your class folder (CIS 101, in this case) in the navigation pane to expand the folder.
- Tap or click the Publisher folder in the navigation pane to display its contents in the file list.
- With the Publisher folder selected, press and hold or right-click an open area in the file list to display a shortcut menu.
- Tap or point to New on the shortcut menu to display the New submenu (Figure 75).

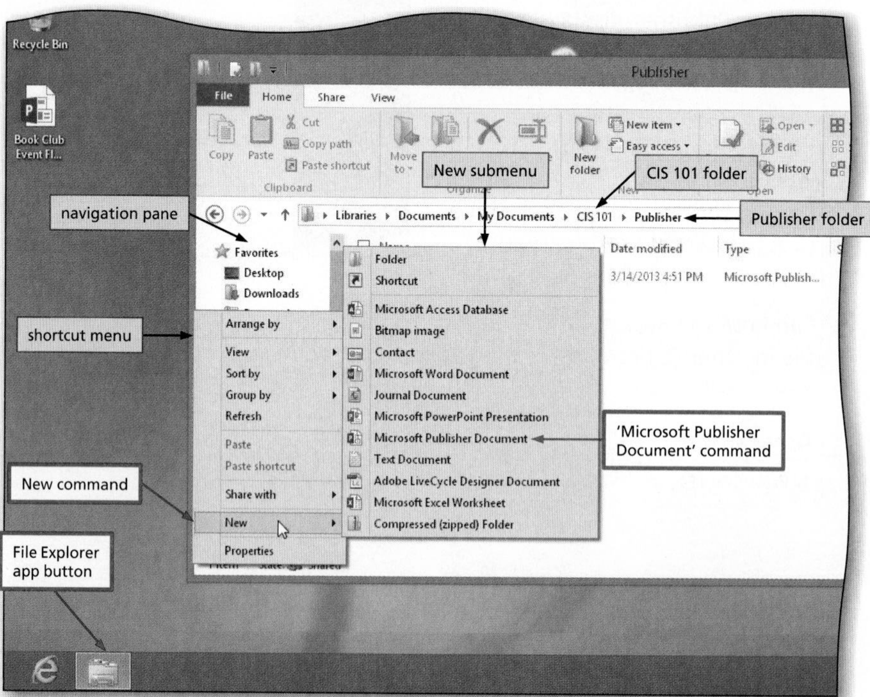

Figure 75

2

- Tap or click 'Microsoft Publisher Document' on the New submenu to display an icon and text box for a new file in the current folder window with the file name, New Microsoft Publisher Document, selected (Figure 76).

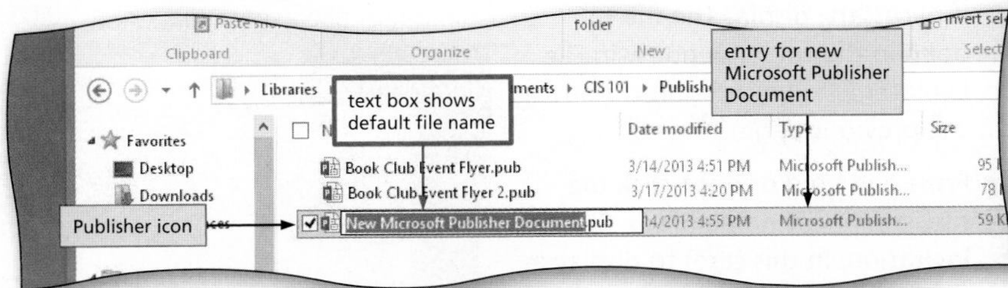

Figure 76

- Type **`Book Club Invitation`** in the text box and then press the ENTER key to assign a new name to the new file in the current folder (Figure 77).

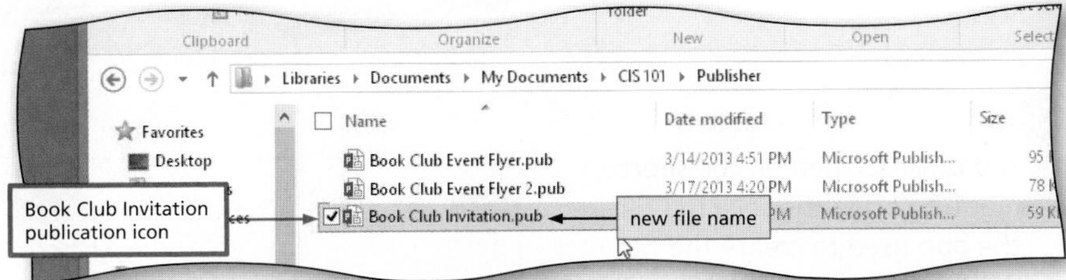

Figure 77

To Create a New Blank Publication from Windows Explorer Using Windows 7

If you are using Windows 7, perform these steps to create a new blank Office document from Windows Explorer instead of the previous steps that use Windows 8.

1. If necessary, click the Windows Explorer button on the taskbar to make the folder window the active window.
2. If necessary, double-click the Documents library in the navigation pane to expand the Documents library.
3. If necessary, double-click the My Documents folder in the navigation pane to expand the My Documents folder.
4. If necessary, double-click your class folder (CIS 101, in this case) in the navigation pane to expand the folder.
5. Click the Publisher folder in the navigation pane to display its contents in the file list.
6. With the Publisher folder selected, right-click an open area in the file list to display a shortcut menu.
7. Point to New on the shortcut menu to display the New submenu.
8. Click 'Microsoft Publisher Document' on the New submenu to display an icon and text box for a new file in the current folder window with the name, New Microsoft Publisher Document, selected.
9. Type **`Book Club Invitation`** in the text box and then press the ENTER key to assign a new name to the new file in the current folder.

To Run an App from File Explorer and Open a File

1 SIGN IN | 2 USE WINDOWS | 3 USE APPS | 4 FILE MANAGEMENT | 5 SWITCH APPS | 6 SAVE FILES
7 CHANGE SCREEN RESOLUTION | 8 EXIT APPS | **9 USE ADDITIONAL APP FEATURES** | **10 USE HELP**

Previously, you learned how to run Publisher using the Start screen and the Search charm. The following steps, which assume Windows is running, use File Explorer to run Publisher based on a typical installation. ***Why?*** *Another way to run an Office app is to open an existing file from File Explorer, which causes the app in which the file was created to run and then open the selected file.* You may need to ask your instructor how to run Publisher for your computer. If you are using Windows 7, follow the steps in the yellow box that immediately follows these Windows 8 steps.

- If necessary, display the file to open in the folder window in File Explorer (shown in Figure 77 on the previous page).
- Press and hold or right-click the file icon or file name (Book Club Invitation, in this case) to display a shortcut menu (Figure 78).

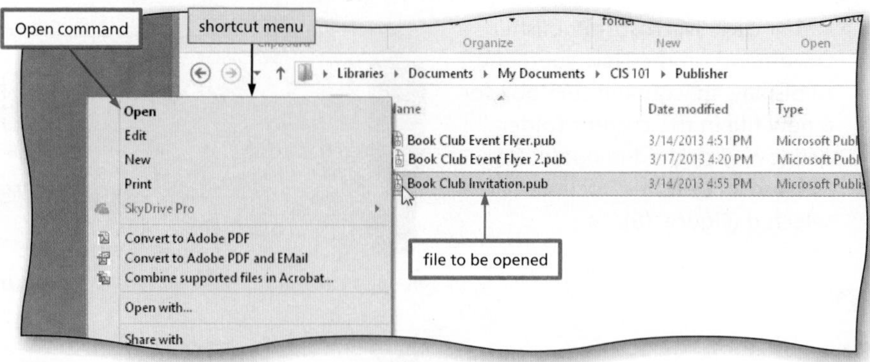

Figure 78

- Tap or click Open on the shortcut menu to open the selected file in the app used to create the file, Publisher in this case (Figure 79).
- If the Publisher window is not maximized, tap or click the Maximize button on the title bar to maximize the window.

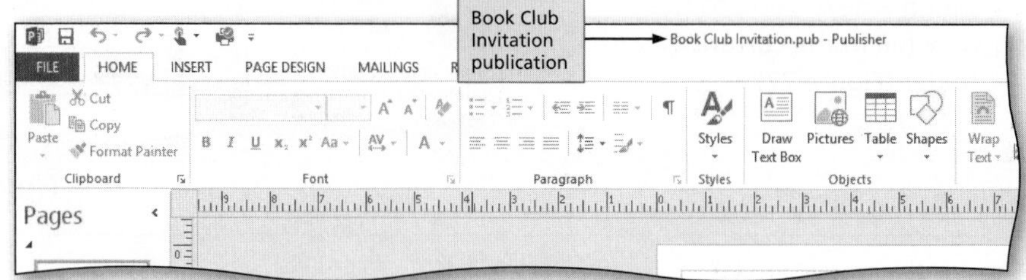

Figure 79

To Run an App from Windows Explorer and Open a File Using Windows 7

If you are using Windows 7, perform these steps to run an app from Windows Explorer and open a file instead of the previous steps that use Windows 8.

1. Display the file to open in the folder window in Windows Explorer.
2. Right-click the file icon or file name (Book Club Invitation, in this case) to display a shortcut menu.
3. Click Open on the shortcut menu to open the selected file in the app used to create the file, Publisher in this case.
4. If the Publisher window is not maximized, click the Maximize button on the title bar to maximize the window.

To Enter Text in a Publication

The next step is to enter text in this blank Publisher publication. The following step enters a line of text.

1 Draw a text box and then type `Book Club Invitation` and then press the ENTER key to move the insertion point to the beginning of the next line (shown in Figure 80).

To Save an Existing File with the Same File Name

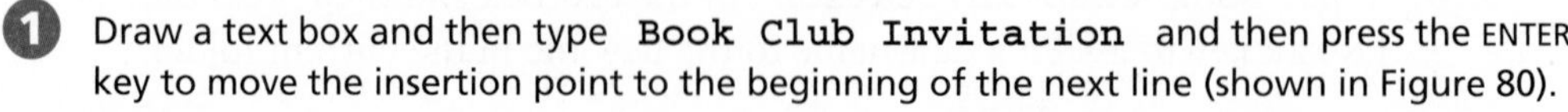

Saving frequently cannot be overemphasized. ***Why?*** *You have made modifications to the file (publication) since you created it. Thus, you should save again. Similarly, you should continue saving files frequently so that you do not lose the changes you have made since the time you last saved the file.* You can use the same file name, such as Book Club Invitation, to save the changes made to the publication. The following step saves a file again with the same file name.

1

- Tap or click the Save button on the Quick Access Toolbar to overwrite the previously saved file (Book Club Invitation, in this case) in the Publisher folder (Figure 80).

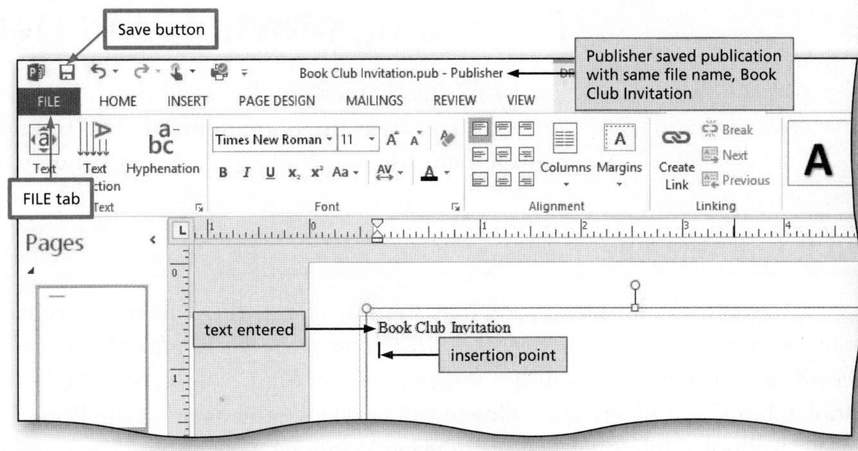

Figure 80

Other Ways

1. Press CTRL+S or press SHIFT+F12

To Save a File with a New File Name

You might want to save a file with a different name or to a different location. For example, you might start a homework assignment with a data file and then save it with a final file name for submission to your instructor, saving it to a location designated by your instructor. The following steps save a file with a different file name.

1. Tap or click the FILE tab to open the Backstage view.
2. Tap or click the Save As tab to display the Save As gallery.
3. If necessary, tap or click Computer to display options in the right pane related to saving on your computer.
4. Tap or click the Browse button in the right pane to display the Save As dialog box.
5. Type **`Book Club Invitation List`** in the File name box (Save As dialog box) to change the file name. Do not press the ENTER key after typing the file name because you do not want to close the dialog box at this time.
6. If necessary, navigate to the desired save location (in this case, the Publisher folder in the CIS 101 folder [or your class folder] in the My Documents folder in the Documents library). For specific instructions, perform the tasks in Steps 4a and 4b on page OFF 30.
7. Tap or click the Save button (Save As dialog box) to save the publication in the selected folder on the selected drive with the entered file name.

To Exit an Office App

You are finished using Publisher. The following steps exit Publisher. You would use similar steps to exit other Office apps.

1. Because you have multiple Publisher publications open, press and hold or right-click the app button on the taskbar and then tap or click 'Close all windows' on the shortcut menu to close all open publications and exit Publisher.
2. If a dialog box appears, tap or click the Save button to save any changes made to the file since the last save.

Renaming, Moving, and Deleting Files

Earlier in this chapter, you learned how to organize files in folders, which is part of a process known as **file management**. The following sections cover additional file management topics including renaming, moving, and deleting files.

To Rename a File

1 SIGN IN | 2 USE WINDOWS | 3 USE APPS | **4 FILE MANAGEMENT** | 5 SWITCH APPS | 6 SAVE FILES
7 CHANGE SCREEN RESOLUTION | 8 EXIT APPS | 9 USE ADDITIONAL APP FEATURES | **10 USE HELP**

In some circumstances, you may want to change the name of, or rename, a file or a folder. ***Why?*** *You may want to distinguish a file in one folder or drive from a copy of a similar file, or you may decide to rename a file to better identify its contents.* The Publisher folder shown in Figure 64 on page OFF 40 contains the Publisher publication, Book Club Event Flyer. The following steps change the name of the Book Club Event Flyer file in the Publisher folder to Book Club Flyer. If you are using Windows 7, skip these steps and instead perform the steps in the yellow box that immediately follows these Windows 8 steps.

1

- If necessary, tap or click the File Explorer app button on the taskbar to make the folder window the active window.
- If necessary, navigate to the location of the file to be renamed (in this case, the Publisher folder in the CIS 101 [or your class folder] folder in the My Documents folder in the Documents library) to display the file(s) it contains in the file list.
- Press and hold or right-click the Book Club Event Flyer icon or file name in the file list to select the Book Club Event Flyer file and display a shortcut menu that presents a list of commands related to files (Figure 81).

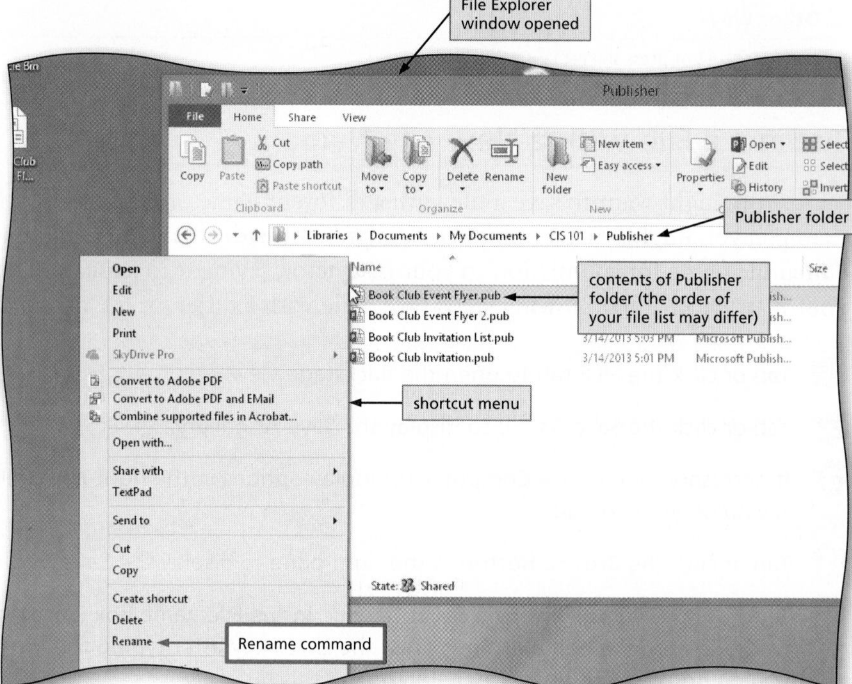

Figure 81

2

- Tap or click Rename on the shortcut menu to place the current file name in a text box.
- Type `Book Club Flyer` in the text box and then press the ENTER key (Figure 82).

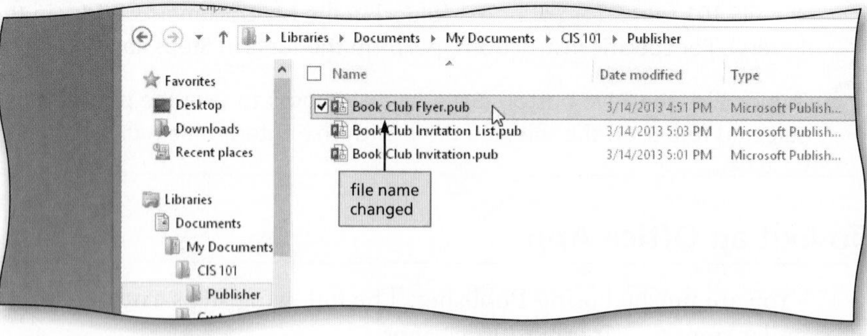

Figure 82

Q&A

Are any risks involved in renaming files that are located on a hard disk?
If you inadvertently rename a file that is associated with certain apps, the apps may not be able to find the file and, therefore, may not run properly. Always use caution when renaming files.

Can I rename a file when it is open?
No, a file must be closed to change the file name.

Other Ways

1. Select file, press F2, type new file name, press ENTER 2. Select file, tap or click Rename (Home tab | Organize group), type new file name, press ENTER

To Rename a File Using Windows 7

If you are using Windows 7, perform these steps to rename a file instead of the previous steps that use Windows 8.

1. If necessary, click the Windows Explorer app button on the taskbar to make the folder window the active window.
2. Navigate to the location of the file to be renamed (in this case, the Publisher folder in the CIS 101 [or your class folder] folder in the My Documents folder in the Documents library) to display the file(s) it contains in the file list.
3. Right-click the Book Club Event Flyer icon or file name in the file list to select the Book Club Event Flyer file and display a shortcut menu that presents a list of commands related to files.
4. Click Rename on the shortcut menu to place the current file name in a text box.
5. Type **`Book Club Flyer`** in the text box and then press the ENTER key.

To Move a File

1 SIGN IN | 2 USE WINDOWS | 3 USE APPS | **4 FILE MANAGEMENT** | 5 SWITCH APPS | 6 SAVE FILES
7 CHANGE SCREEN RESOLUTION | 8 EXIT APPS | 9 USE ADDITIONAL APP FEATURES | **10 USE HELP**

Why? *At some time, you may want to move a file from one folder, called the source folder, to another, called the destination folder.* When you move a file, it no longer appears in the original folder. If the destination and the source folders are on the same media, you can move a file by dragging it. If the folders are on different media, then you will need to press and hold and then drag, or right-drag the file, and then click Move here on the shortcut menu. The following step moves the Book Club Flyer file from the Publisher folder to the CIS 101 folder. If you are using Windows 7, skip these steps and instead perform the steps in the yellow box that immediately follows these Windows 8 steps.

- In File Explorer, if necessary, navigate to the location of the file to be moved (in this case, the Publisher folder in the CIS 101 folder [or your class folder] in the Documents library).
- If necessary, tap or click the Publisher folder in the navigation pane to display the files it contains in the right pane.
- Drag the Book Club Flyer file in the right pane to the CIS 101 folder in the navigation pane and notice the ScreenTip as you drag the mouse (Figure 83).

- Click the CIS 101 folder in the navigation pane to verify that the file was moved.

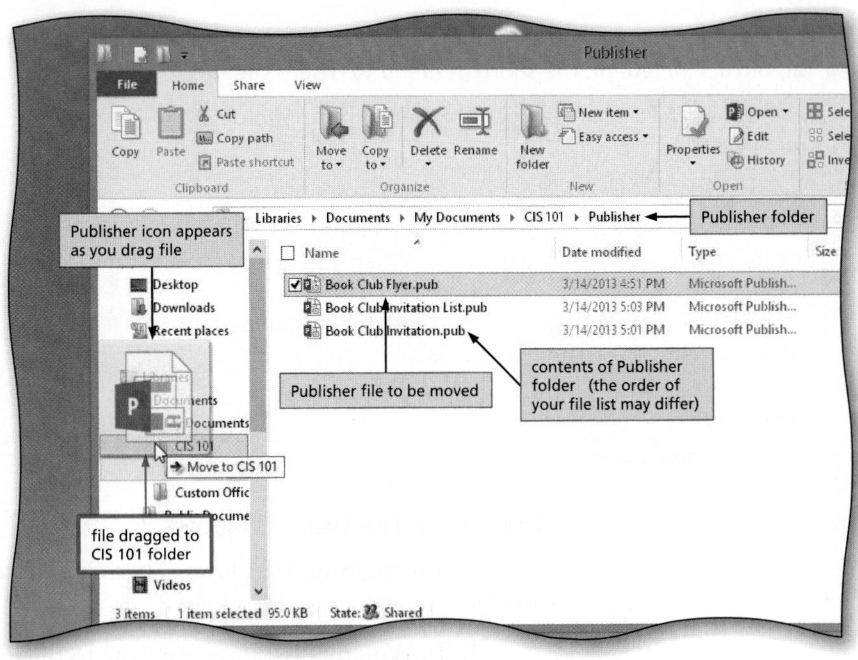

Figure 83

Other Ways

1. Press and hold or right-click file to move, tap or click Cut on shortcut menu, press and hold or right-click destination folder, tap or click Paste on shortcut menu
2. Select file to move, press CTRL+X, select destination folder, press CTRL+V

To Move a File Using Windows 7

If you are using Windows 7, perform these steps to move a file instead of the previous steps that use Windows 8.

1. In Windows Explorer, navigate to the location of the file to be moved (in this case, the Publisher folder in the CIS 101 folder [or your class folder] in the Documents library).
2. Click the Publisher folder in the navigation pane to display the files it contains in the right pane.
3. Drag the Book Club Flyer file in the right pane to the CIS 101 folder in the navigation pane.

To Delete a File

1 SIGN IN | 2 USE WINDOWS | 3 USE APPS | **4 FILE MANAGEMENT** | 5 SWITCH APPS | 6 SAVE FILES
7 CHANGE SCREEN RESOLUTION | 8 EXIT APPS | 9 USE ADDITIONAL APP FEATURES | **10 USE HELP**

A final task you may want to perform is to delete a file. Exercise extreme caution when deleting a file or files. When you delete a file from a hard disk, the deleted file is stored in the Recycle Bin where you can recover it until you empty the Recycle Bin. If you delete a file from removable media, such as a USB flash drive, the file is deleted permanently. The next steps delete the Book Club Flyer file from the CIS 101 folder. ***Why?*** *When a file no longer is needed, you can delete it to conserve space in your storage location.* If you are using Windows 7, skip these steps and instead perform the steps in the yellow box that immediately follows these Windows 8 steps.

- In File Explorer, navigate to the location of the file to be deleted (in this case, the CIS 101 folder [or your class folder] in the Documents library).
- Press and hold or right-click the Book Club Flyer icon or file name in the right pane to select the file and display a shortcut menu (Figure 84).

- Tap or click Delete on the shortcut menu to delete the file.
- If a dialog box appears, tap or click the Yes button to delete the file.

Q&A Can I use this same technique to delete a folder?
Yes. Press and hold or right-click the folder and then tap or click Delete on the shortcut menu. When you delete a folder, all of the files and folders contained in the folder you are deleting, together with any files and folders on lower hierarchical levels, are deleted as well.

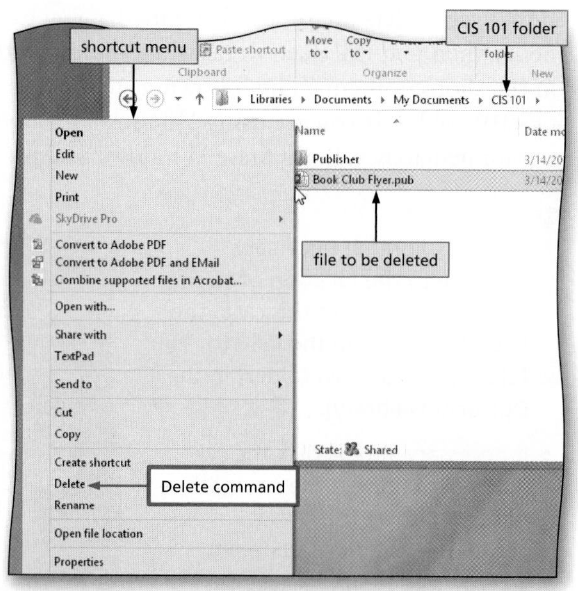

Figure 84

Other Ways

1. Select icon, press DELETE

To Delete a File Using Windows 7

If you are using Windows 7, perform these steps to delete a file instead of the previous steps that use Windows 8.

1. In Windows Explorer, navigate to the location of the file to be deleted (in this case, the CIS 101 folder [or your class folder] in the Documents library).
2. Right-click the Book Club Flyer icon or file name in the right pane to select the file and display a shortcut menu.
3. Click Delete on the shortcut menu to delete the file.
4. If a dialog box appears, click the Yes button to delete the file.

Microsoft Office and Windows Help

At any time while you are using one of the Office apps, such as Publisher, you can use Office Help to display information about all topics associated with the app. This section illustrates the use of Publisher Help. Help in other Office apps operates in a similar fashion.

In Office, Help is presented in a window that has browser-style navigation buttons. Each Office app has its own Help home page, which is the starting Help page that is displayed in the Help window. If your computer is connected to the Internet, the contents of the Help page reflect both the local help files installed on the computer and material from Microsoft's website.

To Open the Help Window in Publisher

1 SIGN IN | 2 USE WINDOWS | 3 USE APPS | 4 FILE MANAGEMENT | 5 SWITCH APPS | 6 SAVE FILES
7 CHANGE SCREEN RESOLUTION | 8 EXIT APPS | 9 USE ADDITIONAL APP FEATURES | **10 USE HELP**

The following step opens the Publisher Help window. ***Why?*** *You might not understand how certain commands or operations work in Publisher, so you can obtain the necessary information using help.* The step to open a Help window in other Office programs is similar.

- Run Publisher and open a blank file.
- Tap or click the Microsoft Publisher Help button near the upper-right corner of the app window to open the Publisher Help window (Figure 85).

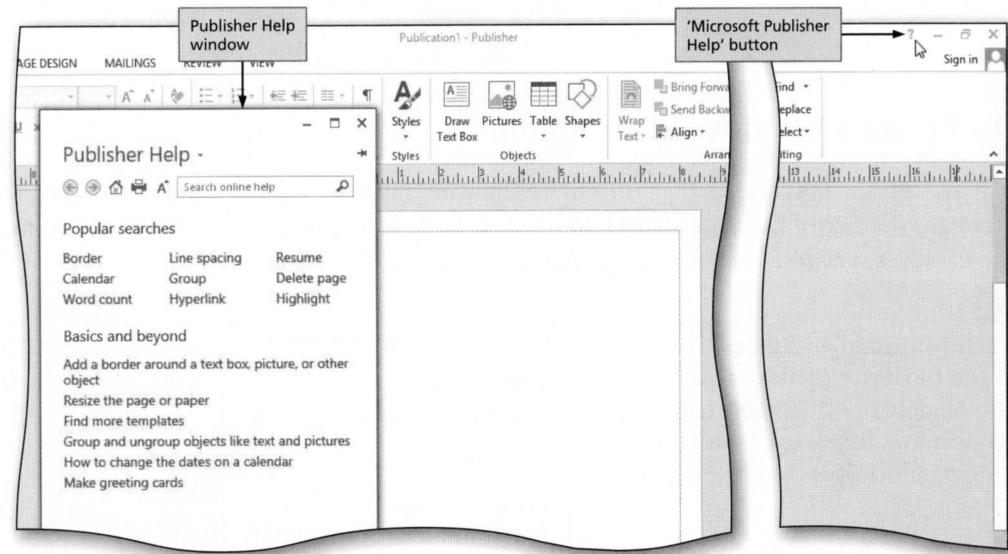

Figure 85

Other Ways

1. Press F1

Moving and Resizing Windows

At times, it is useful, or even necessary, to have more than one window open and visible on the screen at the same time. You can resize and move these open windows so that you can view different areas of and elements in the window. In the case of the Help window, for example, it could be covering publication text in the Publisher window that you need to see.

To Move a Window by Dragging

1 SIGN IN | 2 USE WINDOWS | 3 USE APPS | 4 FILE MANAGEMENT | 5 SWITCH APPS | 6 SAVE FILES
7 CHANGE SCREEN RESOLUTION | 8 EXIT APPS | 9 USE ADDITIONAL APP FEATURES | **10 USE HELP**

You can move any open window that is not maximized to another location on the desktop by dragging the title bar of the window. ***Why?*** *You might want to have a better view of what is behind the window or just want to move the window so that you can see it better.* The following step drags the Publisher Help window to the upper-left corner of the desktop.

- Drag the window title bar (the Publisher Help window title bar, in this case) so that the window moves to the upper-left corner of the desktop, as shown in Figure 86.

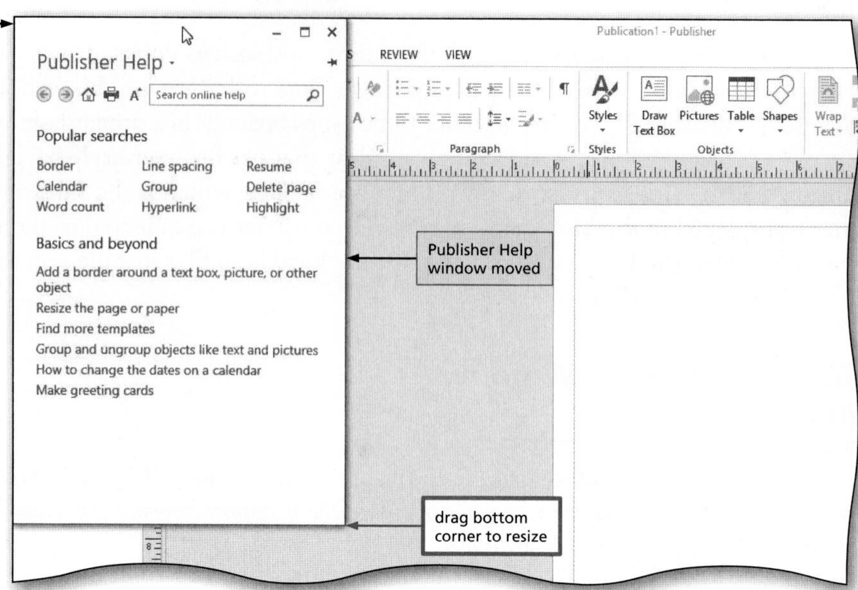

Figure 86

To Resize a Window by Dragging

1 SIGN IN | 2 USE WINDOWS | 3 USE APPS | 4 FILE MANAGEMENT | 5 SWITCH APPS | 6 SAVE FILES
7 CHANGE SCREEN RESOLUTION | 8 EXIT APPS | 9 USE ADDITIONAL APP FEATURES | 10 USE HELP

A method used to change the size of the window is to drag the window borders. The following step changes the size of the Publisher Help window by dragging its borders. ***Why?*** *Sometimes, information is not visible completely in a window, and you want to increase the size of the window.*

- If you are using a mouse, point to the lower-right corner of the window (the Publisher Help window, in this case) until the pointer changes to a two-headed arrow.
- Drag the bottom border downward to display more of the active window (Figure 87).

Q&A

Can I drag other borders on the window to enlarge or shrink the window?
Yes, you can drag the left, right, and top borders and any window corner to resize a window.

Will Windows remember the new size of the window after I close it?
Yes. When you reopen the window, Windows will display it at the same size it was when you closed it.

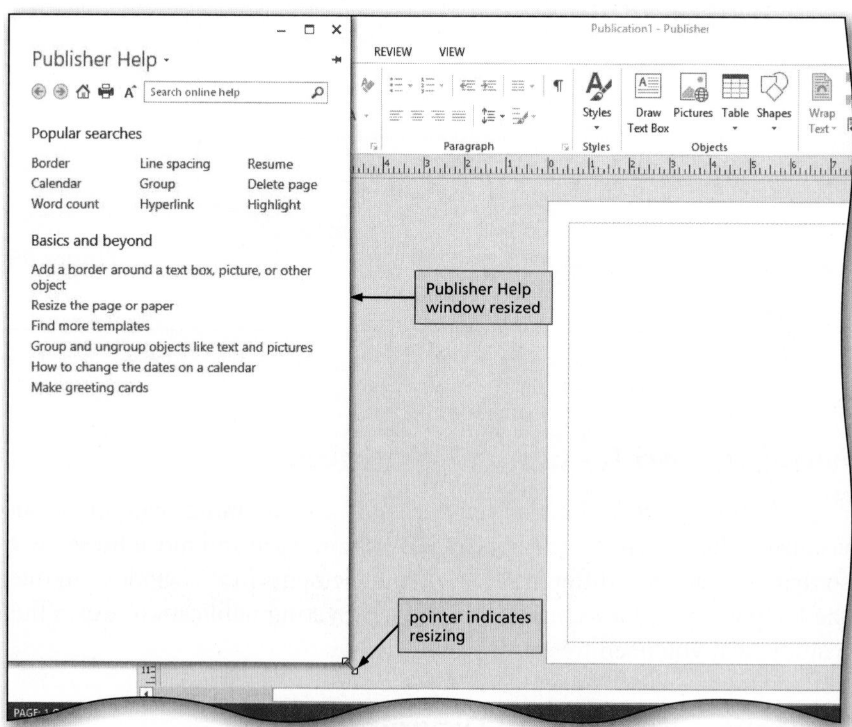

Figure 87

Using Office Help

Once an Office app's Help window is open, several methods exist for navigating Help. You can search for help by using any of the three following methods from the Help window:

1. Enter search text in the 'Search online help' text box.
2. Click the links in the Help window.
3. Use the Table of Contents.

To Obtain Help Using the 'Search online help' Text Box

1 SIGN IN | 2 USE WINDOWS | 3 USE APPS | 4 FILE MANAGEMENT | 5 SWITCH APPS | 6 SAVE FILES
7 CHANGE SCREEN RESOLUTION | 8 EXIT APPS | 9 USE ADDITIONAL APP FEATURES | **10 USE HELP**

Assume for the following example that you want to know more about cropping. The following steps use the 'Search online help' text box to obtain useful information about cropping by entering the word, crop, as search text. ***Why?*** *You may not know the exact help topic you are looking to find, so using keywords can help narrow your search.*

1

- Type **crop** in the 'Search online help' text box at the top of the Publisher Help window to enter the search text.
- Tap or click the 'Search online help' button to display the search results (Figure 88).

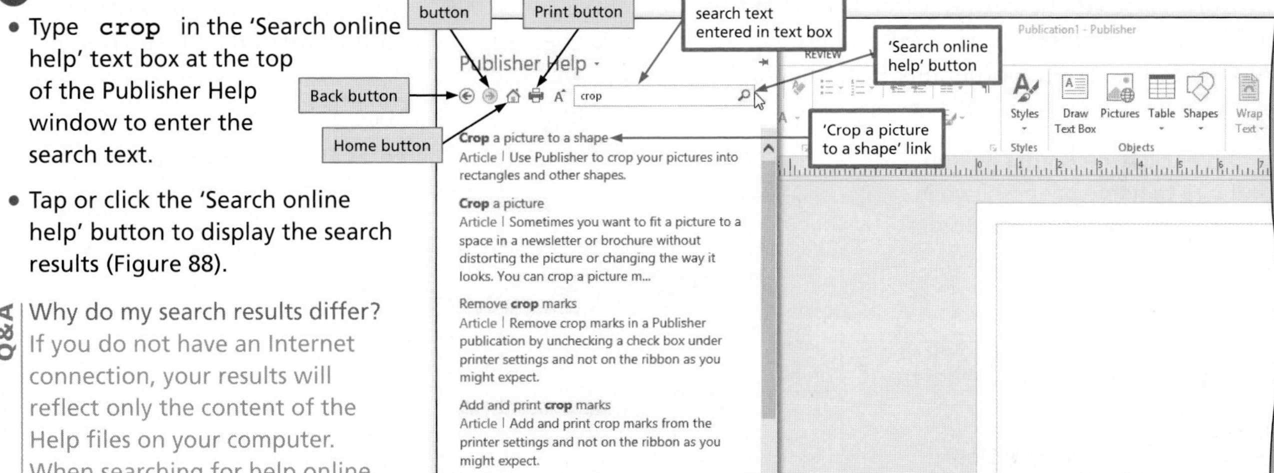

Figure 88

Q&A

Why do my search results differ?
If you do not have an Internet connection, your results will reflect only the content of the Help files on your computer. When searching for help online, results also can change as material is added, deleted, and updated on the online Help webpages maintained by Microsoft.

Why were my search results not very helpful?
When initiating a search, be sure to check the spelling of the search text; also, keep your search specific to return the most accurate results.

2

- Tap or click the 'Crop a picture to a shape' link to display the Help information associated with the selected topic (Figure 89).

Q&A

What is the purpose of the Use Large Text button?
When you tap or click the Use Large Text button, the Help topics text displays in a larger font.

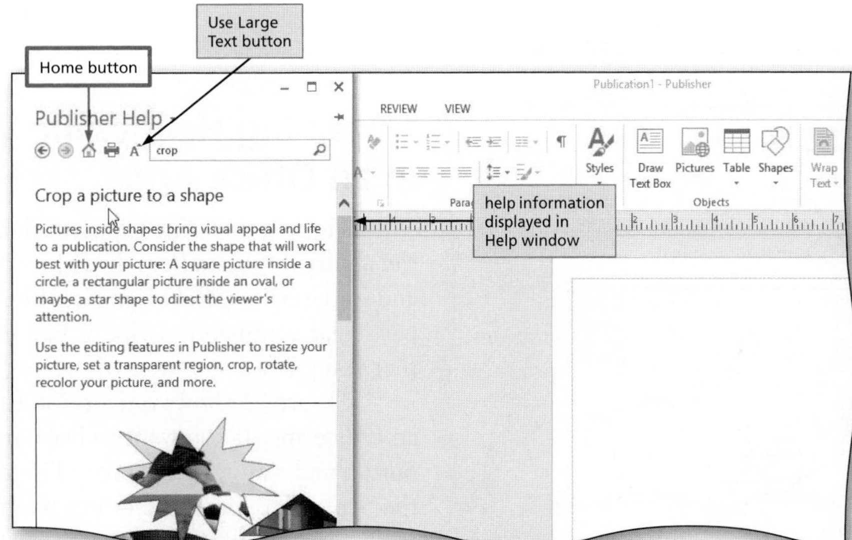

Figure 89

- Tap or click the Home button in the Help window to clear the search results and redisplay the Help home page (Figure 90).

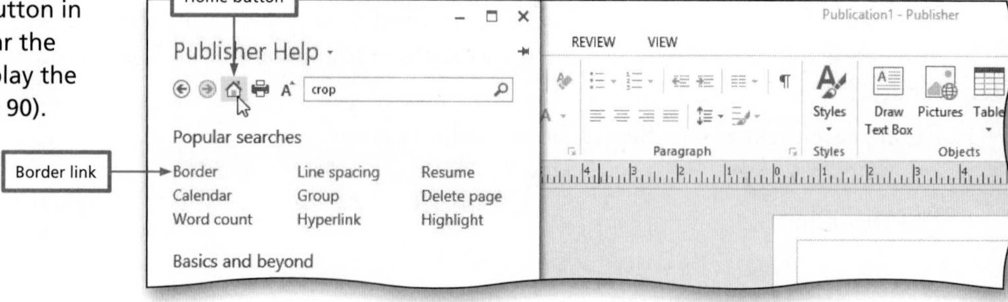

Figure 90

To Obtain Help Using Help Links

1 SIGN IN | 2 USE WINDOWS | 3 USE APPS | 4 FILE MANAGEMENT | 5 SWITCH APPS | 6 SAVE FILES
7 CHANGE SCREEN RESOLUTION | 8 EXIT APPS | 9 USE ADDITIONAL APP FEATURES | **10 USE HELP**

If your topic of interest is listed in the Help window, you can click the link to begin browsing the Help categories instead of entering search text. ***Why?*** *You browse Help just as you would browse a website. If you know which category contains your Help information, you may wish to use these links.* The following step finds the Border information using the Border link from the Publisher Help home page.

- Tap or click the Border link on the Help home page (shown in Figure 90) to display the Border help links (Figure 91).

- After reviewing the page, tap or click the Close button to close the Help window.
- Tap or click Publisher's Close button to exit Publisher.

Q&A Why does my Help window display different links?
The content of your Help window may differ because Microsoft continually updates its Help information.

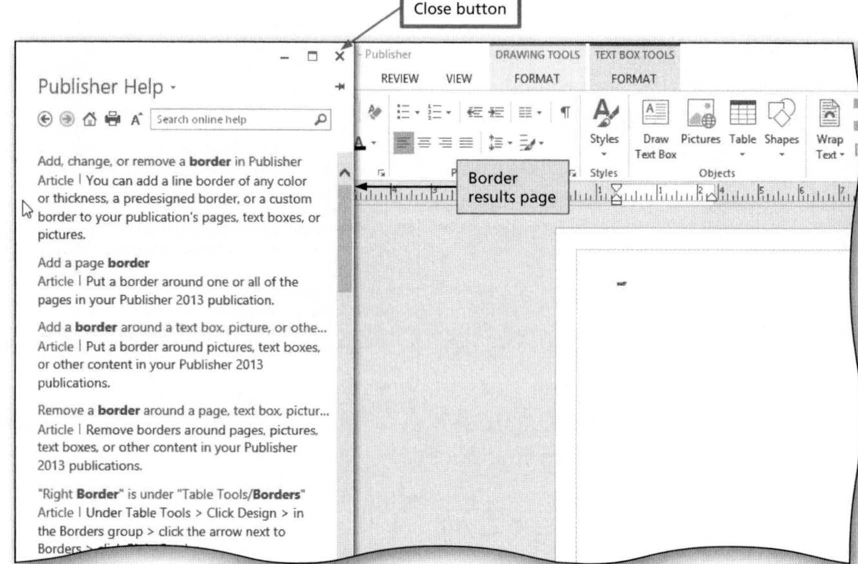

Figure 91

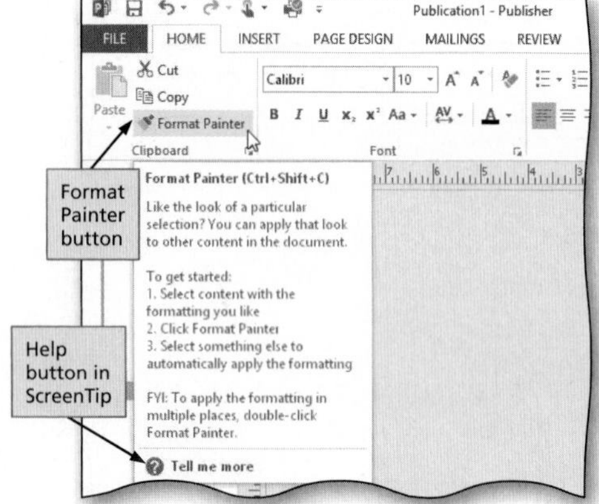

Figure 92

Obtaining Help while Working in an Office App

Help in the Office apps, such as Publisher, provides you with the ability to obtain help directly, without opening the Help window and initiating a search. For example, you may be unsure about how a particular command works, or you may be presented with a dialog box that you are not sure how to use.

Figure 92 shows one option for obtaining help while working in an Office app. If you want to learn more about a command, point to its button and wait for the ScreenTip to appear. If the Help icon appears in the ScreenTip, press the F1 key while pointing to the button to open the Help window associated with that command.

Figure 93 shows a dialog box that contains a Help button. Pressing the F1 key while the dialog box is displayed opens a Help window. The Help window contains help about that dialog box, if available. If no help file is available for that particular dialog box, then the main Help window opens.

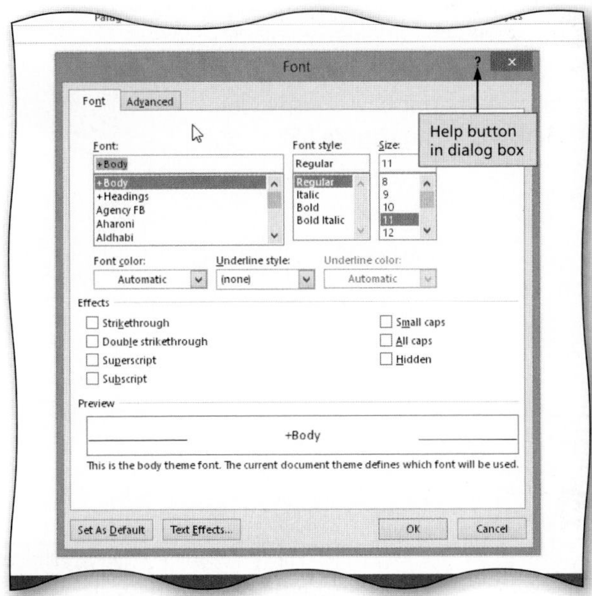

Figure 93

Using Windows Help and Support

One of the more powerful Windows features is Windows Help and Support. **Windows Help and Support** is available when using Windows or when using any Microsoft app running in Windows. The same methods used for searching Microsoft Office Help can be used in Windows Help and Support. The difference is that Windows Help and Support displays help for Windows, instead of for Microsoft Office.

To Use Windows Help and Support

1 SIGN IN | 2 USE WINDOWS | 3 USE APPS | 4 FILE MANAGEMENT | 5 SWITCH APPS | 6 SAVE FILES
7 CHANGE SCREEN RESOLUTION | 8 EXIT APPS | 9 USE ADDITIONAL APP FEATURES | **10 USE HELP**

The following steps use Windows Help and Support and open the Windows Help and Support window, which contains links to more information about Windows. ***Why?*** *This feature is designed to assist you in using Windows or the various apps.* If you are using Windows 7, skip these steps and instead perform the steps in the yellow box that immediately follows these Windows 8 steps.

- Swipe in from the right edge of the screen or point to the upper-right corner of the screen to display the Charms bar (Figure 94).

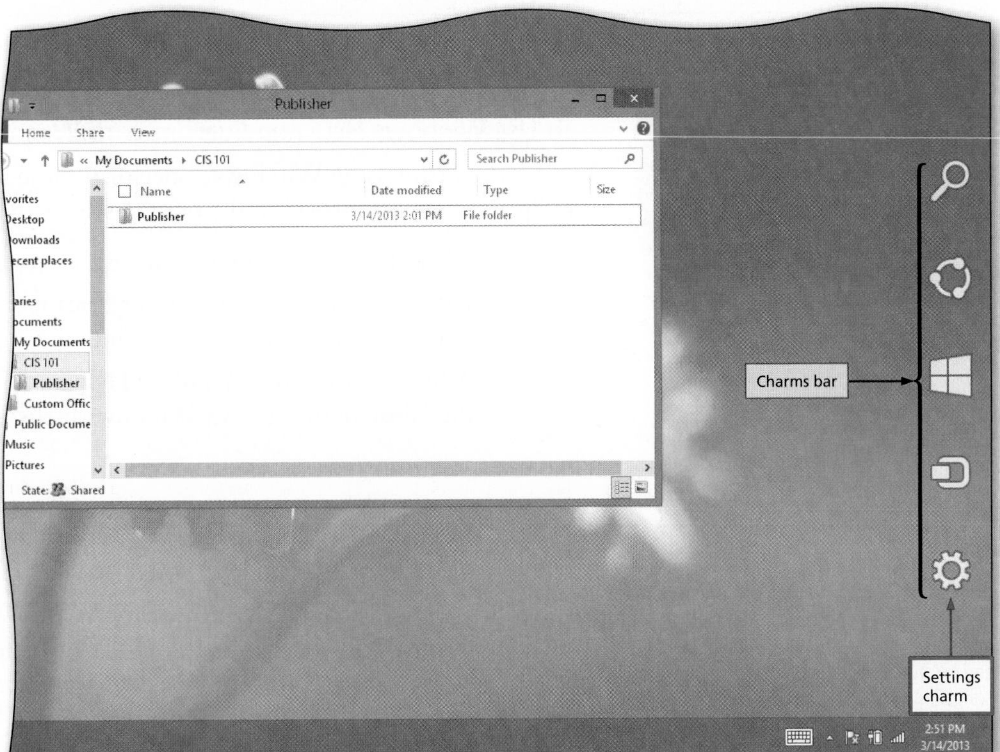

Figure 94

- Tap or click the Settings charm on the Charms bar to display the Settings menu (Figure 95).

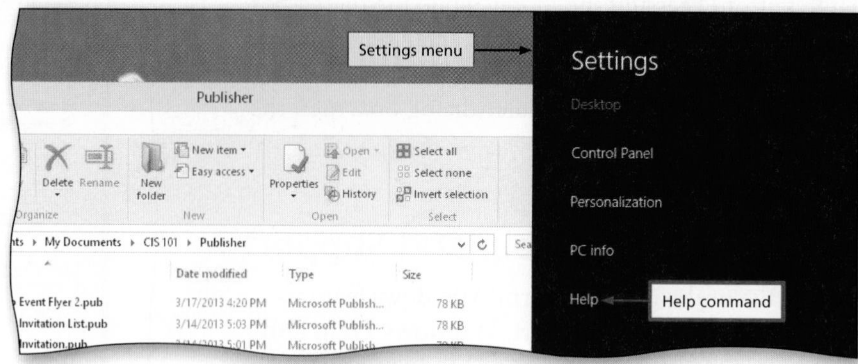

Figure 95

- Tap or click Help to open the Windows Help and Support window (Figure 96).

- After reviewing the Windows Help and Support window, tap or click the Close button to close the Windows Help and Support window.

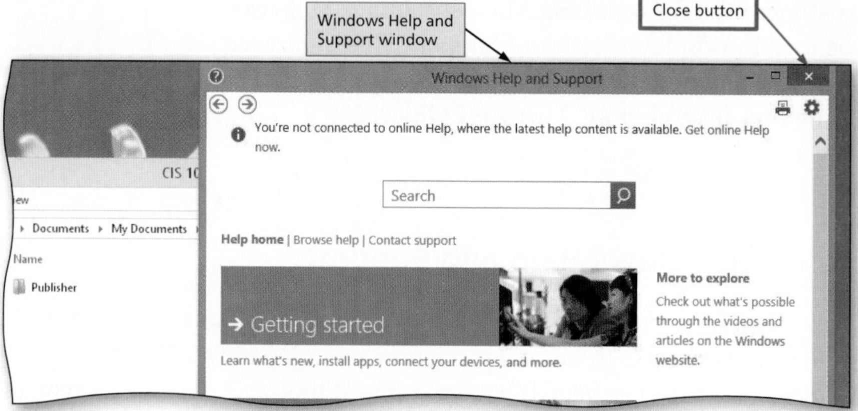

Figure 96

Other Ways

1. Press WINDOWS+F1

BTW

Certification

The Microsoft Office Specialist (MOS) program provides an opportunity for you to obtain a valuable industry credential — proof that you have the Microsoft Office 2013 skills required by employers. For more information, visit the Certification resource on the Student Companion Site located on www.cengagebrain.com. For detailed instructions about accessing available resources, visit www.cengage.com/ct/studentdownload or contact your instructor for information about accessing the required files.

BTW

Quick Reference

For a table that lists how to complete the tasks covered in this book using touch gestures, the mouse, ribbon, shortcut menu, and keyboard, see the Quick Reference Summary at the back of this book, or visit the Quick Reference resource on the Student Companion Site located on www.cengagebrain.com. For detailed instructions about accessing available resources, visit www.cengage.com/ct/studentdownload or contact your instructor for information about accessing the required files.

To Use Windows Help and Support with Windows 7

If you are using Windows 7, perform these steps to start Windows Help and Support instead of the previous steps that use Windows 8.

1. Click the Start button on the taskbar to display the Start menu.
2. Click Help and Support on the Start menu to open the Windows Help and Support window.
3. After reviewing the Windows Help and Support window, click the Close button to exit Windows Help and Support.

Chapter Summary

In this chapter, you learned how to use the Windows interface, several touch screen and mouse operations, and file and folder management. You also learned some basic features of Publisher and discovered the common elements that exist among Microsoft Office apps. The items listed below include all of the new Windows and Publisher skills you have learned in this chapter, with the tasks grouped by activity.

File Management

Create a Folder (OFF 24)
Create a Folder within a Folder (OFF 26)
Expand a Folder, Scroll through Folder Contents, and Collapse a Folder (OFF 27)
Copy a Folder to a USB Flash Drive (OFF 39)
Rename a File (OFF 50)
Move a File (OFF 51)
Delete a File (OFF 52)

Use Help

Open the Help Window in Publisher (OFF 53)
Obtain Help Using the 'Search online help' Text Box (OFF 55)
Obtain Help Using Help Links (OFF 56)
Use Windows Help and Support (OFF 57)

Use Windows

Sign In to an Account (OFF 7)
Run an App from the Start Screen (OFF 11)
Switch between an App and the Start Screen (OFF 13)
Maximize a Window (OFF 14)
Switch from One App to Another (OFF 29)
Minimize and Restore a Window (OFF 32)
Change the Screen Resolution (OFF 37)
Move a Window by Dragging (OFF 53)
Resize a Window by Dragging (OFF 54)

Use Publisher

Display a Different Tab on the Ribbon (OFF 18)
Collapse and Expand the Ribbon and Use Full Screen Mode (OFF 19)
Use a Shortcut Menu to Relocate the Quick Access Toolbar (OFF 20)
Customize the Quick Access Toolbar (OFF 21)
Enter Text in a Publication (OFF 22)
Save a File in a Folder (OFF 29)
Save a File on SkyDrive (OFF 33)
Sign Out of a Microsoft Account (OFF 35)
Exit an App with One Document Open (OFF 38)
Run an App Using the Search Box (OFF 40)
Open an Existing File (OFF 42)
Create a New Publication from the Backstage View (OFF 43)
Close a File Using the Backstage View (OFF 45)
Open a Recent File Using the Backstage View (OFF 45)
Create a New Blank Publication from File Explorer (OFF 46)
Run an App from File Explorer and Open a File (OFF 40)
Save an Existing File with the Same File Name (OFF 48)

CONSIDER THIS: PLAN AHEAD

What guidelines should you follow to plan your projects?

The process of communicating specific information is a learned, rational skill. Computers and software, especially Microsoft Office 2013, can help you develop ideas and present detailed information to a particular audience and minimize much of the laborious work of drafting and revising projects. No matter what method you use to plan a project, it is beneficial to follow some specific guidelines from the onset to arrive at a final product that is informative, relevant, and effective. Use some aspects of these guidelines every time you undertake a project, and others as needed in specific instances.

1. Determine the project's purpose.
   a) Clearly define why you are undertaking this assignment.
   b) Begin to draft ideas of how best to communicate information by handwriting ideas on paper; composing directly on a laptop, tablet, or mobile device; or developing a strategy that fits your particular thinking and writing style.
2. Analyze your audience.
   a) Learn about the people who will read, analyze, or view your work.
   b) Determine their interests and needs so that you can present the information they need to know and omit the information they already possess.
   c) Form a mental picture of these people or find photos of people who fit this profile so that you can develop a project with the audience in mind.
3. Gather possible content.
   a) Locate existing information that may reside in spreadsheets, databases, or other files.
   b) Conduct a web search to find relevant websites.
   c) Read pamphlets, magazine and newspaper articles, and books to gain insights of how others have approached your topic.
   d) Conduct personal interviews to obtain perspectives not available by any other means.
   e) Consider video and audio clips as potential sources for material that might complement or support the factual data you uncover.

4. Determine what content to present to your audience.
   a) Write three or four major ideas you want an audience member to remember after reading or viewing your project.
   b) Envision your project's endpoint, the key fact you wish to emphasize, so that all project elements lead to this final element.
   c) Determine relevant time factors, such as the length of time to develop the project, how long readers will spend reviewing your project, or the amount of time allocated for your speaking engagement.
   d) Decide whether a graph, photo, or artistic element can express or enhance a particular concept.
   e) Be mindful of the order in which you plan to present the content, and place the most important material at the top or bottom of the page, because readers and audience members generally remember the first and last pieces of information they see and hear.

CONSIDER THIS

How should you submit solutions to questions in the assignments identified with a ✱ symbol?
Every assignment in this book contains one or more questions identified with a ✱ symbol. These questions require you to think beyond the assigned file. Present your solutions to the questions in the format required by your instructor. Possible formats may include one or more of these options: write the answer; create a document that contains the answer; present your answer to the class; discuss your answer in a group; record the answer as audio or video using a webcam, smartphone, or portable media player; or post answers on a blog, wiki, or website.

Apply Your Knowledge

Reinforce the skills and apply the concepts you learned in this chapter.

Creating a Folder and a Publication

Instructions: You will create a new folder and then create a publication and save it in the folder.

Perform the following tasks:

1. Open the File Explorer app and then double-tap or double-click to open the Documents library.
2. Tap or click the New folder button on the File Explorer Quick Access Toolbar to display a new folder icon and text box for the folder name.
3. Type **`Apply Publisher`** in the text box to name the folder. Press the ENTER key to create the folder in the Documents library.
4. Run Publisher.
5. Draw a text box and then enter the name(s) of the course(s) you are taking this semester (Figure 97).
6. If requested by your instructor, enter your name in the Publisher publication.
7. Tap or click the Save button on the Publisher Quick Access Toolbar. Navigate to the Apply Publisher folder in the Documents library and then save the publication using the file name, Apply 1 Class List.

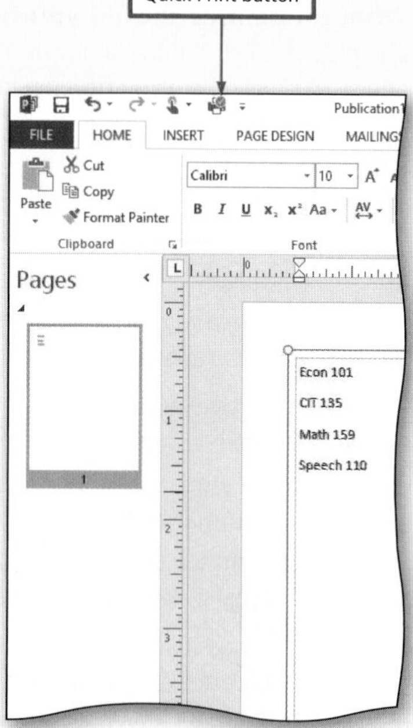

Figure 97

8. If your Quick Access Toolbar does not show the Quick Print button, add the Quick Print button to the Quick Access Toolbar. Print the publication using the Quick Print button on the Quick Access Toolbar (Figure 97). When you are finished printing, remove the Quick Print button from the Quick Access Toolbar.
9. Submit the printout to your instructor and exit Publisher.
10. ✱ What other commands might you find useful to include on the Quick Access Toolbar?

Extend Your Knowledge

Extend the skills you learned in this chapter and experiment with new skills. You will use Help to complete the assignment.

Using Help

Instructions: Use Publisher Help to perform the following tasks.

Perform the following tasks:

1. Run Publisher.
2. Tap or click the Microsoft Publisher Help button to open the Publisher Help window (Figure 98).
3. Search Publisher Help to answer the following questions.
   a. What are three features new to Publisher 2013?
   b. What type of training courses are available through Help?
   c. What are the steps to add a new group to the ribbon?
   d. What are Building Blocks?
   e. How do you insert clip art?
   f. What is a template?
   g. How do you insert a new page?
   h. What is a SmartArt graphic?
   i. What is cropping?
   j. Where is the Measurement toolbar?

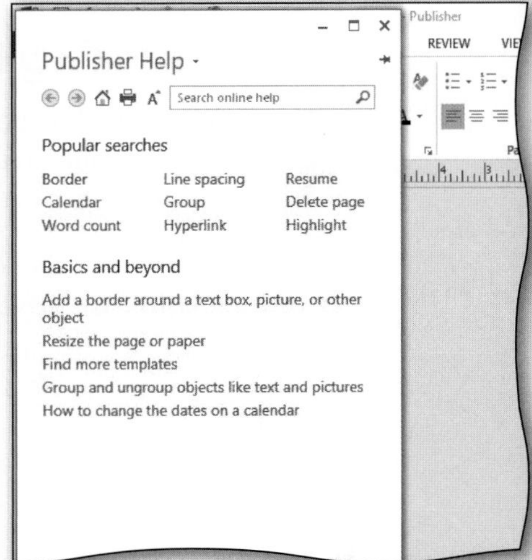

Figure 98

4. Type the answers from your searches in a new blank Publisher publication. If requested by your instructor, enter your name in the Publisher publication.
5. Save the publication with a new file name and then submit it in the format specified by your instructor.
6. Exit Publisher.
7. What search text did you use to perform the searches above? Did it take multiple attempts to search and locate the exact information for which you were searching?

Analyze, Correct, Improve

Analyze a file structure, correct all errors, and improve the design.

Organizing Vacation Photos

Note: To complete this assignment, you will be required to use the Data Files for Students. Visit www.cengage.com/ct/studentdownload for detailed instructions or contact your instructor for information about accessing the required files.

Instructions: Traditionally, you have stored photos from past vacations together in one folder. The photos are becoming difficult to manage, and you now want to store them in appropriate folders. You will create the folder structure shown in Figure 99. You then will move the photos to the folders so that they will be organized properly.

1. Correct Create the folder structure in Figure 99 so that you are able to store the photos in an organized manner. If requested by your instructor, add another folder using your last name as the folder name.

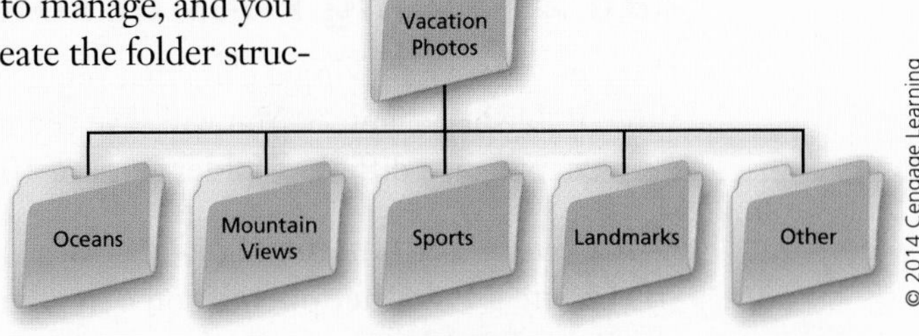

Figure 99

2. Improve View each photo and drag it to the appropriate folder to improve the organization. Submit the assignment in the format specified by your instructor.

3. In which folder did you place each photo? Think about the files you have stored on your computer. What folder hierarchy would be best to manage your files?

© 2014 Cengage Learning

In the Labs

Use the guidelines, concepts, and skills presented in this chapter to increase your knowledge of Windows 8 and Publisher 2013. Labs 1 and 2, which increase in difficulty, require you to create solutions based on what you learned in the chapter; Lab 3 requires you to create a solution, which uses cloud and web technologies, by learning and investigating on your own from general guidance.

Lab 1: Creating Folders for a Video Store

Problem: Your friend works for Ebaird Video. He would like to organize his files in relation to the types of videos available in the store. He has six main categories: drama, action, romance, foreign, biographical, and comedy. You are to create a folder structure similar to Figure 100.

Instructions: Perform the following tasks:

1. Insert a USB flash drive in an available USB port and then open the USB flash drive window.
2. Create the main folder for Ebaird Video.
3. Navigate to the Ebaird Video folder.
4. Within the Ebaird Video folder, create a folder for each of the following: Drama, Action, Romance, Foreign, Biographical, and Comedy.

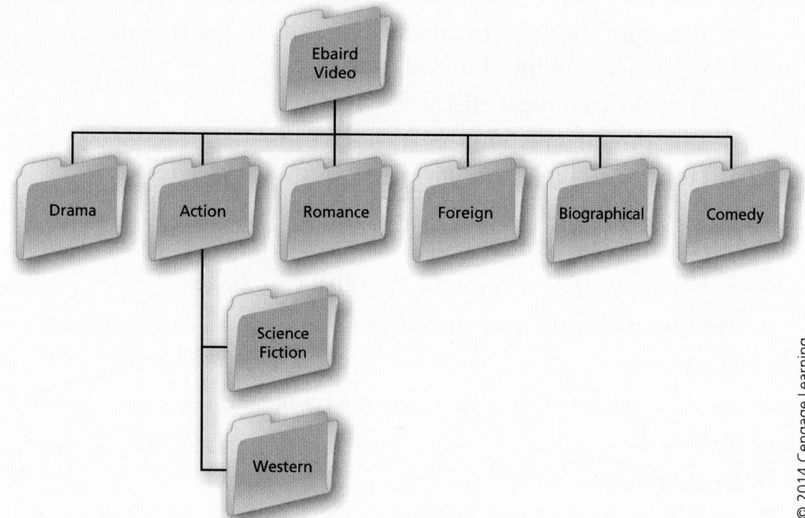

Figure 100

© 2014 Cengage Learning

5. Within the Action folder, create two additional folders, one for Science Fiction and the second for Western.
6. If requested by your instructor, add another folder using your last name as the folder name.
7. Submit the assignment in the format specified by your instructor.
8. Think about how you use your computer for various tasks (consider personal, professional, and academic reasons). What folders do you think will be required on your computer to store the files you save?

Lab 2: Saving Files in Folders

Problem: You are taking a class that requires you to complete three Publisher chapters. You will save the work completed in each chapter in a different folder (Figure 101).

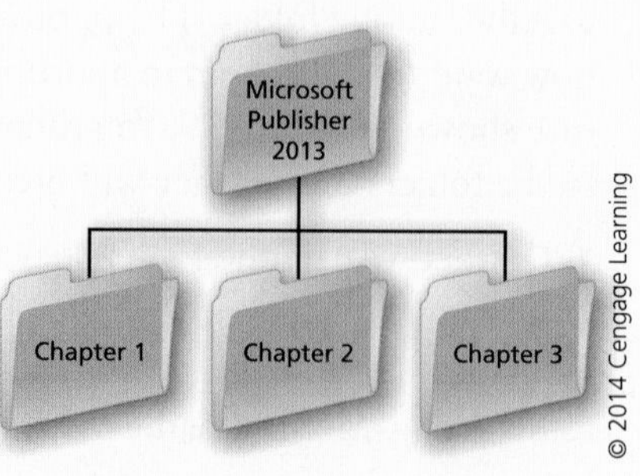

Figure 101

© 2014 Cengage Learning

Instructions: Perform the following tasks:

1. Create a Publisher publication containing the text, First Publisher Chapter.
2. In the Backstage view, tap or click Save As and then tap or click Computer.

3. Tap or click the Browse button to display the Save As dialog box.
4. Tap or click Documents to open the Documents library. Next, create the folder structure shown in Figure 101 using the New folder button.
5. Navigate to the Chapter 1 folder and then save the file in the Chapter 1 folder using the file name, Publisher Chapter 1 Publication.
6. Create another Publisher publication containing the text, Second Publisher Chapter, and then save it in the Chapter 2 folder using the file name, Publisher Chapter 2 Publication.
7. Create a third Publisher publication containing the text, Third Publisher Chapter, and then save it in the Chapter 3 folder using the file name, Publisher Chapter 3 Publication.
8. If requested by your instructor, add your name to each of the three Publisher files.
9. Submit the assignment in the format specified by your instructor.
10. Based on your current knowledge of Windows and Publisher, how will you organize folders for assignments in this class? Why?

Lab 3: Expand Your World: Cloud and Web Technologies

Creating Folders on SkyDrive

Problem: You are taking a class that requires you to create folders on SkyDrive (Figure 102).

Instructions: Perform the following tasks:

1. Sign in to SkyDrive in your browser.
2. Use the Create button to create the folder structure shown in Figure 102.
3. Create a blank publication. Draw a text box and enter the steps in this assignment.
4. If requested by your instructor, add your name to the publication.
5. Save the publication in the Word folder and then exit the app.
6. Submit the assignment in the format specified by your instructor.
7. Based on your current knowledge of SkyDrive, do you think you will use it? What about the Publisher Web App?

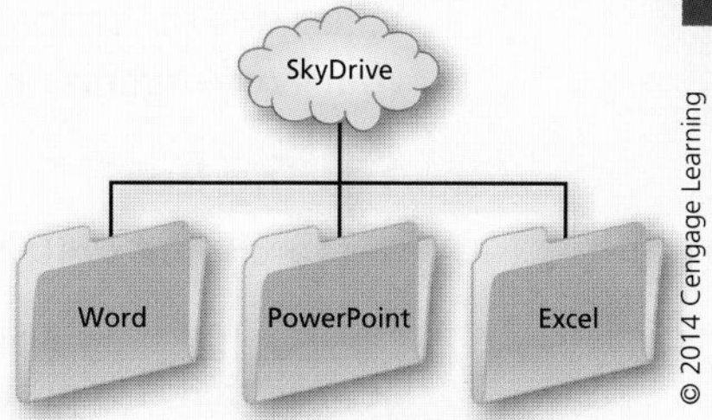

© 2014 Cengage Learning

Figure 102

Consider This: Your Turn

Apply your creative thinking and problem solving skills to design and implement a solution.

1: Creating Beginning Files for Classes

Personal

Part 1: You are taking the following classes: Introduction to Sociology, Chemistry, Calculus, and Marketing. Create folders for each of the classes. Create a folder structure that will store the documents for each of these classes. Use Publisher to create a separate publication for each class. Each publication should contain the name of each class and the class meeting locations and times: Introduction to Sociology meets on Mondays and Wednesdays from 8:00 a.m. to 10:00 a.m.; Chemistry meets on Tuesdays and Thursdays from 11:00 a.m. to 1:00 p.m.; Calculus meets on Mondays, Wednesdays, and Fridays from 1:30 p.m. to 3:00 p.m.; and Marketing meets on Tuesdays from 5:00 p.m. to 8:00 p.m. If requested by your instructor, add your name to each of the Publisher

Continued >

Consider This: Your Turn *continued*

publications. Use the concepts and techniques presented in this chapter to create the folders and files, and store the files in their respective locations. Submit your assignment in the format specified by your instructor.

Part 2: You made several decisions while determining the folder structure in this assignment. What was the rationale behind these decisions? Are there any other decisions that also might have worked?

2: Creating Folders

Professional

Part 1: Your boss at the media store where you work part-time has asked for help with organizing his files. After looking through the files, you decided upon a file structure for her to use, including the following folders: CDs, DVDs, and general merchandise. Use Publisher to create separate publications that list examples in each category. For example, CDs include music [blues, rock, country, new age, pop, and soundtracks], blank discs, books, and games; DVDs include movies [action, documentary, music videos, mystery, and drama], television series, and blank discs; and general merchandise includes clothing, portable media players, cases, earbuds, chargers, and cables. If requested by your instructor, add your name to each of the Publisher publications. Use the concepts and techniques presented in this chapter to create the folders. Submit your assignment in the format specified by your instructor.

Part 2: You made several decisions while determining the folder structure in this assignment. What was the rationale behind these decisions? Justify why you feel this folder structure will help your boss organize her files.

3: Using Help

Research and Collaboration

Part 1: You have just installed a new computer with the Windows operating system and want to be sure that it is protected from the threat of viruses. You ask two of your friends to help research computer viruses, virus prevention, and virus removal. In a team of three people, each person should choose a topic (computer viruses, virus prevention, and virus removal) to research. Use the concepts and techniques presented in this chapter to use Help to find information regarding these topics. Create a Publisher publication that contains steps to properly safeguard a computer from viruses, ways to prevent viruses, as well as the different ways to remove a virus should your computer become infected. Submit your assignment in the format specified by your instructor.

Part 2: You made several decisions while searching Windows Help and Support for this assignment. What decisions did you make? What was the rationale behind these decisions? How did you locate the required information about viruses in help?

Learn Online

Reinforce what you learned in this chapter with games, exercises, training, and many other online activities and resources.

Student Companion Site Reinforcement activities and resources are available at no additional cost on www.cengagebrain.com. Visit www.cengage.com/ct/studentdownload for detailed instructions about accessing the resources available at the Student Companion Site.

Office 365 Essentials

Microsoft product screen shots used with permission from Microsoft Corporation.

Objectives

You will have mastered the material in this chapter when you can:

- Describe the components of Office 365
- Compare Office 2013 to Office 365 subscription plans
- Understand the productivity tools of Office 365
- Sync multiple devices using Office 365
- Describe how business teams collaborate using SharePoint
- Describe how to use a SharePoint template to design a public website
- Describe how to conduct an online meeting with Lync

Explore Office 365

Introduction to Office 365

Microsoft Office 365 uses the cloud to deliver a subscription-based service offering the newest Office suite and much more. The Microsoft cloud provides Office software and information stored on remote servers all over the world. Your documents are located online or on the cloud, which provides you access to your information anywhere using a PC, Mac, tablet, mobile phone, or other device with an Internet connection. For businesses and students alike, Office 365 offers significant cost savings compared to the traditional cost of purchasing Microsoft Office 2013. In addition to the core desktop Office suite, Office 365 provides access to email, calendars, conferencing, file sharing, and website design, which sync across multiple devices.

Cloud Computing

Cloud computing refers to a collection of computer servers that house resources users access through the Internet (Figure 1). These resources include email messages, schedules, music, photos, videos, games, websites, programs, apps, servers, storage, and more. Instead of accessing these resources on your computer or mobile device, you access them on the cloud.

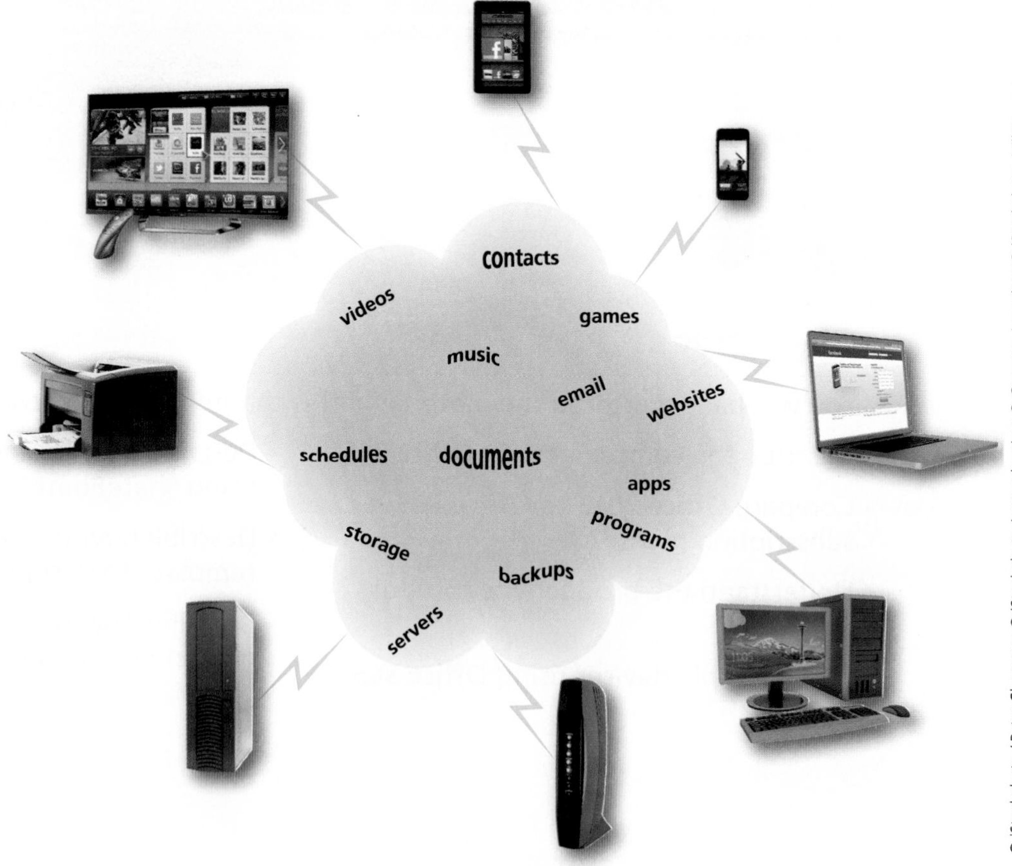

© iStockphoto / Petar Chernaev; © iStockphoto / cotesebastien; © Cengage Learning; © iStockphoto / Jill Fromer; © Cengage Learning; © iStockphoto / 123 render; © Cengage Learning; © Pablo Eder / Shutterstock.com; © Peter Gudella / Shutterstock.com; © Mr.Reborn55 / Shutterstock.com; Courtesy of LG Electronics USA Inc.; © Cengage Learning

Figure 1

Cloud computing can help businesses be more efficient and save them money by shifting usage and the consumption of resources, such as servers and programs, from a local environment to the Internet. For example, an employee working during the day in California could use computing resources located in an office in London that is closed for the evening. When the company in California uses the computing resources, it pays a fee that is based on the amount of computing time and other resources it consumes, much in the same way that consumers pay utility companies for the amount of electricity they use.

Cloud computing is changing how users access and pay for software applications. Fading fast are the days when software packages were sold in boxes at a physical store location with a one-time purchase software license fee. Instead, the new pricing structure is a subscription-based model, where users pay a monthly or annual fee for the software that you can use on multiple devices. The cloud-based Office 365 offers the Office suite with added features that allow you to communicate and collaborate with others in real time.

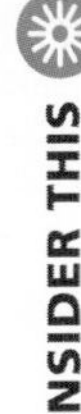

When you create a free Microsoft account, do you get free cloud storage space?
Yes, when you create a free Microsoft account at Outlook.com, you have access to 7 GB of cloud storage for any type of files.

What Is Office 365?

Office 365 (Office365.com) is a collection of programs and services, which includes the Microsoft Office 2013 suite, file storage, online collaboration, and file synchronization, as shown in Figure 2 on the next page. You can access these services using your computer, browser, or supported mobile device. For example, a business has two options for providing Office to their employees. A business could purchase Office 2013 and install the software on company computers and servers; however, this traditional Office 2013 package with perpetual licensing does not include the communication and collaboration tools. Employees could not access the Office software if they were not using their work computers. In contrast, if the business purchases a monthly subscription to Office 365, each employee has access to the Office suite on up to five different computers, whether at home or work; company-wide email; web conferencing; website creation capabilities; cloud storage; and shared files. For a lower price, Office 365 provides many more features. In addition, a business may prefer a subscription plan with predictable monthly costs and no up-front infrastructure costs.

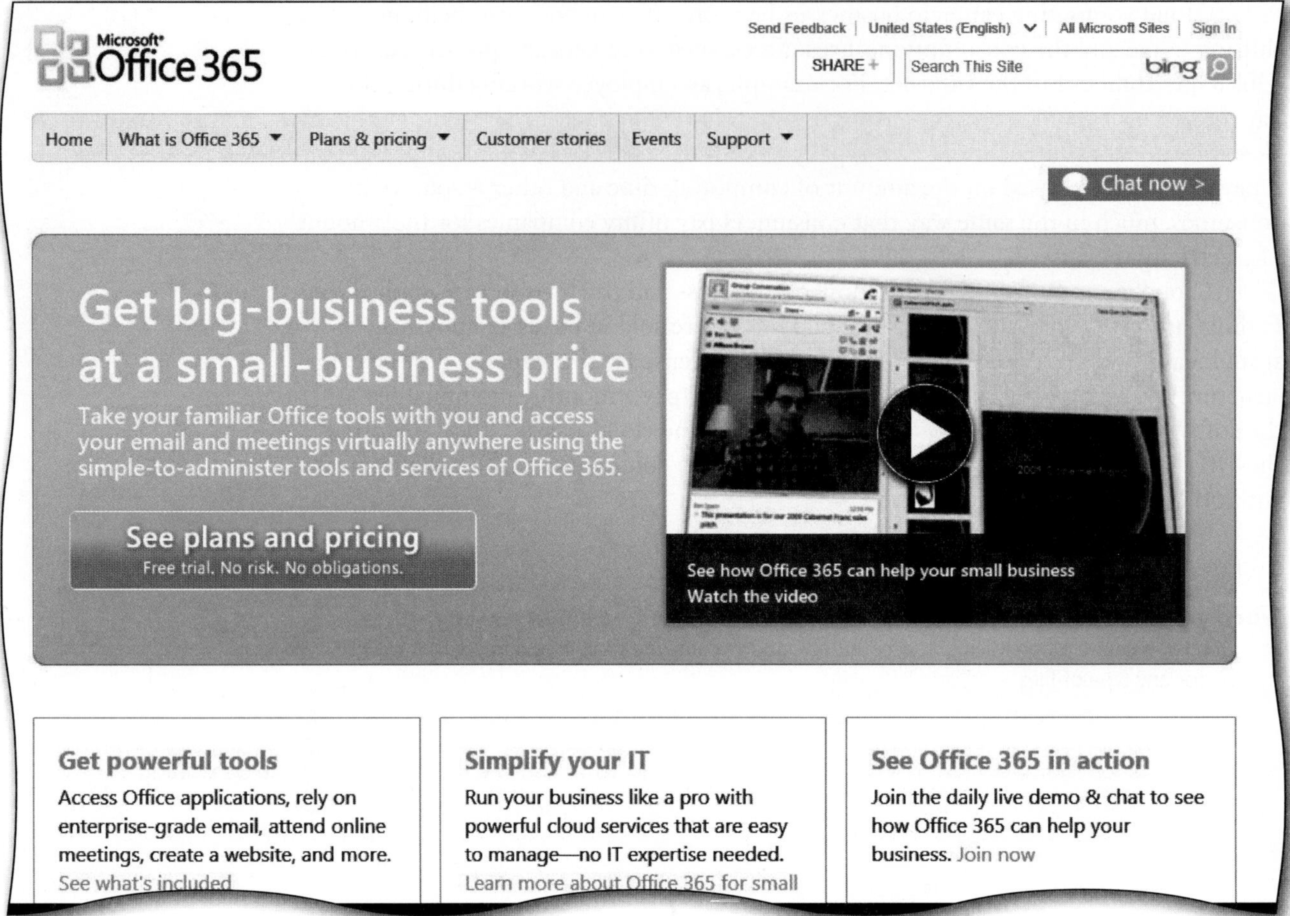

Figure 2

Office 2013 and Office 365 Features Comparison

Office 2013 is the name of the perpetual software package that includes individual applications that can be installed on a single computer. An Office 365 subscription comes with a license to install the software on multiple PCs or Macs at the same time, giving you more flexibility to use your Office products in your home, school, or workplace, whether on a computer or a mobile device. Office 365 provides the Office 2013 programs as part of a subscription service that includes online storage, sharing, and syncing via Microsoft cloud services as shown in Table 1.

Office 365 is available in business, consumer, education, and government editions. Office 365 combines the full version of the Microsoft Office desktop suite with cloud-based versions of Microsoft's communications and collaboration services. The subscription package includes:

- Microsoft Exchange online for shared email and calendars
- Microsoft SharePoint Online for shared file access and public website creation
- Microsoft Office Web apps for browser viewing
- Microsoft Lync Online for communication services

Table 1 Office 2013 and Office 365 Feature Comparison

Office 2013 Professional (Installed on a single device)	Office 365 Subscription (Installed on 2 to 5 devices)
Microsoft Word	Microsoft Word
Microsoft Excel	Microsoft Excel
Microsoft PowerPoint	Microsoft PowerPoint
Microsoft Access	Microsoft Access
Microsoft Outlook	Microsoft Outlook
Microsoft Publisher	Microsoft Publisher
Microsoft OneNote	Microsoft OneNote
	email and calendars (Exchange Online)
	file sharing (SharePoint Online)
	public website design and publishing (SharePoint Online)
	browser-based Office Web Apps
	instant messaging (Lync Online)
	audio and video web conferencing (Lync Online)
	screen sharing with shared control (Lync Online)
	technical support

© 2014 Cengage Learning

Subscription-Based Office 365 Plans

Microsoft provides various subscription plans for Office 365 with different benefits for each individual or organization. Subscription plans include Office 365 Home Premium for home users, Office 365 University for students, Office 365 Small Business, Office 365 Small Business Premium, Office 365 Midsize Business, and Office 365 Enterprise and Government. During the Office 365 sign-up process, you create a Microsoft email address and password to use on your multiple devices. A single subscription to an Office 365 Home Premium account can cover an entire household. The Office 365 Home Premium subscription allows up to five concurrent installations by using the same email address and password combination. This means that your mother could be on the main family computer while you use your tablet and smartphone at the same time. You each can sign in with your individual Microsoft accounts using your settings and accessing your own documents using a single Office 365 subscription.

The Office 365 University subscription plan is designed for higher-education full-time and part-time students, faculty, and staff. By submitting the proper credentials, such as a school email address, students and faculty can purchase Office 365 University, including Word, PowerPoint, Excel, Access, Outlook, Publisher, and OneNote. A one-time payment covers a four-year subscription. In addition, Office 365 University provides users with 27 GB of SkyDrive cloud storage rather than the free 7 GB provided by a Microsoft account, and 60 Skype world minutes per month for videoconferencing. Students have the option of renewing for another four years, for a total of eight years. The Office 365 University edition is limited to two computers (PC or Mac).

The Microsoft Office 365 Business Plans can provide full support for employees to work from any location, whether they are in their traditional business office, commuting to and from work across the country, or working from a home office. Office 365 small business plans (Small Business and Small Business Premium) are best for companies with up to 10 employees, but can accommodate up to 25 users. Office 365 Midsize Business accommodates from 11 to 300 users. Office 365 Enterprise Plan fits organizations ranging in size from a single employee to 50,000-plus users. Each employee can install Microsoft Office 365 on five different computers.

First Look at Office 365

Microsoft Office 365 subscription plans offer all the same applications that are available in the Microsoft Office Professional 2013 suite in addition to multiple communication and collaboration tools. With Office 365 you can retrieve, edit, and save Office documents on the Office 365 cloud, coauthor documents in real time with others, and quickly initiate computer-based calls, instant messages, and web conferences with others.

Productivity Tools

Whether you are inserting audio and video into a Word document to create a high-impact business plan proposal or utilizing the visualization tools in Excel to chart the return on investment of a new mobile marketing program, Office 365 premium plans deliver the full Office product with the same features as the latest version of Microsoft Office. Office 365 uses a quick-start installation technology, called **Click-to-Run**, that downloads and installs the basics within minutes, so that users are able to start working almost immediately. It also includes **Office on Demand**, which streams Office to Windows 7- and Windows 8-based PCs for work performed on public computers. The single-use copy that is installed temporarily on the Windows computer does not count toward the device limit. No installation is necessary when using Office on Demand, and the applications disappear from the computer once you are finished using them. If you have a document on a USB drive or on SkyDrive that you need to edit on another PC, you can use Office on Demand to get the full version of Word in just a few minutes.

In effect, the Office 365 subscription provides access to the full Office applications wherever you are working. When you access your Office 365 account management panel, three choices are listed: 32- and 64-bit versions of Office 2013, and Office for Mac. Selecting the third option will initiate a download of an installer that must be run in the standard OS X fashion. When you install Office 365 on a Mac, the most current Mac version of Office is installed.

CONSIDER THIS

Unlike Google, which offers online documents, spreadsheets, and presentations called Google Docs, Microsoft Office 365 installs locally on your computer in addition to being available online. Google Docs is entirely browser based, which means if you are not connected to the Internet, you cannot access your Google Docs files.

Email and Calendars

In business, sharing information is essential to meeting the needs of your customers and staff. Office 365 offers shared access to business email, calendars, and contacts using **Exchange Online** from a computer, tablet, phone, and browser. The cloud-based Exchange Online enables business people to access Outlook information from anywhere at any time, while eliminating the cost of purchasing and maintaining servers to store data. If you need to meet with a colleague about a new project, you can compare calendars to view availability, confirm conference room availability, share project contacts, search email messages related to the project, and send email invitations to the project meeting. Exchange Online also allows you to search and access your company's address list.

Online Meetings

When you are working with a team on a project that requires interaction, email and text communications can slow the communications process. Microsoft Lync connects you with others by facilitating real-time, interactive presentations and meetings over the Internet using both video and audio calling. As shown in Figure 3, you can conduct an online meeting with a team member or customer that includes an instant messaging conversation, audio, high-definition video, virtual whiteboards, and screen sharing. If the customer does not have an Office 365 subscription, they still can join the meeting through the invitation link, which runs the Lync Web App.

Skype is another tool in the Office 365 subscription, which enables users to place video calls to computers and smartphones and voice calls to landlines. Skype also supports instant message and file sharing to computers and mobile devices. While Skype may be adequate for simple communication, Lync provides for more robust, comprehensive communications. These robust features include high-definition (HD) videoconferencing capabilities, a whiteboard, and a larger audience. Using Lync, meeting attendees simultaneously can view up to five participants' video, identify the active speaker, and associate names with faces. Lync supports up to 250 attendees per meeting. Unlike Skype, Lync meetings can be recorded for replaying at a later time. This enables businesses and schools to schedule meetings or organize online classes using Lync capabilities.

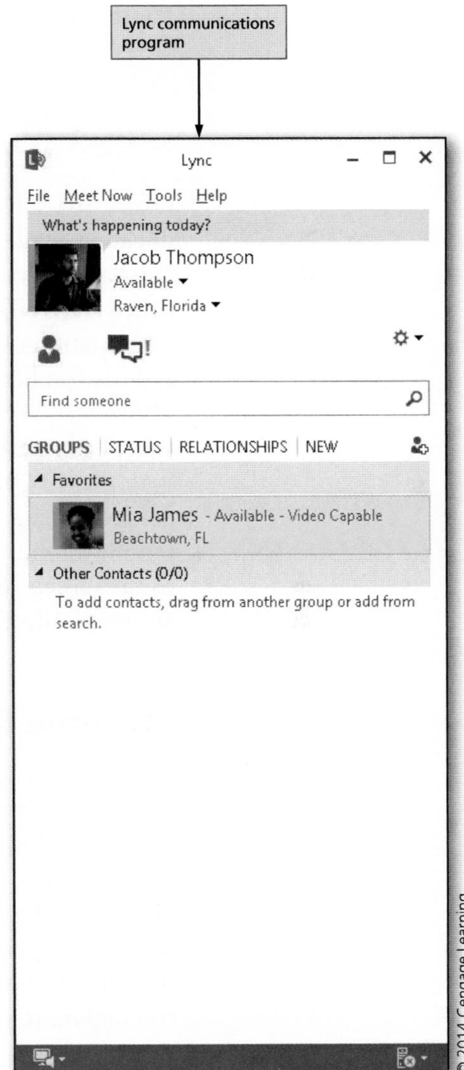

© 2014 Cengage Learning

Figure 3

File Sharing

Office 365 includes a team site, which is a password-protected portal that supports sharing of large, difficult-to-email files and provides a single location for the latest versions of documents. In business, for example, colleagues working on common projects can save valuable time by being able to access instantly the latest master copy of each document. Security can be managed through different levels of user access so that users see only what they are supposed to see. Office 365 provides access to shared files using the cloud, making writing, editing, and sharing documents easier. If a construction company creates a commercial bid for a building project, the customers can be invited to view an Excel spreadsheet bid, construction timetable with a shared calendar, and an Access database of all the materials needed using the file sharing feature online.

Website Creation

Office 365 business plan subscriptions include a built-in hosted public website, where customers and clients can find an online storefront of a company. This public website, called the Website, can be customized to market a company by using various templates within the Office 365 cloud. The website creation tools include those for adding a theme, graphics, fonts, maps, directions, blogs, stock tickers, slide shows, PayPal, weather, and videos to interact with the website's visitors.

Synchronization

Office 365 subscription plans provide a central place to store and access your documents and business information. A feature of Office 365 ensures the original and backup computer files in two or more locations are identical through a process called **Active Directory Synchronization**. For example, if you open a PowerPoint presentation on your smartphone while you are riding a city bus and then add a new slide as you head to school, the PowerPoint presentation automatically is synced with Office 365. When you arrive on campus and open the PowerPoint presentation on a school computer, your new slide already is part of the finished slide show. By storing your files in Office 365, you can access your files on another computer if your home computer fails, with no loss of time or important information. When using your mobile phone's data plan, you do not need to search for a Wi-Fi hot spot to connect to the Office 365 cloud. Computer labs in schools can be configured to synchronize automatically all student files to Office 365 online.

Multiple Device Access to Office 365

With a single sign-in process, Office 365 provides access to multiple computers and mobile devices, including Android smartphones and tablets, Apple iPhones and iPads, Windows phones, and Blackberry phones. After you configure your devices' email settings, you can view your Microsoft account calendar, contacts, and email. Your personalized settings, preferences, and documents can be synchronized among all the different devices included in your Office 365 premium subscription. With the mobility of Office 365, students and employees can work anywhere, accessing information and responding to email requests immediately. If you lose your phone, Office 365 includes a feature that allows you to remotely wipe your phone clean of any data. By wiping your phone's data, you can prevent any unauthorized access to sensitive information, such as your banking information, passwords, and contacts, as well as discourage identity theft. Because your phone contacts and other information are stored on the Microsoft cloud, damaged or lost equipment is never a problem.

CONSIDER THIS

A thief can be quite resourceful if he or she steals your phone. Before you can alert your parents or spouse to the theft, they might receive a text from "you" asking for your ATM or credit card PIN number. Your parents or spouse might then reply with the PIN number. Your bank account could be emptied in minutes.

Teams Using Office 365 in Business

In the business world, rarely does an employee work in isolation. Companies need their employees to collaborate, whether they work in the same office or in locations around the world. Telecommuters working from home can communicate as if they were on-site by using a common team website and conferencing software. SharePoint Online and Lync Online provide seamless communication.

Small business subscription plans as low as $6.00 per user per month allow employees to create and store Word documents, Excel spreadsheets, and PowerPoint presentations online and communicate with one another via email, instant messaging, or video chat as they work on projects together. As shown in Figure 4, a team portal page is shown when you subscribe at https://portal.microsoftonline.com. Larger companies and those requiring more features can take advantage of the Office 365 business premium package, which, in addition to the features listed above, provides access to the Office 365 portal website and eliminates the effort and cost of the users maintaining their own costly computer servers.

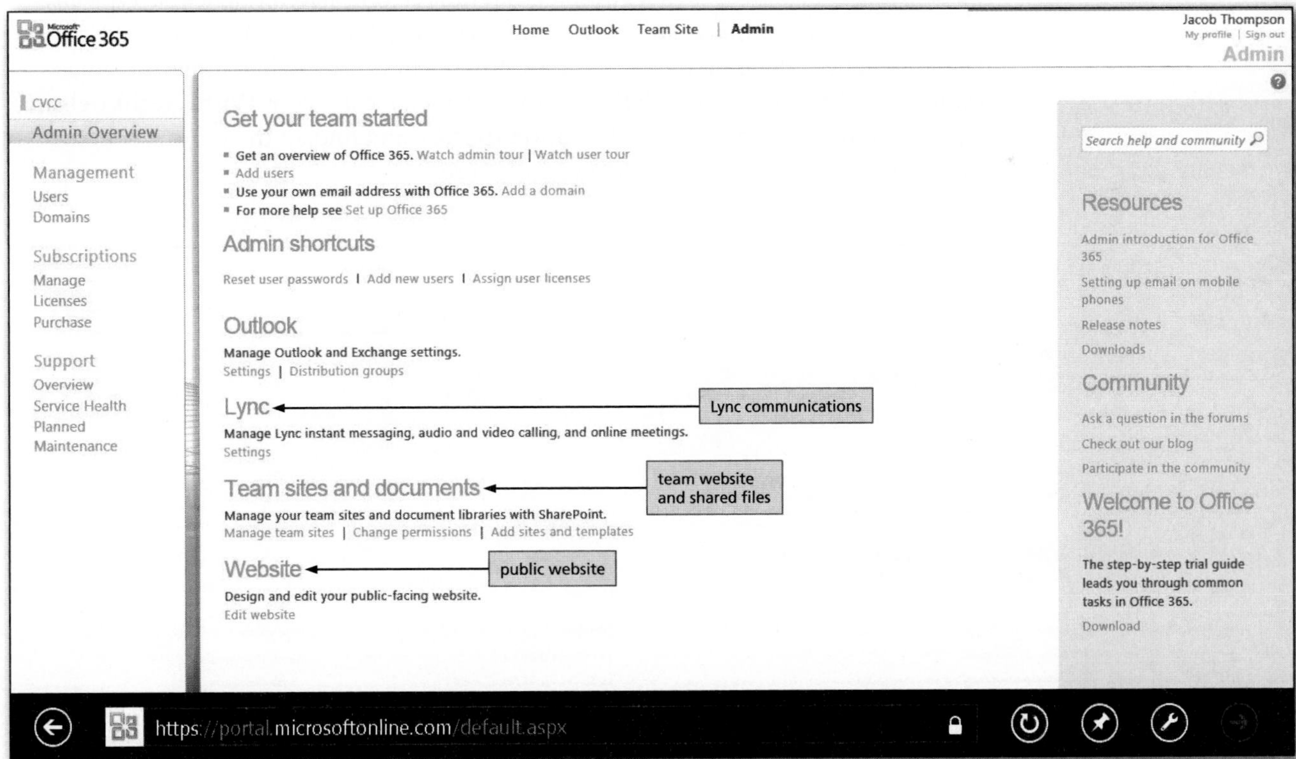

Figure 4

Email Communication Using Exchange

Office 365 includes Exchange Online, an email-based collaborative communications server for business. Exchange enables employees to be more productive by effectively managing email across multiple devices and facilitating teamwork.

Collaboration Using SharePoint

SharePoint Online, a part of Office 365 subscription plans, allows employees to collaborate with one another, share documents, post announcements, and track tasks, as shown in Table 2.

Table 2 Office 365 SharePoint Features

Team Site Feature	Description
Calendar	Track important dates
Shared Document Library	Store related documents according to topic; picture, report, and slide libraries often are included
Task List	Track team tasks according to who is responsible for completion
Team Discussion Board	Discuss the topics at hand in an open forum
Contacts List	Share contact lists of employees, customers, contractors, and suppliers

© 2014 Cengage Learning

Office 365 provides the tools to plan meetings. Users can share calendars side by side, view availability, and suggest meeting times from shared calendars. Typically, a SharePoint team administrator or website owner establishes a folder structure to share and manage documents. The team website is fully searchable online, making locating and sharing data more efficient than using a local server. With a team website, everyone on the team has a central location to store and find all the information for a project, client, or department, as shown in Figure 5.

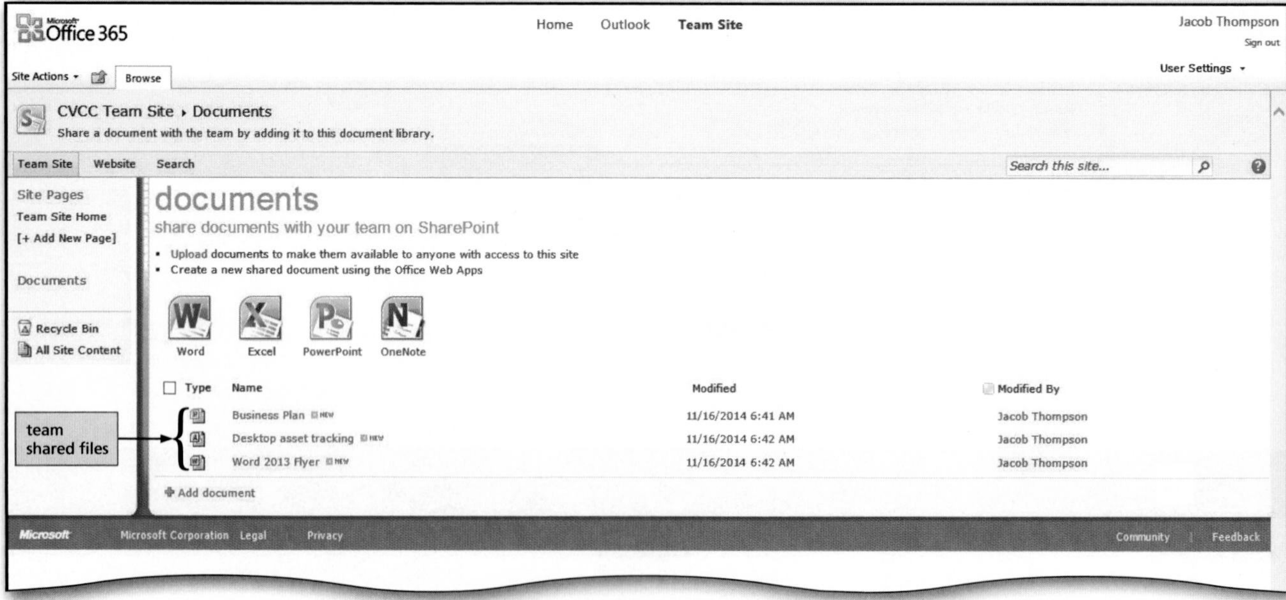

Figure 5

Website Design Using SharePoint

SharePoint provides templates to create a professional looking, public website for an online presence to market your business. As shown in Figure 6, a local pet sitting business is setting up a business website by customizing a SharePoint template. SharePoint Public Website includes features within the Design Manager that you use to customize and design your website by adding your own images, forms, style sheets, maps, themes, and social networking tools. When you finish customizing your business site, you can apply your own domain name to the site. A **domain** is a unique web address that identifies where your website can be found. Office 365 SharePoint hosts your website as part of your subscription. Your customers easily can find your business online and learn about your services.

BTW

Creating SharePoint Intranet Sites

A SharePoint website also can be customized to serve as an internal company website for private communications within the company.

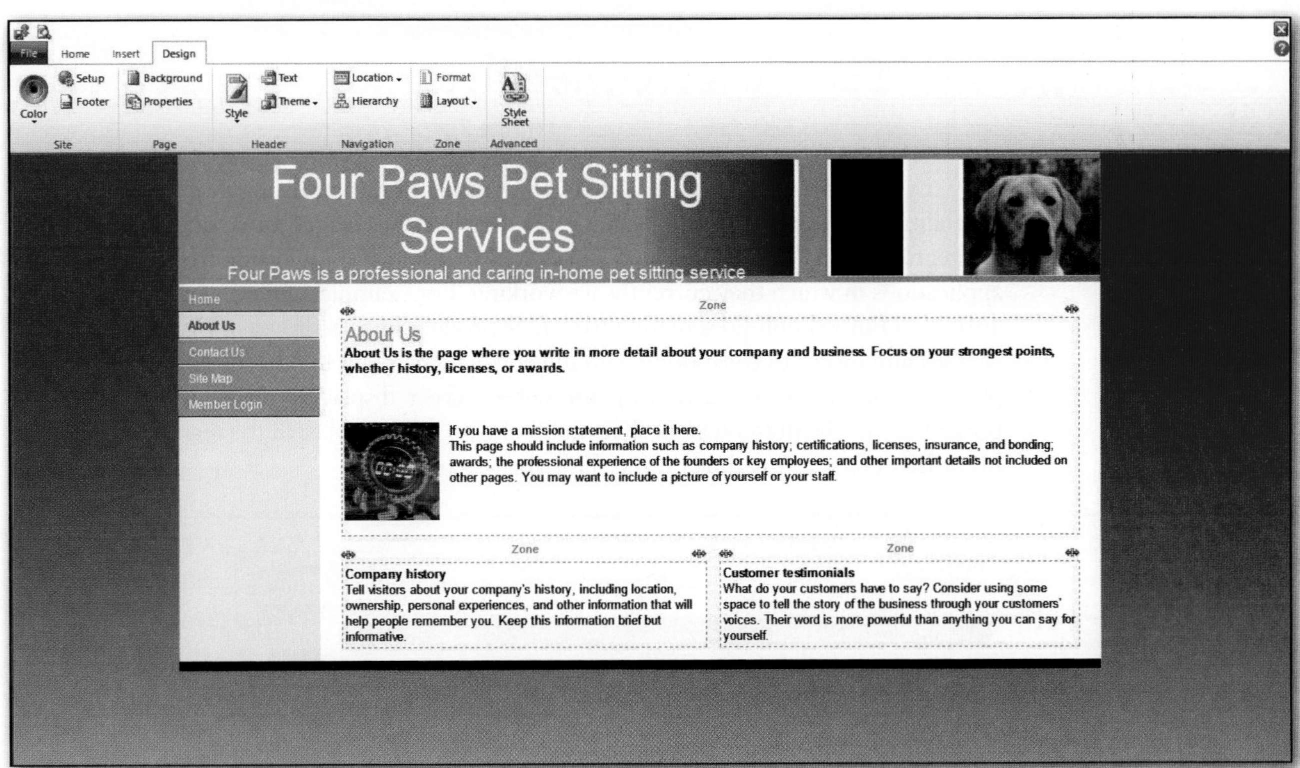

Figure 6

Real-Time Communications Using Lync

Lync Online is Microsoft's server platform for online team communications and comes bundled with Office 365 business subscriptions. As shown in Figure 7, Lync connects in real time to allow instant messaging, videoconferencing, and voice communications; it also integrates with email and Microsoft Office applications.

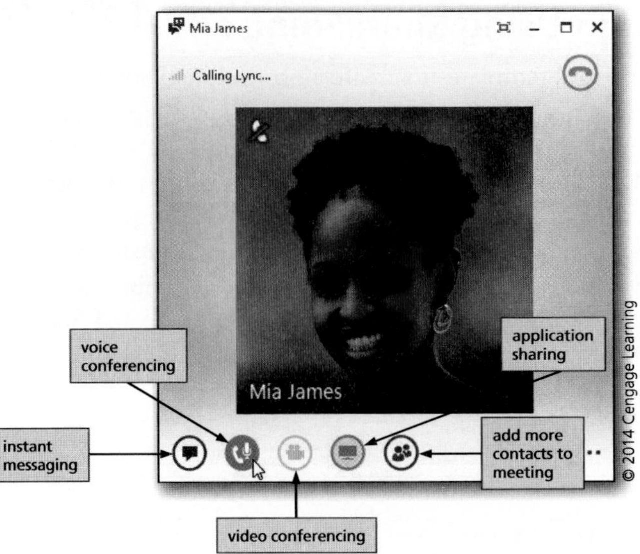

Figure 7

Lync allows you to connect with staff at remote locations using instant messaging capabilities, desktop sharing, videoconferencing, and shared agendas or documents. Lync is integrated into Office 365, which allows staff to start communicating from within the applications in which they currently are working. For example, while an employee is creating a PowerPoint presentation for a new product line, as shown in Figure 8, Lync enables him or her to collaborate with the entire team about the details of the product presentation. The team can view the presenter's screen displaying the PowerPoint presentation. The presenter can share control with any member of the team and can share his or her screen at any time during the Lync meeting.

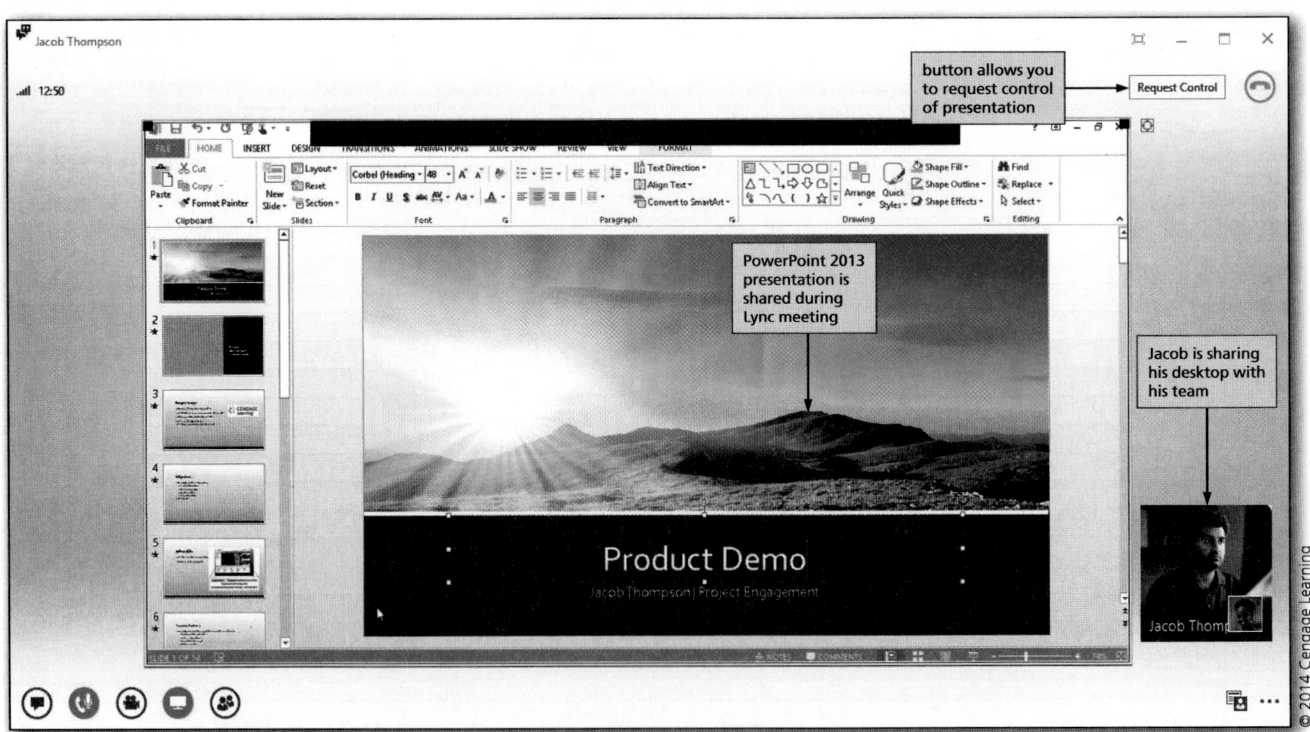

Figure 8

Users can send a Lync meeting request to schedule a team meeting, or an impromptu conversation can be started immediately using the Meet Now feature. Participants receive a Lync meeting request link via an email message, and when they click the meeting request link, Lync automatically connects them to the online conference. If the participant does not have Lync installed, the Lync Web App automatically connects to the Lync meeting through the user's PC or Mac OS X browser. If a participant is away from his or her computer, he or she still can participate using the Lync Mobile apps for Windows Phone, iOS, and Android. As shown in Figure 9, Lync utilizes **instant messaging** (IM), allowing two or more people to share text messages. They can communicate in real time, similar to a voice conversation. In addition to a simple instant message, Lync provides a feature called **persistent chat**, which allows end-users to participate in a working session of instant messages that is persistent or sustained over a specified amount of time in a moderated chat room. Consider having an instant messaging session with a group of colleagues in different parts of your organization, regardless of geographic region, where you all are working on the same project. Over the course of the project, different people post questions and concerns, and others are able to respond to all those who have subscribed to your topic or been admitted to the chat room. Instead of a long trail of email messages, a team can keep information in a controlled environment with a full history of the discussion in one location.

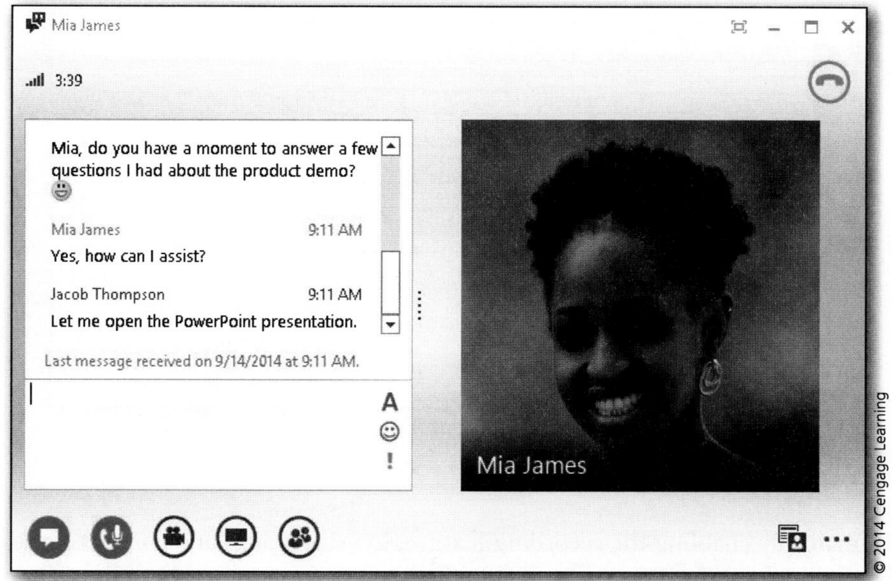

Figure 9

Lync also delivers support for full high-definition (HD) videoconferencing, so that a team can have a clear view of the participants, products, and demos. Before you join the video feed, you can preview your video feed to make sure your video camera is at the correct angle, your image is centered within the video frame, and that your room lighting provides for a clear image. The Lync preview option is important in creating a positive first impression over video. Your audio devices can be tested for clarity to make sure your headset, microphone, and speakers are functioning properly.

Lync provides a polling feature that presenters can use to ask the participants' opinions during a meeting (Figure 10). The poll question can consist of up to seven possible choices. The presenter has the option to view the results privately or share the results with the entire group.

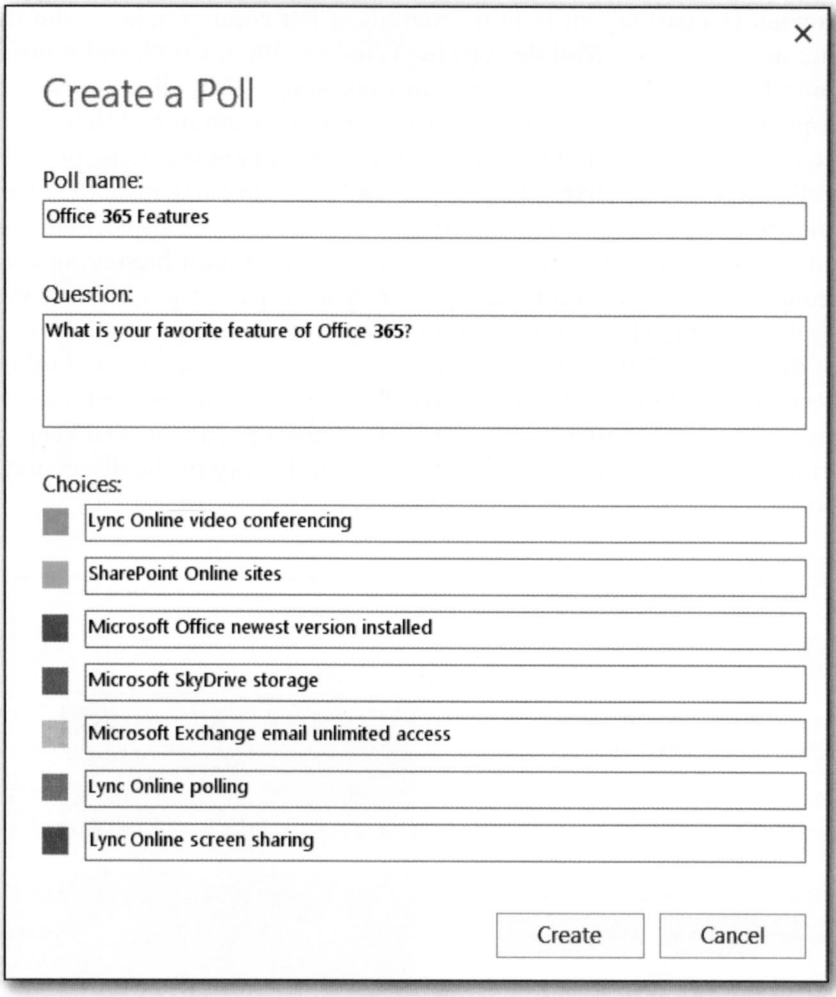

© 2014 Cengage Learning

Figure 10

Finally, by enabling the recording feature, Lync meetings and conversations can be captured for viewing at a later time. For instance, you can capture the audio, video, instant messaging (IM), screen sharing, Microsoft PowerPoint presentations, whiteboard, and polling portions of the Lync session and then play them back just as they transpired during the live Lync event. The meeting recordings can be made available to others so that they can view all or part of the Lync event. Instructors can record Lync online class sessions for students who were unable to attend the original presentation. The recording starts in Microsoft Lync; recordings then can be viewed within the Recording Manager feature.

Chapter Summary

In this chapter, you have learned how to subscribe to Office 365, which provides local and online access to Office applications, email, document sharing, web conferencing, and business websites. You also learned how a business can utilize Office 365 features on the cloud to facilitate teamwork. Finally, you learned about the features of SharePoint and Lync, which provide collaboration and communications for business teams using Office 365.

Consider This: Your Turn

Apply your creative thinking and problem solving skills to design and implement a solution.

1: Comparing Office 365 Personal Plans

Personal

Part 1: You are a freshman in college living at home with your family. You are considering if it would be a better value to subscribe to Office 365 University or Office 365 Home Premium. Write a one-page document comparing the pros and cons of the two subscription plans. Research the different subscriptions in detail at Office365.com. Submit your assignment in the format specified by your instructor.

Part 2: Which type of computer and/or devices would you use with your Office 365 subscription? If you are at a friend's home that does not have Office 365, how could you access your Office files if you do not have your computer or mobile device with you?

2: Upgrading a Local Business to Office 365

Professional

Part 1: You are an employee at Impact Digital Marketing, a small marketing firm with 12 employees. The firm is setting up an Office 365 Small Business subscription next week, and you need to compose an email message with multiple paragraphs to explain the features of this new subscription plan to the members of your firm. Research the Office 365 Small Business subscription plan in detail at Office365.com, and compile your findings in an email message. Submit your assignment in the format specified by your instructor.

Part 2: Give three examples of how a marketing firm could use Lync. How could a marketing firm use the SharePoint Websites feature?

3: Conducting a Lync Meeting

Research and Collaboration

* Students need an Office 365 subscription to complete the following assignment.

Part 1: Using your Office 365 subscription, conduct a meeting using Lync. Working with a partner, use your Office 365 subscription to research how to use Lync. Then, conduct a 15-minute Lync meeting, including instant messaging, to discuss the features of Lync. Use the concepts and techniques presented in this chapter to create the Lync meeting. Submit your assignment in the format specified by your instructor.

Part 2: When using Lync in business, when would the video feature best be utilized?

1 Creating a Flyer

Microsoft product screenshots used with permission from Microsoft Corporation.
QR code © 2014 Cengage Learning; Guitar clip art courtesy of Joy Starks.

Objectives

You will have mastered the material in this chapter when you can:

- Choose Publisher template options
- Describe the Publisher window
- Select objects and zoom
- Replace Publisher placeholder text
- Check spelling as you type
- Delete objects
- Format text and autofit
- Insert and format a photo
- Move, align, and resize objects
- Print a publication
- Open and modify a publication
- Create a hyperlink
- Change the background
- Save a print publication as a web publication

1 | Creating a Flyer

Introduction

To publicize an event, advertise a sale or service, promote a business, or convey a message to the community, you may want to create a flyer and post it in a public location. A **flyer** is a single-page publication, which may be printed on various sizes of paper, announcing personal items for sale or rent (car, boat, apartment); garage or block sales; services being offered (housecleaning, lessons, carpooling); membership, sponsorship, or donation requests (club, religious organization, charity); and other messages. Flyers are an inexpensive means of reaching the community, yet many go unnoticed because they are designed poorly. A good flyer, or any publication, must deliver a message in the clearest, most attractive and effective way possible. You must clarify your purpose and know your target audience. You need to gather ideas and plan for the printing. Finally, you must edit, proofread, and then publish your flyer. Flyers must stand out to be noticed.

Flyers also can be posted on the web. Electronic bulletin boards, social networking sites, and online auction websites are good places to reach people with flyers, advertising everything from a bake sale to a part-time job.

To illustrate the features of Publisher, this book presents a series of projects that create publications similar to those you will encounter in academic and business environments.

Project—Concert Flyer

The project in this chapter uses Publisher and a flyer template to create the flyer shown in Figure 1–1. This attractive flyer advertises a concert on campus. The **headline** clearly identifies the purpose of the flyer, using large, bold letters. Below that, to maintain consistency, the same font is used for the ticket information, date, time, and location. In the upper-right portion of the flyer, the phone number and title of the series appear. The photo of the guitar is formatted to be eye-catching and entices people to stop and look at the flyer. The QR code graphic allows mobile devices to access the band's webpage quickly. The tear-offs, aligned at the bottom of the flyer, include the name, phone number, and website of the band. Finally, the font and color schemes support the topic and make the text stand out.

555-TICKETS

Campus Concerts

Shadows Blue

Live! In Concert!

For tickets, visit www.utix.biz

Saturday, October 4

8:00 p.m. at the Campus Auditorium

Shadows Blue 555-TICKETS
Online at www.utix.biz

Shadows Blue 555-TICKETS
Online at www.utix.biz

Shadows Blue 555-TICKETS
Online at www.utix.biz

Shadows Blue 555-TICKETS
Online at www.utix.biz

Shadows Blue 555-TICKETS
Online at www.utix.biz

Shadows Blue 555-TICKETS
Online at www.utix.biz

Shadows Blue 555-TICKETS
Online at www.utix.biz

Shadows Blue 555-TICKETS
Online at www.utix.biz

Shadows Blue 555-TICKETS
Online at www.utix.biz

Shadows Blue 555-TICKETS
Online at www.utix.biz

Figure 1–1

QR code © 2014 Cengage Learning; Guitar clip art courtesy of Joy Starks

Roadmap

In this chapter, you will learn how to create the flyer shown in Figure 1–1 on the previous page. The following roadmap identifies general activities you will perform as you progress through this chapter:

1. CUSTOMIZE the TEMPLATE options such as choice, color scheme, and font scheme.
2. NAVIGATE the interface and SELECT objects.
3. REPLACE placeholder TEXT.
4. DELETE OBJECTS you do not plan to use in the publication, if any.
5. FORMAT the TEXT in the flyer.
6. INSERT GRAPHICS in placeholders and in other locations, as necessary.
7. FORMAT PICTURES by adding borders and styles.
8. ENHANCE the PAGE by repositioning and aligning objects.
9. PRINT and EXIT the publication.
10. OPEN and REVISE the publication.

At the beginning of step instructions throughout the chapter, you will see an abbreviated form of this roadmap. The abbreviated roadmap uses colors to indicate chapter progress: gray means the chapter is beyond that activity, blue means the task being shown is covered in that activity, and black means that activity is yet to be covered. For example, the following abbreviated roadmap indicates the chapter would be showing a task in the Format Text activity.

1 CUSTOMIZE TEMPLATES | 2 NAVIGATE & SELECT | 3 REPLACE TEXT | 4 DELETE OBJECTS | **5 FORMAT TEXT**
6 INSERT GRAPHICS | 7 FORMAT PICTURE | 8 ENHANCE PAGE | 9 PRINT & EXIT | 10 OPEN & REVISE

Use the abbreviated roadmap as a progress guide while you read or step through the instructions in this chapter.

To Run Publisher

If you are using a computer to step through the project in this chapter and you want your screens to match the figures in this book, you should change your screen's resolution to 1366 × 768. For information about how to change a computer's resolution, refer to the Office and Windows chapter at the beginning of this book.

The following steps, which assume Windows 8 is running, use the Start screen or the search box to run Publisher based on a typical installation. You may need to ask your instructor how to run Publisher on your computer. For a detailed example of the procedure summarized below, refer to the Office and Windows chapter.

For an introduction to Windows 8 and instruction about how to perform basic Windows 8 tasks, read the Office and Windows chapter at the beginning of this book, where you can learn how to resize windows, change screen resolution, create folders, move and rename files, use Windows Help, and much more.

1. Scroll the Start screen and search for a Publisher 2013 tile. If your Start screen contains a Publisher 2013 tile, tap or click it to run Publisher and then proceed to Step 5. If the Start screen does not contain the Publisher 2013 tile, proceed to the next step to search for the Publisher app.
2. Swipe in from the right edge of the screen or point to the upper-right corner of the screen to display the Charms bar and then tap or click the Search charm on the Charms bar to display the Search menu.
3. Type `Publisher` as the search text in the Search box and watch the search results appear in the Apps list.
4. Tap or click Publisher 2013 in the search results to run Publisher.
5. If the Publisher window is not maximized, tap or click the Maximize button on its title bar to maximize the window (Figure 1–2).

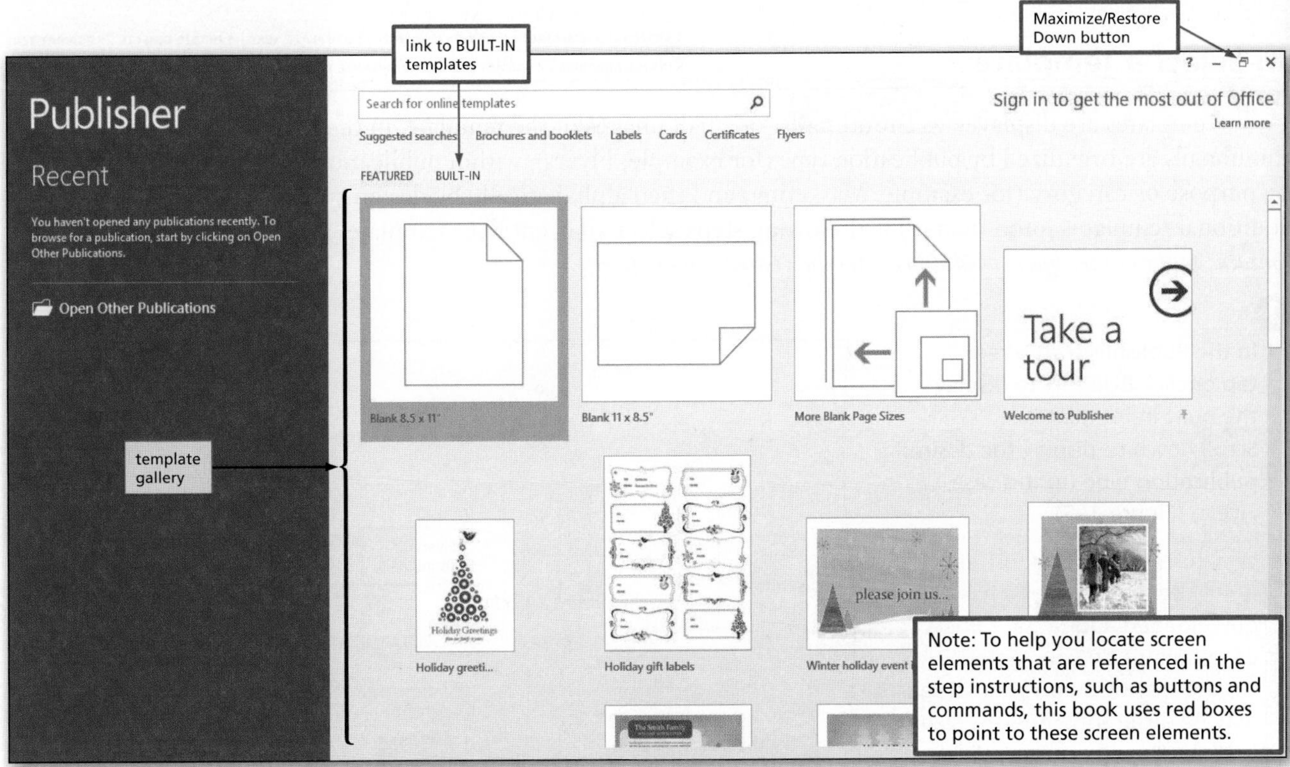

Figure 1–2

Creating a Flyer

Publisher provides many ways to begin the process of creating and editing a publication. You can:

- Create a new publication from a design template.
- Create a new publication or a webpage from scratch.
- Create a new publication based on an existing one.
- Open an existing publication.

Choosing the appropriate method depends on your experience with desktop publishing and on how you have used Publisher in the past.

BTW
Featured Template Gallery
You may have to wait a few minutes for Publisher to populate the FEATURED template gallery, as the gallery is updated from Microsoft every day.

Templates

Because many people find that composing and designing from scratch is a difficult process, Publisher provides templates to assist in publication preparation. Publisher has hundreds of templates to create professionally designed and unique publications. A template is a tool that helps you through the design process by offering you publication options and changing your publication accordingly. A **template** is similar to a blueprint you can use over and over, filling in the blanks, replacing prewritten text as necessary, and changing the art to fit your needs. In this first project, as you begin to learn about the features of Publisher, a series of steps is presented to create a publication using a design template.

When you run Publisher or when you tap or click the New tab in the Backstage view, Publisher displays the **template gallery**. Publisher provides two kinds of templates. Featured templates are downloaded from Office.com and customized for specific situations. Built-in templates are more generic and require no downloading. If you choose a template from the BUILT-IN template gallery, Publisher displays the **template information pane** on the right, with a larger preview of the selected template, along with some customization options.

BTW
Templates
Choose a template that suits the purpose of the publication, with headline and graphic placement that attracts your audience. Choose a style that has meaning for the topic.

To Select a Template

Templates are displayed as **thumbnails,** or small images of the template, in the template gallery. The thumbnails are organized by publication type (for example, Flyers); within publication type, they are organized by purpose or category (for example, Marketing) and then alphabetically by design type. Publisher groups additional templates into folders. The following steps select an event flyer template. ***Why?*** *An event flyer template contains many of the objects needed to create the desired concert flyer.*

- In the Publisher start screen, tap or click BUILT-IN to display the built-in templates.
- Scroll down to display the desired publication type (in this case, Flyers) (Figure 1–3).

Q&A Why does my list look different?
It may be that someone has downloaded additional folders of templates on your system. Or, the resolution on your screen may be different. Thus, the size and number of displayed folders may vary.

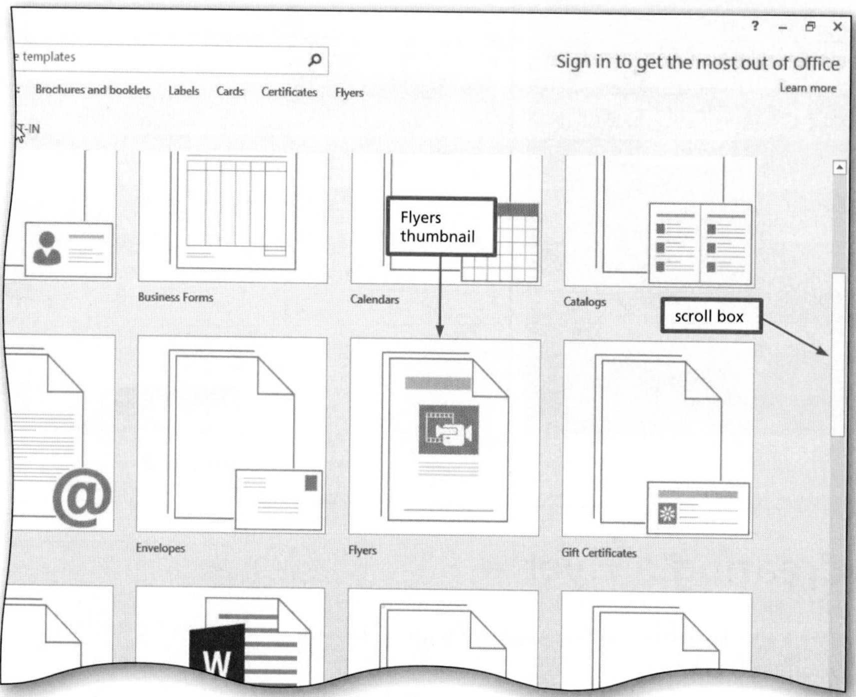

Figure 1–3

- Tap or click the Flyers thumbnail to display the Flyer templates and folders of additional templates (Figure 1–4).

Q&A Can I go back and choose a different category of templates?
Yes, you can tap or click the Back button in the upper-left corner of the template gallery, or you can tap or click Home or Flyers in the breadcrumb trail to move back to those previous locations.

Experiment

- Scroll through the available templates and tap or click various flyers in the list. Watch the preview change in the template information pane.

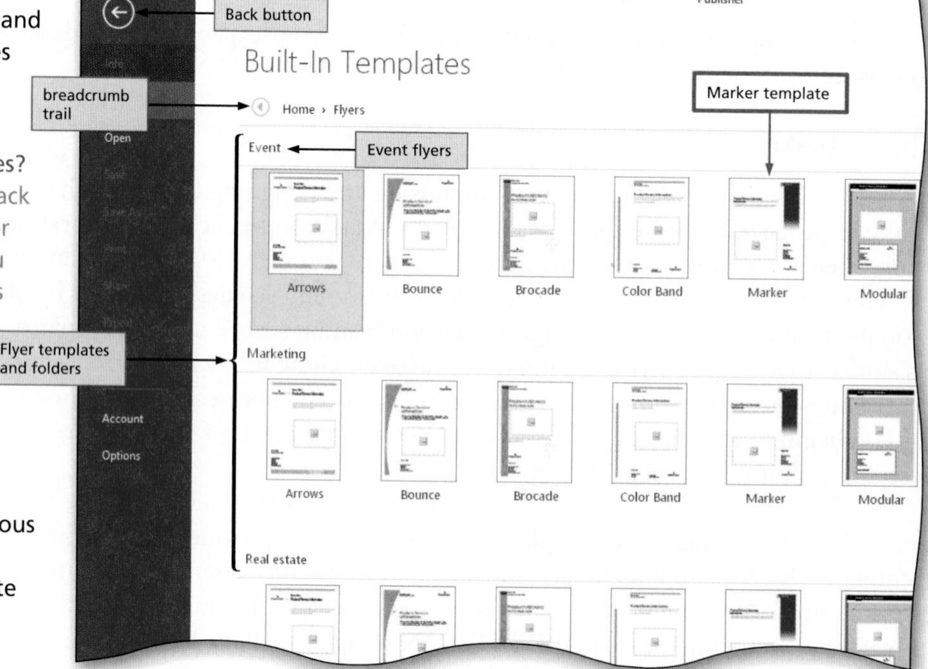

Figure 1–4

3

- Tap or click the Marker thumbnail in the Event category (Figure 1–5).

Q&A Could I use a different template?
You could, but it does not have the same features as the template used in this chapter.

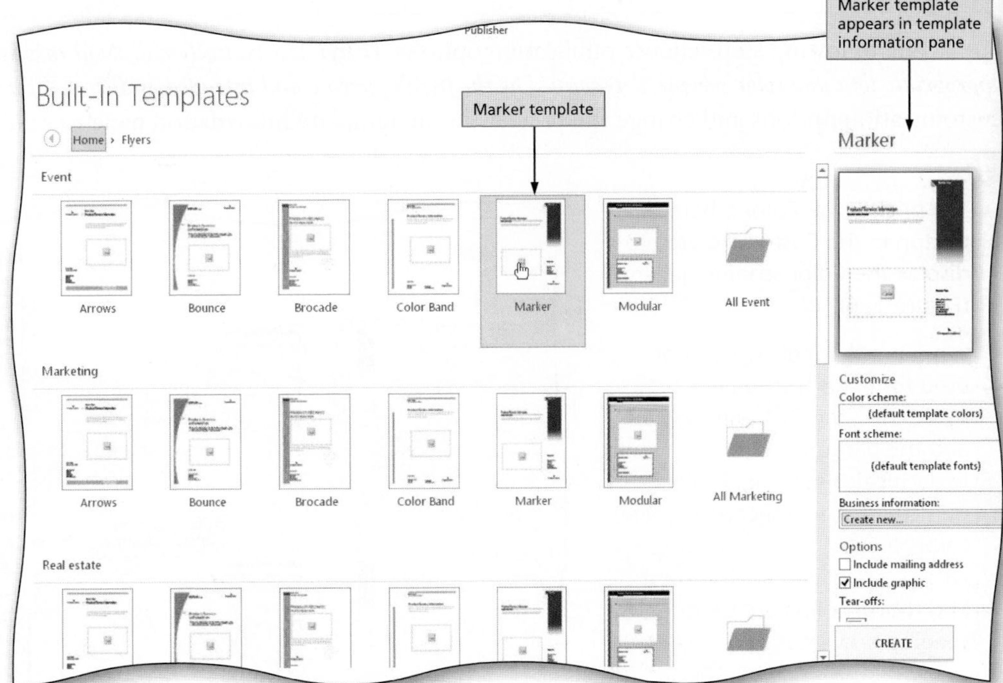

Figure 1–5

CONSIDER THIS

Does it make any difference which color scheme and font scheme you use?

Yes. The choice of an appropriate template, font, and color scheme is determined by the flyer's purpose and intended audience. For example, in this concert flyer about a blues band, the Navy color scheme helps connect the audience with the name of the band. The Flow font scheme uses a Calibri rounded font for the heading. Calibri is a sans serif font, meaning it has no flourishes on individual letters, and is suitable for print publications.

Customizing Templates

Once you choose a template, you should make choices about the color scheme, font scheme, and other components of the publication. A **color scheme** is a defined set of colors that complement each other when used in the same publication. Each Publisher color scheme provides four complementary colors. A **font scheme** is a defined set of fonts associated with a publication. A **font**, or typeface, defines the appearance and shape of the letters, numbers, and special characters. A font scheme contains one font for headings and another font for body text and captions. Font schemes make it easy to change all the fonts in a publication to give it a new look. Other customization options allow you to choose to include business information, a mailing address, a graphic, or tear-offs.

BTW

Font Schemes

Choose a font scheme that gives your flyer a consistent, professional appearance and characterizes your subject. Make intentional decisions about the font style and type. Avoid common reading fonts such as Arial, Times New Roman, and Helvetica that are used in other kinds of print publications. Flyers are more effective with stronger or unusual font schemes.

To Choose Publication Options

The following steps choose publication options. ***Why?*** *You typically will want to customize a template with an appropriate font and color scheme, determined by the flyer's purpose and intended audience.* The following steps choose customization options and change the preview in the template information pane to reflect your choices.

1

- Tap or click the Color scheme button in the Customize area to display the Color scheme gallery (Figure 1–6).

Q&A What are the individual colors used for in each scheme?
By default, the text will be black and the background will be white in each color scheme. Publisher uses the first and second scheme colors for major color accents within a publication. The third and fourth colors are used for shading and secondary accents.

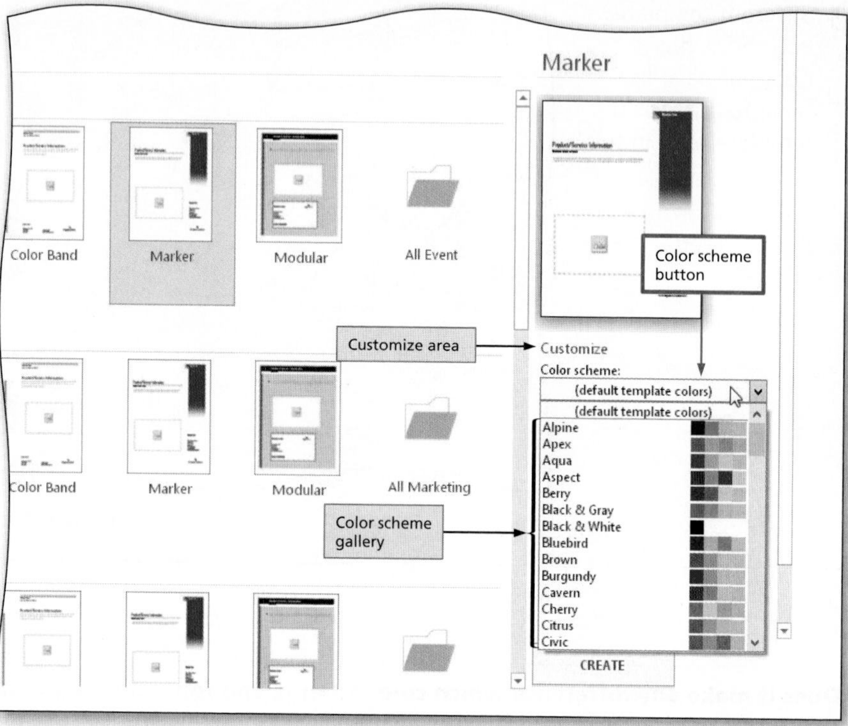

Figure 1–6

2

- Scroll as necessary and then tap or click Navy in the Color scheme gallery to select it (Figure 1–7).

Experiment

- Tap or click various color schemes and watch the changes in all of the thumbnails. When you finish experimenting, tap or click the Navy color scheme.

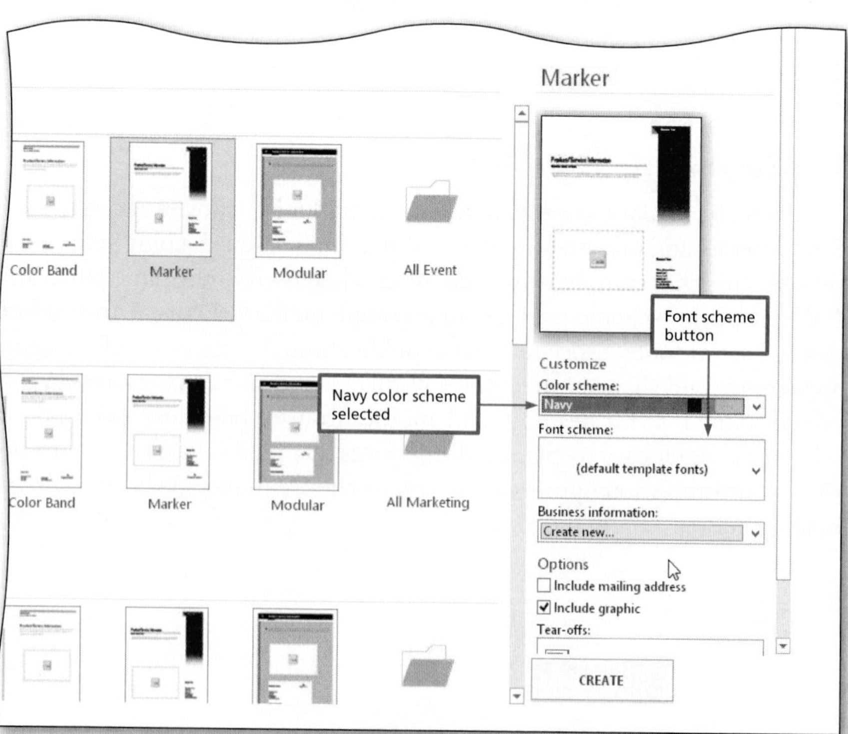

Figure 1–7

3

- Tap or click the Font scheme button in the Customize area to display the Font scheme gallery (Figure 1–8).

Q&A What are the three items listed in each scheme?
The first line is the generic name of the scheme. Below that, both a major font and a minor font are specified. Generally, a major font is used for titles and headings, and a minor font is used for body text.

Figure 1–8

4

- If necessary, scroll in the list and then tap or click Flow in the Font scheme gallery to select it.
- If necessary, scroll to display the Options area of the template information pane (Figure 1–9).

Q&A How are the font schemes organized?
The font schemes are organized alphabetically by the generic name of the scheme.

 **Experiment**

- Tap or click various font schemes and watch the changes in all of the thumbnails. When you finish experimenting, tap or click the Flow font scheme.

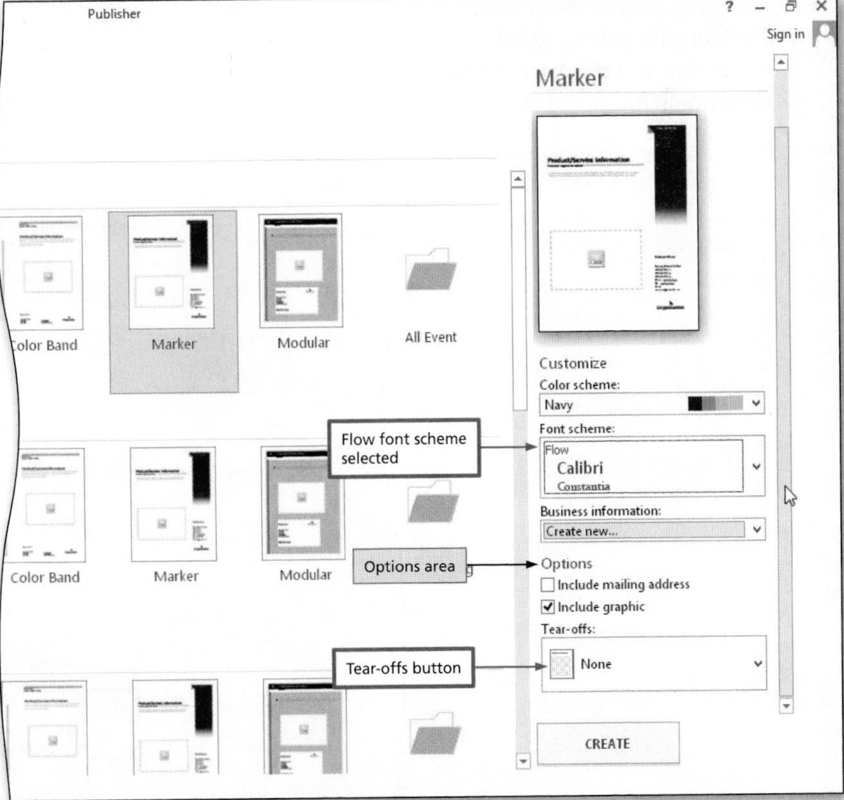

Figure 1–9

- Tap or click the Tear-offs button in the Options area to display the Tear-offs gallery (Figure 1–10).

Q&A What are the other kinds of tear-offs?
You can choose to display tear-offs for coupons, order forms, response forms, and sign-up forms.

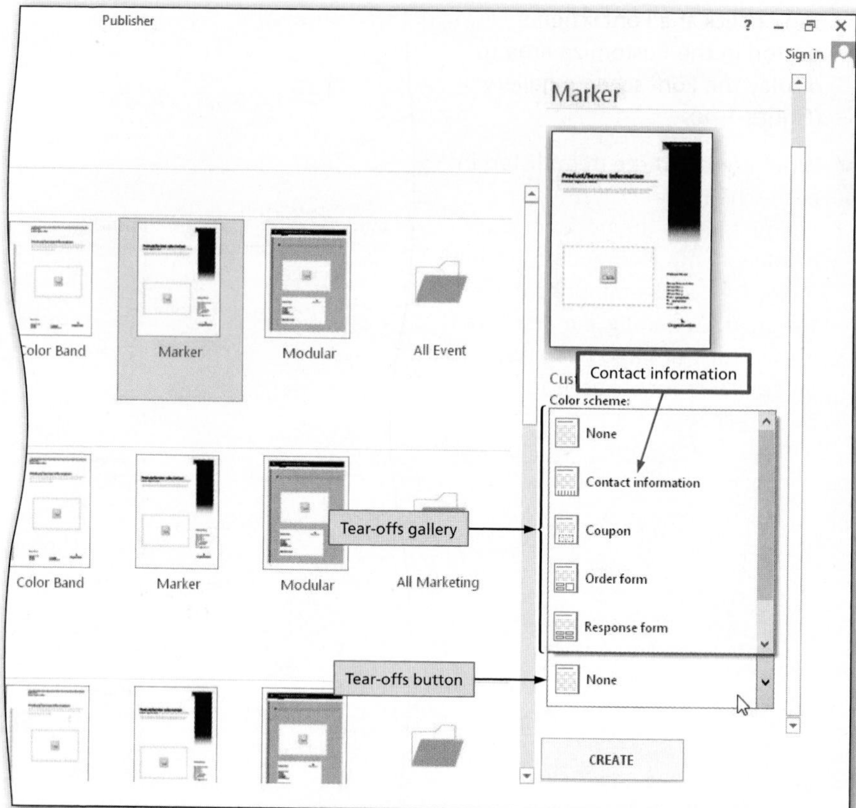

Figure 1–10

- Tap or click Contact information in the Tear-offs gallery to select tear-offs that will display contact information (Figure 1–11).

Q&A Should I change the check boxes?
No, the flyer you create in this chapter uses the default value of no mailing address, but includes a graphic.

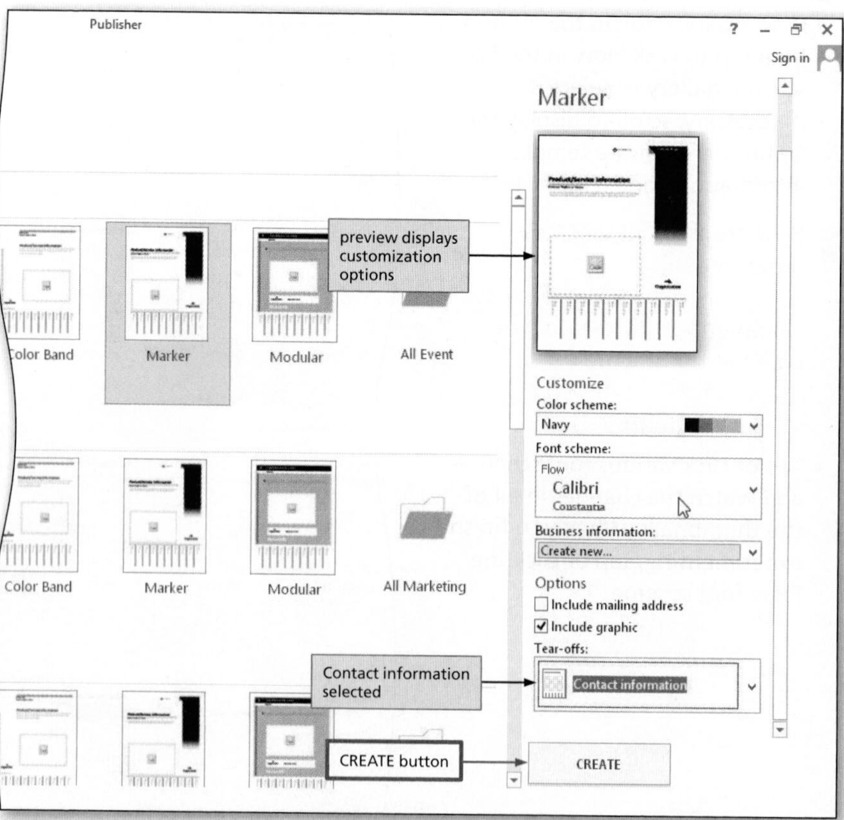

Figure 1–11

7

- Tap or click the CREATE button to create the publication using the selected template and options (Figure 1–12).

Q&A Is there a way to go back if I change my mind?
You can tap or click FILE on the ribbon and start a new publication, or you can make changes to the template, font scheme, color scheme, and other options using the ribbon, as you will see in this and subsequent chapters.

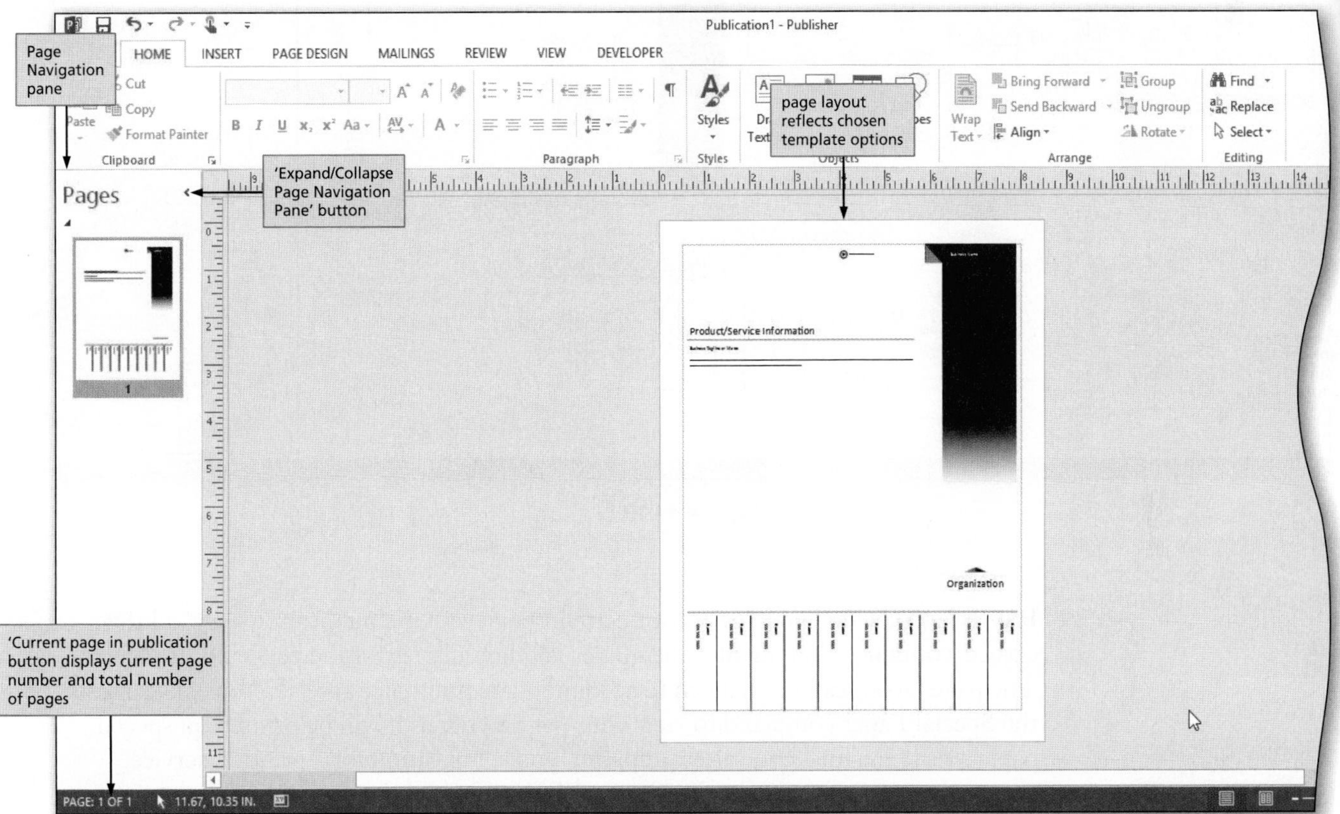

Figure 1–12

The Publisher Window

The Publisher window consists of a variety of components to make your work more efficient and your publication more professional. The following sections discuss these components.

The Workspace

The **workspace** contains several elements similar to the document windows of other applications, as well as some elements unique to Publisher. For more information on common window elements, read the Office and Windows chapter at the beginning of this book. In Publisher, as you create a publication, the page layout, rulers, scroll bars, guides, the Page Navigation pane, and the status bar are displayed in the gray workspace (Figure 1–13 on the next page). Objects can be placed on the page layout or in the light gray workspace.

For an introduction to Office and instruction about how to perform basic tasks in Office apps, read the Office and Windows chapter at the beginning of this book, where you can learn how to run an application, use the ribbon, save a file, open a file, exit an application, use Help, and much more.

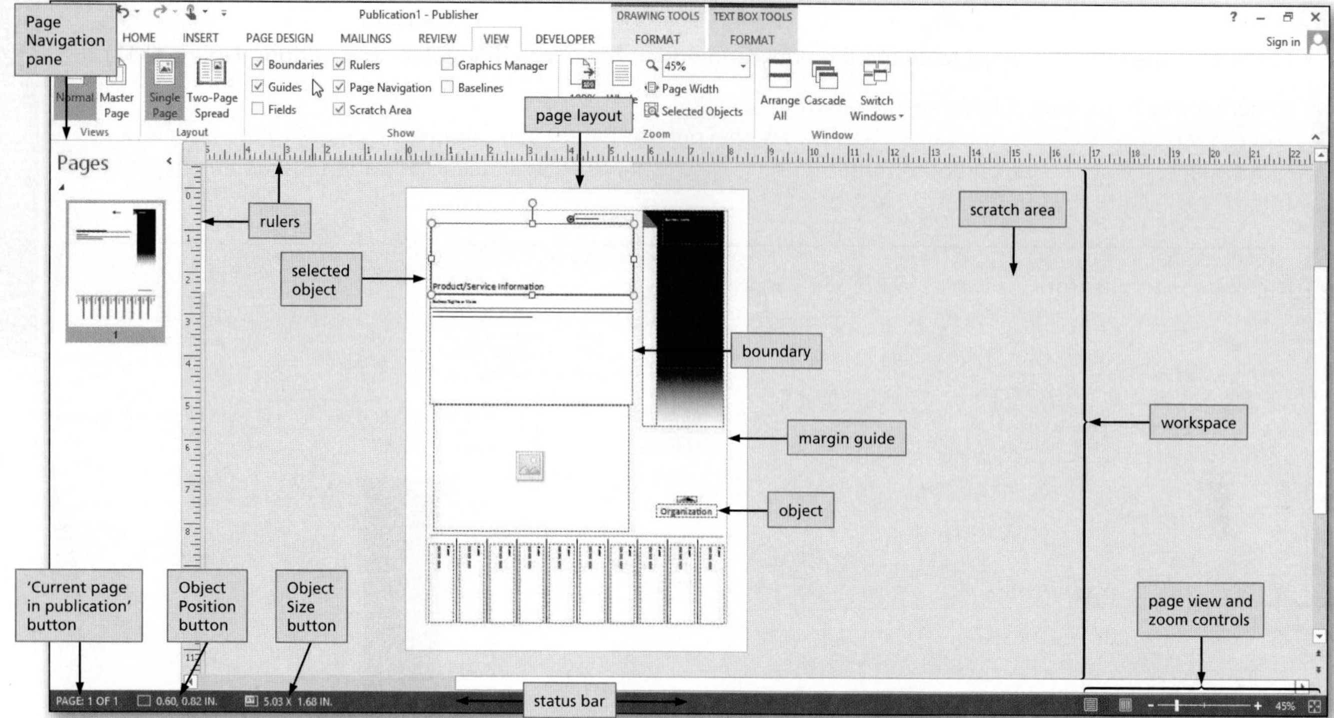

Figure 1–13

PAGE LAYOUT The **page layout** contains a view of the publication page, all the objects contained therein, plus the guides and boundaries for the page and its objects. The page layout can be changed to accommodate multipage spreads. You also can use the Special Paper command to view your page layout as it will be printed on special paper or see the final copy after preparing your publication for a printing service.

RULERS Two rulers outline the workspace at the top and left. A **ruler** is used to measure and place objects on the page. Although the vertical and horizontal rulers are displayed at the left and top of the workspace, they can be moved and placed anywhere you need them. You use the rulers to measure and align objects on the page, set tab stops, adjust text frames, and change margins. Additionally, the rulers can be hidden to show more of the workspace. You will learn more about rulers in a later chapter.

One of the few differences between Windows 7 and Windows 8 occurs in the steps to run Publisher. If you are using Windows 7, click the Start button, type `Publisher` in the 'Search programs and files' box, click Publisher 2013, and then, if necessary, maximize the Publisher window. For detailed steps to run Publisher in Windows 7, refer to the Office and Windows chapter at the beginning of this book. For a summary of the steps, refer to the Quick Reference located at the back of this book.

OBJECTS The elements you want to place in your publication are called **objects**, including, text, WordArt, tear-offs, graphics, pictures, bookmarks, bullets, lines, and web tools.

GUIDES AND BOUNDARIES Publisher's page layout displays guides and boundaries of the page and selected objects. A **boundary** is the gray, dotted line surrounding an object. Boundaries are useful when you want to move or resize objects on the page. Boundaries and guides can be turned on and off using the VIEW tab. They do not display on printed copies. **Margin guides** automatically are displayed in blue at all four margins. Other guides include grid guides, which you can turn on to help organize objects in rows and columns, visual layout guides that display as you move objects, and baseline guides that help you align text horizontally across text boxes.

STATUS BAR As with other Office 2013 applications, Publisher displays a status bar at the bottom of the workspace. The Publisher status bar contains the 'Current page in publication' button, the Object Position button, and the Object Size button on the left; on the right side of the status bar, Publisher includes buttons and controls you can use to change the view of a publication and adjust the size of the displayed publication.

The **Object Position button** and **Object Size button** serve as guidelines for lining up objects from the left and top margins. The exact position and size of a selected object is displayed in inches as you create or move it. You may choose to have the measurement displayed in pica, points, or centimeters. If no object is selected, the Object Position button displays the location of the pointer. Tapping or clicking either button will display the Measurements toolbar. You will learn more about the Measurements toolbar in a later chapter.

The right side of the status bar includes the Single Page, 'Two-Page Spread', and 'Show Whole Page' buttons, as well as the zoom controls. If you press and hold or right-click the status bar, you can choose which controls to display.

BTW

The Ribbon and Screen Resolution

Publisher may change how the groups and buttons within the groups appear on the ribbon, depending on the computer's screen resolution. Thus, your ribbon may look different from the ones in this book if you are using a screen resolution other than 1366 × 768.

PAGE NAVIGATION PANE The Page Navigation pane displays all of the current pages in the publication as thumbnails in a panel on the left side of the workspace. Tapping or clicking a thumbnail displays that page in the workspace.

To Hide the Page Navigation Pane

1 CUSTOMIZE TEMPLATES | 2 NAVIGATE & SELECT | 3 REPLACE TEXT | DELETE OBJECTS | FORMAT TEXT
6 INSERT GRAPHICS | 7 FORMAT PICTURE | 8 ENHANCE PAGE | 9 PRINT & EXIT | 10 OPEN & REVISE

Because the flyer contains only one page, you will hide the Page Navigation pane using the 'Current page in publication' button on the status bar. ***Why?*** *Hiding the pane gives you more room on the screen for viewing and editing the flyer.* The following step hides the Page Navigation pane.

1

- Tap or click the 'Current page in publication' button on the status bar to hide the Page Navigation pane (Figure 1–14).

I do not see the Page Navigation pane. What did I do wrong?

It may be that someone has hidden the Page Navigation pane already. The 'Current page in publication' button opens and closes the Page Navigation pane. Tap or click it again.

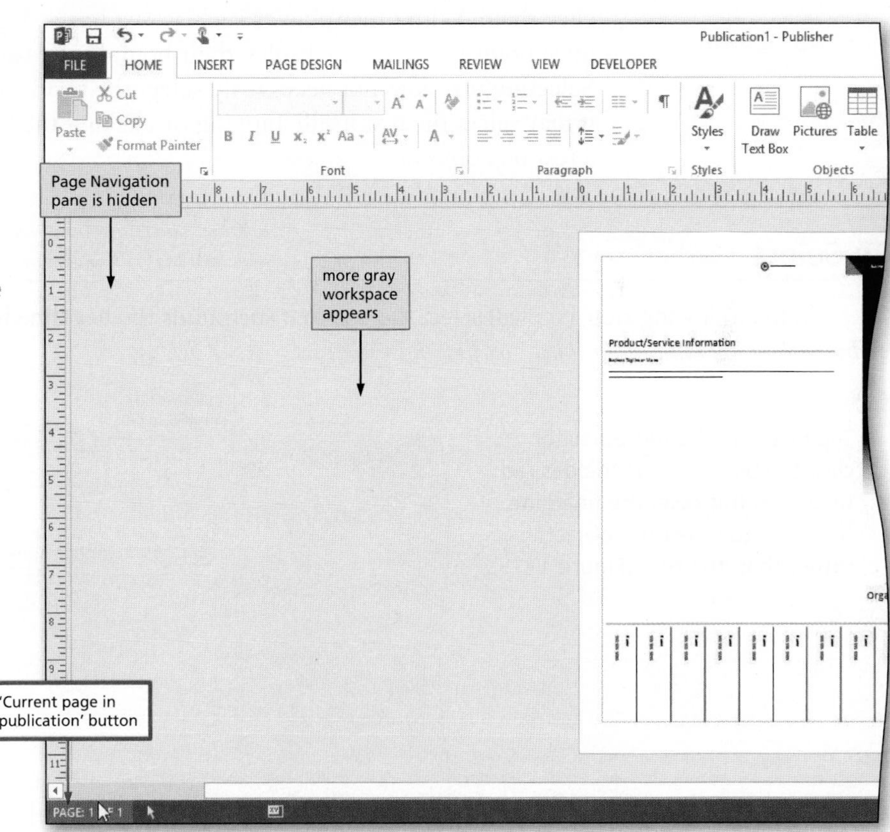

Figure 1–14

Other Ways

1. Tap or click Page Navigation check box (VIEW tab | Show group)

BTW
Boundaries
If you want to see all object boundaries, tap or click the Boundaries check box (VIEW tab | Show group).

To Collapse and Expand the Page Navigation Pane

An alternative to hiding the Page Navigation pane is to collapse or minimize it. If you wanted to collapse the Page Navigation pane, you would perform the following steps.

1. If the Page Navigation pane is not open, click the 'Current page in publication' button on the status bar to display the Page Navigation pane.
2. Tap or click the 'Collapse Page Navigation Pane' button in the upper-right corner of the pane.
3. If you want to expand a collapsed Page Navigation pane, click the 'Expand Page Navigation Pane' button in the upper-right corner of the pane.

Selecting Objects and Zooming

BTW
Selecting
If your screen normally displays dark letters on a light background, which is the default setting in Publisher, then selected text displays as light letters on a dark background.

Pointing to an object in Publisher causes the object to display its boundary, helping you to determine the edges and general shape of the object. When you **select** an object by clicking it, the object appears surrounded by a solid **selection rectangle**, which has small squares and circles, called **handles**, at each corner and middle location. Many objects also display a green **rotation handle** connected to the top of the object or a yellow **adjustment handle** used to change the shape of some objects. A selected object can be resized, rotated, moved, deleted, or grouped with other objects. Often it is easier to select and edit objects by zooming.

Objects such as photos, clip art, and shapes are easy to select. You simply tap or click them. With other objects such as text boxes, logos, and placeholders, you first must point to them—to display their boundaries—and then tap or click the boundary. Selecting text does not necessarily select the text box object that holds the text; rather, it may select the text itself. Tapping or clicking the boundary is the best way to select a text box object.

To Select

1 CUSTOMIZE TEMPLATES | 2 NAVIGATE & SELECT | 3 REPLACE TEXT | 4 DELETE OBJECTS | 5 FORMAT TEXT
6 INSERT GRAPHICS | 7 FORMAT PICTURE | 8 ENHANCE PAGE | 9 PRINT & EXIT | 10 OPEN & REVISE

In the following step, you will select the box that surrounds the headline in the flyer by tapping or clicking it. ***Why?*** *Before you can edit an object, you first must select it.*

- Tap near the desired object or click the boundary of the desired object (in this case, the headline text box) to select the object rather than the text (Figure 1–15).

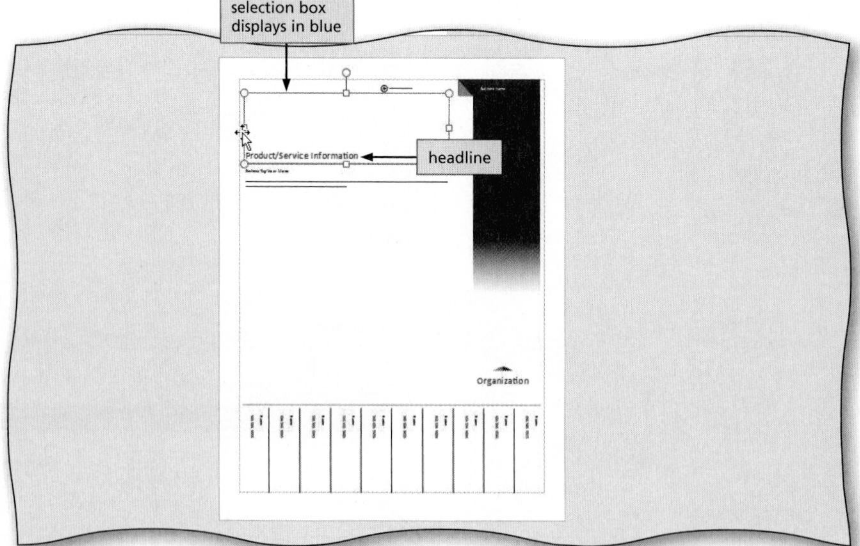

Figure 1–15

Other Ways

1. With no object selected, press TAB until desired object is selected

Zooming

Once selected, the size of the object might be small and, therefore, difficult to edit. Publisher provides several ways to **zoom**, or change the magnification of an object, to facilitate viewing and editing.

Table 1–1 shows several zoom methods.

Table 1–1 Zoom Methods

Tool	Method	Result
function key	To zoom in on an object, press the F9 key on the keyboard, press the F9 key again to return to the previous magnification.	Selected object appears centered in the workspace at 100% magnification.
mouse wheel	To change the magnification, press and hold the CTRL key and then move the mouse wheel down or up.	Page layout appears 20% smaller or larger.
Page Width button	To zoom to page width, tap or click the Page Width button (VIEW tab | Zoom group).	Page layout expands to fill the workspace horizontally.
ribbon	To use the ribbon, tap or click the VIEW tab. In the Zoom group, tap or click the desired button.	Page layout appears at selected magnification.
Selected Objects button	To zoom to objects, tap or click the Selected Objects button (VIEW tab | Zoom group).	Selected object is magnified as large as possible to fit on the screen.
shortcut keys	To zoom to page width, press CTRL+SHIFT+L.	Page layout is magnified as large as possible in the workspace.
shortcut menu	To zoom in on an object, press and hold or right-click the object, tap or point to Zoom on the shortcut menu, tap or click the desired magnification.	Object appears at selected magnification.
Show Whole Page button	To zoom to whole page, tap or click the Show Whole Page button on the status bar.	Page layout is magnified as large as possible in the workspace.
Whole Page button	To zoom to whole page, tap or click the Whole Page button (VIEW tab | Zoom group).	Page layout is magnified as large as possible in the workspace.
Zoom box	To change the magnification, enter a magnification percentage in the Zoom box (VIEW tab | Zoom group).	Page layout appears at entered magnification.
Zoom arrow	To change the magnification, tap or click Zoom box arrow (VIEW tab | Zoom group) and then tap or click desired magnification.	Page layout appears at selected magnification.
Zoom Out button Zoom In button	To increment or decrement magnification, tap or click the Zoom Out or Zoom In button on the status bar.	Page layout appears 10% smaller or larger with each tap or click.
Zoom slider	To change the magnification of the entire page, drag the Zoom slider on the status bar.	Objects appear at selected magnification.
100% button	To zoom to page width, tap or click the 100% button (VIEW tab | Zoom group).	Page layout is magnified to 100%.

© 2014 Cengage Learning

To Zoom

When viewing an entire printed page, 8½ by11 inches, the magnification is approximately 45%, which makes reading small text difficult. If your keyboard has function keys, you press the F9 key to enlarge selected objects to 100% and center them in the Publisher window. Pressing the F9 key a second time returns the layout to its previous magnification. If you are using touch gestures, you can stretch to zoom in. The following step zooms in on the headline. ***Why?*** *Editing small areas of text is easier if you use zooming techniques to enlarge the view of the publication.*

- Stretch the text box or press the F9 key to zoom the selected object to approximately 100% (Figure 1–16).

Q&A What is the best way to zoom to 100%?
If you have a keyboard with function keys, pressing the F9 key toggles between a zoom of 100% and the previous zoom percentage. You also can tap or click settings in the Zoom group on the VIEW tab on the ribbon.

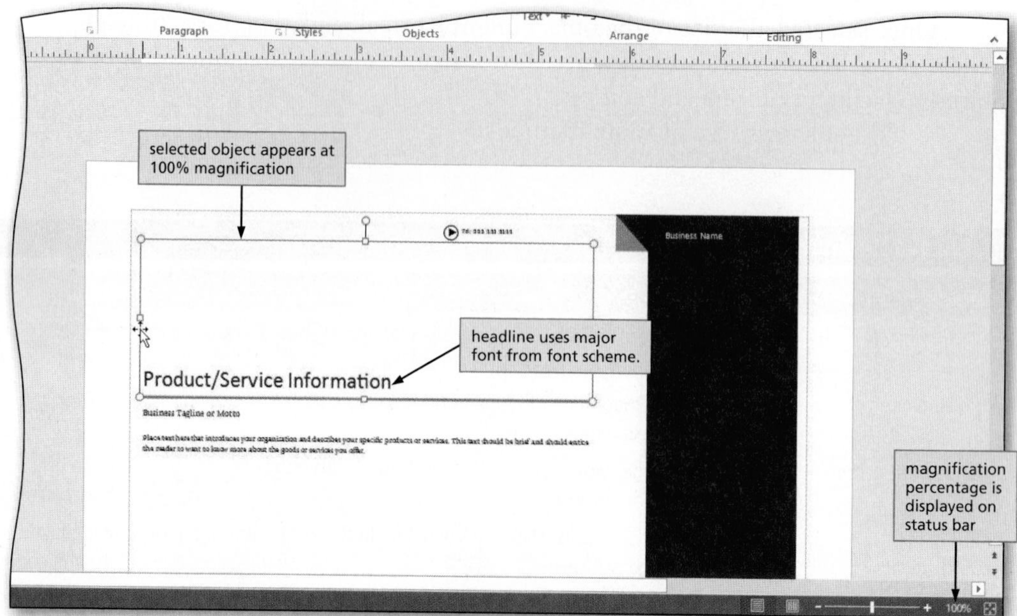

Figure 1–16

Other Ways

1. Press and hold or right-click object, tap or point to Zoom on shortcut menu, tap or click desired magnification on Zoom menu
2. Tap or click Zoom arrow (VIEW tab | Zoom group), tap or click desired magnification
3. Tap or click 100% button (VIEW tab | Zoom group)
4. Tap or click Selected Objects button (VIEW tab | Zoom group)
5. Drag Zoom slider on status bar
6. Tap or click Zoom In button or Zoom Out button on status bar

BTW
Q&As
For a complete list of the Q&As found in many of the step-by-step sequences in this book, visit the Q&A resource on the Student Companion Site located on www.cengagebrain.com. For detailed instructions about accessing available resources, visit www.cengage.com/ct/studentdownload or see the inside back cover of this book.

Selecting and Entering Text

The first step in editing a publication template is to replace its text by typing on the keyboard. You may have to scroll and zoom in the page layout to make careful edits. In a later section of this chapter, you will learn how to format, or change the appearance of the entered text.

Text Boxes

Most of Publisher's templates come with text already inserted into text boxes. A **text box** is an object in a publication designed to hold text in a specific shape, size, and style. Text boxes also can be drawn on the page using the Draw Text Box button (HOME tab | Objects group). Text boxes can be formatted using the ribbon, the mini toolbar, or the shortcut menu. A text box has changeable properties. A **property** is an attribute or characteristic of an object. Within text boxes, you can **edit**, or make changes to, many properties such as font, spacing, alignment, line/border style, fill color, and margins, among others. As you type, if you make a mistake you can backspace or use the DELETE key as you do in word processing. You also can **undo** by clicking the Undo button on the Quick Access Toolbar or by pressing CTRL+Z.

To Replace Placeholder Text

Publisher templates use two types of text in template text boxes. You select **placeholder text,** such as that in the flyer headline, with a single tap or click. ***Why?*** *Tapping or clicking once to select text allows you to begin typing immediately without having to select the text or press the* DELETE *key.* Other text, such as the business name, address, or tag line, is selected by dragging through the text, double-tapping or double-clicking specific words, or by pressing CTRL+A to select all of the text in the text box. Then, you simply type to replace the text.

The following steps select and replace placeholder text in the headline.

1

- Tap or click the headline text to select it (Figure 1–17).

Q&A What are the extra tabs on the ribbon?

Those additional tabs appear when performing certain tasks with objects such as text boxes, pictures, or tables. You will use tool tabs later in this chapter and in subsequent chapters.

What toolbar was displayed when I selected the text?

Recall from the Office 2013 and Windows 8 chapter that the mini toolbar appears automatically and contains commands related to changing the appearance of text in a publication. If you do not use the mini toolbar, it disappears from the screen.

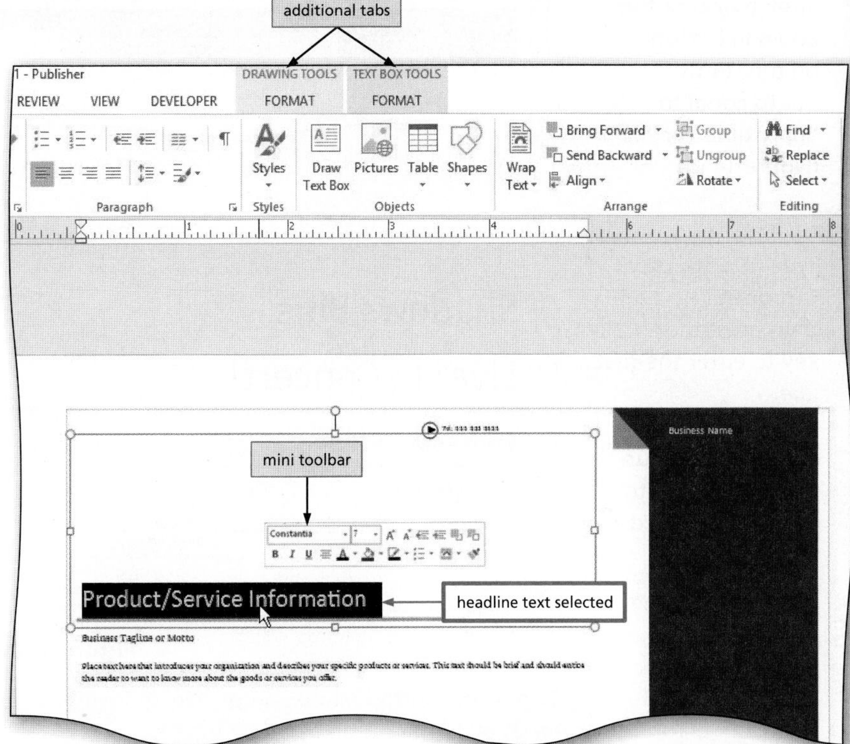

Figure 1–17

2

- Type **Shadows Blue** and then press the ENTER key to enter the first line of the heading.
- Type **Live! In Concert!** to complete the text (Figure 1–18).

Q&A What if I make an error while typing?

Common word processing techniques work in Publisher text boxes. For example, you can press the BACKSPACE key until you have deleted the text in error and then retype the text correctly.

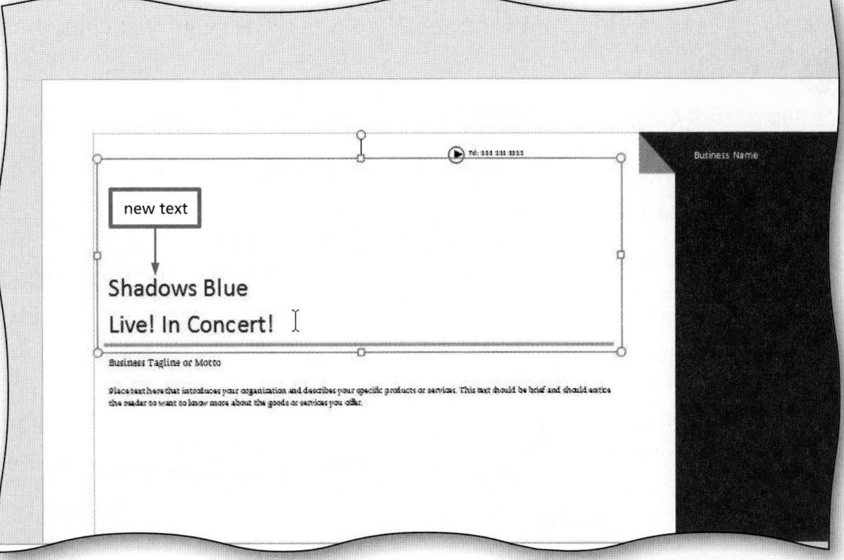

Figure 1–18

- Below the Business Tagline or Motto box, tap or click the text in the introduction text box to select the placeholder text.
- Stretch or click the Zoom In button on the status bar to zoom to approximately 200% (Figure 1–19).

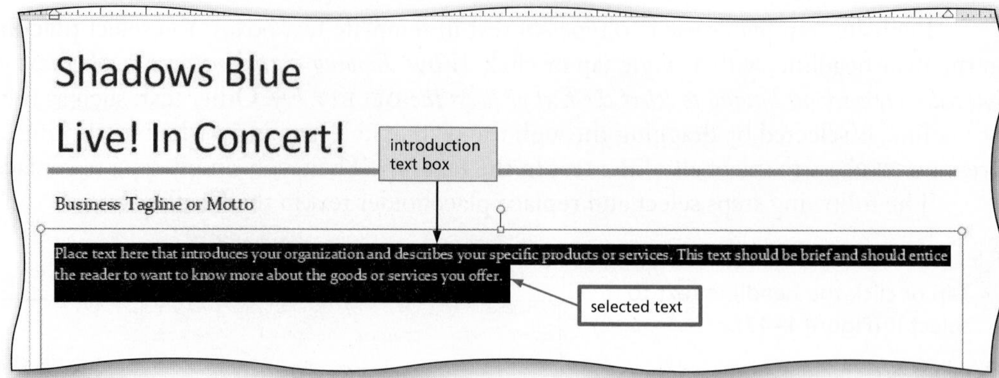

Figure 1–19

- Type **`Saturday, October 4`** and then press the ENTER key to enter the first line.
- Type **`8:00 p.m. at the Campus Auditorium`** to complete the text (Figure 1–20).

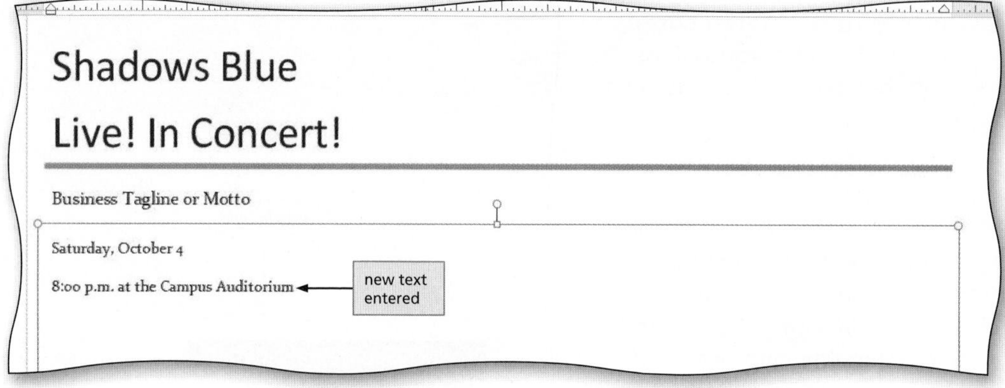

Figure 1–20

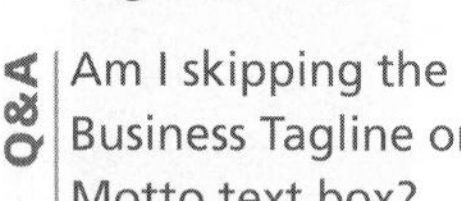

Q&A Am I skipping the Business Tagline or Motto text box?
The text in the Business Tagline or Motto text box is not selected with a single tap or click. You will edit that text later in the chapter.

To Deselect an Object

1 CUSTOMIZE TEMPLATES | 2 NAVIGATE & SELECT | 3 REPLACE TEXT | 4 DELETE OBJECTS | 5 FORMAT TEXT
6 INSERT GRAPHICS | 7 FORMAT PICTURE | 8 ENHANCE PAGE | 9 PRINT & EXIT | 10 OPEN & REVISE

When a Publisher object is selected, scrolling is limited. ***Why?*** *Publisher assumes you would not want to scroll past the end of the object.* The following step deselects the object by clicking outside of its boundaries.

- Tap or click outside of the selected object (in this case, the text box) to deselect it (Figure 1–21).

Q&A Exactly where should I click?
As long as you do not select another object, anywhere in the workspace is fine. You may want to click just to the right of the text box selection rectangle.

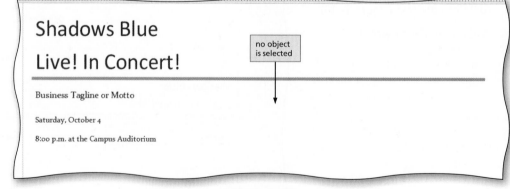

Figure 1–21

Other Ways

1. Press ESC

To Replace More Placeholder Text

1 Scroll to the upper portion of the template and then tap or click the text in the phone number text box to select the placeholder text

2 Type `555-TICKETS` to replace the text (Figure 1–22).

Figure 1–22

To Replace Other Text

In the following steps, you replace the **default**, or preset, text in other template text boxes by selecting all of the text and then typing the new text. ***Why?*** *Default text is different from placeholder text that is selected with a single click.*

1

- Scroll down and then tap or click the text in the Business Tagline or Motto text box to position the insertion point inside the text box (Figure 1–23).

Q&A What is the button that displays the letter, i?

It is a smart tag button. If you click it, Publisher offers to fill in the text for you with various options. **Smart tag buttons** appear when you point to certain text boxes that are part of the business information set or when you click a logo.

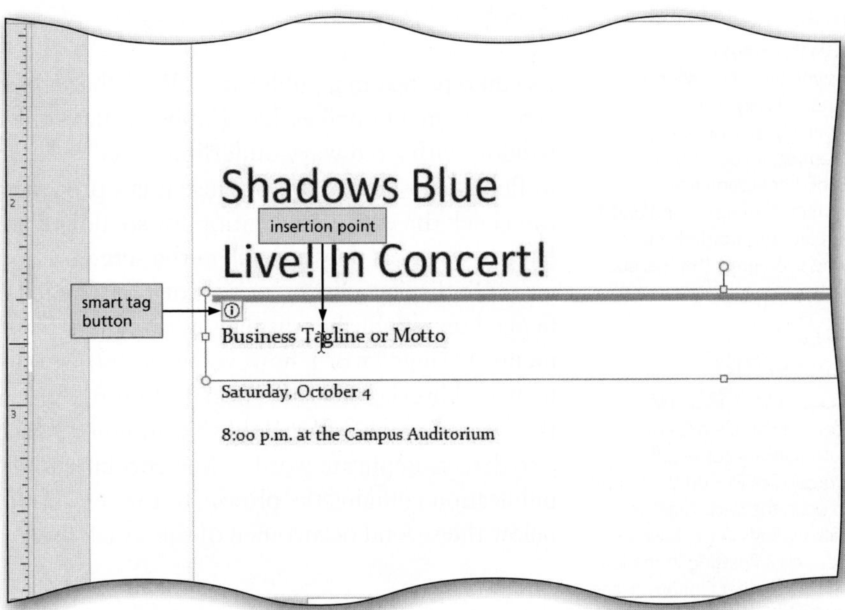

Figure 1–23

- Drag through the text in the Business Tagline or Motto text box to select all of the text in the text box (Figure 1–24).

Q&A Could I press CTRL+A?
Yes, as long as the insertion point is positioned inside the text box, CTRL+A will select all of the text in the text box.

Figure 1–24

- Type **`For tickets, visit www.utix.biz`** to complete the text (Figure 1–25).

Q&A Should I press the DELETE key before typing?
It is not necessary to press the DELETE key; the text you type deletes the selected text automatically.

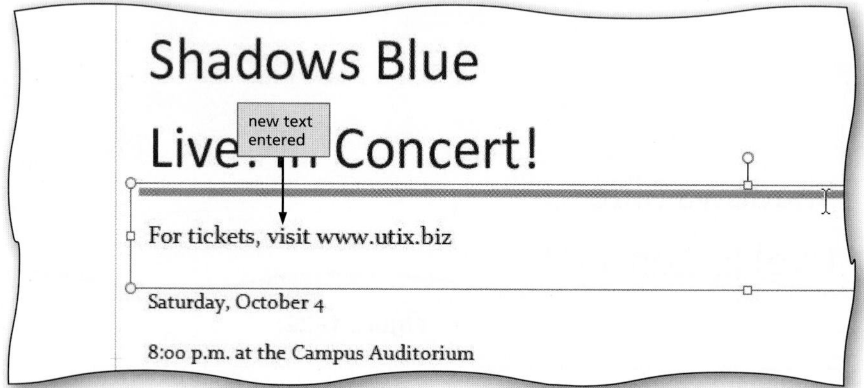

Figure 1–25

- Deselect the text box by tapping or clicking outside of its boundary.

Other Ways

1. Select text box, tap or click Select button (HOME tab | Editing group), tap or click Select All Text in Text Box, type new text

BTW
Automatic Spelling Correction
As you type, Publisher automatically corrects some misspelled words. For example, if you type, recieve, Publisher automatically corrects the misspelling and displays the word, receive, when you press the spacebar or type a punctuation mark.

BTW
Automatically Corrected Words
To see a complete list of automatically corrected words, click FILE on the ribbon to open the Backstage view, click Options in the Backstage view, click Proofing in the left pane (Publisher Options dialog box), click the AutoCorrect Options button, and then scroll through the list near the bottom of the dialog box.

Checking the Spelling

As you type text in a publication, Publisher checks your typing for possible spelling errors. As mentioned earlier, Publisher **flags** the potential error in the publication window with a red wavy underline. A red wavy underline means the flagged text is not in Publisher's dictionary (because it is a proper name or misspelled). Although you can check the entire publication for spelling errors at once, you also can check these flagged errors as they appear on the screen.

To display a list of corrections for flagged text, press and hold or right-click the flagged text. Publisher displays a list of suggested spelling corrections on the shortcut menu. A flagged word, however, is not necessarily misspelled. For example, many names, abbreviations, and specialized terms are not in Publisher's main dictionary. In these cases, you instruct Publisher to ignore the flagged word. As you type, Publisher also detects duplicate words while checking for spelling errors. For example, if your publication contains the phrase, to the the store, Publisher places a red wavy underline below the second occurrence of the word, the.

To Check Spelling as You Type

In the following steps, the word, Concerts, has been misspelled intentionally as Conerts to illustrate Publisher's check spelling as you type feature. If you are doing this project on a computer, your flyer may contain different misspelled words. ***Why?*** *You may have made spelling or typographical errors, if your typing was not accurate.*

- Scroll to the upper-right portion of the flyer.
- Tap or click the text in the Business Name text box to position the insertion point inside the text box.
- Drag through the text, or press CTRL+A, to select all of the text in the text box (Figure 1–26).

Q&A Why does my template list a different business name?
The person who installed Microsoft Office 2013 on your computer or network may have set or customized the field.

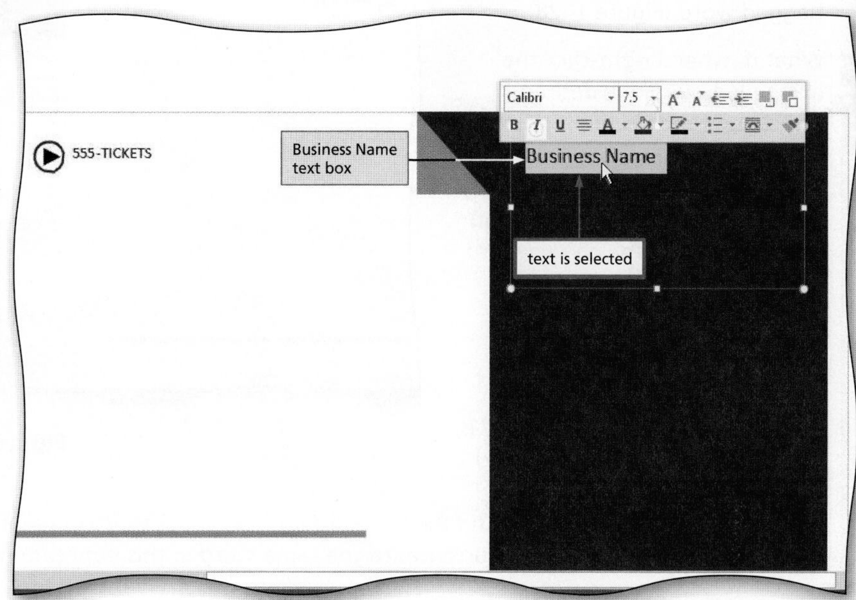

Figure 1–26

- Type **`Campus Conerts`** and then press the SPACEBAR so that a red wavy line appears below the misspelled word (Figure 1–27).

Q&A What if Publisher does not flag my spelling errors with wavy underlines?
To verify that the check spelling as you type features are enabled, click FILE on the ribbon to open the Backstage view and then click Options. When the Publisher Options dialog box is displayed, click Proofing in the left pane, and then ensure the 'Check spelling as you type' check box contains a check mark. Also ensure the 'Hide spelling and grammar errors' check box does not have a check mark. Tap or click the OK button.

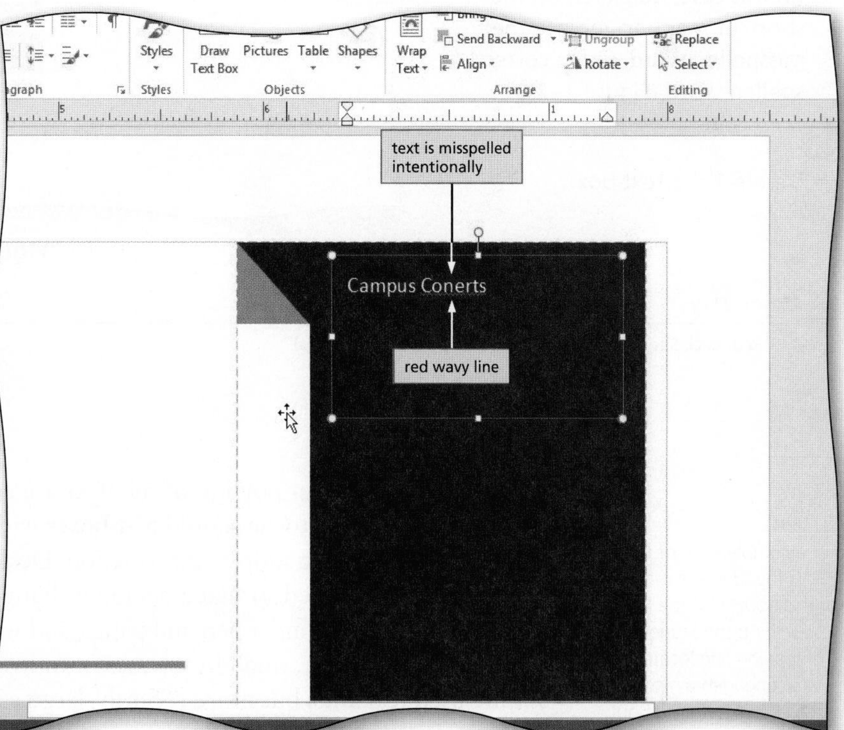

Figure 1–27

- Press and hold or right-click the flagged word (Conerts, in this case) to display a shortcut menu that presents a list of suggested spelling corrections for the flagged word (Figure 1–28).

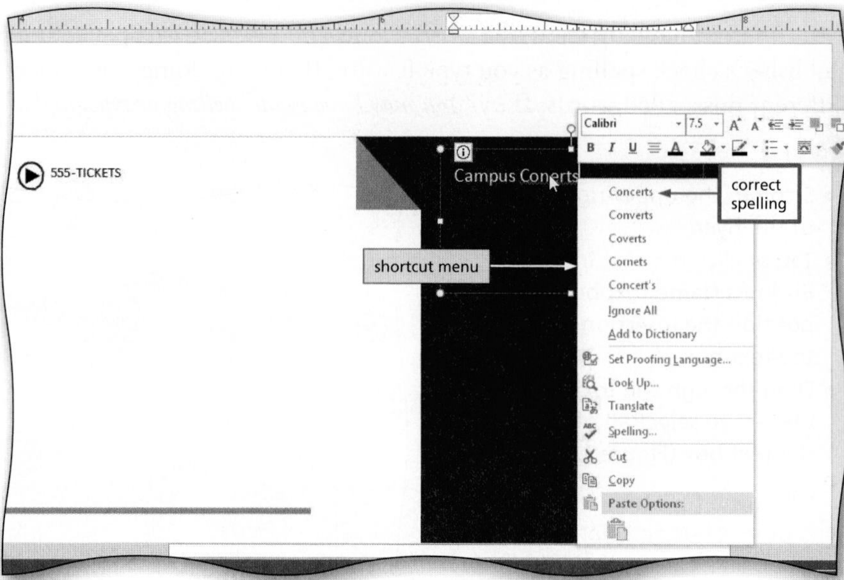

Figure 1–28

Q&A

What if, when I right-click the misspelled word, my desired correction is not in the list on the shortcut menu?

You can click outside the shortcut menu to close the shortcut menu and then retype the correct word, or you can click Spelling on the shortcut menu to display the Spelling dialog box. Chapter 2 discusses the Spelling dialog box.

What if a flagged word actually is, for example, a proper name and spelled correctly?

Press and hold or right-click it and then click Ignore All on the shortcut menu to instruct Publisher not to flag future occurrences of the same word in this publication.

- Tap or click the correct spelling (in this case, Concerts) on the shortcut menu to replace the misspelled word with a correctly spelled word (Figure 1–29).

- Deselect the text box.

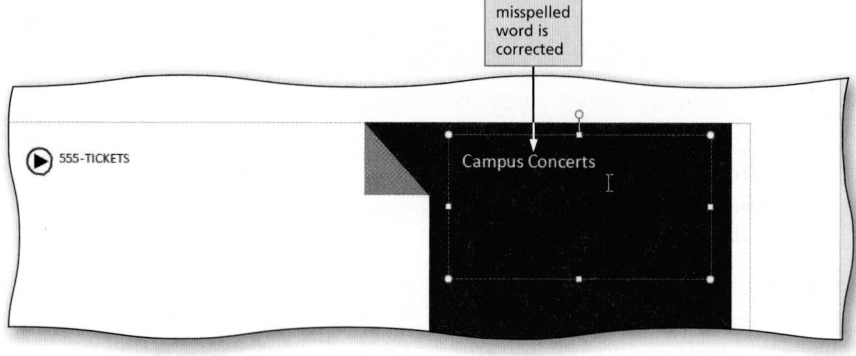

Figure 1–29

Other Ways

1. Tap or click Spelling button (REVIEW tab | Proofing group)

Tear-Offs

BTW

BTWs

For a complete list of the BTWs found in the margins of this book, visit the BTW resource on the Student Companion Site located on www.cengagebrain.com. For detailed instructions about accessing available resources, visit www.cengage.com/ct/studentdownload or see the inside back cover of this book.

Across the lower portion of the flyer are contact information tear-offs. **Tear-offs** are small, ready-to-be scored text boxes with some combination of name, phone number, fax, email, or address information. Designed for customer use, tear-offs typically are perforated so that a person walking by can tear off a tab to keep, rather than having to stop, find a pen and paper, and write down the name and phone number. Traditionally, small businesses or individuals wanting to advertise something locally used tear-offs, but more recently, large companies are mass-producing advertising flyers with tear-offs to post at shopping centers, display in offices, and advertise on college campuses.

Publisher tear-offs contain placeholder text and are **synchronized**, which means when you finish editing one of the tear-off text boxes, the others change to match it automatically.

To Enter Tear-Off Text

The following steps edit the tear-off text boxes. ***Why?*** *The tear-offs must contain information to contact the flyer's creator or to request more information.*

1

- Scroll to display the lower portion of the flyer.
- Tap or click the text in one of the tear-off text boxes to select it (Figure 1–30).

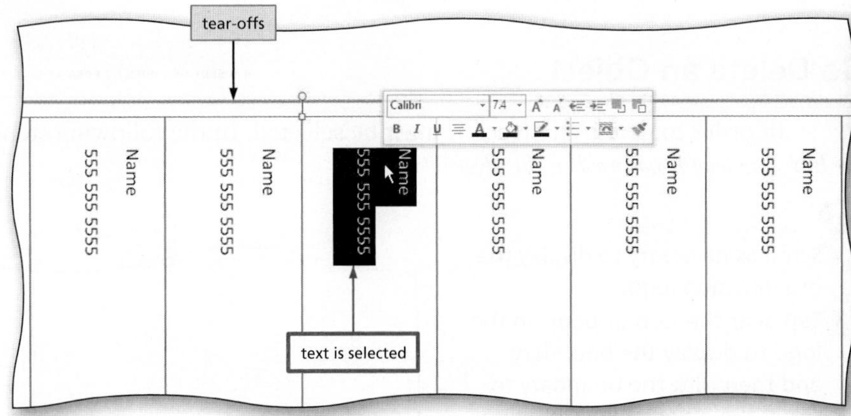

Figure 1–30

2

- Type **Shadows Blue 555-TICKETS** and then press the ENTER key.
- Type **Online at www.utix.biz** to complete the tear-off (Figure 1–31).

If requested by your instructor, enter your phone number instead of 555-TICKETS in the tear-off.

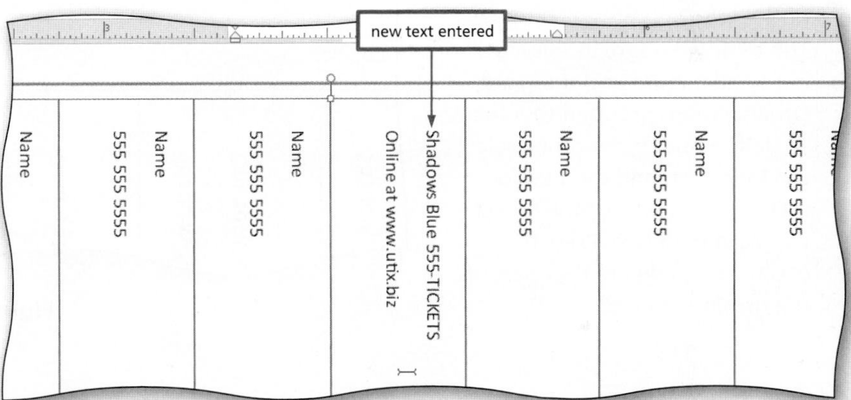

Figure 1–31

3

- Tap or click outside of the text box to synchronize the other tear-offs (Figure 1–32).

Q&A What if I want to make each tear-off different?

Typically, all of the tear-offs are the same, but you can undo synchronization by tapping or clicking the Undo button on the Quick Access Toolbar and then entering the text for other tear-offs.

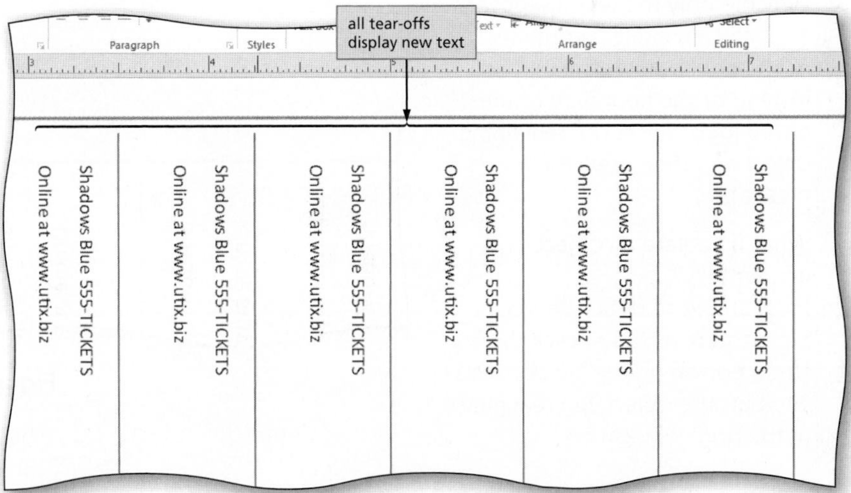

Figure 1–32

Deleting Objects

Templates may display objects in the page layout that you do not wish to use. In those cases, or when you change your mind about including an inserted object, you must delete objects.

To Delete an Object

1 CUSTOMIZE TEMPLATES | 2 NAVIGATE & SELECT | 3 REPLACE TEXT | **4 DELETE OBJECTS** | **5 FORMAT TEXT**
6 INSERT GRAPHICS | **7 FORMAT PICTURE** | **8 ENHANCE PAGE** | **9 PRINT & EXIT** | **10 OPEN & REVISE**

In order to delete an object, it must be selected. In the following steps, you delete the organization logo. ***Why?*** *The logo is not used in this flyer.*

1

- Scroll as necessary to display the organization logo.
- Tap near the icon or point to the logo to display the boundary and then click the boundary to select the object. Avoid tapping or clicking the text in the logo (Figure 1–33).

Q&A What if I want to delete just part of the logo?
The template logo, in this case, is a small picture and the word, Organization, grouped together. To delete one or the other, select the logo first, and then tap or click only the part of the object you wish to delete. Press the DELETE key to delete that part of the grouped object.

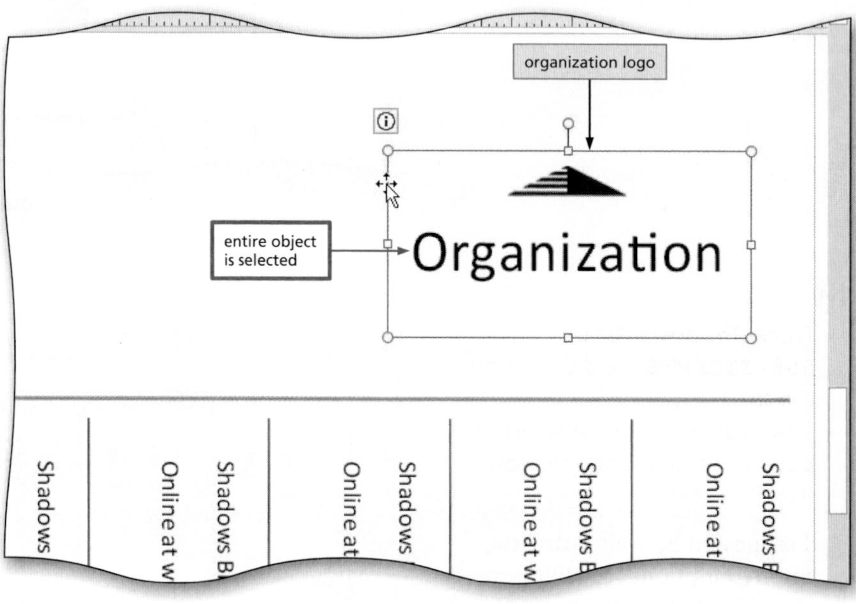

Figure 1–33

2

- Press the DELETE key to delete the selected object (Figure 1–34).

Q&A Why did only the text disappear?
You may have selected the text, or the boundary of the text box, instead of the boundary of the entire logo. Select the remaining object and then press the DELETE key.

What if I delete an object accidentally?
Press CTRL+Z to undo the most recent step, or tap or click the Undo button on the Quick Access Toolbar. The object will reappear in the original location.

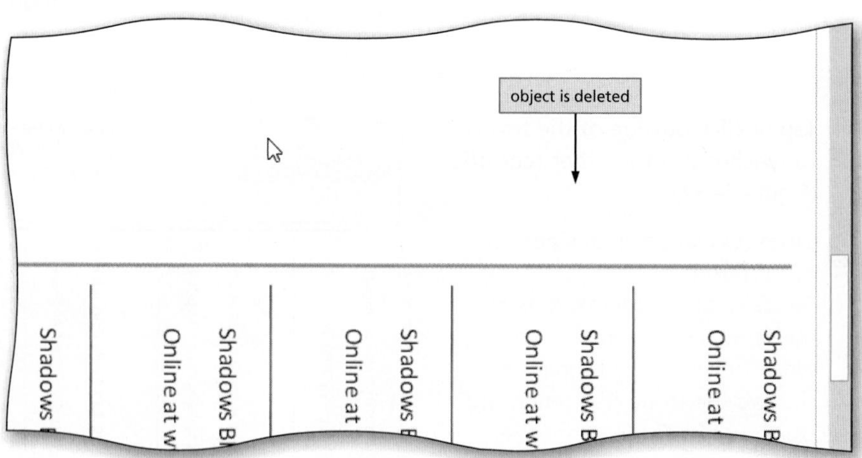

Figure 1–34

Other Ways

1. Press and hold or right-click, tap or click Delete Object on shortcut menu
2. Select object, press BACKSPACE

To Save a Publication with a New File Name

You have performed many tasks while creating this publication and do not want to risk losing work completed thus far. Accordingly, you should save the publication on your hard disk, SkyDrive, or a location that is most appropriate to your situation.

The following steps assume you already have created folders for storing your files, for example, a CIS 101 folder (for your class) that contains a Publisher folder (for your assignments). Thus, these steps save the publication in the Publisher folder in the CIS 101 folder on your desired save location. For a detailed example of the procedure for saving a file in a folder or saving a file on SkyDrive, refer to the Office and Windows chapter at the beginning of this book.

1. Tap or click the Save button on the Quick Access Toolbar, which depending on settings, will display either the Save As gallery in the Backstage view or the Save As dialog box.

2. To save on a hard disk or other storage media on your computer, proceed to Step 2a. To save on SkyDrive, proceed to Step 2b.

2a. If your screen opens the Backstage view and you want to save on storage media on your computer, tap or click Computer in the left pane, if necessary, to display options in the right pane related to saving on your computer. If your screen already displays the Save As dialog box, proceed to Step 3.

2b. If your screen opens the Backstage view and you want to save on SkyDrive, tap or click SkyDrive in the left pane to display SkyDrive saving options or a Sign In button. If your screen displays a Sign In button, tap or click it and then sign in to SkyDrive.

3. Tap or click the Browse button in the right pane to display the Save As dialog box associated with the selected save location (i.e., Computer or SkyDrive).

4. Type `Concert Flyer` in the File name text box to change the file name. Do not press the ENTER key after typing the file name because you do not want to close the dialog box at this time.

5. Navigate to the desired save location (in this case, the Publisher folder in the CIS 101 folder [or your class folder] on your computer or SkyDrive).

6. Tap or click the Save button (Save As dialog box) to save the file in the selected save folder on the selected location with the entered file name.

BTW

Organizing Files and Folders

You should organize and store files in folders so that you easily can find the files later. For example, if you are taking an introductory computer class called CIS 101, a good practice would be to save all Publisher files in a Publisher folder in a CIS 101 folder. For a discussion of folders and detailed examples of creating folders, refer to the Office and Windows chapter at the beginning of this book.

Break Point: If you wish to take a break, this is a good place to do so. To resume at a later time, run Publisher, open the file called Concert Flyer, and continue following the steps from this location forward.

Formatting Text

Although you can format text before you type, many Publisher users enter text first and then format the existing text. Publisher provides many ways to modify the appearance, or **format**, of selected text. Some formatting options include editing the font, paragraph, alignment, typography, copy fitting, and text effects. The more common formatting commands are shown in the Font group on the HOME tab on the ribbon (Figure 1–35) or on the TEXT BOX TOOLS FORMAT tab. These include the capability to change the font size, color, style, and effects. You will learn more about each of the formatting options in the Font group as you use them.

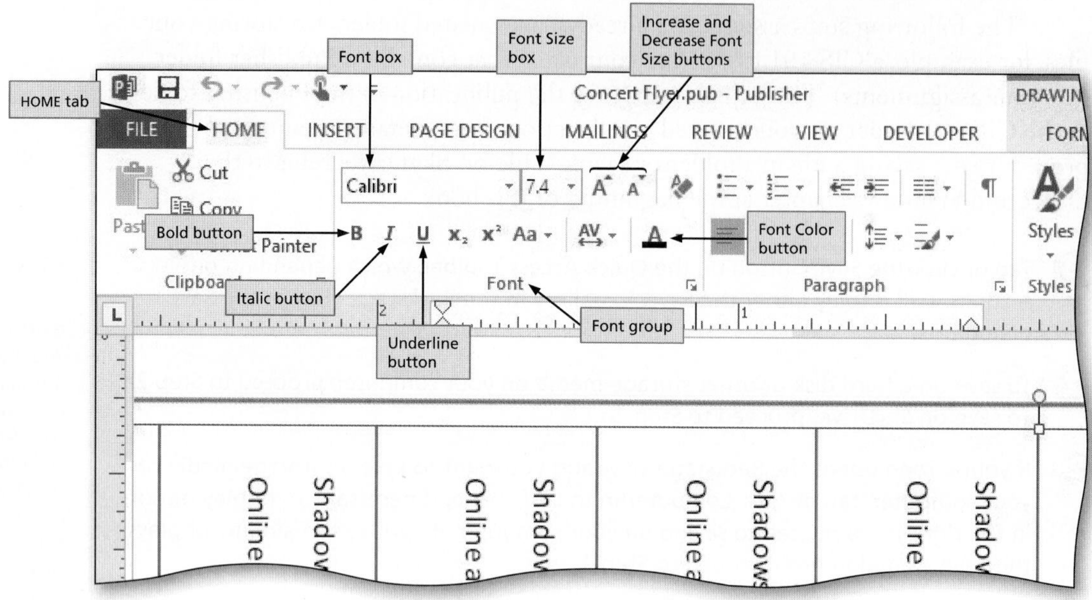

Figure 1–35

BTW
Touch Screen Differences
The Office and Windows interfaces may vary if you are using a touch screen. For this reason, you might notice that the function or appearance of your touch screen differs slightly from this chapter's presentation.

Many of these formatting tools also appear on a mini toolbar when you point to text. Recall that the mini toolbar, which appears automatically based on the tasks you perform, contains commands related to changing the appearance of text or graphics in a publication. The purpose of the mini toolbar is to minimize mouse movement.

A third way to format text involves using the shortcut menu, which appears when you press and hold or right-click an object, or when you press SHIFT+F10. The shortcut menu is a list of frequently used commands that relate to the selected object. If you press and hold or right-click some items, Publisher displays both the mini toolbar and a shortcut menu.

Formatting Text

Characters that appear on the screen are a specific shape and size, determined by the template you choose or the settings you apply. Recall that the font, or typeface, defines the appearance and shape of the letters, numbers, and special characters. The name of the font appears in the Font box (HOME tab | Font group). You can leave characters in the default font or change them to a different font. **Font size** specifies the size of the characters and is determined by a measurement system called points. A single **point** is about 1/72 of one inch in height. Thus, a character with a font size of 12 is about 12/72 or 1/6 of one inch in height. You can increase or decrease the font size of characters in a publication, as well as change the capitalization.

In addition to the common bold, italic, and underline formatting options, Publisher also allows you to apply special text effects and highlights.

Formatting Single versus Multiple Characters and Words

To format a single character, the character must be selected. To format a word, however, you simply can position the insertion point in the word, to make it the current word, and then format the word. You will learn in a later chapter that paragraph formatting, such as alignment and bullets, also can be applied without first selecting it; however, if you want to format multiple characters or words, you first must select the words you want to format and then format the selection.

To Bold Text

Bold characters appear somewhat thicker and darker than those that are not bold. To format the name of the band, you first will select the line. ***Why?*** *Multiple words or lines must be selected in order to apply formatting.* The following steps add bold formatting to the name of the band.

- Deselect any selected object, if necessary.
- Scroll to the upper portion of the flyer.
- Swipe or drag through the text you wish to format (in this case, the name of the band).
- With the text selected, tap or click the Bold button (HOME tab | Font group) to bold the selected text (Figure 1–36).

Q&A How would I remove a bold format?
You would click the Bold button a second time, or you immediately could tap or click the Undo button on the Quick Access Toolbar, or press CTRL+Z.

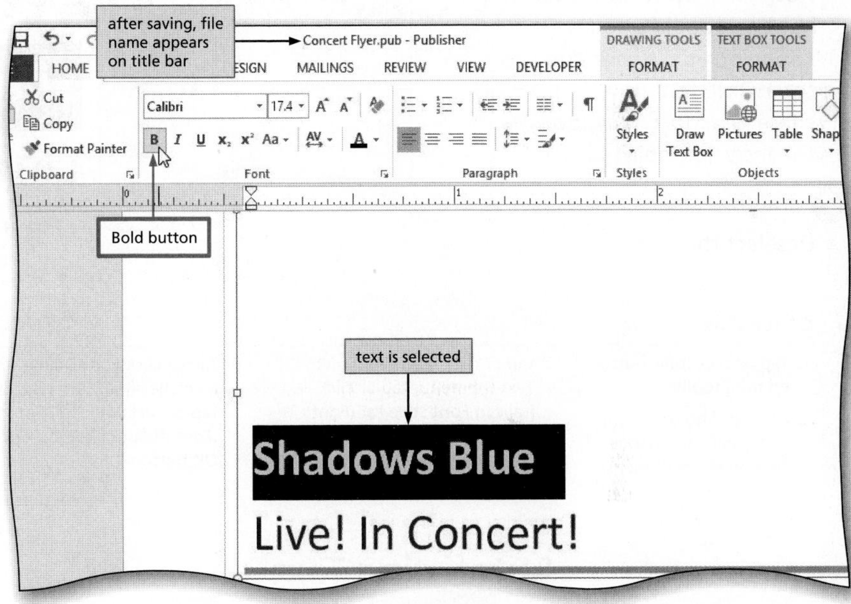

Figure 1–36

- Do not deselect the text.

Other Ways

1. Tap or click Bold button on mini toolbar
2. Press and hold or right-click selected text, tap or point to Change Text on shortcut menu, tap or click Font, tap or click Bold in Font style list (Font dialog box), tap or click OK button
3. Tap or click Font Dialog Box Launcher (HOME tab | Font group), tap or click Bold in Font style list (Font dialog box), tap or click OK button
4. Press CTRL+B

To Italicize Text

Italic text has a slanted appearance. The following steps format a word in italic. ***Why?*** *The italicized text draws attention and makes the text stand out.*

1

- With the text selected (Shadows Blue in this case), tap or click the Italic button (HOME tab | Font group) to italicize the selected text (Figure 1–37).

Q&A

How would I remove an italic format?
You would tap or click the Italic button a second time, or you immediately could tap or click the Undo button on the Quick Access Toolbar, or press CTRL+Z.

How can I tell what formatting has been applied to text?
The selected buttons and boxes on the HOME tab show formatting characteristics of the location of the insertion point.

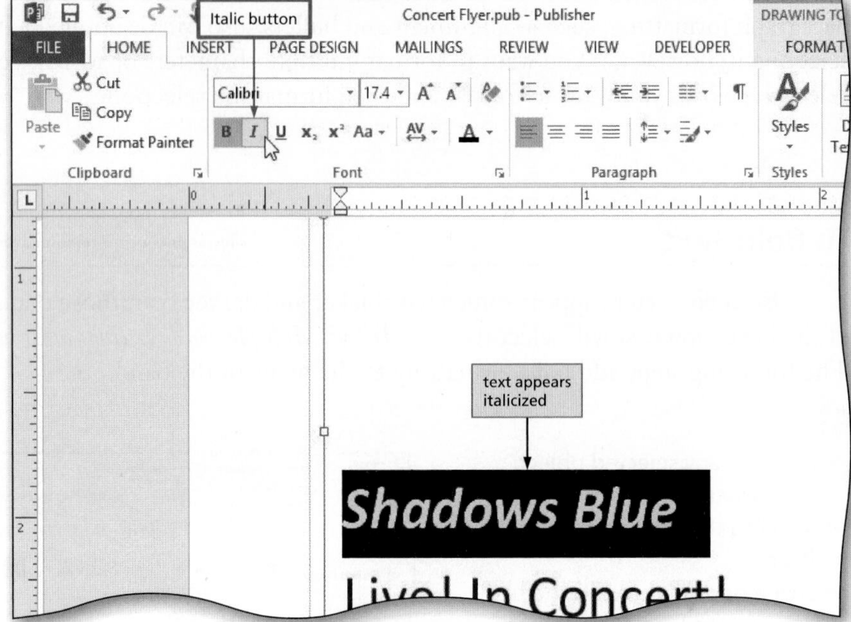

Figure 1–37

2

- Deselect the text.

Other Ways

1. Tap or click Italic button on mini toolbar
2. Press and hold or right-click, point to Change Text on shortcut menu, tap or click Font on Change Text submenu, tap or click Italic in Font style list (Font dialog box), tap or click OK button
3. Tap or click Font Dialog Box Launcher (HOME tab | Font group), tap or click Italic in Font style list (Font dialog box), tap or click OK button
4. Press CTRL+I

Autofitting Text

Other advanced text formatting commands are located on the TEXT BOX TOOLS FORMAT tab that is displayed when a text box is selected. You can autofit text, change the text direction, and hyphenate, as well as make changes to the alignment, styles, and typography.

Sometimes, the replacement text that you enter into a template does not fit the same way as the original template text—there might be too much text to fit, or too little text to fill the box. In those cases, you may want **autofit**, or **copy fit**, the text to adjust the way the text fits into the text box. Publisher autofitting choices are listed in Table 1–2.

Table 1–2 Autofitting Choices

Type of Autofitting	Result
Best Fit	Shrinks or expands text to fit in the text box, even when the text box is resized
Shrink Text On Overflow	Reduces the point size of text until no text is in overflow
Grow Text Box to Fit	Enlarges text box to fit all of the text at its current size
Do Not Autofit	Text appears at its current size

© 2014 Cengage Learning

To Autofit Text

The following steps autofit the text in the headline. ***Why?*** *You want the headline to appear as large as possible.*

1

- If necessary, click the text in the desired text box (in this case the headline text) to position the insertion point in the text box.
- Tap or click TEXT BOX TOOLS FORMAT on the ribbon to display the TEXT BOX TOOLS FORMAT tab.
- Tap or click the Text Fit button (TEXT BOX TOOLS FORMAT tab | Text group) to display the Text Fit menu (Figure 1–38).

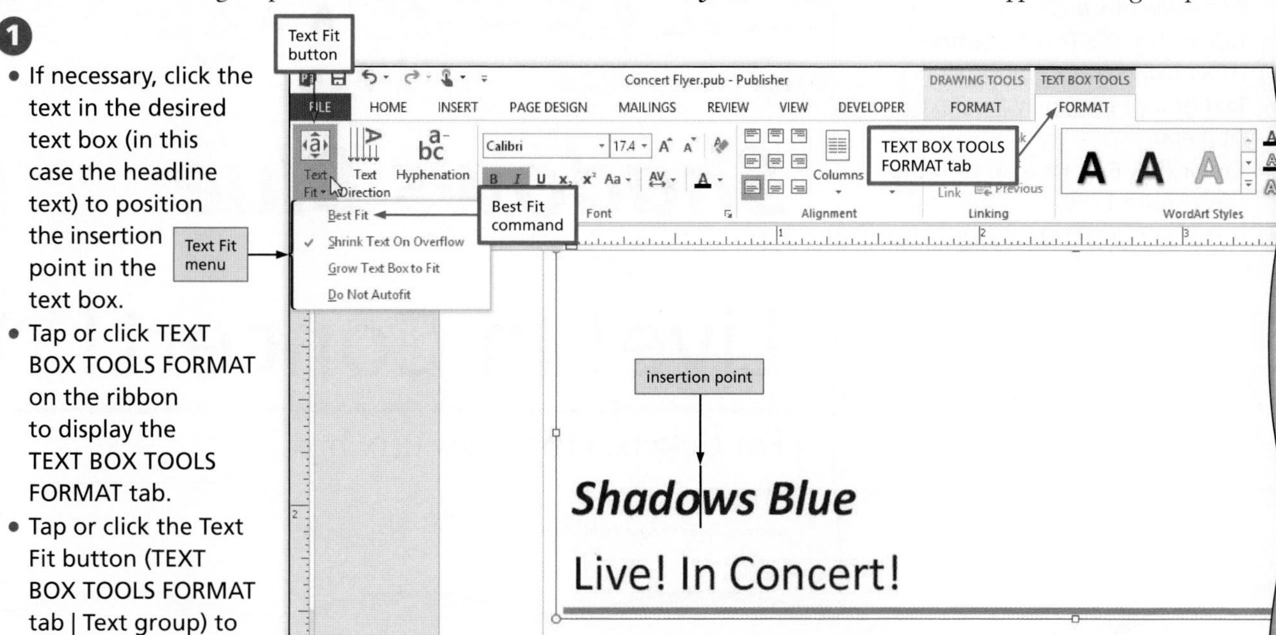

Figure 1–38

Q&A Do I have to select all of the text in a text box in order to autofit it?
No. Because all of the text in the text box is included automatically in autofitting, you do not need to select the text in order to autofit it.

2

- Tap or click Best Fit to autofit the text in the text box (Figure 1–39).

Q&A Could I use the Increase Font Size button to make the headline larger?
Yes, but you would have to estimate how big to make the text. Autofitting is different from using the Increase Font Size button. With autofitting, the text is increased, or decreased, to fit the given size of the text box automatically.

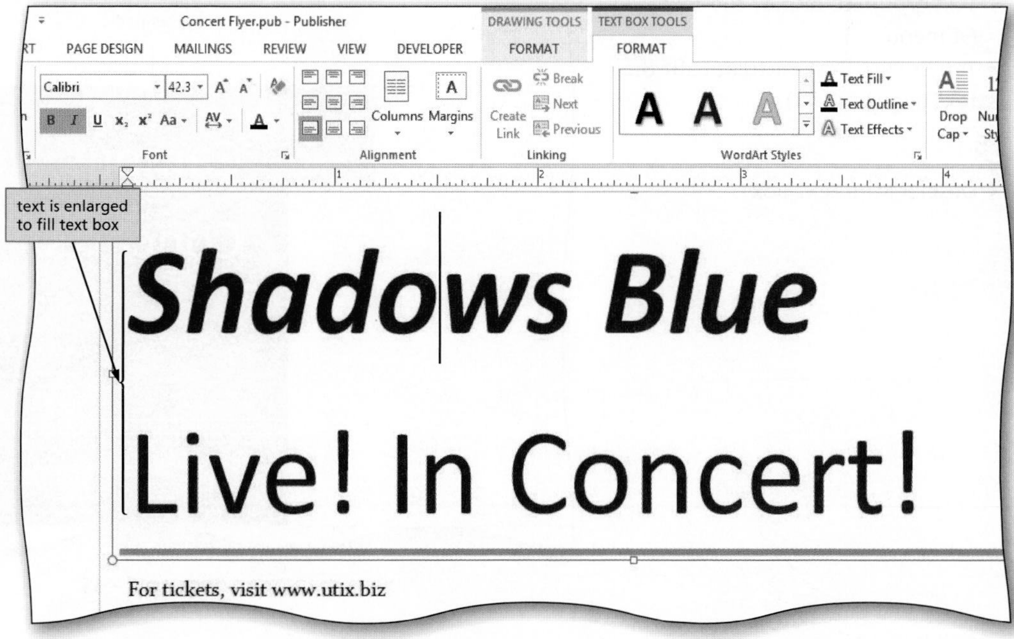

Figure 1–39

- Tap or click the text, For tickets, visit www.utix.biz.
- Tap or click the Text Fit button (TEXT BOX TOOLS FORMAT tab | Text group) to display the Text Fit menu.
- Tap or click Best Fit to autofit the text (Figure 1–40).

Figure 1–40

- Scroll if necessary and then tap or click the text, Campus Concerts, in the upper-right portion of the page.
- Tap or click the Text Fit button (TEXT BOX TOOLS FORMAT tab | Text group) to display the Text Fit menu.
- Tap or click Best Fit to autofit the text (Figure 1–41).

- Deselect the text box.

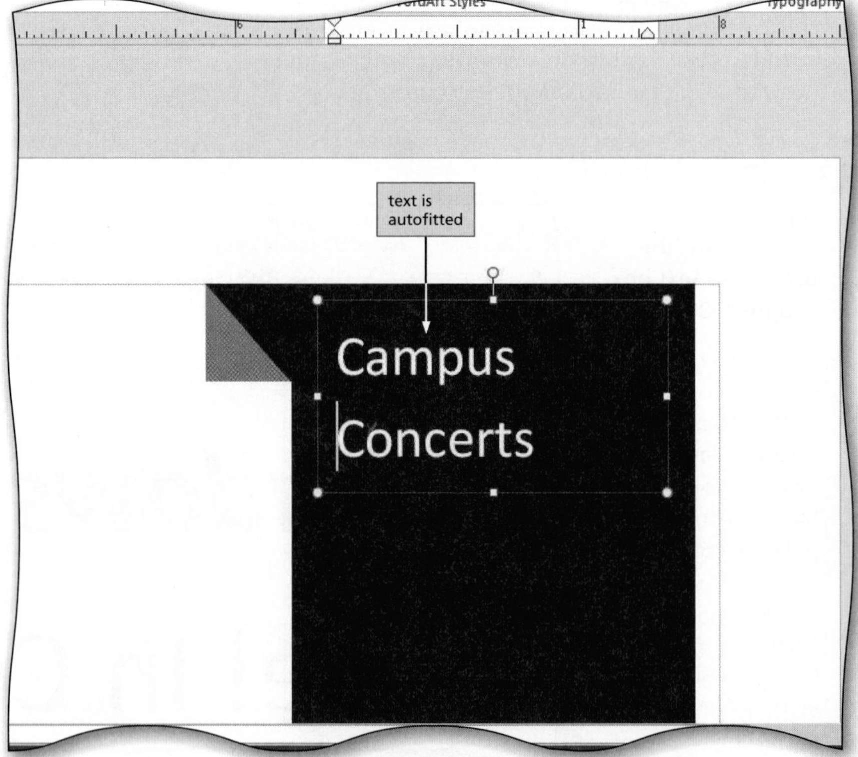

Figure 1–41

Other Ways

1. Press and hold or right-click selected text, tap or click Best Fit on shortcut menu

To Increase the Font Size

1 CUSTOMIZE TEMPLATES | 2 NAVIGATE & SELECT | 3 REPLACE TEXT | 4 DELETE OBJECTS | **5 FORMAT TEXT**
6 INSERT GRAPHICS | 7 FORMAT PICTURE | 8 ENHANCE PAGE | 9 PRINT & EXIT | 10 OPEN & REVISE

The following steps use the Increase Font Size button to enlarge the date and place text to make it easier to read. ***Why not use autofit?*** *The Best Fit command would fill the large text box, making the text even larger than the headline.*

1

- Scroll as necessary to display the text in the date and place text box.
- Tap or click the text and then press CTRL+A to select all of the text in the text box.
- Tap or click the 'Increase Font Size' button (HOME tab | Font group) several times until the text fills the text box without wrapping to a third line. If the line wraps, click the 'Decrease Font Size' button (HOME tab | Font group) (Figure 1–42).

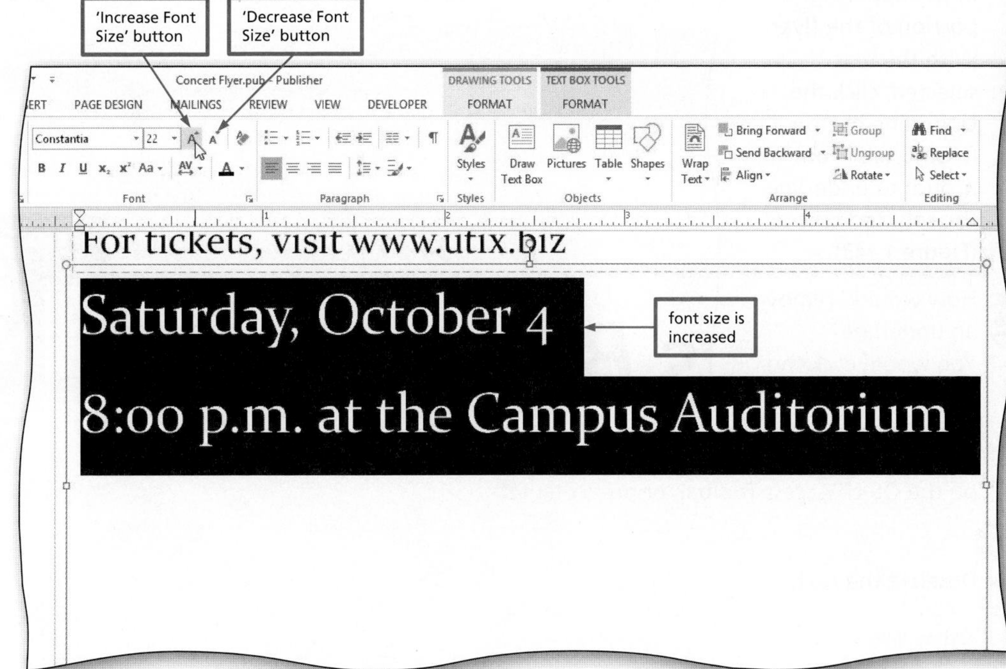

Figure 1–42

Q&A Why did the ribbon change back to the HOME tab?
In the previous steps, you deselected the Campus Concerts text box. When no object is selected, Publisher redisplays the HOME tab.

2

- Deselect the text box.

Other Ways

1. Tap or click Increase Font Size button on mini toolbar
2. Tap or click Font Size arrow (HOME tab | Font group), tap or click larger font size
3. Press SHIFT+CTRL+>

To Underline Text

1 CUSTOMIZE TEMPLATES | 2 NAVIGATE & SELECT | 3 REPLACE TEXT | 4 DELETE OBJECTS | **5 FORMAT TEXT**
6 INSERT GRAPHICS | 7 FORMAT PICTURE | 8 ENHANCE PAGE | 9 PRINT & EXIT | 10 OPEN & REVISE

Underlines are used to emphasize or draw attention to specific text. **Underlined** text prints with an underscore (_) below each character. ***Why?*** *Underlining the spaces between words provides continuity.* In the flyer, the name of the series, Campus Concerts, is emphasized with an underline. The steps on the next page select the text and format it with an underline.

- Scroll as necessary and select the text, Campus Concerts, in the upper-right portion of the flyer.
- With the text selected, click the Underline button (HOME tab | Font group) to underline the selected text (Figure 1–43).

Q&A How would I remove an underline?

You would click the Underline button a second time, or you immediately could tap or click the Undo button on the Quick Access Toolbar, or press CTRL+Z.

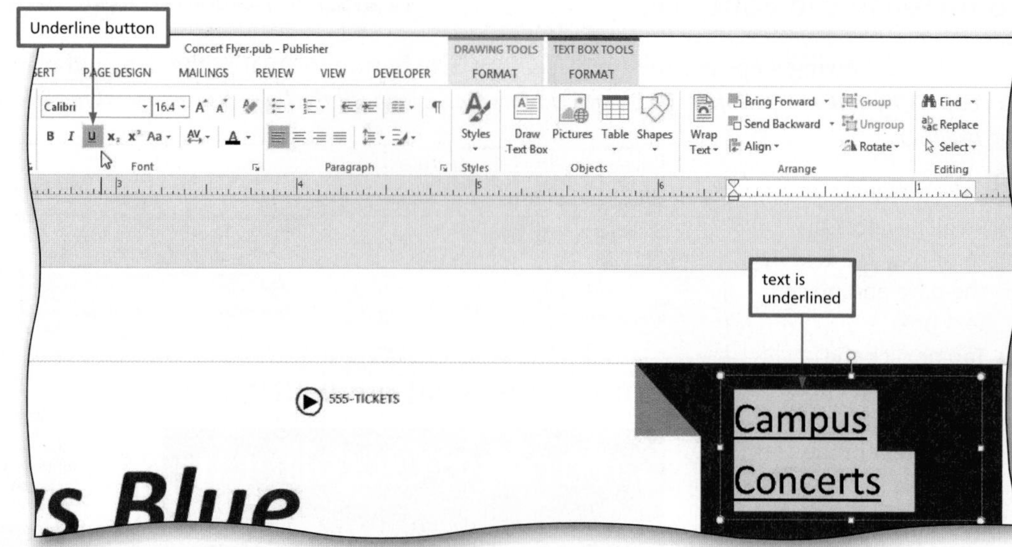

Figure 1–43

- Deselect the text.

Other Ways

1. Tap or click Underline button on mini toolbar
2. Press and hold or right-click selected text, point to Change Text on shortcut menu, tap or click Font on Change Text submenu, tap or click Underline arrow (Font dialog box), tap or click desired underline style, tap or click OK button
3. Tap or click Font Dialog Box Launcher (HOME tab | Font group), tap or click Underline arrow (Font dialog box), tap or click desired underline style, tap or click OK button
4. Press CTRL+U

To Change Text Direction

1 CUSTOMIZE TEMPLATES | 2 NAVIGATE & SELECT | 3 REPLACE TEXT | 4 DELETE OBJECTS | **5 FORMAT TEXT**
6 INSERT GRAPHICS | 7 FORMAT PICTURE | 8 ENHANCE PAGE | 9 PRINT & EXIT | 10 OPEN & REVISE

The next step is to change the direction of the text in the upper-right portion of the flyer. ***Why?*** *Changing the direction adds interest.* Later in the chapter, you will enlarge the text box to make the text appear on one line. The following step changes direction of the text.

- Tap or click the text to be changed (in this case, Campus Concerts).
- If necessary, tap or click TEXT BOX TOOLS FORMAT on the ribbon to display the TEXT BOX TOOLS FORMAT tab.
- Tap or click the Text Direction button (TEXT BOX TOOLS FORMAT tab | Text group) to change the text direction (Figure 1–44).

Q&A Do I have to select the text first?

No. As with single-word formatting, Publisher will apply the text direction to all of the text in the text box.

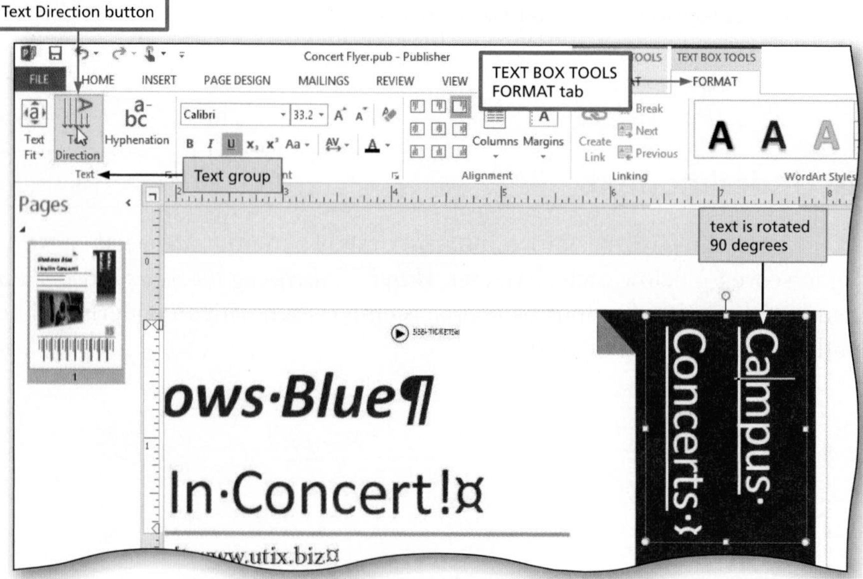

Figure 1–44

To View Whole Page

The following step views the entire page layout. ***Why?*** *Before you save the publication again, you may want to see how it looks so far.*

- Tap or click the 'Show Whole Page' button on the status bar to view the entire page (Figure 1–45).

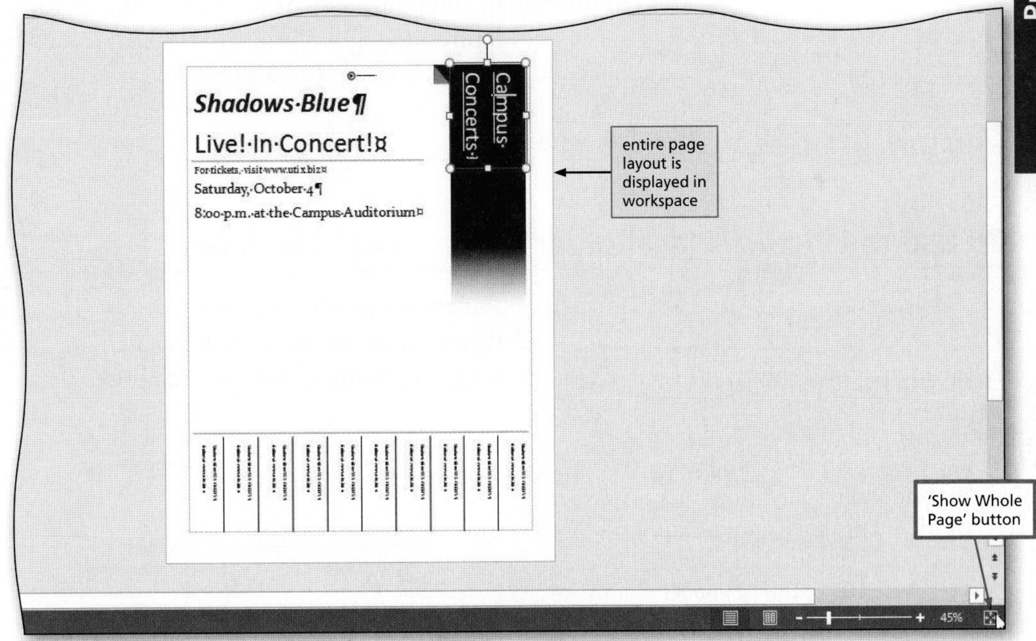

Figure 1–45

Other Ways

1. Tap or click Whole Page button (VIEW tab | Zoom group)
2. Press SHIFT+CTRL+L

To Save an Existing Publication with the Same File Name

You have made several modifications to the publication since you last saved it. Thus, you should save it again. The following step saves the publication again. For an example of the step listed below, refer to the Office and Windows chapter at the beginning of this book.

Tap or click the Save button on the Quick Access Toolbar to overwrite the previously saved file.

Break Point: If you wish to take a break, this is a good place to do so. To resume at a later time, run Publisher, open the file called Concert Flyer, and continue following the steps from this location forward.

Using Graphics

Files containing graphical images, also called **graphics**, are available from a variety of sources. Publisher provides access to Office.com Clip Art, a series of royalty-free, predefined graphics, such as drawings, photos, sounds, videos, and other media files, called clips. A **clip** is a single media file, such as art, sound, or animation, that you can insert and use in print publications, web publications, and other Microsoft Office documents. You also can insert pictures stored on your computer or storage location, or search for pictures on the web. **Picture** is a generic term for photos and clip art. You will learn about other kinds of graphics and illustrations in future chapters.

Many templates have picture placeholders that provide a size and shape to hold selected pictures. A **picture placeholder** has boundaries and a picture icon that is displayed only when you point to it. You can click the picture icon in a template to access the Insert Pictures dialog box. You also can insert an empty picture frame to reserve space for pictures you want to add later.

To Use the Picture Placeholder

Many templates contain picture placeholders whose size and shape fit in with the template style. ***Why?*** *Publications with pictures attract attention and add a sense of realism; most users want pictures in their publications.* The following steps use the picture placeholder to access photos from Office.com Clip Art.

1

- Tap or click the area above the tear-offs to display the boundary of the picture placeholder and the picture placeholder icon.
- Stretch or press the F9 key to zoom to 100% (Figure 1–46).

Q&A Can I turn on the boundary so that I can see it without pointing to it?
Yes. Tap or click the Boundaries check box (VIEW tab | Show group), which will display the boundaries on all objects.

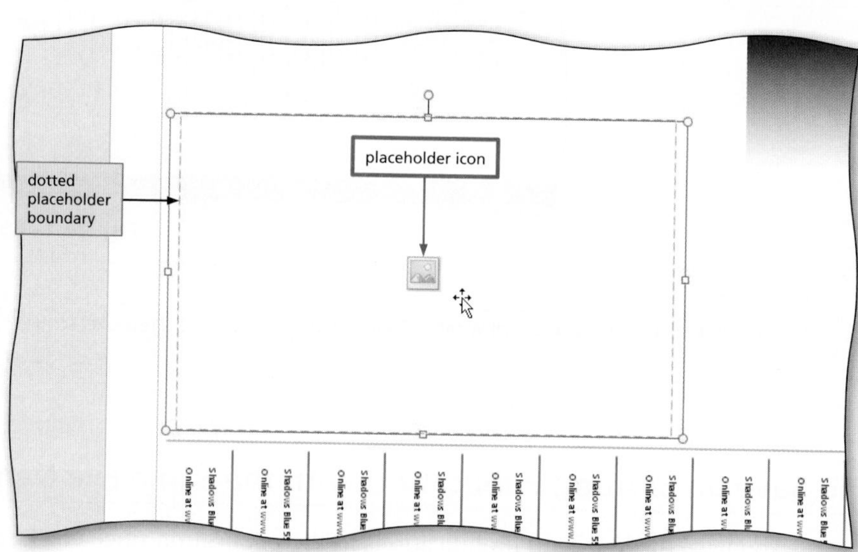

Figure 1–46

2

- Tap or click the placeholder icon to display the Insert Pictures dialog box.
- Tap or click Office.com Clip Art to place the insertion point in the search box.
- Type the desired search term (in this case, guitar) in the search box (Figure 1–47).

Q&A If I decide not to add a picture, will the placeholder print?
No. Graphic placeholders do not print. Placeholder text will print, however.

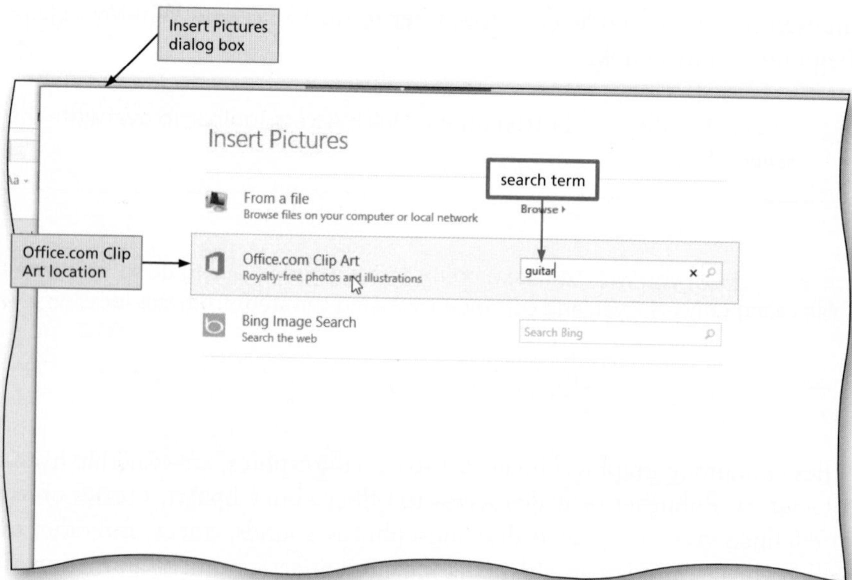

Figure 1–47

3

- Press the ENTER key to begin the search.
- When the results appear, tap or click the picture shown in Figure 1–48 or a similar picture.

Experiment

- Scroll through the clip art gallery and notice it includes photos, drawings, and traditional clip art graphics. When you are finished, tap or click the desired picture.

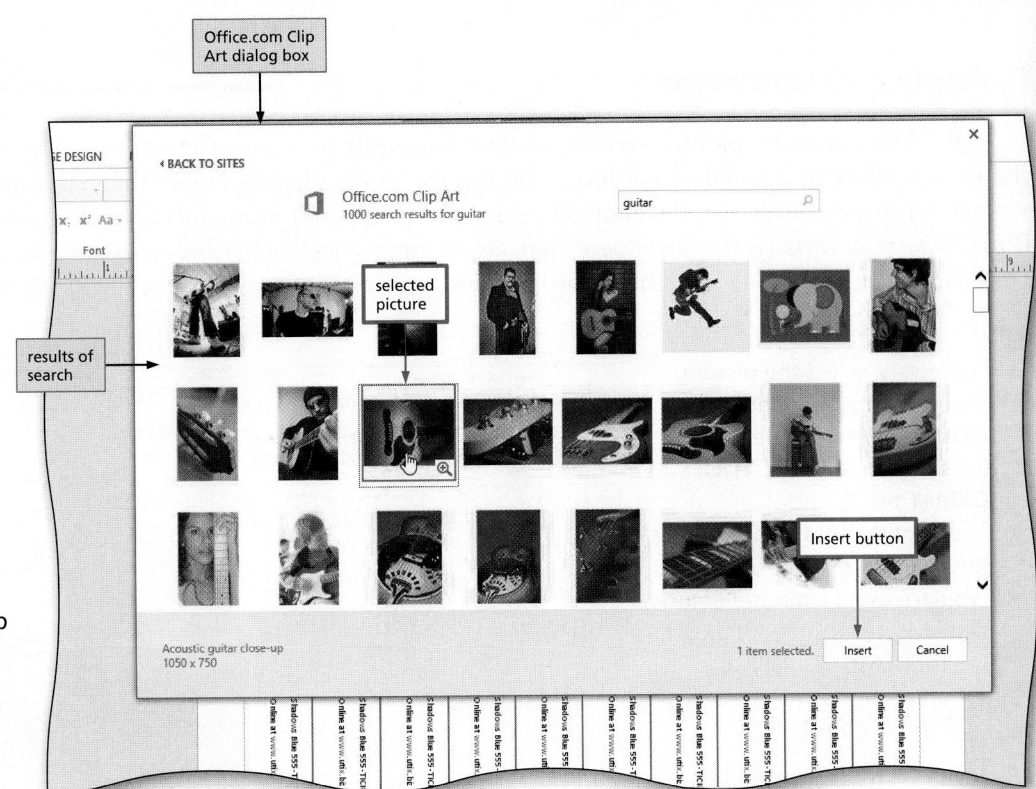

Figure 1–48

4

- Tap or click the Insert button (Office.com Clip Art dialog box) to insert the chosen picture into the publication (Figure 1–49).

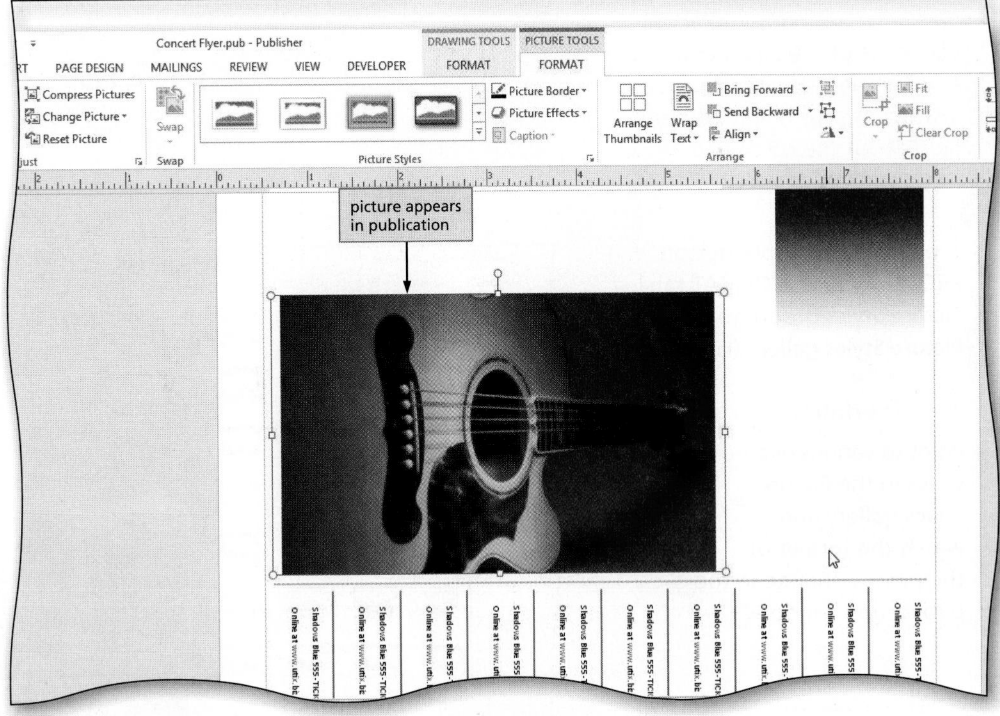

Figure 1–49

To Apply a Picture Style

Publisher provides **picture styles** that allow you easily to change the basic rectangle format to a more visually appealing style and designer look. The Picture Style gallery has more than 20 picture styles that include a variety of shapes, borders, and scallops. The flyer in this chapter uses a picture style slanting up and right. ***Why?*** *Some researchers say that an upward slant adds energy to a publication and directs the reader's eye toward the center of the publication with a 3-D look.* The following steps apply a picture style to the picture in the flyer.

1

- If necessary, select the picture.
- If necessary, tap or click PICTURE TOOLS FORMAT on the ribbon to display the PICTURE TOOLS FORMAT tab.
- Scroll slightly right to adjust the page layout.
- If you are using a mouse, point to the More button (PICTURE TOOLS FORMAT tab | Picture Styles group) to display the Enhanced ScreenTip (Figure 1–50).

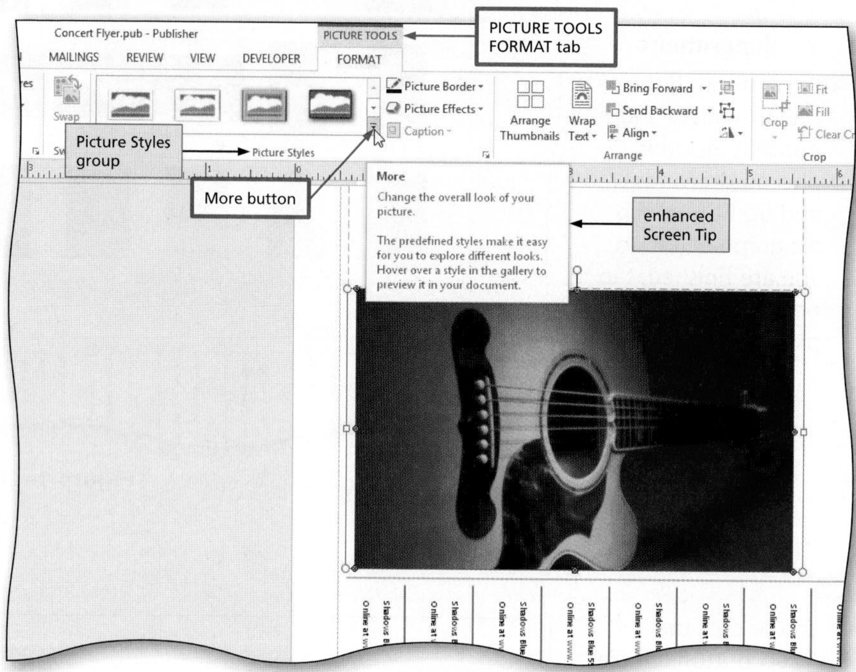

Figure 1–50

Q&A

Why did I scroll the page layout?

By scrolling, the Picture Styles gallery will not cover up the graphic in the next step.

What is an Enhanced ScreenTip?

An **Enhanced ScreenTip** is an on-screen note that provides the name of the command, a description, and sometimes instructions for how to obtain help about the command.

2

- Tap or click the More button (PICTURE TOOLS FORMAT tab | Picture Styles group) to display the Picture Styles gallery (Figure 1–51).

Experiment

- Point to various picture styles in the Picture Styles gallery and watch the format of the picture change in the publication window.

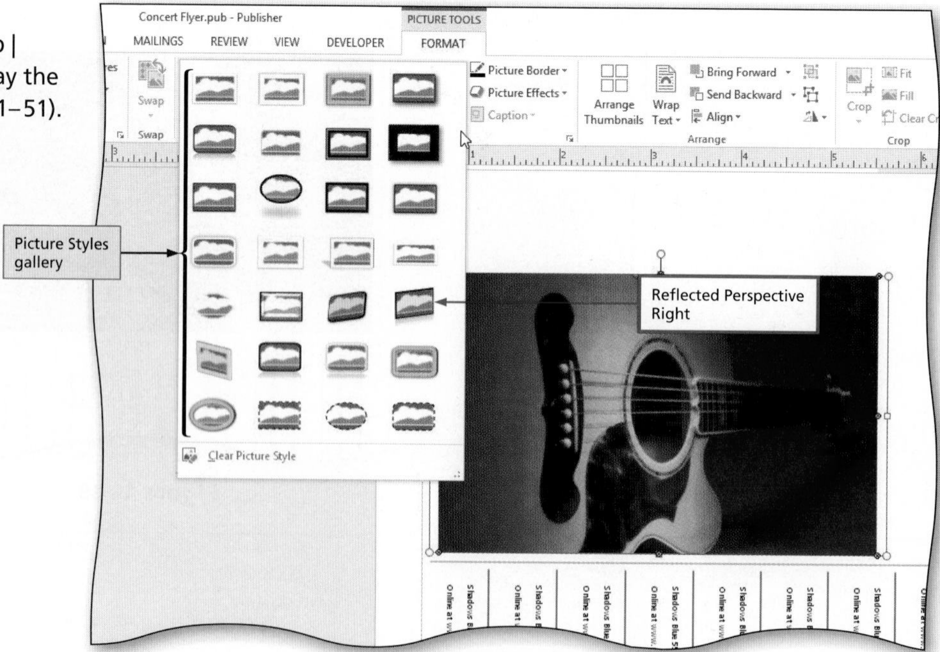

Figure 1–51

3

- Tap or click Reflected Perspective Right in the Picture Styles gallery to apply the selected style to the picture (Figure 1–52).

Q&A Should I be concerned that the picture overlaps the tear-offs slightly?

No. You will move the picture later in the chapter.

Figure 1–52

Borders

Similar to a frame around a picture on the wall, a **border** helps define the edge of an object on the page. Not only can you choose a color for the border, but Publisher also allows you to set a weight or size of the border and choose a tint, dashed line, or pattern.

To Set the Weight of a Border

1 CUSTOMIZE TEMPLATES | 2 NAVIGATE & SELECT | 3 REPLACE TEXT | 4 DELETE OBJECTS | 5 FORMAT TEXT
6 INSERT GRAPHICS | 7 FORMAT PICTURE | 8 ENHANCE PAGE | 9 PRINT & EXIT | 10 OPEN & REVISE

You will change the weight of the line around the picture to create a border. ***Why?*** *Adding a border defines the edges of a picture, makes it stand out from the background, and eliminates the perception of floating.* The following steps add a border to the picture in the flyer.

1

- If necessary, select the picture.
- Tap or click the Picture Border button (PICTURE TOOLS FORMAT tab | Picture Styles group) to display the Picture Border gallery.
- Tap or click Weight to display the Weight gallery (Figure 1–53).

Experiment

- Point to various weights in the list and watch the border size change in the publication window.

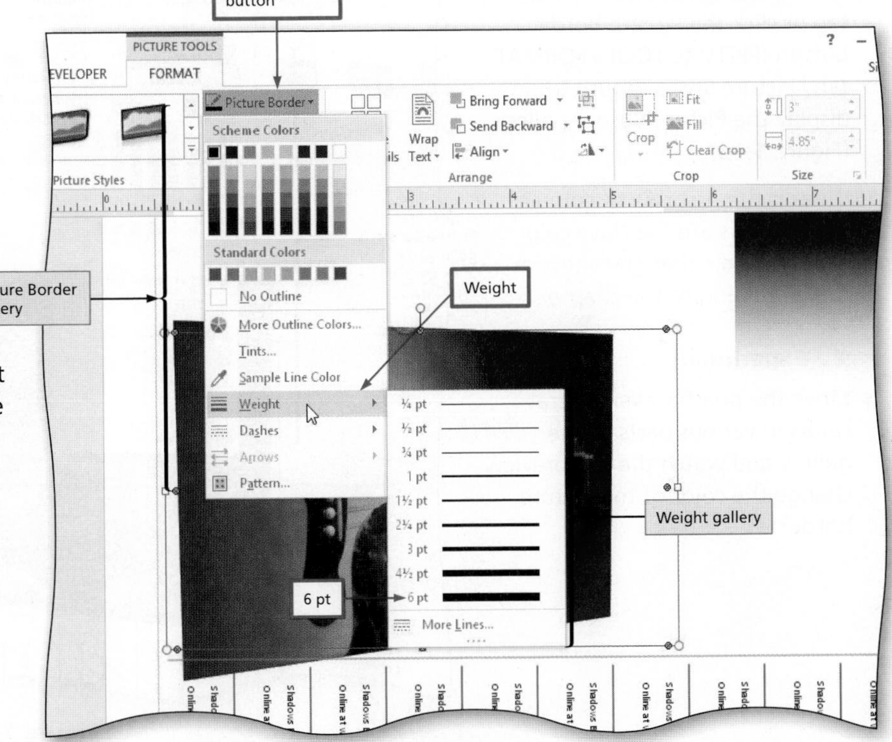

Figure 1–53

- Tap or click 6 pt to apply a 6-point line (Figure 1–54).

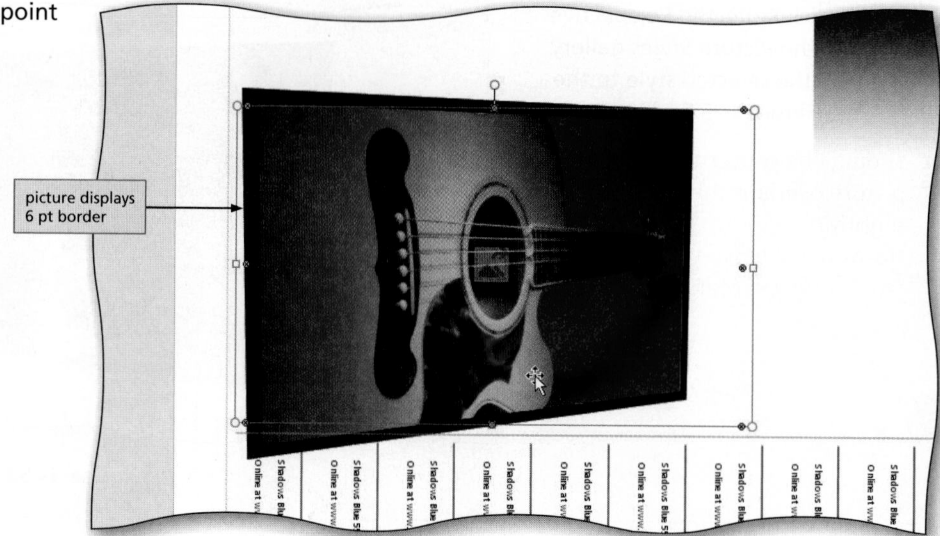

Figure 1–54

Other Ways

1. Press and hold or right-click selected picture, tap or click Format Picture on shortcut menu, tap or click Colors and Lines tab, enter width
2. Tap or click Format Shape Dialog Box Launcher (PICTURE TOOLS FORMAT tab | Picture Styles group), tap or click Colors and Lines tab, enter width

To Change the Border Color

1 CUSTOMIZE TEMPLATES | 2 NAVIGATE & SELECT | 3 REPLACE TEXT | 4 DELETE OBJECTS | 5 FORMAT TEXT
6 INSERT GRAPHICS | 7 FORMAT PICTURE | 8 ENHANCE PAGE | 9 PRINT & EXIT | 10 OPEN & REVISE

The following steps change the border color to gray. ***Why?*** *The picture is dark; gray helps define the border better than the default black color.*

- With the picture still selected, tap or click the Picture Border button (PICTURE TOOLS FORMAT tab | Picture Styles group) to display the Picture Border gallery (Figure 1–55).

Q&A What is the first row of colors?
Those colors are the Navy color scheme colors that you chose at the beginning of the chapter.

Experiment

- Move the pointer over several colors in various parts of the gallery and watch the live preview change the color of the picture border.

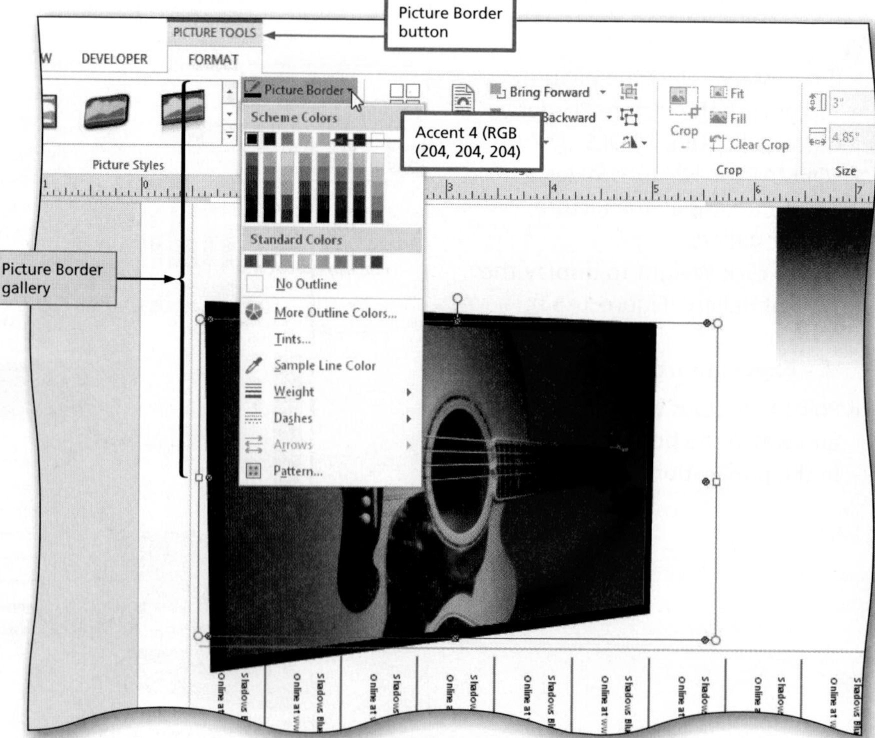

Figure 1–55

2

- Tap or click Accent 4 (RGB (204, 204, 204)) (first row, fifth column) to choose the gray color from the color scheme (Figure 1–56).

Q&A What do the numbers in the button name signify?
Those are the intensity values of red, green, and blue that define the color, gray.

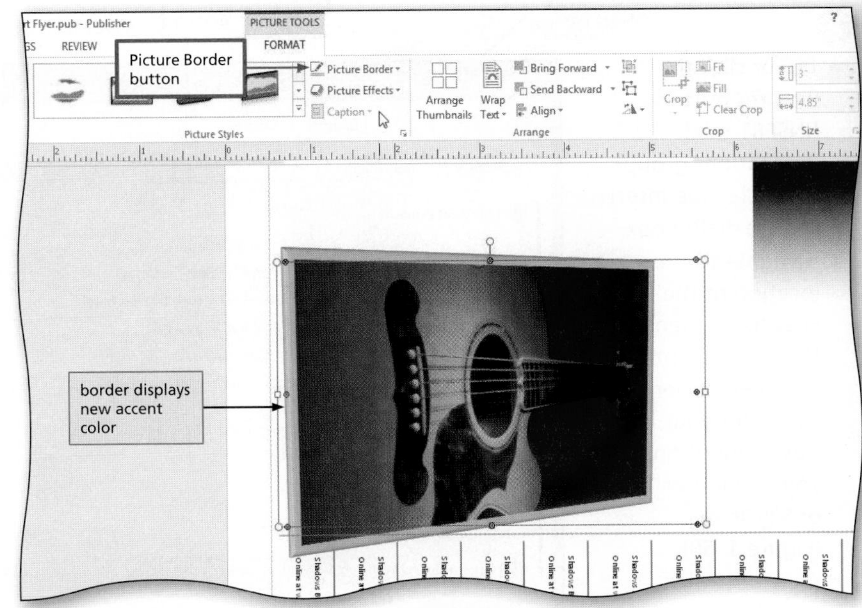

Figure 1–56

Other Ways

1. Tap or click Format Picture on shortcut menu, on Colors and Lines sheet, tap or click Color box in Line area, tap or click desired color
2. Tap or click Format Shape Dialog Box Launcher (PICTURE TOOLS FORMAT tab | Picture Styles group), on Colors and Lines sheet, tap or click Color box in Line area, tap or click desired color

To Insert a Picture from a Storage Device

1 CUSTOMIZE TEMPLATES | 2 NAVIGATE & SELECT | 3 REPLACE TEXT | 4 DELETE OBJECTS | 5 FORMAT TEXT
6 INSERT GRAPHICS | 7 FORMAT PICTURE | 8 ENHANCE PAGE | 9 PRINT & EXIT | 10 OPEN & REVISE

You do not have to have a picture placeholder to insert pictures into a publication. ***Why?*** *You may want to use a picture as is and not have it conform to the size of the placeholder.* You can insert both online pictures and those from storage, using the Publisher ribbon.

The following steps insert a picture from a storage device. To complete this assignment, you will be required to use the Data Files for Students. Visit www.cengage.com/ct/studentdownload for detailed instructions or contact your instructor for information about accessing the required files.

1

- Tap or click outside the page layout so that no object is selected.
- Tap or click INSERT on the ribbon to display the INSERT tab (Figure 1–57).

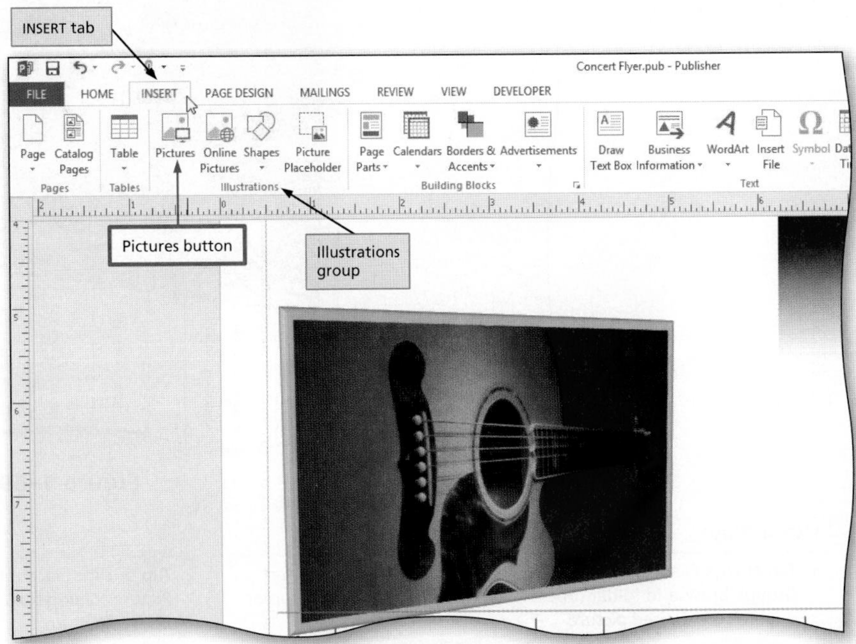

Figure 1–57

2

- Tap or click the Pictures button (INSERT tab | Illustrations group) to display the Insert Picture dialog box.
- Navigate to the location of the Data Files for Students (in this case, Chapter 01 in the Publisher folder [or your class folder]) on your computer or SkyDrive (Figure 1–58).

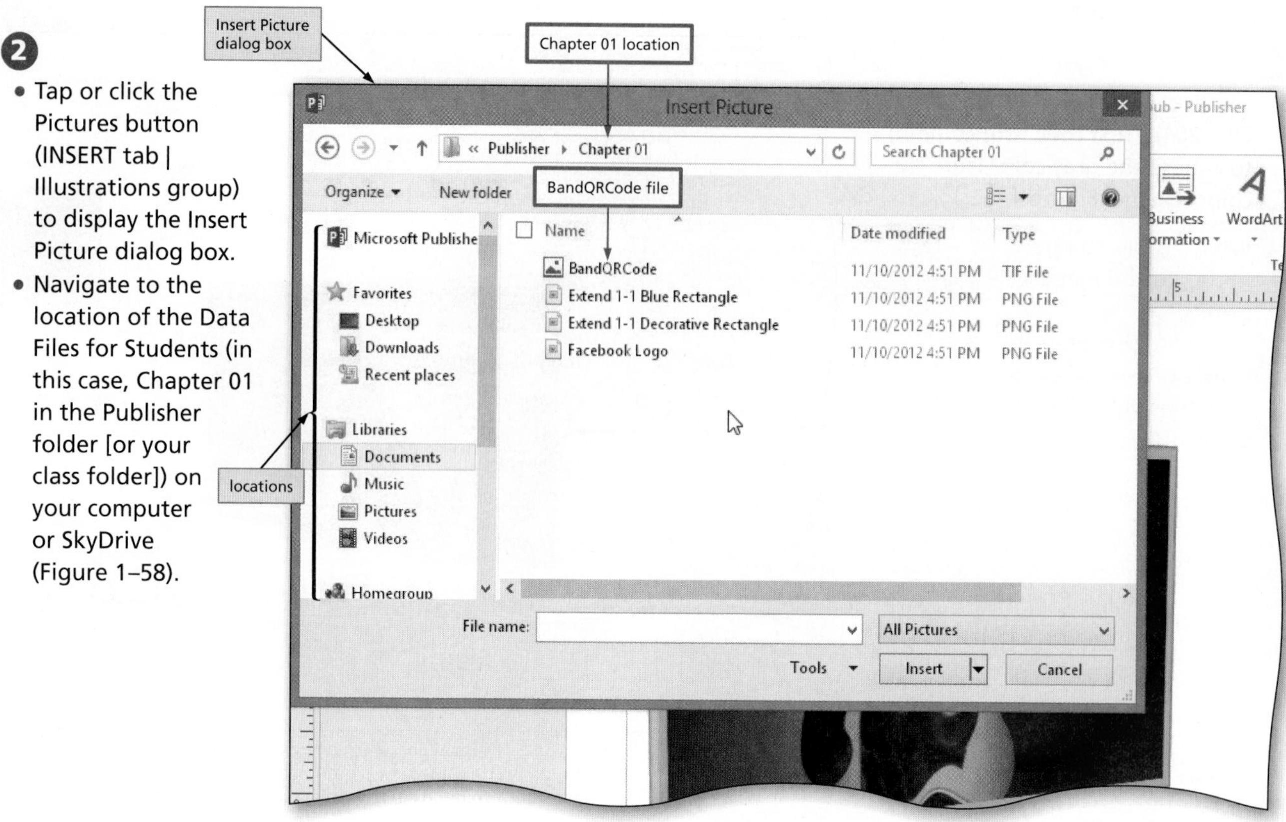

Figure 1–58

- Double-tap or double-click the desired picture (in this case, the BandQRCode file) to insert the file into the publication (Figure 1–59).

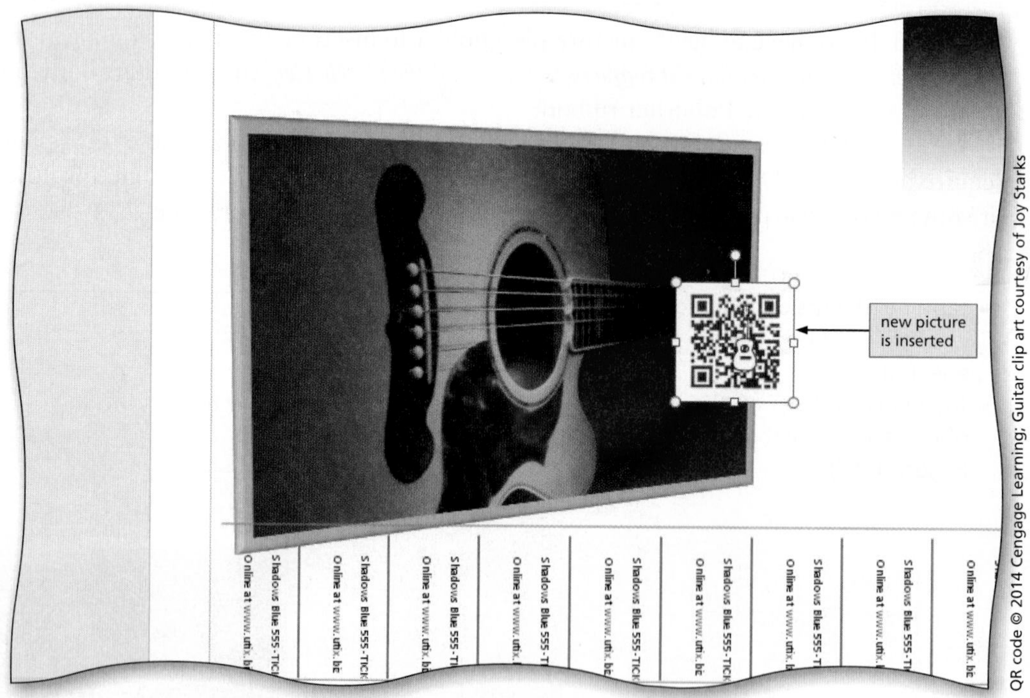

QR code © 2014 Cengage Learning; Guitar clip art courtesy of Joy Starks

Figure 1–59

Other Ways

1. Tap or click Pictures button (PICTURE TOOLS FORMAT tab | Insert Group), browse to folder (Insert Picture dialog box), double-tap or double-click desired picture
2. Tap or click placeholder icon, tap or click Browse button (Insert Pictures dialog box), browse to folder, double-tap or double-click desired picture

Moving, Aligning, and Resizing Objects

Many times, even when using a template, you will want to enhance the page by moving objects around on the page layout; or, you may want to change the size of objects as you did with the size of text. To move an object, it must be selected. The pointer changes to a double two-headed arrow, and you then drag the object to the new location or to the scratch area. If you press and hold the SHIFT key while dragging, the object moves in a straight line. Pressing the CTRL key while dragging creates a copy of the object. As you move an object, Publisher displays **visual layout guides** to help you place and align the object to other objects on the page layout. When you **align** an object to another object, its edge or center lines up, either vertically or horizontally. The visual layout guides display as pink lines that move from object to object as you drag. Visual layout guides appear when aligning to the left, right, top, bottom, or middle of objects.

Sometimes pictures and graphics are not the right size. In that case, you need to resize the object. To **resize** any object in Publisher, select the object, and then drag a handle. Recall that a handle is one of several small shapes displayed around an object when the object is selected. To resize by dragging, position the pointer over one of the handles and then drag the mouse. Pressing the CTRL key while dragging (CTRL+drag) keeps the center of the graphic in the same place during resizing. Pressing the SHIFT key while dragging (SHIFT+drag) maintains the graphic's proportions during resizing. Finally, pressing the SHIFT and CTRL keys while dragging (SHIFT+CTRL+drag) maintains the proportions and keeps the center in the same place.

BTW
QR Codes
A QR code, or Quick Reference code, can be generated by a variety of programs on the web. If a company wants to include a graphic in its QR code, the graphic designer needs to maintain the integrity of the code by inserting a graphic that covers less than 30% of the space.

To Move an Object

1 CUSTOMIZE TEMPLATES | 2 NAVIGATE & SELECT | 3 REPLACE TEXT | 4 DELETE OBJECTS | 5 FORMAT TEXT
6 INSERT GRAPHICS | 7 FORMAT PICTURE | 8 ENHANCE PAGE | 9 PRINT & EXIT | 10 OPEN & REVISE

While text boxes need to be moved by dragging their borders, graphics can be moved by dragging from anywhere within the graphic. ***Why?*** *If you drag the text inside a text box, you may move the text, rather than the entire text box object.* The following steps move the QR code from its current location, the center, to a location above the tear-offs on the right.

- If necessary, select the object (in this case, the QR code).
- Drag the graphic to its new location (in this case, above the tear-offs on the right) until both the horizontal and vertical pink visual layout lines appear (Figure 1–60).

Q&A The graphic does not appear to be aligned. Did I do something wrong?
This particular graphic has a thick white border, which makes it hard to see the alignment.

- Release the mouse button to finish moving the object.

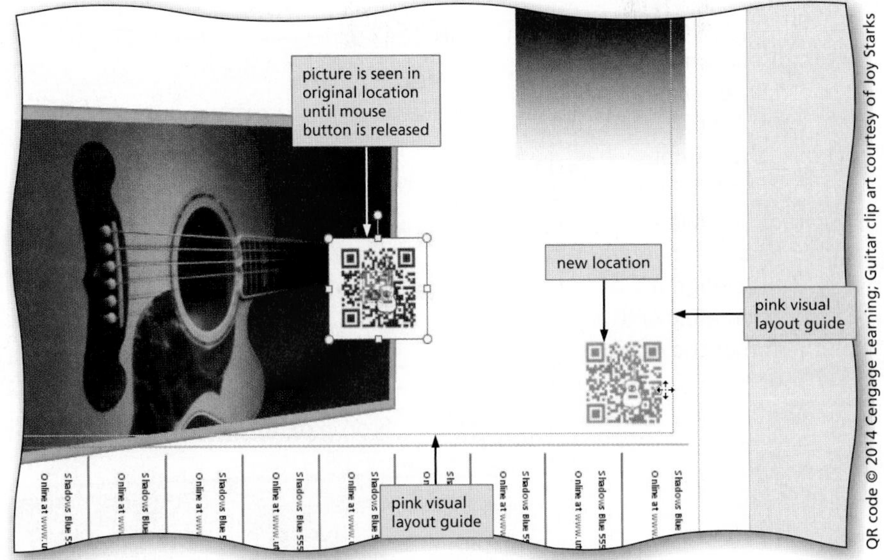

Figure 1–60

QR code © 2014 Cengage Learning; Guitar clip art courtesy of Joy Starks

Other Ways

1. Select object, press ARROW key
2. Tap or click Object Position button on status bar, enter new x and y coordinates on Measurement toolbar

To Align an Object

The following steps align the guitar with the left margin as it is moved up on the page layout. ***Why?*** *Moving the graphic up gives it a more prominent place in the flyer and keeps it from overlapping the tear-offs.*

- Select the object you wish to move (in this case, the guitar photo) by tapping or clicking it.
- Drag the object to its new location and align it using the visual layout guides. In this case, drag the guitar up and align it with the left margin (Figure 1–61).

- Deselect the picture.

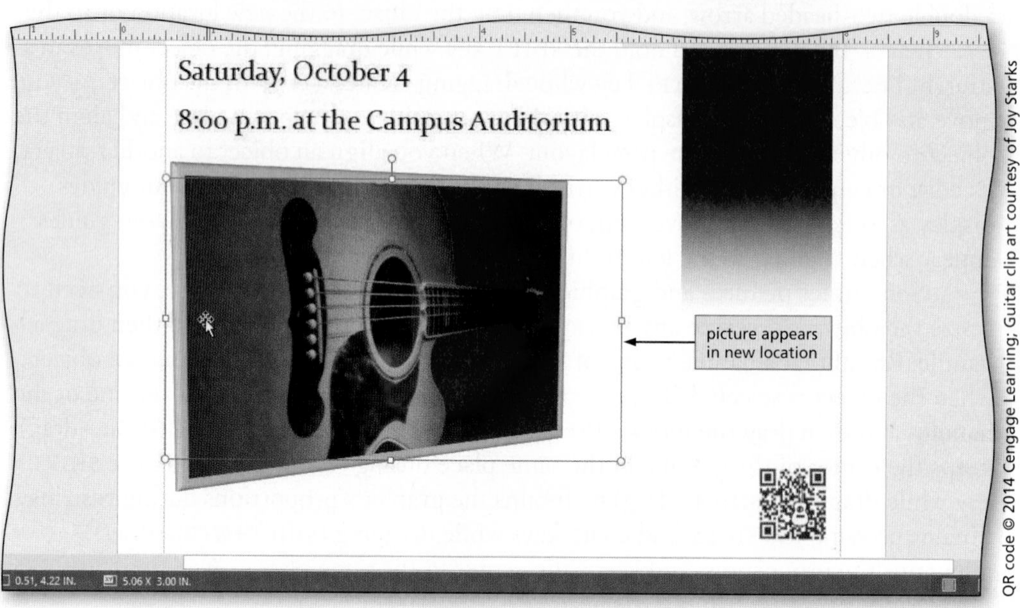

Figure 1–61

QR code © 2014 Cengage Learning; Guitar clip art courtesy of Joy Starks

To Resize an Object

The next step resizes the Campus Concerts text box to make it larger. ***Why?*** *Enlarging the text box causes the text to appear on one line.* Recall that selecting a text box involves clicking its border rather than its text.

- Scroll as necessary to display and then select the object to be resized (in this case, the Campus Concerts text box).
- Drag the lower-center sizing handle down to align it approximately with the top of the guitar (Figure 1–62).

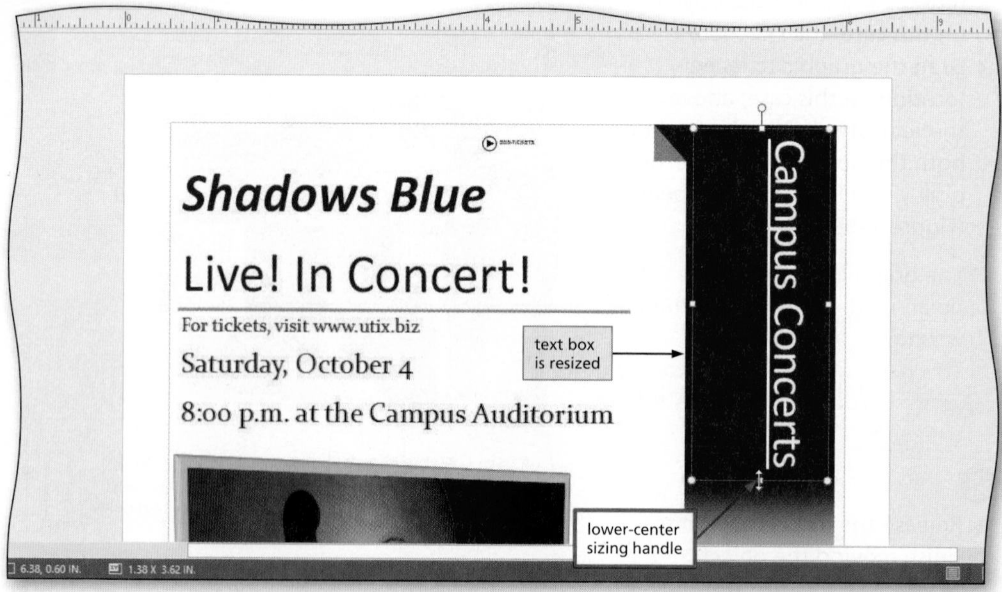

Figure 1–62

Other Ways

1. Tap or click Object size button on status bar, enter dimensions on Measurement toolbar

Publication Properties

Publisher helps you organize and identify your files by using **publication properties**, which are the details about a file, such as the project author, title, and subject. For example, a class name or publication topic can describe the file's purpose or content.

CONSIDER THIS

Why would you want to assign publication properties to a publication?
Publication properties are valuable for a variety of reasons:

- Users can save time locating a particular file because they can view a file's document properties without opening the publication.
- By creating consistent properties for files having similar content, users can better organize their publications.
- Some organizations require Publisher users to add document properties so that other employees can view details about these files.

The more common document properties are standard and automatically updated properties. **Standard properties** are associated with all Microsoft Office files and include author, title, and subject. **Automatically updated properties** include file system properties, such as the date you create or change a file, and statistics, such as the file size.

BTW
Publisher Properties Keywords
Assigning keywords to a print publication allows you to search for publications based on those keywords. For example, you might enter the word, marketing, as a keyword in a flyer. In the future, you could search for all marketing publications on your company's storage device.

To Change Publication Properties

To change publication properties, you would follow these steps.

1. Tap or click FILE on the ribbon to open the Backstage view and then, if necessary, tap or click the Info tab in the Backstage view to display the Info gallery.

2. Tap or click the Publication Properties button in the right pane to display the Properties menu and then tap or click Advanced Properties on the Publication Properties menu to display the Publication Properties dialog box.

Q&A Why are some of the publication properties already filled in?
The person who installed Office 2013 on your computer or network may have set or customized the properties.

3. Type the desired text in the appropriate property text boxes in the Summary sheet.

Q&A What if the property I want to change is not displayed in the Document Information Panel?
Tap or click the Document Properties button in the Document Information Panel and then tap or click Advanced Properties on the menu to display the Properties dialog box. If necessary, tap or click the Summary tab (Properties dialog box) to display the Summary sheet, fill in the appropriate text boxes, and then tap or click the OK button.

4. Tap or click the OK button (Publication Properties dialog box) to save the properties.

To Save an Existing Publication with the Same File Name

You have made several modifications to the publication since you last saved it. Thus, you should save it again. The following step saves the publication again. For an example of the step listed below, refer to the Office and Windows chapter at the beginning of this book.

1 Tap or click the Save button on the Quick Access Toolbar to overwrite the previously saved file.

Break Point: If you wish to take a break, this is a good place to do so. To resume at a later time, run Publisher, open the file called Concert Flyer, and continue following the steps from this location forward.

Printing a Publication

After creating a publication, you may want to print it. Printing a publication enables you to distribute it to others in a form that can be read or viewed but typically not edited. It is a good practice to save a publication before printing it, in case you experience difficulties printing.

CONSIDER THIS

What is the best method for distributing a publication?

The traditional method of distributing a publication uses a printer to produce a hard copy. A **hard copy** or **printout** is information that exists on a physical medium such as paper. Hard copies can be useful for the following reasons:

- Some people prefer proofreading a hard copy of a publication rather than viewing it on the screen to check for errors and readability.
- Hard copies can serve as a backup reference if your storage medium is lost or becomes corrupted and you need to recreate the publication.

Instead of distributing a hard copy of a publication, users can distribute the publication as an electronic image that mirrors the original publication's appearance. The electronic image of the publication can be sent as an email attachment, posted on a website, or copied to a portable storage medium such as a USB flash drive. Two popular electronic image formats, sometimes called fixed formats, are PDF by Adobe Systems and XPS by Microsoft. In Publisher, you can create electronic image files through the Save As dialog box and the Export, Share, and Print tabs in the Backstage view. Electronic images of publications, such as PDF and XPS, can be useful for the following reasons:

- Users can view electronic images of publications without the software that created the original publication (e.g., Publisher). Specifically, to view a PDF file, you use a program called Adobe Reader, which can be downloaded free from Adobe's website. Similarly, to view an XPS file, you use a program called XPS Viewer, which is included in the latest versions of Windows and Internet Explorer.
- Sending electronic publications saves paper and printer supplies. Society encourages users to contribute to **green computing**, which involves reducing the electricity consumed and environmental waste generated when using computers, mobile devices, and related technologies.

To Print a Publication

1 CUSTOMIZE TEMPLATES | 2 NAVIGATE & SELECT | 3 REPLACE TEXT | 4 DELETE OBJECTS | 5 FORMAT TEXT
6 INSERT GRAPHICS | 7 FORMAT PICTURE | 8 ENHANCE PAGE | **9 PRINT & EXIT** | **10 OPEN & REVISE**

With the completed publication saved, you may want to print it. ***Why?*** *Because this flyer is being posted, you will print a hard copy on a printer.* The following steps print a hard copy of the contents of the saved Concert Flyer publication.

1

- Tap or click FILE on the ribbon to open the Backstage view.
- Tap or click the Print tab in the Backstage view to display the Print gallery.
- Verify the printer name listed on the Printer Status button will print a hard copy of the publication. If necessary, click the Printer Status button to display a list of available printer options and then click the desired printer to change the currently selected printer (Figure 1–63).

Q&A

How can I print multiple copies of my publication?
Increase the number in the Copies box in the Print gallery.

What if I decide not to print the publication at this time?
Tap or click the Back button in the upper-left corner of the Backstage view to return to the publication window.

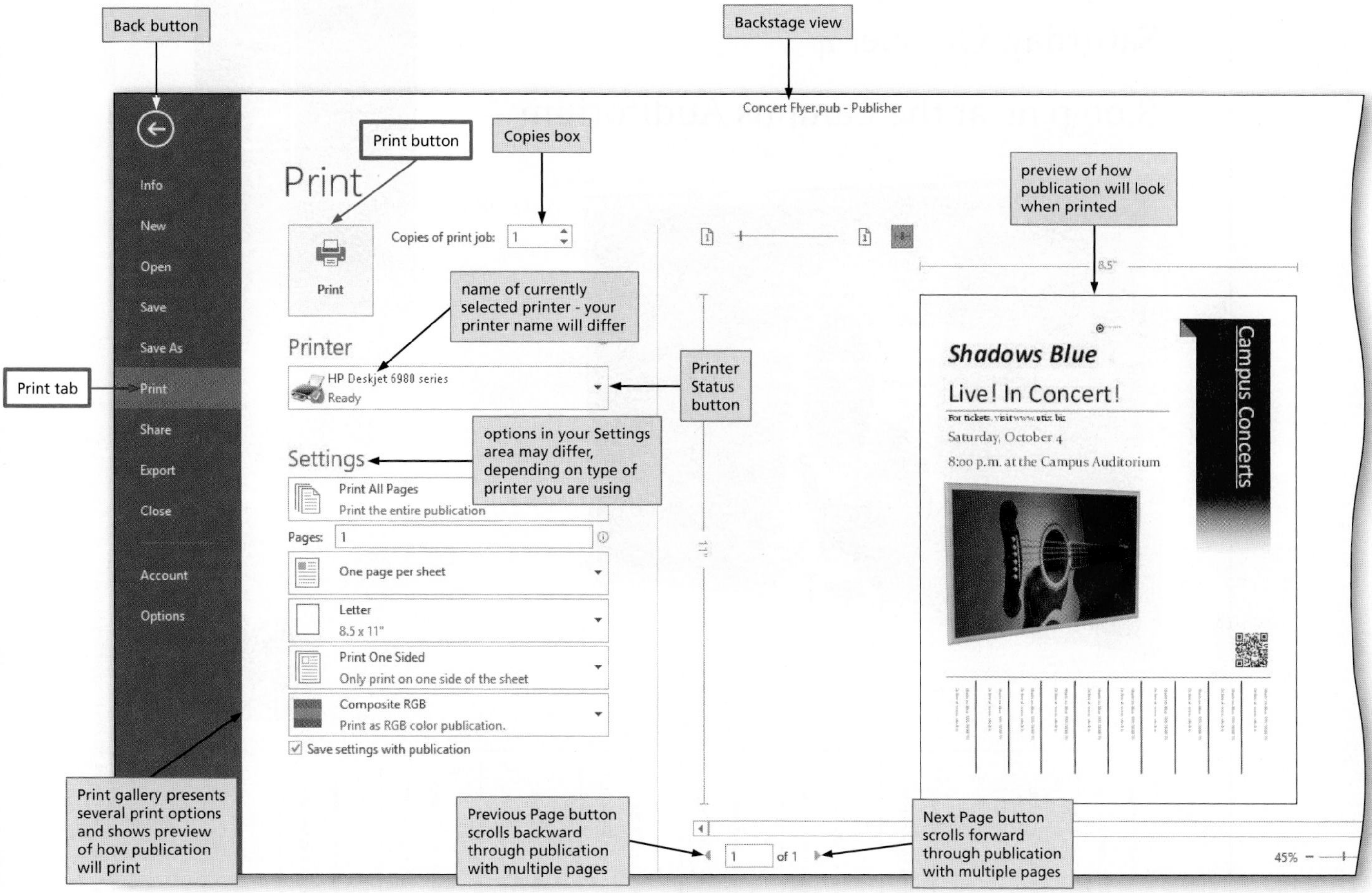

Back button
Backstage view
Concert Flyer.pub - Publisher
Print button
Copies box
preview of how publication will look when printed
Print
Copies of print job: 1
name of currently selected printer - your printer name will differ
Printer
HP Deskjet 6980 series
Ready
Print tab
Printer Status button
options in your Settings area may differ, depending on type of printer you are using
Settings
Print All Pages
Print the entire publication
Pages: 1
One page per sheet
Letter
8.5 x 11"
Print One Sided
Only print on one side of the sheet
Composite RGB
Print as RGB color publication.
Save settings with publication
Info
New
Open
Save
Save As
Print
Share
Export
Close
Account
Options
Shadows Blue
Live! In Concert!
Saturday, October 4
8:00 p.m. at the Campus Auditorium
Campus Concerts
Print gallery presents several print options and shows preview of how publication will print
Previous Page button scrolls backward through publication with multiple pages
Next Page button scrolls forward through publication with multiple pages
1 of 1
45%

QR code © 2014 Cengage Learning; Guitar clip art courtesy of Joy Starks

Figure 1–63

- Tap or click the Print button in the Print gallery to print the publication on the currently selected printer.
- When the printer stops, retrieve the hard copy (Figure 1–64 on the next page).

Q&A

Do I have to wait until my publication is complete to print it?
No, you can follow these steps to print a publication at any time while you are creating it.

What if I want to print an electronic image of a publication instead of a hard copy?
In a later chapter, you will learn how to export the file to the PDF format; or, if it is installed, you can select Adobe PDF from the list of printers.

555-TICKETS

Shadows Blue

Live! In Concert!

For tickets, visit www.utix.biz

Saturday, October 4

8:00 p.m. at the Campus Auditorium

Campus Concerts

Shadows Blue 555-TICKETS
Online at www.utix.biz

Shadows Blue 555-TICKETS
Online at www.utix.biz

Shadows Blue 555-TICKETS
Online at www.utix.biz

Shadows Blue 555-TICKETS
Online at www.utix.biz

Shadows Blue 555-TICKETS
Online at www.utix.biz

Shadows Blue 555-TICKETS
Online at www.utix.biz

Shadows Blue 555-TICKETS
Online at www.utix.biz

Shadows Blue 555-TICKETS
Online at www.utix.biz

Shadows Blue 555-TICKETS
Online at www.utix.biz

Shadows Blue 555-TICKETS
Online at www.utix.biz

QR code © 2014 Cengage Learning; Guitar clip art courtesy of Joy Starks

Figure 1–64

Other Ways

1. Press CTRL+P, press ENTER

To Exit Publisher

The print flyer is complete. The following steps exit Publisher. For a detailed example of the procedure summarized below, refer to the Office and Windows chapter at the beginning of this book.

1a If you have one Publisher publication open, tap or click the Close button on the right side of the title bar to close the open publication and exit Publisher.

1b If you have multiple Publisher publications open, press and hold or right-click the Publisher app button on the taskbar and then tap or click 'Close all windows' on the shortcut menu, or press ALT+F4 to close all open publications and exit Publisher.

Q&A Could I press and hold or repeatedly click the Close button to close all open publications and exit Publisher?
Yes.

2 If a Microsoft Publisher dialog box appears, tap or click the Save button to save any changes made to the publication since the last save.

BTW
Conserving Ink and Toner
If you want to conserve ink or toner, you can instruct Publisher to print draft quality documents by tapping or clicking FILE on the ribbon to open the Backstage view, tapping or clicking Print in the Backstage view to display the Print gallery. Tap or click the Printer Properties link, and then, depending on your printer, click the Print Quality button and choose Draft in the list. Close the Printer Properties dialog box and then tap or click the Print button as usual.

BTW
Publisher Help
At any time while using Publisher, you can find answers to questions and display information about various topics through Publisher Help. Used properly, this form of assistance can increase your productivity and reduce your frustrations by minimizing the time you spend learning how to use Publisher. For instruction about Publisher Help and exercises that will help you gain confidence in using it, read the Office and Windows chapter at the beginning of this book.

Starting Publisher and Opening a Publication

Once you have created and saved a publication, you may need to retrieve it from your storage medium. For example, you might want to revise the publication or reprint it. Opening a publication requires that Publisher is running on your computer.

To Run Publisher

The following steps, which assume Windows 8 is running, use the Start screen or the search box to run Publisher based on a typical installation. You may need to ask your instructor how to run Publisher on your computer. For a detailed example of the procedure summarized below, refer to the Office and Windows chapter.

1 Scroll the Start screen and search for a Publisher 2013 tile. If your Start screen contains a Publisher 2013 tile, tap or click it to run Publisher and then proceed to Step 5. If the Start screen does not contain the Publisher 2013 tile, proceed to Step 2 to search for the Publisher app.

2 Swipe in from the right edge of the screen or point to the upper-right corner of the screen to display the Charms bar and then tap or click the Search charm on the Charms bar to display the Search menu.

3 Type `Publisher` as the search text in the Search text box and watch the search results appear in the Apps list.

4 Tap or click Publisher 2013 in the search results to run Publisher.

5 If the Publisher window is not maximized, tap or click the Maximize button on its title bar to maximize the window.

To Open a Publication from Publisher

Earlier in this chapter, you saved your publication using the file name, Concert Flyer. The following steps open the Concert Flyer file from the Publisher folder in the CIS 101 folder. For a detailed example of the procedure summarized below, refer to the Office and Windows chapter at the beginning of this book.

1. If the file you wish to open is displayed in the Recent Publications list, tap or click the file name to open the file and display the opened publication in the Publisher window; then, skip the remaining steps. If the file you wish to open is not displayed in the Recent Publications list, proceed to the next step to locate the file.
2. Tap or click Open Other Publications and then navigate to the location of the file to be opened (in this case, the Publisher folder in the CIS 101 folder).
3. Tap or click Concert Flyer to select the file to be opened.
4. Tap or click the Open button (Open dialog box) to open the selected file and display the opened publication in the Publisher window.

Changing a Publication

After creating a publication, you often will find that you must make changes to it. Changes can be required because the publication contains an error or because of new circumstances. The types of changes made to publications normally fall into one of the three following categories: deletions, additions, or modifications.

BTW
Print Publications
When creating a print publication, you must consider paper type, color options, number of copies, and the plan for publishing. Does the publication have to be in print to reach the target audience? How will readers find the printed publication? Keep the limitations of printed material in mind when deciding what to include in the layout.

DELETIONS Sometimes deletions are necessary in a publication because objects are incorrect or no longer are needed. For example, to place this advertising flyer on a website, the tear-offs no longer are needed. In that case, you would delete them from the page layout.

ADDITIONS Additional text, objects, or formatting may be required in the publication. For example, in the Concert Flyer you may want to insert a text box that could be displayed when the flyer is published to the web.

MODIFICATIONS If you make modifications to text or graphics, normal techniques of inserting, deleting, editing, and formatting apply. Publisher provides several methods for detecting problems in a publication and making modifications, including spell checking and design checking.

In the following sections, you will make changes to the flyer to prepare it for publishing to the web.

To Insert a Hyperlink

1 CUSTOMIZE TEMPLATES | 2 NAVIGATE & SELECT | 3 REPLACE TEXT | 4 DELETE OBJECTS | 5 FORMAT TEXT
6 INSERT GRAPHICS | 7 FORMAT PICTURE | 8 ENHANCE PAGE | 9 PRINT & EXIT | **10 OPEN & REVISE**

A **hyperlink**, or hypertext, is a computer link or reference to another location. A hyperlink can link to a page on the Internet, to an email address, to a location on a storage device, or another location within a publication. Users click links to navigate or browse to the location. The following steps create a hyperlink to the ticket website. ***Why?*** *This version of the flyer will be seen on the web, where users may want to click to buy tickets.*

1

- Select the text you wish to make a hyperlink (in this case, the web address) and then zoom to 100% (Figure 1–65).

Figure 1–65

2

- Tap or click INSERT on the ribbon to display the INSERT tab.
- Tap or click the 'Add a Hyperlink' button (INSERT tab | Links group) to display the Insert Hyperlink dialog box.
- If necessary, click the Address text box to position the insertion point and then type **`www.utix.biz`** to enter the web address (Figure 1–66).

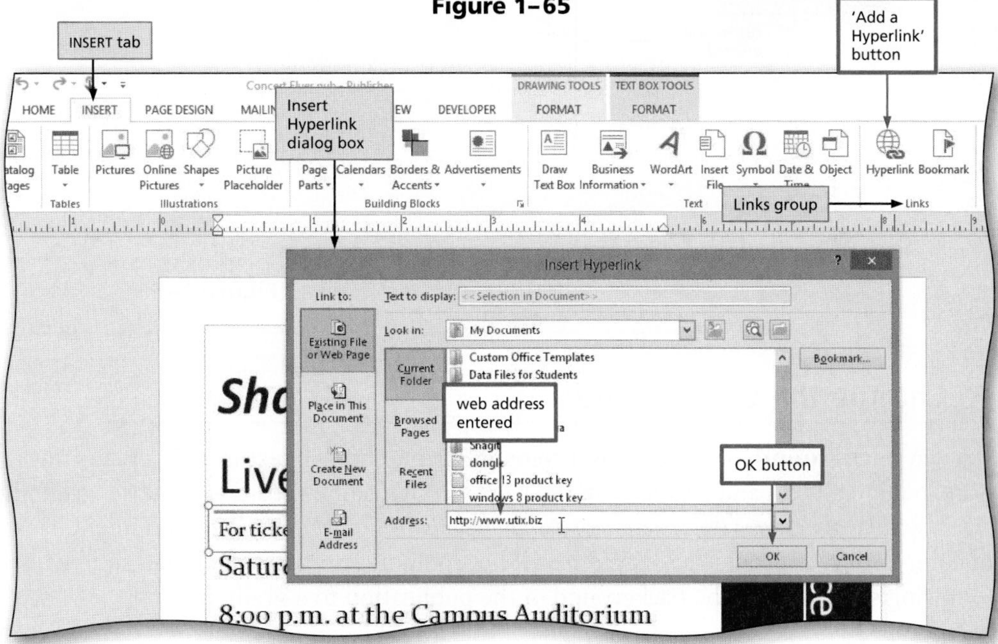

Figure 1–66

3

- Tap or click the OK button (Insert Hyperlink dialog box) to assign the hyperlink.
- Deselect the text to reveal the hyperlink (Figure 1–67).

Figure 1–67

Other Ways

1. Select text, press CTRL+K, enter web address in Address text box (Insert Hyperlink dialog box), click OK button

To Delete the Tear-Offs

If this flyer is displayed on a website, the tear-offs are unnecessary and should be deleted. The following steps delete the tear-offs using the shortcut menu.

1. Scroll to the lower portion of the flyer.
2. Press and hold or right-click any one of the tear-offs to display the shortcut menu and then tap or click Delete Object on the shortcut menu to delete the tear-offs (Figure 1–68).

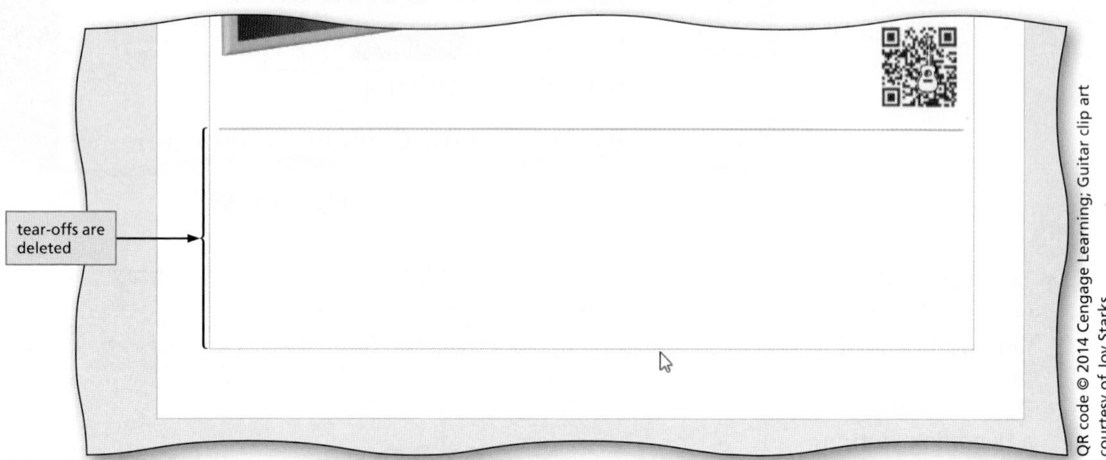

Figure 1–68

QR code © 2014 Cengage Learning; Guitar clip art courtesy of Joy Starks

To Change the Background

1 CUSTOMIZE TEMPLATES | 2 NAVIGATE & SELECT | 3 REPLACE TEXT | 4 DELETE OBJECTS | 5 FORMAT TEXT
6 INSERT GRAPHICS | 7 FORMAT PICTURE | 8 ENHANCE PAGE | 9 PRINT & EXIT | 10 OPEN & REVISE

A **background**, or page fill, is a color, gradient, pattern, texture, picture, or tint that fills the entire page, behind all text and graphics on the page layout. Many websites use a background to add interest. ***Why?*** *A background eliminates the sometimes harsh glare of a bright white webpage.* Gradient backgrounds use a progression of color shades to provide a subtle effect. They look more professional than solid colors or pictures. The following steps change the background of the publication to a gradient.

1

- Tap or click the 'Show Whole Page' button on the status bar to display the entire page layout.
- Tap or click PAGE DESIGN on the ribbon to display the PAGE DESIGN tab.
- Tap or click the Background button (PAGE DESIGN tab | Page Background group) to display the Background gallery (Figure 1–69).

Experiment

- Point to each of the backgrounds and watch the live preview.

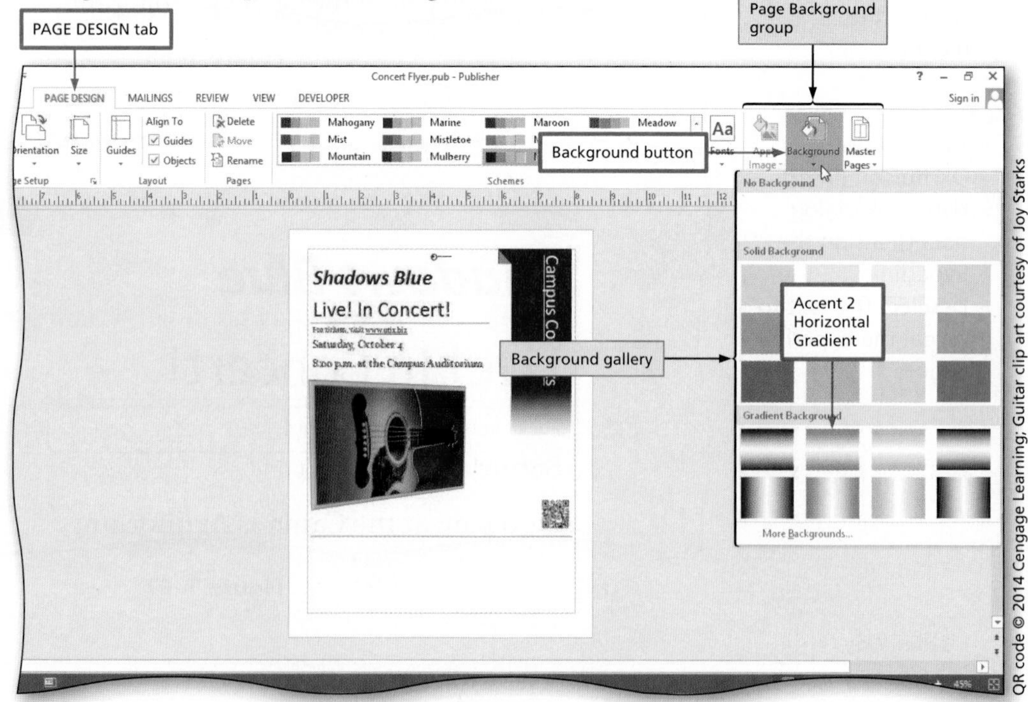

Figure 1–69

QR code © 2014 Cengage Learning; Guitar clip art courtesy of Joy Starks

2

- Tap or click Accent 2 Horizontal Gradient to select a blue and white gradient for the webpage background (Figure 1–70).

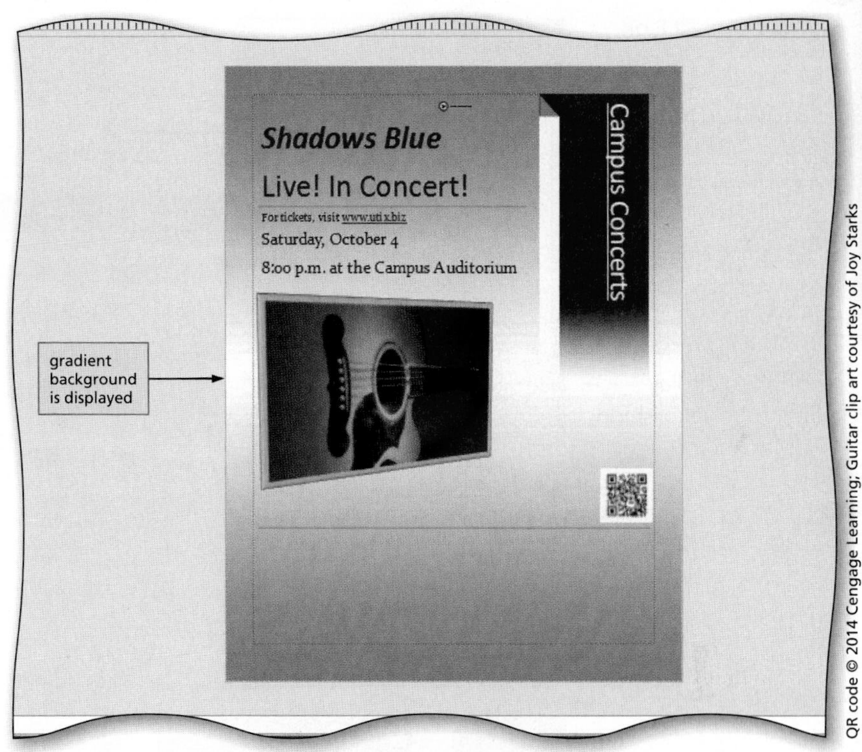

QR code © 2014 Cengage Learning; Guitar clip art courtesy of Joy Starks

Figure 1–70

Creating a Webpage from a Publication

You can create several types of publications with Microsoft Publisher, other than standard print publications. A **web publication** is one suitable for publishing to the web, containing certain objects, formatting options, hyperlinks, and other features specific to webpages. You can create a web publication from scratch, or you can save the print publication as a web publication. The following sections create a web version of the flyer that might be posted on a campus website or social networking site.

BTW

Web publications
When converting to a web publication, determine which objects will work effectively on the web and which ones will not, modifying the publication as necessary. Will the publication be accessible on the web? Is the target audience common web users? If so, determine whether an email or website would be the most efficient means of communication.

To Save a Print Publication as a Web Publication

The Export tab in the Backstage view includes a group of commands that allow you to save publications as different file types or to package publications for sending to other users. In the following steps, you will export the publication by publishing it to the web. **Publishing HTML** or **publishing to the web** is the process of making webpages available to others, for example, on the World Wide Web or on a company's intranet. Files intended for use on the web, however, need a different format. A **Hypertext Markup Language (HTML)** file is a file capable of being stored and transferred electronically on a file server in order to display on the web.

In the steps on the next page, you will save the publication as a web flyer by publishing it as **MHTML** (Mime Hypertext Markup Language), a small single-file file format that does not create a supporting folder of resources. ***Why?*** *The MHTML file can be published to and downloaded from the web quickly.* For a detailed example of the procedure for using the Save As dialog box, refer to the Office 2013 and Windows 8 chapter at the beginning of this book.

- Tap or click FILE on the ribbon to open the Backstage view.
- Tap or click the Export tab to display the Export gallery.
- Tap or click Publish HTML to display its options.
- Tap or click the 'Web Page (HTML)' button to display options for publishing HTML (Figure 1–71).

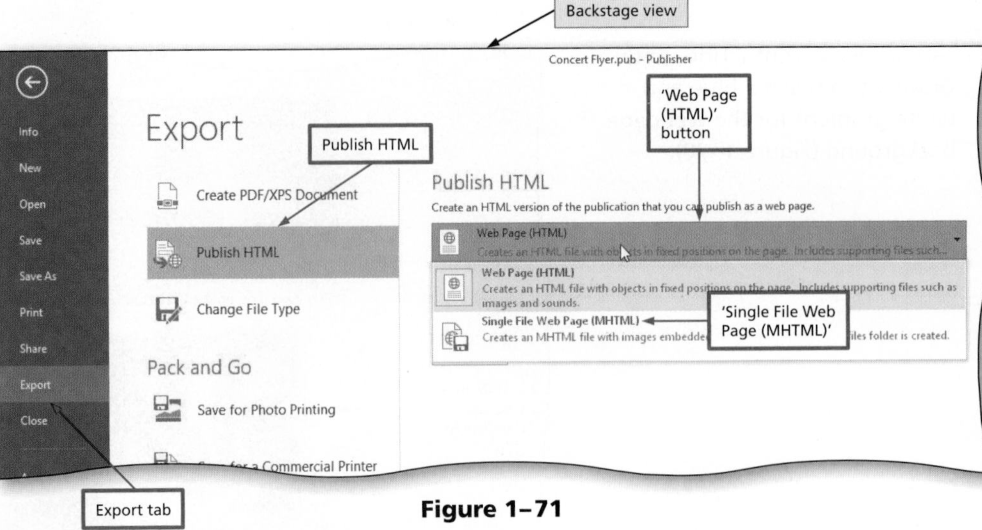

Figure 1–71

- Tap or click 'Single File Web Page (MHTML)' to select it (Figure 1–72).

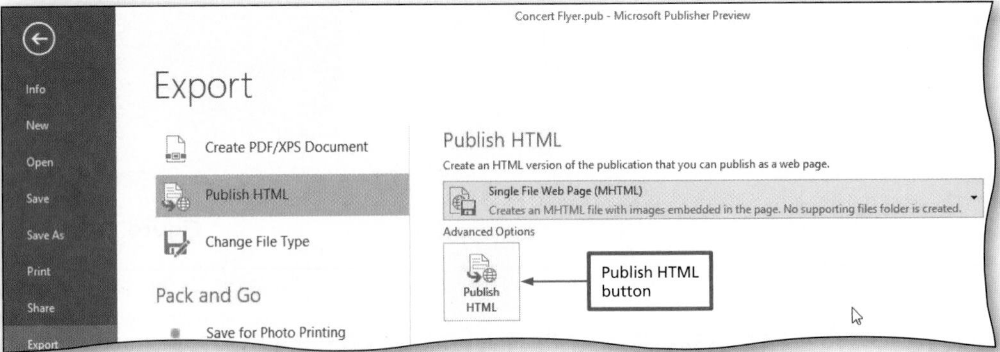

Figure 1–72

- Tap or click the Publish HTML button to display the Save As dialog box.
- Type `Concert Web Flyer` in the File name text box. Do not press the ENTER key after typing the file name.
- Navigate to your storage location (in this case, the Chapter 01 Folder of the Publisher Folder) (Figure 1–73).

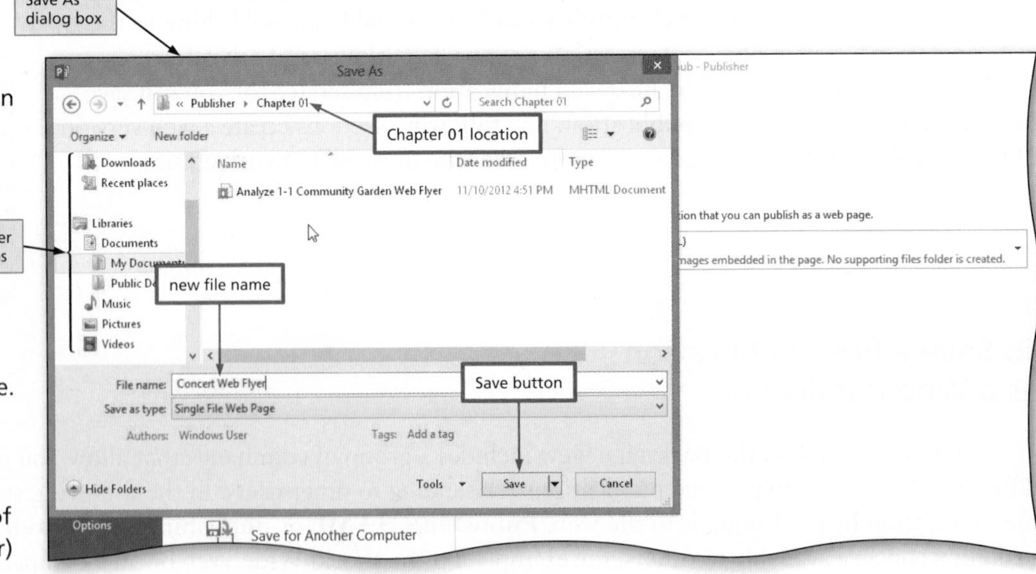

Figure 1–73

- Tap or click the Save button (Save As dialog box) to save the publication.

Other Ways

1. Tap or click Save As in Backstage view, tap or click storage location, enter file name, tap or click 'Save as type' button, tap or click 'Single File Web Page', tap or click Save button (Save As dialog box)

To Preview the Web Publication in a Browser

The following steps preview the web publication. ***Why?*** *Previewing is the best way to test the look and feel of the webpage and to test the hyperlink.* You will open the MHTML file from its storage location. For a detailed example of the procedure for navigating to a storage location, refer to the Office 2013 and Windows 8 chapter at the beginning of this book.

1

- Run the File Explorer app and navigate to your storage location (in this case, the Chapter 01 Folder of the Publisher Folder) (Figure 1–74).

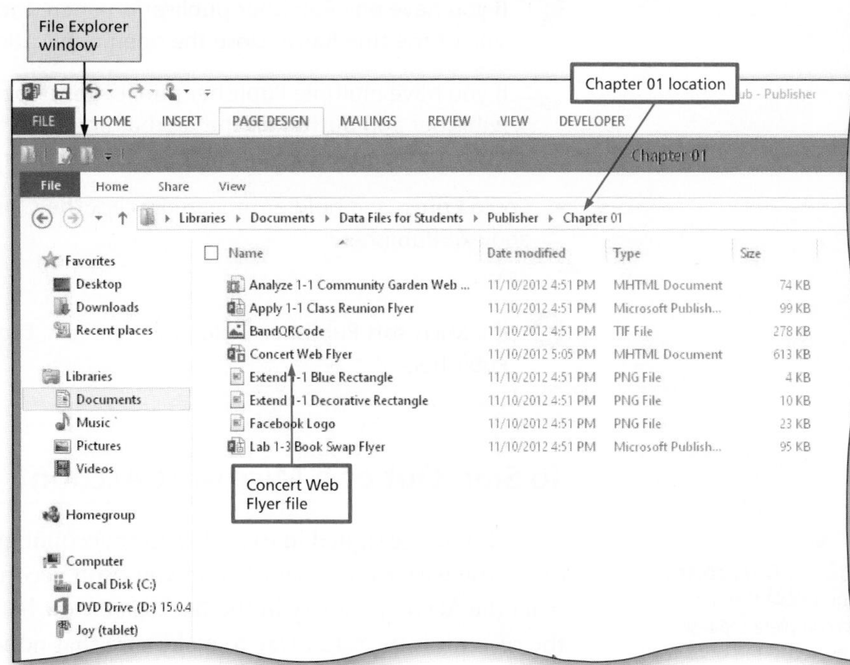

Figure 1–74

- Double-tap or double-click the Concert Web Flyer file.
- When the browser window opens, if necessary, maximize the window (Figure 1–75).

Q&A Why does my display look different?
Each brand and version of browser software displays information in a slightly different manner. Additionally, your browser settings, such as text size and zoom level, may differ.

- Tap or click the Close button on the browser window's title bar.
- Tap or click the Close button on the File Explorer window's title bar.

Figure 1–75

QR code © 2014 Cengage Learning; Guitar clip art courtesy of Joy Starks

To Exit Publisher

This web flyer is complete. The following steps exit Publisher. For a detailed example of the procedure summarized below, refer to the Office and Windows chapter at the beginning of this book. The web flyer and print flyer were saved in previous steps, so you do not need to save the file again.

1a If you have one Publisher publication open, tap or click the Close button on the right side of the title bar to close the open publication and exit Publisher.

1b If you have multiple Publisher publications open, press and hold or right-click the Publisher app button on the taskbar and then tap or click 'Close all windows' on the shortcut menu, or press ALT+F4 to close all open publications and exit Publisher.

Q&A Could I press and hold or repeatedly click the Close button to close all open documents and exit Publisher?
Yes.

2 If a Microsoft Publisher dialog box appears, tap or click the Don't Save button to exit Publisher.

To Sign Out of a Microsoft Account

BTW
Quick Reference
For a table that lists how to complete the tasks covered in this book using touch gestures, the mouse, ribbon, shortcut menu, and keyboard, see the Quick Reference Summary at the back of this book, or visit the Quick Reference resource on the Student Companion Site located on www.cengagebrain.com. For detailed instructions about accessing available resources, visit www.cengage.com/ct/studentdownload or see the inside back cover of this book.

If you are signed in to a Microsoft account and are using a public computer or otherwise wish to sign out of your Microsoft account, you should sign out of the account from the Account gallery in the Backstage view before exiting Publisher. Signing out of the account is the safest way to make sure that nobody else can access SkyDrive files or settings stored in your Microsoft account. The following steps sign out of a Microsoft account from Publisher. For a detailed example of the procedure summarized below, refer to the Office and Windows chapter at the beginning of this book.

1 If you wish to sign out of your Microsoft account, tap or click FILE on the ribbon to open the Backstage view and then tap or click the Account tab to display the Account gallery.

2 Tap or click the Sign out link, which displays the Remove Account dialog box. If a Can't remove Windows accounts dialog box appears instead of the Remove Account dialog box, click the OK button and skip the remaining steps.

Q&A Why does a Can't remove Windows accounts dialog box appear?
If you signed in to Windows using your Microsoft account, then you also must sign out from Windows, rather than signing out from within Publisher. When you are finished using Windows, be sure to sign out at that time.

3 Tap or click the Yes button (Remove Account dialog box) to sign out of your Microsoft account on this computer.

Q&A Should I sign out of Windows after signing out of my Microsoft account?
When you are finished using the computer, you should sign out of your account for maximum security.

4 Tap or click the Back button in the upper-left corner of the Backstage view to return to the publication.

Chapter Summary

In this chapter, you learned to choose a publication template, set font and color schemes, enter text in a publication, delete objects in a publication, insert a picture with a style and border, print a publication, and save a print publication as a web publication. The items listed below include all the new Publisher skills you have learned in this chapter, with the tasks grouped by activity.

Enter and Format Text

Autofit Text (PUB 28)
Bold Text (PUB 27)
Change Text Direction (PUB 32)
Check Spelling as You Type (PUB 21)
Enter Tear-Off Text (PUB 23)
Increase the Font Size (PUB 31)
Italicize Text (PUB 28)
Replace Other Text (PUB 19)
Replace Placeholder Text (PUB 17)
Underline Text (PUB 31)

Graphics

Apply a Picture Style (PUB 36)
Change the Border Color (PUB 38)
Insert a Picture from a Storage Device (PUB 39)
Set the Weight of a Border (PUB 37)
Use the Picture Placeholder (PUB 34)

Prepare a Web Publication

Change Document Properties (PUB 43)
Change the Background (PUB 50)
Insert a Hyperlink (PUB 48)
Preview the Web Publication in a Browser (PUB 53)
Save a Print Publication as a Web Publication (PUB 51)

Print

Print a Publication (PUB 44)

Select, Zoom, and Manipulate Objects

Align an Object (PUB 42)
Collapse and Expand the Page Navigation Pane (PUB 14)
Delete an Object (PUB 24)
Deselect an Object (PUB 18)
Hide the Page Navigation Pane (PUB 13)
Move an Object (PUB 41)
Resize an Object (PUB 42)
Select an Object (PUB 14)
View Whole Page (PUB 15)
Zoom (PUB 15)

Templates

Choose Publication Options (PUB 8)
Select a Template (PUB 6)

CONSIDER THIS

What decisions will you need to make when creating your next publication?

Use these guidelines as you complete the assignments in this chapter and create your own publications outside of this class.

1. Select template options.
   a) Select a template that matches your need.
   b) Choose font and color schemes determined by the flyer's purpose and audience.
2. Choose words for the text.
   a) Replace all placeholder and default text.
   b) Add other text boxes as necessary; delete unused items.
3. Identify how to format various objects in the flyer.
   a) Use bold, underline, and italics for emphasis.
   b) Autofit the text to make the flyer easy to read.
4. Find the appropriate graphic(s).
5. Determine whether the flyer will be more effective as a print publication, web publication, or both.
   a) Insert any necessary hyperlinks.
   b) Consider creating a background for web publication.

CONSIDER THIS

How should you submit solutions to questions in the assignments identified with a ✲ symbol?

Every assignment in this book contains one or more questions identified with a ✲ symbol. These questions require you to think beyond the assigned publication. Present your solutions to the questions in the format required by your instructor. Possible formats may include one or more of these options: write the answer; create a document that contains the answer; present your answer to the class; discuss your answer in a group; record the answer as audio or video using a webcam, smartphone, or portable media player; or post answers on a blog, wiki, or website.

Apply Your Knowledge

Reinforce the skills and apply the concepts you learned in this chapter.

Editing a Flyer with Text, Graphic, and Tear-Offs

Note: To complete this assignment, you will be required to use the Data Files for Students. Visit www.cengage.com/ct/studentdownload for detailed instructions or contact your instructor for information about accessing the required files.

Instructions: Your brother is in charge of advertising his 10-year class reunion. He has asked you to help him with editing the text, graphic, and tear-offs. You produce the flyer shown in Figure 1–76.

Perform the following tasks:

1. Run Publisher and open the file Apply 1-1 Class Reunion Flyer from the Data Files for Students.
2. Tap or click the Major Heading default text and drag to select it. Type **`10-Year Reunion Gym Party!`** to replace the text.
3. Tap or click the Subheading default text box and then drag the text to select it. Type **`05/21/15`** to replace the text.
4. Tap or click the default bulleted text and then press CTRL+A to select all of the text. Type the following text, pressing the ENTER key at the end of each line.

   `Wear your letter jacket!`

   `Show your school spirit!`

   `High School Gym!`

   `7:00 p.m.!`

   `RSVP to Jesse by 05/07/15!`
5. Tap or click one of the tear-offs, type **`Jesse`** and then press the ENTER key. Type **`402-555-1306`** to finish entering the text. Tap or click outside the tear-offs to synchronize them. If requested by your instructor, use your name in the tear-offs.
6. Select the text in the attention getter sunburst shape and replace it with the text shown in Figure 1–76.
7. Select the attention getter and change the border weight to 6 point, using the Shape Outline button (DRAWING TOOLS FORMAT tab | ShapeStyles group).
8. At the top of the flyer, select the picture placeholder. Tap or click the picture placeholder icon to display the Insert Pictures dialog box. Use Office.com Clip Art to search for a picture related to academics, similar to the one shown in Figure 1–76.

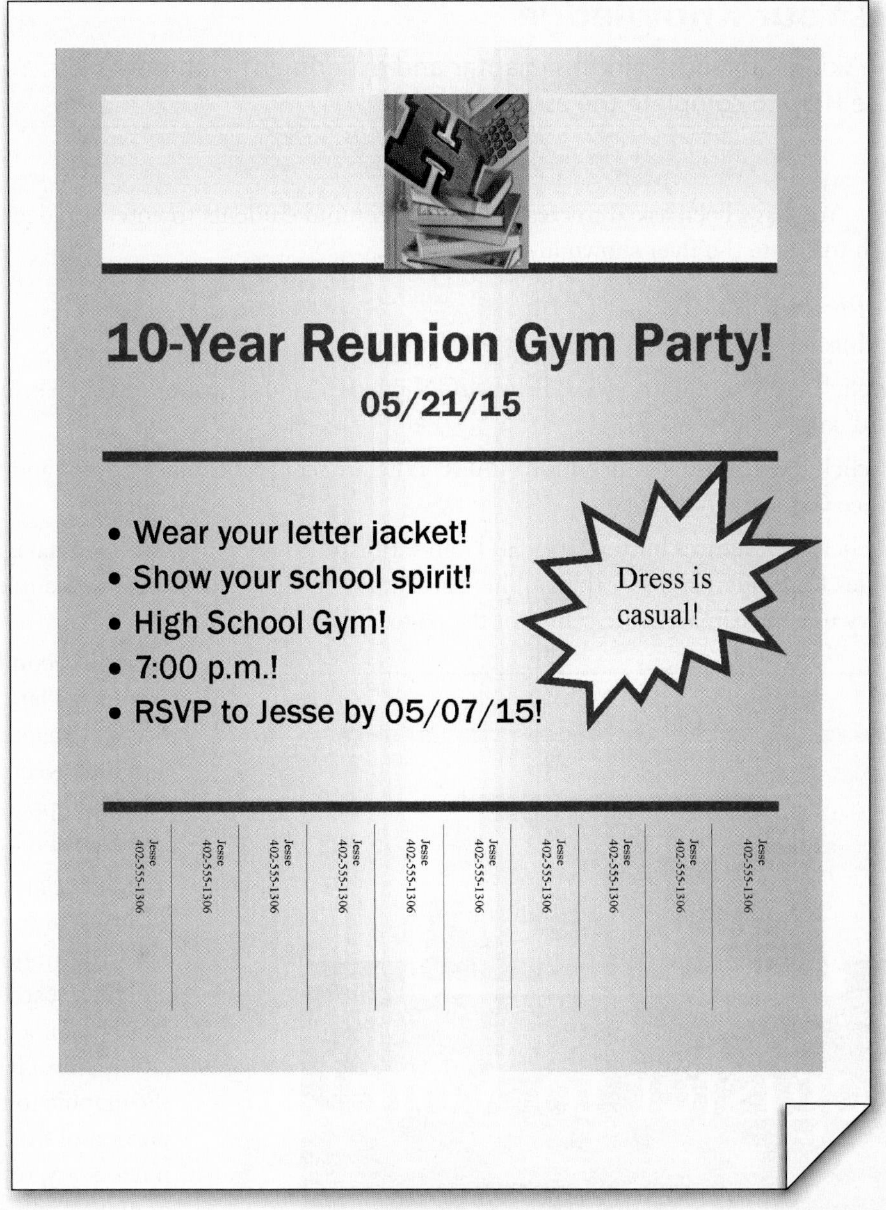

Figure 1–76

9. Tap or click the Background button (PAGE DESIGN tab | Page Background group) to display the Background gallery. Choose the Accent 3 Vertical Gradient.
10. Save the flyer on your storage device with the file name, Apply 1-1 Class Reunion Flyer Complete.
11. Print a hardcopy of the flyer by performing the following steps:
    a. Tap or click FILE on the ribbon to open the Backstage view and then tap or click the Print tab in the Backstage view to display the Print gallery.
    b. Verify the printer name that appears on the Printer Status button will print a hard copy of the publication. If necessary, click the Printer Status button to display a list of available printer options and then click the desired printer to change the currently selected printer.
    c. Tap or click the Print button in the Print gallery to print the publication on the currently selected printer. When the printer stops, retrieve the hard copy.
12. Submit the revised document in the format specified by your instructor.
13. What would you add or delete if you were to publish this flyer in the MHTML format on the web? Why?

Extend Your Knowledge

Extend the skills you learned in this chapter and experiment with new skills. You may need to use Help to complete the assignment.

Creating a Flyer from Scratch

Instructions: You have been asked to create a flyer to remind students to vote. You decide to start from scratch to create the flyer shown in Figure 1–77.

Perform the following tasks:

1. Run Publisher and select the Blank 8.5 × 11" template.
2. Tap or click the More button (PAGE DESIGN tab | Schemes group) and then select the Bluebird color scheme.
3. Tap or click the Scheme Fonts button (PAGE DESIGN tab | Schemes group) and then select the Office Classic 1 font scheme.
4. Tap or click the Pictures button (INSERT tab | Illustrations group) and then navigate to the Data Files for Students. Insert the graphic named, Extend 1-1 Decorative Rectangle. Move it as necessary to approximately the center of the page.
5. Insert a second picture from the Data Files for Students named, Extend 1-1 Blue Rectangle. Move it to the upper-center as shown in Figure 1–77.
6. Tap or click the Online Pictures button (INSERT tab | Illustrations group) and then search Office.com Clip Art for a graphic of an American flag. Move the graphic to the upper portion of the flyer and, if necessary, resize the graphic. Apply a picture style, such as Relaxed Perspective, White.
7. Use Help to read about drawing text boxes and then perform the following tasks:
   a. Use the Draw Text box button (HOME tab | Objects group) to create a text box on top of the blue rectangle, filling the area below the flag graphic.

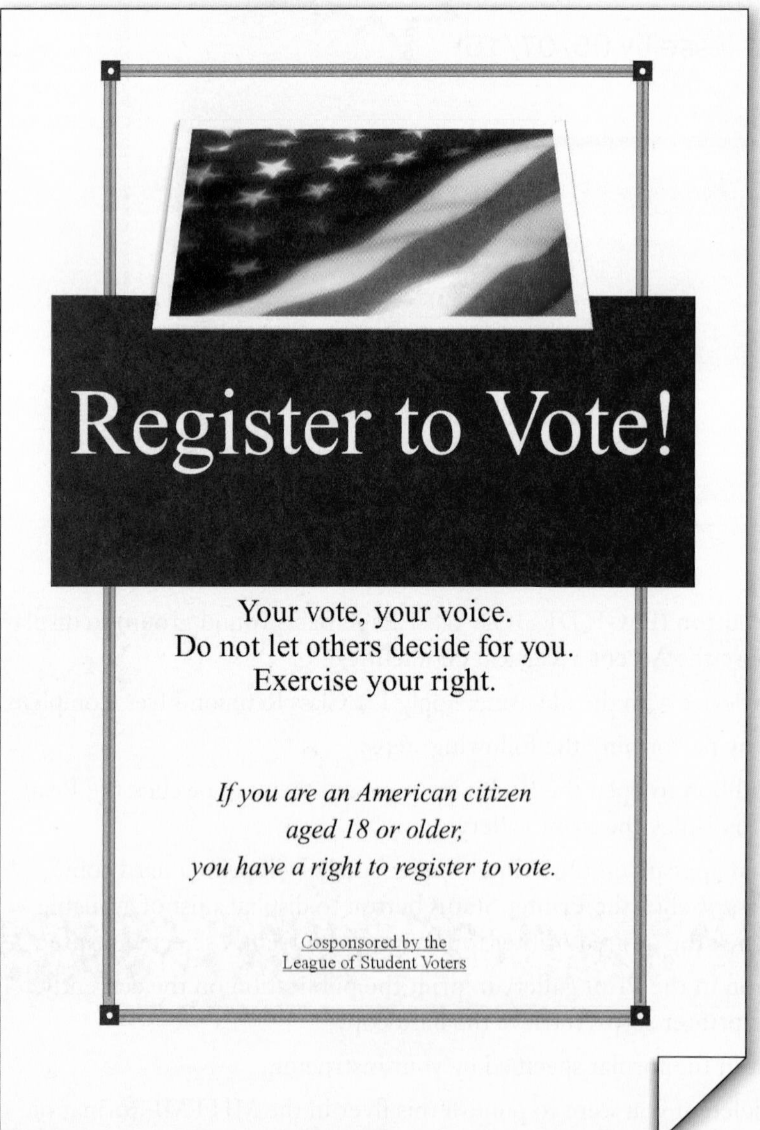

Figure 1–77

b. Before typing the text, click the Font Color arrow (HOME tab | Font group) and then choose a white color. Type the text, `Register to Vote!` and then autofit it.

c. Draw another text box below the first one. Tap or click the Font Color arrow (HOME tab | Font group) and then choose a black color. Tap or click the Bold button (HOME tab | Font group). Tap or click the Center button (HOME tab | Paragraph group) and then type the text shown in Figure 1–77.

d. Repeat Step 7c for the next text box and format the text italic.

e. Repeat Step 7c for the last text box and format the text underlined.

f. If requested to do so by your instructor, add the name of your voting location to the flyer.

8. Save the file with the file name, Extend 1-1 Vote Flyer Complete.
9. Submit the file in the format specified by your instructor.
10. When would you use a template instead of creating a flyer from scratch that contains only the fields you need? Was formatting the font before you typed easier than selecting text and formatting it afterward?

Analyze, Correct, Improve

Analyze a publication, correct all errors, and improve the design.

Making Changes to a Web Flyer

Note: To complete this assignment, you will be required to use the Data Files for Students. Visit www.cengage.com/ct/studentdownload for detailed instructions or contact your instructor for information about accessing the required files.

Instructions: Your community is trying to promote its community garden. A former gardener created the website shown in Figure 1–78 using Publisher, but it has several issues. You decide to improve the flyer. Run Publisher and open the file, Analyze 1-1 Community Garden Web Flyer.

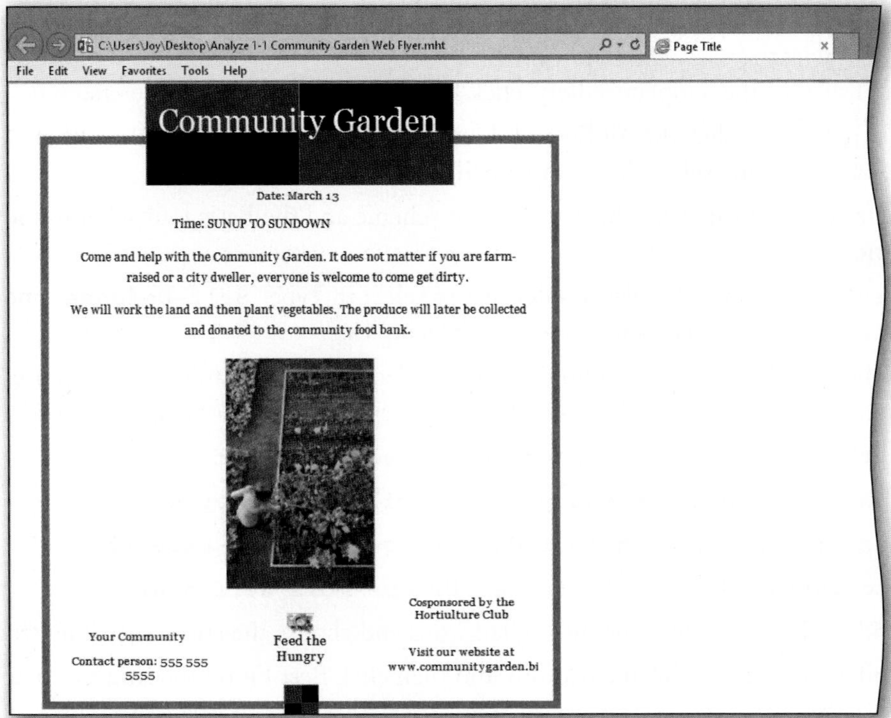

Figure 1–78

Continued >

Analyze, Correct, Improve *continued*

1. Correct Correct the date on the flyer. This year's event is March 25. The flyer still has default text in the lower-left corner. If requested to do so by your instructor, insert your community and your phone number. The website listed in the lower-right corner should be a hyperlink. Resize any text boxes whose text wraps awkwardly.

2. Improve Each of the text boxes seems to be a different font size. Choose a large size for the main heading. Change the description text to best fit and then increase or decrease the fonts in the lower text boxes so that they all match. Choose to make them all bold. Align objects horizontally with each other and with the margins. Correct the misspelled word. Change the color scheme to an all green color scheme such as Green or Floral. Experiment with different font schemes. Save the document using the file name, Analyze 1-1 Community Garden Flyer Complete. Submit the revised document in the format specified by your instructor.

3. What errors existed in the starting file? How did creating consistency in font sizes enhance the publication? Did changing the color scheme improve the effectiveness of the flyer? What other improvements would you make?

In the Labs

Design, create, modify, and/or use a publication following the guidelines, concepts, and skills presented in this chapter. Labs 1 and 2, which increase in difficulty, require you to create solutions based on what you learned in the chapter; Lab 3 requires you to create a solution, which uses cloud and web technologies, by learning and investigating on your own from general guidance.

Lab 1: Creating a Sign-Up Sheet

Problem: The Self-Defense Club on campus would like you to create a sign-up sheet for students who want to take classes in the Fall semester. You decide to look through Publisher's templates for an appropriate flyer to use as a starting point. You create the flyer shown in Figure 1–79.

Perform the following tasks:

1. Run Publisher. In the template gallery, click BUILT-IN and then click Flyers.
2. In the Event group, click the All Event folder to open it. Scroll down to the Other category at the end of the list and select the Company Sign Up template.
3. Customize the template with the Alpine color scheme and the Basis font scheme and create the publication.
4. Tap or click the Event Title placeholder text to select it. Type `Self-Defense` and then press the ENTER key. Type `Classes` to finish replacing the text.
5. Tap or click the description placeholder text to select it. Type the following text, pressing the ENTER key at the end of each line. The last line purposefully has a misspelled word.

   `Learn the techniques you need to protect yourself.`

   `Prepare now, for the event you hope will never happen.`

   `Classes will be held on Thursdays throughout the semester.`

   `Easy to learn. Gain confidfence. Become more self-aware.`
6. Press and hold or right-click the misspelled word and choose the correct spelling from the list.
7. Press and hold or right-click the text box and then click Best Fit on the shortcut menu.
8. Change the Date text, Date: 00/00/00, to `Fall Semester` to replace the text.
9. Change the Time text, Time: 00:00, to `7:00-8:00 p.m.` to replace the text.

10. Change the text, Contact person:, to `Aaron Gilbert` to replace the text. If requested by your instructor, type your name as the contact person.
11. Change the phone number to 303 555 9753.
12. Tap or click the boundary of the Sign up heading text box select the text box. Press the DELETE key to delete the object.
13. Select the graphic. Press the DELETE key to delete the object.
14. Tap or click the Online Pictures button (INSERT tab | Illustrations group). Use the concepts in the chapter to search for a self-defense graphic, similar to the one shown in Figure 1–79, from Office.com Clip Art. Insert the graphic.
15. Using Figure 1–79 as a guide, move the graphic up and align it with the right margin. If necessary, resize the graphic by SHIFT+dragging the upper-left corner toward the center of the graphic, so that no text wraps in the description text box.
16. Save the flyer on your storage device with the file name, Lab 1-1 Self-Defense Flyer.
17. Print a hardcopy of the flyer.
18. Submit the file as directed by your instructor.
19. Would a page background make this flyer easier to read or harder to read? Which elements would you change if this were a flyer on the web?

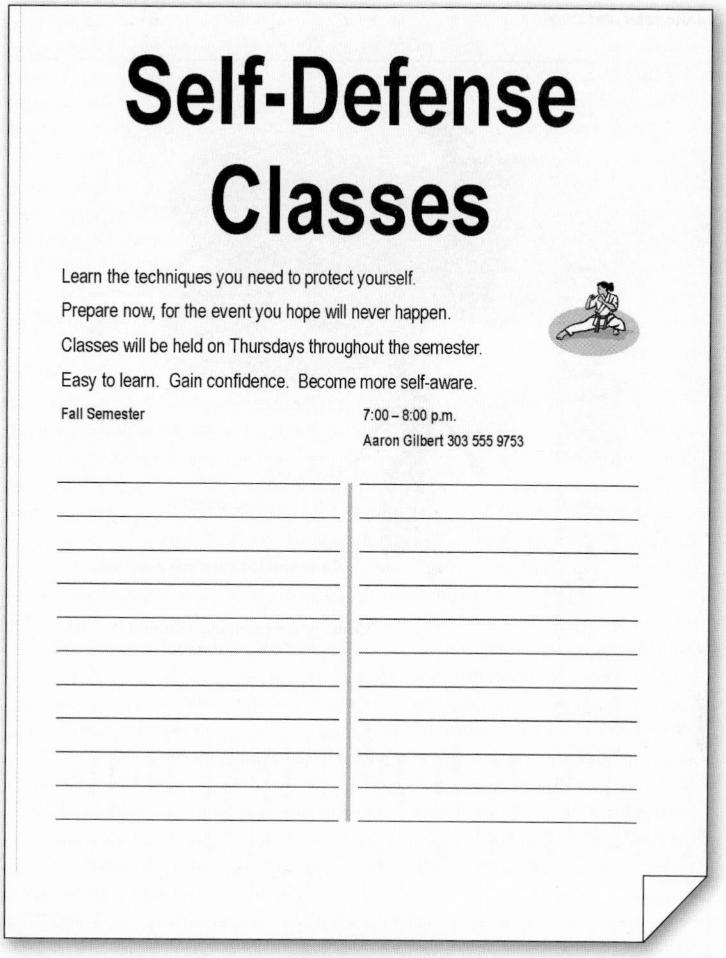

Figure 1–79

Lab 2: Creating an Event Flyer

Problem: You have been asked to create a flyer for a flash mob event. A flash mob, usually triggered by a text message or web posting, describes a group of people who come together suddenly in a specified place to perform an unusual and sometimes pointless act for a brief time, often for the purpose of entertainment, parody, or artistic expression. You create the flyer shown in Figure 1–80 on the next page.

1. Run Publisher. In the template gallery, tap or click BUILT-IN and then tap or click Flyers.
2. In the Marketing group, tap or click the All Marketing folder to open it. Scroll down to the Other category and then select the Baby-Sitting template.
3. Customize the template with the Parrot color scheme and the Foundry font scheme and create the publication.
4. Select the text, Baby-Sitting. Type `Flash Mob` to replace the text. Autofit the text.
5. Select the description placeholder text. Type `Come on!` and then press the ENTER key. Type `You know you want to!` to replace the text.

Continued >

In the Labs *continued*

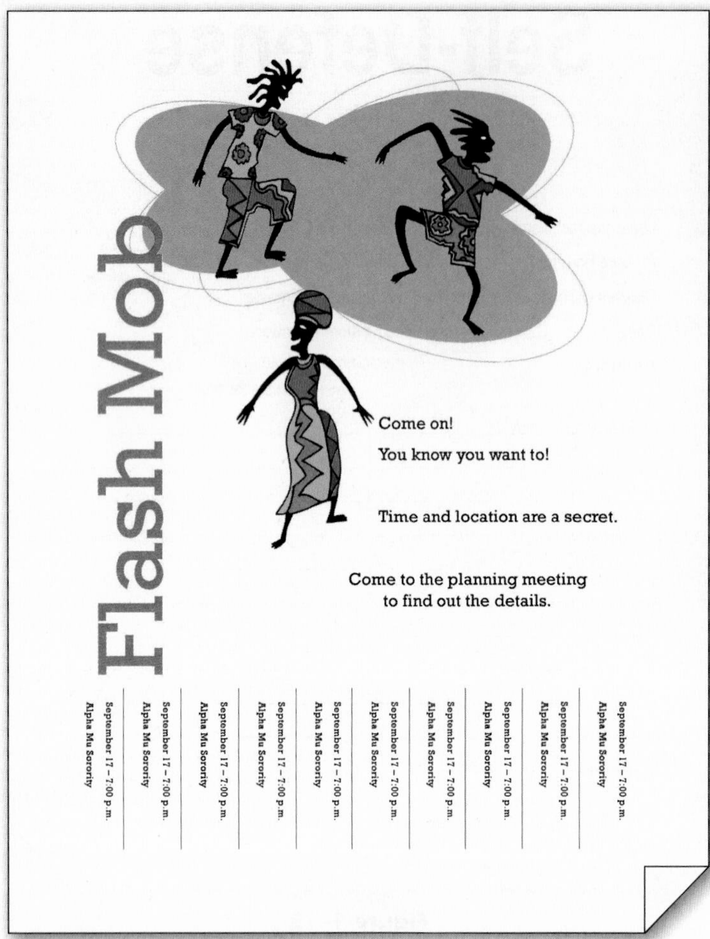

Figure 1–80

6. Select the hourly rate text. Type `Time and location area secret.` and then press the ENTER key twice. Resize the text box as necessary and type `Come to the planning meeting to find out the details.` to replace the text. Delete the $00.00 placeholder text.
7. Delete the Contact person text box.
8. Tap or click a tear-off. Type `September 17 - 7:00 p.m.` and then press the ENTER key. Type `Alpha Mu Sorority` to complete the tear-offs. If requested by your instructor, type the name of your (or a campus) sorority or fraternity in the text box.
9. Delete the two child graphics.
10. Tap or click the Online Pictures button (INSERT tab | Illustrations group). Use the concepts in the chapter to search Office.com Clip Art for a graphic similar to the first one shown in Figure 1–80. Search for dancers. Insert the graphic. Resize the graphic. Repeat the process to find two more graphics.
11. Save the flyer on your storage device with the file name, Lab 1-2 Flash Mob Flyer.
12. Print a hardcopy of the flyer.
13. Submit the file as directed by your instructor.
14. How did the Baby-Sitting flyer template work for you? Would it have been easier to choose a template with a picture placeholder rather than one with default pictures? Could you have found a different template and made the changes, such as text direction, yourself? Would that have been easier?

Lab 3: Expand Your World: Cloud and Web Technologies
Modifying and Exporting a Publication

Note: To complete this assignment, you will be required to use the Data Files for Students. Visit www.cengage.com/ct/studentdownload for detailed instructions or contact your instructor for information about accessing the required files.

Problem: Your school library is planning a book swap and has asked you to create a flyer. You want to share the final product with the library staff, so you have decided to store the file on SkyDrive so that the staff can access it easily. You are going to modify the flyer you have created thus far shown in Figure 1–81 and save on SkyDrive.

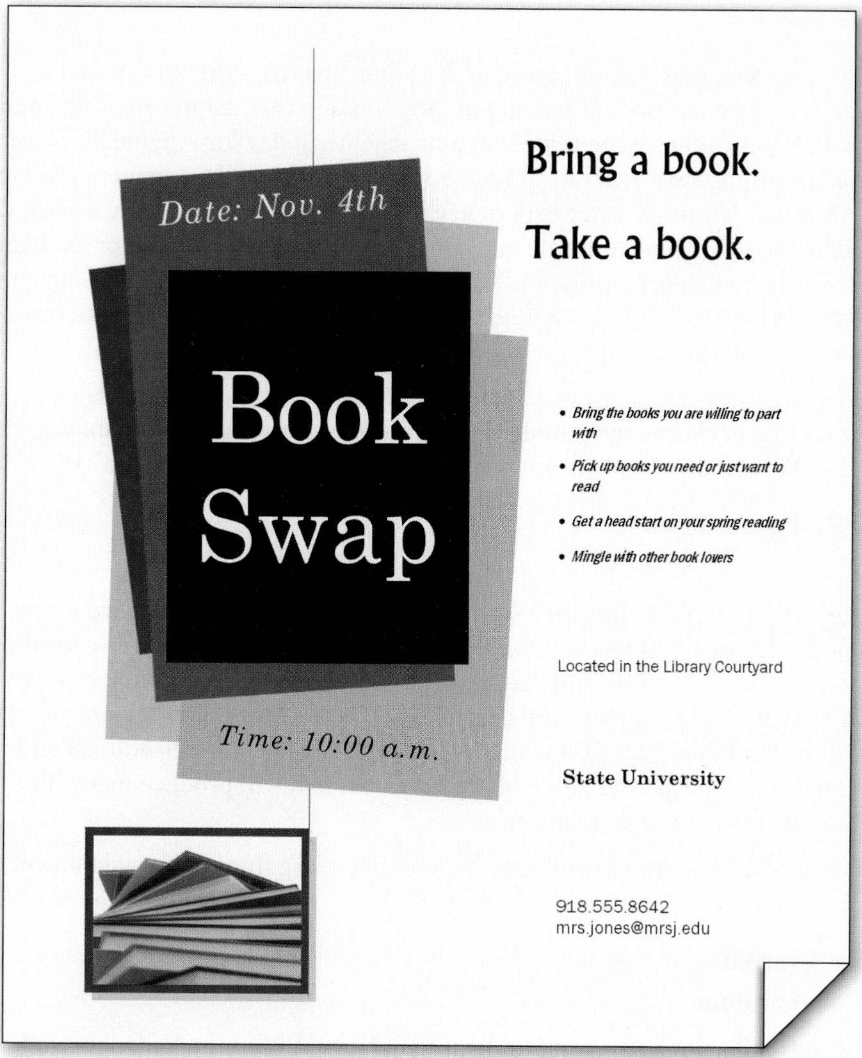
Bring a book.
Take a book.
Date: Nov. 4th
Book Swap
• Bring the books you are willing to part with
• Pick up books you need or just want to read
• Get a head start on your spring reading
• Mingle with other book lovers
Located in the Library Courtyard
Time: 10:00 a.m.
State University
918.555.8642
mrs.jones@mrsj.edu

Figure 1–81

Instructions:

1. Open the file named, Lab 1-3 Book Swap Flyer, from the Data Files for Students.
2. Insert a picture and format it as shown in Figure 1–81.
3. If requested to do so by your instructor, change the email address to your email address.
4. Save the presentation on SkyDrive in the Publisher folder using the file name, Lab 1–3 Book Swap Flyer Complete.
5. Submit the assignment in the format specified by your instructor.
6. When would you save one of your files for school or your job on SkyDrive? Do you think using SkyDrive enhances collaboration efforts? Why?

Consider This: Your Turn

Apply your creative thinking and problem solving skills to design and implement a solution.

1: Creating an Advertisement

Personal/Academic

Part 1: You attend a college that is famous for its Department of Dance. Students who major in dance are required to complete internships as dance instructors. Because you are a computer

Continued >

Consider This: Your Turn *continued*

technology major, they have asked you to create a flyer that advertises the lessons and includes a social media logo. Use the concepts and techniques presented in this chapter to design and create an advertising flyer. Use an appropriate template, font scheme, and color scheme. Replace placeholder text. Include wording such as, "The graduate students from the Department of Dance will teach Ballroom Dancing. No prior dance experience is necessary. Come and have a great time—it is a great date night, guys!!" Include the date and time of the dance lessons. Tap or click the picture placeholder icon for the template graphic, and search for a graphic related to ballroom dancing. Insert the social media logo from the Data Files for Students and use an appropriate text reference. Submit your assignment in the format specified by your instructor.

Part 2: You made several decisions while determining the appropriate template, schemes, text, and graphics. How did you choose the template? What did you consider when choosing the color and font schemes? Did you choose a ballroom dancing clip art graphic or a photo? Why?

2: Creating a Workplace Flyer

Professional

Part 1: Your Internet service provider (ISP) maintains an electronic bulletin board where customers may post one-page business announcements. Create an advertising flyer for the place you work or where you want to work. You may use one of Publisher's Flyer templates, or you can design one from scratch. Replace all text and graphics. Use font colors and font sizes to attract attention. Instead of tear-offs, draw a text box that includes the company's web address and phone number. Assign publication properties and include keywords that will produce many hits during web searches. Save the flyer as a web publication.

Part 2: You made several decisions while creating the advertising flyer in this assignment. How did your choices complement the topic? Would you use Publisher to create websites? Why or why not?

3: Researching Templates

Research and Collaboration

Part 1: Publisher has online templates and built-in templates. Within the built-in templates, each folder has a section of tailored templates labeled Other. Get together with your group and scroll through the template gallery. One at a time, click each of the built-in Flyer category folders and scroll down to the bottom of each list. Make a list of the Other flyer templates that are tailored toward a specific event, marketing advertisement, or real estate project. Ask your group if anyone recalls seeing any of these flyers or similar flyers posted around campus.

Part 2: How are these Other flyer templates different from the Built-in templates and the online Featured templates? When would you use each?

Learn Online

Reinforce what you learned in this chapter with games, exercises, training, and many other online activities and resources.

Student Companion Site Reinforce chapter terms and concepts using review questions, flash cards, practice tests, and interactive learning games, such as a crossword puzzle. These and other online activities and resources are available at no additional cost on www.cengagebrain.com. Visit www.cengage.com/ct/studentdownload for detailed instructions about accessing the resources available at the Student Companion Site.

2 Publishing a Trifold Brochure

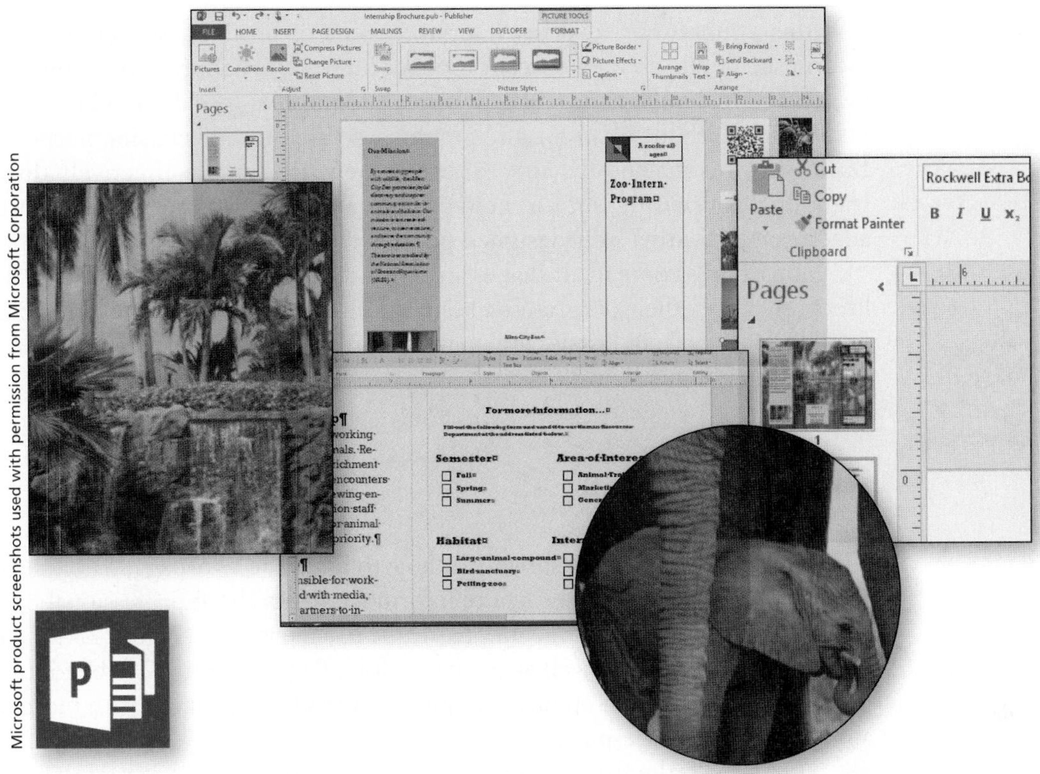

Microsoft product screenshots used with permission from Microsoft Corporation

Objectives

You will have mastered the material in this chapter when you can:

- Discuss advantages of the brochure medium
- Choose brochure options
- Copy and paste with paste options
- Wordwrap text
- Swap pictures using the scratch area and arrange thumbnails
- Use a picture as a background
- Copy formatting with the Format Painter
- Employ typography such as stylistic sets, ligatures, and drop caps
- Edit captions and caption styles
- Check the spelling of the entire publication
- Run the Design Checker
- Choose appropriate printing services, paper, and color libraries
- Package a publication for a printing service
- Explain the use of PostScript files

2 | Publishing a Trifold Brochure

Introduction

Whether you want to advertise a service, event, or product, or merely want to inform the public about a current topic of interest, brochures are a popular type of promotional publication. A **brochure**, or pamphlet, usually is a high-quality publication with lots of color and graphics, created for advertising purposes. Businesses that may not be able to reach potential clientele effectively through traditional advertising, such as newspapers and radio, can create a long-lasting advertisement with a well-designed brochure.

Brochures come in all shapes and sizes. Colleges and universities produce brochures about their programs. The travel industry uses brochures to entice tourists. In addition, service industries and manufacturers display their products using this visual, hands-on medium.

Project—Brochure

The project in this chapter shows you how to build the two-page, trifold brochure shown in Figure 2–1. The brochure informs students about professional internships at a zoo. Each side of the brochure has three panels. Page 1 (Figure 2–1a) contains the front and back panels, as well as the inside fold. Page 2 (Figure 2–1b) contains a three-panel display that, when opened completely, provides the reader with more details about the zoo and a response form.

On page 1, the front panel contains shapes, text boxes, a graphic, and a background designed to draw the reader's attention and inform the reader of the intent of the brochure. The back panel, which displays in the middle of page 1, contains the name of the business, the address, phone and fax numbers, and an email address. The inside fold, on the left, contains the zoo's mission statement.

The three inside panels on page 2 contain more information about the internships and a form the reader may use to request more information.

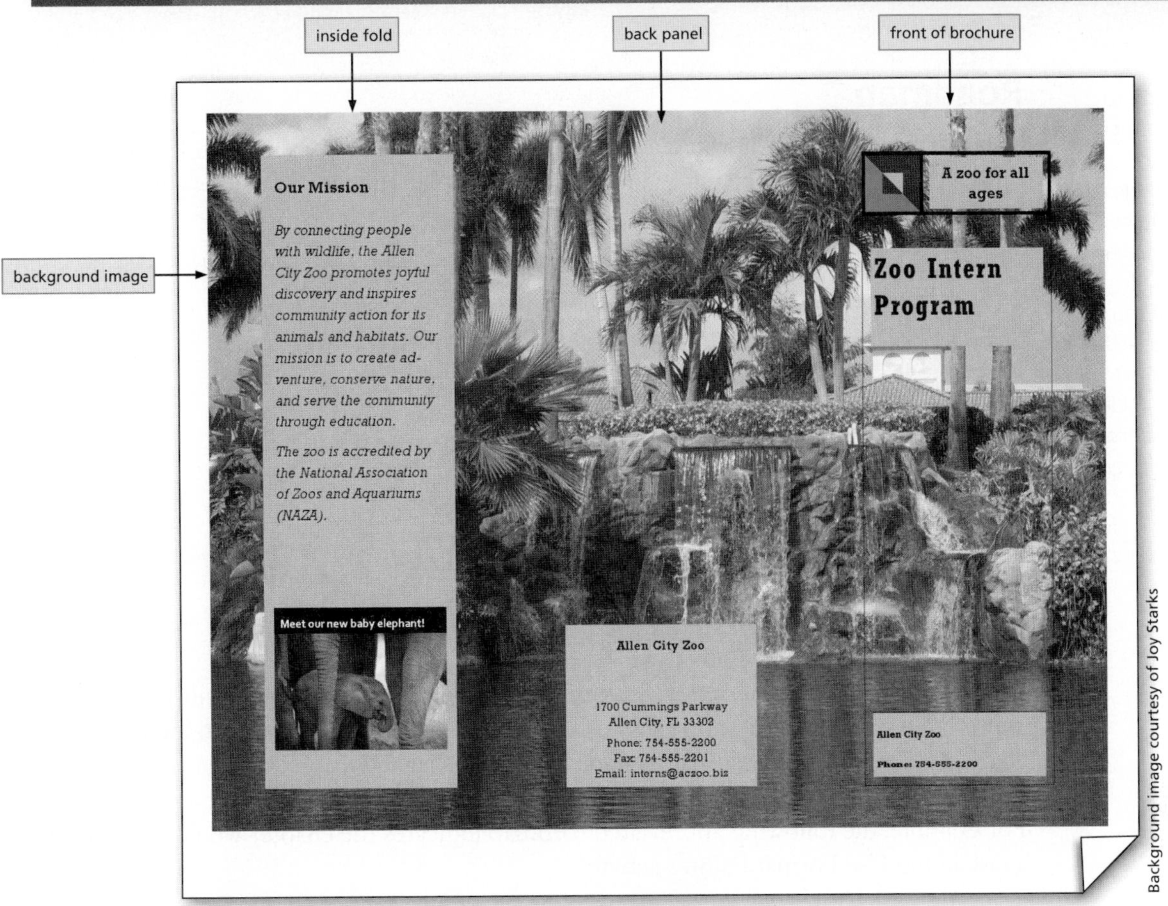

(a) Page 1

inside of brochure

Internships

Learn how to "pinken" up the flamingos!

Our internship experience is an exciting and educational opportunity for students to participate in various departments at Allen City Zoo. Our interns achieve learning goals associated with their field of study.

Interns are monitored carefully by their managers to ensure that they have active opportunities to participate in a wide variety of learning experiences. The zoo works to meet the academic credit requirements of the intern's educational institution. The program features a learning agenda complete with objectives, observation, reflection, evaluation, assessment, and periodic performance evaluations. Internships last 12 weeks.

Animal Training Internship
Animal training interns establish a working relationship with the animals. Responsibilities include providing enrichment for the animals, presenting animal encounters to the public, researching and reviewing enrichment data, and assisting education staff with the show animals. Interns with prior animal handling experience will be given priority.

Marketing Internship
Marketing interns are responsible for working in all areas of the zoo, and with media, corporate, and community partners to increase public awareness, promote programs, plan special events, and coordinate corporate engagement. Allen City Zoo is seeking motivated individuals with good communication, computer, and writing skills.

General Education Internship
General education interns work to develop and improve educational opportunities for zoo patrons by contributing to the development and evaluation of new curriculum, including distance learning, outreach, and on-grounds programming.

Giraffes in the large animal compound

For more information...

response form

Fill out the following form and send it to our Human Resources Department at the address listed below.

Semester
- ☐ Fall
- ☐ Spring
- ☐ Summer

Area of Interest
- ☐ Animal Training
- ☐ Marketing
- ☐ General Education

Habitat
- ☐ Large animal compound
- ☐ Bird sanctuary
- ☐ Petting zoo

Internship Type
- ☐ For credit only
- ☐ Paid only
- ☐ No preference

Comments:

Name

Address

Phone

Allen City Zoo

1700 Cummings Parkway
Allen City, FL 33302
Phone: 754-555-2200
Fax: 754-555-2201
Email: interns@aczoo.biz

(b) Page 2

Figure 2–1

Background image courtesy of Joy Starks

QR code © 2014 Cengage Learning
Scott Dunlap/iStock Vectors/Getty Images

For an introduction to Windows and instruction about how to perform basic Windows tasks, read the Office and Windows chapter at the beginning of this book, where you can learn how to resize windows, change screen resolution, create folders, move and rename files, use Windows Help, and much more.

Roadmap

In this chapter, you will learn how to create the brochure shown in Figure 2–1 on the previous page. The following roadmap identifies general activities you will perform as you progress through this chapter:

1. CUSTOMIZE the BROCHURE template options such as choice, color scheme, and font scheme.
2. EDIT template TEXT and OBJECTS.
3. SWAP PICTURES and use picture backgrounds.
4. USE the FORMAT PAINTER.
5. EDIT a Publisher FORM.
6. USE TYPOGRAPHY to enhance brochure text.
7. INSERT CAPTIONS for each photo.
8. CHECK the PUBLICATION for errors.
9. PACK the PUBLICATION for a printing service.

At the beginning of step instructions throughout the chapter, you will see an abbreviated form of this roadmap. The abbreviated roadmap uses colors to indicate chapter progress: gray means the chapter is beyond that activity, blue means the task being shown is covered in that activity, and black means that activity is yet to be covered. For example, the following abbreviated roadmap indicates the chapter would be showing a task in the Use Format Painter activity.

1 CUSTOMIZE BROCHURE | 2 EDIT TEXT & OBJECTS | 3 SWAP PICTURES | **4 USE FORMAT PAINTER**
5 EDIT FORM | 6 USE TYPOGRAPHY | 7 INSERT CAPTIONS | 8 CHECK PUBLICATION | 9 PACK PUBLICATION

Use the abbreviated roadmap as a progress guide while you read or step through the instructions in this chapter.

One of the few differences between Windows 7 and Windows 8 occurs in the steps to run Publisher. If you are using Windows 7, click the Start button, type Publisher in the 'Search programs and files' box, click Publisher 2013, and then, if necessary, maximize the Publisher window. For detailed steps to run Publisher in Windows 7, refer to the Office and Windows chapter at the beginning of this book. For a summary of the steps, refer to the Quick Reference located at the back of this book.

To Run Publisher

If you are using a computer to step through the project in this chapter and you want your screens to match the figures in this book, you should change your screen's resolution to 1366 × 768. For information about how to change a computer's resolution, refer to the Office and Windows chapter at the beginning of this book.

The following steps, which assume Windows 8 is running, use the Start screen or the search box to run Publisher based on a typical installation. You may need to ask your instructor how to run Publisher on your computer. For a detailed example of the procedure summarized below, refer to the Office and Windows chapter.

1. Scroll the Start screen and search for a Publisher 2013 tile. If your Start screen contains a Publisher 2013 tile, tap or click it to run Publisher and then proceed to Step 5. If the Start screen does not contain the Publisher 2013 tile, proceed to the next step to search for the Publisher app.
2. Swipe in from the right edge of the screen or point to the upper-right corner of the screen to display the Charms bar and then tap or click the Search charm on the Charms bar to display the Search menu.
3. Type `Publisher` as the search text in the Search box, and watch the search results appear in the Apps list.
4. Tap or click Publisher 2013 in the search results to run Publisher.
5. If the Publisher window is not maximized, tap or click the Maximize button on its title bar to maximize the window.

CONSIDER THIS

How do you decide on the purpose, shelf life, and layout of a brochure?
Spend time brainstorming ideas for the brochure. Think about why you want to create one. Decide on the purpose of the brochure. Is it to inform, sell, attract, or advertise an event? Adjust your template, fonts, colors, and graphics to match that purpose. Brochures commonly have a wider audience than flyers. They need to last longer, so carefully consider whether to add dated material or prices. Create a timeline of effectiveness and plan to have the brochure ready far in advance. Decide how many panels your brochure should be and how often you are going to produce it. If you are working for someone, draw a storyboard and get it approved before you begin. Think about alignment of objects, proximity of similar data, contrast, and repetition.

The Brochure Medium

Professionals commonly print brochures on special paper to provide long-lasting documents and to enhance the graphics. The brochure medium intentionally is tactile. Brochures are meant to be touched, carried home, passed along, and looked at, again and again. Newspapers and flyers usually have short-term readership on paper that readers throw away or recycle. Brochures, on the other hand, frequently use a heavier stock of paper so that they can stand better in a display rack.

The content of a brochure needs to last longer, too. On occasion, the intent of a brochure is to educate, such as a brochure on health issues in a doctor's office. More commonly, though, the intent is to market a product or sell a service. Prices and dated materials that are subject to frequent change affect the usable life of a brochure.

Typically, brochures use a great deal of color, and they include actual photos instead of drawings or clip art. Photos give a sense of realism to a publication and show people, places, or objects that are real, whereas images or drawings more appropriately are used to convey concepts or ideas.

Brochures, designed to be in circulation for longer periods as a type of advertising, ordinarily are published in greater quantities and on more expensive paper than other single-page publications, so they can be more costly. The cost, however, is less prohibitive when produced **in-house** using desktop publishing rather than hiring an outside service. The cost per copy is lower when producing brochures in mass quantities.

Table 2–1 lists some benefits and advantages of using the brochure medium.

For an introduction to Office and instruction about how to perform basic tasks in Office apps, read the Office and Windows chapter at the beginning of this book, where you can learn how to run an application, use the ribbon, save a file, open a file, exit an application, use Help, and much more.

BTW
How Brochures Differ
Each brochure template produces two pages of graphics, business information text boxes, and story boxes. Brochures are differentiated by the look and feel of the front panel, the location and style of the shapes and graphics, the design of any panel dividers, and the specific kind of decorations unique to each publication set.

Table 2–1 Benefits and Advantages of Using the Brochure Medium

EXPOSURE	An attention getter in displays
	A take-along document encouraging second looks
	A long-lasting publication due to paper and content
	An easily distributed publication — mass mailings, advertising sites
INFORMATION	An in-depth look at a product or service
	An opportunity to inform in a nonrestrictive environment
	An opportunity for focused feedback using forms
AUDIENCE	Interested clientele and potential customers
COMMUNICATION	An effective medium to highlight products and services
	A source of free information to build credibility
	An easier method to disseminate information than a magazine

© 2014 Cengage Learning

Creating a Trifold Brochure

BTW
Brochures
Brochures commonly have a wider audience than flyers. They need to last longer. Carefully consider whether to add dated material or prices. Create a timeline of effectiveness and plan to have the brochure ready far in advance.

Publisher-supplied templates use proven design strategies and combinations of objects, which are placed to attract attention and disseminate information effectively. The options for brochures differ from other publications in that they allow you to choose from page sizes, special kinds of forms, and panel/page layout options.

Making Choices about Brochure Options

For the Internship Brochure publication, you will use an informational brochure template, named Accent Box, making changes to its color scheme, font scheme, page size, and forms. **Page size** refers to the number of panels in the brochure. **Form options**, which appear on page 2 of the brochure, include Order form, Response form, and Sign-up form, or no form at all. The **Order form** displays fields for the description of items ordered as well as types of payment information, including blank fields for entering items, quantities, and prices. The **Response form** displays check box choices for up to four multiple-choice questions and a comment section. The **Sign-up form** displays check box choices, fields for time and price, and payment information. All three forms are meant to be detached as turnaround documents.

To Select a Brochure Template

1 CUSTOMIZE BROCHURE | 2 EDIT TEXT & OBJECTS | 3 SWAP PICTURES | 4 USE FORMAT PAINTER
5 EDIT FORM | 6 USE TYPOGRAPHY | 7 INSERT CAPTIONS | 8 CHECK PUBLICATION | 9 PACK PUBLICATION

The following step selects the Accent Box brochure template. ***Why?*** *You should use a template until you are more experienced in designing brochures.*

- In the template gallery, tap or click BUILT-IN to display the built-in templates.
- Tap or click the Brochures thumbnail within the BUILT-IN templates to display the Brochure templates.
- Scroll to the section labeled, More Installed Templates. Below that heading, in the Informational area, tap or click the Accent Box thumbnail (Figure 2–2).

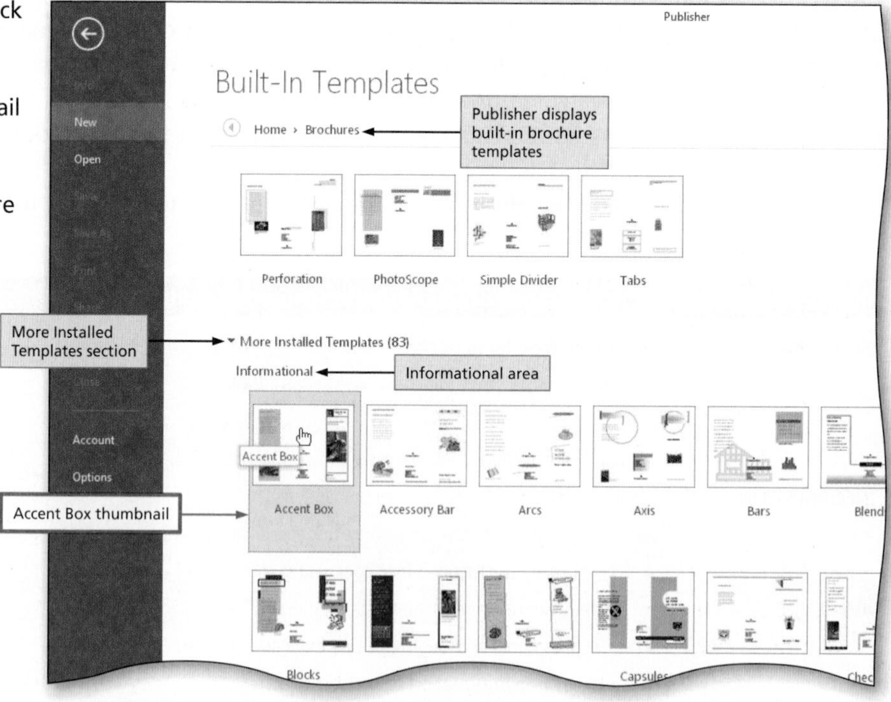

Figure 2–2

To Choose Brochure Options

The following steps choose brochure options.

1. Tap or click the Color scheme button in the template information pane. Scroll as necessary to tap or click Rain Forest to choose the color scheme.
2. Tap or click the Font scheme button, and then tap or click Foundry to choose the font scheme.
3. Do not tap or click the Business information button because it is not used in this publication.
4. Tap or click the Page size button in the Options area and then, if necessary, tap or click 3-panel to choose the number of panels.
5. If necessary, tap or click to remove the check mark in the 'Include customer address' check box.
6. Scroll down and then tap or click the Form button in the Options area. Tap or click Response form to choose the type of form (Figure 2–3).
7. Tap or click the CREATE button to create the publication based on the template settings.

BTW
Color Scheme
Choose a color scheme that is consistent with your company, client, or purpose. Do you need color, or black and white? Think about the plan for printing and the number of copies, in order to select a manageable color scheme. Remember that you can add more visual interest and contrast by bolding the color of text in the scheme; however, keep in mind that too many colors can detract from the flyer and make it difficult to read.

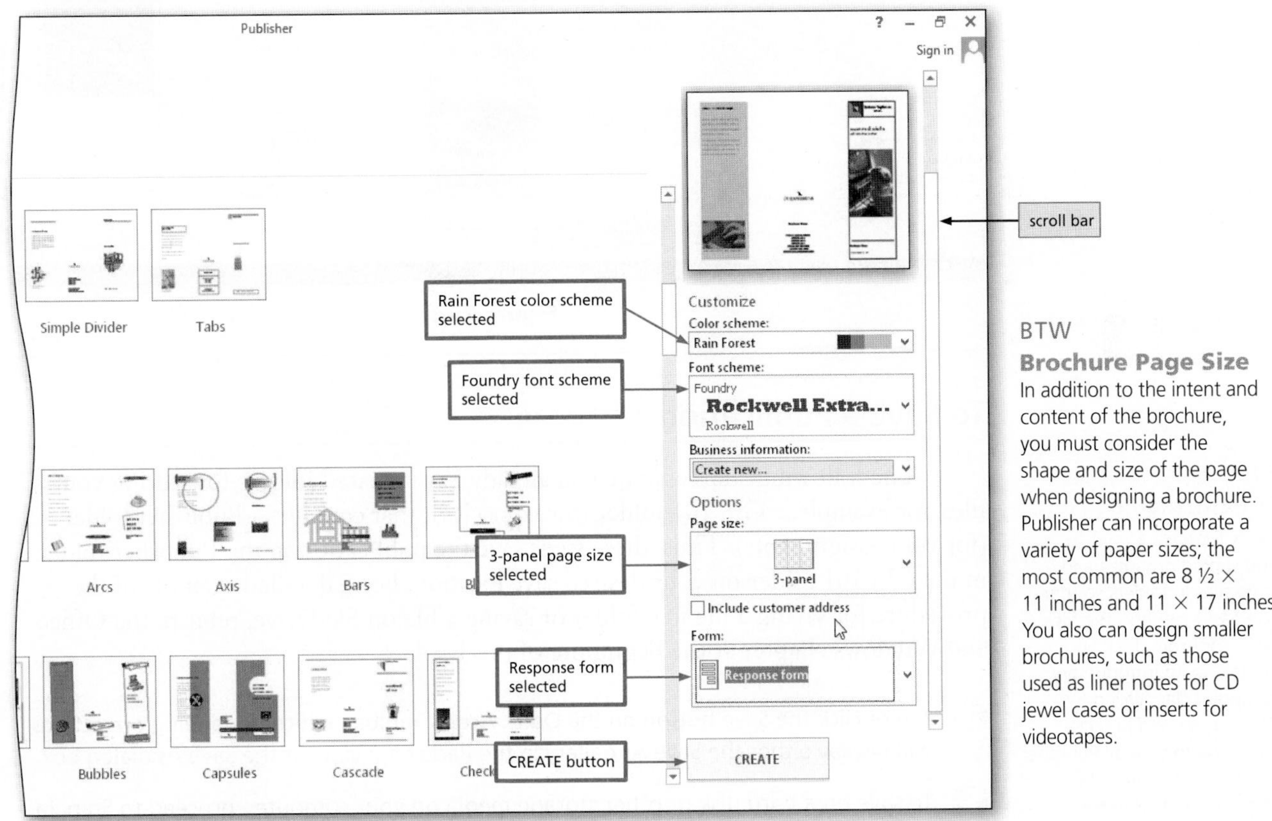

Figure 2–3

BTW
Brochure Page Size
In addition to the intent and content of the brochure, you must consider the shape and size of the page when designing a brochure. Publisher can incorporate a variety of paper sizes; the most common are 8 ½ × 11 inches and 11 × 17 inches. You also can design smaller brochures, such as those used as liner notes for CD jewel cases or inserts for videotapes.

BTW
Other Options
The template information pane contains additional options for brochures. Decide if you need a graphic or tear-offs. Will the publication need to be mailed? Might any specific information be difficult for your audience to remember? What kind of tear-off makes sense for your topic and message?

If you are using your finger on a touch screen and are having difficulty completing the steps in this chapter, consider using a stylus. Many people find it easier to be precise with a stylus rather than with a finger. In addition, with a stylus you see the pointer. If you still are having trouble completing the steps with a stylus, try using a mouse.

To Open the Page Navigation Pane

The following step opens the Page Navigation pane to display both pages of the brochure.

1. If the Page Navigation pane is not displayed, tap or click the 'Current page in publication' button on the status bar to open the Page Navigation pane. If the Page Navigation pane is minimized, tap or click the 'Expand Page Navigation Pane' button to maximize it (Figure 2–4).

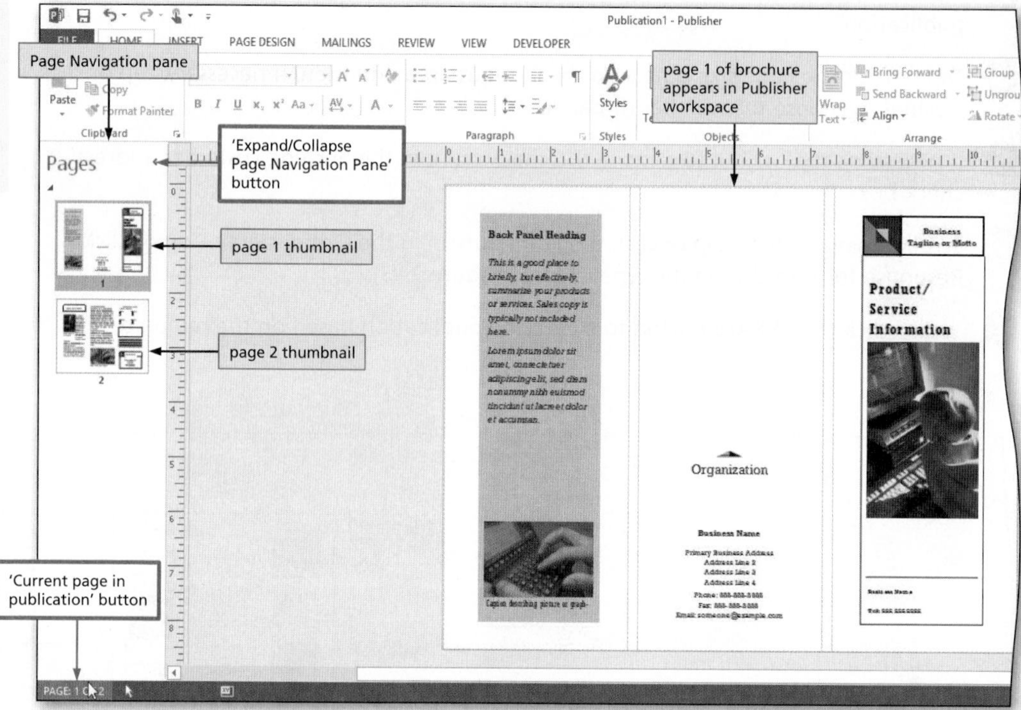

Figure 2–4

To Save a Publication

BTW
Organizing Files and Folders
You should organize and store files in folders so that you easily can find the files later. For example, if you are taking an introductory computer class called CIS 101, a good practice would be to save all Publisher files in a Publisher folder in a CIS 101 folder. For a discussion of folders and detailed examples of creating folders, refer to the Office and Windows chapter at the beginning of this book.

The following steps assume you already have created folders for storing your files, for example, a CIS 101 folder (for your class) that contains a Publisher folder (for your assignments). Thus, these steps save the publication in the Publisher folder in the CIS 101 folder on your desired save location. For a detailed example of the procedure for saving a file in a folder or saving a file on SkyDrive, refer to the Office and Windows chapter at the beginning of this book.

1. Tap or click the Save button on the Quick Access Toolbar, which depending on settings, will display either the Save As gallery in the Backstage view or the Save As dialog box.

2. To save on a hard disk or other storage media on your computer, proceed to Step 2a. To save on SkyDrive, proceed to Step 2b.

2a. If your screen opens the Backstage view and you want to save on storage media on your computer, tap or click Computer in the left pane, if necessary, to display options in the right pane related to saving on your computer. If your screen already displays the Save As dialog box, proceed to Step 4.

2b. If your screen opens the Backstage view and you want to save on SkyDrive, tap or click SkyDrive in the left pane to display SkyDrive saving options or a Sign In button. If your screen displays a Sign In button, tap or click it and then sign in to SkyDrive.

3. Tap or click the Browse button in the right pane to display the Save As dialog box associated with the selected save location (i.e., Computer or SkyDrive).

4. Type **Internship Brochure** in the File name text box to change the file name. Do not press the ENTER key after typing the file name because you do not want to close the dialog box at this time.

5. Navigate to the desired save location (in this case, the Publisher folder in the CIS 101 folder [or your class folder] on your computer or SkyDrive).

6. Tap or click the Save button (Save As dialog box) to save the publication in the selected folder on the selected save location with the entered file name.

To Delete Objects

You will not use some of the objects in the brochure template. The following steps delete the unused objects.

1. Tap or click the picture in the right panel of page 1 to select it. Press the DELETE key to delete the object.

2. Tap or click the boundary of the Organization logo in the middle panel to select it. Press the DELETE key to delete the object (Figure 2–5).

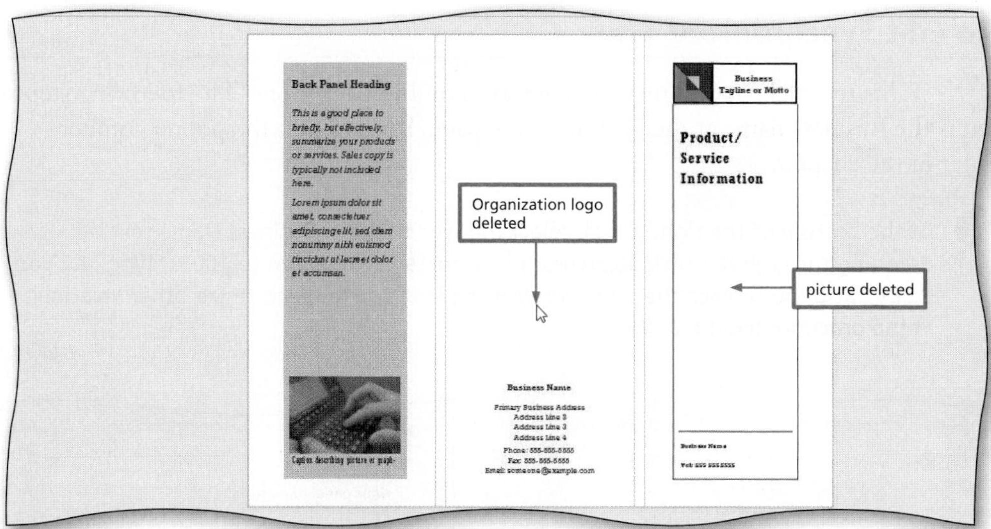

Figure 2–5

BTW
Automatic Saving
Publisher can save your publication at regular intervals for you. In the Backstage view, tap or click Options, and then tap or click Save (Publisher Options dialog box). Select the 'Save AutoRecover information every *10* minutes' check box. In the minutes box, specify how often you want Publisher to save files. Do not use AutoRecover as a substitute for regularly saving your work.

To Edit Text in the Right Panel

The front of the brochure displays in the right panel of page 1 and contains default text, placeholder text, and synchronized text. Recall that default text must be selected by dragging or pressing CTRL+A. Placeholder text is selected with a single tap or click. The following steps edit various text boxes on the front panel.

1. In the right panel, select the Business Tagline or Motto by dragging through the text. Type **A zoo for all ages** to replace the text.

BTW
The Ribbon and Screen Resolution
Publisher may change how the groups and buttons within the groups appear on the ribbon, depending on the computer's screen resolution. Thus, your ribbon may look different from the ones in this book if you are using a screen resolution other than 1366 × 768.

BTW
BTWs
For a complete list of the BTWs found in the margins of this book, visit the BTW resource on the Student Companion Site located on www.cengagebrain.com. For detailed instructions about accessing available resources, visit www.cengage.com/ct/studentdownload or see the inside back cover of this book.

2. Tap or click the Product/Service Information headline placeholder text to select it. Type `Zoo Intern Program` to replace the text (Figure 2–6).

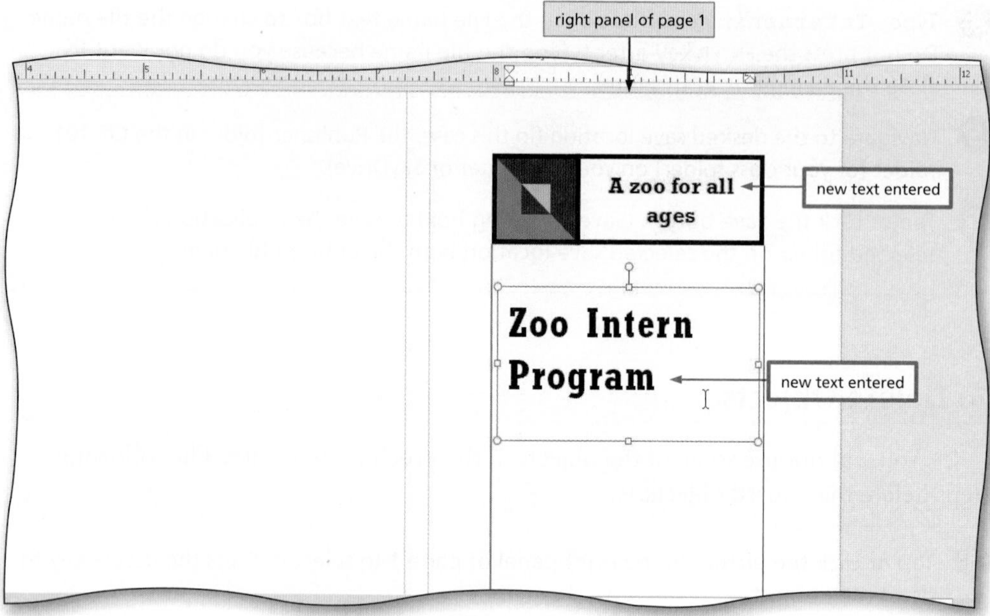

Figure 2–6

To Edit Synchronized Text

BTW
Brochure Features
Many brochures incorporate newspaper features, such as columns and a masthead, and add eye appeal with logos, sidebars, shapes, and graphics. Small brochures typically have folded panels. Larger brochures resemble small magazines, with multiple pages and stapled bindings.

Edits to synchronized text change text in multiple locations. The following step edits the Business name at the bottom of the page. You will edit the phone number later in the chapter.

1. At the bottom of the right panel, select the synchronized Business Name text by dragging through the text. Stretch or press the F9 key to zoom to 100%. Type `Allen City Zoo` to replace the text. Deselect the text box to synchronize other locations in the brochure (Figure 2–7).

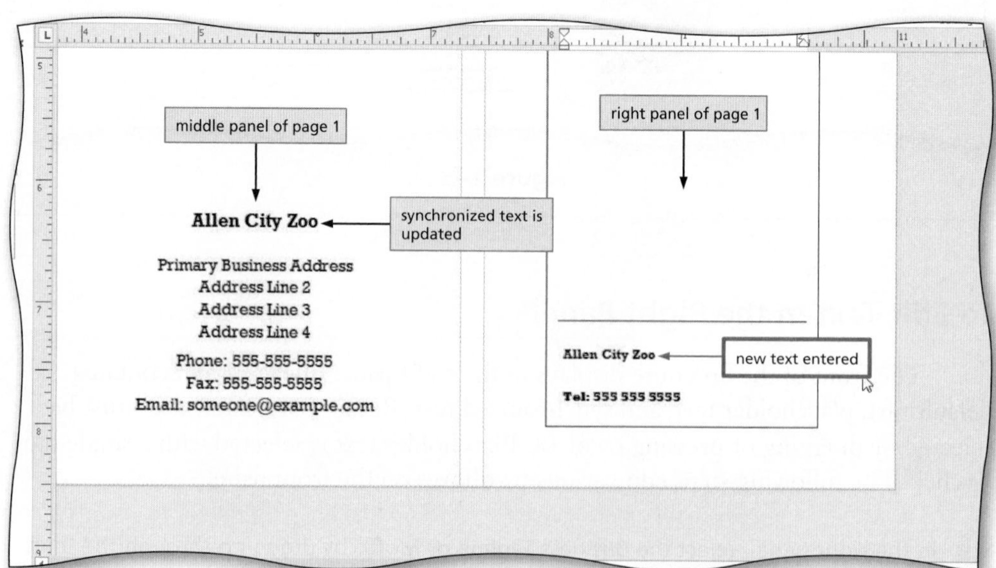

Figure 2–7

To Edit Text in the Middle Panel

When folded, the middle panel will display on the back of the trifold brochure. It contains text boxes for the business address, phone numbers, and email address. The following steps edit the text in the middle panel.

1. Scroll as necessary to display the middle panel. If necessary, stretch or press the F9 key to zoom to 100%.

2. Drag to select the all of the text in the Primary Business Address text box. Type **`1700 Cummings Parkway`** and then press the ENTER key to finish the first line of the address and advance to the next address line. Type **`Allen City, FL 33302`** to finish entering the address text.

   If requested by your instructor, enter your address, city and state instead of the address in Step 2. Do not press the ENTER key after the last line.

3. Drag to select the phone and fax numbers and the email address text. Type **`Phone: 754-555-2200`** and then press the ENTER key to finish entering the first line. Type **`Fax: 754-555-2201`** and then press the ENTER key to finish entering the second line. Type **`Email: interns@aczoo.biz`** to finish entering the text. Do not press the ENTER key after the last line (Figure 2–8).

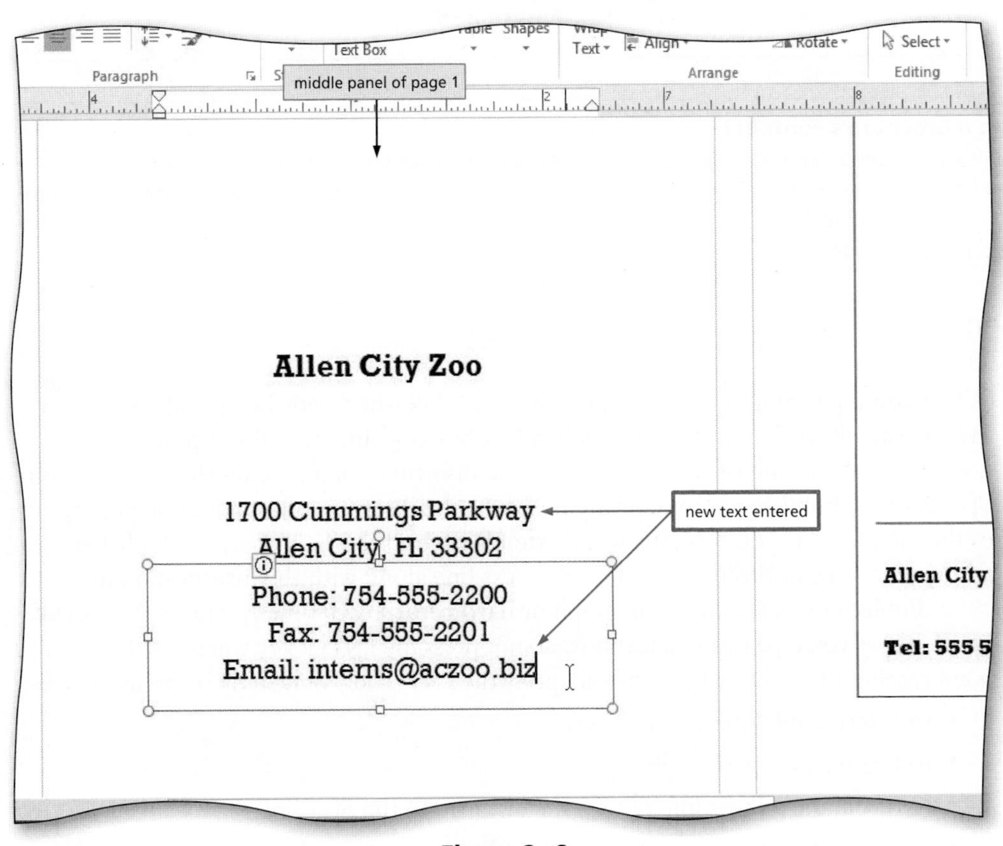

Figure 2–8

BTW

Publisher Help

At any time while using Publisher, you can find answers to questions and display information about various topics through Publisher Help. Used properly, this form of assistance can increase your productivity and reduce your frustrations by minimizing the time you spend learning how to use Publisher. For instruction about Publisher Help and exercises that will help you gain confidence in using it, read the Office and Windows chapter at the beginning of this book.

BTW
Superscripts and Subscripts
Two special font effects are superscript and subscript. A superscript is a character that appears slightly higher than other text on a line, such as that used in footnotes (reference[1]). A subscript is text that is slightly lower than other text on a line, such as that used in scientific formulas ($H_2 0$).

To Edit Heading Text in the Left Panel

The left panel will appear when the brochure is first opened. It contains text boxes for a heading and summary text. The following steps edit the heading text.

1. Scroll to the top of the left panel and zoom to 100%.
2. In the left panel, tap or click to select the Back Panel Heading placeholder text. Type `Our Mission` to replace the text (Figure 2–9).

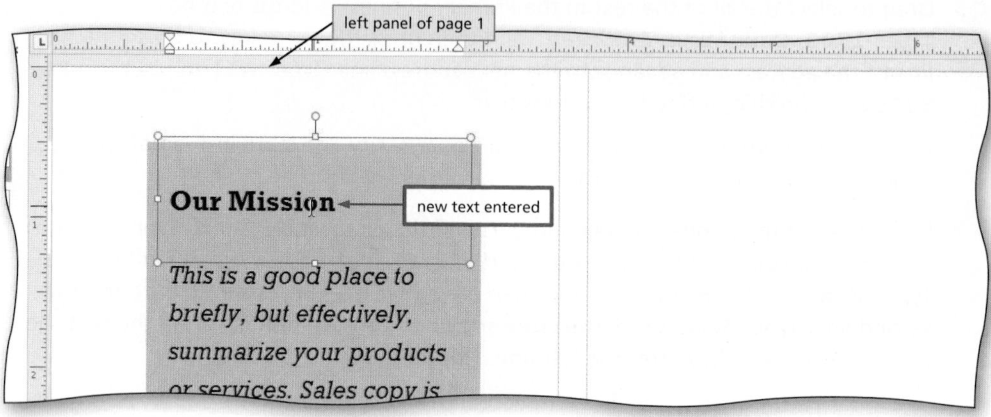
left panel of page 1
Our Mission
new text entered
This is a good place to
briefly, but effectively,
summarize your products
or services. Sales copy is

Figure 2–9

CONSIDER THIS

How do you decide on a brochure's content?
Gather all the information, such as stories, graphics, logos, colors, shapes, style information, and watermarks. Save copies or versions along the way. If you have to create objects from scratch, have someone else evaluate your work and give you constructive feedback. If you are using forms in your brochure, verify the manner in which the viewer will return the form. Check and double-check all prices, addresses, and phone numbers.

Typing Paragraphs of Text

BTW
Gate Folds
A gatefold is a 4-panel brochure where both ends fold toward the center. Gatefolds, also called foldouts, commonly are used in advertising, for menus, or as inserts in magazines.

When you type paragraphs of text, you will use Publisher's wordwrap feature. **Wordwrap** allows you to type words in a text box continually without pressing the ENTER key at the end of each line. When the insertion point reaches the right margin of a text box, Publisher automatically positions the insertion point at the beginning of the next line. As you type, if a word extends beyond the right margin, Publisher automatically positions that word on the next line along with the insertion point.

Publisher creates a new paragraph or **hard return** each time you press the ENTER key. Thus, as you type text in a text box, do not press the ENTER key when the insertion point reaches the right margin. Instead, press the ENTER key only in these circumstances:

- To insert blank lines in a text box
- To begin a new paragraph
- To terminate a short line of text and advance to the next line
- To respond to questions or prompts in Publisher dialog boxes, panes, and other on-screen objects

To view where in a publication you pressed the ENTER key or SPACEBAR key, you may find it helpful to display formatting marks. A **formatting mark**, sometimes called a **nonprinting character**, is a special character that Publisher displays on the screen, but one that is not visible on a printed publication. For example, the paragraph mark (¶) is a formatting mark that indicates where you pressed the ENTER key. A raised dot (·) appears where you pressed the spacebar. An end of field marker (¤) is displayed to indicate the end of text in a text box. Other formatting marks are discussed as they appear on the screen.

To Display Formatting Marks

The following step displays formatting marks, if they do not show already on the screen. ***Why?*** *The formatting marks help you see where you pressed the* ENTER *key and the* SPACEBAR *key, among other things.*

1

- If it is not selected already, tap or click the Special Characters button (HOME tab | Paragraph group) to display formatting marks (Figure 2–10).

Q&A What if I do not want formatting marks to show on the screen?
If you feel the formatting marks clutter the screen, you can hide them by tapping or clicking the Special Characters button again. The figures presented in the rest of this chapter show the formatting marks.

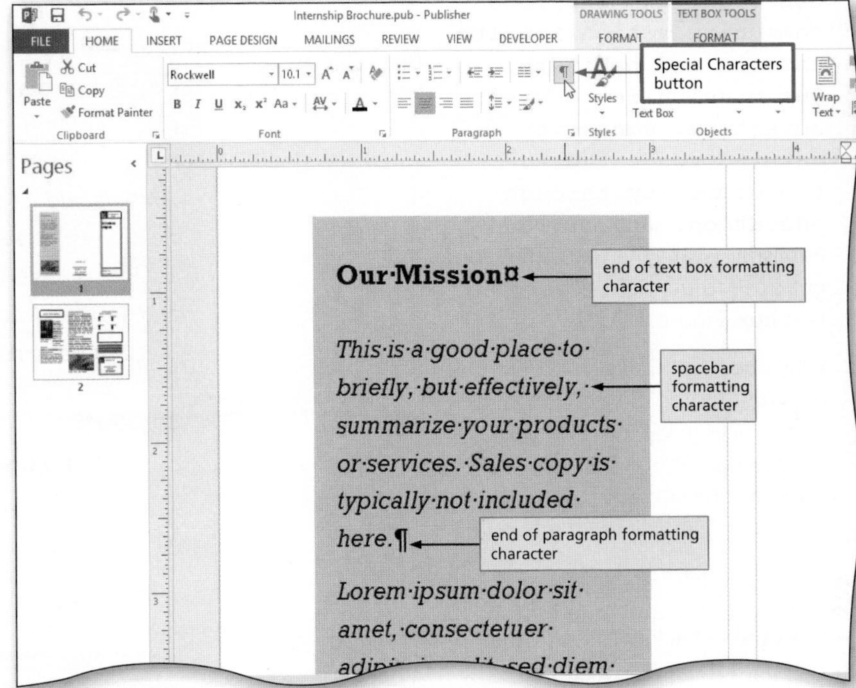

Figure 2–10

Other Ways

1. Press CTRL+SHIFT+Y

To Wordwrap Text as You Type

The next step in creating the flyer is to type the text in the left panel. The following steps wordwrap the text in the text box. ***Why?*** *Using wordwrap ensures consistent margins.*

1

- Tap or click to select the placeholder text in the text box below the title, Our Mission (Figure 2–11).

Q&A Should I delete the text before typing?
No, it is placeholder text that will disappear automatically when you begin to type.

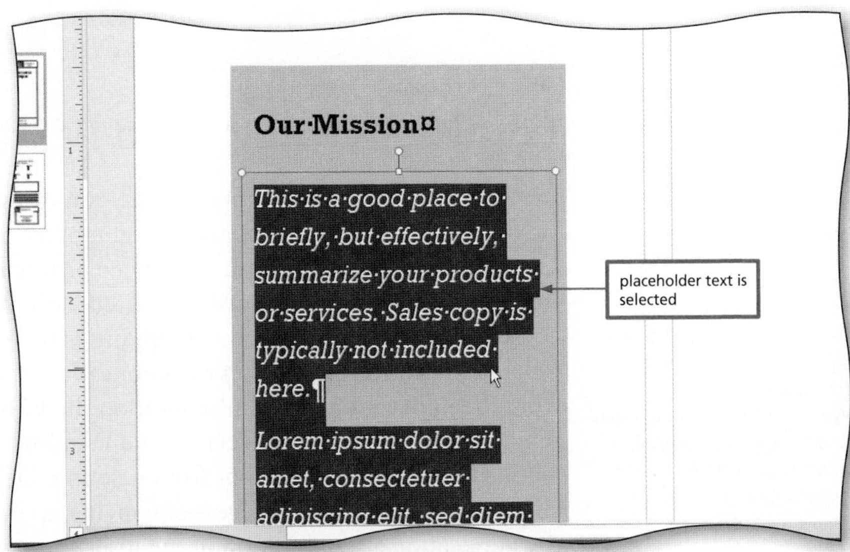

Figure 2–11

2

- Type **By connecting people with wildlife, the Allen City Zoo promotes joyful discovery and inspires community action for its animals and habitats. Our mission is to create adventure, conserve nature, and serve the community through education.** and notice that Publisher wraps the text when you get close to the right edge of the text box (Figure 2–12).

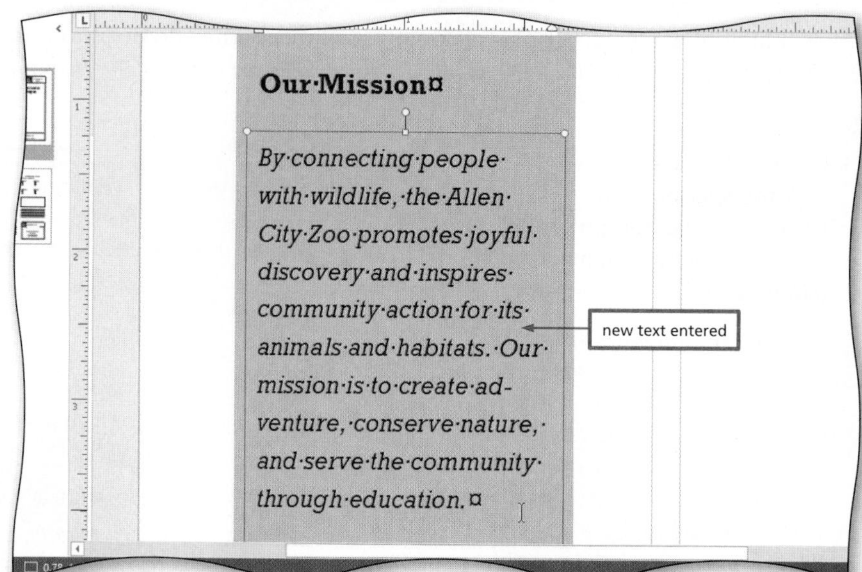

Figure 2–12

Q&A Why does my publication wrap on different words?
Differences in wordwrap relate to your printer. It is possible that the same publication could wordwrap differently if printed on different printers.

3

- Press the ENTER key to finish the first paragraph.
- Type **The zoo is accredited by the National Association of Zoos and Aquariums (NAZA).** to finish the text (Figure 2–13).

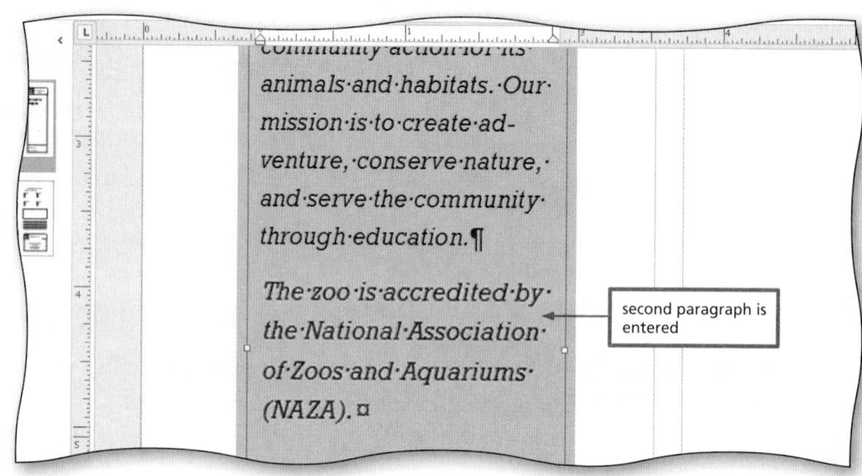

Figure 2–13

Copying, Cutting, and Pasting

BTW
Touch Galleries
If you are using a mouse or stylus, galleries such as the Font color gallery, display their choices in small colored squares. If you are touching to display the gallery, Windows 8 senses that touch and displays the gallery with much larger colored squares, making it easier to tap the one you want.

In each of the Office 2013 applications, you can store or copy text and objects for later use. The **Office Clipboard** is a temporary storage area that holds up to 24 items (text or graphics) copied from any Office program. The Office Clipboard is different from the **Windows Clipboard** associated with the operating system, which can contain only one item at a time. **Copying** is the process of placing items on the Office Clipboard, leaving the item in the publication. **Cutting**, by contrast, removes the item from the publication before placing it on the Office Clipboard. The copy and cut functions transfer text or objects to the Windows Clipboard as well as to the Office Clipboard. Cutting is different from deleting. Deleted items are not placed on either clipboard. **Pasting** is the process of copying an item from the Office Clipboard into the publication at the location of the insertion point or selection.

Table 2–2 describes various methods to copy, cut, paste, and delete selected text.

Table 2–2 Copy, Cut, Paste, and Delete Text

Method	Copy	Cut	Paste	Delete
shortcut menu	Press and hold or right-click to display the shortcut menu and then tap or click Copy	Press and hold or right-click to display the shortcut menu and then tap or click Cut	Press and hold or right-click to display the shortcut menu and then tap or click Paste	Press and hold or right-click to display the shortcut menu and then tap or click Delete Text
ribbon	Tap or click the Copy button (HOME tab | Clipboard group)	Tap or click the Cut button (HOME tab | Clipboard group)	Tap or click the Paste button (HOME tab | Clipboard group)	not available
keyboard	Press CTRL+C	Press CTRL+X	Press CTRL+V	Press the DELETE key or BACKSPACE key

© 2014 Cengage Learning

In Publisher, you can copy, cut, paste, and delete objects as well as text. If you are copying text, it is advisable to select from the beginning letter of the text and include any ending spaces, tabs, punctuation, or paragraph marks. That way, when you cut or paste, the text will be spaced properly. If you are copying, cutting, pasting, and deleting objects, the object must be selected. Publisher normally pastes objects from either clipboard into the center of the displayed page layout if no object is selected.

The next step in editing the brochure is to replace the phone number at the bottom of the right panel. One way to enter this information in the brochure is to type it. Recall, however, that you already typed this information on the center panel. Thus, a timesaving alternative would be to copy and paste the text.

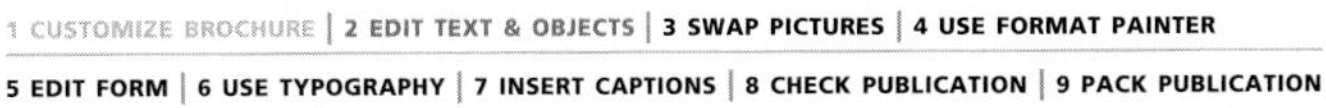

To Copy and Paste

In the brochure, you want to copy the phone number from one panel to the other. ***Why?*** *Copying and pasting reduces errors that might result from retyping information.* The following steps copy and paste the phone number.

1

- Scroll to the lower portion of the middle panel.
- Tap or click the phone number text box to select it.
- Drag to select the item to be copied (the word, Phone, and the phone number in this case).
- Tap or click the Copy button (HOME tab | Clipboard group) to copy the selected item in the publication to the Office Clipboard (Figure 2–14).

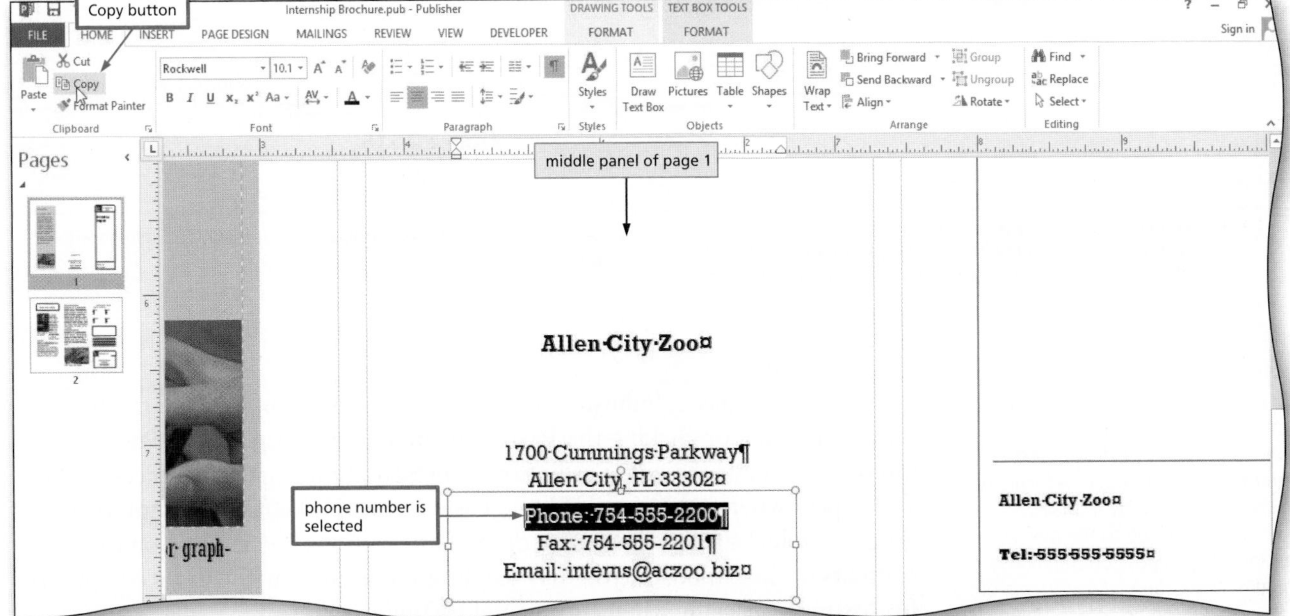

Figure 2–14

- Tap or click the text in the phone number text box on the right panel to select it (Figure 2–15).

Q&A Do I always have to select text before pasting?
No. If you are not replacing text, you position the insertion point at the desired location and then paste.

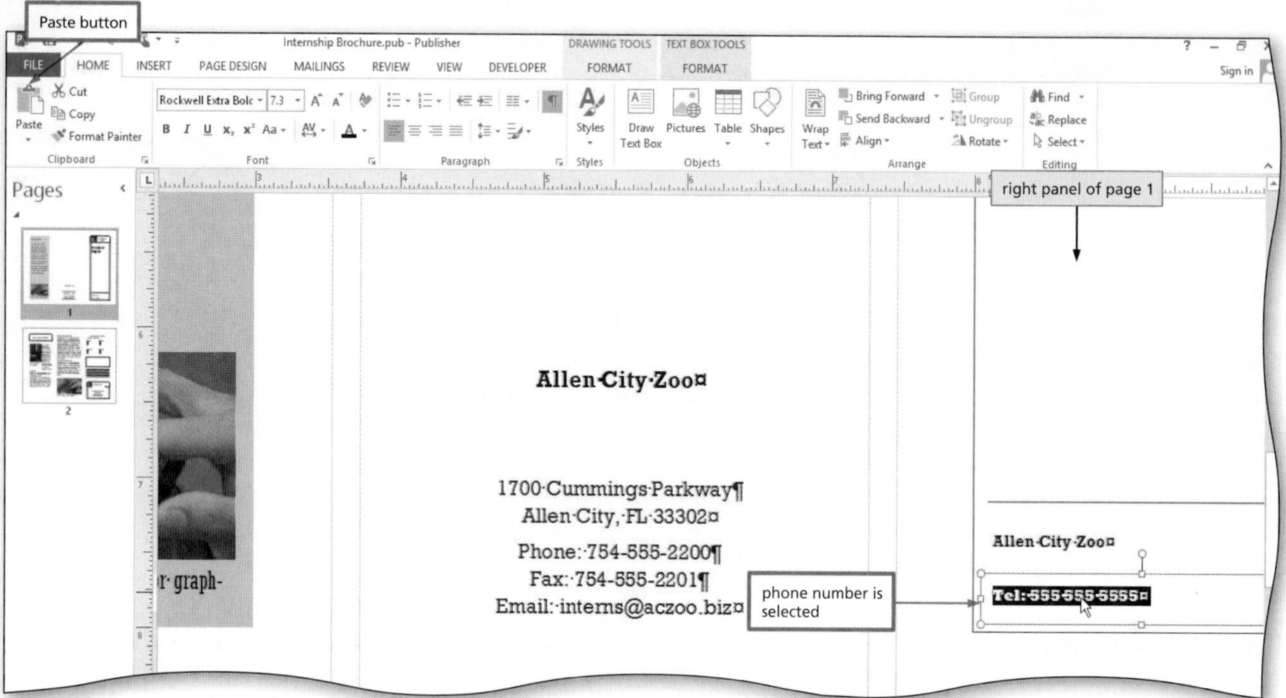

Figure 2–15

- Tap or click the Paste button (HOME tab | Clipboard group) to paste the copied item in the publication and replace the selected phone number. Do not press any other keys (Figure 2–16).

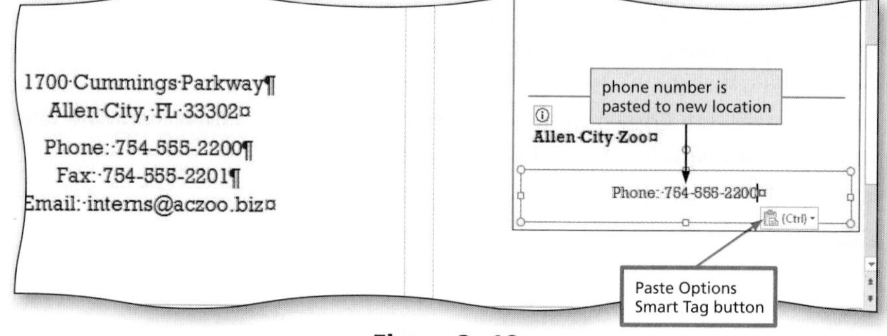

Figure 2–16

Other Ways

1. Press and hold or right-click selected item, tap or click Copy on shortcut menu, press and hold or right-click at paste location, tap or click desired formatting in Paste Options area on shortcut menu
2. Select item, press CTRL+C, position insertion point at paste location, press CTRL+V

BTW
Moving Text
If you want to use your mouse to move text from one location to another, you can select the text and the drag it to the new location. Publisher will display a small rectangle attached to the mouse pointer as you position the mouse in the new location. Moving text or objects also can be accomplished by cutting and then pasting.

Paste Options Button

After you paste, Publisher may display the Paste Options Smart Tag button. Tapping or clicking the **Paste Options** button displays the Paste Options menu, which contains buttons representing formatting choices. They also appear when you tap or click the Paste arrow (HOME tab | Clipboard group). Table 2–3 describes some of the Paste options. Depending on the contents of the clipboard, you may see different buttons with advanced options for pasting, especially when cutting and pasting graphics.

Table 2–3 Paste Options

Button	Option	Result
	Paste	Pastes the copied content as is, without any formatting changes
	Keep Source Formatting	Pastes the copied content as is, without any formatting changes
	Merge Formatting	Changes the formatting so that it matches the text around it
	Keep Text Only	Pastes the copied text as plain unformatted text and removes any styles or hyperlinks

© 2014 Cengage Learning

To Select a Paste Option

The following steps select the Keep Text Only Paste Option. ***Why?*** *The phone number should match the font style in the right panel.*

1

- Tap or click the Paste Options Smart Tag button that appears below the pasted information to display the Paste Options menu (Figure 2–17).

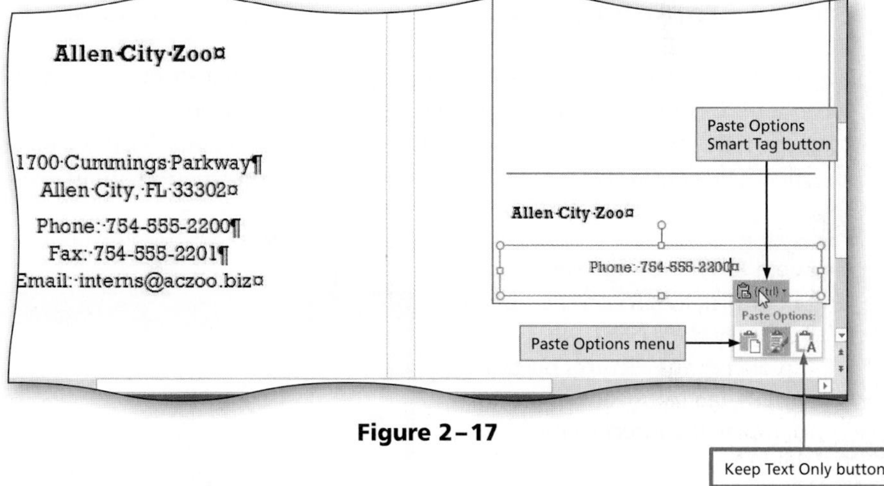

Figure 2–17

Experiment

- Point to each of the Paste Options buttons to see their ScreenTips.

2

- Tap or click the Keep Text Only button to paste using the destination formatting (Figure 2–18).

Q&A Can I change my mind and choose a different paste option?

Yes, if you change it before typing anything else. Otherwise you would have to delete and paste again.

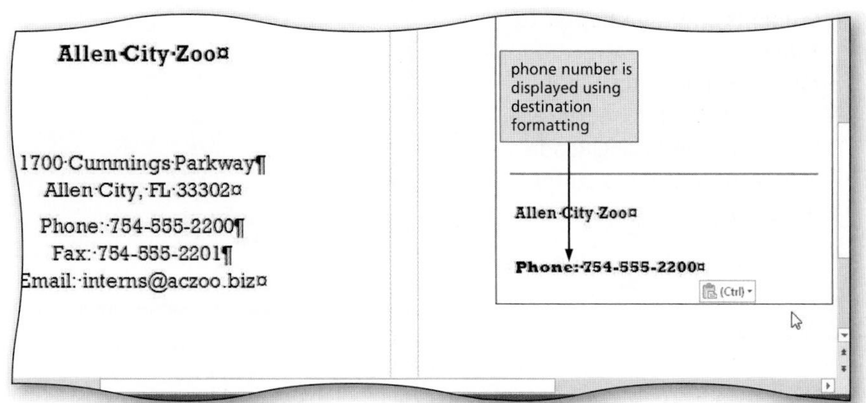

Figure 2–18

Other Ways

1. Press CTRL key, tap or click Paste Options button
2. Tap or click Paste arrow (HOME tab | Clipboard group), tap or click Paste Options button
3. Press and hold or right-click pasted text, tap or click desired paste option button on shortcut menu.

Swapping Pictures

BTW
Q&As
For a complete list of the Q&As found in many of the step-by-step sequences in this book, visit the Q&A resource on the Student Companion Site located on www.cengagebrain.com. For detailed instructions about accessing available resources, visit www.cengage.com/ct/studentdownload or see the inside back cover of this book.

A new feature in Publisher 2013 is the use of the scratch area to manipulate and swap pictures. The **scratch area** is the gray area that appears outside the publication page. It is used as a temporary holding area; if you are not sure where you want to move an item, you can drag it to the scratch area. When inserting a single picture, you can drag it to the scratch area. When you insert multiple pictures at one time, Publisher arranges the thumbnails or puts them in a column in the scratch area, instead of on top of one another on your page. Unlike the clipboard, the scratch area is saved with the publication. The pictures in the scratch area will still be there the next time you open the publication. The scratch area does not print and contains the same items, regardless of which page of the publication is displayed.

Many templates include picture placeholders, each with a placeholder icon. After the placeholder is replaced with a picture, the icon changes to a **swap icon**. Pictures in the scratch area also have swap icons. You can drag the swap icon to swap pictures with one another, or press and hold or right-click the swap icon to display a shortcut menu with more options.

To Insert Multiple Pictures from a Storage Device

1 CUSTOMIZE BROCHURE | 2 EDIT TEXT & OBJECTS | 3 SWAP PICTURES | 4 USE FORMAT PAINTER
5 EDIT FORM | 6 USE TYPOGRAPHY | 7 INSERT CAPTIONS | 8 CHECK PUBLICATION | 9 PACK PUBLICATION

The following steps insert multiple pictures from a storage device. ***Why?*** *Selecting and placing multiple pictures in the scratch area allows you to see what different pictures might look like in the publication.* To complete these steps, you will be required to use the Data Files for Students. Visit www.cengage.com/ct/studentdownload for detailed instructions or contact your instructor for information about accessing the required files.

- Zoom to Whole Page view.
- Tap or click INSERT on the ribbon to display the INSERT tab.
- Tap or click the Pictures button (INSERT tab | Illustrations group) to display the Insert Picture dialog box.
- Navigate to the Data Files for Students and the Chapter 02 folder.
- One at a time, CTRL+tap or CTRL+click the files, Social Media, Zoo Scene, and ZooQRcode to select the three pictures (Figure 2–19).

Q&A Why do I have to use the CTRL key?
CTRL+tapping or CTRL+clicking allows you to select multiple items, rather than selecting them one at a time.

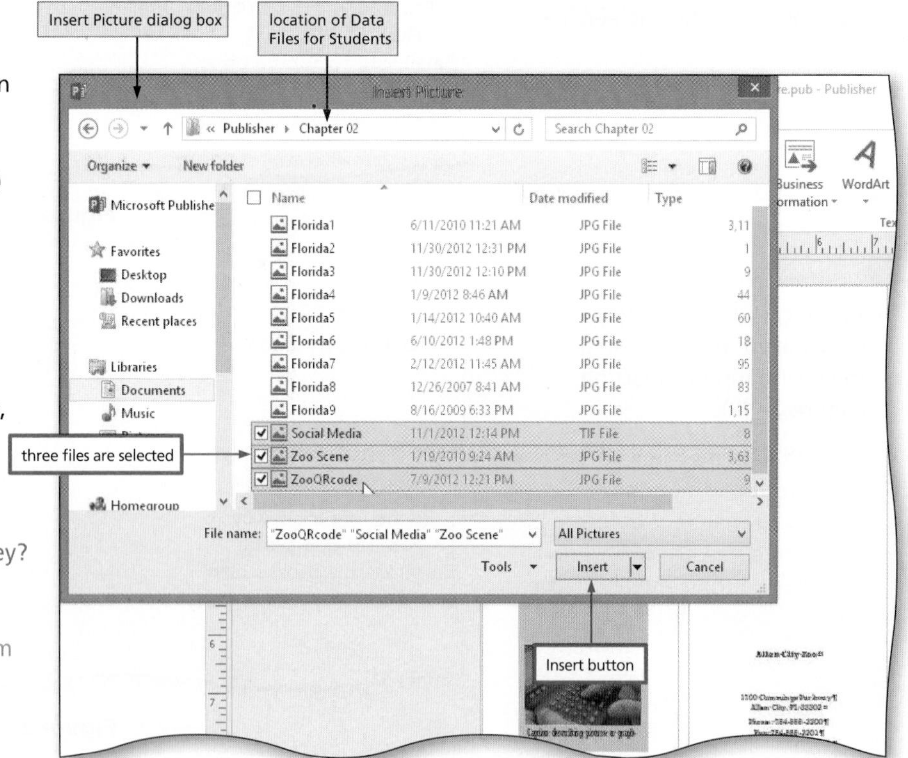

Figure 2–19

2

- Tap or click the Insert button (Insert Picture dialog box) to place the pictures in the scratch area (Figure 2–20).

Q&A My picture displays in the middle of the publication rather than scratch area. What did I do wrong?

If you choose just one picture, it is displayed in the middle of the publication. Multiple selections appear in the scratch area. You can drag your picture to the scratch area, if necessary.

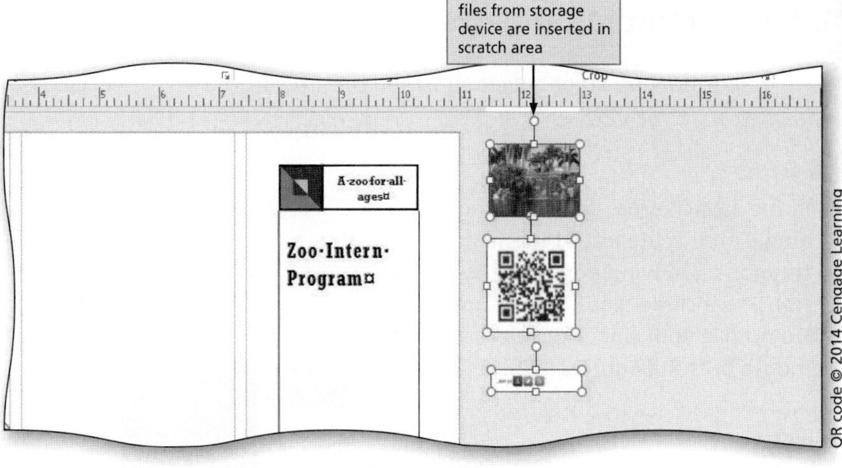

Figure 2–20

To Insert Online Pictures

The following steps select pictures from Office.com Clip Art and place them in the Publisher scratch area. The size of your pictures may vary.

BTW

Clip Art Sources

In addition to the clip art images included with Publisher, other sources for clip art include retailers specializing in computer software, the Internet, bulletin board systems, and online information systems. A bulletin board system is a computer service that allows users to communicate with each other and share files.

1. Tap or click the scratch area, away from the pictures to deselect them.
2. Pinch or use the zoom controls on the status bar to zoom to approximately 40%.
3. If necessary, tap or click the INSERT tab and then, with no object selected, tap or click the Online Pictures button (INSERT tab | Illustrations group) to display the Insert Pictures dialog box.
4. Type `giraffes` in the Office.com Clip Art search box to enter the search term. Press the ENTER key to display pictures of giraffes. Tap or click a picture of giraffes similar to the one shown in Figure 2–21.
5. Tap or click the Insert button (Office.com Clip Art dialog box) to place the selected picture in the publication.
6. Drag the picture to the scratch area.
7. Repeat Steps 3 through 6 to insert a picture of elephants and a picture of flamingos. Scroll as necessary to view all of the pictures (Figure 2–21).

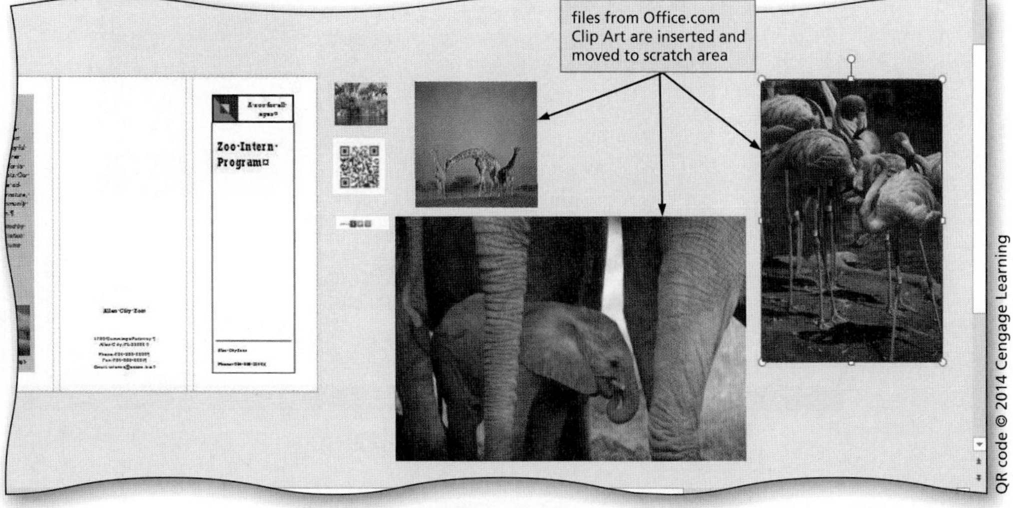

Figure 2–21

To Select Multiple Objects

The following steps select all of the pictures in the scratch area. ***Why?*** *They must be selected in order to arrange them in the next series of steps.*

- In the scratch area, drag, starting above and to the left of the first thumbnail, moving down and to the right, to include all of the pictures. Do not lift your finger or release the mouse button (Figure 2–22).

Figure 2–22

- Release the drag to select all of the pictures (Figure 2–23).

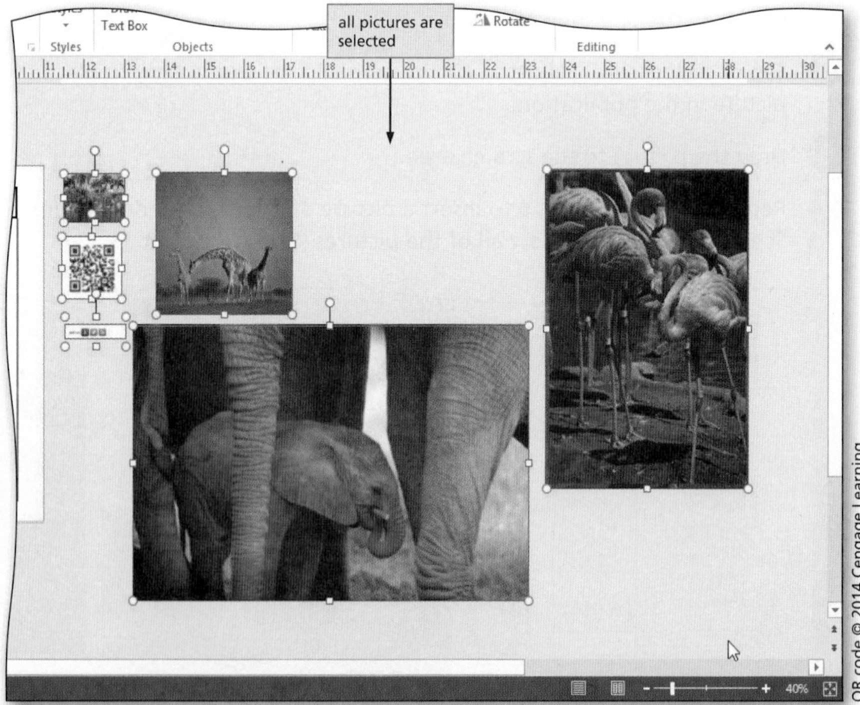

Figure 2–23

Other Ways

1. CTRL+tap or CTRL+click each picture in scratch area

To Arrange Thumbnails

The scratch area displays pictures as thumbnails. ***Why?*** *A* **thumbnail** *is a reduced-size version of a larger graphic image used to help recognize and organize pictures, and to save space.* When you **arrange thumbnails**, all of the pictures are reduced to thumbnail size and are aligned in rows and columns. The following step arranges thumbnails.

1

- If necessary, tap or click PICTURE TOOLS FORMAT on the ribbon to display the PICTURE TOOLS FORMAT tab.
- Tap or click the Arrange Thumbnails button (PICTURE TOOLS FORMAT tab | Arrange group) to arrange the thumbnails (Figure 2–24).

Q&A My tab disappeared. Did I do something wrong?

No. The PICTURE TOOLS FORMAT tab displays only when a picture is selected. Arranging the thumbnails may have deselected the pictures.

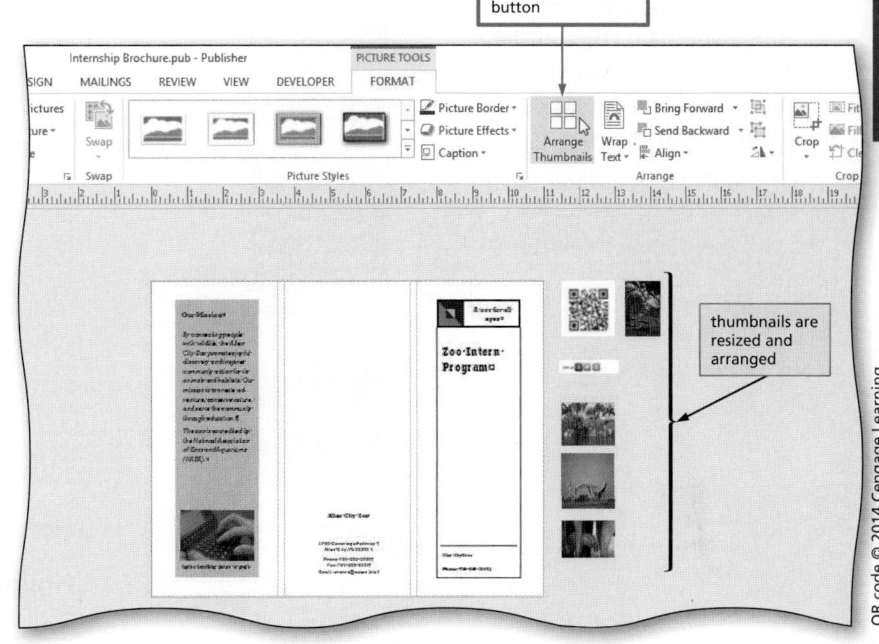

Figure 2–24

Other Ways

1. Select pictures in scratch area, press and hold or right-click any picture, tap or click Arrange Thumbnails on shortcut menu

To Swap Pictures

When you decide to swap one picture for another, you drag the new picture toward the old picture. When Publisher displays a pink boundary, lift your finger away from the screen or release the mouse button. It is a good idea to swap pictures that have the same orientation. ***Why?*** *Pictures with the same orientation as the template fit the area better and are not scaled disproportionately.* **Portrait** pictures are taller than they are wide. Pictures that are **landscape** oriented are wider than they tall. The following steps swap the picture on the left panel of page 1 in the brochure.

1

- Zoom to Whole Page view.
- In the scratch area, tap or click the photo you wish to use in the brochure (in this case the picture of the elephants) to display the swap icon. (Figure 2–25).

Q&A The swap icon disappeared. Did I do something wrong?

You may have moved your finger or the pointer away from the picture. Tap the picture or move the pointer back over the top of the selected picture to display the swap icon.

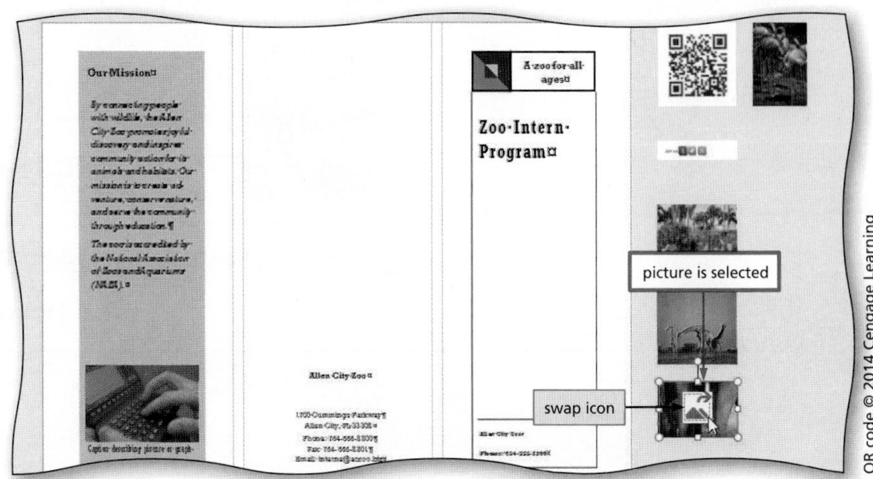

Figure 2–25

QR code © 2014 Cengage Learning

QR code © 2014 Cengage Learning

2

- From the scratch area, drag the swap icon of the photo you wish to swap to a location over a current graphic on the page. In this case, you are dragging the picture of the elephant to a location over the picture of the keyboard in the left panel. Do not lift your finger or release the mouse button (Figure 2–26).

Q&A What should I do with the other pictures?
You will use them later in the project.

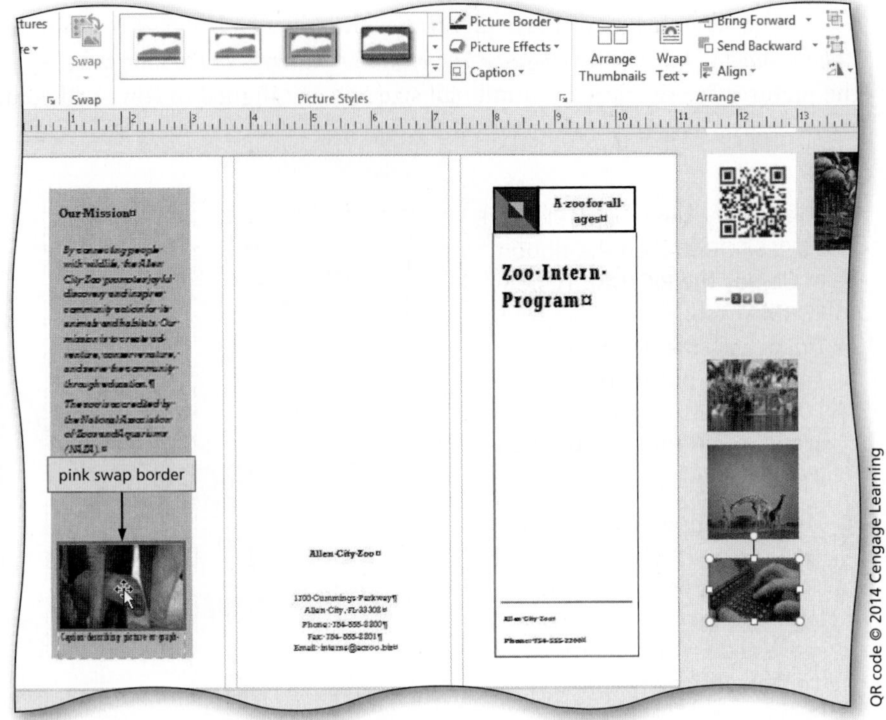

QR code © 2014 Cengage Learning

Figure 2–26

3

- When the pink boundary is displayed, lift your finger or release the mouse button to swap the pictures (Figure 2–27).

Q&A Should I edit the caption?
No, you will edit the caption later in the chapter.

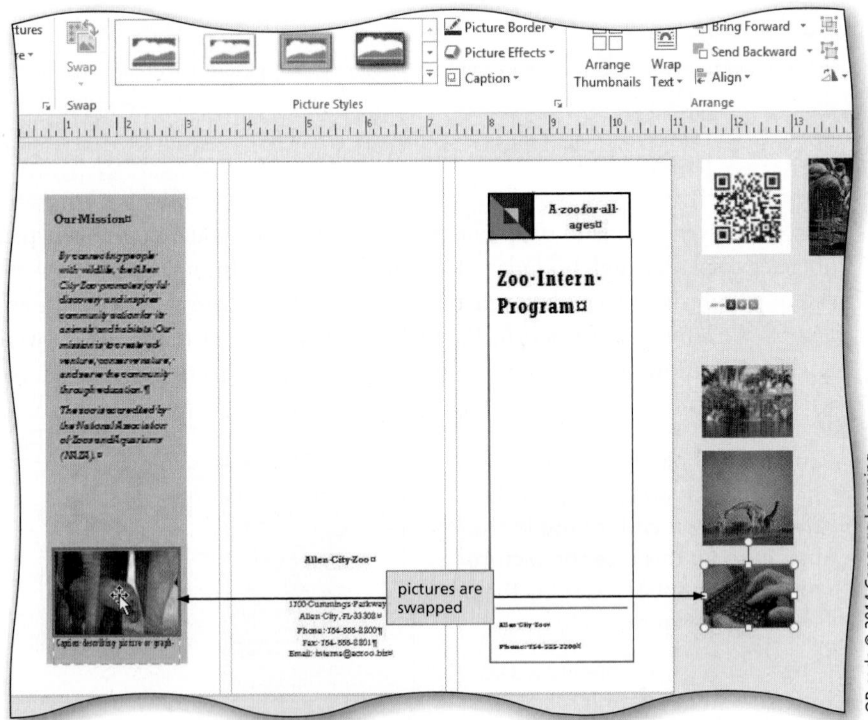

QR code © 2014 Cengage Learning

Figure 2–27

To Use a Picture as a Background

1 CUSTOMIZE BROCHURE | 2 EDIT TEXT & OBJECTS | 3 SWAP PICTURES | 4 USE FORMAT PAINTER
5 EDIT FORM | 6 USE TYPOGRAPHY | 7 INSERT CAPTIONS | 8 CHECK PUBLICATION | 9 PACK PUBLICATION

Many brochures use pictures in the background. ***Why?** A picture adds interest and removes the stark white color around objects in the brochure.* Recall that in Chapter 1 you used a gradient background for the web flyer. In this brochure, you will apply a picture to the background, using a picture from the scratch area and the shortcut menu. The following steps apply a picture to the background of page 1 of the brochure.

1

- Press and hold or right-click the picture you wish to use as a background (in this case, the Zoo Scene picture) to display the shortcut menu.
- Tap or click 'Apply to Background' to display the Apply to Background submenu (Figure 2–28).

Q&A Will the picture also be placed on page 2?
No, not unless you go to page 2 and apply it there. Each page of a publication has a unique background area.

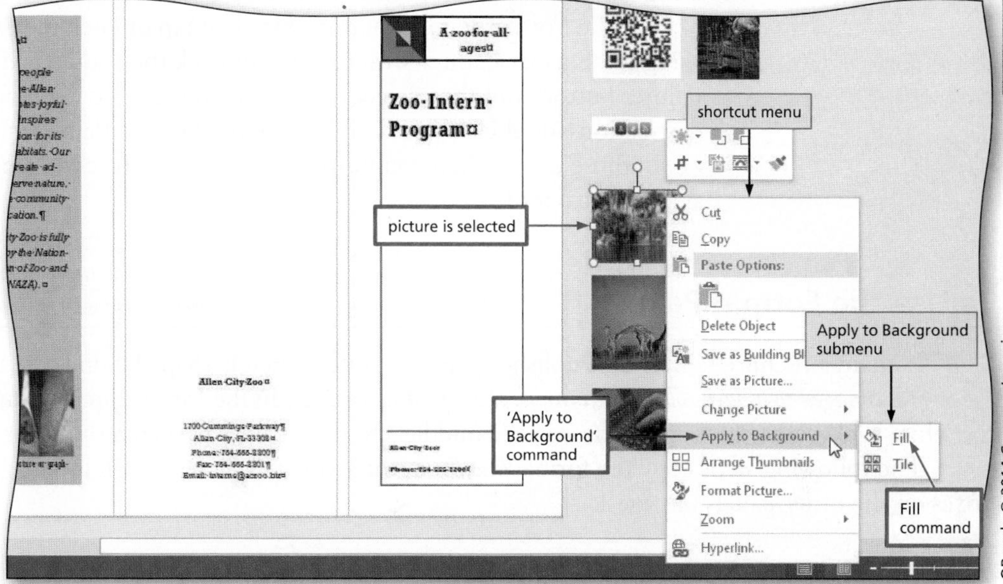

Figure 2–28

QR code © 2014 Cengage Learning

2

- Tap or click Fill on the Apply to Background submenu to place the picture in the background of the page (Figure 2–29).

Q&A Should I change the white background behind the text boxes?
You will format that later in the chapter.

Should I delete the extra vertical lines on the right panel?
The vertical lines are a rectangle that helps keep the two text box concepts together. They do not need to be deleted.

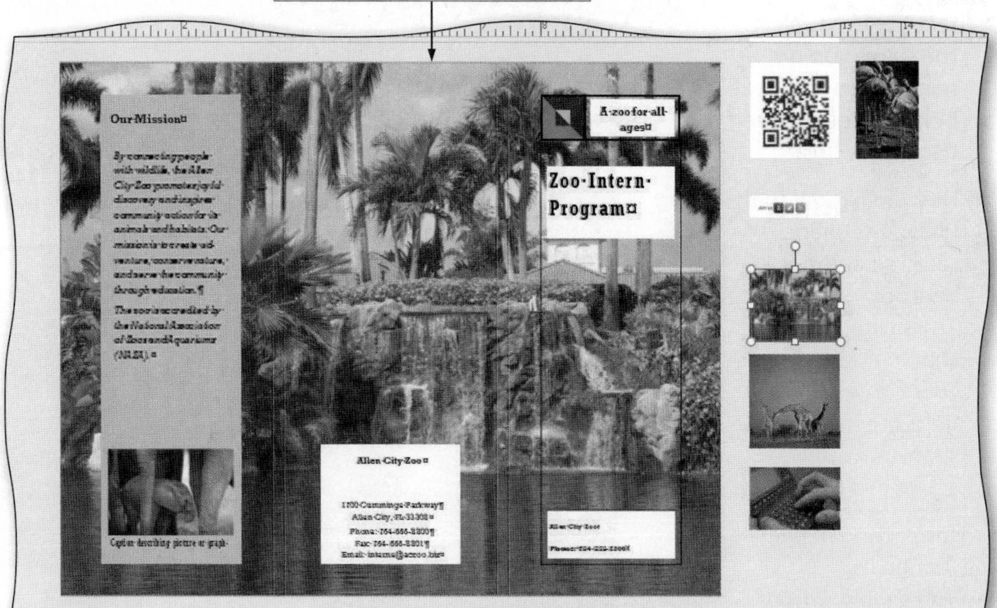

Figure 2–29

QR code © 2014 Cengage Learning
Background image courtesy of Joy Starks

Other Ways

1. Tap or click Background button (PAGE DESIGN tab | Page Background group), tap or click More Backgrounds in Background gallery, tap or click 'Picture or texture fill', tap or click File, navigate to picture, double-tap or double-click picture, tap or click OK button (Format Background dialog box)

Using the Format Painter

A convenient way to apply specific formatting is to copy the formatting from existing text or objects using the Format Painter button (HOME tab | Clipboard group). The **Format Painter** copies formatting such as color, border, font, font size, and special effects, from a **source** object (the object whose formatting you wish to copy) to a **destination** object (the object that will be reformatted to match the source). When using the Format Painter with objects, tap or click anywhere in the source object, tap or click the Format Painter button, and then tap or click the destination object. When using the Format Painter with text, tap or click the source text, tap or click the Format Painter button, and then select the destination text. To apply formatting to multiple destinations, double-tap or double-click the Format Painter button so that it stays on. In those cases, when you finish formatting, tap or click the Format Painter button again to turn it off.

To Use the Format Painter

1 CUSTOMIZE BROCHURE | 2 EDIT TEXT & OBJECTS | 3 SWAP PICTURES | **4 USE FORMAT PAINTER**
5 EDIT FORM | 6 USE TYPOGRAPHY | 7 INSERT CAPTIONS | 8 CHECK PUBLICATION | 9 PACK PUBLICATION

In many brochure templates, Publisher places a white rectangle shape behind text. ***Why?*** *If the background of the page is changed to a dark color, for example, the text still is visible.* In the Internship Brochure, you decide to change the white background of the text boxes in the middle and right panels to match the color of the left panel.

The following steps copy the formatting from the left panel shape, which is pale green, to the white text boxes on the other panels of page 1.

- In the left panel, tap or click the edge of the rectangle shape behind the text boxes to select the shape. Do not select any of the text boxes or the picture (Figure 2–30).

Q&A How do I know that I have the shape selected and not a text box?

The sizing handles should appear at the four corners of the light green rectangle shape.

Could I copy the formatting of the text box?

You should not. Besides the color, text boxes have font, font sizes, and perhaps other formatting that would be copied. In this case, you want to copy only the color from the shape.

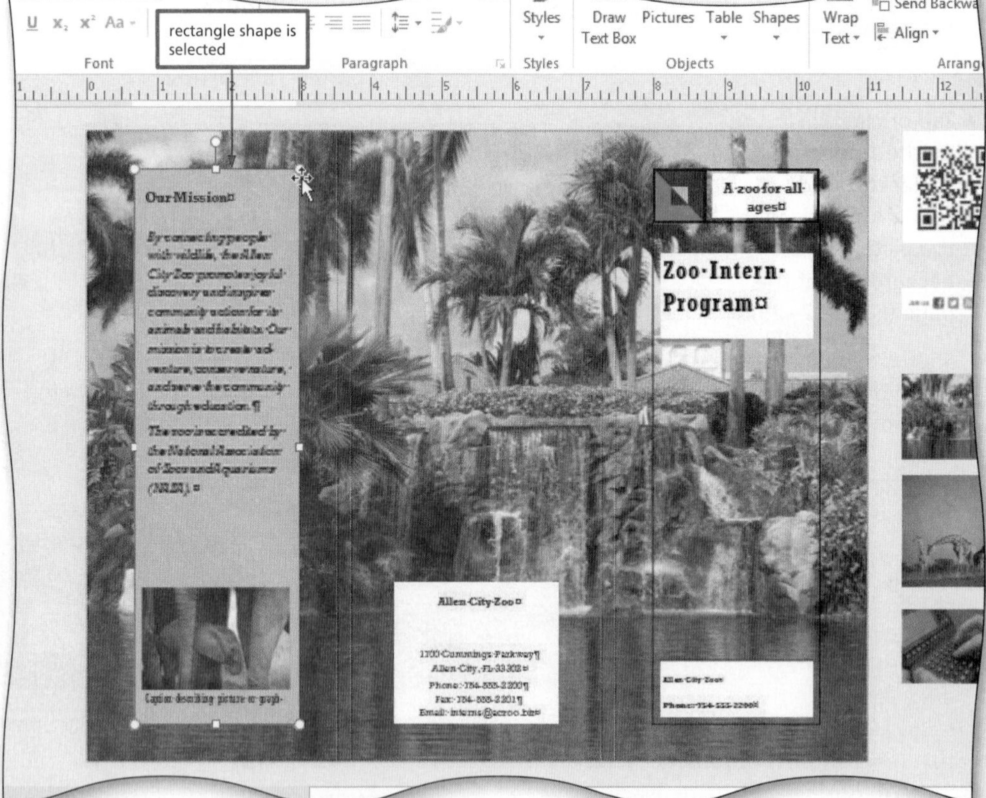

Figure 2–30

QR code © 2014 Cengage Learning
Background image courtesy of Joy Starks

2

- Double-tap or double-click the Format Painter button (HOME Tab | Clipboard group) to copy the formatting.
- Move the pointer into the workspace (Figure 2–31).

Q&A Why does the pointer display a paintbrush icon?
The pointer changes when a format has been copied. Once you turn off the Format Painter, the paintbrush icon will disappear.

Do I always have to double-tap or double-click the Format Painter button?
No. You only double-tap or double-click to apply the format to multiple locations. If you have only one place to format, a single click will do. After a single click application of formatting, the Format Painter turns off automatically.

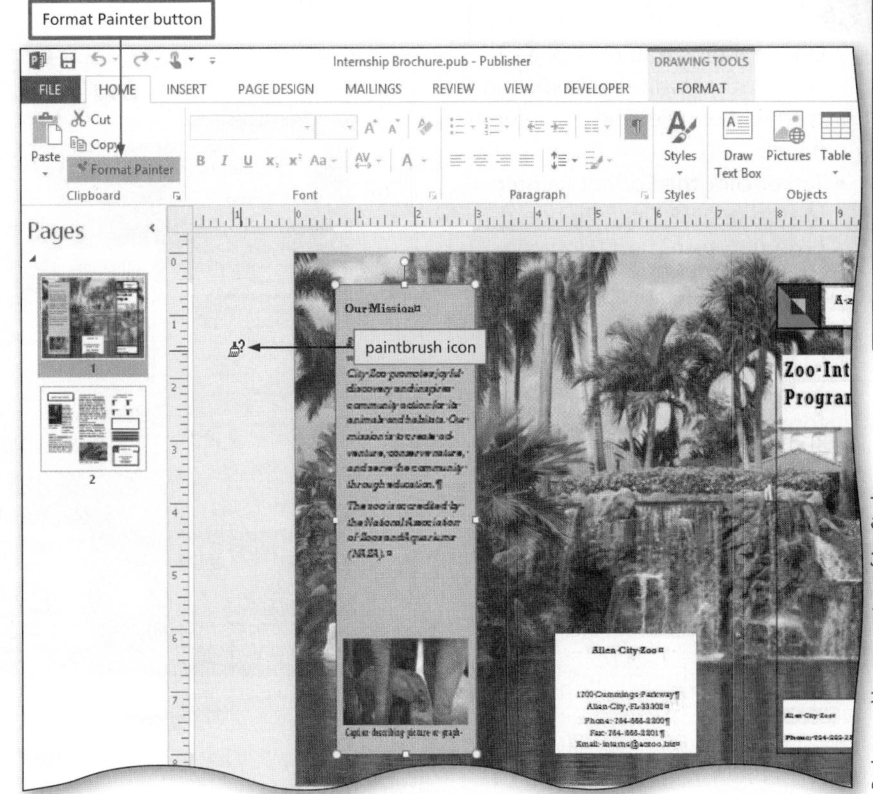

Figure 2–31

3

- Tap or click one of the white text boxes in the middle panel (Figure 2–32).

Q&A Should I try to tap or click the shape behind the text box?
Ideally, yes; however, the text boxes in the middle panel completely fill the shape behind them, making it nearly impossible to tap or click the shape alone. Formatting the text boxes with the color will achieve the same effect.

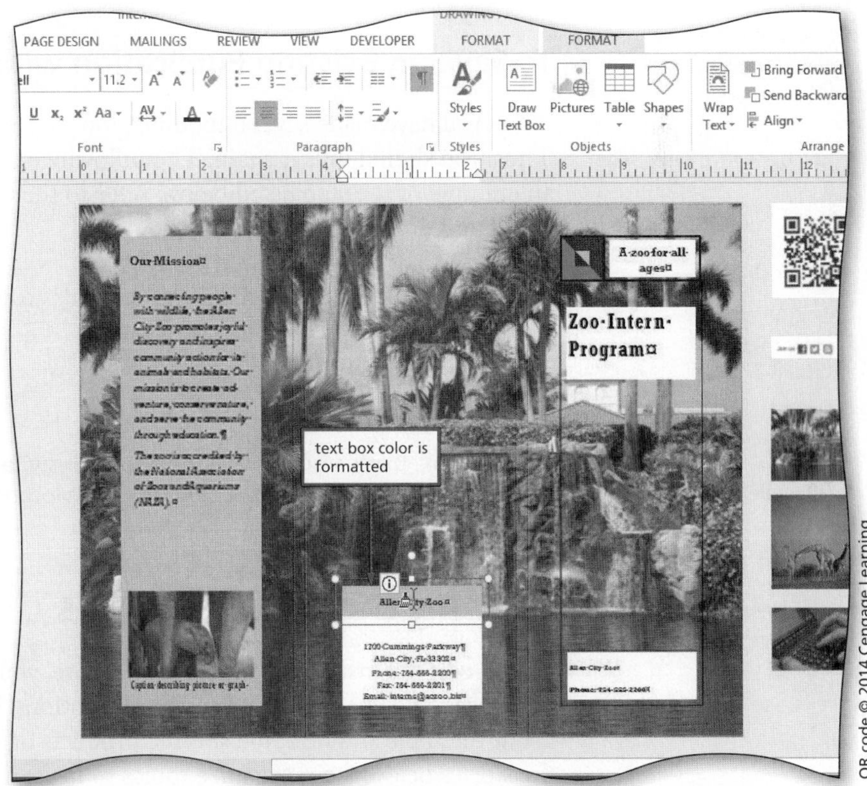

Figure 2–32

Background image courtesy of Joy Starks

QR code © 2014 Cengage Learning
Background image courtesy of Joy Starks

- One at a time, tap or click each of the other white text boxes in the middle panel and in the right panel.
- Tap or click the Format Painter button (HOME Tab | Clipboard group) to turn it off (Figure 2–33).

Q&A Can I use the Format Painter button on objects other than shapes?
Yes. You can copy applied formatting of text, a graphic, WordArt, shapes, fills, or any object from the Design Gallery. If you can change an object's style or set its formatting options, you can copy the formatting from that object to another.

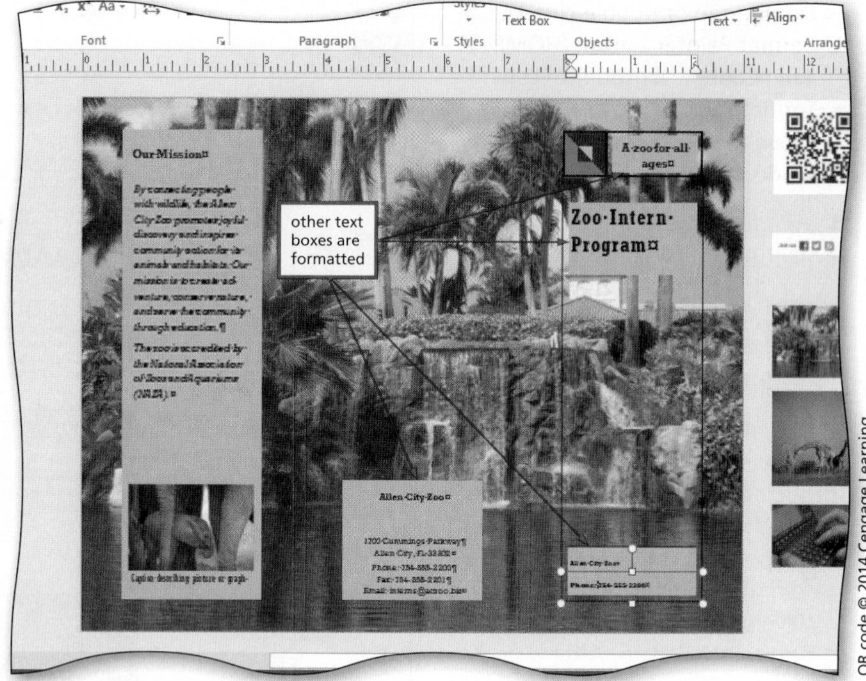

Figure 2–33

QR code © 2014 Cengage Learning
Background image courtesy of Joy Starks

Other Ways

1. Select source, press and hold or right-click selection, tap or click Format Painter button on mini toolbar, tap or click destination

To Save an Existing Publication with the Same File Name

You have made several modifications to the publication since you last saved it. Thus, you should save it again. The following step saves the publication again. For an example of the step listed below, refer to the Office and Windows chapter at the beginning of this book.

 Tap or click the Save button on the Quick Access Toolbar to overwrite the previously saved file.

Break Point: If you wish to take a break, this is a good place to do so. To resume at a later time, run Publisher, open the file called Internship Brochure, and continue following the steps from this location forward.

Editing the Inside Panels of a Brochure

As you edit the inside panels of the brochure, you will change text, edit the form text boxes, and change the pictures and captions. Headings introduce information about the topic and describe specific products or services. Secondary headings and the stories below them organize topics to make it easier for readers to understand the information.

To Switch to Page 2

The following step uses the Page Navigation pane to move to page 2. ***Why?*** *The Page Navigation pane is the only way to move among pages by tapping or clicking; however, you can press the* F5 *key and enter the new page number.*

1

- Tap or click the Page 2 icon in the Page Navigation pane to display page 2.
- If necessary, zoom to Whole Page view (Figure 2–34).

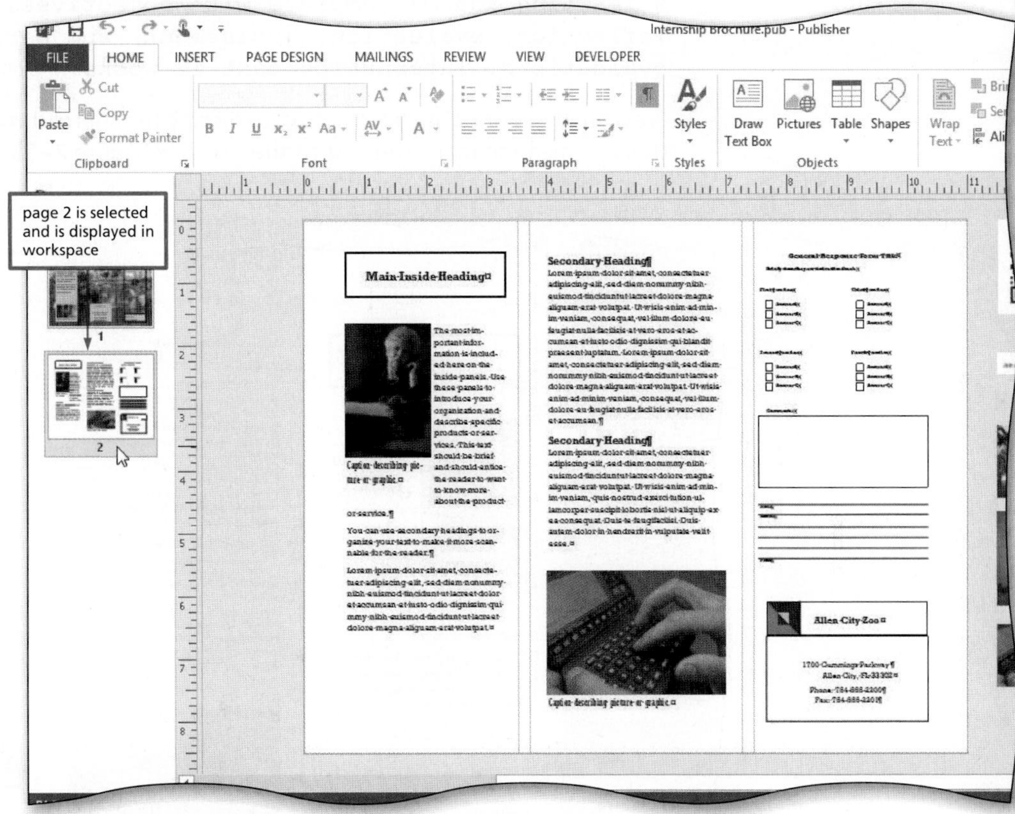

Figure 2–34

Other Ways

1. Press F5, enter page number, tap or click OK button

To Edit the Left Panel on Page 2

The following steps edit the text on the left panel of page 2. As you edit the text, zoom and scroll as necessary to view the text.

1. In the left panel of page 2, tap or click the placeholder text in the Main Inside Heading text box to select it.
2. Type **`Internships`** to complete the heading.
3. Tap or click the placeholder text for the story in the left panel.
4. Type **`Our internship experience is an exciting and educational opportunity for students to participate in various departments at Allen City Zoo. Our interns achieve learning goals associated with their field of study.`** and then press the ENTER key to create the first paragraph.

5. Type `Interns are monitored carefully by their managers to ensure that they have active opportunities to participate in a wide variety of learning experiences. The zoo works to meet the academic credit requirements of the intern's educational institution. The program features a learning agenda complete with objectives, observation, reflection, evaluation, assessment, and periodic performance evaluations. Internships last 12 weeks.`

6. Press and hold or right-click the text to display the shortcut menu. Click Best Fit on the shortcut menu to make the text fit the text box (Figure 2–35).

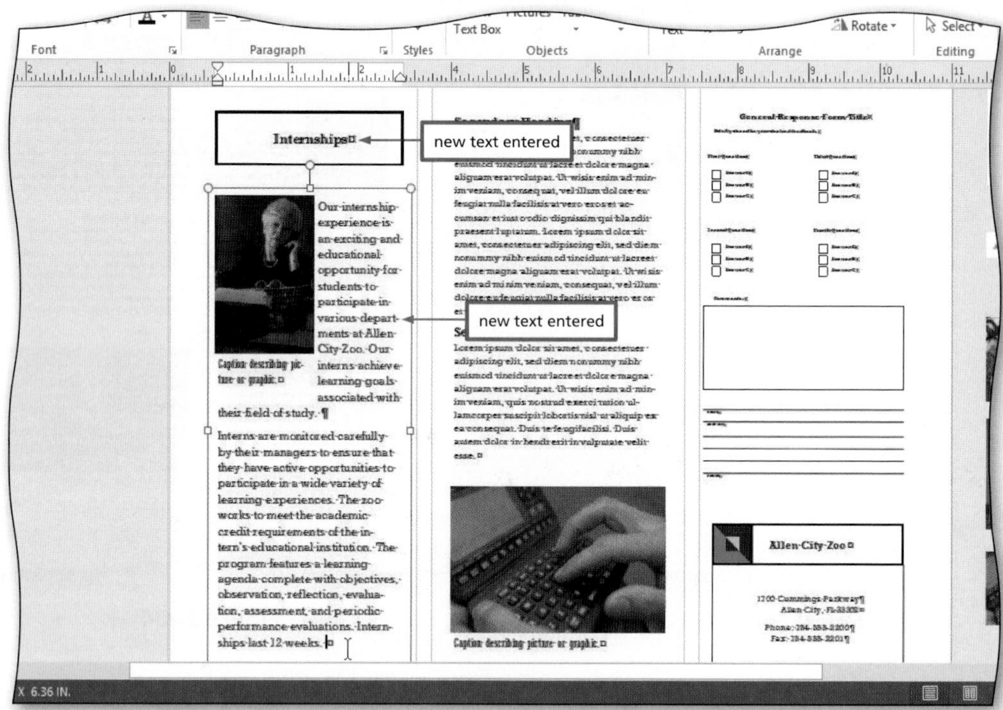

Figure 2–35

To Edit the Middle Panel on Page 2

The following steps edit the text in the middle panel of page 2. As you edit the text, zoom and scroll as necessary to view the text. Later in the chapter, you will format the text.

1. In the middle panel of page 2, tap or click the first Secondary Heading placeholder text in the middle panel to select it.

2. Type `Animal Training Internship` to complete the text.

3. Tap or click the story below the heading to select the placeholder text.

4. Type `Animal training interns establish a working relationship with the animals. Responsibilities include providing enrichment for the animals, presenting animal encounters to the public, researching and reviewing enrichment data, and assisting education staff with the show animals. Interns with prior animal handling experience will be given priority.`

5. Tap or click the second Secondary Heading placeholder text on the middle panel to select it.

6. Type `Marketing Internship` to complete the text.

7. Tap or click the story below the heading to select the placeholder text.

8. Type `Marketing interns are responsible for working with all areas of the zoo, and with media, corporate, and community partners to increase public awareness, promote programs, plan special events, and coordinate corporate engagement. Allen City Zoo is seeking motivated individuals with good communication, computer, and writing skills.` and then press the ENTER key to finish the paragraph.

9. Type `General Education Internship` and then press the ENTER key to create a third heading.

10. Type `General education interns work to develop and improve educational opportunities for zoo patrons by contributing to the development and evaluation of new curriculum, including distance learning, outreach, and on-grounds programming.` (Figure 2–36).

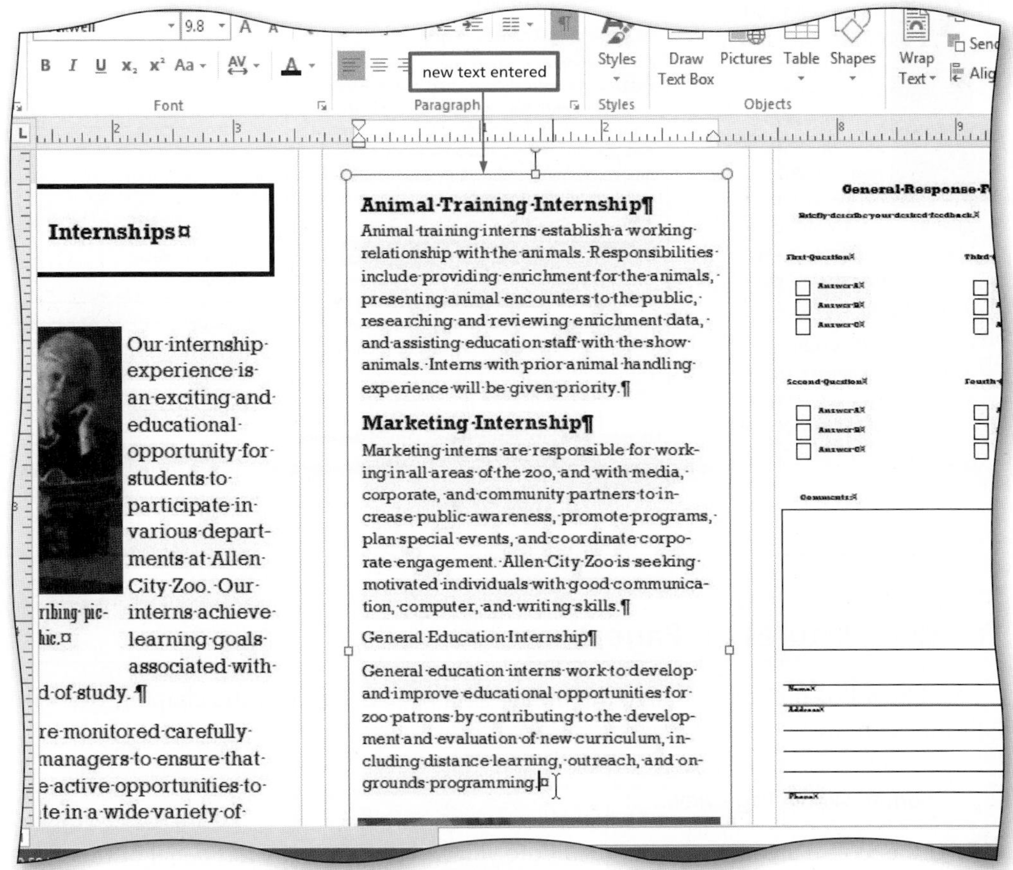

Figure 2–36

BTW

Touch Screen Differences

The Office and Windows interfaces may vary if you are using a touch screen. For this reason, you might notice that the function or appearance of your touch screen differs slightly from this chapter's presentation.

To Copy the Heading Format

The following steps use the Format Painter to copy the heading format to the third heading in the middle panel.

1. Tap or click the heading, Animal Training Internship, to specify the source of the formatting style.
2. Tap or click the Format Painter button (HOME Tab | Clipboard group) to copy the formatting.
3. Drag through the text, General Education Internship, to paste the formatting to the third heading (Figure 2–37).

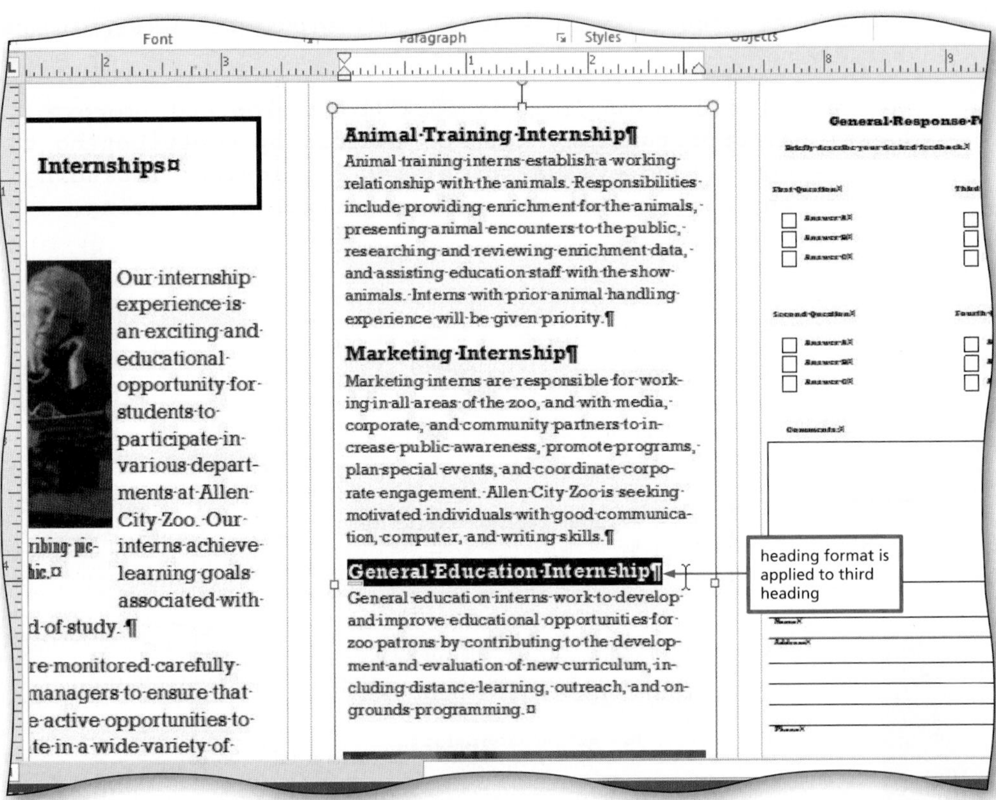

Figure 2–37

BTW

Quick Reference

For a table that lists how to complete the tasks covered in this book using touch gestures, the mouse, ribbon, shortcut menu, and keyboard, see the Quick Reference Summary at the back of this book, or visit the Quick Reference resource on the Student Companion Site located on www.cengagebrain.com. For detailed instructions about accessing available resources, visit www.cengage.com/ct/studentdownload or see the inside back cover of this book.

To Swap Pictures on Page 2

The following steps change the pictures on page 2. Later in the chapter, you will edit the captions.

1. Zoom to Whole Page view.
2. In the scratch area, tap or click the photo you wish to use in the left panel of the brochure (in this case, the picture of the flamingos) to display the swap icon.
3. From the scratch area, drag the swap icon of the photo to a location over the graphic in the left panel. When you see a pink boundary, drop the picture.
4. Repeat steps 2 and 3 swapping the giraffes picture with the picture of the keyboard in the middle panel (Figure 2–38).

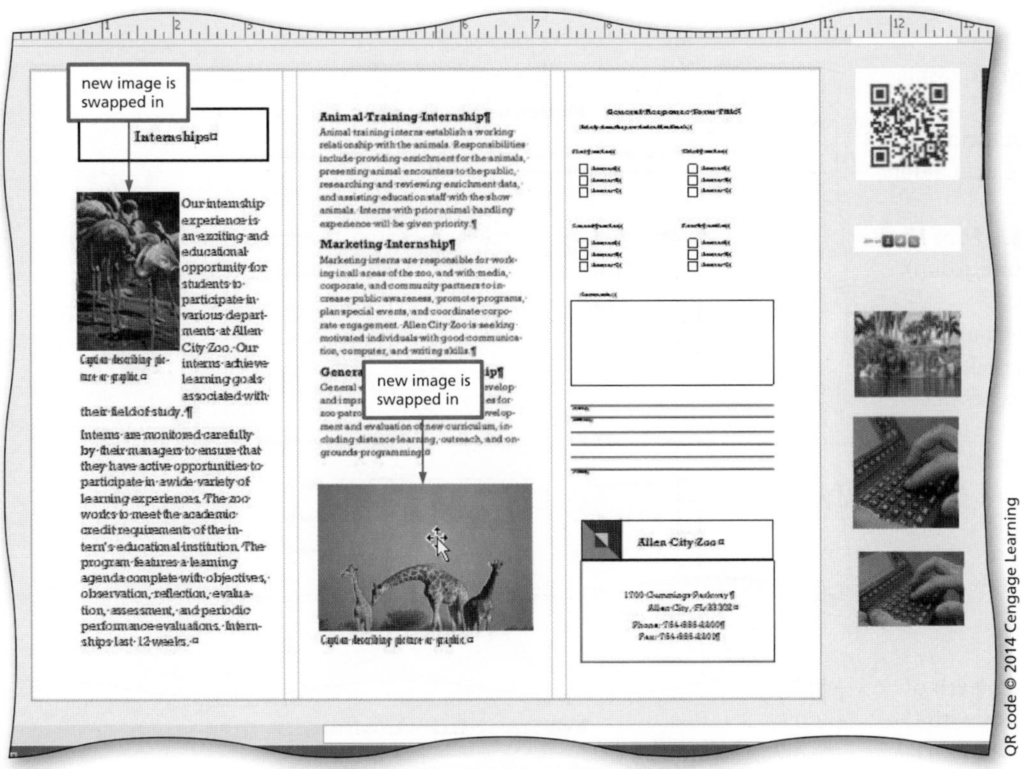

Figure 2–38

BTW

Using Forms

Each form contains blanks for the name and address of prospective customers or clients. A company not only verifies the marketing power of its brochure, it also is able to create a customer database with the information.

To Edit the Form

Publisher forms consist of text boxes, graphic boxes, and lines grouped together in an attractive and usable format. As you edit the text in the text boxes, you may have to tap or click the check box text twice to select the placeholder text. ***Why?*** *The check boxes consist of a graphic and a text box grouped together; if you tap or click the text, the placeholder text will be selected. However, if you tap or click on the square shape, the check box will be selected. You will have to tap or click the text again to select the placeholder text.*

The following steps edit the text boxes and check boxes in the form in the right panel of page 2.

1

- On the right panel of page 2, tap or click the text in the General Response Form Title text box to select the placeholder text.
- Stretch or click the Zoom In button on the status bar to zoom to approximately 200%.
- Type **For more information...** to complete the text.
- Tap or click the instruction text box below the heading to select the placeholder text.
- Type **Fill out the following form and send it to our Human Resources Department at the address listed below.** to finish entering the text (Figure 2–39).

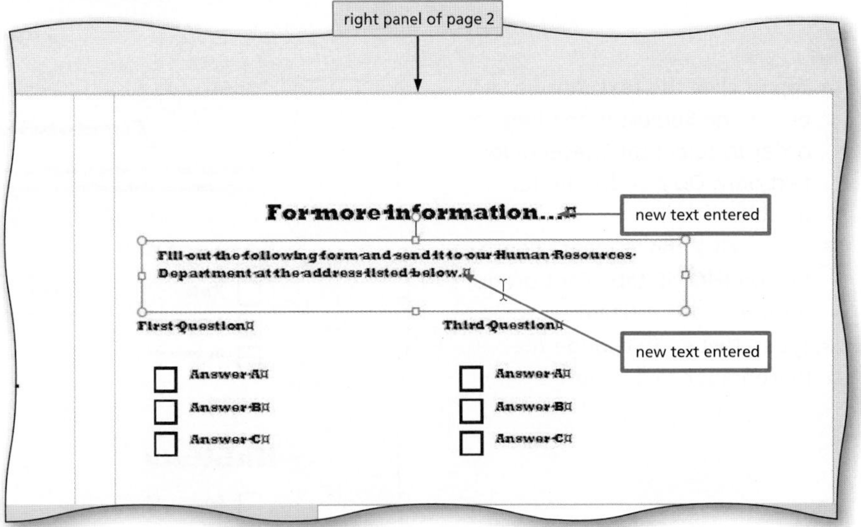

Figure 2–39

2

- If necessary, scroll down to display the check box area.
- Tap or click the First Question heading to select the placeholder text.
- Tap or click the 'Increase Font Size' button (HOME tab | Font group) until the font is size 9.
- Type `Semester` to change the heading and then click outside the text box to deselect it (Figure 2–40).

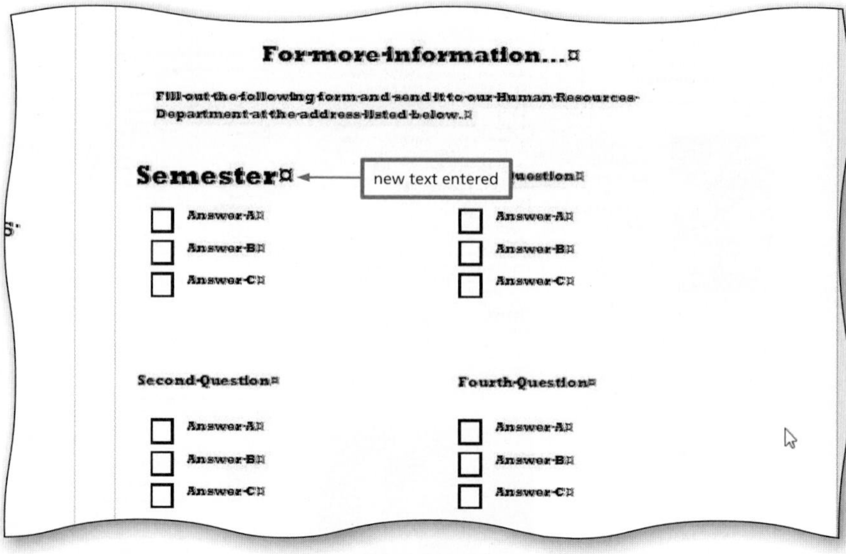

Figure 2–40

3

- Repeat Step 2 to replace each of the other three headings with the headings shown in Figure 2–41.

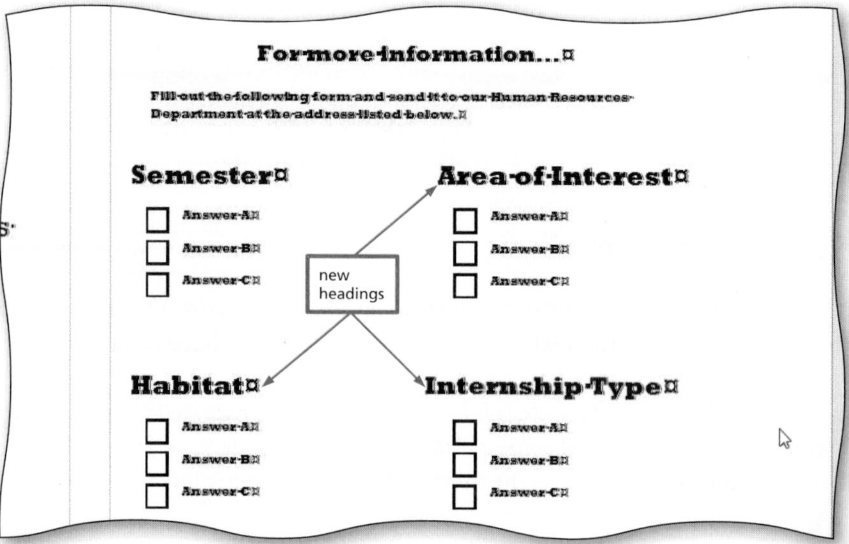

Figure 2–41

4

- Tap or click the text, Answer A, below the Semester heading, in order to select the placeholder text only. Do not double-tap or double-click.
- Tap or click the 'Increase Font Size' button (HOME tab | Font group) until the font is size 6.
- Type `Fall` to change the placeholder text (Figure 2–42).

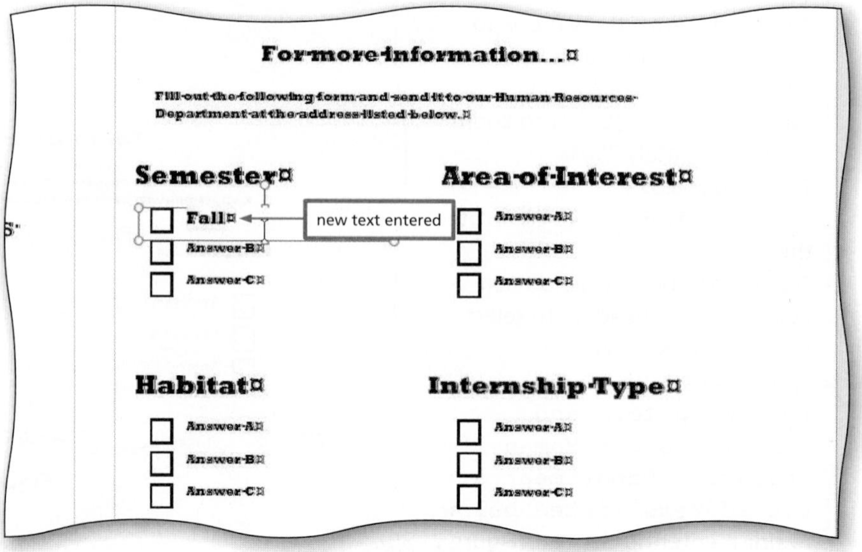

Figure 2–42

5

- Repeat Step 4 for each of the other 11 choices as shown in Figure 2–43. If necessary, resize the Large animal compound text box, so that all of the text is displayed.

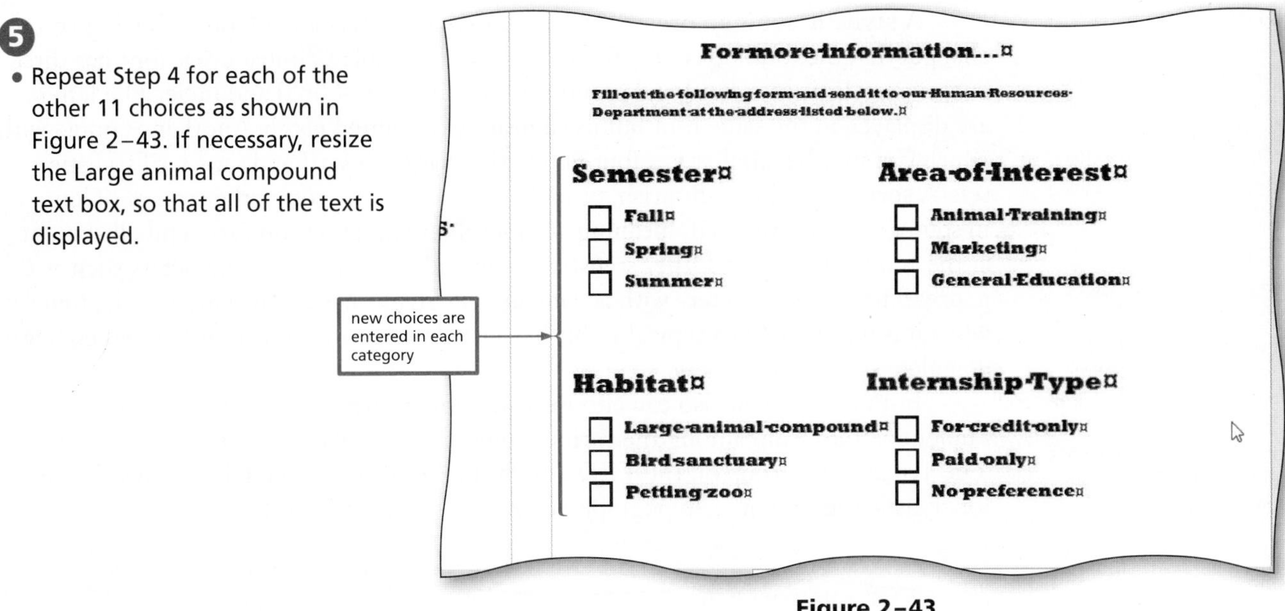

Figure 2–43

To Save an Existing Publication with the Same File Name

You have made several modifications to the publication since you last saved it. Thus, you should save it again. The following step saves the publication again. For an example of the step listed below, refer to the Office and Windows chapter at the beginning of this book.

1 Tap or click the Save button on the Quick Access Toolbar to overwrite the previously saved file.

BTW
Character Typography
Typography also includes scaling, tracking, and kerning of characters. You will learn about these spacing options in a future chapter.

Break Point: If you wish to take a break, this is a good place to do so. To resume at a later time, run Publisher, open the file called Internship Brochure, and continue following the steps from this location forward.

Typography

In Publisher, **typography** refers to specialized effects and fonts, including stylistic sets, drop caps, number styles, and glyphs. A **glyph** is a special stroke that appears in text that is not part of the normal font set. Diacritical marks, such as the umlaut (ä) or cedilla (ç), use glyphs. Ligatures, stylistic sets, swashes, and stylistic alternates, as well as some alphabetic characters that are not part of the English language, also are created with glyphs (Figure 2–44).

BTW
Swashes
A swash is an exaggerated serif or glyph that typically runs into the space above or below the next letter. Some swashes can cause an unattractive appearance when used with adjacent descending letters such as g, j, or y; however, when used correctly, a swash produces a flowing, linear appearance that adds interest to the font.

Figure 2–44

BTW
Serif Fonts
Serif fonts are considered Oldstyle when they display a slanted serif. Fonts are considered Modern when they use horizontal serifs.

BTW
Stylistic Alternate Sets
If you use a script font that looks like cursive writing, a stylistic alternate can simulate handwriting by using of a set of randomly chosen glyphs with slight differences in appearance.

A **stylistic set** is an organized set of alternate letters and glyphs, allowing you to change what the font looks like. Besides its regular display, almost every font has three common stylistic sets: bold, italic, and the combination of bold and italic. The letters are displayed in the same font but use a heavier or slanted glyph. Another example with which you may be familiar is a font family that has both serif and sans serif stylistic sets. A **serif** is small line, flourish, or embellishment, that crosses the strokes of letters in some fonts. A **sans serif**, meaning without flourish, set has no extra embellishment at the end of characters. Other stylistic sets include alternates for characters such as e, j, g, or y. The extra characters with accompanying glyphs have to be a part of the font set when it is installed. On a typical Publisher installation only a few font families contain complete stylistic sets.

In Publisher, you also can choose a **stylistic alternate** set, which creates a random pattern from among the various stylistic sets available for the current font. The Typography group on the TEXT BOX TOOLS FORMAT tab displays choices for stylistic sets and other typography commands (Figure 2–45).

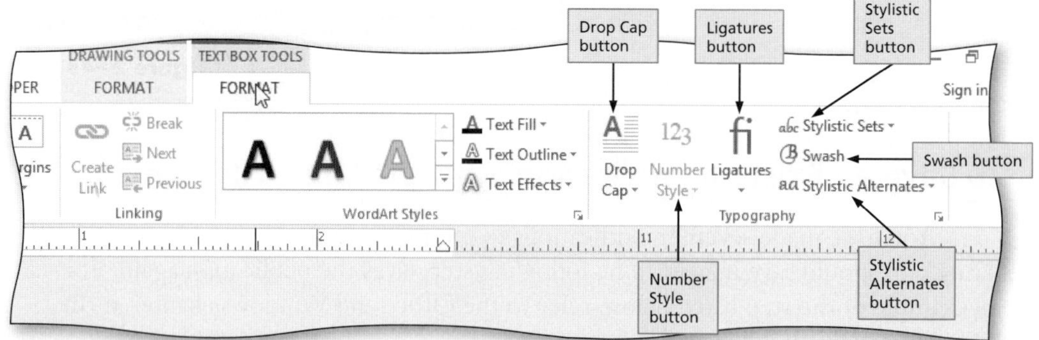

Figure 2–45

To Edit the Font Family

1 CUSTOMIZE BROCHURE | 2 EDIT TEXT & OBJECTS | 3 SWAP PICTURES | 4 USE FORMAT PAINTER
5 EDIT FORM | 6 USE TYPOGRAPHY | 7 INSERT CAPTIONS | 8 CHECK PUBLICATION | 9 PACK PUBLICATION

Recall that in Chapter 1 you formatted text with bold, underline, and italics. You also increased the font size of text. In the following steps you will change the font itself. ***Why?*** *The Gabriola font family has a wide variety of stylistic sets.*

1

- On page 2, drag to select the heading, For more information..., in the right panel.
- Tap or click the Font arrow (HOME tab | Font group) to display the Font gallery (Figure 2–46).

Experiment

- Point to each of the font names and watch the live preview.

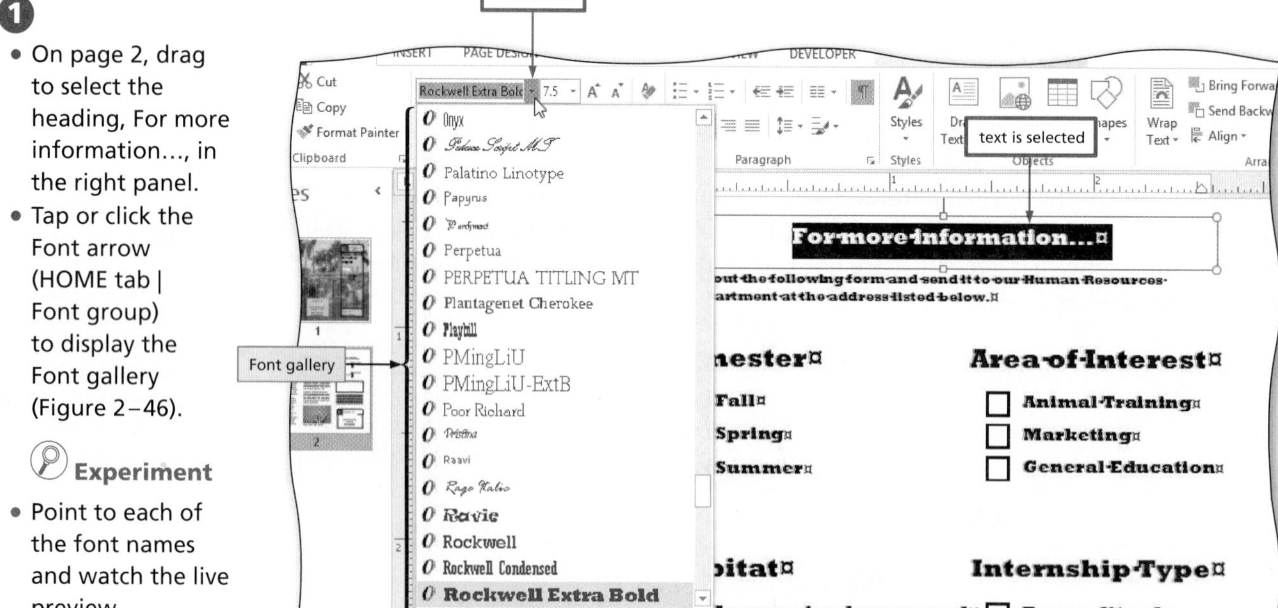

Figure 2–46

2

- Scroll to display the desired font (in this case, Gabriola), and then tap or click the font name to choose the font.
- Do not deselect the heading text (Figure 2–47).

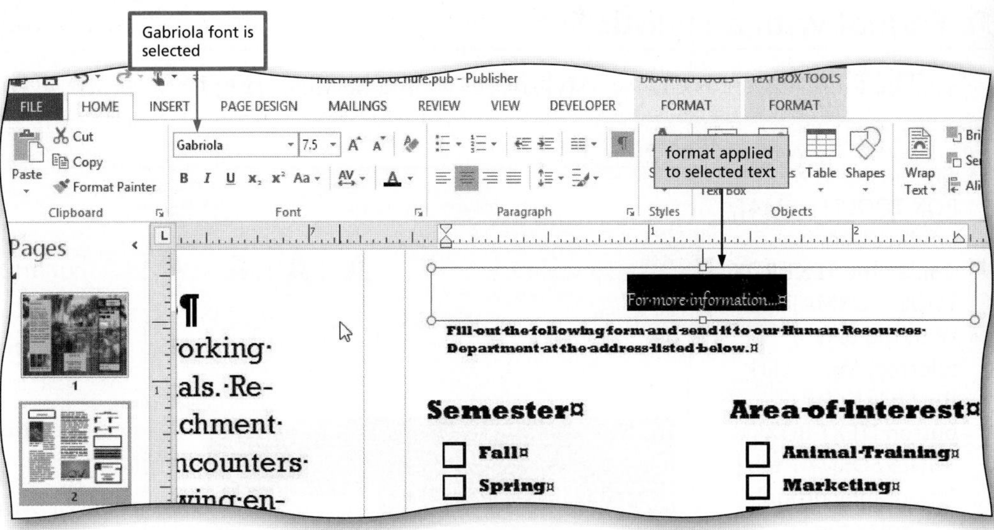

Figure 2–47

Other Ways

1. Tap or click Font arrow on mini toolbar, select desired font
2. Press and hold or right-click selected text, tap or click Change Text on shortcut menu, tap or click Font on Change Text menu, tap or click desired font in Font list (Font dialog box), tap or click OK button
3. Tap or click Font Dialog Box Launcher (HOME tab | Font group), tap or click desired font in Font list (Font dialog box), tap or click OK button

To Resize the Text Box and the Font

The following steps resize the text box and increase the font size in preparation for typography changes.

1. With the text still selected, drag the upper-center sizing handle up to approximately the 1/8 inch mark on the vertical ruler to increase the size of the box.
2. Tap or click the 'Increase Font Size' button (HOME tab | Font group) several times until the Font Size box displays 22.
3. Do not deselect the text (Figure 2–48).

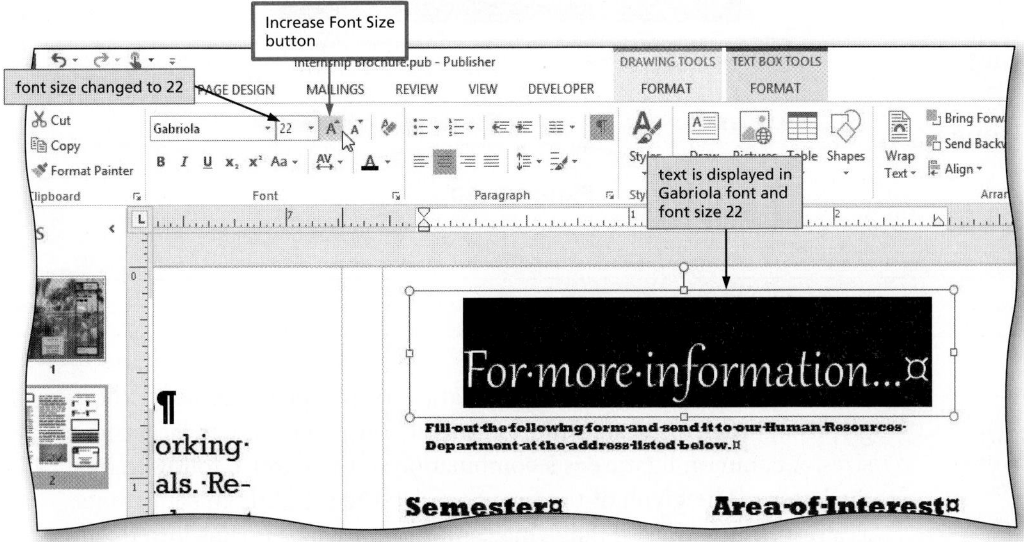

Figure 2–48

To Format with a Stylistic Set

The following steps choose a stylistic set for the heading. ***Why?*** *Stylistic sets add interest and flair to headings.*

1

- Tap or click TEXT BOX TOOLS FORMAT on the ribbon to display the TEXT BOX TOOLS FORMAT tab.
- With the text selected, tap or click the Stylistic Sets button (TEXT BOX TOOLS FORMAT tab | Typography group) to display the Stylistic Sets gallery. Scroll in the gallery to display more stylistic sets (Figure 2–49).

Experiment

- Point to each stylistic set and watch the live preview in the text box.

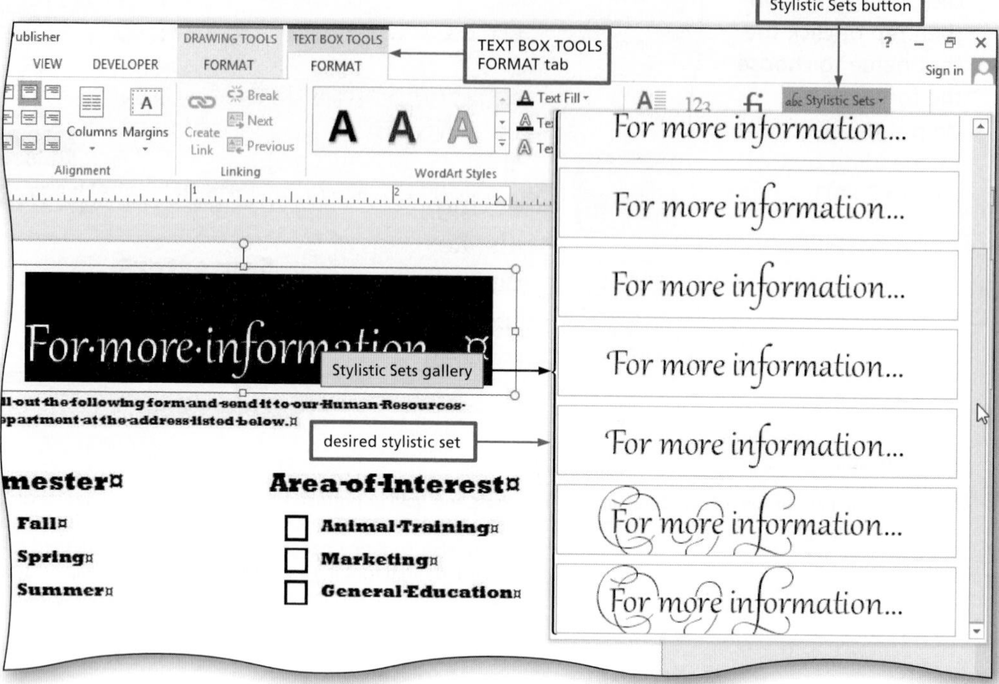

Figure 2–49

Q&A Do all fonts have fancy stylistic sets?
No, usually only **OpenType** or scalable fonts contain stylistic sets other than bold and italic.

2

- Tap or click the desired set (in this case, the third one from the bottom) to apply the stylistic set to the selected text (Figure 2–50).

Q&A Could I use one of the fancier stylistic sets?
You could, but the fancier stylistic sets with large glyphs will not fit in with the style of the brochure.

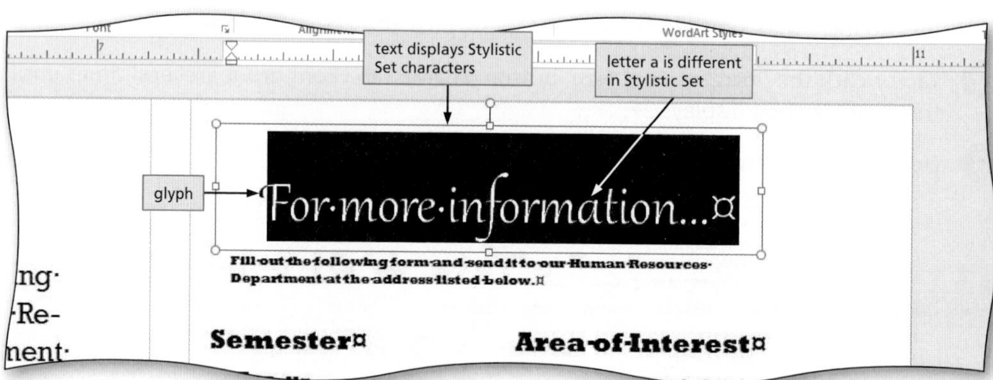

Figure 2–50

Ligatures

Ligatures are two or more characters grouped together without glyphs in order to create a more readable font, especially in larger font sizes. A common ligature is a combination of the letter f, followed by the letter i. The glyph of the f may overlap the i slightly in some fonts; as a result, an awkward bulge may appear on the f as it runs into the dot of the i. The fi ligature creates a cleaner line. Figure 2–51 shows the

BTW

Other Ligatures

The standard ligatures are fi, ffi, and fl; however, in some font families, Publisher offers discretionary ligatures that you may create, including all of the ascending letters that might follow the letter, f, as well as ligatures such as ki, th, or ae.

fi combination, first without the ligature and then with the ligature. Most ligatures turn off glyphs to improve readability. Because stylistic sets have more glyphs than standard fonts, they also have more ligatures. By default, ligatures are **enabled,** or turned on.

BTW
Ligatures
When a program automatically changes a typed fraction, for example, 1/2 to ½, it is creating a ligature for you. The 1/2 requires three spaces, whereas the ½ requires only one.

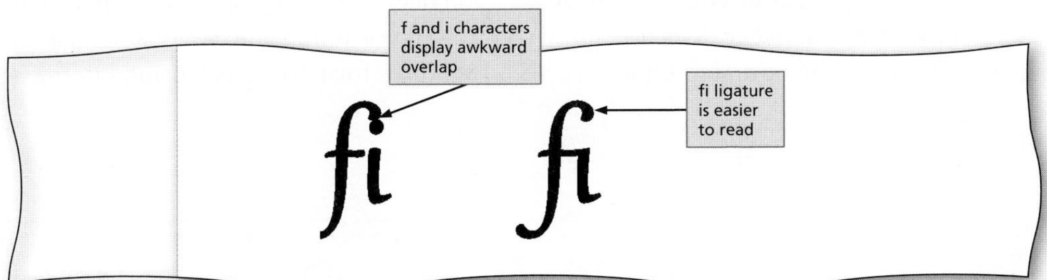

Figure 2–51

To Examine Ligatures

1 CUSTOMIZE BROCHURE | 2 EDIT TEXT & OBJECTS | 3 SWAP PICTURES | 4 USE FORMAT PAINTER
5 EDIT FORM | 6 USE TYPOGRAPHY | 7 INSERT CAPTIONS | 8 CHECK PUBLICATION | 9 PACK PUBLICATION

The following steps look at letters with ligatures disabled. ***Why?*** *Examining ligature letters and the same letters with glyphs helps you understand the concept.*

1

- In the form heading, select the letters, atio, in the word, information.
- Tap or click the Ligatures button (TEXT BOX TOOLS FORMAT tab | Typography group) to display the Ligatures gallery (Figure 2–52).

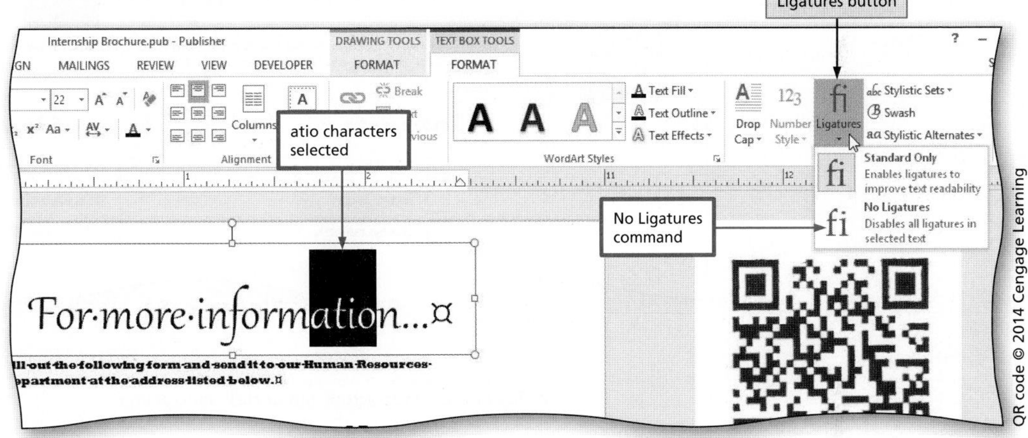

QR code © 2014 Cengage Learning

Figure 2–52

2

- Tap or click No Ligatures to disable the ligature.
- Deselect the letters to better view the effect of no ligatures (Figure 2–53).

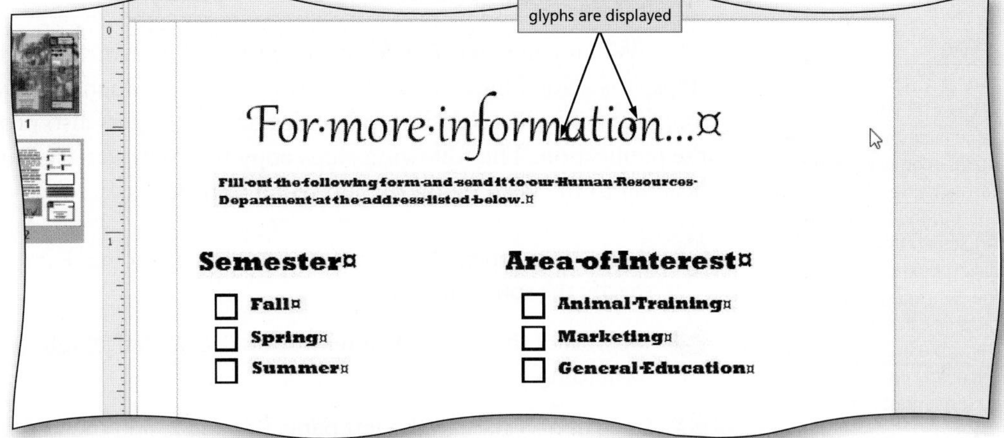

Figure 2–53

Q&A
What changed?
Without ligatures, all of the glyphs for those letters display. They run into each other, making the text more difficult to read.

Other Ways

1. Tap or click Symbol button (INSERT tab | Text group), tap or click More Symbols, tap or click desired ligature, tap or click Insert button (Symbol dialog box)

To Undo an Action

Publisher provides a means of canceling your recent command(s) or action(s). ***Why?*** *If you format text incorrectly, you can undo the format and try it again.* When you point to the Undo button, Publisher displays the action you can undo as part of a ScreenTip. If, after you undo an action, you decide you did not want to perform the undo, you can redo the undone action. Publisher does not allow you to undo or redo some actions, such as copying, saving, or printing a publication. The next step undoes the No Ligatures formatting performed in the previous steps.

1

- Click the Undo button on the Quick Access Toolbar to reverse your most recent action (in this case, disabling the ligatures) (Figure 2–54).

Experiment

- Tap or click the Undo arrow to view recent actions.

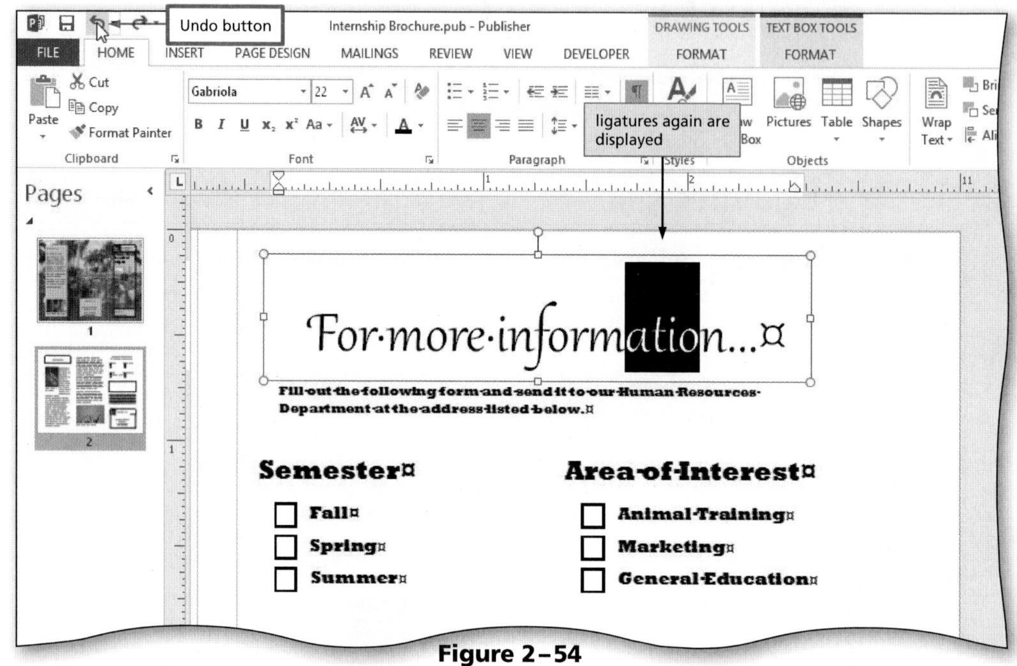

Figure 2–54

Other Ways

1. Press CTRL+Z
2. Tap or click Undo arrow, tap or click undo action

To Copy the Stylistic Set Formatting

BTW
Drop Caps
Microsoft's collection of clip art includes stylized letters that can be used as drop caps. Simply type the desired letter in the Office.com Clip Art search box (Insert Pictures dialog box) and then press the ENTER key. The selected graphic can serve as the Drop Cap for a line of text, which is placed very close to a text box that contains the rest of the text.

When you make a major change to the formatting of text, as you did in previous steps, it is a good idea to use that formatting more than once, so that it does not look like a mistake. Reusing font styles or stylistic sets also provides continuity in the publication. The following steps copy the stylistic set formatting from the form heading to the heading on the left panel of page 2.

1. If necessary, tap or click the text in the form heading, For more information... to specify the source formatting.
2. Tap or click the Format Painter button (HOME tab | Clipboard group) to copy the formatting.
3. Scroll as necessary to the left panel of page 2, and then drag to select and apply the copied format to the heading, Internships.
4. If necessary, tap or click the Center button (HOME tab | Paragraph group) to center the heading (Figure 2–55).

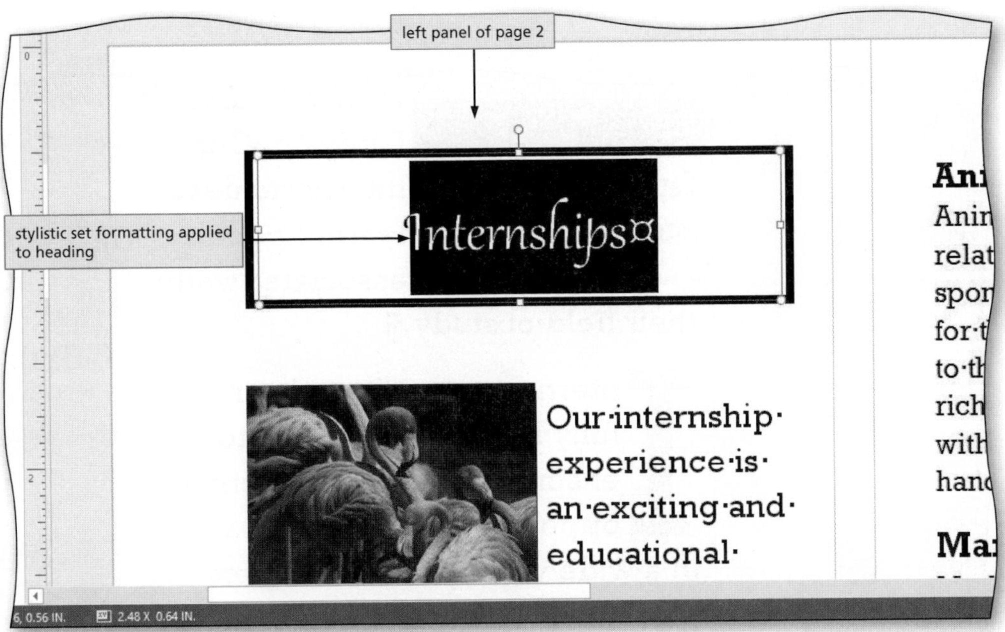

Figure 2–55

To Create a Drop Cap

A dropped capital letter, or **drop cap**, is a decorative large initial capital letter extending down below the other letters in the line. If the text wraps to more than one line, the paragraph typically wraps around the dropped capital letter. The following steps create a dropped capital letter I to begin the word, Interns, in the second paragraph. ***Why?*** *A drop cap will set off the paragraph and draw the reader's eye toward an important part of the brochure.*

1

- If necessary, scroll to the middle portion of the left panel and then tap or click to the left of the letter, I, at the beginning of the second paragraph.
- Tap or click TEXT BOX TOOLS FORMAT on the ribbon to display the TEXT BOX TOOLS FORMAT tab.
- Tap or click the Drop Cap button (TEXT BOX TOOLS FORMAT tab | Typography group) to display the Drop Cap gallery (Figure 2–56).

 **Experiment**

- Point to each of the available drop caps to preview the different styles.

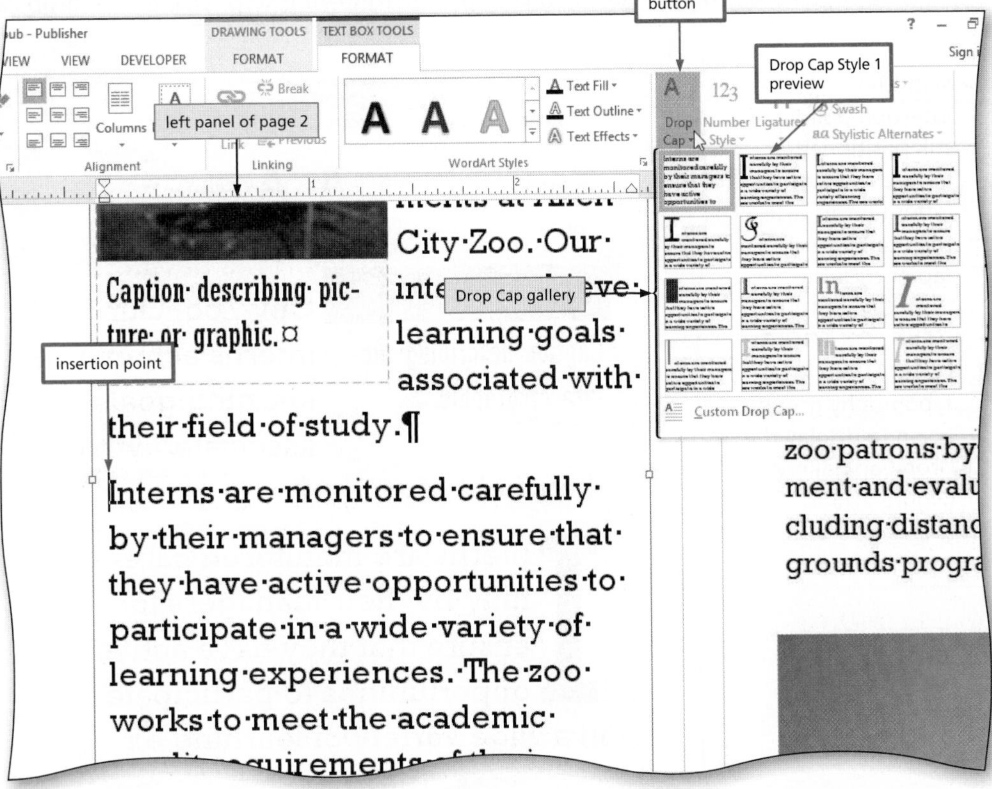

Figure 2–56

2

- Tap or click the Drop Cap Style 1 preview to select it (Figure 2–57).

Q&A Will this drop cap look inconsistent with the other fonts on the page?
The font is still Rockwell, which will match the rest of the paragraph.

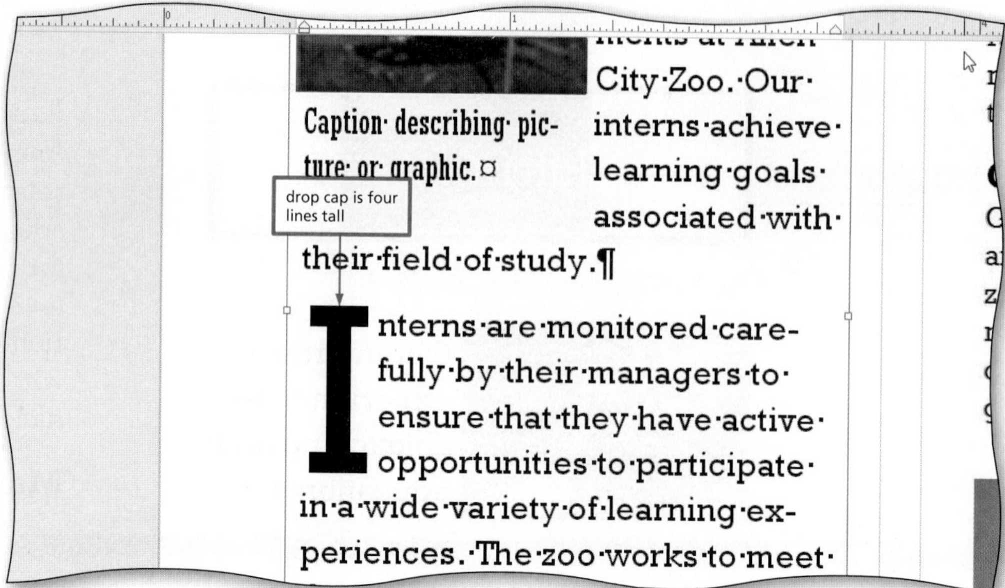

Figure 2–57

To Customize a Drop Cap

1 CUSTOMIZE BROCHURE | 2 EDIT TEXT & OBJECTS | 3 SWAP PICTURES | 4 USE FORMAT PAINTER
5 EDIT FORM | 6 USE TYPOGRAPHY | 7 INSERT CAPTIONS | 8 CHECK PUBLICATION | 9 PACK PUBLICATION

The Drop Cap dialog box allows you to customize the drop cap. You can format the number of lines in the drop cap or even change it to an **up cap**, in which the larger letter extends up above the rest of the text. You also can change the font, font style, and color of the text.

Once created, the customized style is added to the Available drop caps list. ***Why?*** *Publisher makes it available to use in other portions of the publication, if desired.* The following steps change the drop cap size to two lines.

1

- With the insertion point still positioned before the desired letter (in this case, the I of Interns), tap or click the Drop Cap button (TEXT BOX TOOLS FORMAT tab | Typography group) again to display the Drop Cap gallery (Figure 2–58).

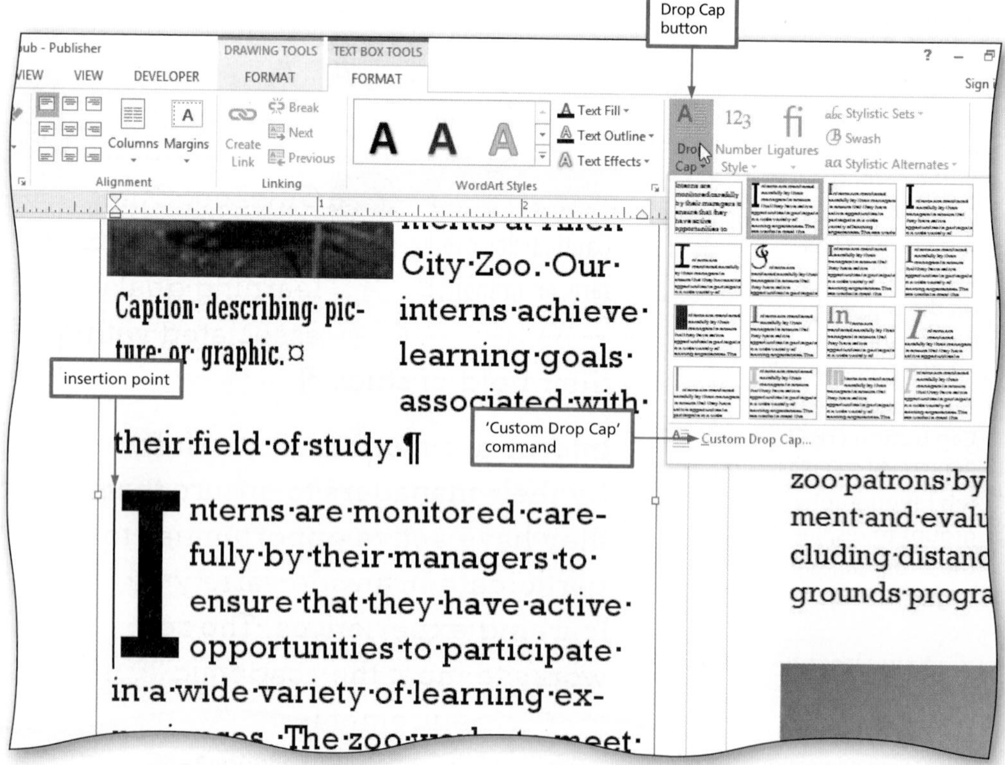

Figure 2–58

2

- Tap or click Custom Drop Cap at the bottom of the gallery to display the Drop Cap dialog box.
- Tap or click the 'Size of letters' down arrow twice, to change the height of the drop cap to 2 lines of text (Figure 2–59).

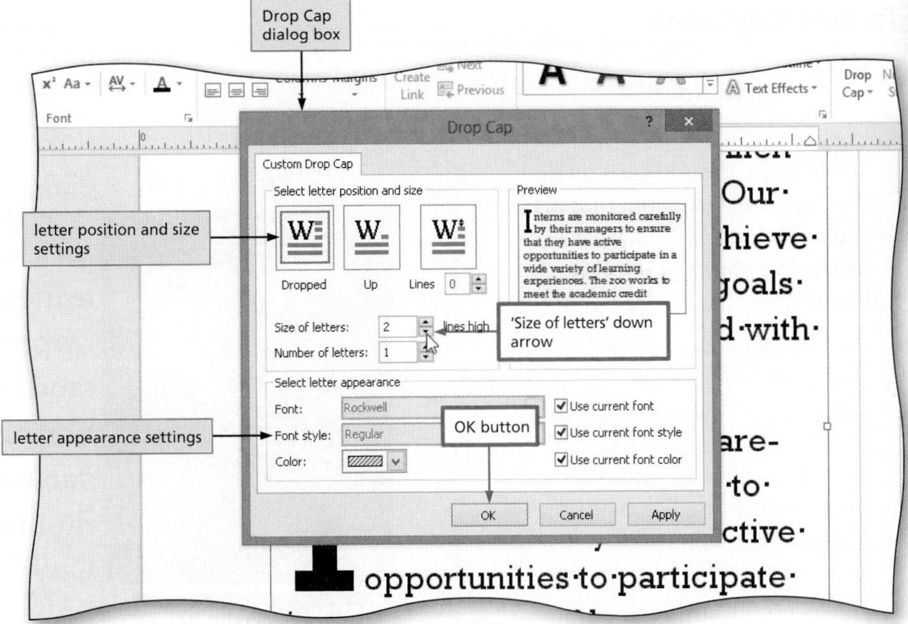

Figure 2–59

3

- Tap or click the OK button (Drop Cap dialog box) to apply the formatting (Figure 2–60).

Q&A Is a drop cap limited to a single letter?

No, you can format up to 15 contiguous letters and spaces as drop caps at the beginning of each paragraph.

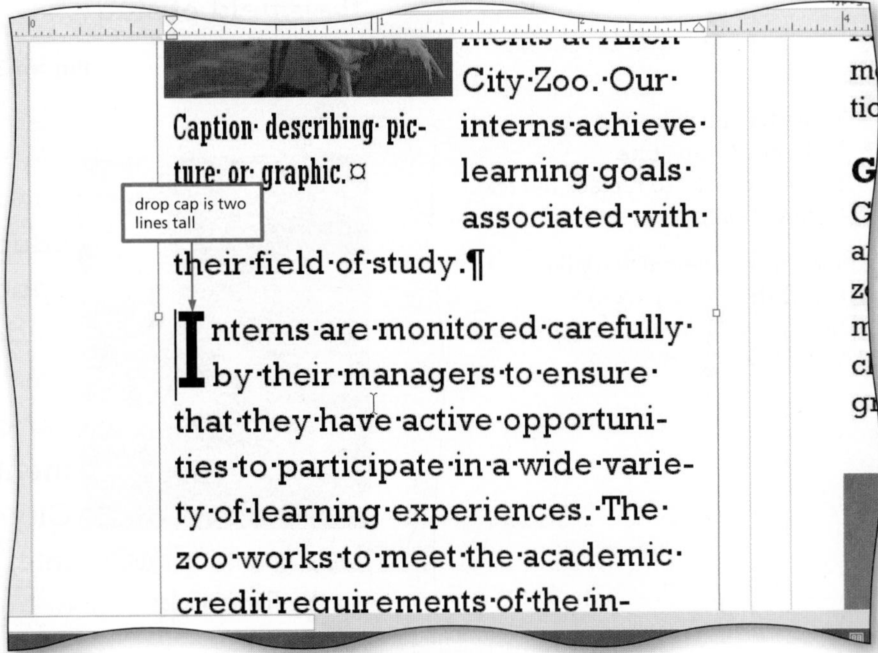

Figure 2–60

Captions

A **caption** is explanatory or identification text or a title that accompanies a graphic, figure, or photo. A caption can be as simple as a figure number, as you see in the figures of this book, or a caption can identify people, places, objects, or actions occurring in the graphic. When using Publisher templates, some captions already exist near a graphic. In those cases, the caption is a text box grouped with a graphic. If a graphic or photo does not have a caption, you can add one using the Caption gallery.

BTW

OpenType Fonts

Stylistic sets are more common in OpenType fonts. An **OpenType** font is a cross-platform, scalable font format with a wider range of characters than TrueType or PostScript fonts. If your printer can support them, OpenType fonts display a small computer icon or an uppercase O next to the font name when you tap or click the Font arrow (TEXT BOX TOOLS FORMAT tab | Font group).

To Edit Captions

The following steps edit the text in the captions on page 2. ***Why?*** *A caption explains the graphic to the reader.*

1

- Scroll to the desired caption (in this case, the left panel of page 2).
- Tap or click the caption text below the photo to select it (Figure 2–61).

Q&A Can you delete a caption?
Yes, but be sure to delete the text box as well as the text. If the caption is part of a group, tap or click once to select the group, then point to the border of the text box and tap or click to select it. Finally, press the DELETE key to delete the caption text box.

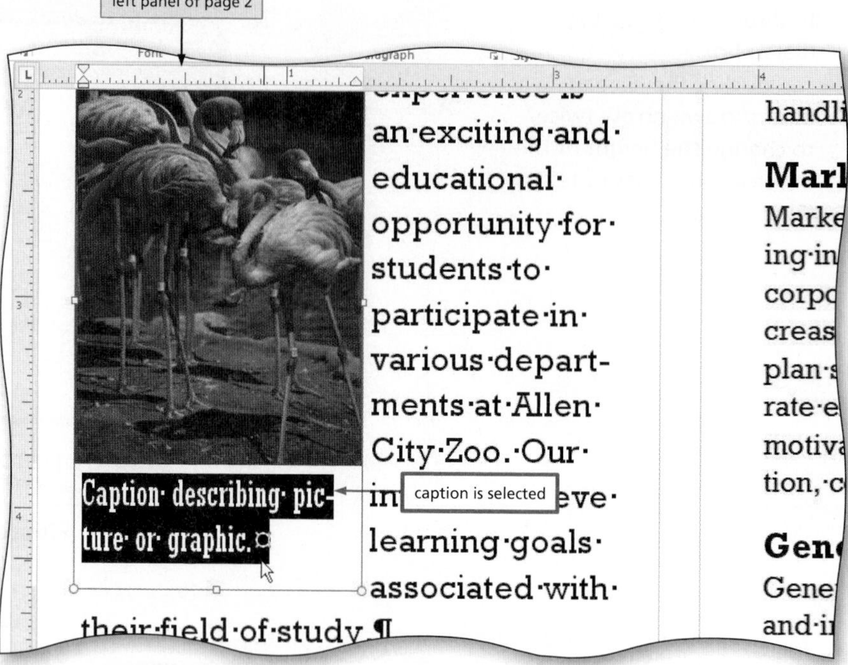

Figure 2–61

2

- Type `Learn how to "pinken" up the flamingos!` to replace the text (Figure 2–62).

Q&A Should I fix the red wavy line below the word, pinken?
No. You will run the spell checker later in the chapter.

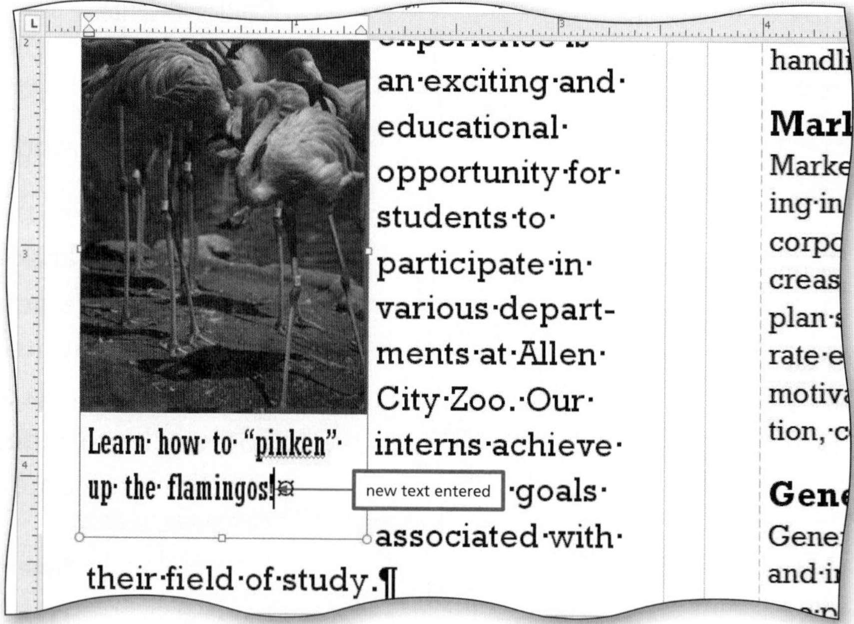

Figure 2–62

To Edit Other Captions

The following steps edit the other captions in the brochure.

1. Scroll to the caption on the middle panel of page 2.
2. Tap or click the caption text below the photo to select it.
3. Type `Giraffes in the large animal compound` to complete the caption.

4 Go to page 1 of the brochure, and select the caption text in the left panel. Zoom as necessary.

5 Type **Meet our new baby elephant!** to replace the caption. If necessary, delete the paragraph mark at the end of the caption, so that the caption contains just one line of text (Figure 2–63).

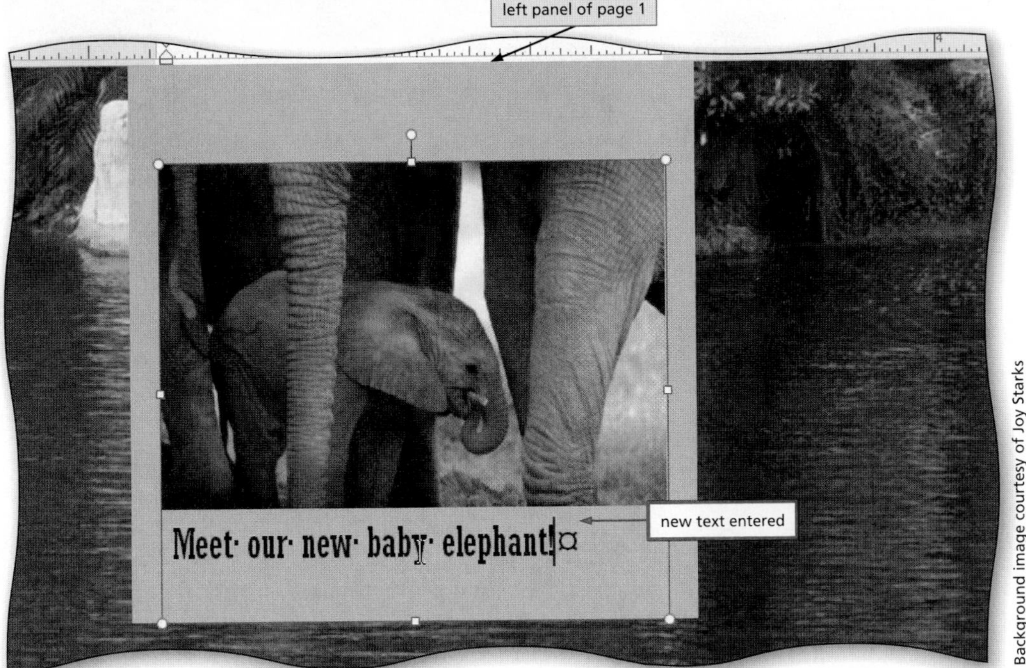

Figure 2–63

To Use the Caption Gallery

1 CUSTOMIZE BROCHURE | 2 EDIT TEXT & OBJECTS | 3 SWAP PICTURES | 4 USE FORMAT PAINTER
5 EDIT FORM | 6 USE TYPOGRAPHY | 7 INSERT CAPTIONS | **8 CHECK PUBLICATION** | **9 PACK PUBLICATION**

The following step adds a decorative caption to an existing photo using the Caption gallery. ***Why?*** *A decorative caption adds interest and color to the back panel.*

1

- Select the elephant photo above the newly added caption.
- Tap or click PICTURE TOOLS FORMAT on the ribbon to display the PICTURE TOOLS FORMAT tab.
- Tap or click the Caption button (PICTURE TOOLS FORMAT tab | Picture Styles group) to display its gallery (Figure 2–64).

Experiment

- Point to each caption style in the gallery to see its effect on the publication.

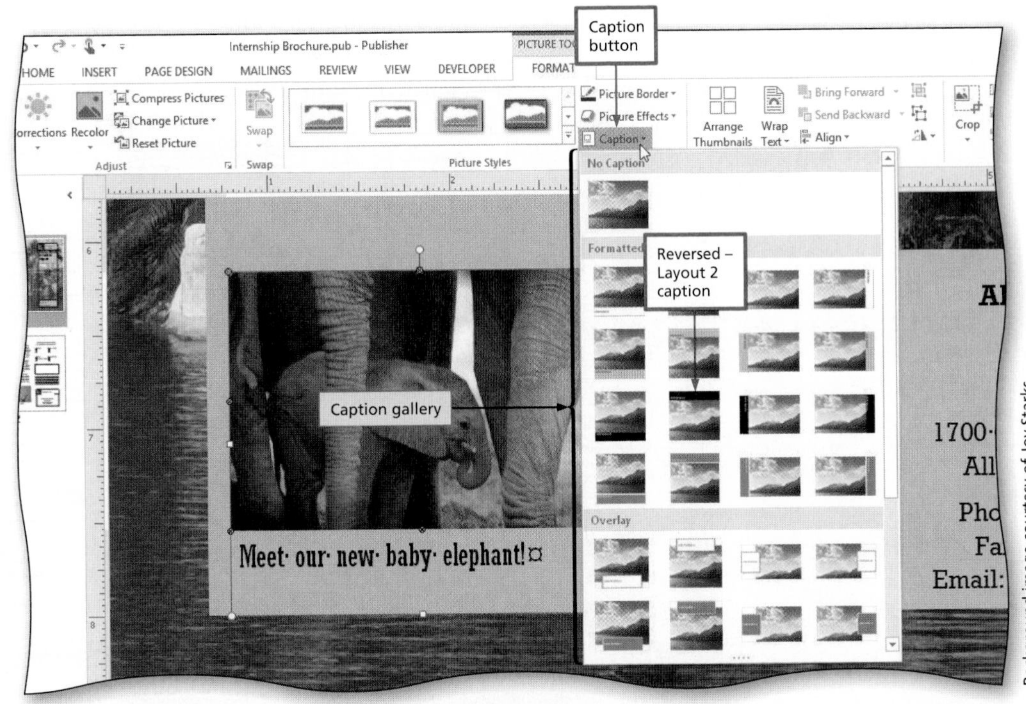

Figure 2–64

- Tap or click the Reversed – Layout 2 thumbnail (column 2, row 3) to apply the caption style to the picture (Figure 2–65).

Background image courtesy of Joy Starks

Figure 2–65

To Insert Graphics

The final new content will be to add two graphics to page 2 of the brochure as shown in the following steps.

BTW

The Undo Button
The Undo button on the Quick Access Toolbar displays different ScreenTips depending upon the previous task. For example, if you have just changed the font scheme, the ScreenTip will say Undo Font Schemes. In Figure 2–66, the button's ScreenTip will read Undo Move Object. The same is true of the Redo button.

1. Go to page 2 and zoom to Whole Page view.
2. Drag the QR code to a location on the right panel, just above the name of the zoo and aligned with the right side as shown in Figure 2–66. SHIFT+drag a corner sizing handle of the picture to resize it to approximately one inch square.
3. Drag the social media graphic to a location on the middle panel, on top of the current picture. As you drag, you can center the graphic by releasing the drag when you see the pink vertical guide as shown in Figure 2–66.

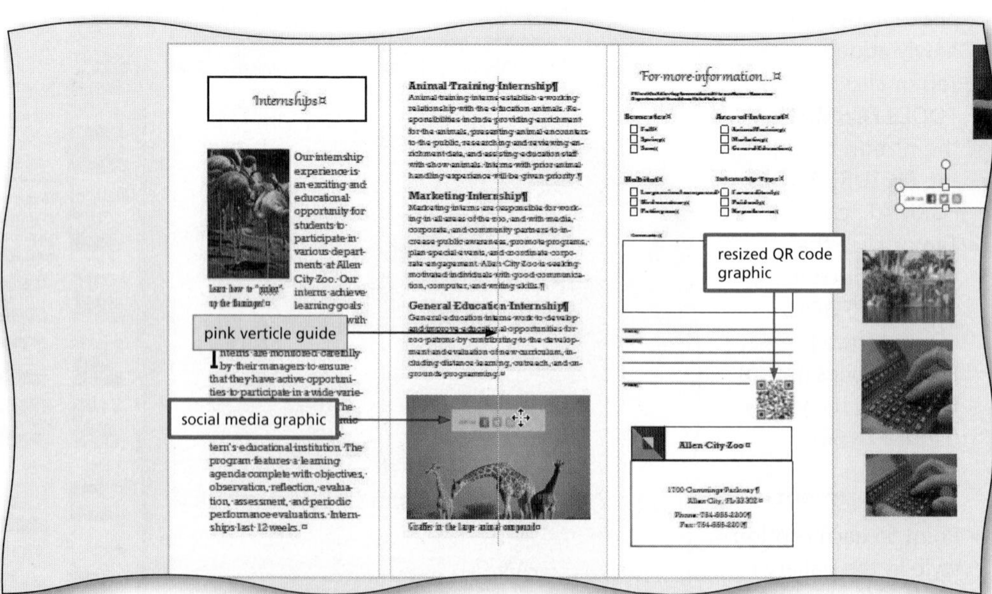

Figure 2–66

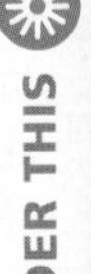

CONSIDER THIS

What is the best way to eliminate errors in the brochure?
If possible, proofread the brochure with a fresh set of eyes, that is, at least one to two days after completing the first draft. Insert repeated elements and special objects, such as watermarks and logos, which need to be placed around, or behind, other objects. Look at text wrapping on every graphic. Ask someone else to proofread the brochure and give you suggestions for improvements. Revise it as necessary and then use the spelling and design checking features of the software.

Checking the Publication

Recall that you checked a publication for spelling errors as you typed in Chapter 1. A wavy, red line indicated a word that was not in Publisher's dictionary. You then used the shortcut menu to choose the correct word. Additionally, Publisher can check the entire publication once you have finished editing it. The process of checking your entire publication for spelling errors, moves from text box to text box and offers suggestions for words it does not find in its dictionary. Publisher does not look for grammatical errors.

A second kind of publication check is called the Design Checker. The **Design Checker** finds potential design problems in the publication such as objects hidden behind other objects, text that does not fit in its text box, or a picture that is scaled disproportionately. As with the spelling check, you can choose to correct or ignore each design problem.

BTW
Proper Nouns, Titles, and Headings
If a flagged word is spelled correctly, tap or click the Ignore button to ignore the flag, or tap or click the Ignore All button if the word occurs more than once.

To Check the Spelling of the Entire Publication

1 CUSTOMIZE BROCHURE | 2 EDIT TEXT & OBJECTS | 3 SWAP PICTURES | 4 USE FORMAT PAINTER
5 EDIT FORM | 6 USE TYPOGRAPHY | 7 INSERT CAPTIONS | **8 CHECK PUBLICATION** | **9 PACK PUBLICATION**

The following steps check the entire publication for spelling errors. ***Why?*** *You should check the spelling on every publication after you finish editing it.*

1

- Click REVIEW on the ribbon to display the REVIEW tab.
- Tap or click the Spelling button (REVIEW tab | Spelling group) to begin the spelling check in the current location, which in this case, is inside the caption text box (Figure 2–67).

Q&A Can I check spelling of just a section of a publication?
Yes, select the text before starting the spelling check.

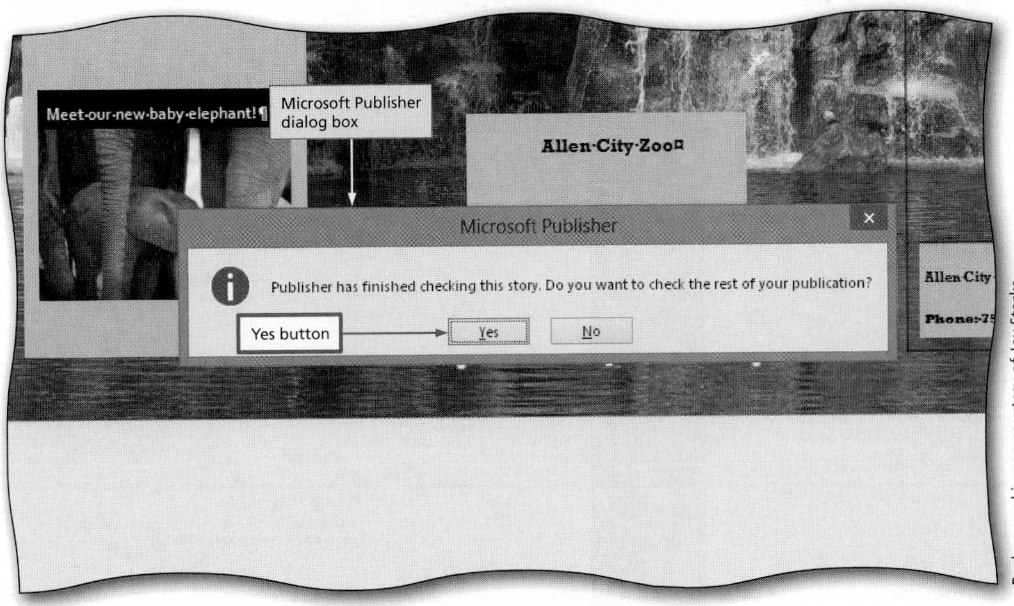

Figure 2–67

2

- Tap or click the Yes button (Microsoft Publisher dialog box) to tell Publisher to check the rest of the publication. If your publication displays a different error, accept or ignore it as necessary (Figure 2–68).

3

- Tap or click the Ignore button (Check Spelling dialog box) to ignore the misspelled word (in this case, pinken).

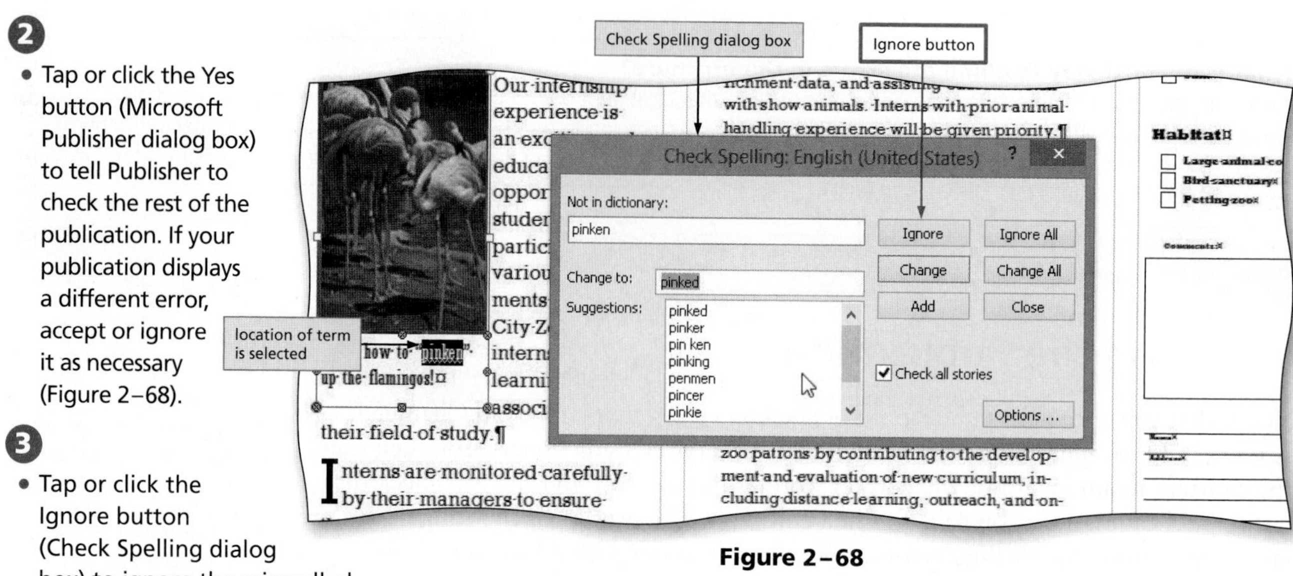

Figure 2–68

4

- If Publisher flags any other words, choose the correct spelling in the Suggestions list, click the Change button, and then continue the spelling check until the next error is identified or the end of the publication is reached. Tap or click the OK button to close the dialog box.

Other Ways

1. Press the F7 key
2. Press and hold or right-click flagged word, tap or click Spelling on shortcut menu

To Run the Design Checker

The following steps run the Design Checker. ***Why?*** *The Design Checker troubleshoots and identifies potential design problems in the publication.*

1

- Tap or click FILE on the ribbon to open the Backstage view and, by default, select the Info tab (Figure 2–69).

Q&A Will the Design Checker fix the problems automatically?
In some cases, you will have the option of choosing an automatic fix for the issue; in other cases, you will have to fix the problem manually.

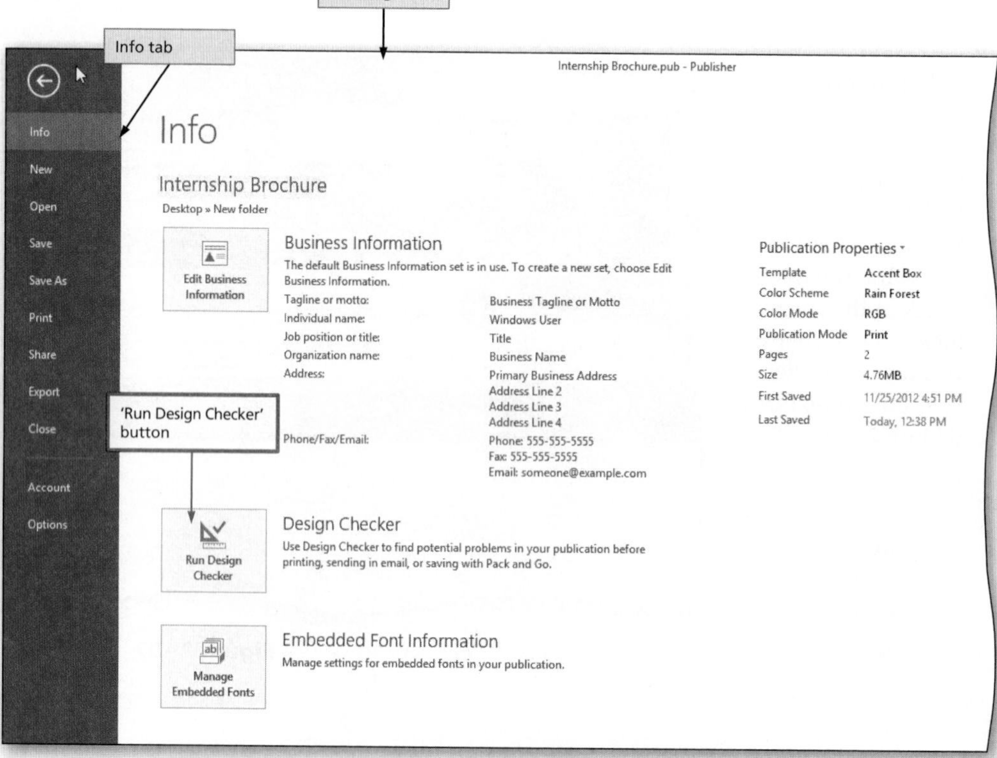

Figure 2–69

2

- Tap or click the Run Design Checker button in the Info gallery to display the Design Checker task pane (Figure 2–70).

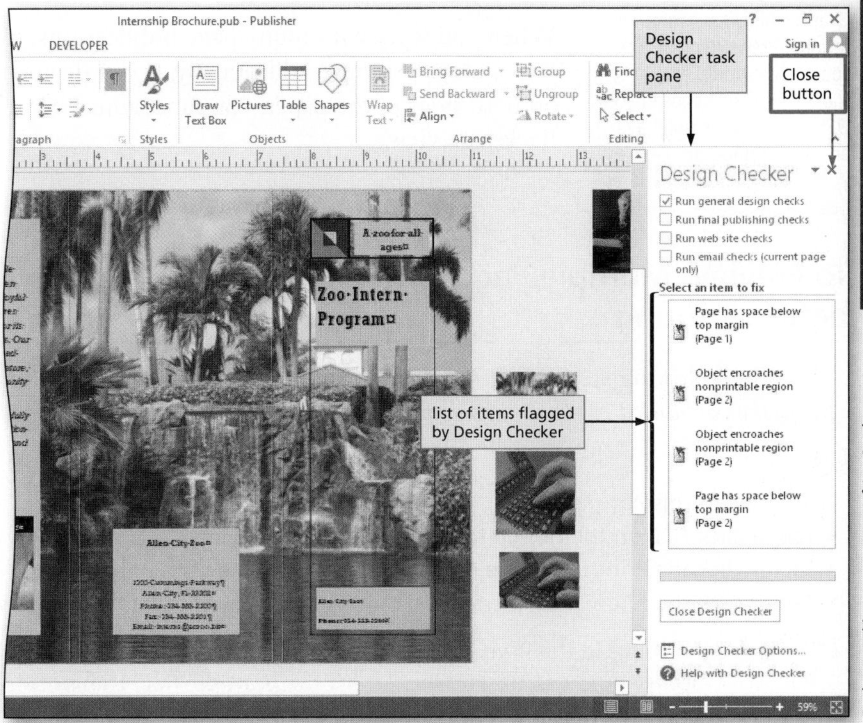

Figure 2–70

Background image courtesy of Joy Starks

Q&A What are the links at the bottom of the Design Checker task pane?
You can tap or click the link, Design Checker Options, to specify the order in which the Design Checker checks the pages of your publication, or to specify which kinds of design issues to include. The second link offers tips from the Publisher Help system about running the Design Checker.

What are the listed design problems?
A small amount of space appears between the margin of the page and the closest object to the margin. This is intentional and was part of the template, but the Design Checker notes the problem for your information only. Two of the publication objects are close to the printable area margin. This also is just a warning. The brochure will print correctly.

3

- If your publication has problems other than margin spacing or objects near the margin, point to the problem in the 'Select an item to fix' box. When a button appears on the right side of the problem, tap or click the button and then tap or click the provided Fix command.

4

- Tap or click the Close button on the Design Checker task pane to close the Design Checker and return to the publication.

To Save an Existing Publication with the Same File Name

You have made several modifications to the publication since you last saved it. Thus, you should save it again. The following step saves the publication again. For an example of the step listed below, refer to the Office and Windows chapter at the beginning of this book.

 Tap or click the Save button on the Quick Access Toolbar to overwrite the previously saved file.

BTW
Design Problems
If you want to learn more about specific design problems, tap or click the problem in the 'Select an item to fix' box (Design Checker task pane). Tap or click the arrow that appears, and then tap or click Explain to obtain more information.

CONSIDER THIS

How do you make wise, professional printing choices?
Make a firm decision that quality matters, and consult with several commercial printers ahead of time. Get prices, color modes, copies, paper, and folding options in writing before you finish your brochure. Brochures are more effective on heavier paper, with strong colors and a glossy feel. Together with the commercial printer, select a paper that is going to last. Check to make sure the commercial printer can accept Microsoft Publisher 2013 files.

BTW
Storage
Graphic files and fonts require a great deal of disk space, but should fit on most USB flash drives. If your USB flash drive is full, have another storage device ready. Publisher will prompt you to insert it.

Previewing and Printing

When you work with multi-page publications, it is a good idea to preview each page before printing. Additionally, if you decide to print on special paper, or print on both sides of the paper, you must adjust certain settings on the Print tab in the Backstage view.

To Preview Multiple Pages before Printing

1 CUSTOMIZE BROCHURE | 2 EDIT TEXT & OBJECTS | 3 SWAP PICTURES | 4 USE FORMAT PAINTER
5 EDIT FORM | 6 USE TYPOGRAPHY | 7 INSERT CAPTIONS | **8 CHECK PUBLICATION** | **9 PACK PUBLICATION**

The following steps preview both pages of the brochure before printing. ***Why?*** *Previewing is the first step in getting the publication ready for outside printing as you examine what the printed copy will look like from your desktop.*

- If necessary, display page 1.
- Tap or click FILE on the ribbon to open the Backstage view.
- Tap or click the Print tab in the Backstage view to display the Print gallery.
- Tap or click the 'View Multiple Sheets' button to display the Multiple Sheets gallery (Figure 2–71).

Q&A

What are the rulers in the Print gallery?
Publisher displays rulers at the top and left of the print preview to help you verify the size of the printed page. You can turn off the ruler display by tapping or clicking the Ruler button.

If the brochure has only two pages, why do all of those preview grids exist?
Publisher allows for more pages in every kind of publication, should you decide to add them. If you tap or click a button in the grid for more than two pages — either horizontally or vertically — the size of the preview is reduced.

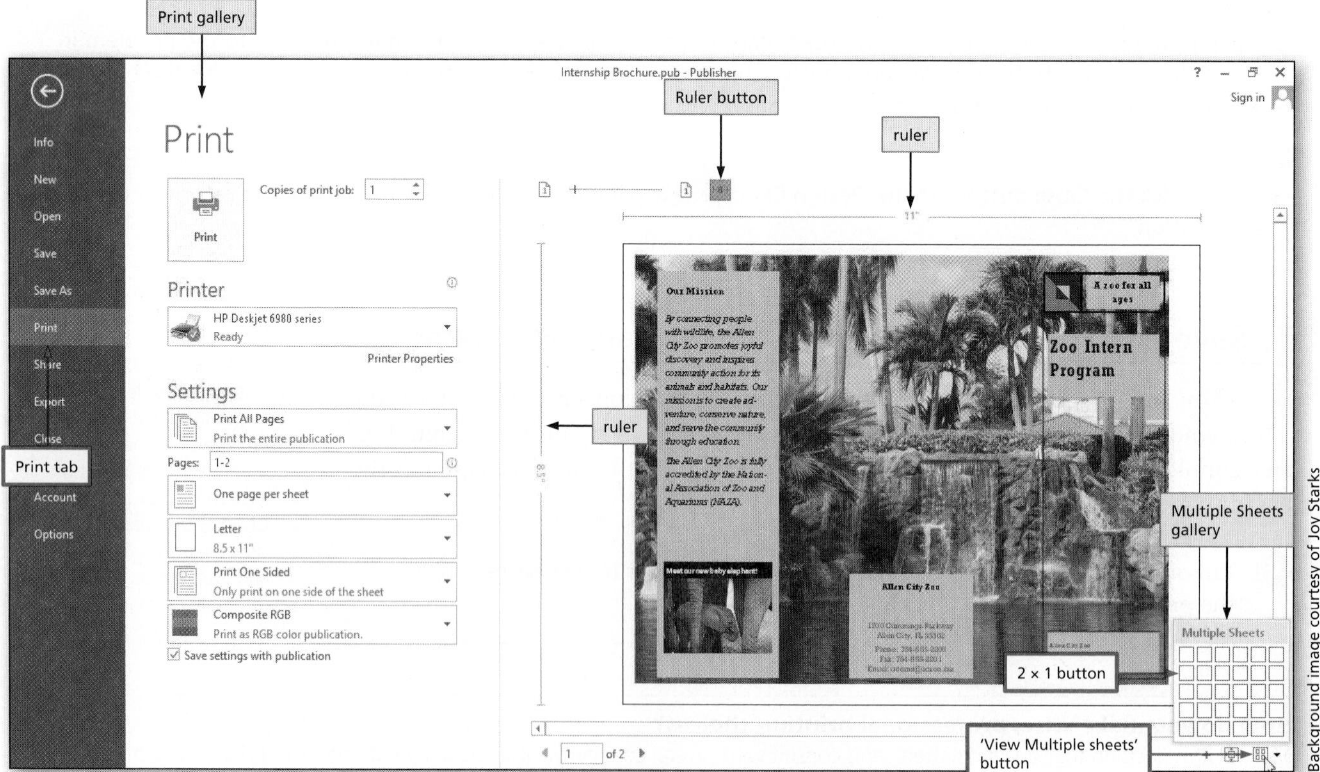

Background image courtesy of Joy Starks

Figure 2–71

2

- Tap or click the 2 × 1 button to display the pages above one another (Figure 2–72).

Q&A

Is that the best way to preview the brochure?

Viewing two full pages with intensive graphics and text may give you a good overview of the publication; however, do not substitute the preview for checking the publication for errors by reading the content carefully and running the spelling and design checking tools.

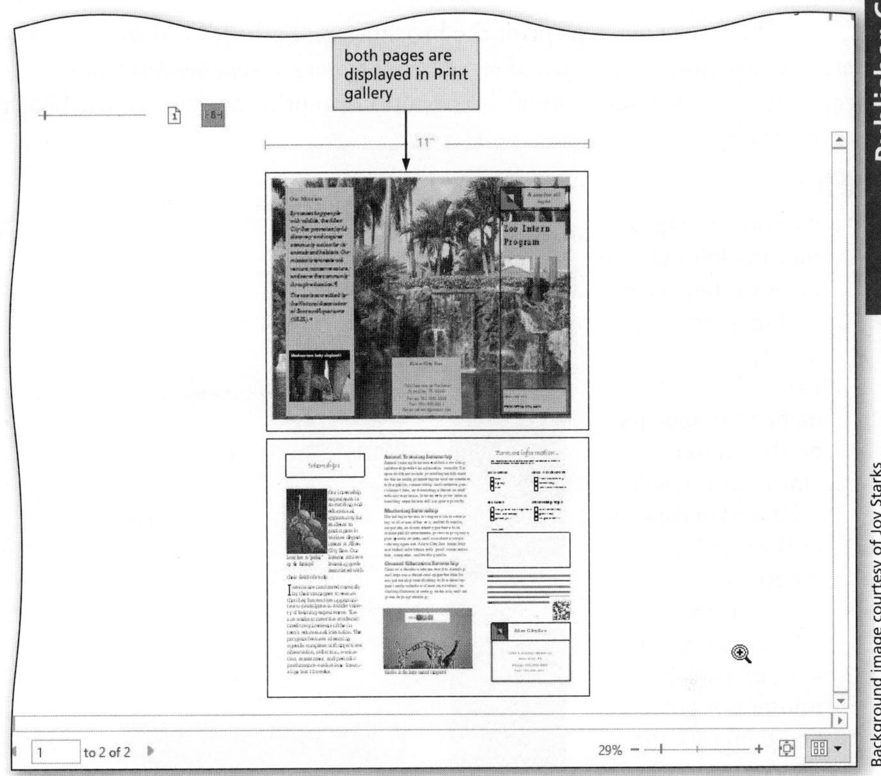

Figure 2–72

Background image courtesy of Joy Starks

Other Ways

1. Press CTRL+P, tap or click 'View Multiple Sheets' button, tap or click desired preview

Print Settings

Printing the brochure on a high grade of paper results in a professional look. A heavier stock paper helps the brochure to stand up better in display racks, although any paper will suffice. **Brochure paper** is a special paper with creases that create a professional-looking fold, and with a paper finish that works well with color and graphics.

BTW
Distributing a Document
Instead of printing and distributing a hard copy of a document, you can distribute the document electronically. Options include sending the document via email; posting it on cloud storage (such as SkyDrive) and sharing the file with others; posting it on a social networking site, blog, or other website; and sharing a link associated with an online location of the document. You also can create and share a PDF or XPS image of the document, so that users can view the file in Acrobat Reader or XPS Viewer instead of in Publisher.

To Print on Special Paper

If you have special paper, you would perform the following steps to choose that special paper before printing. See your instructor for assistance in choosing the correct option associated with your printer.

1. Open the Backstage view and then tap or click the Print tab.
2. Tap or click the Printer Properties link below the Printer Status box to display your printer's Properties dialog box.
3. Find the paper or quality setting and then choose your paper.
4. Tap or click the OK button in that dialog box to return to the Backstage view.

BTW
Printer Memory
Some printers do not have enough memory to print a wide variety of images and colors. In these cases, the printer prints up to a certain point on a page and then stops — resulting in only the top portion of the publication printing. Check with your instructor to see if your printer has enough memory to work with colors.

To Print on Both Sides

The following steps print the brochure on both sides. ***Why?*** *Printing on both sides gives you the opportunity to check your panels and folds and to view the brochure as your readers will view it.* If your printer does not have that capability, follow your printer's specifications to print one side of the brochure, turn it over, and then print the reverse side.

- If necessary, tap or click the Print tab in the Backstage view to display the Print gallery.
- Verify the printer name that appears on the Printer Status button will print a hard copy of the publication. If necessary, click the Printer Status button to display a list of available printer options and then click the desired printer to change the currently selected printer.
- Tap or click the 'Print One Sided' button to display the list of options (Figure 2–73).

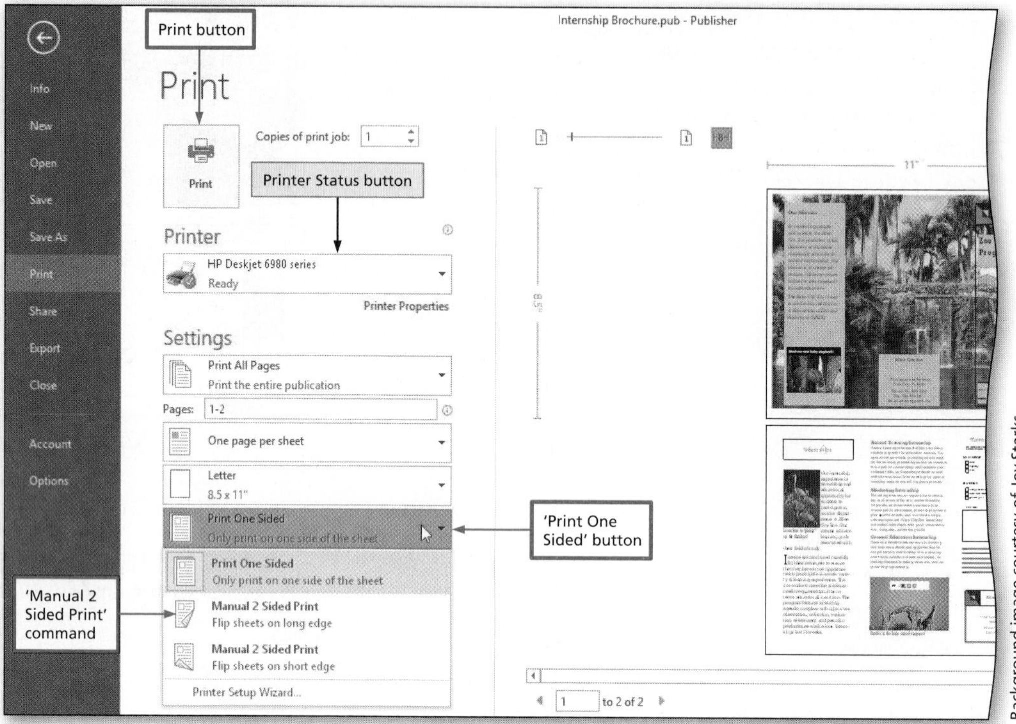

Figure 2–73

- If your list displays a Print On Both Sides (Flip sheets on long edge) command, tap or click it to select automatic printing of both sides.
- If your list displays a Manual 2 Sided Print (Flip sheets on long edge) command, tap or click it to select manual printing.
- Tap or click the Print button to print the brochure.
- When the printer stops, retrieve the printed publication.

Other Ways

1. Press CTRL+P, choose settings, tap or click Print button (Print gallery)

BTW

Conserving Ink and Toner

If you want to conserve ink or toner, you can instruct Publisher to print draft quality documents by tapping or clicking FILE on the ribbon to open the Backstage view, and then tapping or clicking Print in the Backstage view to display the Print gallery. Tap or click the Printer Properties link, and then, depending on your printer, click the Print Quality button and choose Draft in the list. Close the Printer Properties dialog box and then tap or click the Print button as usual.

Printing Considerations

When they need mass quantities of publications, businesses generally **outsource**, or submit their publications to an outside printer, for duplicating. You must make special considerations when preparing a publication for outside printing.

If you start a publication from scratch, it is best to **set up** the publication for the type of printing you want before you place objects on the page. Otherwise, you may be forced to make design changes at the last minute. You also may set up an existing publication for a printing service. In order to provide you with experience in setting up a publication for outside printing, this project guides you through the preparation steps — even if you are submitting this publication only to your instructor.

Printing options, such as whether to use a copy shop or commercial printer, have advantages and limitations. You may have to make some trade-offs before deciding on the best printing option. Table 2–4 shows some of the questions you can ask yourself about printing.

Table 2–4 Choosing a Printing Option

Consideration	Questions to Ask	Desktop Option	Professional Options
Color	Is the quality of photos and color a high priority?	Low to medium quality	High quality
Convenience	Do I want the easy way?	Very convenient and familiar	Time needed to explore different methods, unfamiliarity
Cost	How much do I want to pay?	Printer supplies and personal time	High-resolution color/high quality is expensive; the more you print, the less expensive the per-copy price
Quality	How formal is the purpose of my publication?	Local event; narrow, personal audience	Business, marketing, professional services
Quantity	How many copies do I need?	1 to 10 copies	10 to 500 copies: use a copy shop; 500+ copies: use a commercial printer
Turnaround	How soon do I need it?	Immediate	Rush outside printing is probably an extra cost

© 2014 Cengage Learning

Paper Considerations

Professional brochures are printed on a high grade of paper to enhance the graphics and provide a longer lasting document. Grades of paper are based on weight. Desktop printers commonly use **20 lb. bond paper**, which means they use a lightweight paper intended for writing and printing. A commercial printer might use 60 lb. glossy or linen paper.

The finishing options and their costs are important considerations that may take additional time to explore. **Glossy paper** is a coated paper, produced using a heat process with clay and titanium. **Linen paper**, with its mild texture or grain, can support high-quality graphics without the shine and slick feel of glossy paper. Users sometimes choose a special stock of paper, such as cover stock, card stock, or text stock. This textbook is printed on 45 lb., blade-coated paper. **Blade-coated paper** is coated and then skimmed and smoothed to create the pages you see here.

These paper and finishing options may seem burdensome, but they are becoming conveniently available to desktop publishers. Local office supply stores have shelf after shelf of special computer paper specifically designed for laser and ink-jet printers. Some of the paper you can purchase has been prescored for special folding.

BTW

CMYK Colors

When Process Colors are selected, Publisher converts all colors in text, graphics, and other objects to CMYK values and then creates four plates, regardless of the color scheme originally used to create the publication. Some RGB colors, including some of Publisher's standard colors, cannot be matched exactly to a CMYK color. After setting up for process-color printing, be sure to evaluate the publication for color changes. If a color does not match the color you want, you will have to include the new color library when you pack the publication.

Color Considerations

When printing colors, Publisher uses a color scheme called RGB. **RGB** stands for the three colors — red, green, and blue — that are used to print the combined colors of your publication. RGB provides the best color matching for graphics and photos. Desktop printers may convert the RGB specifications to CMYK, which stands for Cyan, Magenta, Yellow, and Key (black). Professional printers, on the other hand, can print your publication using color scheme processes, or **libraries**. These processes include black and white, spot color, and process color.

In **black-and-white printing**, the printer uses only one color of ink (usually black, but you can choose a different color if you want). You can add accent colors to your publication by using different shades of gray or by printing on colored paper. Your publication can have the same range of subtleties as a black-and-white photo.

BTW

Embedding Font Sets

To embed the fonts for a commercial printing service, tap or click Info in Backstage view, and then tap or click the Manage Embedded Fonts button. Select the 'Embed TrueType fonts when saving publication' check box (Fonts dialog box) Deselect any other check boxes.

BTW

Spot Colors

If you choose black plus one spot color in a publication, Publisher converts all colors except for black to tints of the selected spot color. If you choose black plus two spot colors, Publisher changes only exact matches of the second spot color to 100 percent of the second spot color. All other colors in the publication, other than black, are changed to tints of the first spot color. You then can apply, manually, tints of the second spot color to objects in the publication.

A **spot color** is used to accent a black-and-white publication. Newspapers, for example, may print their masthead in a bright, eye-catching color on page 1 but print the rest of the publication in black and white. A printing service may apply up to two spot colors with a color matching system called **Pantone**. **Spot-color printing** uses semitransparent, premixed inks typically chosen from standard color-matching guides, such as Pantone. Choosing colors from a **color-matching library** helps ensure high-quality results, because printing professionals who license the libraries agree to maintain the specifications, control, and quality.

In a spot-color publication, each spot color is **separated** on its own plate and printed on an offset printing press. The use of spot colors has become more creative in the last few years. Printing services use spot colors of metallic or florescent inks, as well as screen tints, to provide color variations without increasing the number of color separations and cost. If your publication includes a logo with one or two colors, or if you want to use color to emphasize line art or text, then consider using spot-color printing.

Process-color printing means your publication can include color photos and any color or combination of colors. One of the process-color libraries, called **CMYK**, or **four-color printing**, is named for the four semitransparent process inks — cyan, magenta, yellow, and key (black). CMYK process-color printing can reproduce a full range of colors on a printed page. The CMYK color model defines color as it is absorbed and reflected on a printed page rather than in its liquid state.

Process-color printing is the most expensive proposition; black-and-white printing is the cheapest. Using color increases the cost and time it takes to process the publication. When using either the spot-color or process-color method, the printer first must output the publication to film on an **image setter**, which recreates the publication on film or photographic paper. The film then is used to create color **printing plates**. Each printing plate transfers one of the colors in the publication onto paper in an offset process. Publisher can print a preview of these individual sheets showing how the colors will separate before you take your publication to the printer.

A new printing technology called **digital printing** uses toner instead of ink to reproduce a full range of colors. Digital printing does not require separate printing plates. Although not yet widely available, digital printing promises to become cheaper than offset printing without sacrificing any quality.

Publisher supports all three kinds of printing and provides the tools commercial printing services need to print the publication. You should ask your printing service which color-matching system it uses.

Packaging the Publication for the Printing Service

The publication file can be packaged for the printing service in two ways. The first way is to give the printing service the Publisher file in Publisher format using the Pack and Go Wizard. The second way is to save the file in a format called Encapsulated PostScript. Both of these methods are discussed in the following sections.

To Use the Pack and Go Wizard

1 CUSTOMIZE BROCHURE | 2 EDIT TEXT & OBJECTS | 3 SWAP PICTURES | 4 USE FORMAT PAINTER
5 EDIT FORM | 6 USE TYPOGRAPHY | 7 INSERT CAPTIONS | 8 CHECK PUBLICATION | **9 PACK PUBLICATION**

The **Pack and Go Wizard** guides you through the steps to collect and pack all the files the printing service needs and then compresses the files. ***Why?*** *Publisher checks for and embeds the TrueType fonts used in the publication, in case the printing service does not have those fonts available.* The following steps use the Pack and Go Wizard to ready the publication for submission to a commercial printing service. These steps create a compressed, or zipped, folder on your storage device.

1

- Click FILE on the ribbon to open the Backstage view.
- Tap or click the Export tab in the Backstage view to display the Export gallery.
- In the 'Pack and Go' area, tap or click the 'Save for a Commercial Printer' tab (Figure 2–74).

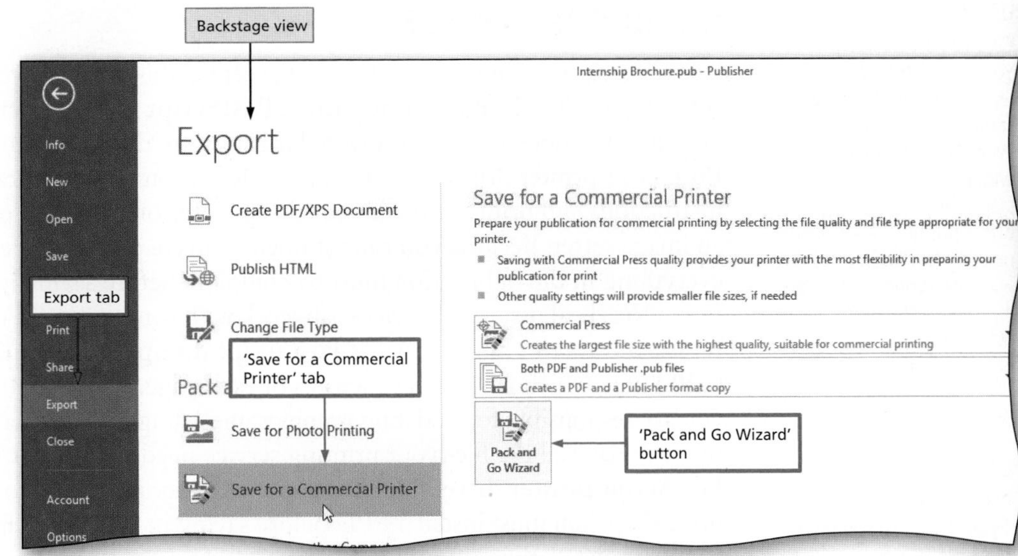

Figure 2–74

Q&A Should I save my file first?

You do not have to save it again; however, if you plan to store the publication on a storage device other than the one on which you previously saved the brochure, save it again on the new medium before beginning the process.

- Tap or click the 'Pack and Go Wizard' button to begin the Pack and Go Wizard.
- If necessary, browse to your storage location (Figure 2–75).

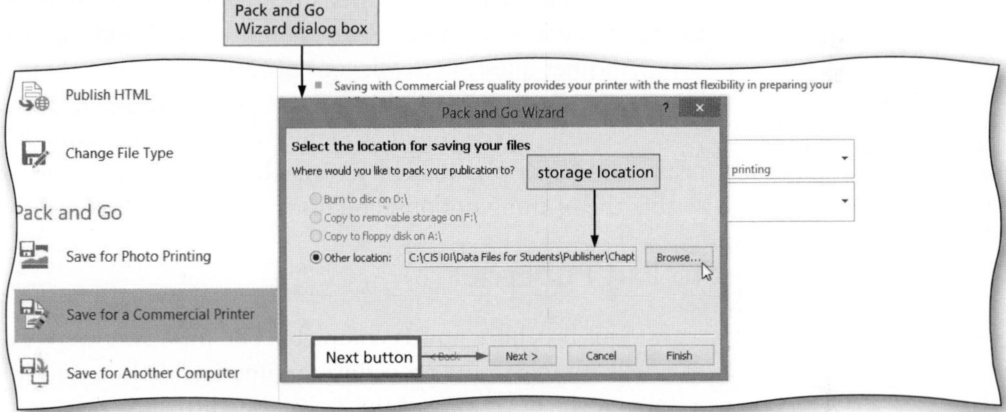

Figure 2–75

3

- Tap or click the Next button to save the file.
- When the final dialog box is displayed, remove the check mark in the 'Print a composite proof' check box (Figure 2–76).

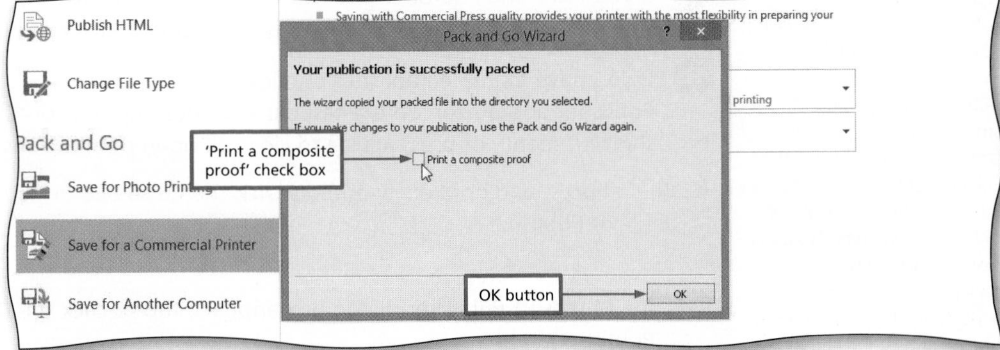

Figure 2–76

Q&A What if I make a change to the publication after running the Pack and Go Wizard?

The file is saved in a compressed format on your storage location, with the same file name as your Publisher file. If you make changes to the publication after packing the files, be sure to run the Pack and Go Wizard again so that the changes are part of the packed publication.

- Tap or click the OK button to close the Pack and Go Wizard dialog box.

Using PostScript Files

If your printing service does not accept Publisher files, you can hand off, or submit, your files in PostScript format. **PostScript** is a page definition language that describes the document to be printed in language that the printer can understand. The PostScript printer driver includes a page definition language translator to interpret the instructions and print the document on a printer or a PostScript output device, such as an image setter. Because you cannot open or make changes directly to a PostScript file, everything in the publication must be complete before saving it.

Nearly all printing services can work with some type of PostScript file, either regular PostScript files, known as **PostScript dumps**, or **Encapsulated PostScript (EPS)** files, which are graphic pictures of each page. If you hand off a PostScript file, you are responsible for updating graphics, including the necessary fonts, and ensuring that you have all the files your printing service needs. Publisher includes several **PostScript printer drivers (PPDs)** and their description files to facilitate printing at the print shop. You must install a PPD before saving in PostScript form. Because the most common installation of Publisher is for a single user in a desktop environment, this project does not provide the steps involved in installing a PostScript printer driver. That process would require using original operating system disks and advanced knowledge of PostScript printers. Ask your printing service representative for the correct printer driver, and refer to your Windows documentation installation instructions. Then, use the Save As dialog box to save the publication in PostScript format.

Another question to ask your printing service is whether it performs the **prepress tasks** or a **preflight check**. These kinds of checks include the typesetting process, checking the page layout and other tasks performed before the publication is printed on paper. You may be responsible for making color corrections, separations, setting the printing options, and other printing tasks.

BTW
Offset Printing
Your printing service may use the initials SWOP, which stand for Standard for Web Offset Printing — a widely accepted set of color standards used in web offset printing. Web offset printing has nothing to do with the World Wide Web. It is merely the name for an offset printing designed to print thousands of pieces in a single run from a giant roll of paper.

BTW
PostScript Files
If you decide to submit a PostScript dump, or file, to an outside printer or service bureau, include a copy of the original document as well — for backup purposes. Many shops slowly are changing over from Macintosh-based to cross-platform based operations. If an error occurs, the printer technician can correct the error from the original document without requiring you to make another trip to the print shop.

To Exit Publisher

This brochure now is complete. The following steps exit Publisher. For a detailed example of the procedure summarized below, refer to the Office and Windows chapter at the beginning of this book. The brochure was saved in previous steps, so you do not need to save the file again.

1a If you have one Publisher publication open, tap or click the Close button on the right side of the title bar to close the open publication and exit Publisher.

1b If you have multiple Publisher publications open, press and hold or right-click the Publisher app button on the taskbar and then tap or click 'Close all windows' on the shortcut menu, or press ALT+F4 to close all open publications and exit Publisher.

Q&A Could I press and hold or repeatedly click the Close button to close all open publications and exit Publisher?
Yes.

2 If a Microsoft Publisher dialog box appears, tap or click the Don't Save button to exit Publisher.

BTW
Subsetting
A file prepared for submission to a commercial printer includes all fonts from the publication. If you use only a small number of characters from a font, such as for drop caps or for headlines, you can instruct Publisher to embed only the characters you used from the font. Embedding only part of a font is called subsetting. The advantage of font subsetting is that it decreases the overall size of the file. The disadvantage is that it limits the ability to make corrections at the printing service. If the printing service does not have the full font installed on its computer, corrections can be made only by using the characters included in the subset.

To Sign Out of a Microsoft Account

If you are signed in to a Microsoft account and are using a public computer or otherwise wish to sign out of your Microsoft account, you should remove the account from the Account gallery in the Backstage view before exiting Publisher. Signing out of the account is the safest way to make sure that nobody else can access SkyDrive files or settings stored in your Microsoft account. The following steps sign out of a Microsoft account from Publisher. For a detailed example of the procedure summarized below, refer to the Office and Windows chapter at the beginning of this book.

1. If you wish to sign out of your Microsoft account, tap or click FILE on the ribbon to open the Backstage view and then tap or click the Account tab to display the Account gallery.

2. Tap or click the Sign out link, which displays the Remove Account dialog box. If a Can't remove Windows accounts dialog box appears instead of the Remove Account dialog box, click the OK button and skip the remaining steps.

Q&A Why does a Can't remove Windows accounts dialog box appear?
If you signed in to Windows using your Microsoft account, then you also must sign out from Windows, rather than signing out from within Publisher. When you are finished using Windows, be sure to sign out at that time.

3. Tap or click the Yes button (Remove Account dialog box) to sign out of your Microsoft account on this computer.

Q&A Should I sign out of Windows after signing out of my Microsoft account?
When you are finished using the computer, you should sign out of your account for maximum security.

4. Tap or click the Back button in the upper-left corner of the Backstage view to return to the publication.

Chapter Summary

In this chapter, you have learned how to choose make choices about brochures and brochure templates, edit headings and paragraphs, swap pictures, edit Publisher forms, use Publisher typography tools, insert captions, check the publication for errors, and pack the publication for a printing service. The items listed below include all the new Publisher skills you have learned in this chapter.

Editing Text and Options
Copy and Paste (PUB 79)
Display Formatting Marks (PUB 77)
Select a Brochure Template (PUB 70)
Select a Paste Option (PUB 81)
Switch to Page 2 (PUB 91)
Undo an Action (PUB 102)
Use the Format Painter (PUB 88)
Wordwrap Text as You Type (PUB 77)

Forms
Edit the Form (PUB 95)

Graphics
Arrange Thumbnails (PUB 85)
Insert Multiple Pictures from a Storage Device (PUB 82)
Select Multiple Objects (PUB 84)
Swap Pictures (PUB 82)
Use a Picture as a Background (PUB 87)

Publication Checking and Packing
Check the Spelling of the Entire Publication (PUB 109)
Preview Multiple Pages before Printing (PUB 112)
Print on Special Paper (PUB 113)
Print on Both Sides (PUB 114)
Run the Design Checker (PUB 110)
Use the Pack and Go Wizard (PUB 116)

Typography
Create a Drop Cap (PUB 103)
Customize a Drop Cap (PUB 104)
Edit Captions (PUB 106)
Edit the Font Family (PUB 98)
Examine Ligatures (PUB 101)
Format with a Stylistic Set (PUB 100)
Use the Caption Gallery (PUB 107)

CONSIDER THIS

What decisions will you need to make when creating your next publication?

Use these guidelines as you complete the assignments in this chapter and create your own publications outside of this class.

1. Decide on the purpose, shelf life, and layout.
   a) Select a template that matches your need.
   b) Choose font and color schemes determined by the brochure's purpose and audience.
2. Create the brochure.
   a) Replace all placeholder and default text.
   b) Copy and paste text when possible to prevent the introduction of new errors.
   c) Edit forms.
   d) Use appropriate pictures with captions.
   e) Swap pictures when possible so they will fit in the space.

3. Identify how to format various objects in the brochure.
    a) Use the Format Painter to copy formats for consistency.
    b) Use typography tools to enhance the brochure.
4. Proofread and check the publication.
    a) Read the brochure.
    b) Ask another person to read it.
    c) Use the spell checking feature.
    d) Use the Design Checker.
5. Plan for printing and packaging.
    a) Choose correct printing options.
    b) Consult with a commercial printing service.
    c) Use the Pack and Go Wizard.

CONSIDER THIS

How should you submit solutions to questions in the assignments identified with a symbol?
Every assignment in this book contains one or more questions identified with a symbol. These questions require you to think beyond the assigned publication. Present your solutions to the questions in the format required by your instructor. Possible formats may include one or more of these options: write the answer; create a document that contains the answer; present your answer to the class; discuss your answer in a group; record the answer as audio or video using a webcam, smartphone, or portable media player; or post answers on a blog, wiki, or website.

Apply Your Knowledge

Reinforce the skills and apply the concepts you learned in this chapter.

Swapping Graphics

Note: To complete this assignment, you will be required to use the Data Files for Students. Visit www.cengage.com/ct/studentdownload for detailed instructions or contact your instructor for information about accessing the required files.

Instructions: You decide to create a collage of pictures from your recent Florida vacation. You produce the publication shown in Figure 2–77.

Perform the following tasks:

1. Run Publisher and open the file Apply 2-1 Picture Collage from the Data Files for Students.
2. Tap or click the Pictures button (INSERT tab | Illustrations group). Navigate to the Data Files for Students and CTRL-tap or CTRL-click each of the Florida pictures to select them. Tap or click the Insert button to insert the multiple pictures into the scratch area.

All images Courtesy of Joy Starks

Figure 2–77

3. One at a time, swap the pictures for the empty picture placeholders.
4. Arrange the pictures on the page layout as desired.
5. Choose one picture for the background. To apply it, press and hold or right-click its swap icon, tap or click 'Apply to Background', and then tap or click Fill.
6. Save the collage on your storage device with the file name, Apply 2-1 Picture Collage Complete.
7. Submit the revised document in the format specified by your instructor.
8. Do you think a caption on each picture would make the publication look cluttered? Why or why not?

Extend Your Knowledge

Extend the skills you learned in this chapter and experiment with new skills. You may need to use Help to complete the assignment.

Creating a Brochure from Scratch

Instructions: The local county park provides a stargazing program for families and those interested in learning more about astronomy. They need a brochure to promote the event. They have supplied you with the content for page 1. You decide to start from scratch to create the brochure shown in Figure 2–78.

Perform the following tasks:

1. Run Publisher. Tap or click BUILT-IN, and then tap or click Brochures. Scroll to the Blank Sizes area, and then tap or click the Letter (Landscape) thumbnail.
2. Choose the Office color scheme and the Office 1 font scheme. Tap or click the CREATE button to create the publication.
3. Use Help to read about creating guides and then perform the following tasks:
   a. To create panel guides, drag from the vertical ruler into the publication creating a non-printing guide, stopping at 3 5/8" as measured on the horizontal ruler. Drag another guide from the vertical ruler into the publication, stopping at 7 3/8".
   b. In the Page Navigation pane, press and hold or right-click the page 1 icon, and then click Insert Duplicate Page on the shortcut menu. You will leave page 2 blank for future content.
   c. If necessary, tap or click the page 1 icon to return to page 1 in the brochure.
   d. Save the publication on your storage device with the file name, **`Extend 2-1 Night Sky Tours Brochure`**.

Figure 2–78

4. Tap or click the Online Pictures button (INSERT tab | Illustrations group). Use Office.com Clip Art to insert a picture of the moon. Drag the picture to the scratch area and then tap or click the Arrange Thumbnails button (PICTURE TOOLS FORMAT tab | Arrange group) to reduce the size of the thumbnail.
5. Repeat Step 4 to insert five or six photos of stars, meteors, and constellations.
6. To create the right panel, which serves as the front of the brochure, do the following:
   a. Drag an appropriate picture to the right panel. Position it in the center, vertically; resize it so that it almost fills the panel horizontally. Deselect the picture.
   b. Tap or click the Draw Text Box button (HOME tab | Objects group). Drag to create a text box at the top of the right panel, approximately ½" tall. Stay within the margin and guides. Tap or click the Shape Fill arrow (DRAWING TOOLS FORMAT tab | Shape Styles group), and then click a black color in the gallery. Tap or click the Font Color arrow (HOME tab | Font group) and then click a white color in the gallery. Type **`Clay County Park`** to enter the text. Press and hold or right-click the text, and then tap or click Best Fit on the shortcut menu.
   c. Tap or click the Draw Text Box button (HOME tab | Objects group). Drag to create another text box to fill the area between the previous text box and the picture. Type **`Night Sky Tours`** to enter the text. Press and hold or right-click the text, and then tap or click Best Fit on the shortcut menu. Format the text bold.

Continued >

Extend Your Knowledge *continued*

d. Create another text box below the graphic. Type **Tours available on clear Saturday nights in April, May, and June.** Format the text italic and use Best Fit to make the text fill the text box.

7. On the middle panel of page 1, create a text box with the name, address, and phone number of the park. If requested to do so by your instructor, use your name and address in the brochure.

   Clay County Park
   540 County Line Road
   Mayfield, OK 74109
   Phone: (918) 555-PARK

8. To create the left panel of page 1:

   a. Drag an appropriate picture onto the left panel. Position it in the lower portion of the left panel; resize it so that it almost fills the panel horizontally.

   b. Click the Caption button (PICTURE TOOLS FORMAT tab | Picture Styles group) and choose an appropriate caption style. Edit the caption to say **Meteor showers are most prevalent in the spring!**

   c. Create a text box above the picture. Type the following text and format it appropriately:

   Night Sky Tours
   Unique, memorable, fascinating!
   An evening out under the blanket of the heavens above - bring a blanket for the earth below. We meet at approximately 10:00 p.m. to learn about the universe and see it up close.
   Your Night Sky Tour is accompanied by a personalized, educational, inspirational, and humorous dialogue with an astronomy professor and longtime astronomer, making it a truly stellar experience.

9. Using the techniques presented in this chapter, select all of the pictures in the scratch area. Press the DELETE key to delete the extra pictures.

10. Check the brochure for spelling errors and design errors and fix them as necessary. Save the file again.

11. Submit the file in the format specified by your instructor.

12. When would you use a template instead of creating a brochure from scratch? Would formatting the font before you type be easier than selecting text and formatting it afterward?

Analyze, Correct, Improve

Analyze a publication, correct all errors, and improve the design.

Making Typography Changes

Note: To complete this assignment, you will be required to use the Data Files for Students. Visit www.cengage.com/ct/studentdownload for detailed instructions or contact your instructor for information about accessing the required files.

Instructions: You have been given page 1 of the proposed brochure for a campus fraternity, Sigma Sigma. The brochure is shown in Figure 2–79, but it has several issues. You decide to improve the brochure. Run Publisher and open the file, Analyze 2–1 Fraternity Brochure.

1. Correct The publication has spelling and design errors. Use Publisher tools to help you correct those errors. The text in the left panel uses too many different font sizes. Use the Format Painter to standardize the font. Use the address of your school and your phone number.

2. Improve The graphic in the left panel is not very exciting. Search for a replacement picture using Office.com Clip Art. Insert an appropriate caption and caption style. In the right panel, the picture border helps set off the picture. Use the Format Painter to copy the formatting of that picture to the graphics in the center panel. Check the publication for spelling errors and design errors. Ignore any errors about space below the top margin. Save the document using the file name, Analyze 2-1 Fraternity Brochure Complete. Submit the revised document in the format specified by your instructor.

3. What errors existed in the starting file? How did creating consistency in font sizes enhance the publication? Did changing the graphic improve the effectiveness of the brochure? What other improvements would you make? Why?

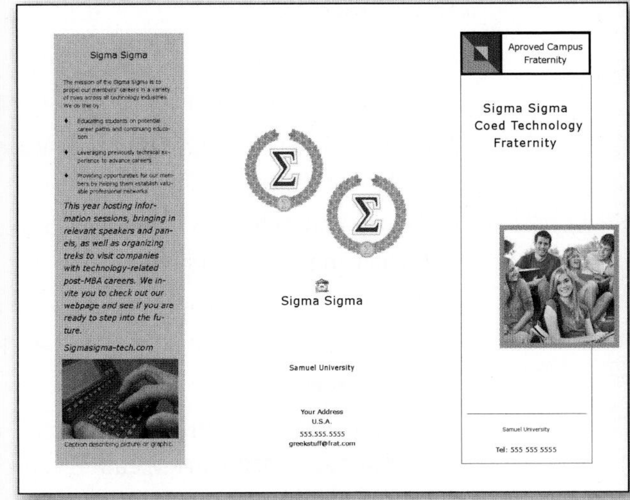

Figure 2–79

In the Labs

Design, create, or modify a publication using the guidelines, concepts, and skills presented in this chapter. Labs 1 and 2, which increase in difficulty, require you to create a solution based on what you learned in the chapter; Lab 3 requires you to create a solution, which uses cloud and web technologies, by learning and investigating on your own from general guidance.

Lab 1: Creating a Brochure

Problem: The Students Against Bullying group has asked you to create a brochure they can distribute to students, teachers, and parents. You create the brochure shown in Figure 2–80.

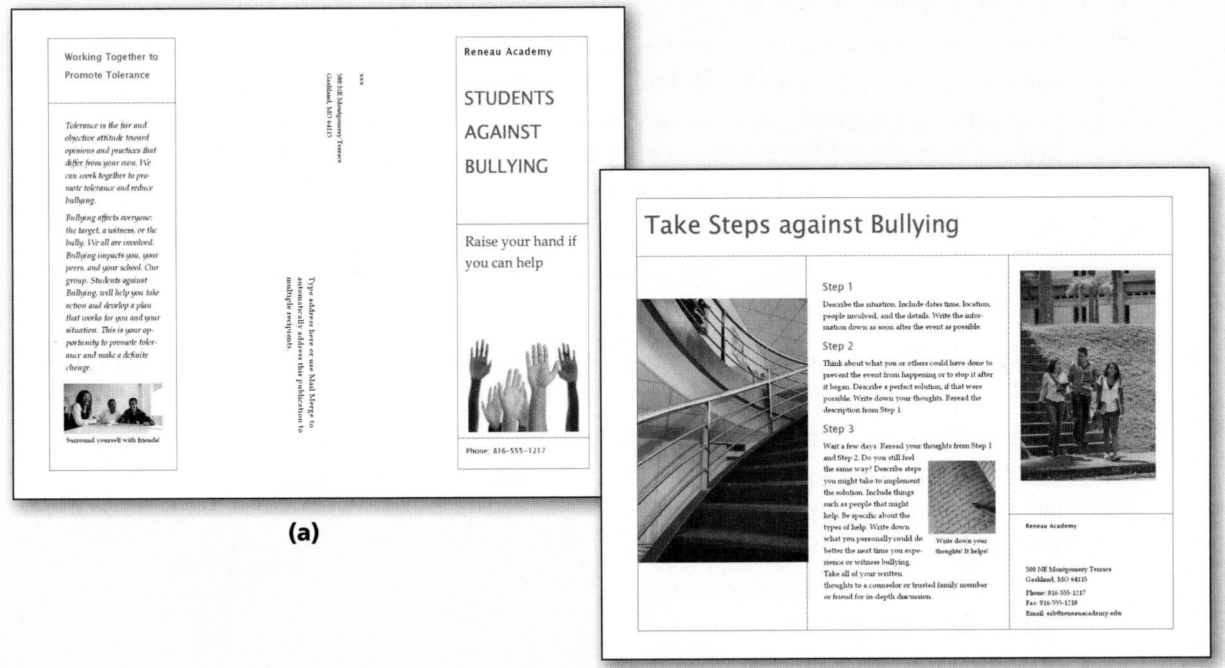

(a)

(b)

Figure 2–80

Continued >

In the Labs *continued*

1. Run Publisher. In the template gallery, click BUILT-IN and then click Brochures.
2. In the More Installed Templates section, choose the Frames template in the Informational area.
3. Select a 3-panel design with the Sunset color scheme and the Apex font scheme. Choose to include a customer address but no form. Create the publication.
4. As you make changes to the brochure, scroll and zoom as necessary. Turn on the display of formatting characters if desired.
5. To edit the text on page 1:
   a. On the right panel, drag through the Business Name text to select it. Type `Reneau Academy.` Tap or click outside the text box to synchronize the text.
   b. Tap or click the Product/Service Information placeholder text to select it. Type `STUDENTS AGAINST BULLYING,` all in capital letters.
   c. Drag through the Business Tagline or Motto text to select it. Type `Raise your hand if you can help.`
   d. Do not change the phone number; you will copy and paste it later in the steps.
   e. On the left panel, tap or click the Back Panel Heading placeholder text to select it. Type `Working Together to Promote Tolerance.`
   f. Use wordwrap as you replace the text in the story on the left panel. Type `Tolerance is the fair and objective attitude toward opinions and practices that differ from your own. We can work together to promote tolerance and reduce bullying.` and then press the ENTER key to complete the first paragraph.
   g. Type `Bullying affects everyone: the target, a witness, or the bully. We all are involved. Bullying impacts you, your peers, and your school. Our group, Students Against Bullying, will help you take action and develop a plan that works for you and your situation. This is your opportunity to promote tolerance and make a definitive change.` to complete the text.
6. To edit the graphics on page 1:
   a. On the left panel of page 1, tap or click the picture twice to select only the picture. Press and hold or right-click the picture, and then tap or click Change Picture on the shortcut menu to display the submenu. Tap or click Change Picture on the submenu to display the Insert Pictures dialog box. Search Office.com Clip Art for the term, students, and insert a picture similar to Figure 2–80 on the previous page. Edit the caption to say `Surround yourself with friends!`
   b. Repeat the process for the picture on the right panel, using the search term, raise hands.
7. Go to page 2 of the brochure. To edit the text on page 2, do the following:
   a. Replace the Main Inside Heading placeholder text with the text, `Take Steps against Bullying.`
   b. On the right panel, select the text in the Primary Business Address text box. Type the following text, pressing the ENTER key after the first line. It will synchronize with the middle panel on page 1. If requested by your instructor, replace the mailing address text box with your address.

      `500 NE Montgomery Terrace`
      `Gashland, MO 64115`

c. Select the text in the Phone, Fax, and Email text box. Type the following text, pressing the ENTER key after each line, except the last.

`Phone: 816-555-1217`

`Fax: 816-555-1218`

`Email: sab@reneauacademy.edu`

d. On the middle panel, replace the first Secondary Heading with the text, **`Step 1.`**

Replace the story under the Step 1 heading with the text, **`Describe the situation. Include dates, time, location, people involved, and the details. Write the information down as soon after the event as possible.`**

f. Replace the second Secondary Heading with the text, **`Step 2.`**

g. Replace the story under the Step 2 heading with the text, **`Think about what you or others could have done to prevent the event from happening or to stop it after it began. Describe a perfect solution, if that were possible. Write down your thoughts. Reread the description from Step 1.`** and then press the ENTER key to finish the paragraph.

h. Type **`Step 3`** and then press the ENTER key to finish the third heading. You will format it later.

i. Type **`Wait a few days. Reread your thoughts from Step 1 and Step 2. Do you still feel the same way? Describe steps you might take to implement the solution. Include things such as people that might help. Be specific about the types of help. Write down what you personally could do better the next time you experience or witness bullying. Take all of your written thoughts to a counselor or trusted family member or friend for in-depth discussion.`**

j. Tap or click the Step 1 text. Tap or click the Format Painter button (HOME tab | Clipboard group). Drag through the text, Step 3, to apply the formatting.

8. Replace the graphic on the middle panel with a picture from Office.com searching for the term, **`pen.`** Edit the caption to say, **`Write down your thoughts! It helps!`**

9. Delete the text, text box, graphic, and caption on the left panel. Replace it with a picture from Office.com Clip Art, searching for the term, **`staircase.`** Choose a portrait-oriented picture. Move the inserted graphic to the left panel and resize it to fit the panel as necessary. Repeat the process to insert a picture in the upper portion of the right panel. Use the search term, **`students.`**

10. Use the copy and paste techniques presented in the chapter to copy the phone number from the right panel of page 2 to the right panel of page 1. Use the Keep Text Only button on the Paste Options menu.

11. Check your publication for spelling and design errors, and fix or ignore the flagged items as necessary.

12. Save the brochure on your storage device with the file name, Lab 2-1 Students Against Bullying Brochure.

13. Submit the file as directed by your instructor.

14. Would a page background make this brochure easier to read or harder to read? Would you use a picture background, or a gradient as you did in Chapter 1? Why?

Lab 2: Editing an Order Form

Note: To complete this assignment, you will be required to use the Data Files for Students. Visit www.cengage.com/ct/studentdownload for detailed instructions or contact your instructor for information about accessing the required files.

Problem: The Biology Club is selling poinsettias and wreaths for the Christmas season. The members started a form, but they would like you to make it more appealing. You create the form shown in Figure 2–81.

1. Run Publisher and open the file Lab 2-2 Order Form from the Data Files for Students.
2. Tap or click the heading. Type `Biology Club Order Form` to replace the text. Change the font to Gabriola. Change the font size to 22. Change the font color to red. Resize the text box as necessary to display all of the text.
3. With the heading text still selected, tap or click the Stylistic Sets button (TEXT BOX TOOLS FORMAT tab | Typography group). Select a fancy stylistic set. Resize the text box as necessary to display all of the glyphs.

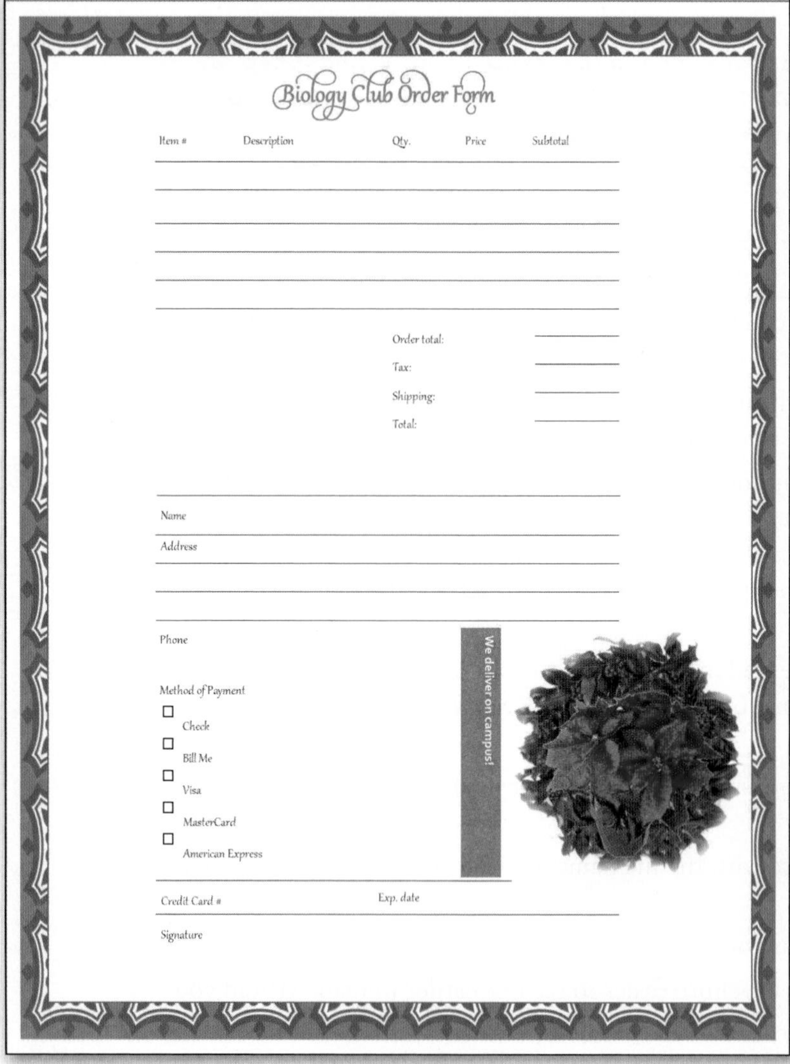

Figure 2–81

4. Select the text in the Item # text box. Change the font to Gabriola and the font size to 11. Double-tap or double-click the Format Painter (HOME tab | Clipboard group) to copy the formatting.
5. One at a time, select each of the other text boxes on the form to apply the formatting. It is OK if the alignment changes. If necessary, resize any text boxes that are too small to accommodate the font change.
6. Select the picture. Tap or click the Caption button (PICTURE TOOLS FORMAT tab | Picture Styles group) to display the Caption gallery. Choose the Offset – Layout 3 caption style. Edit the caption to say `We deliver on campus!`
7. Check the brochure for spelling errors and design errors, and fix them as necessary. Save the order form on your storage device with the file name, Lab 2-2 Order Form Complete.
8. Submit the file as directed by your instructor.
9. How might you have created this order form from scratch? Does Publisher have the individual components that you could add? Would that have been easier than trying to customize a built-in form?

Lab 3: Expand Your World: Cloud and Web Technologies

Creating a Google Drive

Problem: Many company websites include a link to download a print copy of various brochures. You would like to create a webpage with a link to download one of your brochures stored on the cloud.

Instructions:

1. If you do not have a SkyDrive account, create one. For a detailed example of the procedure, refer to the Office and Windows chapter.
2. Save one of your brochures on SkyDrive.
3. Run the Notepad app or other text editor app on your computer. Enter the code from Figure 2–82, leaving the ninth line blank, as shown.
4. If requested to do so by your instructor, change the words, My Web Page, to your name in line five.

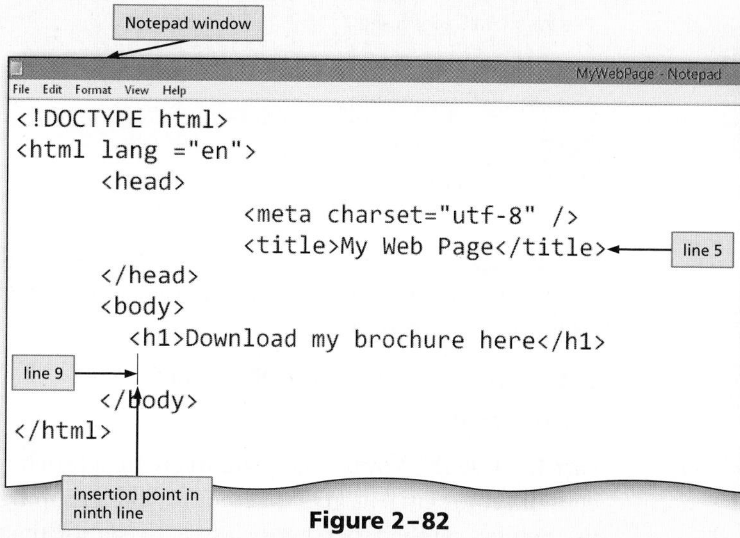

Notepad window

MyWebPage - Notepad

File Edit Format View Help

```
<!DOCTYPE html>
<html lang ="en">
      <head>
               <meta charset="utf-8" />
               <title>My Web Page</title>
      </head>
      <body>
        <h1>Download my brochure here</h1>

      </body>
</html>
```

line 5

line 9

insertion point in ninth line

Figure 2–82

5. Save the file on your storage device, using **`MyWebPage.html`** as the file name. Do not close the text editor window.
6. Run a browser and navigate to your SkyDrive account.
7. Press and hold or right-click the stored brochure file to display the shortcut menu. Tap or click Embed on the shortcut menu. When prompted, tap or click the Generate button. When SkyDrive displays the HTML code, press CTRL+C to copy the highlighted code.
8. Go back to the text editor window and position the insertion point on line nine. Press CTRL+V to paste the code into the file. If necessary, click Format on the menu bar and then click Word Wrap to enable the feature. Save the HTML file again, and then close the window.
9. To view your webpage, open a File Explorer window and then navigate to the location of your saved HTML file. Double-tap or double-click the MyWebPage.html file. If your browser asks permission to run the ActiveX content, tap or click the 'Allow blocked content' button.
10. Submit the assignment in the format specified by your instructor.
11. Does your school provide a brochure about its program? Can you download the brochure from the school's website? Do you think it still is good to have a hard copy? Why?

Consider This: Your Turn

Apply your creative thinking and problem solving skills to design and implement a solution.

1: Creating a Youth Baseball League Brochure

Personal/Academic

Part 1: Your brother belongs to a youth baseball league. Use the Ascent Event brochure template to create a brochure announcing the Youth Baseball League. Pick an appropriate color and font scheme, and include a sign-up form. Type **`Preseason Sign-Up`** as the brochure title. Type **`Youth Baseball League`**, to replace the Business Name text. Type your address and phone number in the appropriate text boxes. Delete the logo. Replace all graphics with sports-related clip art. Edit the captions to match. The league commissioner will send you content for the stories at a later date. Edit the sign-up form event boxes as displayed in Table 2–5 on the next page.

Continued >

Consider This: Your Turn *continued*

Table 2–5 Sign-Up Form Check Box Content

Event Name	Time	Price
Preschool T-Ball: ages 4 and 5	10:00 a.m.	$35.00
Pee-Wee T-Ball: ages 6 and 7	11:00 a.m.	$35.00
Coach Pitched: ages 8 and 9	1:00 p.m.	$50.00
Intermediate: ages 10 and 11	2:30 p.m.	$50.00
Advanced: ages 12 and 13	4:00 p.m.	$50.00
City Team: audition only	6:00 p.m.	TBA

© 2014 Cengage Learning

Part 2: On a separate piece of paper, make a table similar to Table 2–1 on page PUB 69, listing the type of exposure, information, audience, and purpose of the communication. Turn in the table with your printout.

2: Creating a Travel Club Brochure

Professional

Part 1: Use the Voyage template to create a brochure for the Seniors Abroad Club. This local club of senior citizens gets together to take group trips. Use the Casual font scheme. For the title, use Seniors on the Go. Choose a stylistic set for the title. On page 2, include an article describing last year's trip to London (you may use the default text in the story itself), and a secondary article heading that tells how to pack lightly for trips overseas. Insert the social media logo from the Data Files for Students. On page 1, replace the story on the left panel with a list of dates for the upcoming trips to Paris, the Caribbean, and Tokyo. Replace the graphics with suitable pictures and caption styles. Submit your assignment in the format specified by your instructor.

Part 2: You made several decisions while creating the travel brochure in this assignment. How did your choices complement the topic?

3: Researching Templates

Research and Collaboration

Part 1: Individually, visit or call several local copy shops or commercial printers in your area, or visit the websites of several commercial printers. Ask them the following questions: What kind of paper stock do your customers choose for brochures? What is the most commonly used finish? Do you support all three color processes? Will you accept files saved with the Microsoft Publisher Pack and Go Wizard or EPS files? What prepress tasks do you perform? Come back together as a group and create a blank Publisher publication to record your answers. Create a table with the Insert Table button (INSERT tab | Tables group). Insert the questions down the left side. Insert the names of the print shops across the top. Fill in the grid with the answers they provide.

Part 2: Which commercial printer would be the best one to print the Internship Brochure created in this chapter? What information made you choose it? How would you recommend finding a commercial printer to someone who has not studied desktop publishing?

Learn Online

Reinforce what you learned in this chapter with games, exercises, training, and many other online activities and resources.

Student Companion Site Reinforce chapter terms and concepts using review questions, flash cards, practice tests, and interactive learning games, such as a crossword puzzle. These and other online activities and resources are available at no additional cost on www.cengagebrain.com. Visit www.cengage.com/ct/studentdownload for detailed instructions about accessing the resources available at the Student Companion Site.

3 Designing a Newsletter

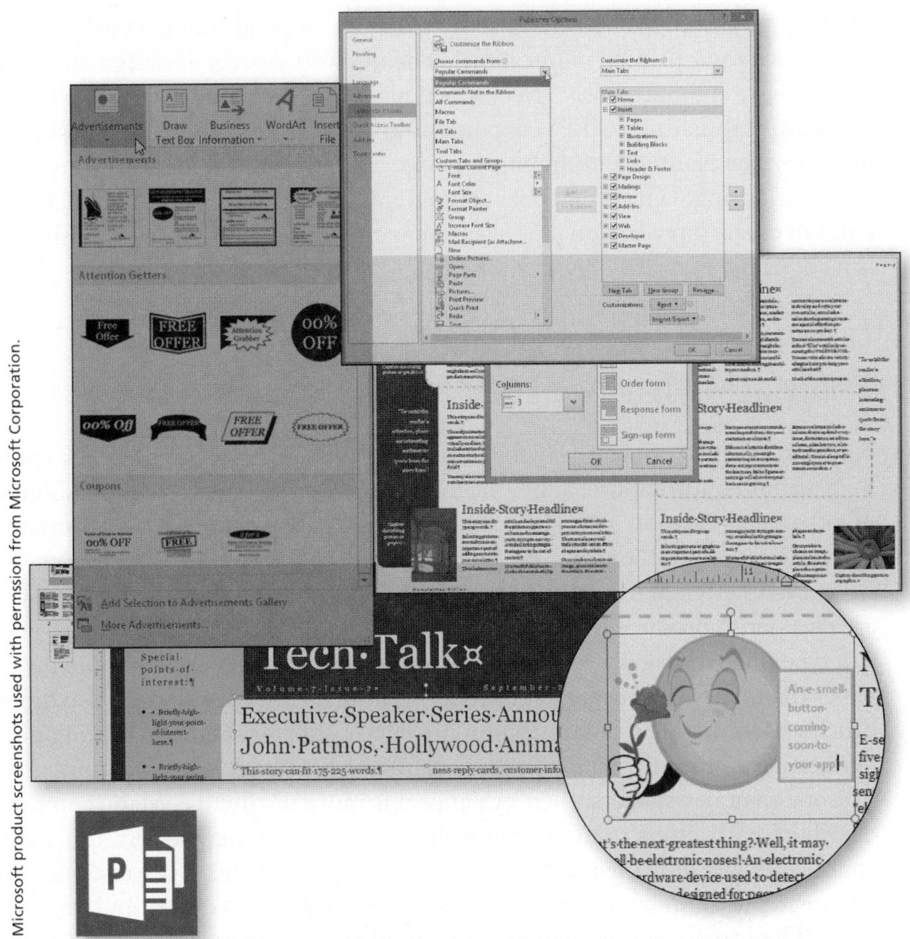

Microsoft product screenshots used with permssion from Microsoft Corporation.

Objectives

You will have mastered the material in this chapter when you can:

- Describe the advantages of using the newsletter medium and identify the steps in its design process
- Edit a newsletter template and navigate pages
- Set page options
- Edit a masthead
- Import text files
- Continue a story across pages and insert continued notices
- Customize the ribbon
- Use Publisher's Edit Story in Microsoft Word feature
- Insert Marginal Elements
- Insert and edit coupons
- Duplicate a graphic
- Revise a newsletter
- Drag-and-drop text
- Check hyphenation in stories
- Create a template with property changes

3 | Designing a Newsletter

Introduction

Desktop publishing is becoming an increasingly popular way for businesses of all sizes to produce their printed publications. The desktop aspects of design and production make it easy and inexpensive to produce high-quality publications in a short time. **Desktop publishing** (DTP) encompasses performing all publishing tasks from a desk, including the planning, designing, writing, and layout, as well as printing, collating, and distributing. With a personal computer and a software program, such as Publisher, you can create a professional publication from your computer without the cost and time of using a professional printer.

Project—Newsletter

Newsletters are a popular way for offices, businesses, schools, and other organizations to distribute information to their clientele. A **newsletter** usually is a double-sided multipage publication with newspaper features, such as columns and a masthead, and the added eye appeal of sidebars, pictures, and other graphics.

Newsletters have several advantages over other publication media. Typically, they are cheaper to produce than brochures. Brochures, designed to be in circulation longer as a type of advertising, are published in greater quantities and on more expensive paper than newsletters, making brochures more costly. Newsletters also differ from brochures in that newsletters commonly have a shorter shelf life, making newsletters a perfect forum for information with dates. Newsletters are narrower and more focused in scope than newspapers; their eye appeal is more distinctive. Many companies distribute newsletters to interested audiences; however, newsletters also are becoming an integral part of many marketing plans to widen audiences, because they offer a legitimate medium by which to communicate services, successes, and issues.

The project in this chapter uses a Publisher newsletter template to produce the Tech Talk newsletter shown in Figure 3–1. This monthly publication informs readers about the Campus Technology Club. The club's four-page newsletter contains a masthead, headings, stories, sidebars, pull quotes, a coupon, and graphics.

Figure 3 – 1

Microsoft product screenshots used with permssion from Microsoft Corporation.

Campus Technology Club Newsletter

School of Technology
Banner Area Community College
8400 Walker Lane
Banner, IL 50024

Phone: 618-555-8662
Fax: 618-555-8663
Email: ctc@bacc.edu

Join us on Facebook!

The **Campus Technology Club** is the premier club for School of Technology students who want to experience all that today's leading technology companies have to offer. The Club sponsors a variety of events with other clubs and campus schools to prepare our members to lead today's technology companies. Members get priority access to round tables with the Executive Speaker Series.

If you have any interest in working in the technology field, the **Campus Technology Club** is for you!

Page 2

Spotlight on Students

This month we are proud to turn the spotlight on Latisha Druze. Latisha is earning her Associate of Science Degree in Health Information Technology and is an active member of the Campus Technology Club.

Latisha wanted to take most classes online so that she could be at home with her small children and save gas. Banner Area Community College was a perfect fit. Also, she knew joining CTC would look good on her resume as well as provide career planning opportunities.

"Health information technology is very marketable," Latisha says. "And, I can use technology while helping people. That's my goal."

Studying online enables her to be a mom, a wife, and a student, allowing her to earn her Health Information Technology degree in a short amount of time.

Way to go Latisha!

What are treks?

Students who have a strong passion for technology should seek professional opportunities beyond the traditional recruiting avenues. To this end, the Campus Technology Club partners with the School of Technology Career Center and the Alumni Office to organize networking 'treks' to areas that have a high concentration of technology-related employers.

Treks provide students the opportunity

to gain a broade[r] information. St[udents] about compan[ies] ni to understand converse with e[mployers] understand tech[nology]. Treks are organi[zed] by students on t[he]

Come to the CT[C meeting to find out] about the next t[rek]

Come to the CTC meeting to find out about the next trek!

It is clear that tech careers are a good choice, with strong potential for growth

Outlook Good for T[ech Jobs]

(Continued from page 1)

on-the-job training, making it a great fit for those who cannot attend college full-time, or temporarily must leave college to work. The work experience will prove invaluable, however, as you complete a degree and seek higher levels of employment.

Those who com[plete] several good em[ployment] programmer ca[n earn a sala-] ry of $71,380 p[er year, and] a system mana[ger can] experience com[parable. The an-]nual salary of $[...] projects an 18% [...] er positions. Th[...] goal for technol[ogy]

Tech Talk

Volume 7 Issue 2

Page 3

New Exciting Web Technologies (NEWT)

E-sensing technology strives to emulate all five senses by using electronic means. While sight and sound are mainstream, the other senses soon will follow. Over the last decade, "electronic sensing" or "e-sensing" technologies have undergone important developments from a technical and commercial point of view. The expression "electronic sensing" re[fers to the capability of reproducing human]

What's the next greatest thing? Well, it may very well be electronic noses! An electronic nose is a hardware device used to detect[...]

An e-small button coming soon to your app!

Campus Technology Club Newsletter

Special points of interest:

- Oct 7 Executive Speaker Series
- Oct [...] CTC [...] Out[...] Yo[...] Smartphon[e]
- Oct 27 Spring registration begins
- Oct 31 Halloween party

Inside this issue:

[Tech] Talk

September 22, 2014

[Executive Speak]er Series Announces [H]ollywood Animator

[...](CTC) [...]ohn [...]ation [...]esday,

with s[...] ing in compu[ter] graphics. Mr. Patmo[s] also will give a presentation entitled "The Moving Picture – Unlocking a Career in Animation," at 3:00 p.m. in Shylock Auditorium, as part of the renowned Executive Speaker Series.

Mr. Patmos is an American animator, film director, and entrepreneur. He founded Revelation Animation Studios in 2010 and still leads the company as

chairman and chief executive. He is best known as the creator of the *Green World* animated cartoon series.

John Patmos of
Revelation Animation Studios

Campus Technology Club members get priority access to the round table with Mr. Patmos. Sign up at ctc_roundtable.edu.

Executive Speaker Series presentations are open to the general public. Arrive early for a good seat.

Revelation Animation Studios, located in La Jacinta Verde, California, employs more than 50 animators in full-time positions.

Outlook Good for Tech Jobs

Students, educators, and employers have been discussing the general worth of a college degree, especially in technology — both in dollars and job growth. After all, college is time-consuming and expensive.

The website of the Bureau of Labor Statistics is a useful source to examine the job and salary outlook problem. At the low end of the scale are computer support specialists. While it is the fastest growth area in

technology (a projected need of 110,000 new positions by 2020), it is one of the lower-paying jobs at $46,000 per year. Only some college education is required, combined with

(Continued on page 2)

Speaker image courtesy of Donna Reneau

For an introduction to Windows and instruction about how to perform basic Windows tasks, read the Office and Windows chapter at the beginning of this book, where you can learn how to resize windows, change screen resolution, create folders, move and rename files, use Windows Help, and much more.

Roadmap

In this chapter, you will learn how to create the newsletter shown in Figure 3–1 on the previous page. The following roadmap identifies general activities you will perform as you progress through this chapter:

1. Select a newsletter template and EDIT publication OPTIONS.
2. IMPORT text from files and CONNECT STORIES across pages.
3. USE CONTINUED NOTICES.
4. CUSTOMIZE the RIBBON.
5. EDIT USING Microsoft WORD when necessary.
6. CREATE sidebars, pull quotes, coupons, and other MARGINAL ELEMENTS.
7. IMPORT GRAPHICS from files and clip art and REVISE.
8. CREATE and change TEMPLATE properties.

At the beginning of step instructions throughout the chapter, you will see an abbreviated form of this roadmap. The abbreviated roadmap uses colors to indicate chapter progress: gray means the chapter is beyond that activity, blue means the task being shown is covered in that activity, and black means that activity is yet to be covered. For example, the following abbreviated roadmap indicates the chapter would be showing a task in the Customize Ribbon activity.

1 EDIT OPTIONS | 2 IMPORT & CONNECT STORIES | 3 USE CONTINUED NOTICES | 4 CUSTOMIZE RIBBON
5 EDIT USING WORD | 6 CREATE MARGINAL ELEMENTS | 7 IMPORT GRAPHICS & REVISE | 8 CREATE TEMPLATE

Use the abbreviated roadmap as a progress guide while you read or step through the instructions in this chapter.

One of the few differences between Windows 7 and Windows 8 occurs in the steps to run Publisher. If you are using Windows 7, click the Start button, type Publisher in the 'Search programs and files' box, click Publisher 2013, and then, if necessary, maximize the Publisher window. For a summary of the steps, refer to the Quick Reference located at the back of this book.

To Run Publisher

If you are using a computer to step through the project in this chapter and you want your screens to match the figures in this book, you should change your screen's resolution to 1366 × 768. For information about how to change a computer's resolution, refer to the Office and Windows chapter at the beginning of this book.

The following steps, which assume Windows 8 is running, use the Start screen or the search box to run Publisher based on a typical installation. You may need to ask your instructor how to run Publisher on your computer. For a detailed example of the procedure summarized below, refer to the Office and Windows chapter.

1. Scroll the Start screen and search for a Publisher 2013 tile. If your Start screen contains a Publisher 2013 tile, tap or click it to run Publisher and then proceed to Step 5; if the Start screen does not contain the Publisher 2013 tile, proceed to the next step to search for the Publisher app.
2. Swipe in from the right edge of the screen or point to the upper-right corner of the screen to display the Charms bar, and then tap or click the Search charm on the Charms bar to display the Search menu.
3. Type `Publisher` as the search text in the Search box, and watch the search results appear in the Apps list.
4. Tap or click Publisher 2013 in the search results to run Publisher.
5. If the Publisher window is not maximized, tap or click the Maximize button on its title bar to maximize the window.

CONSIDER THIS

How do you decide on the purpose and audience of a newsletter?

Designing an effective newsletter involves a great deal of planning in order to deliver a message in the clearest, most attractive, and most effective way possible. Spend time brainstorming ideas for the newsletter with other members of the organization. Ask yourself why you want to create a newsletter in the first place and what message you want to convey. Remember that newsletters both communicate and educate. Identify the scope of the newsletter, and whether you want the topic to be general in nature or more specific — perhaps about only one aspect of the organization. Use the phrase, "I want to tell <audience> about <topic> because <purpose>." Decide on one purpose, and adjust your plans to match that purpose.

As you decide on your audience, ask yourself these questions:

- Who will be reading the stories?
- What are the demographics of this population? That is, what are their characteristics, such as gender, age, educational background, and heritage?
- Why do you want those people to read your newsletter?

Decide if the audience is composed of local, interested clientele, patrons, employees, prospective customers, or family members. Keep in mind the age of your readers and their backgrounds, including both present and future readers.

Benefits and Advantages of Newsletters

Table 3–1 lists some benefits and advantages of using the newsletter medium.

Table 3–1 Benefits and Advantages of Using a Newsletter

Purpose	Benefits and Advantages
Exposure	An easily distributed publication via office mail, by bulk mail, or electronically A pass-along publication for other interested parties A coffee-table reading item in reception areas
Education	An opportunity to inform in a nonrestrictive environment A directed education forum for clientele Increased, focused feedback that is unavailable in most advertising
Contacts	A form of legitimized contact A source of free information to build credibility An easier way to expand a contact database than other marketing tools
Communication	An effective medium to highlight the inner workings of a company A way to create a discussion forum A method to disseminate more information than a brochure
Cost	An easily designed medium using desktop publishing software An inexpensive method of mass production A reusable design using a newsletter template

© 2014 Cengage Learning

Publisher's newsletter templates include stories, graphics, sidebars, and other elements typical of newsletters using a rich collection of intuitive design, layout, typography, and graphic tools. Because Publisher takes care of many of the design issues, using a template to begin a newsletter gives you the advantage of proven layouts with fewer chances of publication errors.

BTW

BTWs

For a complete list of the BTWs found in the margins of this book, visit the BTW resource on the Student Companion Site located on www.cengagebrain.com. For detailed instructions about accessing available resources, visit www.cengage.com/ct/studentdownload or see the inside back cover of this book.

Newsletter Design Choices

Publisher's many design-planning features include more than 100 different newsletter templates from which you may choose, each with its own set of design, color, font, and layout schemes. Each newsletter template produces four pages of stories, graphics, and other objects in the same way. The difference is the location and style of the shapes and graphics, as well as the specific kind of decorations unique to each publication set. A **publication set** is a predefined group of shapes, designed in patterns to create a template style. A publication set is constant across publication

For an introduction to Windows and instruction about how to perform basic Windows tasks, read the Office and Windows chapter at the beginning of this book, where you can learn how to resize windows, change screen resolution, create folders, move and rename files, use Windows Help, and much more.

types; for example, the Bars newsletter template has the same shapes and style of objects as does the Bars brochure template. A publication set helps in branding a company across publication types.

To Choose a Newsletter Template and Options

The following steps choose a newsletter template and change its options.

1. In the template gallery, tap or click BUILT-IN to display the built-in templates.
2. Scroll as necessary and then tap or click the Newsletters thumbnail within the BUILT-IN templates to display the Newsletter templates.
3. Scroll to the section labeled, More Installed Templates, and then tap or click the Banded thumbnail to choose the template.
4. Tap or click the Color scheme button in the template information pane. Scroll as necessary and tap or click Solstice to choose the color scheme.
5. Tap or click the Font scheme button, scroll as necessary, and then tap or click Civic to choose the font scheme.
6. Do not tap or click the Business information button because it is not used in this publication.
7. Tap or click the Page size button in the Options area and then, if necessary, tap or click Two-page spread to choose how the template will display.
8. If necessary, tap or click to remove the check mark in the 'Include customer address' check box (Figure 3–2).

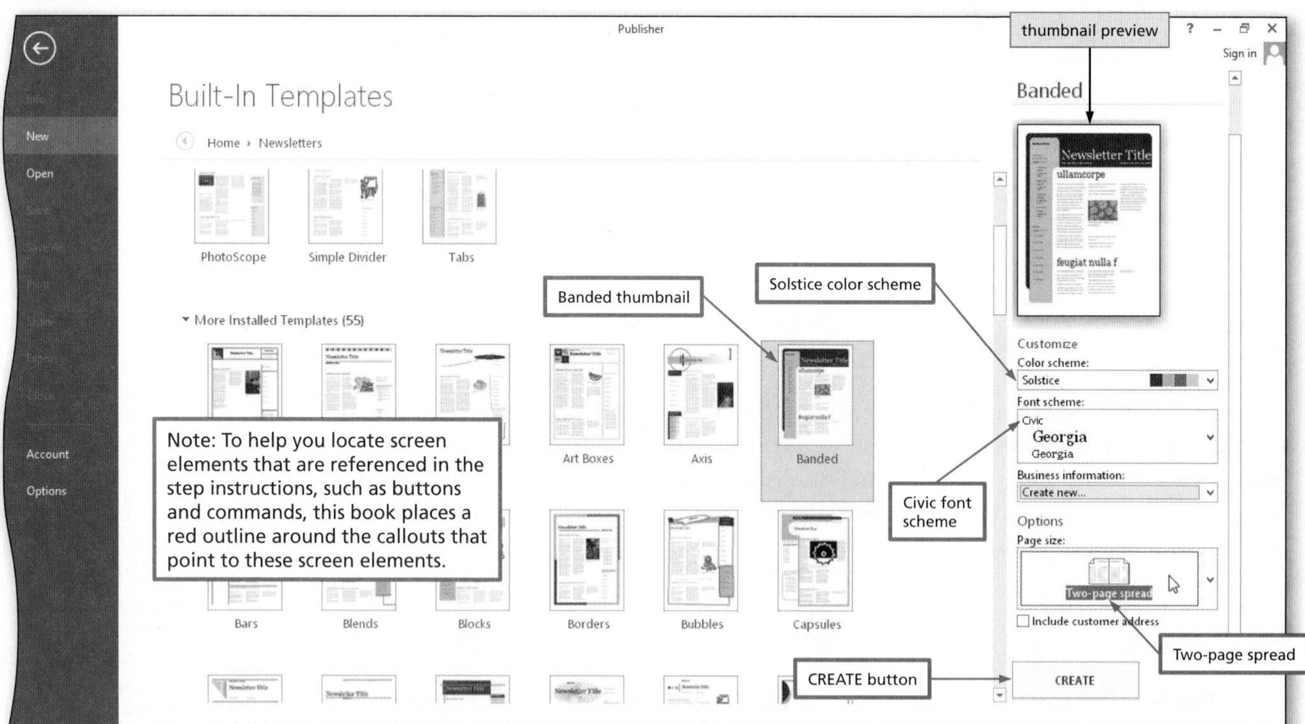

Figure 3–2

9. Tap or click the CREATE button to create the publication based on the template settings.

To Open the Page Navigation Pane

The following step opens the Page Navigation pane to display all of the pages of the newsletter.

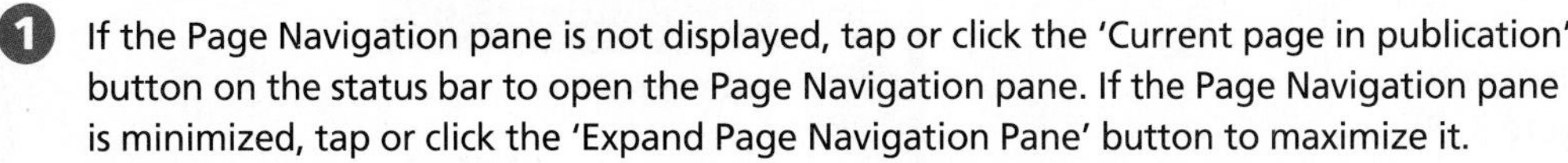

1. If the Page Navigation pane is not displayed, tap or click the 'Current page in publication' button on the status bar to open the Page Navigation pane. If the Page Navigation pane is minimized, tap or click the 'Expand Page Navigation Pane' button to maximize it.

To Display Formatting Marks

As discussed in Chapter 2, it is helpful to display formatting marks, which indicate where in the publication you pressed the ENTER key, the SPACEBAR key, and other keys. The following step displays formatting marks.

1. If the Special Characters button (HOME tab | Paragraph group) is not selected already, tap or click it to display formatting marks on the screen.

CONSIDER THIS

How do you decide about options for the layout and printing?

Choosing a layout and printing options before you even write the stories is a daunting, yet extremely important, task. The kind of printing process and paper you will be using will affect the cost and, therefore, the length of the newsletter. Depending on what you can afford to produce and distribute, the layout may need more or fewer stories, graphics, columns, and sidebars. Base your decisions on content that will be repeated in future newsletters

Make informed decisions about the kind of alignment you plan to use. Choose the paper size and determine how columns, a masthead, and graphics will affect your layout. Decide what kinds of features in the newsletter should be close to each other. A consistent look and feel with simple, eye-catching graphics normally is the best choice for the publication set. Plan to include one graphic with each story. Because newsletters usually are mass-produced, collated, and stapled, you should make a plan for printing and decide if you are going to publish it in-house or externally. Choose a paper that is going to last until the next newsletter.

To Set Page Options

1 EDIT OPTIONS | 2 IMPORT & CONNECT STORIES | 3 USE CONTINUED NOTICES | 4 CUSTOMIZE RIBBON
5 EDIT USING WORD | 6 CREATE MARGINAL ELEMENTS | 7 IMPORT GRAPHICS & REVISE | 8 CREATE TEMPLATE

Publisher newsletters can display one, two, or three columns of story text, or mix the format. ***Why?*** *Changing the number of columns in a story or mixing the format adds visual interest.* The following steps select page options for the various pages in the newsletter.

1

- With Page 1 of the newsletter displayed in the workspace, tap or click PAGE DESIGN on the ribbon to display the PAGE DESIGN tab.
- Tap or click the Options button (PAGE DESIGN tab | Template group) to display the Page Content dialog box.
- Tap or click the Columns button to display its list (Figure 3–3).

Q&A Does the column choice affect the objects down the left side of the newsletter page?

No, the number of columns that you choose will be displayed in the stories only, and the choice affects only the current page.

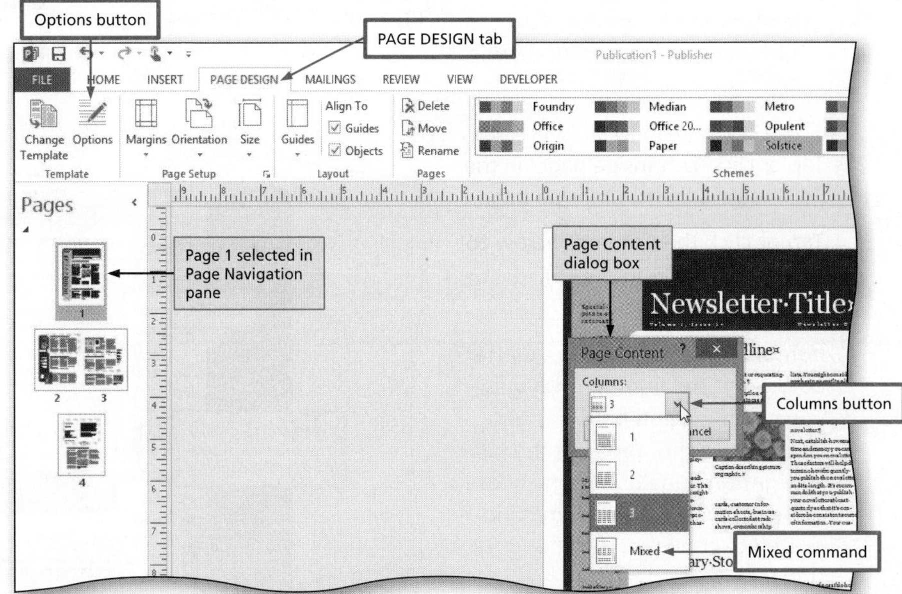

Figure 3–3

2

- Tap or click Mixed in the list to choose a mixed number of columns for the stories on page 1.
- Tap or click the OK button (Page Content dialog box) to change the options for the page (Figure 3–4).

Is one choice better than another one?

No, it is a personal or customer preference. Longer stories may need to be continued at different places, depending upon how many columns of text you have. The more columns you have, the more white space is created on the page.

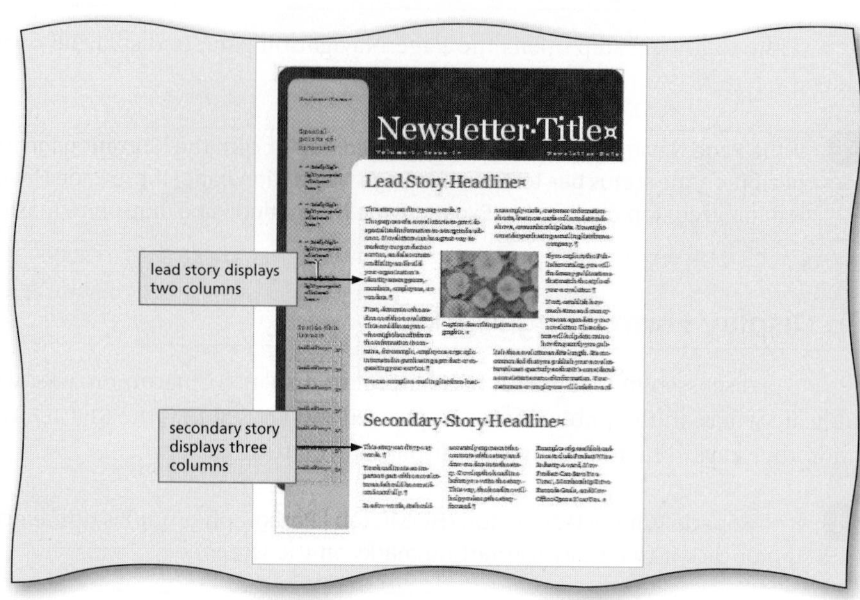

Figure 3–4

3

- Tap or click the 'Page 2 and Page 3' thumbnail in the Page Navigation pane to display the pages in the workspace.
- Tap or click the Options button (PAGE DESIGN tab | Template group) to display the Page Content dialog box.
- Tap or click the 'Select a page to modify' arrow to display its list (Figure 3–5).

What is the Content for page list?

The 'Content for page' list is a list of other objects, including calendars and forms that you might want to use in your newsletter.

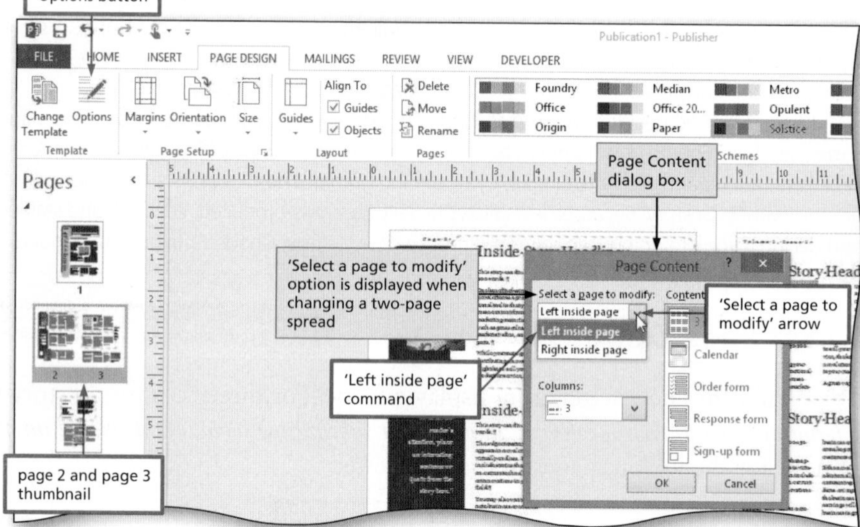

Figure 3–5

4

- Tap or click 'Left inside page' in the list to adjust the columns on page 2.
- Tap or click the Columns arrow to display its list (Figure 3–6).

What if I want to change the number of pages in my newsletter?

To change the number of pages, you can press and hold or right-click a page thumbnail in the Page Navigation pane and then choose either the Insert Page command or Delete command on the shortcut menu.

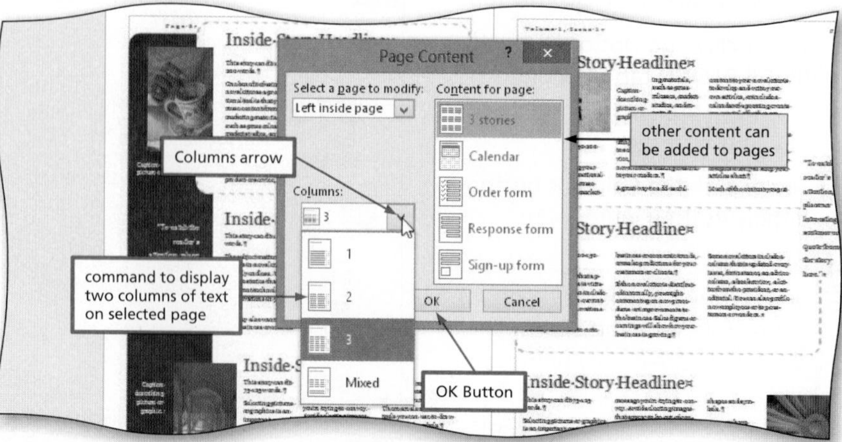

Figure 3–6

5

- Tap or click 2 in the list to choose a two-column format for the stories on page 2.
- Tap or click the OK button (Page Content dialog box) to close the dialog box (Figure 3–7).

Q&A Can I move pages around in my newsletter?

Yes, you can press and hold or right-click in the Page Navigation pane and then choose Move on the shortcut menu. Publisher will display a dialog box, allowing you to specify which page to move and the new location.

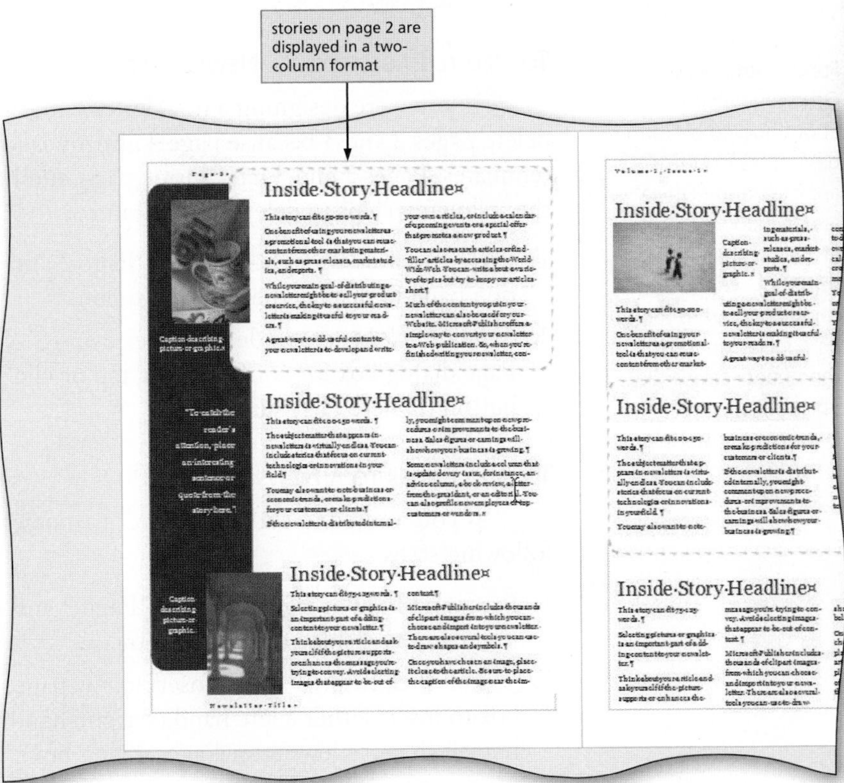

Figure 3–7

6

- Repeat Steps 3 through 5 to set a two-column format for Page 3, the right inside page of the two-page spread (Figure 3–8).

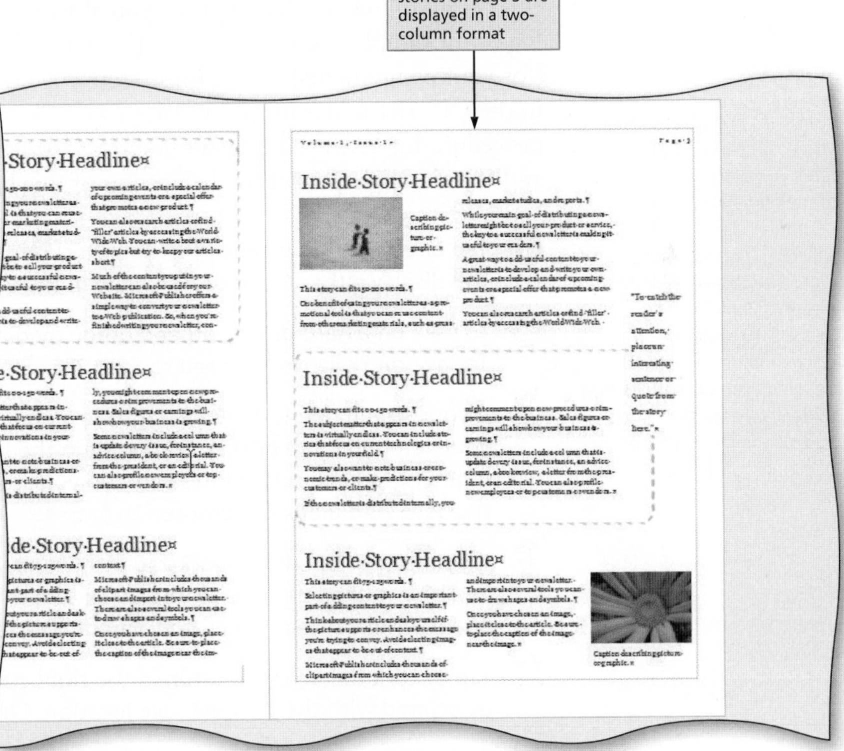

Figure 3–8

Changing the Number of Pages in a Newsletter

Not all newsletters are four pages long. Some will have more or fewer pages. The sections on the next page describe how to add pages to or delete them from a newsletter template.

For an introduction to Office and instruction about how to perform basic tasks in Office apps, read the Office and Windows chapter at the beginning of this book, where you can learn how to run an application, use the ribbon, save a file, open a file, exit an application, use Help, and much more.

To Delete Pages from a Newsletter

If you were designing a newsletter with only two pages, it would be best to delete pages 2 and 3 because page 4 already is formatted to be a back page in most templates. Pages 2 and 3 have inside page numbers and graphics. You would perform the following steps to delete pages 2 and 3.

1. Press and hold or right-click the 'Page 2 and Page 3' thumbnail in the Page Navigation pane to display the shortcut menu.
2. Tap or click Delete to delete pages 2 and 3. When Publisher displays the Delete Page dialog box for confirmation, tap or click Both pages and then click the OK button (Delete Page dialog box).

To Add Pages to a Newsletter

If you wanted to add extra pages to a newsletter, you would perform the following steps.

1. Press and hold or right-click the 'Page 2 and Page 3' thumbnail in the Page Navigation pane to display the shortcut menu.
2. Tap or click Insert Page to insert a new page. Follow the directions in the dialog box to insert either a left-hand or right-hand page, or both, and then click the OK button (Insert Newsletter Pages dialog box).

To Save a Publication

BTW
Organizing Files and Folders
You should organize and store files in folders so that you easily can find the files later. For example, if you are taking an introductory computer class called CIS 101, a good practice would be to save all Publisher files in a Publisher folder in a CIS 101 folder. For a discussion of folders and detailed examples of creating folders, refer to the Office and Windows chapter at the beginning of this book.

The following steps assume you already have created folders for storing your files, for example, a CIS 101 folder (for your class) that contains a Publisher folder (for your assignments). Thus, these steps save the publication in the Publisher folder in the CIS 101 folder on your desired save location. For a detailed example of the procedure for saving a file in a folder or saving a file on SkyDrive, refer to the Office and Windows chapter at the beginning of this book.

1. Tap or click the Save button on the Quick Access Toolbar, which, depending on settings, will display either the Save As gallery in the Backstage view or the Save As dialog box.

2. To save on a hard disk or other storage media on your computer, proceed to Step 2a. To save on SkyDrive, proceed to Step 2b.

2a. If your screen opens the Backstage view and you want to save on storage media on your computer, tap or click Computer in the left pane, if necessary, to display options in the right pane related to saving on your computer. If your screen already displays the Save As dialog box, proceed to Step 4.

2b. If your screen opens the Backstage view and you want to save on SkyDrive, tap or click SkyDrive in the left pane to display SkyDrive saving options or a Sign In button. If your screen displays a Sign In button, tap or click it and then sign in to SkyDrive.

3. Tap or click the Browse button in the right pane to display the Save As dialog box associated with the selected save location (i.e., Computer or SkyDrive).

4. Type `Tech Talk Newsletter` in the File name text box to change the file name. Do not press the ENTER key after typing the file name because you do not want to close the dialog box at this time.

5. Navigate to the desired save location (in this case, the Publisher folder in the CIS 101 folder [or your class folder] on your computer or SkyDrive).

6. Tap or click the Save button (Save As dialog box) to save the publication in the selected folder on the selected save location with the entered file name.

Editing the Masthead

Most newsletters and brochures contain a masthead similar to those used in newspapers. A **masthead** is a box or section printed in each issue that lists information, such as the name, publisher, location, volume, and date. The Publisher-designed masthead, included in the Bars newsletter publication set, contains several text boxes and color-filled shapes that create an attractive, eye-catching graphic to complement the set.

To Edit the Masthead

1 EDIT OPTIONS | 2 IMPORT & CONNECT STORIES | 3 USE CONTINUED NOTICES | 4 CUSTOMIZE RIBBON
5 EDIT USING WORD | 6 CREATE MARGINAL ELEMENTS | 7 IMPORT GRAPHICS & REVISE | 8 CREATE TEMPLATE

The following steps edit text in the masthead, including the volume and issue number. ***Why?*** *Publications typically use volume numbers to indicate the number of years the publication has been in existence. The issue number indicates its sequence. Volume numbers and issue numbers do not necessarily correlate to the calendar year and months. Schools, for example, sometimes start in the fall with Volume 1, Issue 1.*

1

- Tap or click Page 1 in the Page Navigation pane to change the display to page 1.
- Tap or click the text, Newsletter Title, to select it.
- Zoom to 150%.
- Type **`Tech Talk`** to replace the text (Figure 3–9).

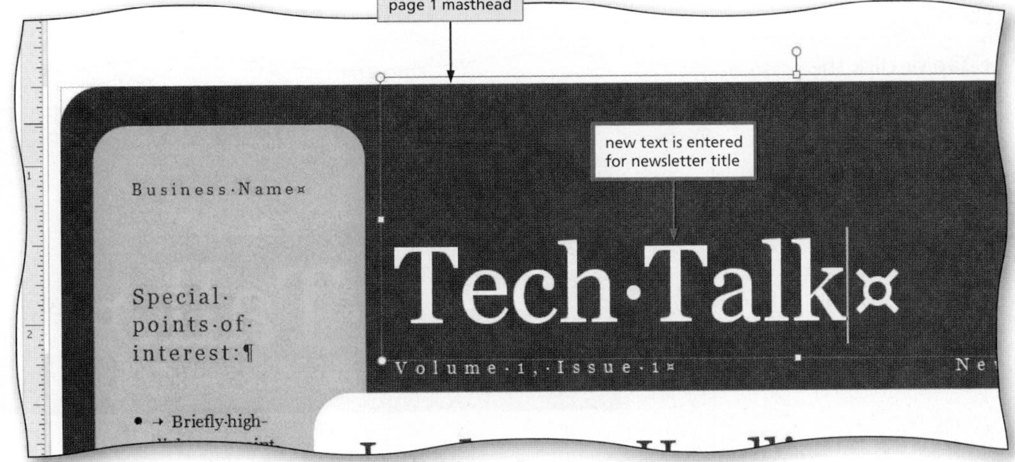

Figure 3–9

Q&A: Why does my font look different?
Publisher replaces the selected text with the font from the publication set. Your font may differ from the one shown.

2

- If necessary, scroll to the left and tap or click the default text in the Business Name text box, and then press CTRL+A to select all of the text.
- Type **`Campus Technology Club Newsletter`** to replace the text (Figure 3–10).

Figure 3–10

Q&A: What if my text does not fit in the box?
Template text boxes for business information components, headlines, and other special boxes use autofitting techniques. Publisher should decrease the font size for longer text as you type. If it does not, someone has turned off the autofitting option; press and hold or right-click the text and then click Best Fit on the shortcut menu to autofit the text.

- Tap or click the placeholder text in the Volume 1, Issue 1 text box to select it.
- Type **Volume 7 Issue 2** to replace the text (Figure 3–11).

Figure 3–11

- Tap or click the placeholder text in the Newsletter Date text box to select it.
- Type **September 22, 2014** to replace the text (Figure 3–12).

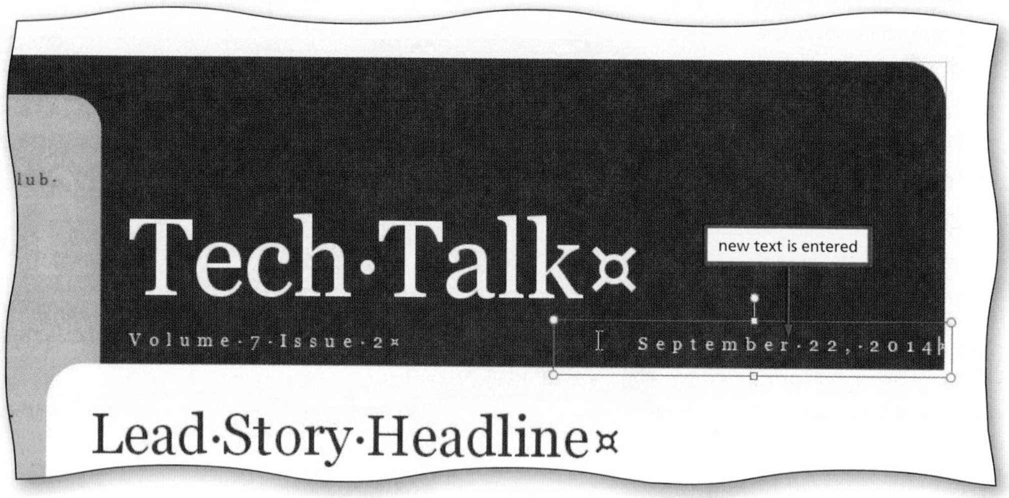

Figure 3–12

BTW
Touch Screen Differences
The Office and Windows interfaces may vary if you are using a touch screen. For this reason, you might notice that the function or appearance of your touch screen differs slightly from this chapter's presentation.

Newsletter Text

Newsletter content may be submitted to you in various ways. Authors may submit their stories in email or as attachments. Others may post a Microsoft Word document or a graphic on the company's common storage drive. Still other authors may handwrite their stories or record them on a recording device. In those cases, you will have to type the story yourself.

Publisher allows users to import text and graphics from many sources, from a variety of different programs, and in many different file formats. Publisher uses the term, **importing**, to describe inserting text or objects from any other source into the Publisher workspace. Publisher uses the term, **story**, when referring to text that is contained within a single text box or a chain of linked text boxes. Each newsletter template provides **linked text boxes**, or text boxes whose text flows from one to another. In the templates, two or three text boxes may be linked automatically; however, if a story is too long to fit in the linked text boxes, Publisher will offer to link even more text boxes for easy reading.

CONSIDER THIS

How do you gather topics and research stories?
Gather credible, relevant information in the form of stories, pictures, dates, figures, tables, and discussion threads. Plan far enough ahead so that you have time to take pictures or gather graphics for each story — even if you end up not using them. Stay organized; keep folders of information and store pictures and stories together. If you have to write a story from scratch, gather your data, do your research, and have an informed reader go over your content.

The same principles of audience, purpose, and topic apply to individual stories, just as they do for the newsletter as a whole. Evaluate your sources for authority, timeliness, and accuracy. Be especially wary of information obtained from the web. Any person, company, or organization can publish a webpage on the Internet. Ask yourself these questions about the source:

- Authority: Does a reputable institution or group support the source? Is the information presented without bias? Are the author's credentials listed and verifiable?
- Timeliness: Is the information up to date? Are the dates of sources listed? What is the last date that the information was revised or updated?
- Accuracy: Is the information free of errors? Is it verifiable? Are the sources clearly identified?

Identify the sources for your text and graphics. Notify all writers of important dates, and allow time for gathering the data. Make a list for each story: include the author's name, the approximate length of the story, the electronic format, and associated graphics. Ask the author for suggestions for headlines. Consult with colleagues about other graphics, features, sidebars, and the masthead.

Acknowledge all sources of information; do not **plagiarize**. Not only is plagiarism unethical, but it also is considered an academic crime that can have severe consequences, such as failing a course or being expelled from school.

When you summarize, paraphrase (rewrite information in your own words), present facts, give statistics, quote exact words, or show a map, chart, or other graphical image, you must acknowledge the source. Information that commonly is known or accessible to the audience constitutes **common knowledge** and does not need to be acknowledged. If, however, you question whether certain information is common knowledge, you should document it — just to be safe.

Replacing Placeholder Text Using an Imported File

Publisher suggests that 175 to 225 words will fit in the space allocated for the lead story. The story is displayed in a two-column text box format that **connects**, or links, the running text from one text box to the next. Publisher links text boxes according to your settings and displays arrow buttons to navigate to the next and previous text boxes.

This edition of Tech Talk contains several stories, some of which have been typed previously and stored using Microsoft Word. The stories, stored on the Data Disk that accompanies this book, are ready to be used in the newsletter. The final story you will type yourself. Each story will include a **headline**, which is a short phrase printed at the top of a story, usually in a bigger font than the story. A headline summarizes the story that follows it.

BTW
Publisher Help
At any time while using Publisher, you can find answers to questions and display information about various topics through Publisher Help. Used properly, this form of assistance can increase your productivity and reduce your frustrations by minimizing the time you spend learning how to use Publisher. For instruction about Publisher Help and exercises that will help you gain confidence in using it, read the Office and Windows chapter at the beginning of this book.

To Edit the Lead Story Headline

The following steps edit the Lead Story Headline placeholder text.

1. Tap or click the placeholder text, Lead Story Headline, on page 1 to select it.
2. Type **`Executive Speaker Series Announces John Patmos, Hollywood Animator`** to replace the text (Figure 3–13).

new headline text is entered
Volume·7·Issue·2
September·22,·2014
Executive·Speaker·Series·Announces·
John·Patmos,·Hollywood·Animator
This·story·can·fit·175-225·words.¶
ness·reply·cards,·customer·information·

Figure 3–13

To Import a Text File

The following steps import a text file to replace the Publisher-supplied placeholder text. ***Why?*** *Importing the story prevents typographical errors created by typing the text.* The text file is included in the Data Files for Students. To complete these steps, you will be required to use the Data Files for Students. Visit www.cengage.com/ct/studentdownload for detailed instructions or contact your instructor for information about accessing the required files.

1

- Scroll down to display the story below the headline.
- Tap or click the placeholder text in the story to select it (Figure 3–14).

Experiment

- Scroll as necessary to read the placeholder text in order to learn about design suggestions related to newsletter publications.

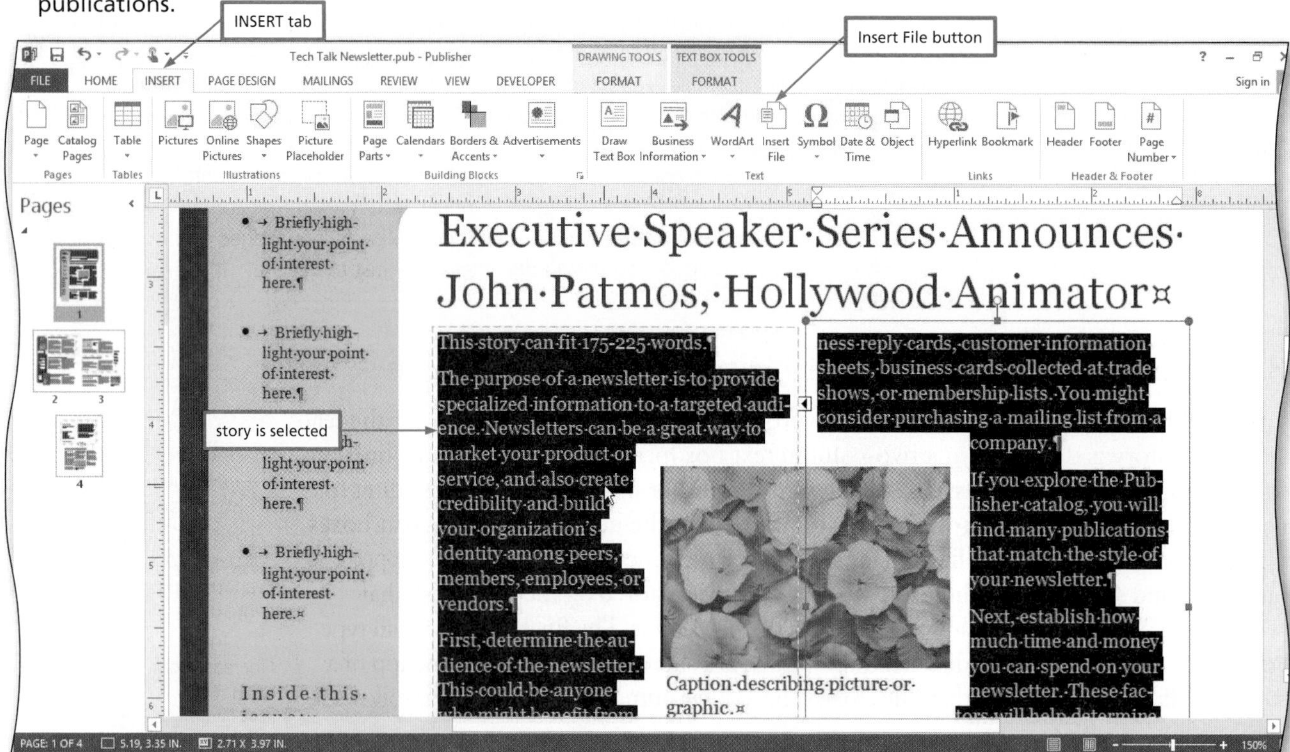

Figure 3–14

2

- Display the INSERT tab.
- Tap or click the Insert File button (INSERT tab | Text group) to display the Insert Text dialog box (Figure 3–15).
- Navigate to the location of the file to be opened (in this case, the Chapter 03 folder in the Publisher folder in the CIS 101 folder).

Q&A What kinds of text files can Publisher import?

Publisher can import files from most popular applications. If you click the 'All Text Formats' button, you can see a list of all of the file types.

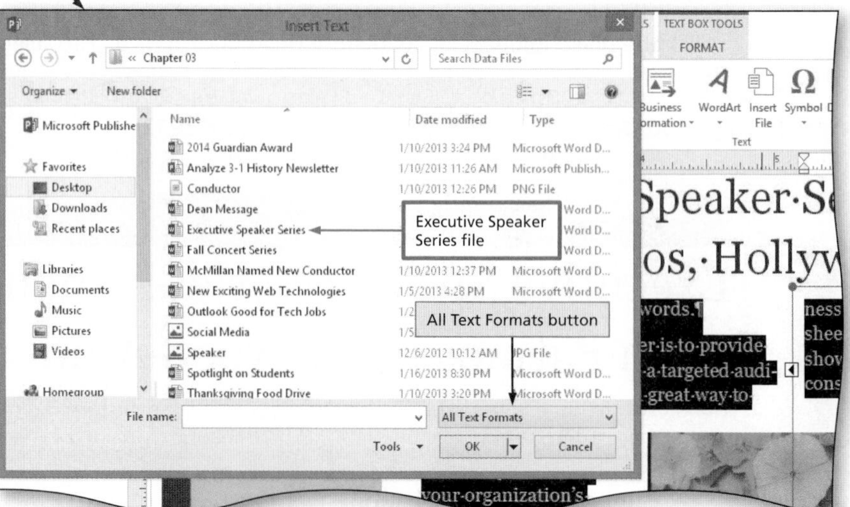

Figure 3–15

- Double-tap or double-click the 'Executive Speaker Series' file to insert the text into the newsletter (Figure 3–16).

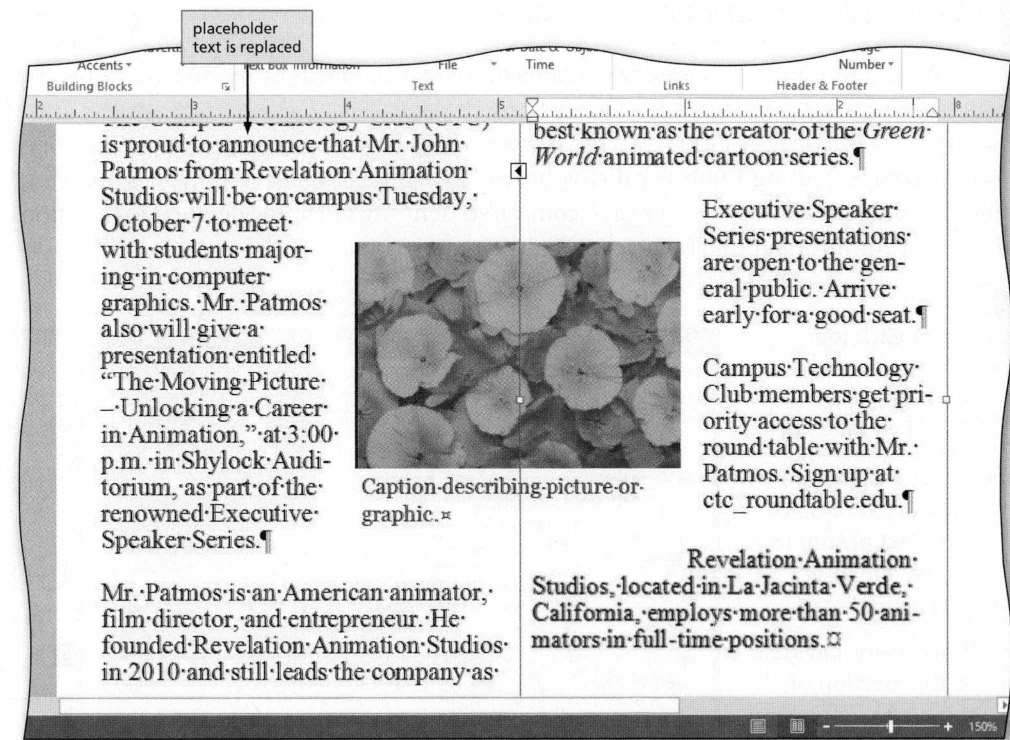
placeholder text is replaced
Building Blocks
Text
Links
Header & Footer
is·proud·to·announce·that·Mr.·John·Patmos·from·Revelation·Animation·Studios·will·be·on·campus·Tuesday,·October·7·to·meet·with·students·majoring·in·computer·graphics.·Mr.·Patmos·also·will·give·a·presentation·entitled·"The·Moving·Picture·–·Unlocking·a·Career·in·Animation,"·at·3:00·p.m.·in·Shylock·Auditorium,·as·part·of·the·renowned·Executive·Speaker·Series.¶
Mr.·Patmos·is·an·American·animator,·film·director,·and·entrepreneur.·He·founded·Revelation·Animation·Studios·in·2010·and·still·leads·the·company·as·
Caption·describing·picture·or·graphic.
best·known·as·the·creator·of·the·Green·World·animated·cartoon·series.¶
Executive·Speaker·Series·presentations·are·open·to·the·general·public.·Arrive·early·for·a·good·seat.¶
Campus·Technology·Club·members·get·priority·access·to·the·round·table·with·Mr.·Patmos.·Sign·up·at·ctc_roundtable.edu.¶
Revelation·Animation·Studios,·located·in·La·Jacinta·Verde,·California,·employs·more·than·50·animators·in·full-time·positions.

Figure 3–16

Other Ways

1. Press and hold or right-click story, tap or click Change Text, tap or click Text File, select File, tap or click OK button (Insert Text dialog box)

To Edit the Secondary Story Headline

The following steps edit the Secondary Story Headline placeholder text.

1. Tap or click the placeholder text, Secondary Story Headline, on page 1 to select it.
2. Type `Outlook Good for Tech Jobs` to replace the text (Figure 3–17).

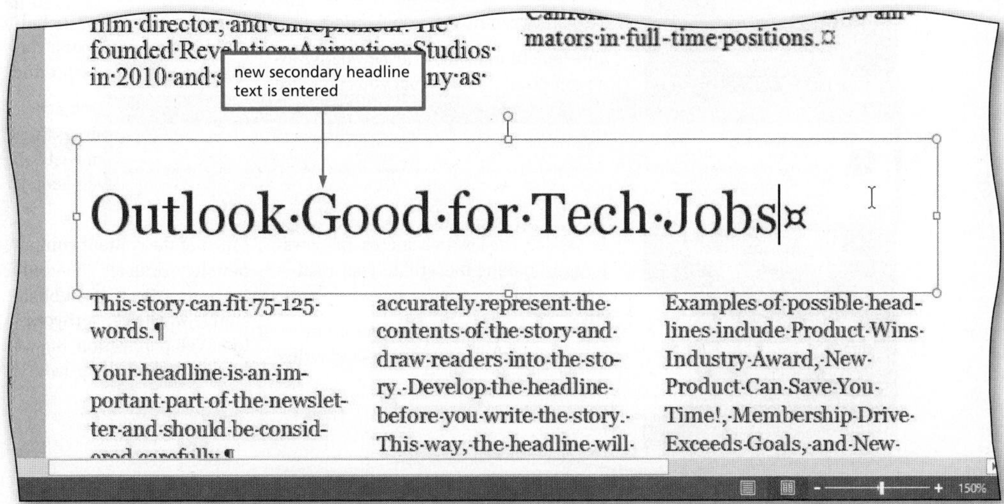
new secondary headline text is entered
Outlook·Good·for·Tech·Jobs
This·story·can·fit·75-125·words.¶
Your·headline·is·an·important·part·of·the·newsletter·and·should·be·considered·carefully.¶
accurately·represent·the·contents·of·the·story·and·draw·readers·into·the·story.·Develop·the·headline·before·you·write·the·story.·This·way,·the·headline·will·
Examples·of·possible·headlines·include·Product·Wins·Industry·Award,·New·Product·Can·Save·You·Time!,·Membership·Drive·Exceeds·Goals,·and·New·

Figure 3–17

To Continue a Story across Pages

As you import text, if a story contains more text than will fit in the default text box, Publisher displays a message to warn you. ***Why?*** *You then have the option to allow Publisher to connect or* **autoflow** *the text to another available text box, or to flow the text yourself, manually.* The following steps import a story and continue it from page 1 to page 2, using Publisher dialog boxes. To complete these steps, you will be required to use the Data Files for Students. Visit www.cengage.com/ct/studentdownload for detailed instructions or contact your instructor for information about accessing the required files.

1

- Tap or click the secondary story placeholder text on page 1 to select it.
- Tap or click the Insert File button (INSERT tab | Text group) to display the Insert Text dialog box.
- If necessary, navigate to the location of the file to be opened (in this case, the Chapter 03 folder in the Publisher folder in the CIS 101 folder) (Figure 3–18).

Figure 3–18

2

- Double-tap or double-click the file named, Outlook Good for Tech Jobs, to insert the text file (Figure 3–19).

Q&A Why did Publisher display a dialog box and move to page 2?
The story was too large to fit in the space provided on page 1. Publisher moved to the first available text box with default or placeholder story text.

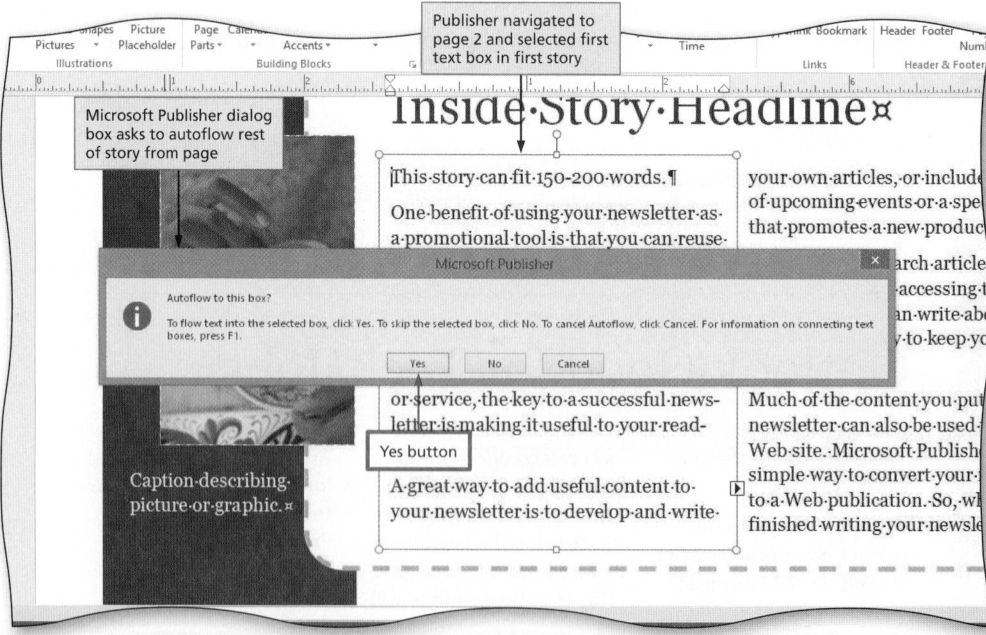

Figure 3–19

3

- In the Microsoft Publisher dialog box, tap or click the Yes button to autoflow the story to the selected text box (Figure 3–20).

Q&A What do the three buttons do?
If you click the Yes button, Publisher will insert the rest of the text in the currently selected text box. If you click the No button, Publisher will move to the next story text box and ask again. If you click the Cancel button, you will have to flow the text manually.

What if I have no more spare text boxes in which to flow the text?
Publisher will ask if you want new text boxes created. If you answer yes, Publisher automatically will create a new page with new text boxes.

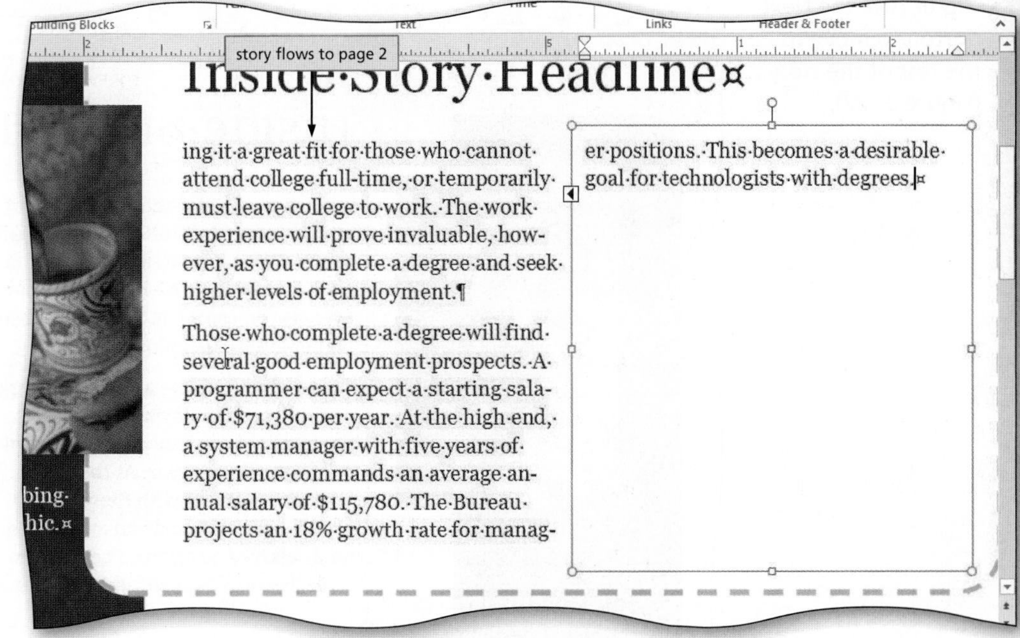
story flows to page 2
Inside·Story·Headline¤
ing·it·a·great·fit·for·those·who·cannot· attend·college·full-time,·or·temporarily· must·leave·college·to·work.·The·work· experience·will·prove·invaluable,·how- ever,·as·you·complete·a·degree·and·seek· higher·levels·of·employment.¶
Those·who·complete·a·degree·will·find· several·good·employment·prospects.·A· programmer·can·expect·a·starting·sala- ry·of·$71,380·per·year.·At·the·high·end,· a·system·manager·with·five·years·of· experience·commands·an·average·an- nual·salary·of·$115,780.·The·Bureau· projects·an·18%·growth·rate·for·manag-
er·positions.·This·becomes·a·desirable· goal·for·technologists·with·degrees.¤

Figure 3–20

To Follow a Story across Pages

1 EDIT OPTIONS | 2 IMPORT & CONNECT STORIES | 3 USE CONTINUED NOTICES | 4 CUSTOMIZE RIBBON
5 EDIT USING WORD | 6 CREATE MARGINAL ELEMENTS | 7 IMPORT GRAPHICS & REVISE | 8 CREATE TEMPLATE

Publisher provides a way to move quickly back and forth through a continued story. ***Why?*** *While reading the story online, you may forget where the rest of the story is located or want to jump to its location quickly.* The following steps use the Next and Previous buttons to follow the story from text box to text box, across pages.

1

- Click Page 1 in the Page Navigation pane and navigate to the Outlook Good for Tech Jobs story at the bottom of the page.
- Tap or click the third text box in the story to display the Previous and Next buttons (Figure 3–21).

Q&A Do all text boxes have Previous and Next buttons?
No. Only text boxes that contain a linked story display the buttons.

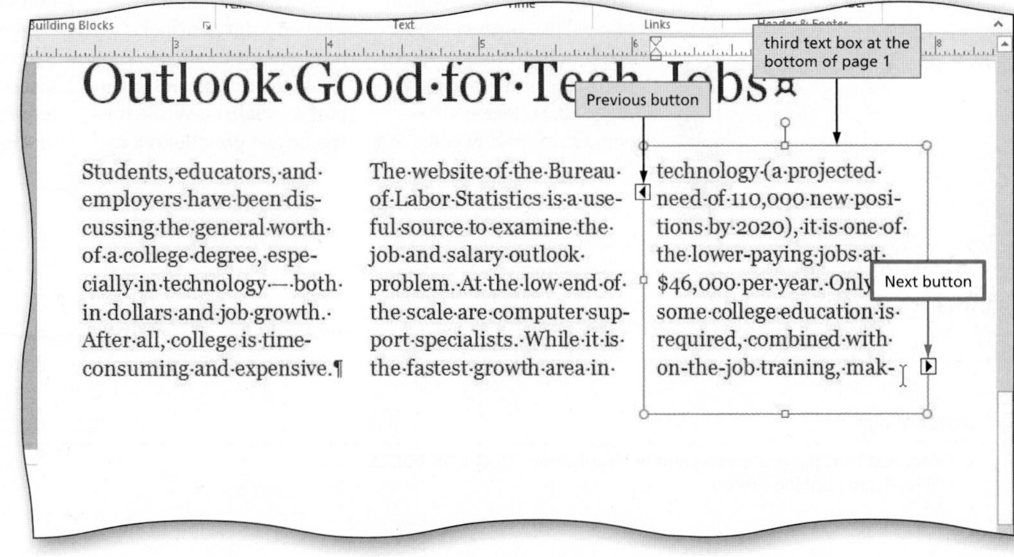
third text box at the bottom of page 1
Previous button
Next button
Outlook·Good·for·Tech·Jobs¤
Students,·educators,·and· employers·have·been·dis- cussing·the·general·worth· of·a·college·degree,·espe- cially·in·technology—both· in·dollars·and·job·growth.· After·all,·college·is·time- consuming·and·expensive.¶
The·website·of·the·Bureau· of·Labor·Statistics·is·a·use- ful·source·to·examine·the· job·and·salary·outlook· problem.·At·the·low·end·of· the·scale·are·computer·sup- port·specialists.·While·it·is· the·fastest·growth·area·in·
technology·(a·projected· need·of·110,000·new·posi- tions·by·2020),·it·is·one·of· the·lower-paying·jobs·at· $46,000·per·year.·Only some·college·education·is· required,·combined·with· on-the-job·training,·mak-

Figure 3–21

- Tap or click the Next button to move to the rest of the story (Figure 3–22).

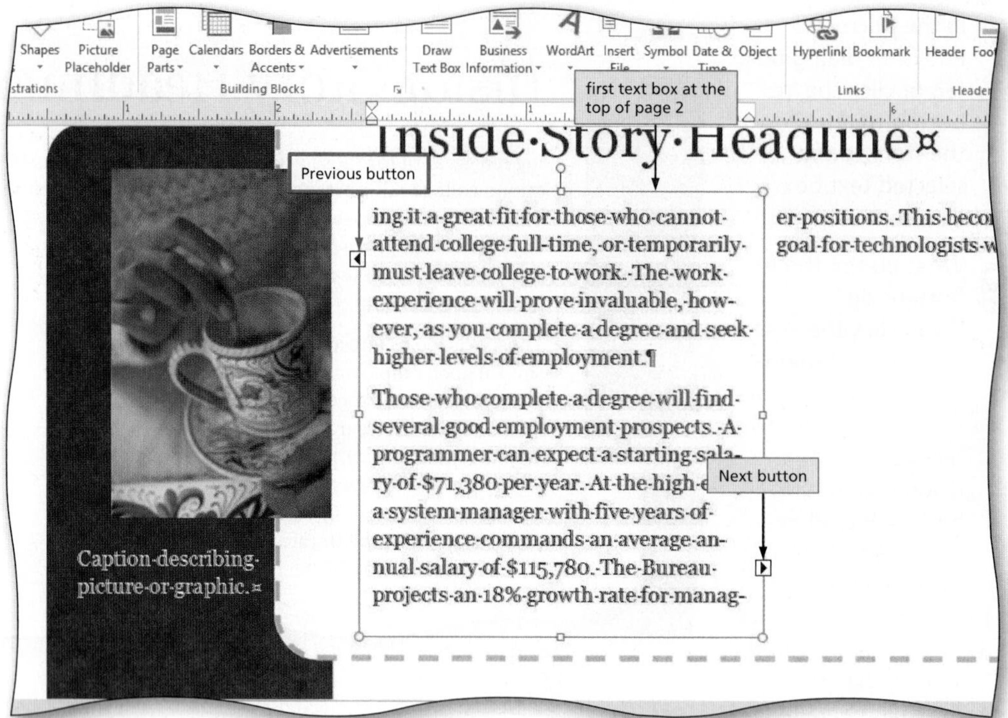

Figure 3 – 22

- Tap or click the Previous button to move back to the first part of the story, the third text box on page 1 (Figure 3–23).

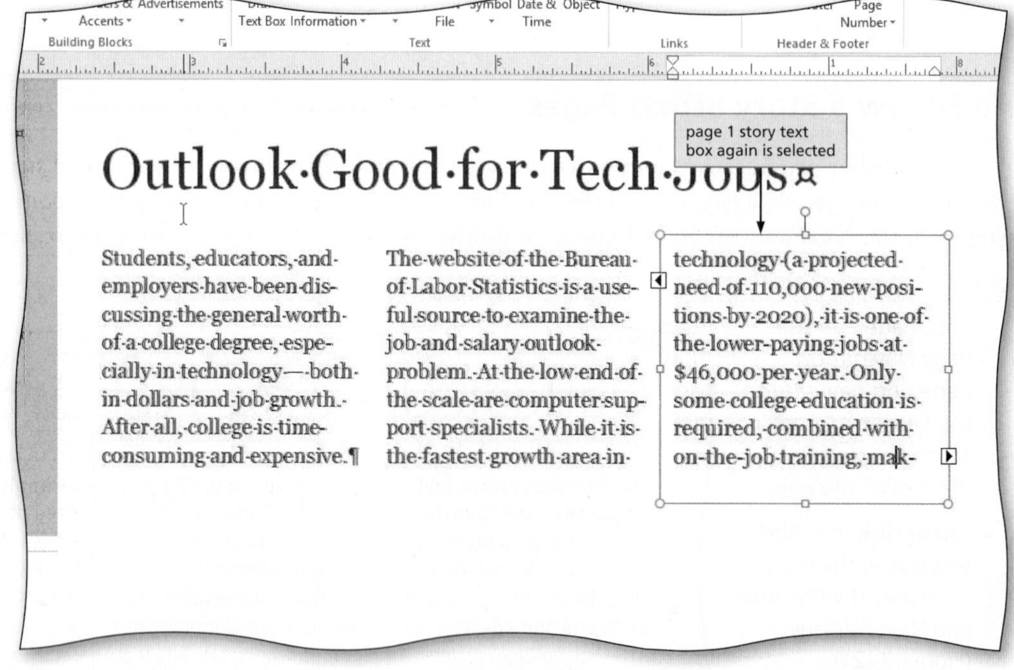

Figure 3 – 23

Other Ways

1. Select text box, tap or click Previous or Next button (TEXT BOX TOOLS FORMAT tab | Linking group)

To Break a Text Box Link

1 EDIT OPTIONS | 2 IMPORT & CONNECT STORIES | 3 USE CONTINUED NOTICES | 4 CUSTOMIZE RIBBON
5 EDIT USING WORD | 6 CREATE MARGINAL ELEMENTS | 7 IMPORT GRAPHICS & REVISE | 8 CREATE TEMPLATE

Sometimes you change your mind about where to continue a story. In that case, you have two choices. You can undo the previous insertion and autoflow again, or you can break the connection and create a manual one. When you break a connection, the extra text that cannot fit in the text box is placed in **overflow**. ***Why?*** *Unlike the Clipboard, the overflow area is maintained when you save the publication, allowing you to access it at any time.* The following step breaks the connection between the story at the bottom of page 1 and its continuation at the top of page 2.

- If necessary, navigate to page 1 and the story at the bottom of the page.
- Tap or click the rightmost column in the story to select the text box.
- Display the TEXT BOX TOOLS FORMAT tab.
- Tap or click the Break button (TEXT BOX TOOLS FORMAT tab | Linking group) to break the connection to the rest of the story (Figure 3–24).

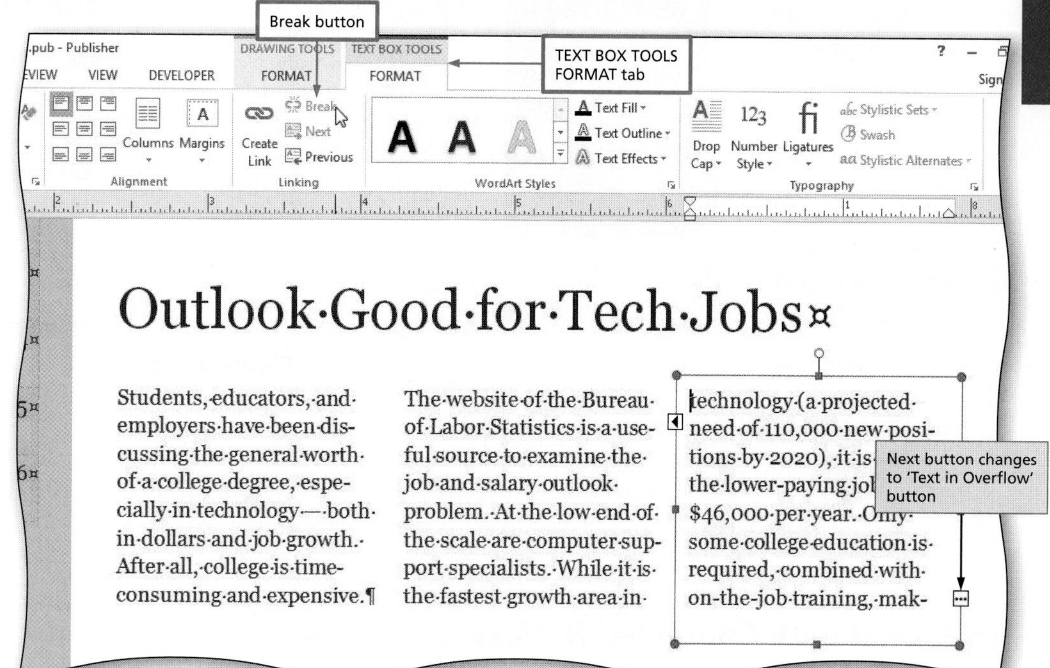

Figure 3–24

Q&A Where is the rest of the story now?
Publisher places it in a special overflow area as indicated by the 'Text in Overflow' button in Figure 3–24. The text box on page 2 becomes blank.

To Manually Continue the Story across Pages

1 EDIT OPTIONS | 2 IMPORT & CONNECT STORIES | 3 USE CONTINUED NOTICES | 4 CUSTOMIZE RIBBON
5 EDIT USING WORD | 6 CREATE MARGINAL ELEMENTS | 7 IMPORT GRAPHICS & REVISE | 8 CREATE TEMPLATE

The following steps manually move the text from the overflow area to another text box. ***Why?*** *You cannot see the text while it is in overflow.*

- If necessary, select the text box that displays the 'Text in Overflow' button.
- Tap or click the 'Text in Overflow' button to display the pitcher mouse pointer (Figure 3–25).

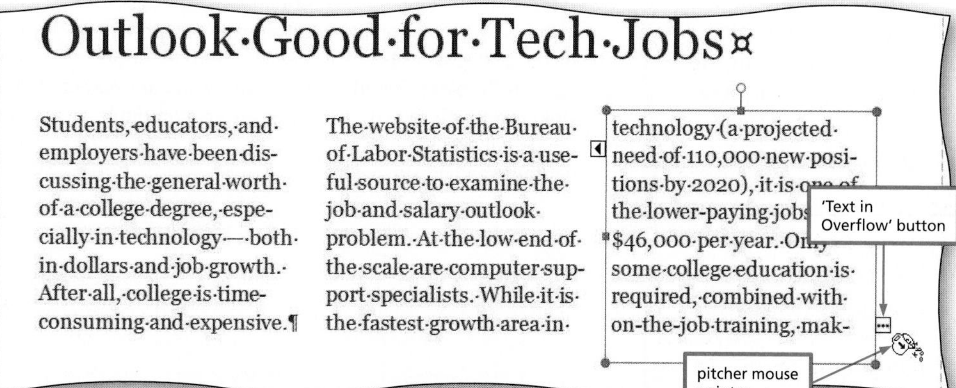

Figure 3–25

Q&A My text wraps at different places. Did I do something wrong?
Your story may wrap differently depending upon your printer's capability of reproducing the font. You will hyphenate all of the stories later in the chapter.

- Tap or click 'Page 2 and Page 3' in the Page Navigation pane to display the pages.
- Scroll as necessary to display the third story on page 2.
- With the pitcher mouse pointer, tap or click the placeholder text in the third story to continue the "Outlook Good for Tech Jobs" text (Figure 3–26).

Figure 3–26

Q&A What if I change my mind and want to continue to a different text box?

You can tap or click the Undo button on the Quick Access Toolbar, or you can tap or click the last column of the story on page 1 and then tap or click the Break button (TEXT BOX TOOLS FORMAT tab | Linking Group). You then can tap or click the 'Text in Overflow' button again.

To Format with Continued Notices

1 EDIT OPTIONS | 2 IMPORT & CONNECT STORIES | 3 USE CONTINUED NOTICES | 4 CUSTOMIZE RIBBON
5 EDIT USING WORD | 6 CREATE MARGINAL ELEMENTS | 7 IMPORT GRAPHICS & REVISE | 8 CREATE TEMPLATE

In print publications for stories that flow from one page to another, it is good practice to add **continued notices**, or **jump lines**, to guide readers through the story. ***Why?*** *A jump line helps readers find the rest of the story easily*. The following steps format the last box on page 1 with a continued on notice. Then, on page 3, the first text box in the rest of the story is formatted with a continued from notice.

- Tap or click the Page 1 icon in the Page Navigation pane, and then navigate to the bottom of the page.
- Press and hold or right-click the third column of text in the lead story to display the shortcut menu (Figure 3–27).

Q&A Will Publisher ask me what page number to use?

The placement of the notices and the page numbering are automatic.

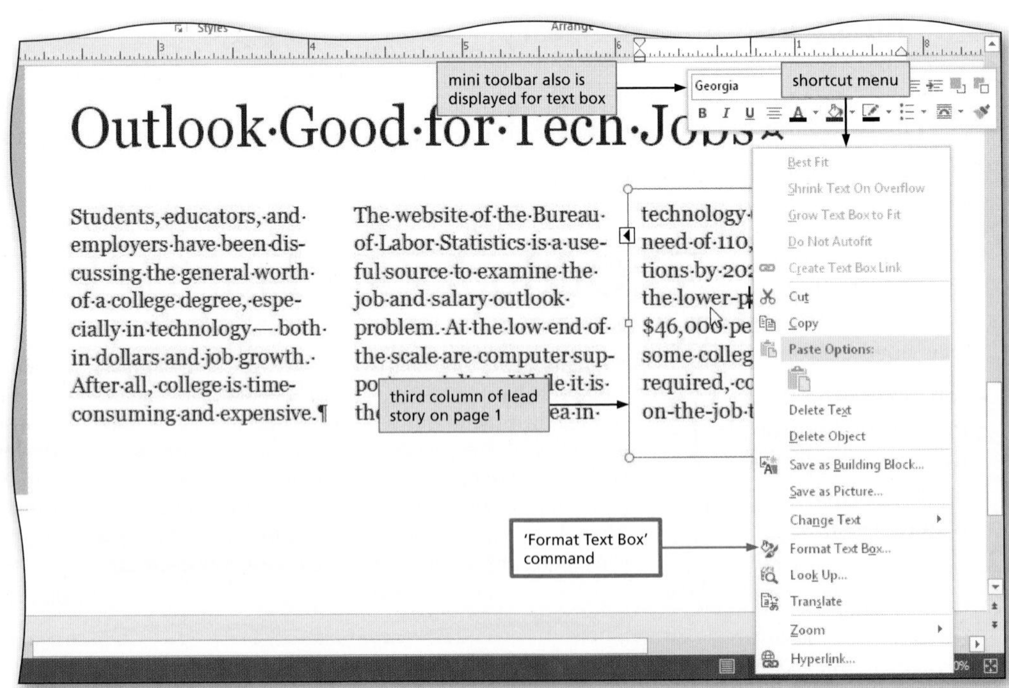

Figure 3–27

2

- Tap or click 'Format Text Box' to display the Format Text Box dialog box.
- Tap or click the Text Box tab to display its settings.
- Tap or click to display a check mark in the 'Include "Continued on page ..."' check box (Figure 3–28).

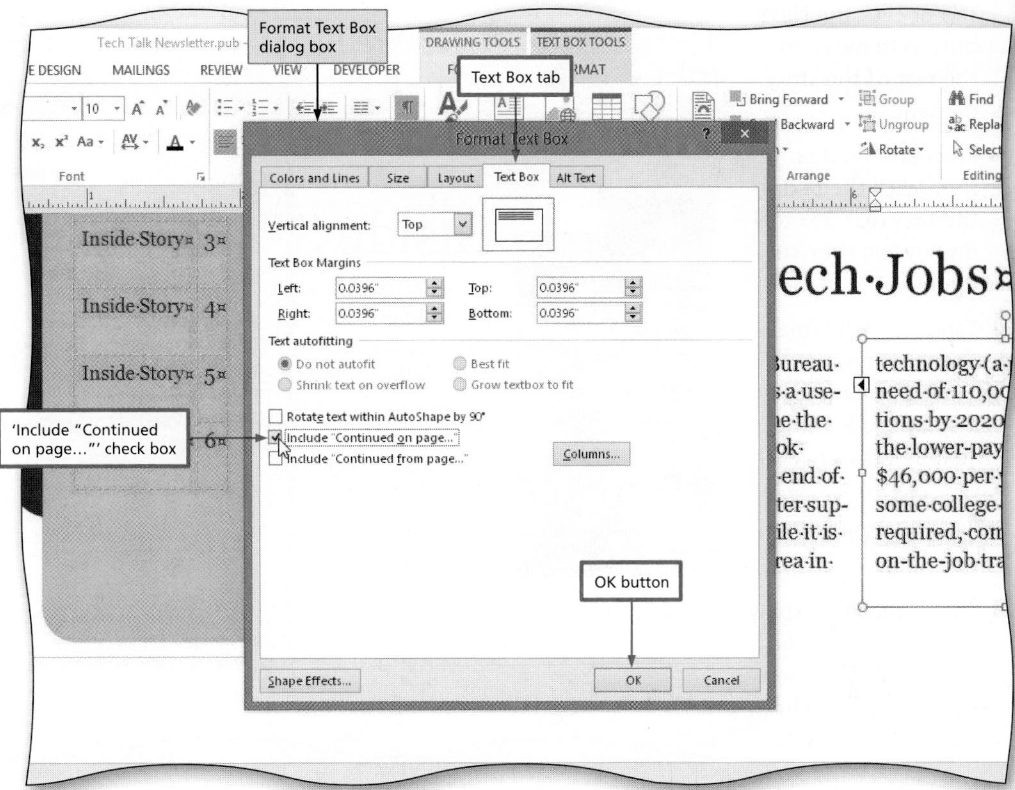

Figure 3–28

3

- Tap or click the OK button (Format Text Box dialog box) to insert the continued notice (Figure 3–29).

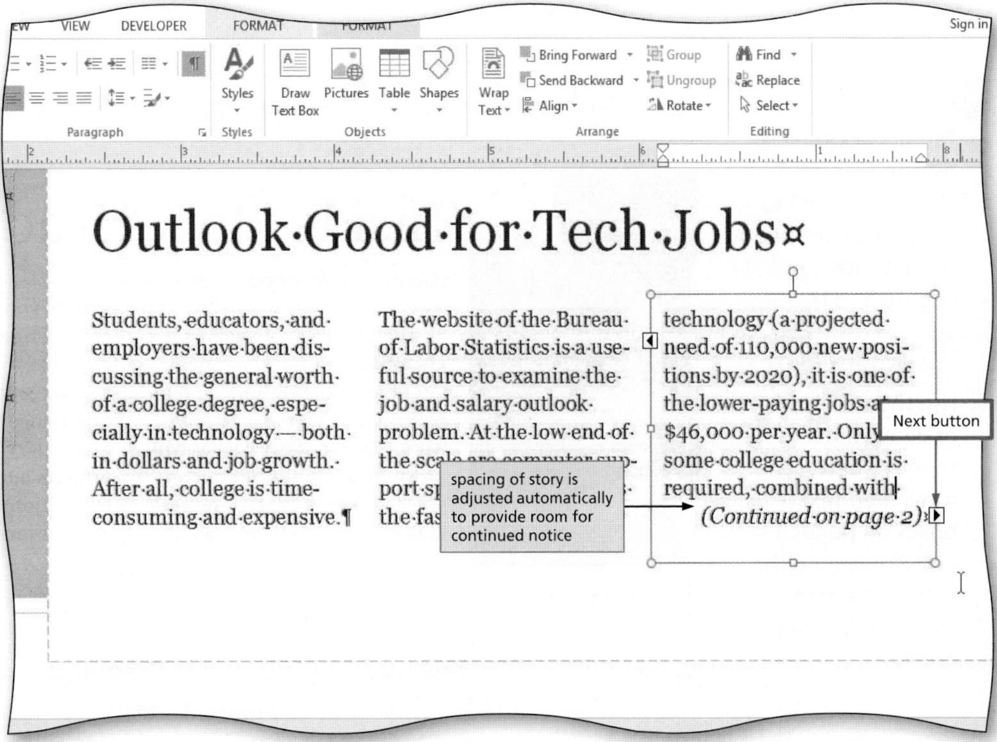

Figure 3–29

4

- Tap or click the Next button to move to the rest of the story on page 2.
- Press and hold or right-click the text in the first text box to display the shortcut menu.
- Tap or click 'Format Text Box' on the shortcut menu to display the Format Text Box dialog box.
- If necessary, tap or click the Text Box tab to display its settings.
- Tap or click to display a check mark in the 'Include "Continued from page ..."' check box (Figure 3–30).

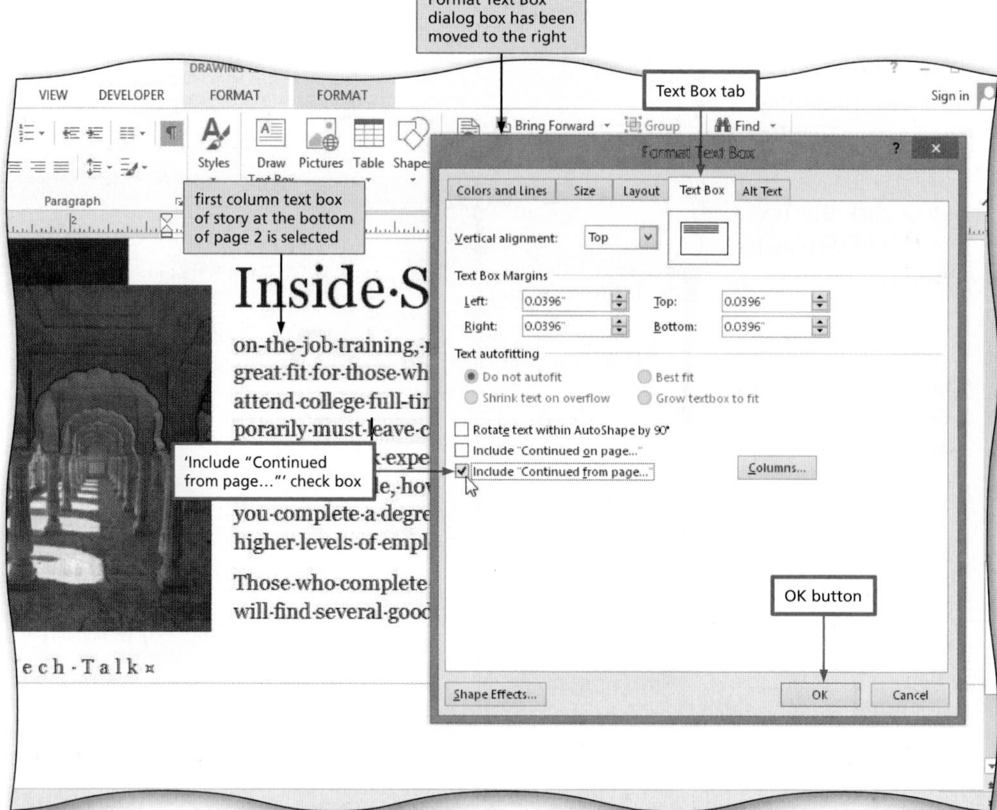

Figure 3–30

Q&A What do I do if my dialog box is covering up the text box?
The setting changes will take place when you click the OK button. If you want to see both the dialog box and the text box, you can drag the title bar of the dialog box to the right, as shown in Figure 3–30.

5

- Tap or click the OK button (Format Text Box dialog box) to insert the continued from notice (Figure 3–31).

Experiment

- Use the next and previous buttons to move between the linked text boxes on pages 1 and 2. Examine the jump lines with the supplied page numbers.

Figure 3–31

Other Ways

1. Select text box, tap or click Format Text Box Dialog Box Launcher (TEXT BOX TOOLS FORMAT tab | Text group), tap or click Text Box tab, tap or click desired continued notice check box

To Edit the Headlines for the Continued Story

The following step edits the inside headlines for the continued story.

1. Tap or click the Inside Story Headline placeholder text to select it, and then type `Outlook Good for Tech Jobs` to replace the text (Figure 3–32).

Figure 3–32

BTW

Text in Overflow

The overflow area is an invisible storage location within a publication that holds extra text. You can move text out of overflow and back into a publication by one of several means: flowing text into a new text box, autofitting text, enlarging the text box, changing the text size, changing the margins within the text box, or deleting some of the text in the text box.

To Import Other Stories on Page 2

The following steps edit the headline and import the text for the second story on page 2. To complete these steps, you will be required to use the Data Files for Students. Visit www.cengage.com/ct/studentdownload for detailed instructions or contact your instructor for information about accessing the required files.

1. Scroll to display the top portion of page 2, and then click the Inside Story Headline placeholder text above the first story to select it. Recall that the first story text box is blank because of the autoflow change.
2. Type `Spotlight on Students` to replace the selected headline.
3. Tap or click inside the empty story text box to position the insertion point.
4. Tap or click the Insert File button (INSERT tab | Text group) to display the Insert Text dialog box.
5. If necessary, navigate to the location of the file to be opened (in this case, the Chapter 03 folder in the Publisher folder in the CIS 101 folder).
6. Double-tap or double-click the file named, Spotlight on Students, to insert the text file.

BTW

The Ribbon and Screen Resolution

Publisher may change how the groups and buttons within the groups appear on the ribbon, depending on the computer's screen resolution. Thus, your ribbon may look different from the ones in this book if you are using a screen resolution other than 1366 × 768.

7. Repeat steps 1 through 6 on the previous page for the second story on the page entitled, What are treks?, inserting the file named, 'What are treks.'

8. Zoom to approximately 80% to display both stories and headlines (Figure 3–33).

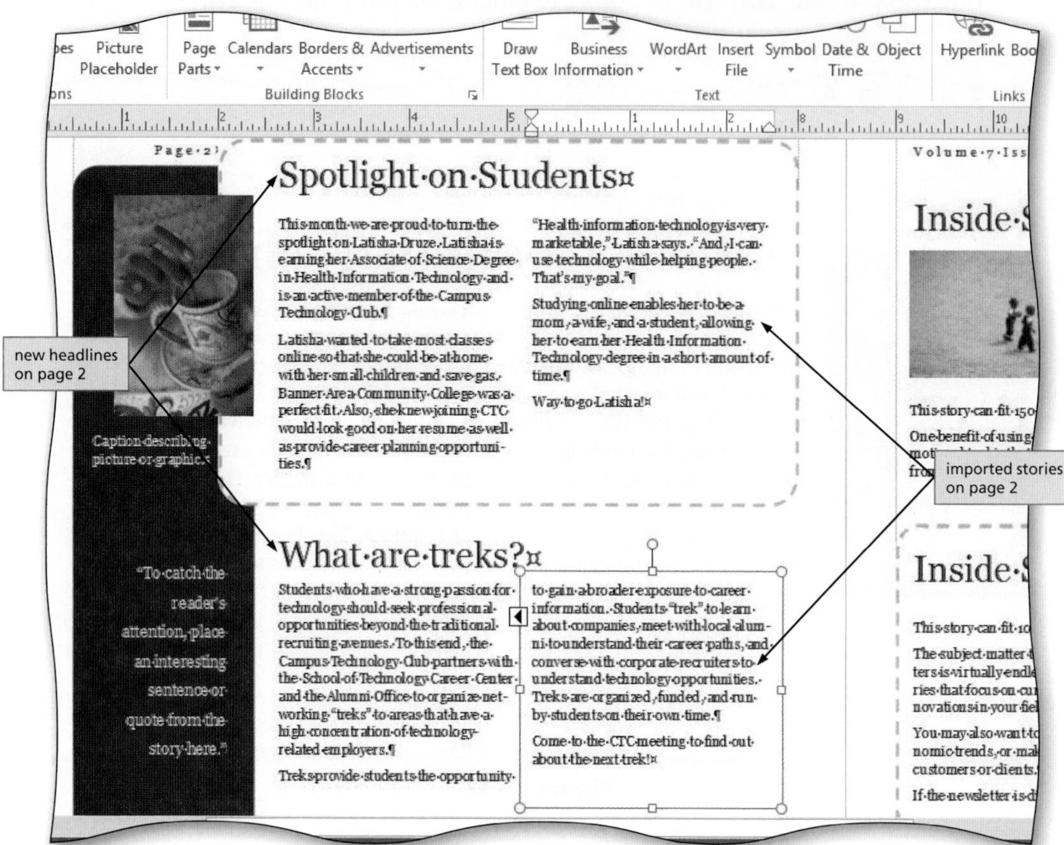

Figure 3–33

To Import a Story on Page 4

BTW
Zooming
Recall that the F9 key toggles between the current page view and 100% magnification or actual size. **Toggle** means the same key will alternate views, or turn a feature on and off. Editing text is easier if you view the text at 100% magnification or higher.

The following steps edit the headline and import the text for the story in the lower portion of page 4. To complete these steps, you will be required to use the Data Files for Students. Visit www.cengage.com/ct/studentdownload for detailed instructions or contact your instructor for information about accessing the required files.

1. Navigate to the lower portion of page 4, and then click the Back Page Story Headline placeholder text to select it.

2. Type `From the desk of the dean...` to replace the selected headline.

3. Tap or click the placeholder text inside the story text box to select it.

4. Tap or click the Insert File button (INSERT tab | Text group) to display the Insert Text dialog box.

5. If necessary, navigate to the location of the file to be opened (in this case, the Chapter 03 folder in the Publisher folder in the CIS 101 folder).

6. Double-tap or double-click the file named, Dean Message to insert the text file (Figure 3–34).

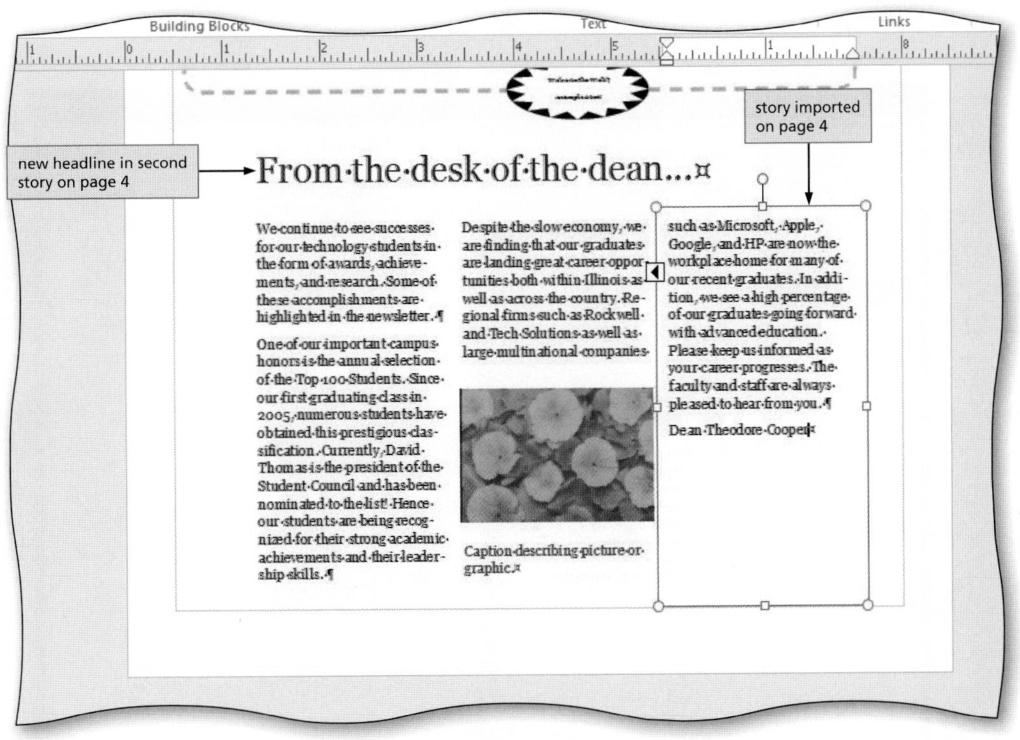

Figure 3–34

Customizing the Ribbon

It is easy to **customize**, or personalize, the ribbon the way that you want it. You can

- Create custom groups and custom tabs to contain frequently used commands
- Rearrange or rename buttons, groups, and tabs to fit your work style
- Rename or remove buttons and boxes from an existing tab and group
- Add new buttons to a custom group

When you add new buttons to the ribbon, you may choose from a list that includes commands that you may use elsewhere in Publisher such as those on shortcut menus, commands from the Backstage view, or other commands that are not on the ribbon. Or, you can create a new button that executes a command or set of commands that you record. You will create such a button later in this book. In this chapter, you will create a custom group on the Review tab and add a command that is not currently on the ribbon. The command will appear as a button in the new custom group.

You can customize the ribbon in all of the Microsoft Office applications, but the customizations are application-specific. The changes you make to the Publisher ribbon will not change the ribbon in any other Microsoft Office application. When you no longer need the customization, it can be removed individually, or the entire ribbon can be reset to its default settings, removing all customizations.

BTW

Whole Page View

The Show Whole Page button on the right side of the Publisher status bar displays the entire page. Page editing techniques such as moving graphics, inserting new objects, and aligning objects are performed more easily in Whole Page view. You also may choose different magnifications and views by clicking the Zoom arrow (VIEW tab | Zoom group).

To Customize the Publisher Ribbon

1 EDIT OPTIONS | 2 IMPORT & CONNECT STORIES | 3 USE CONTINUED NOTICES | **4 CUSTOMIZE RIBBON**
5 EDIT USING WORD | 6 CREATE MARGINAL ELEMENTS | 7 IMPORT GRAPHICS & REVISE | 8 CREATE TEMPLATE

The steps on the next page add the 'Edit Story in Microsoft Word' button to a new group on the Review tab on the ribbon. ***Why?*** *The Review tab has empty space to hold custom groups. The other tabs are full. Adding a custom group to one of the other tabs would compress the existing groups, which might make it more difficult to locate buttons and boxes.*

1

- Tap or click FILE on the ribbon to open the Backstage view, and then click Options to display the Publisher Options dialog box.
- Tap or click Customize Ribbon in the left pane (Publisher Options dialog box) to display the options for customizing the ribbon.
- Tap or click the 'Choose commands from' button to view the list of commands (Figure 3–35).

Publisher Options dialog box

Customize Ribbon

'Choose commands from' button

'Commands Not in the Ribbon' command

Figure 3–35

Q&A Why are some commands not in the ribbon?

Publisher is a powerful program with many commands. Including all of the available commands on the ribbon would be overwhelming to many users. Publisher includes the most used or popular commands in its default set.

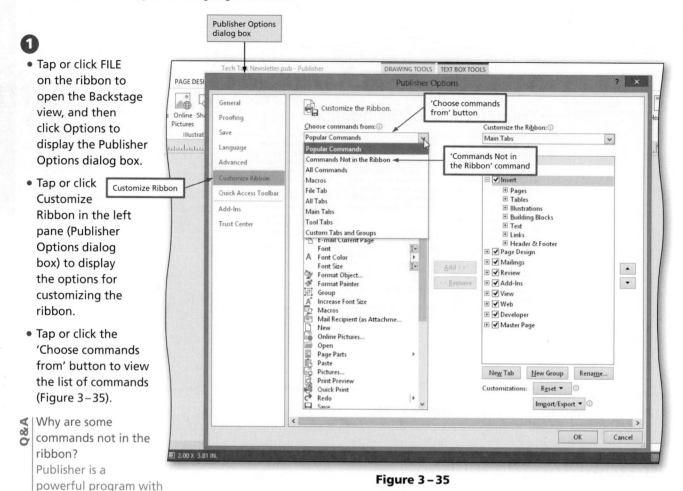

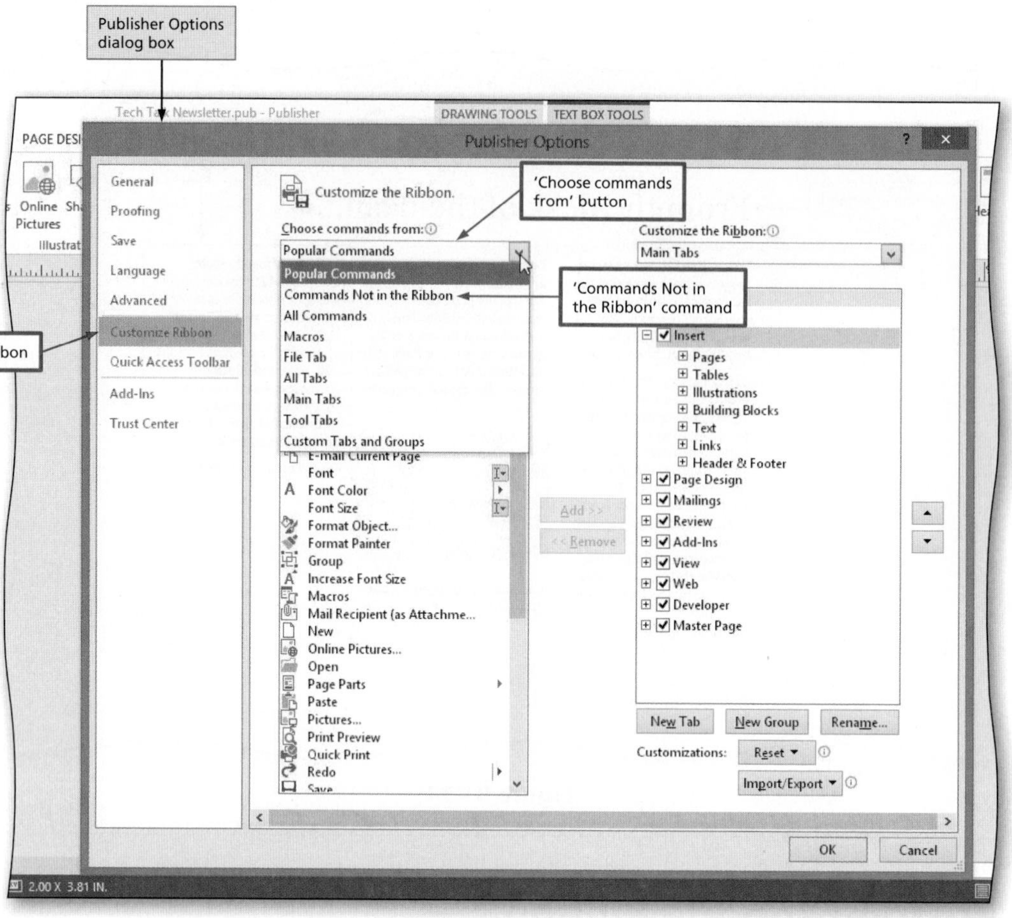

2

- Tap or click 'Commands Not in the Ribbon' to display the list.
- Tap or click the command you want to add (in this case, the 'Edit Story in Microsoft Word' command) (Figure 3–36).

Q&A Can I add more than one command to the ribbon?

Yes, but you have to add them one at a time.

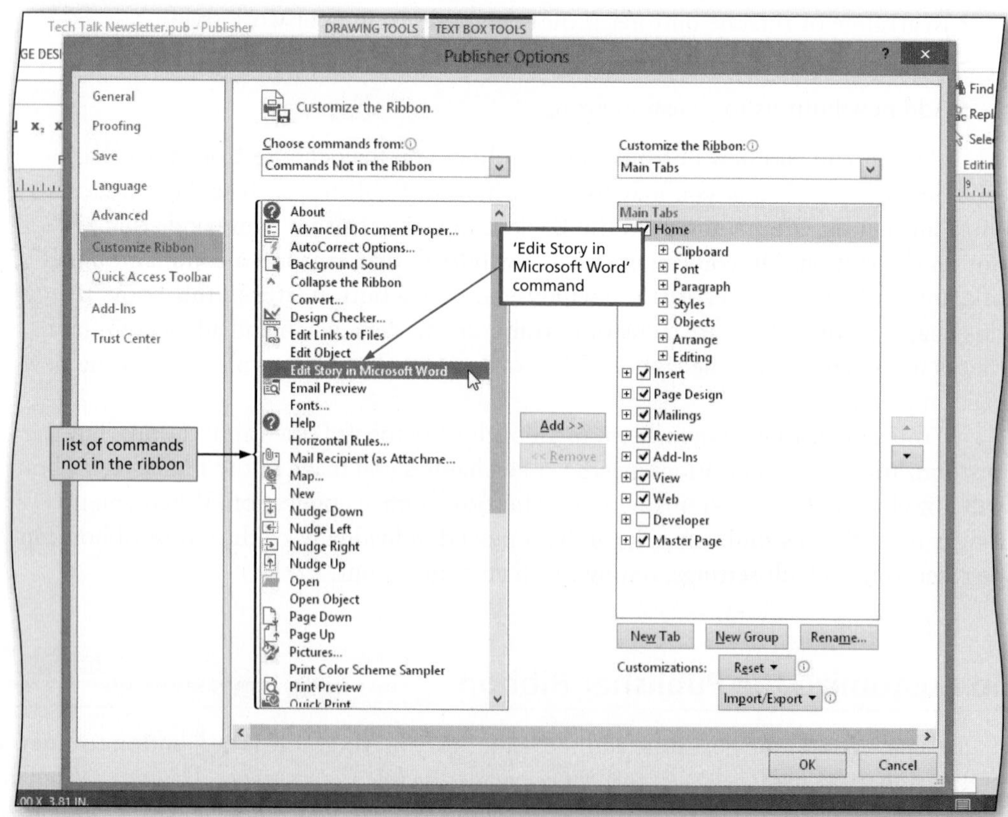

Figure 3–36

- Tap or click Review in the list of Main Tabs to select it.
- Tap or click the New Group button to create a custom group (Figure 3–37).

Q&A Do I have to add commands to a new group?
Yes. Commands only can be added to custom groups. The default tabs and groups cannot be changed.

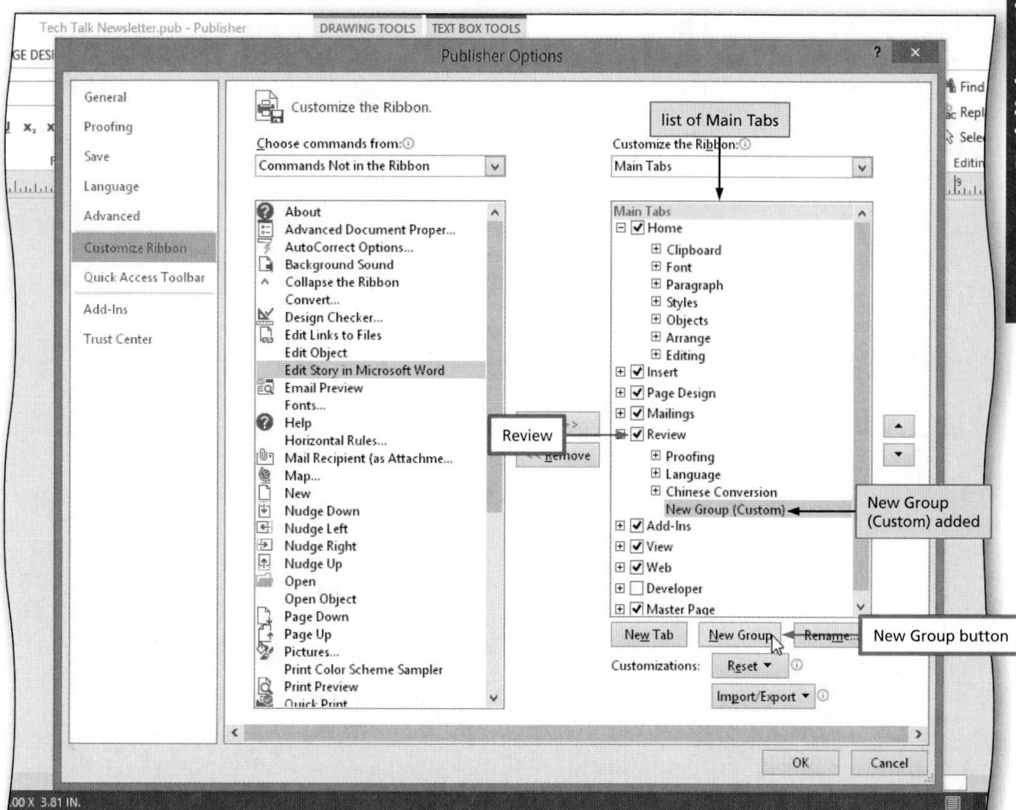

Figure 3–37

- Tap or click the Add button to add the chosen command to the new group (Figure 3–38).

Q&A Can I rename the custom group?
Yes, you can rename any group or command by tapping or clicking the Rename button and then entering a new name in the Rename dialog box. You even can choose an icon for the command.

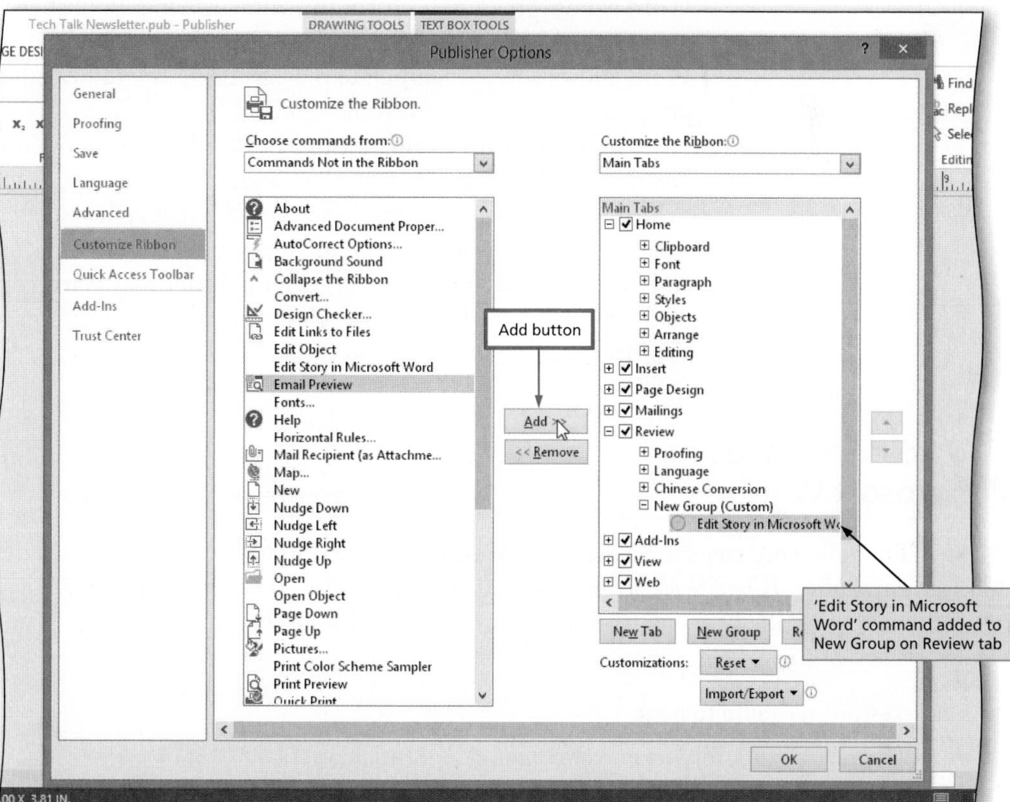

Figure 3–38

- Tap or click the OK button (Publisher Options dialog box) to close the dialog box and create the custom group.
- Tap or click REVIEW on the ribbon to display the REVIEW tab and its new group and button (Figure 3–39).

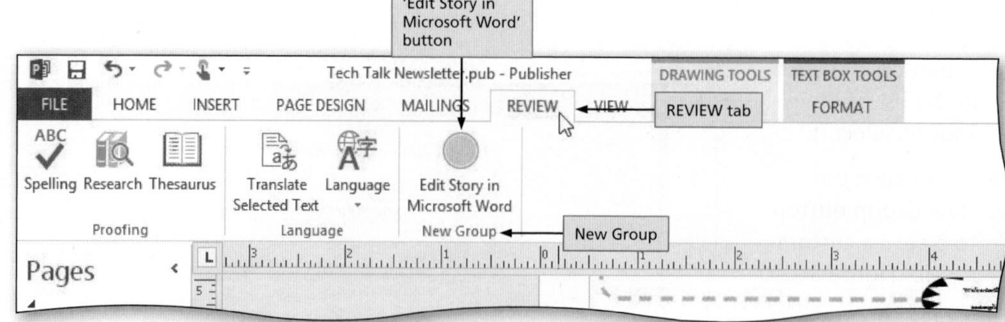

Figure 3–39

Other Ways

1. Press and hold or right-click ribbon, tap or click Customize the Ribbon, choose or create groups, add commands, tap or click OK (Publisher Options dialog box)

Editing Stories in Microsoft Word

You have seen that you can edit text directly in Microsoft Publisher or import text from a previously stored file. A third way to edit text is to use Microsoft Word as your editor. Publisher provides an easy link between the two applications.

If you need to edit only a few words, it is faster to continue using Publisher. If you need to edit a longer story or one that is not available on your storage device, it sometimes is easier to edit the story in Word. Many users are accustomed to working in Word and want to take advantage of available Word features, such as grammar checking and revision tracking. It may be easier to drag-and-drop paragraphs in a Word window than to perform the same task in a Publisher window, especially when it involves moving across pages in a larger Publisher publication. Editing your stories in Word allows you to manipulate the text using the full capabilities of a word processing program.

While you are editing a story in Word, you cannot edit the corresponding text box in Publisher; Publisher displays a gray box instead of the text. When you close Word, control returns to Publisher and the text appears.

Occasionally, if you have many applications running, such as virus protection and other memory-taxing programs, Publisher may warn you that you are low on computer memory. In that case, close the other applications and try editing the story in Word again.

To Edit a Story Using Microsoft Word

1 EDIT OPTIONS | 2 IMPORT & CONNECT STORIES | 3 USE CONTINUED NOTICES | 4 CUSTOMIZE RIBBON
5 EDIT USING WORD | 6 CREATE MARGINAL ELEMENTS | 7 IMPORT GRAPHICS & REVISE | 8 CREATE TEMPLATE

The following steps use Microsoft Word in conjunction with Publisher to create the text on the back page of the newsletter. ***Why?*** *Some people find it easier to edit stories using Microsoft Word.* Microsoft Word version 6.0 or later must be installed on your computer for this procedure to work.

- If necessary, navigate to page 4.
- Scroll to display the story text box in the upper portion of page 4.
- Select all of the text.
- Display the REVIEW tab (Figure 3–40).

'Edit Story in Microsoft Word' button

story text at the top of page 4 is selected

Figure 3–40

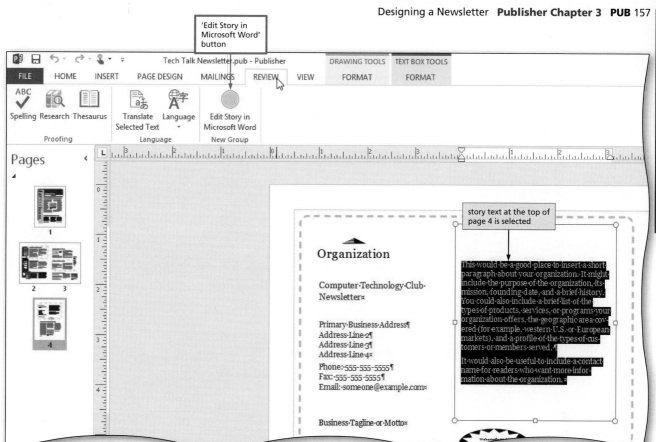

- Tap or click the 'Edit Story in Microsoft Word' button (REVIEW tab | New Group) to start the Word program.
- Press CTRL+A to select all of the text, and then type **`The Campus Technology Club is the premier club for School of Technology students who want to experience all that today's leading technology companies have to offer. The Club sponsors a variety of events with other clubs and campus schools to prepare our members to lead today's technology companies. Members get priority access to round tables with the Executive Speaker Series.`** and then press the ENTER key to finish the first paragraph (Figure 3–41).

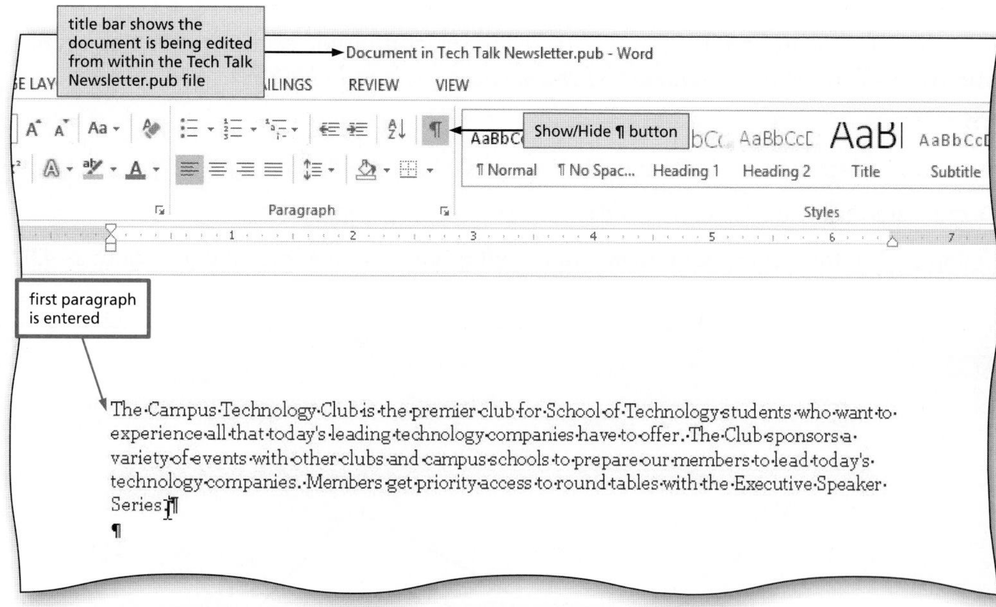

Figure 3–41

Q&A

Why are my formatting marks not showing in Microsoft Word?

It is possible that someone has turned off formatting marks. Tap or click the Show/Hide ¶ button to turn them on and off.

3

- Type **`If you have any interest in working in the technology field, the Campus Technology Club is for you!`** to finish the text (Figure 3–42).

Q&A Why are my fonts different?
Usually, the Word text displays the same formatting as the previous text in Publisher. Your display may differ depending on available fonts.

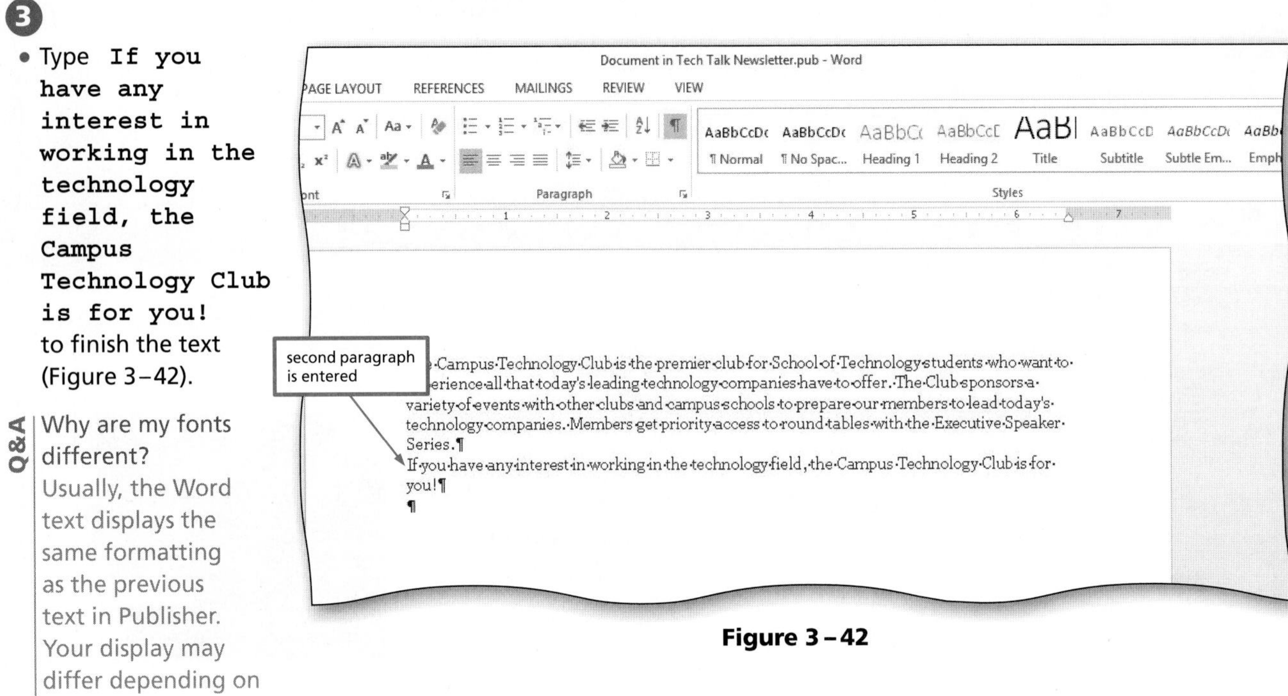

Figure 3–42

To Format while Editing in Microsoft Word

1 EDIT OPTIONS | 2 IMPORT & CONNECT STORIES | 3 USE CONTINUED NOTICES | 4 CUSTOMIZE RIBBON
5 EDIT USING WORD | 6 CREATE MARGINAL ELEMENTS | 7 IMPORT GRAPHICS & REVISE | 8 CREATE TEMPLATE

The following step uses the CTRL key to select multiple sections of nonadjacent text and format them in Microsoft Word. ***Why?*** *You cannot select nonadjacent text in Publisher.*

1

- Drag to select the words, Campus Technology Club, in the first paragraph.
- CTRL+drag to select the same words in the second paragraph.
- Tap or click the Bold button (HOME tab | Font group) on the Word ribbon (Figure 3–43).

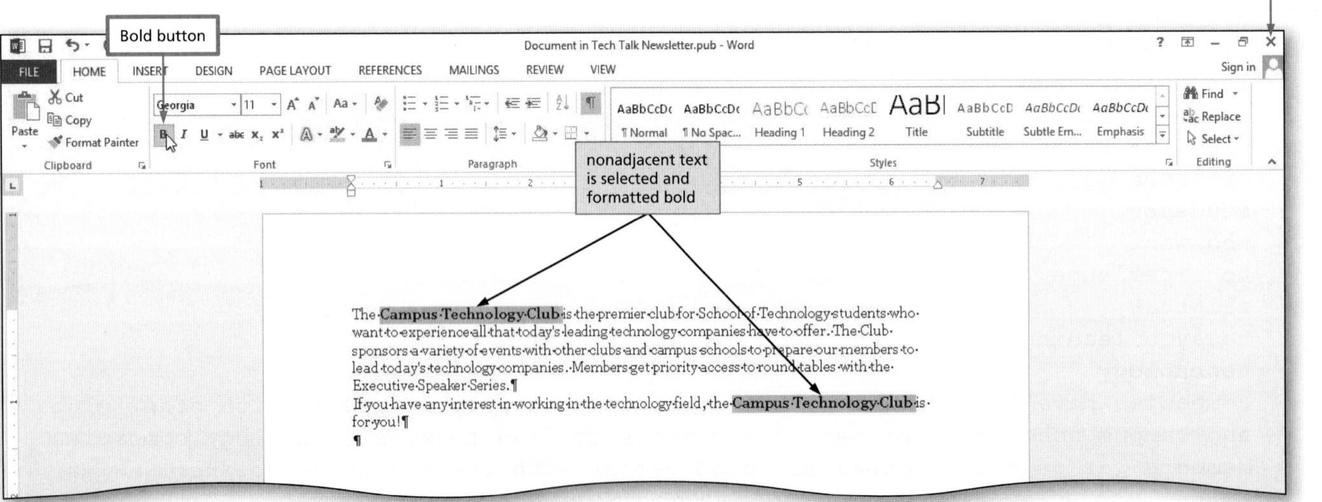

Figure 3–43

To Exit Word and Return to Publisher

The following step exits Word and returns to Publisher. ***Why?*** *You must exit Word in order to edit the text box in Publisher.*

1

- Tap or click the Close button on the title bar of the Document in Tech Talk Newsletter.pub – Word window to quit Word (Figure 3–44).

Q&A Why do I see only gray lines instead of the text?
Starting Microsoft Word from within Microsoft Publisher is a drain on your system's memory and on the refresh rate of your screen. Try navigating to page 1 and then back to page 4 to refresh the screen.

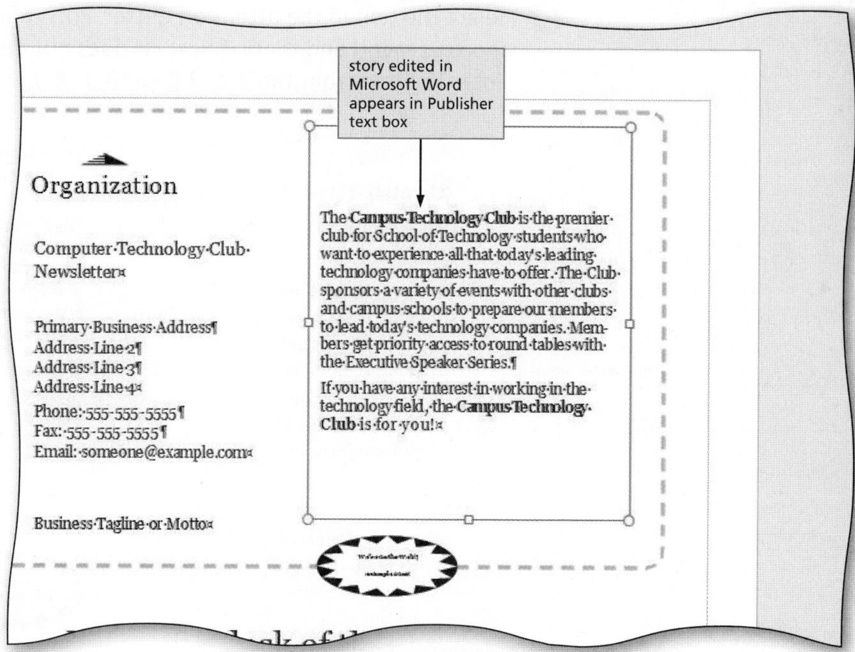

Figure 3–44

To Edit Other Objects on Page 4

Table 3–2 lists text for the other objects on page 4.

Table 3–2 Text for Page 4

Location	Text
Organization logo	<delete>
Primary Business Address	School of Technology Banner Area Community College 8400 Walker Lane Banner, IL 50024
Phone, Fax, Email text box	Phone: 618-555-8662 Fax: 618-555-8663 Email: ctc@bacc.edu
Business Tagline or Motto	Join us on Facebook!
Attention getter	We meet the 2nd Friday of each month

© 2014 Cengage Learning

BTW
Q&As
For a complete list of the Q&As found in many of the step-by-step sequences in this book, visit the Q&A resource on the Student Companion Site located on www.cengagebrain.com. For detailed instructions about accessing available resources, visit www.cengage.com/ct/studentdownload or see the inside back cover of this book.

The following steps delete the logo and edit other text boxes on page 2. As you edit the text boxes, zoom and scroll as necessary.

1 In the upper-left portion of page 4, select the organization logo and delete it.

2 Tap or click the default text in the Primary Business Address text box. Press CTRL+A to select all of the text. Enter the text from Table 3–2.

3. Select the default text in the Phone, Fax, Email text box, and then enter the text from Table 3–2 on the previous page.

4. Select the business tagline or motto placeholder text, and then enter the text from Table 3–2.

5. Select the text in the attention getter. Press and hold or right-click to display the shortcut menu and then, if Best Fit does not display a check mark, tap or click Best Fit. Enter the text from Table 3–2 (Figure 3–45).

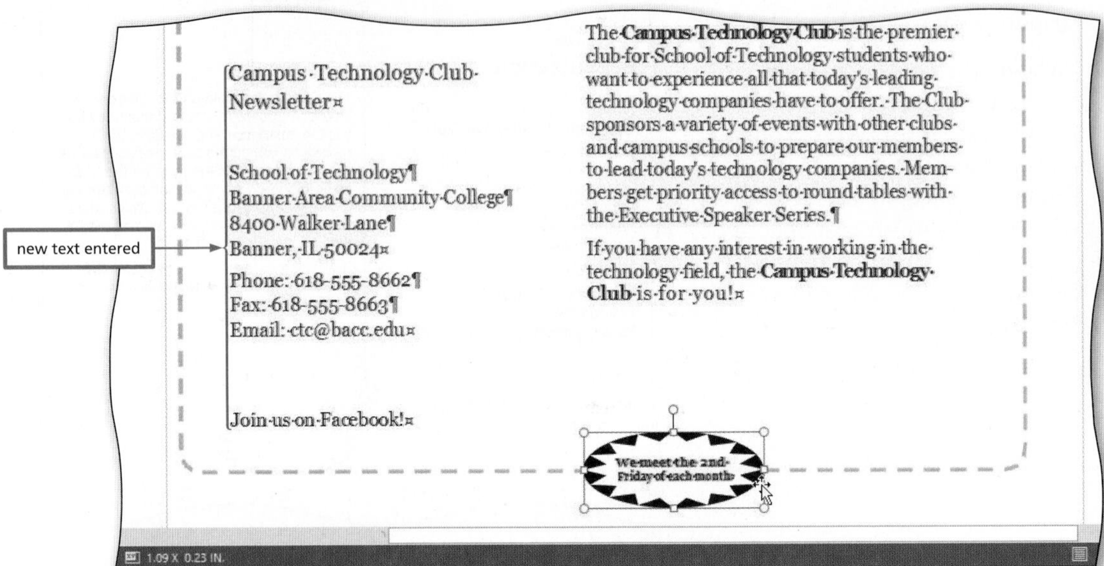
Campus Technology Club Newsletter
School of Technology
Banner Area Community College
8400 Walker Lane
Banner, IL 50024
Phone: 618-555-8662
Fax: 618-555-8663
Email: ctc@bacc.edu
Join us on Facebook!
The Campus Technology Club is the premier club for School of Technology students who want to experience all that today's leading technology companies have to offer. The Club sponsors a variety of events with other clubs and campus schools to prepare our members to lead today's technology companies. Members get priority access to round tables with the Executive Speaker Series.
If you have any interest in working in the technology field, the Campus Technology Club is for you!
We meet the 2nd Friday of each month
new text entered
1.09 X 0.23 IN.

Figure 3–45

To Save the Publication Again

The following step saves the publication again.

1. Tap or click the Save button on the Quick Access Toolbar to save the file again with the same name, and in the same location.

Break Point: If you wish to take a break, this is a good place to do so. Exit Publisher. To resume at a later time, run Publisher, open the file called Tech Talk Newsletter, and continue following the steps from this location forward.

Marginal Elements

BTW

Left and Right Pages

In printing and publishing, the left page of a two-page spread is called **verso**. The right page is called **recto**. Typically the first page of a newsletter, book, or chapter is a recto page; thus, all recto pages will have odd page numbers and all verso pages will have even page numbers.

Publisher newsletter templates include marginal elements and layout features to make the newsletter more attractive and add interest to the page. A **sidebar**, or breakout, is a small piece of text, set off with a box or graphic, and placed beside a story. It contains text that is not vital for understanding the main text but usually adds interest or additional information. Tables of contents, art boxes, and bulleted points of interest are examples of sidebars. A newsletter **table of contents**, or margin table, usually is a narrow, short list that is used to refer readers to specific pages or to present listed or numeric items in the margin area. A **pull quote, or pullout,** is an excerpt from the main story used to highlight the concepts within the story or to attract readers. Pull quotes, like sidebars, can be set off with a box or graphic. Shapes and borders also are used sometimes as marginal elements.

To Edit Sidebars

The Banded newsletter template includes two sidebars on page 1. The first one is a bulleted list about special points of interest. The second is a table of contents. ***Why?*** *Some newsletters use a sidebar table as an index to locate stories in longer newsletters; sidebars also are used to break up a page with lots of text and attract readers to inside pages. Other newsletters use sidebar tables to display numerical data and lists.* Table 3–3 lists the text for the sidebars.

Table 3–3 Text for Sidebars

SPECIAL POINTS OF INTEREST:	Oct. 7 Executive Speaker Series	
	Oct. 10 CTC meeting: Outsmarting Your Smartphone	
	Oct. 27 Spring registration begins	
	Oct.31 Halloween party	
INSIDE THIS ISSUE:	Student Spotlight	2
	Treks	2
	E-smells	3
	Coupon	3
	About Our Club	4
	Dean's Message	4

© 2014 Cengage Learning

The following steps edit the sidebars. Recall that a hard return is created when you press the ENTER key. A hard return also causes a bullet to appear on the next line in a bulleted list. To create a new line within a bulleted item, you will use a **soft return** by pressing the SHIFT+ENTER keys. Neither hard returns nor soft returns print on hard copies.

1

- Navigate to page 1.
- Locate the Special points of interest sidebar, and zoom to approximately 120% magnification.
- Tap or click the bulleted list to select it (Figure 3–46).

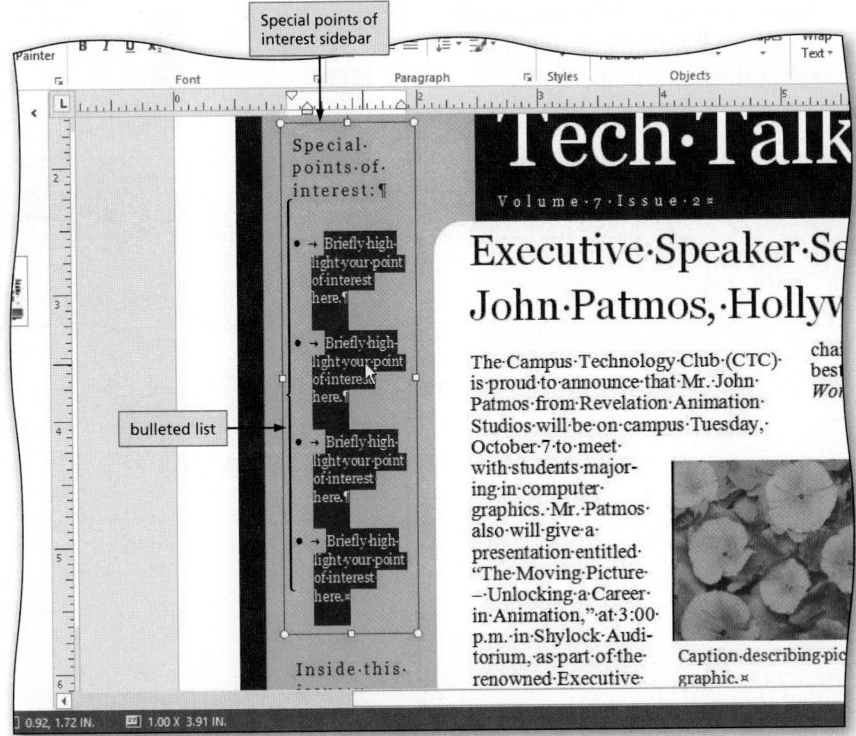

Figure 3–46

2

- Type the list as shown in Table 3–3 on the previous page. Press the SHIFT+ENTER keys after each line within the bullet item to create soft returns. Press the ENTER key at the end of each bulleted item, except the last, to create hard returns (Figure 3–47).

Q&A Why do I need to use soft returns?
The bulleted list is very narrow and might hyphenate awkwardly if you use wordwrap.

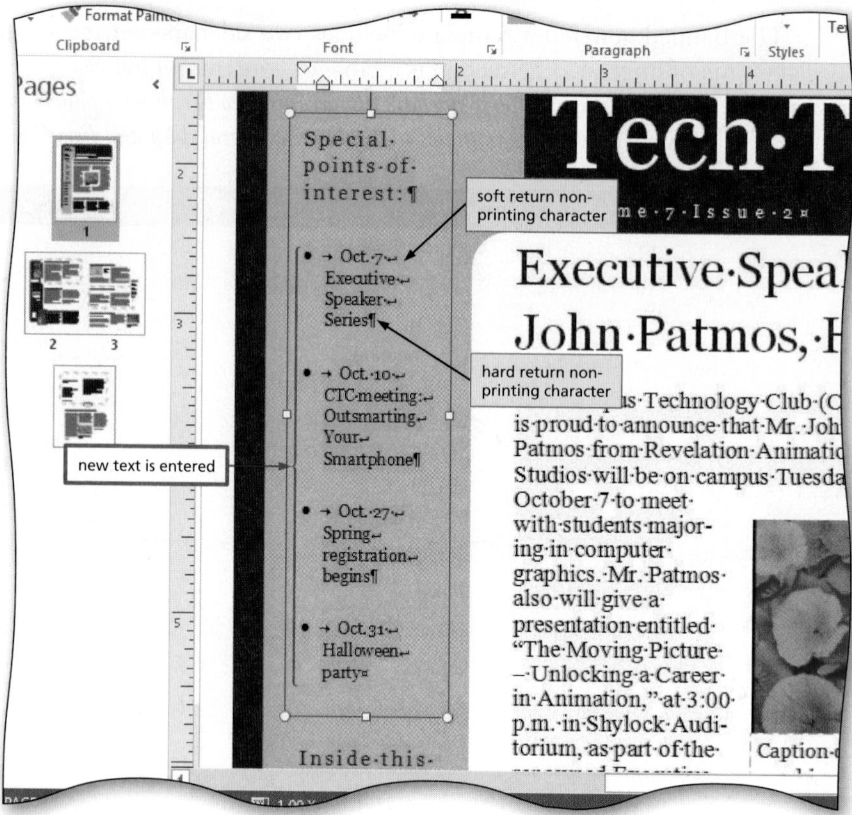

Figure 3–47

3

- Scroll down to the second sidebar, Inside this issue.
- Tap or click the default text, Inside Story, just below the heading to select the text (Figure 3–48).

Q&A Is the heading part of the table?
No, the heading is a text box grouped with subsequent rows, which comprise a table. You will learn more about tables in a future chapter.

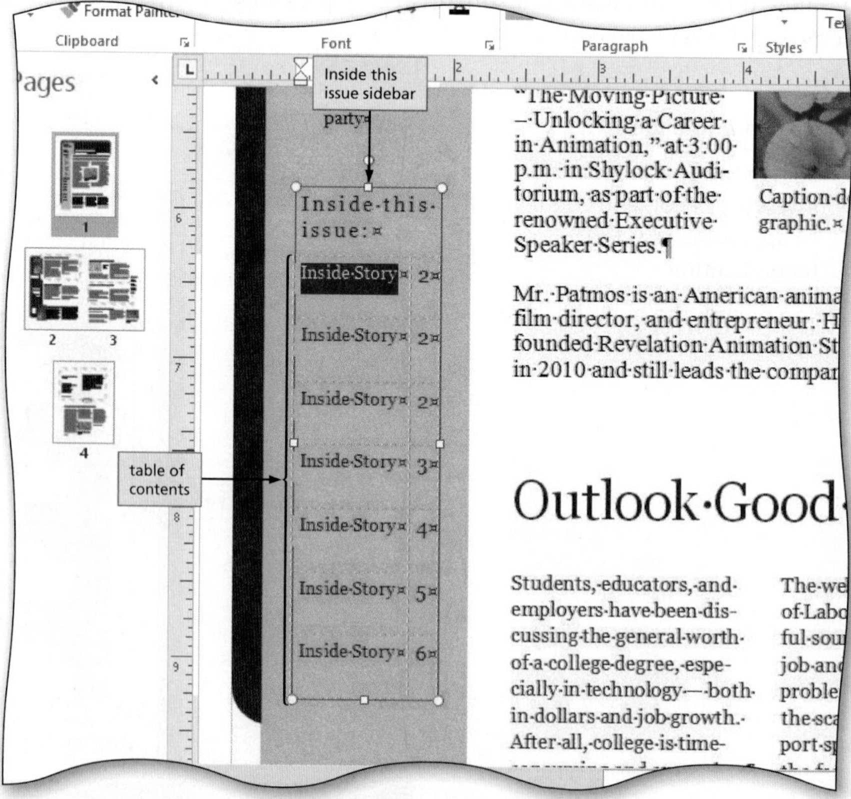

Figure 3–48

4

- Type **Student Spotlight** to replace the text (Figure 3–49).

Q&A What are the dotted gray lines in the table?
Publisher displays dotted gray lines to indicate the size of each cell in the table. A **cell** is the text box located where a table column and table row intersect. The lines do not print.

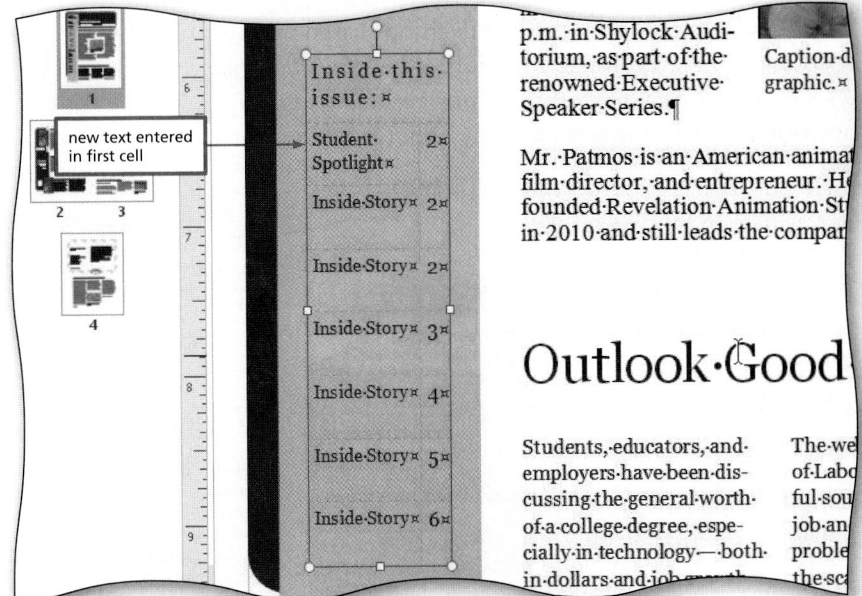

Figure 3–49

5

- If necessary, type 2 to replace the page number just to the right of the Student Spotlight text.
- Complete the table with the data from Table 3–3 on page PUB 161. Use the TAB key to move from cell to cell. Delete the default text in the last row because it will be blank (Figure 3–50). If necessary, add a soft return after the word, Dean's, in Dean's Message, so a hyphen is not created.

Q&A Could I click the next cell instead of using the TAB key?
You could click the cell, but you then would need to select the page number and type to replace it. Pressing the TAB key both advances to and selects the data in the next cell.

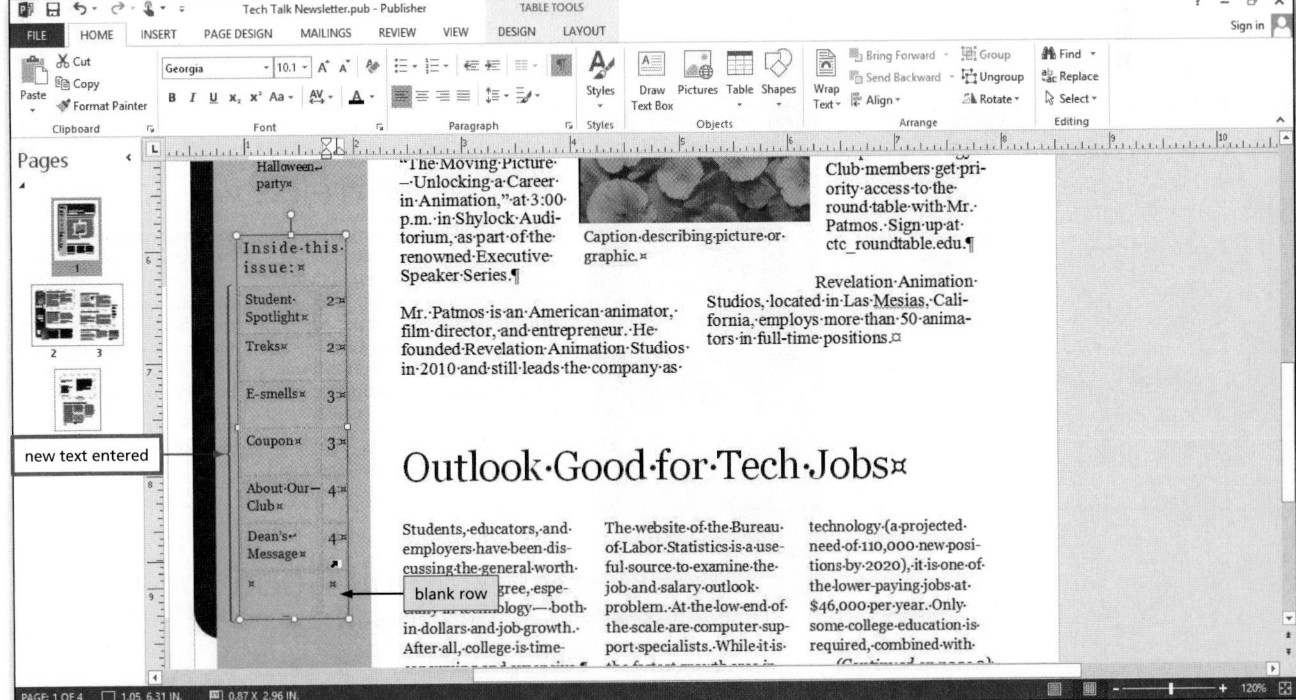

Figure 3–50

To Insert a Pull Quote

People often make reading decisions based on the size of the story. Using a pull quote brings a small portion of the text to their attention. ***Why?*** *Pull quotes invite the reader to read the story, and are useful for breaking the monotony of long columns of text and for adding visual interest.* The following steps insert a pull quote using function keys to copy and paste the quote from the story.

1

- Navigate to the second story, What are treks?, on page 2.
- Drag to select the text in the last sentence.
- Press CTRL+C to copy the sentence to the Clipboard (Figure 3–51).

Q&A How should I choose the text for the pull quote?
Layout specialists say pull quotes should summarize the intended message in one or two sentences.

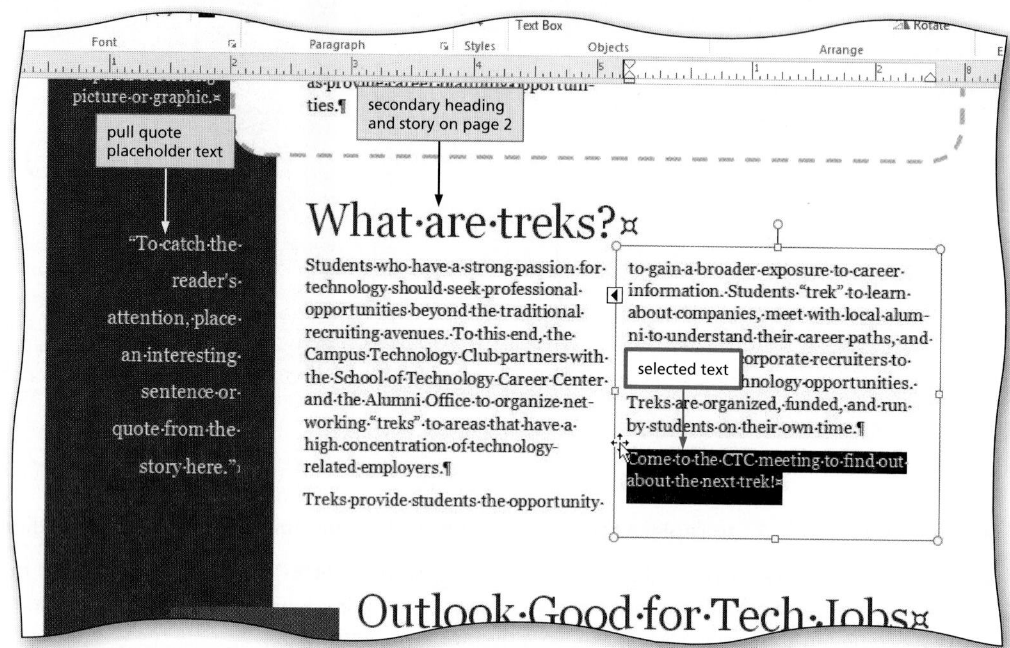

Figure 3–51

2

- Tap or click to select the pull quote placeholder text to the left of the story (Figure 3–52).

Q&A What if there is no pull quote on the page?
You can insert a pull quote from the Page Parts gallery. You will learn about the gallery in a later chapter.

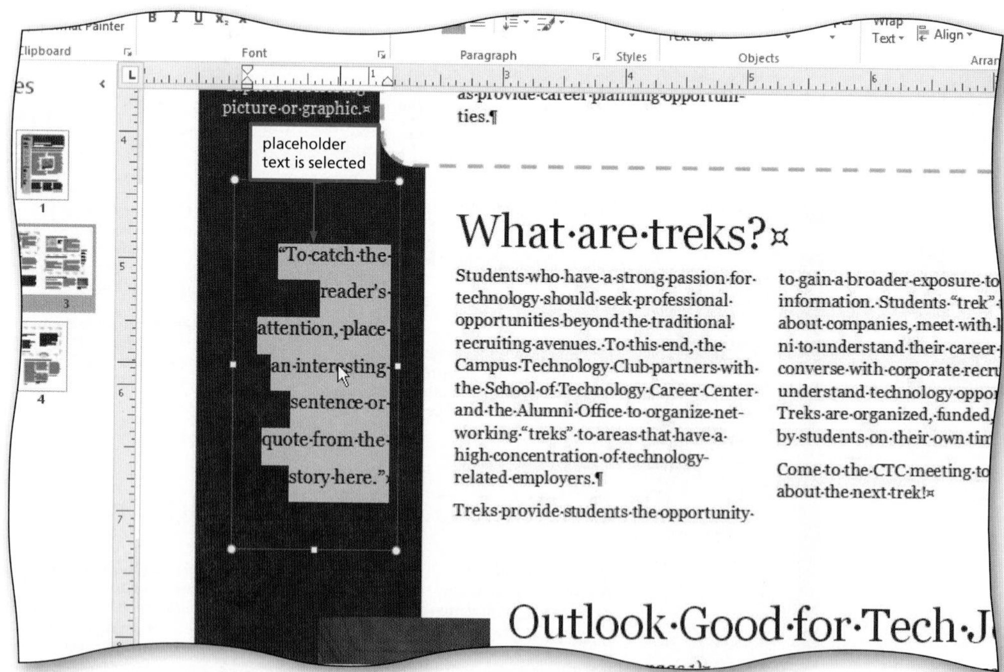

Figure 3–52

- Press CTRL+V to paste the sentence from the Clipboard.
- Tap or click the Paste Options button, and then click the 'Keep Text Only' button to accept the destination formatting (Figure 3–53).

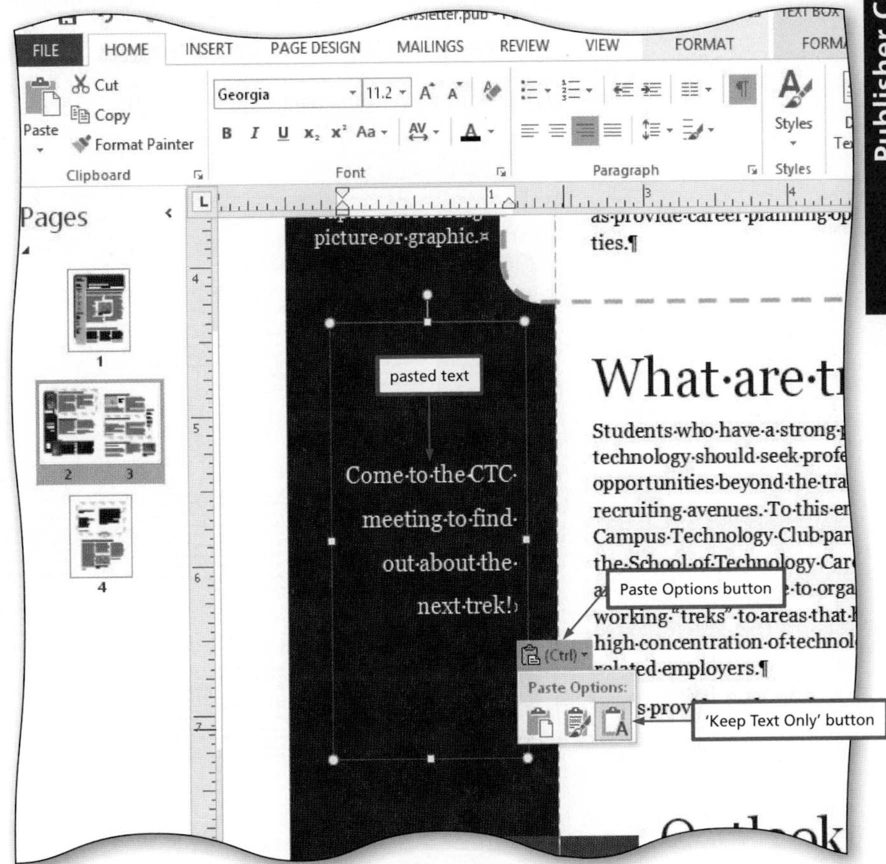

Figure 3–53

Other Ways

1. Tap or click Page Parts button (INSERT tab | Building Blocks group), tap or click desired pull quote, enter pull quote text

To Delete Objects on Page 3

The following steps delete the first and third stories on page 3. Recall that dragging around multiple objects selects them automatically.

1. Navigate to the top of page 3.
2. Tap or click the border of the first heading to select it.
3. Press the DELETE key to delete the text box.
4. Drag around the first story text boxes, graphic, and caption to select them.
5. Press the DELETE key to delete the selected items.
6. Delete the pull quote text box on the right.
7. Scroll to the bottom of the page, and then tap or click the border of the third heading to select it.
8. Press the DELETE key to delete the text box.

BTW

Deleting Objects

If you think there is even a remote possibility that you might use an object again, do not delete it. Simply drag it to the scratch area. That way, it is saved with the publication, but will not appear on the page layout itself, and it will not print. When you are certain that you no longer will need an object, delete it to lower the size of your Publisher file.

9. Drag around the third story text boxes, graphic, and caption to select them all.
10. Press the DELETE key to delete the selected items.
11. Zoom to Whole Page (Figure 3–54).

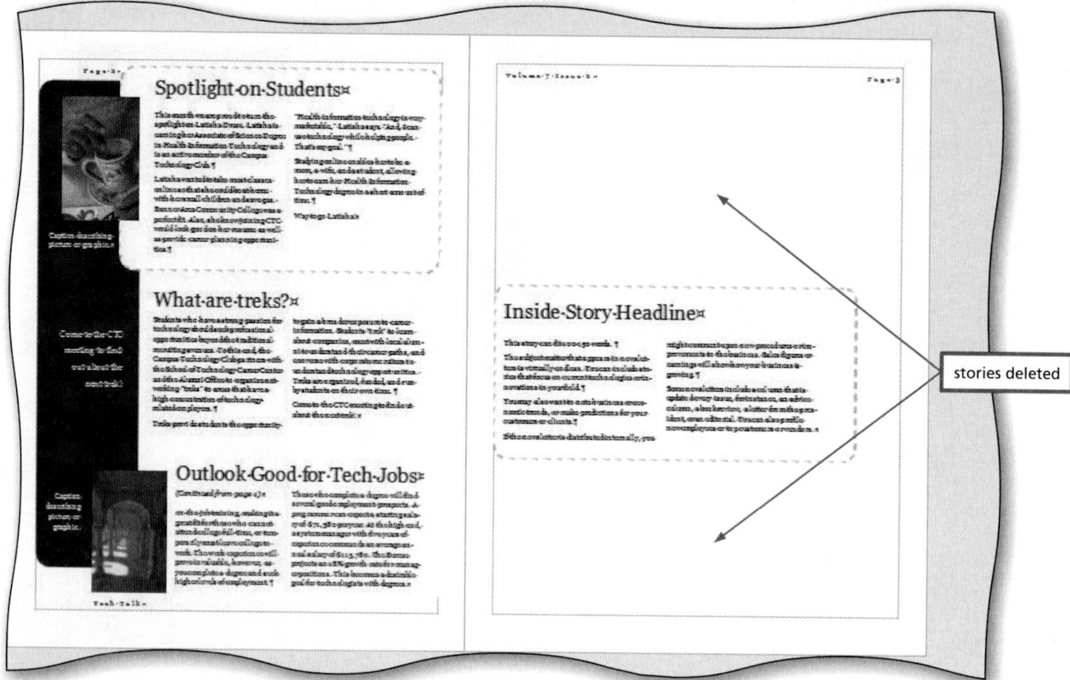

Figure 3–54

To Resize and Move Objects

The following steps move the border, headline, and story on page 3. The border and text boxes also are resized. In the Banded template, the border is a white, rectangular shape with a yellow, dotted line along the edge. You will learn more about creating borders in a later chapter.

1. On page 3, drag around the border, headline text box, and story text boxes to select them.
2. Drag the selection to the top of the page, approximately 1.5 inch from the top of the page.
3. Deselect.
4. Tap or click the border to select it, and then drag the lower-center sizing handle down to approximately the 7-inch mark on the vertical ruler.
5. Drag around the two story text boxes to select them. If you have trouble dragging around only the text boxes, SHIFT+click each one to select them.
6. Drag one of the lower-center sizing handles down to approximately the 6.5-inch mark on the vertical ruler (Figure 3–55).

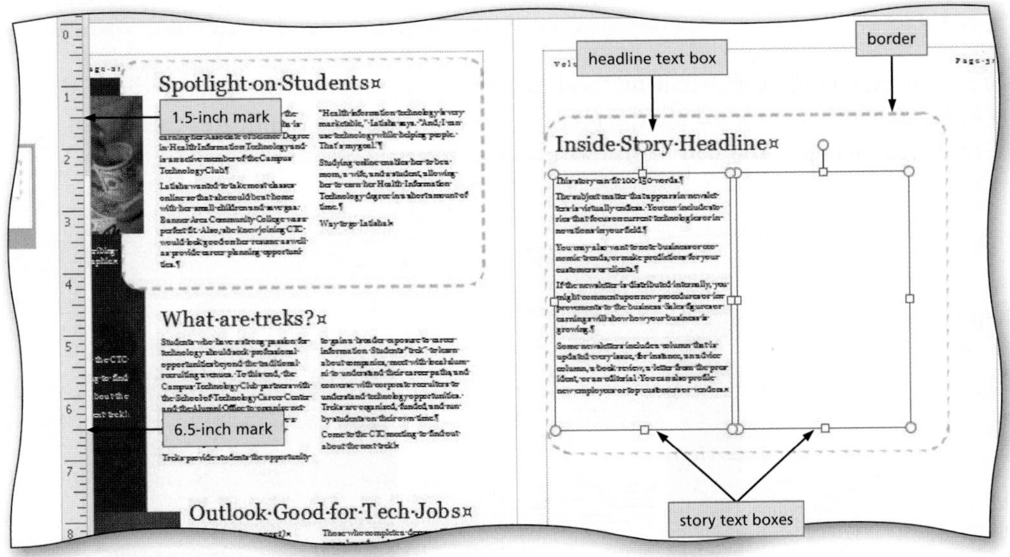

Figure 3–55

To Edit the Story on Page 3

The following steps edit the headline and import the remaining story on page 3. To complete these steps, you will be required to use the Data Files for Students. Visit www.cengage.com/ct/studentdownload for detailed instructions or contact your instructor for information about accessing the required files.

1. On page 3, tap or click the headline placeholder text. Type `New Exciting Web Technologies (NEWT)` to replace the selected headline.
2. Tap or click the placeholder text in the inside story text box to select it.
3. Tap or click the Insert File button (INSERT tab | Text group) to display the Insert Text dialog box.
4. If necessary, navigate to the location of the file to be opened (in this case, the Chapter 03 folder in the Publisher folder in the CIS 101 folder).
5. Double-tap or double-click the file, New Exciting Web Technologies, to insert the text file (Figure 3–56).

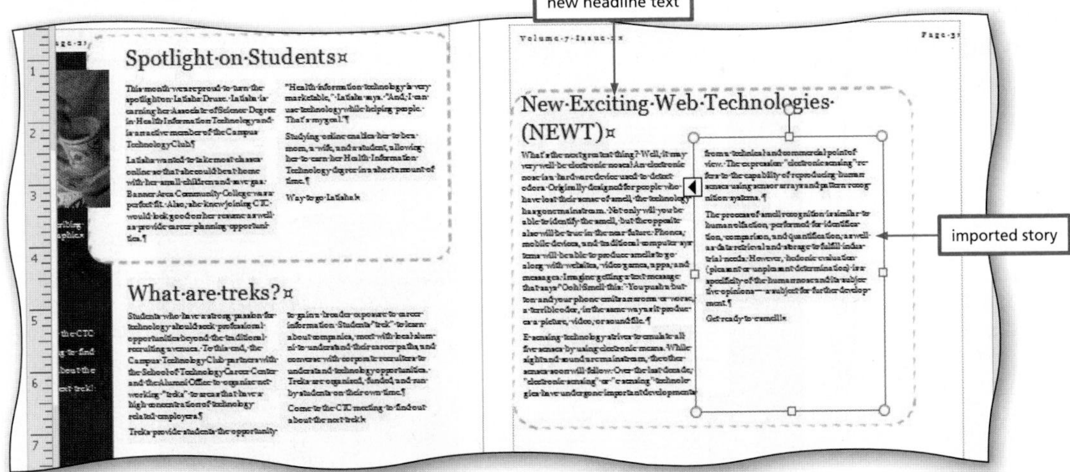

Figure 3–56

To Duplicate an Object

1 EDIT OPTIONS | 2 IMPORT & CONNECT STORIES | 3 USE CONTINUED NOTICES | 4 CUSTOMIZE RIBBON
5 EDIT USING WORD | **6 CREATE MARGINAL ELEMENTS** | **7 IMPORT GRAPHICS & REVISE** | **8 CREATE TEMPLATE**

When you **duplicate** an object, you use a shortcut method to create a copy, rather than the traditional copy-and-paste method. ***Why?*** *A duplicate does not use the Clipboard.* The following step duplicates the brown shape on page 2 to use as a marginal element. You will learn more about shapes in a later chapter.

- Tap or click the brown shape on page 2.
- CTRL+ drag the brown shape from page 2 to the lower-right corner of page 3, within the margin (Figure 3–57).

Q&A Why do I need to press the CTRL the key while dragging?
The CTRL key creates the duplicate copy.

Why is the duplicate copy so much bigger than the original?
It is not bigger. The original shape is partially obscured by the text boxes in front of it.

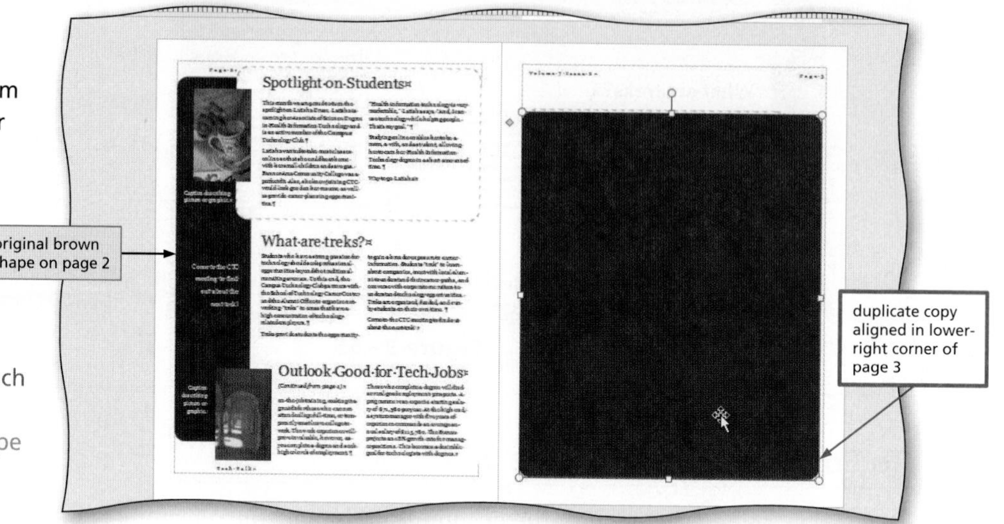

Figure 3–57

To Send an Object to the Back

1 EDIT OPTIONS | 2 IMPORT & CONNECT STORIES | 3 USE CONTINUED NOTICES | 4 CUSTOMIZE RIBBON
5 EDIT USING WORD | **6 CREATE MARGINAL ELEMENTS** | **7 IMPORT GRAPHICS & REVISE** | **8 CREATE TEMPLATE**

Layering involves determining which objects should be displayed in front or behind other objects. Obviously, you do not want to layer an object that would obstruct text or necessary graphics; however, sometimes shapes and colors can be layered to provide interesting backgrounds. On page 2 of the Banded template, the brown shape is layered behind the other text boxes and objects on the page. ***Why?*** *It creates a marginal element of color.* The following steps send the brown shape on page 3 to the back, behind the other objects, creating symmetry across the pages.

- Display the DRAWING TOOLS FORMAT tab.
- Tap or click the Send Backward arrow (DRAWING TOOLS FORMAT tab | Arrange group) to display the list (Figure 3–58).

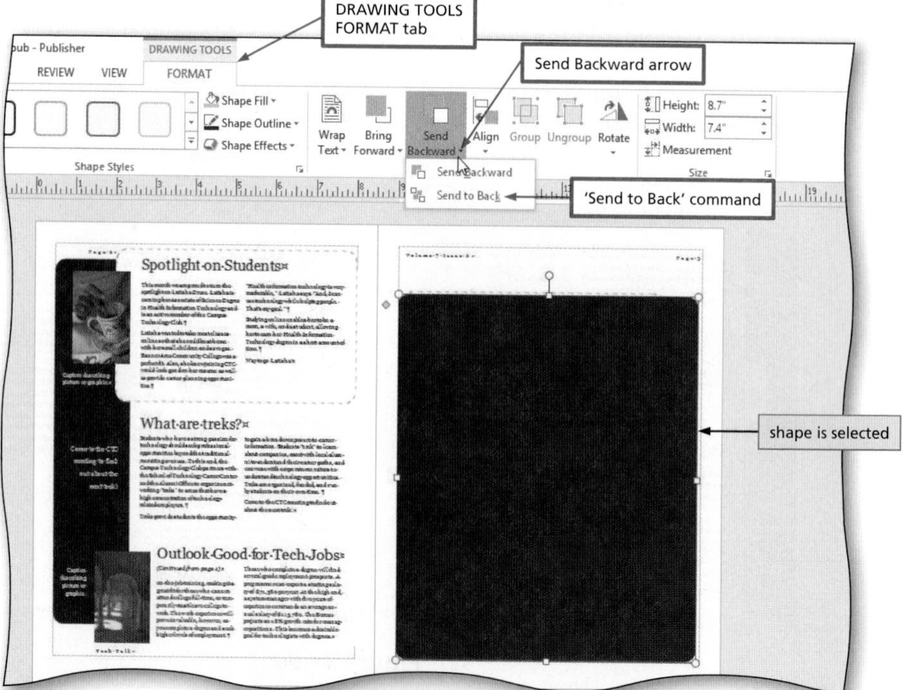

Figure 3–58

- Tap or click the 'Send to Back' command to move the brown shape behind the other objects on the page (Figure 3–59).

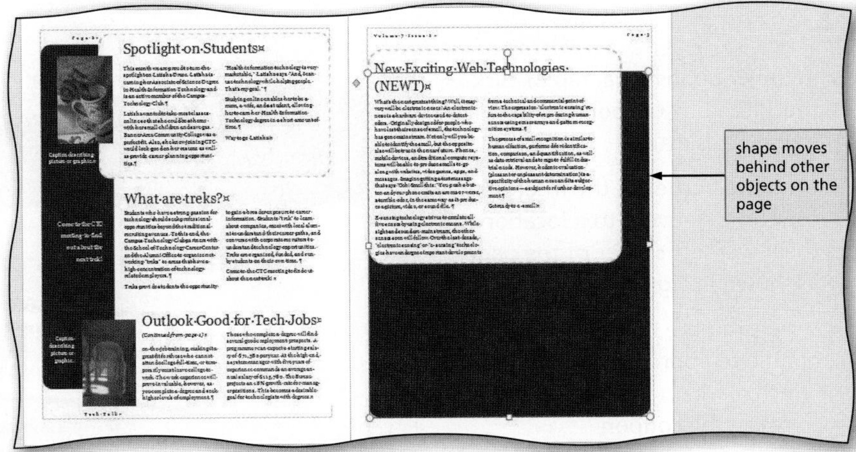

Figure 3–59

Advertisements

Publisher **advertisements** include a group of promotional templates used to market a product or service, including ads that might be placed in newspapers, attention getters, and coupons. Advertisements can be stand-alone publications or inserted as building block items in larger publications. On page 3 of the newsletter, the club will offer a coupon. A **coupon** is a promotional device used to market a product or service. Customers exchange coupons for discounts when purchasing a product. Some coupons offer rebates or free items to attract customers. Coupons often are distributed widely as small printed documents through mail, magazines, newspapers, and newsletters. More recently, however, they are distributed as electronic tags collected through preferred customer cards via the Internet and mobile devices such as cell phones.

To Insert a Coupon

1 EDIT OPTIONS | 2 IMPORT & CONNECT STORIES | 3 USE CONTINUED NOTICES | 4 CUSTOMIZE RIBBON
5 EDIT USING WORD | 6 CREATE MARGINAL ELEMENTS | 7 IMPORT GRAPHICS & REVISE | 8 CREATE TEMPLATE

The following steps insert a coupon on page 3 of the newsletter. ***Why?*** *A coupon is an excellent marketing tool to help track who is reading your publications.*

- Navigate to the lower portion of page 3 in the newsletter and zoom to approximately 150%.
- Display the INSERT tab.
- Tap or click the Advertisements button (INSERT tab | Building Blocks group) to display the Advertisements gallery (Figure 3–60).

Q&A Why does my gallery look different?
Your Advertisements gallery may have an area of recently used items. If necessary, scroll down in the gallery to display the Coupons area.

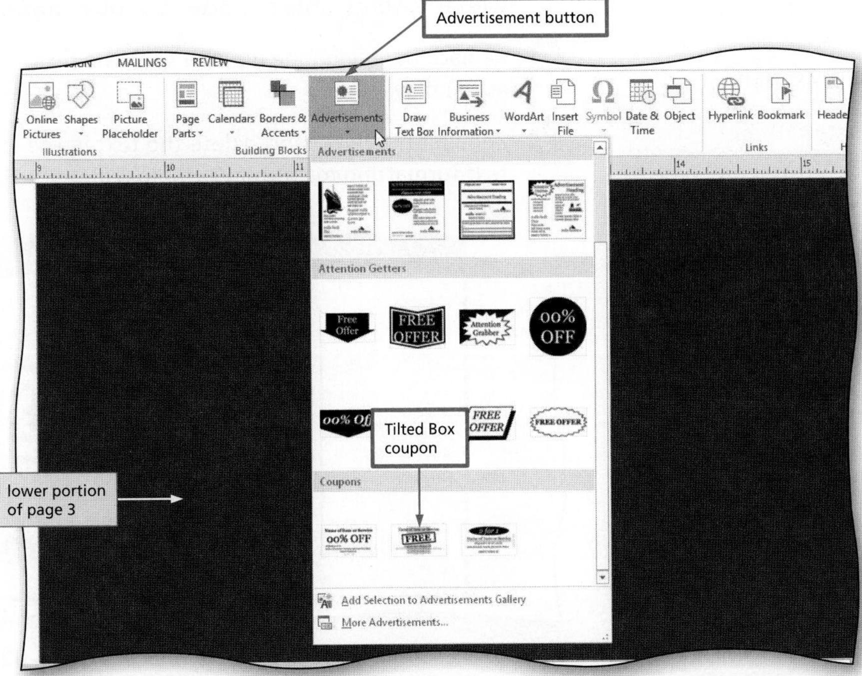

Figure 3–60

2

- In the Coupons area, tap or click the Tilted Box coupon to insert it in the newsletter.
- Drag the border of the inserted coupon to move it to a location in the lower-left corner of the page, as shown in Figure 3–61.
- SHIFT+drag the upper-right sizing handle to approximately the 8-inch mark on the vertical ruler, to resize the coupon.

Q&A My coupon looks different. Did I do something wrong?
No, depending upon your printer and fonts, the coupon may be displayed slightly differently.

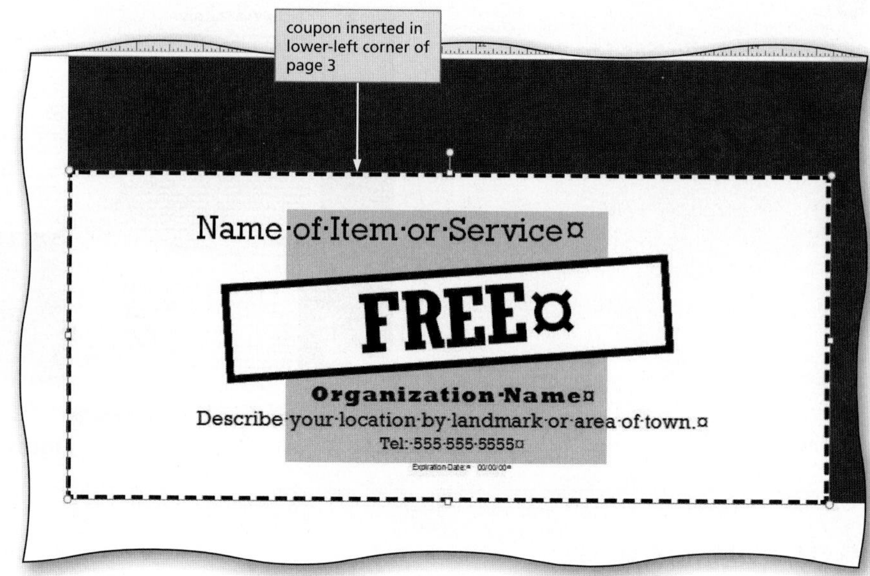

Figure 3–61

Other Ways

1. Tap or click Show Building Block Library Dialog Box Launcher (INSERT tab | Building Blocks group), tap or click Advertisements folder, tap or click desired coupon

To Edit the Coupon

The following steps edit the text boxes in the coupon.

1. Replace the 'Name of Item or Service' placeholder text with the words **`Pizza and Pop`** as the new text
2. Replace the Organization Name placeholder text with the words **`Campus Technology Club`** as the new text.
3. Replace the 'Describe your location by landmark or area of town.' placeholder text with the words **`Just come to our next meeting!`** as the new text.
4. Replace the telephone number with the text, **`October 10, 2014 at 3:00 p.m.`** as the new text.
5. Zoom as necessary and delete the text in the expiration date text boxes. The end of text formatting marks may remain (Figure 3–62).

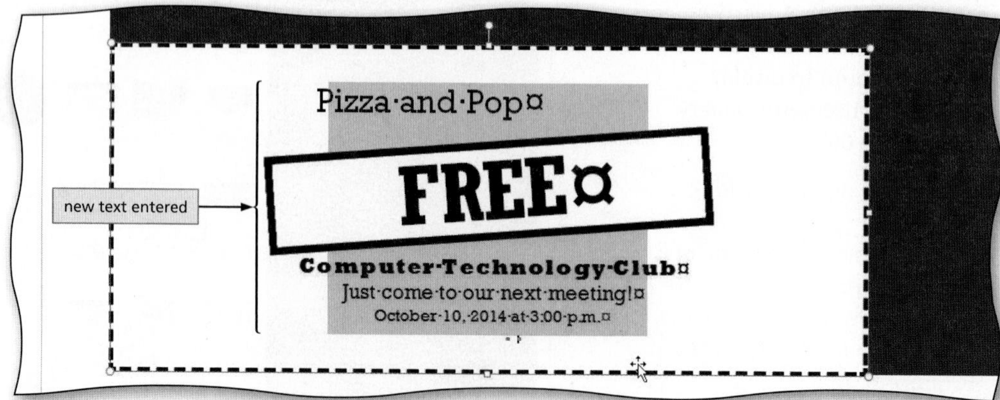

Figure 3–62

Using Graphics in a Newsletter

Most graphic designers employ an easy technique for deciding how many graphics are too many. They hold the publication at arm's length and glance at it. Then, closing their eyes, they count the number of things they remember. Remembering more than five graphics indicates too many; less than two indicates too few. Without question, graphics can make or break a publication. The world has come to expect them. Used correctly, graphics enhance the text, attract the eye, and brighten the look of the publication.

You can use Publisher's clip art images and photos in any publication you create, including newsletters. Publisher also accepts graphics and pictures created by other programs, as well as scanned photos and digital photos. You can import and replace graphics in publications in the same way that you imported stories and replaced template text. Once inserted, graphics can be resized and moved to appropriate locations. In newsletters, you should use photos as true-to-life representations, such as pictures of employees and products. Drawings, on the other hand, can explain, instruct, entertain, or represent images for which you have no picture. The careful use of graphics can add flair and distinction to your publication.

CONSIDER THIS

How do you decide on the best layout?

As you insert graphics and arrange stories, follow any guidelines from the authors or from the company for which you are creating the newsletter. Together, determine the best layout for visual appeal and reliable dissemination of content. Make any required changes. Print a copy and mark the places where sidebars and pull quotes would make sense. Verify that all photos have captions.

The following sections import graphics from the Data Files for Students, edit the captions and sidebar text, and insert a pull quote.

To Replace a Graphic Using the Shortcut Menu

1 EDIT OPTIONS | 2 IMPORT & CONNECT STORIES | 3 USE CONTINUED NOTICES | 4 CUSTOMIZE RIBBON
5 EDIT USING WORD | 6 CREATE MARGINAL ELEMENTS | **7 IMPORT GRAPHICS & REVISE** | **8 CREATE TEMPLATE**

The following steps replace a graphic using the shortcut menu. ***Why?*** *Using the shortcut menu is a quick way to change a picture without having to navigate the ribbon.* To complete these steps, you will be required to use the Data Files for Students. Visit www.cengage.com/ct/studentdownload for detailed instructions or contact your instructor for information about accessing the required files.

- Navigate to page 1.
- Scroll and zoom as necessary to display the graphic in the lead story.
- Press and hold or right-click the graphic to display the shortcut menu and then tap or click Change Picture to display its submenu (Figure 3–63).

Q&A What is the toolbar that appeared on the screen?

When a picture is selected, Publisher displays a mini toolbar in case you want to make changes to the picture.

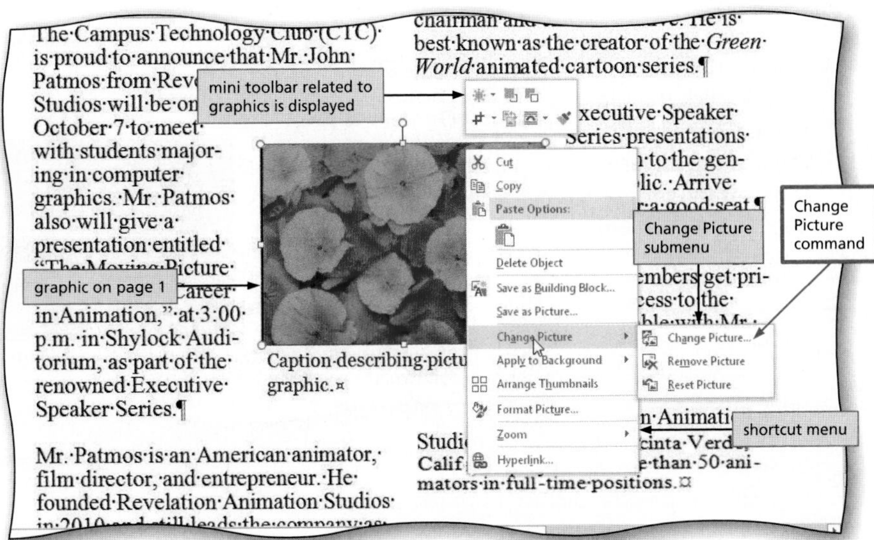

Figure 3–63

- Tap or click Change Picture on the submenu to display the Insert Pictures dialog box (Figure 3–64).

Q&A What do the other choices on the Change Picture submenu do?

The Remove Picture command deletes the picture but retains the picture placeholder. The Reset Picture command removes any previous cropping or resizing.

Insert Pictures dialog box

Browse button

Figure 3 – 64

- Tap or click the Browse button in the From a file area to display the Insert Picture dialog box.
- Navigate to the location of the Data Files for Students (in this case, the Chapter 03 folder in the Publisher folder in the CIS 101 folder) (Figure 3–65).

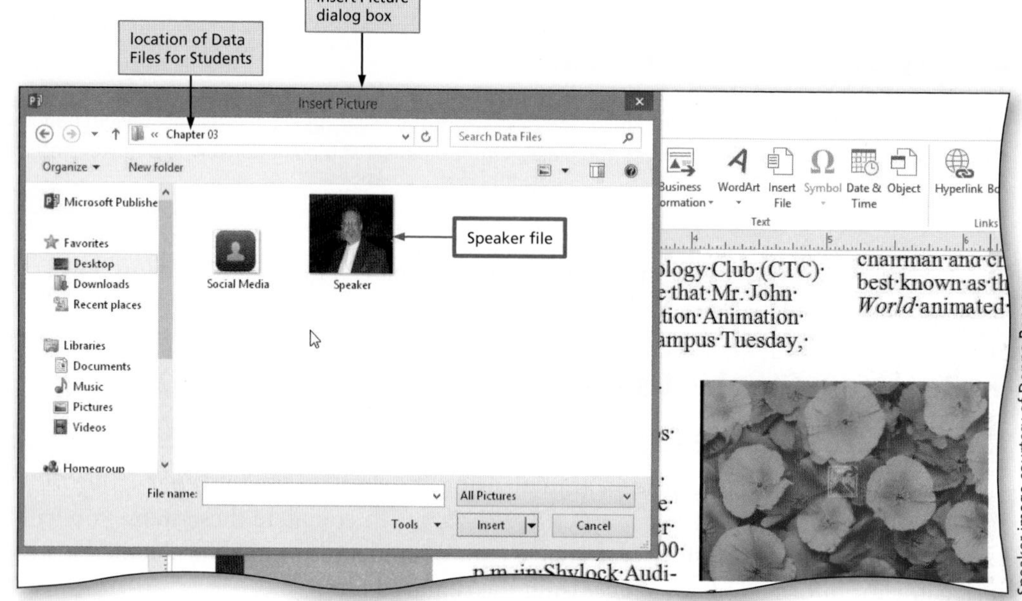

Figure 3 – 65

Speaker image courtesy of Donna Reneau

- Double-tap or double-click the file named, Speaker, to replace the picture. If necessary, zoom to 150% (Figure 3–66).

Q&A What if I choose a bigger or smaller picture?

Because you are replacing the graphic, rather than inserting a picture, Publisher resizes the picture to fit the space. The picture automatically is scaled in proportion.

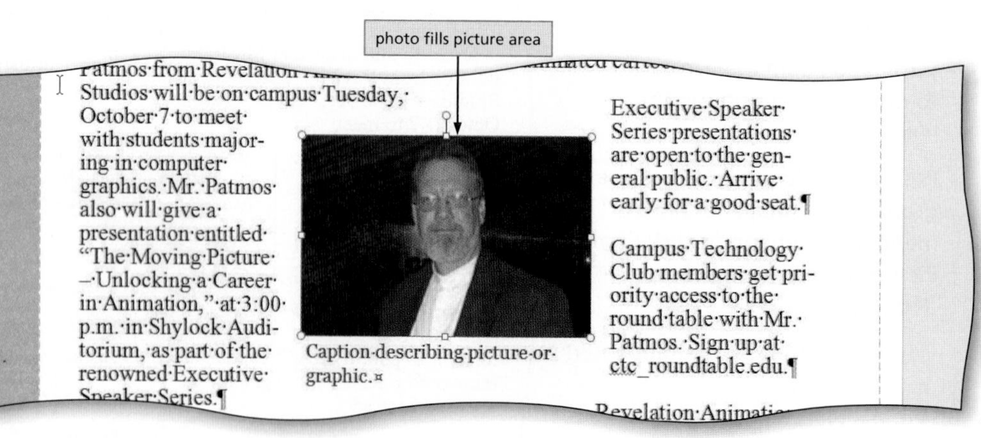

Figure 3 – 66

Speaker image courtesy of Donna Reneau

To Edit the Caption

The following steps edit the picture caption.

1. Select the placeholder text in the caption in order to replace it.
2. Type **John Patmos of** and then press the ENTER key to finish the first line of the caption. Type **Revelation Animation Studios** to finish the caption (Figure 3–67).

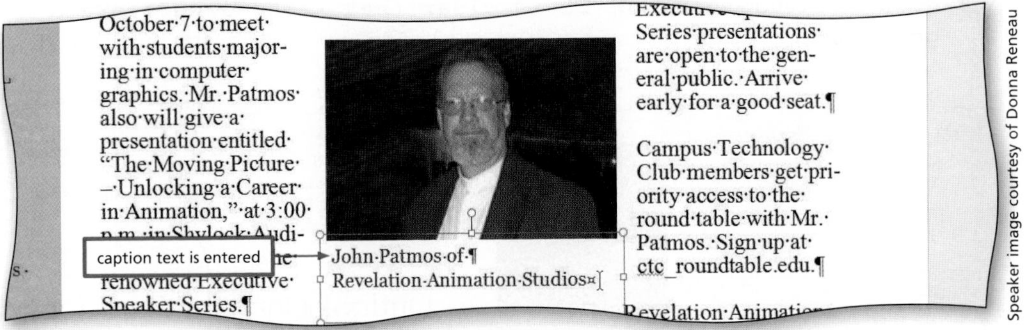
October·7·to·meet·
with·students·major-
ing·in·computer·
graphics.·Mr.·Patmos·
also·will·give·a·
presentation·entitled·
"The·Moving·Picture·
–·Unlocking·a·Career·
in·Animation,"·at·3:00·
caption text is entered
renowned·Executive·
Speaker·Series.¶
John·Patmos·of·¶
Revelation·Animation·Studios¤
Series·presentations·
are·open·to·the·gen-
eral·public.·Arrive·
early·for·a·good·seat.¶
Campus·Technology·
Club·members·get·pri-
ority·access·to·the·
round·table·with·Mr.·
Patmos.·Sign·up·at·
ctc_roundtable.edu.¶
Speaker image courtesy of Donna Reneau

Figure 3–67

To Replace the Graphic on Page 2

The following steps replace other graphics in the newsletter.

1. Navigate to the top of page 2.
2. Press and hold or right-click the graphic beside the first story to display the shortcut menu, and then tap or click Change Picture to display its submenu.
3. Tap or click Change Picture on the submenu to display the Insert Pictures dialog box.
4. Type **spotlight** in the Office.com Clip Art search box, and then press the ENTER key to begin the search.
5. Scroll as necessary in the Office.com Clip Art dialog box, and then double-tap or double-click a picture similar to the one in Figure 3–68 to replace the graphic. If necessary, zoom to 100%.
6. Delete the caption for the picture at the top of page 2.

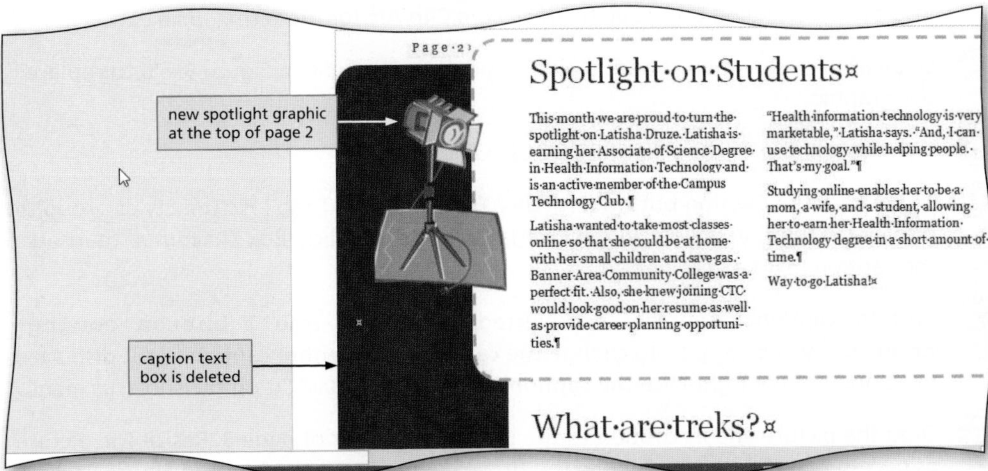
Page·2
Spotlight·on·Students¤
new spotlight graphic at the top of page 2
caption text box is deleted
This·month·we·are·proud·to·turn·the·spotlight·on·Latisha·Druze.·Latisha·is·earning·her·Associate·of·Science·Degree·in·Health·Information·Technology·and·is·an·active·member·of·the·Campus·Technology·Club.¶
Latisha·wanted·to·take·most·classes·online·so·that·she·could·be·at·home·with·her·small·children·and·save·gas.·Banner·Area·Community·College·was·a·perfect·fit.·Also,·she·knew·joining·CTC·would·look·good·on·her·resume·as·well·as·provide·career·planning·opportuni-ties.¶
"Health·information·technology·is·very·marketable,"·Latisha·says.·"And,·I·can·use·technology·while·helping·people.·That's·my·goal."¶
Studying·online·enables·her·to·be·a·mom,·a·wife,·and·a·student,·allowing·her·to·earn·her·Health·Information·Technology·degree·in·a·short·amount·of·time.¶
Way·to·go·Latisha!¤
What·are·treks?¤

Figure 3–68

To Replace the Graphic and Caption on Page 2

The following steps replace other graphics in the newsletter.

1. Navigate to the bottom of page 2.
2. Use the shortcut menu to replace the graphic, searching Office.com Clip Art for the term, **`network`**. Use a graphic similar to the one in Figure 3–69. If necessary, zoom to 100%.
3. Replace the caption by typing, **`It is clear that tech careers are a good choice with strong potential for growth`** as the caption text.

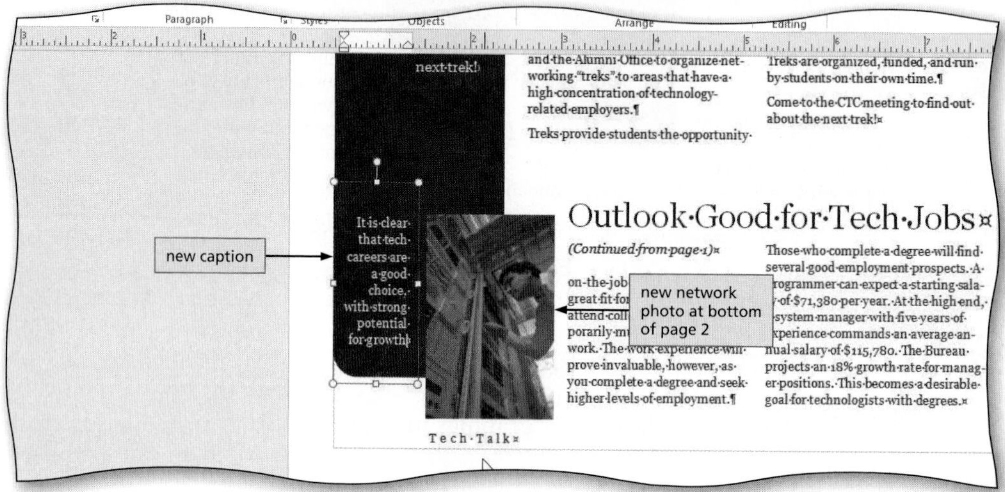

Figure 3–69

To Insert a Graphic and Caption on Page 3

The following steps insert a graphic and caption for the story on page 3 of the newsletter.

1. Navigate to the top of page 3.
2. Display the INSERT tab.
3. Tap or click the Online Pictures button (INSERT tab | Illustrations group) to display the Insert Pictures dialog box. Search Office.com Clip Art for the term, **`smell`**.
4. Scroll as necessary then choose a picture similar to the one in Figure 3–70 to replace the graphic.
5. If necessary, display the PICTURE TOOLS FORMAT tab.
6. Tap or click the Caption button (PICTURE TOOLS FORMAT tab | Picture Styles group) to display the Caption gallery. In the Overlay area, tap or click 'Box - Layout 4' to insert the caption text box.
7. With the caption placeholder text selected, type **`An e-smell button coming soon to your app!`** to change the caption. If the entire caption is not displayed, press and hold or right-click the caption and then click Best Fit on the shortcut menu.
8. Drag the picture and its caption to the upper-left corner of page 3. Resize the picture as necessary to fill the area above the first column of text, as shown in Figure 3–70.

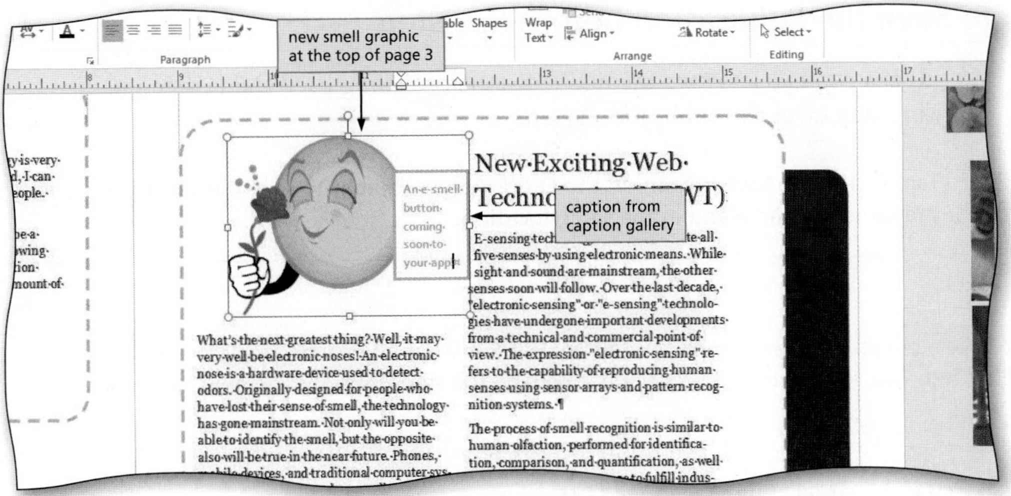

Figure 3–70

To Insert Graphics on Page 4

The following steps insert a graphic and caption for the story on page 4 of the newsletter.

1. Navigate to the top of page 4.
2. Display the INSERT tab.
3. Tap or click the Pictures button (INSERT tab | Illustrations group) to display the Insert Picture dialog box.
4. Navigate to the Data Files for Students, and insert the Social Media graphic.
5. In the publication, drag the graphic to a location near the reference to Facebook.
6. Press and hold or right-click the graphic in the lower portion of Page 4, and use the shortcut menu and Office.com Clip Art to insert a picture related to the search term, `pen`.
7. Delete the caption placeholder text (Figure 3–71).

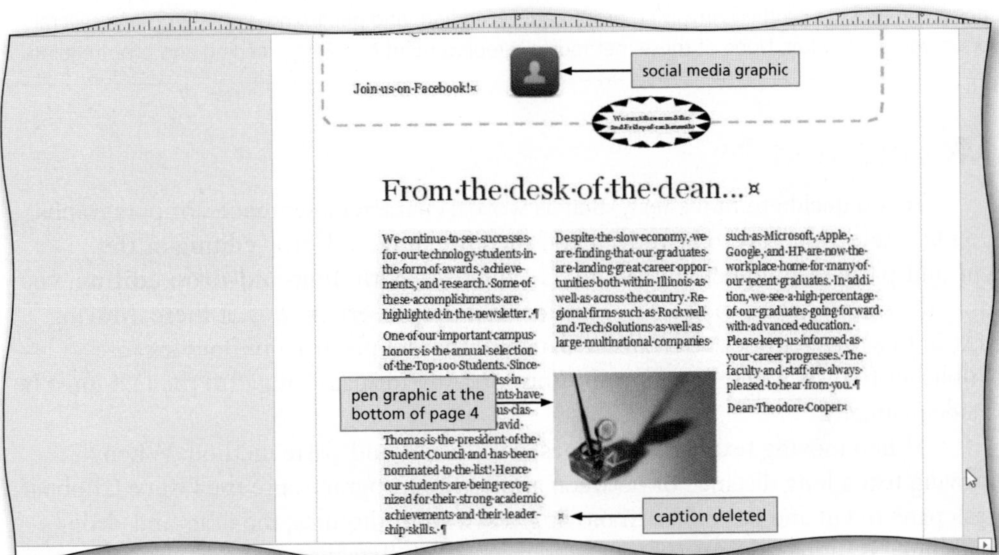

Figure 3–71

To Save the Publication before Revising

It is a good idea to save the newsletter before going back and revising it. The following step saves the publication again.

Tap or click the Save button on the Quick Access Toolbar to save the file again, with the same file name and in the same location.

Break Point: If you wish to take a break, this is a good place to do so. Exit Publisher. To resume at a later time, run Publisher, open the file called Tech Talk Newsletter, and continue following the steps from this location forward.

Revising a Newsletter

As discussed in Chapter 1, once you complete a publication, you may find it necessary to make changes to it. Before submitting a newsletter to a customer or printing service, you should proofread it. While **proofreading**, you look for grammatical errors and spelling errors. You want to be sure the layout, graphics, and stories make sense. If you find errors, you must correct, make changes to, or edit the newsletter. Other readers, perhaps customers or editors, may want to proofread your publication and make changes, such as moving text. You also should check how Publisher has hyphenated your stories.

CONSIDER THIS

How should you proofread and revise a newsletter?

As you proofread the newsletter, look for ways to improve it. Check all grammar, spelling, and punctuation. Be sure the text is logical and transitions are smooth. Where necessary, add text, delete text, reword text, and move text to different locations. Ask yourself these questions:

- Does the title suggest the topic?
- Does the first line of the story entice the reader to continue?
- Is the purpose of the newsletter clear?
- Are all sources acknowledged?

The final phase of the design process is a synthesis involving proofreading, editing, and publishing. Publisher offers several methods to check for errors in your newsletter. None of these methods is a replacement for careful reading and proofreading.

Moving Text

If you decide to move text, such as words, characters, sentences, or paragraphs, you first select the text to be moved and then use drag-and-drop editing or the cut-and-paste technique to move the selected text. With **drag-and-drop editing**, you drag the selected item to the new location and then insert, or *drop*, it there. Moving text in this manner does not transfer data to either Clipboard, nor does it cause Publisher to display the Paste Options button. Any format changes to the text must be made manually.

When moving text between pages, use the cut-and-paste method. When moving text a long distance or between application programs, use the Office Clipboard task pane to cut and paste. When moving text a short distance, the drag-and-drop technique is more efficient. Thus, the steps on the following pages demonstrate drag-and-drop editing.

To Drag-and-Drop Text

1 EDIT OPTIONS | 2 IMPORT & CONNECT STORIES | 3 USE CONTINUED NOTICES | 4 CUSTOMIZE RIBBON
5 EDIT USING WORD | 6 CREATE MARGINAL ELEMENTS | 7 IMPORT GRAPHICS & REVISE | **8 CREATE TEMPLATE**

The editor of the newsletter has decided that two paragraphs on page 3 should be inverted. ***Why?*** *The editor feels that the story will read better with the change.* The following steps move paragraphs by dragging and dropping.

- Navigate to the first story on page 1.
- Triple-tap or triple-click to select the penultimate (next to the last) paragraph (Figure 3–72).

Q&A Could I drag to select the paragraph?
Yes; however, it is more efficient to triple-tap or triple-click, which automatically selects the entire paragraph and the paragraph mark at the end of it.

Speaker image courtesy of Donna Reneau

Figure 3–72

- Drag the selection to the beginning of the previous paragraph. Do not release the mouse button (Figure 3–73).

Q&A My drag is not working. What did I do wrong?
It may be that someone has turned off drag-and-drop editing. Tap or click FILE on the ribbon to open the Backstage view. Tap or click Options and then click Advanced. Tap or click to display a check mark in the 'Allow text to be dragged and dropped' check box.

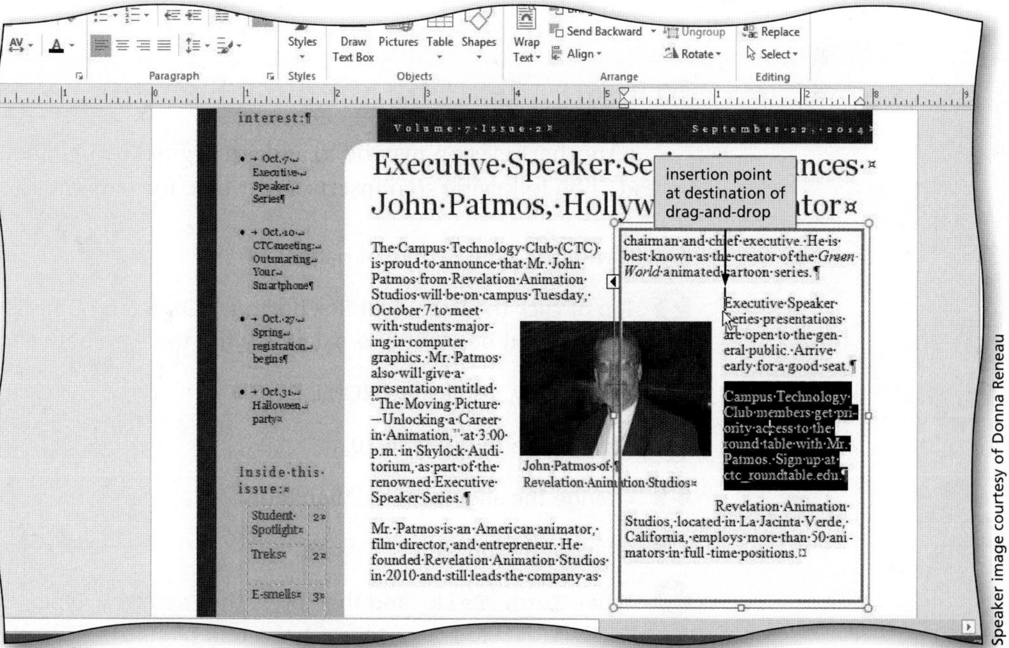

Speaker image courtesy of Donna Reneau

Figure 3–73

- Lift your finger or release the mouse button to move the selected text to the location of the mouse pointer (Figure 3–74).

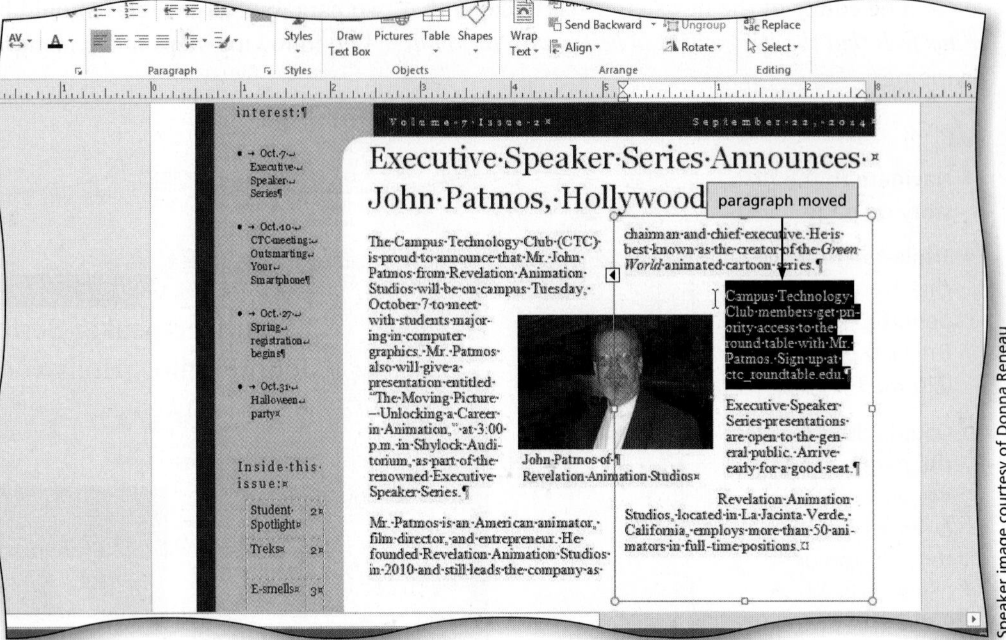

Figure 3–74

Speaker image courtesy of Donna Reneau

Q&A

What if I accidentally drag text to the wrong location?
Tap or click the Undo button on the Quick Access Toolbar, or press CTRL+Z and try again.

Can I use drag-and-drop editing to move any selected item?
Yes, you can select words, sentences, phrases, and graphics and then use drag-and-drop editing to move them.

Other Ways

1. Select item, tap or click Cut button (HOME tab | Clipboard group), tap or click where text is to be pasted, tap or click Paste button (HOME tab | Clipboard group)
2. Press and hold or right-click selected item, tap or click Cut on shortcut menu, press and hold or right-click where text is to be pasted, tap or click Paste Option button on shortcut menu
3. Select item, press CTRL+X, position insertion point where text is to be pasted, press CTRL+V

To Insert a Text Box Marginal Element

Another revision may be to add a marginal text element to balance the two-page spread. The following step inserts a text box, formats the font, and enters the text.

1. Navigate to the middle of page 3.
2. Tap or click the Draw Text Box button (HOME tab | Objects group), and then drag to create a text box that approximately fills the area between the story and the coupon.
3. If necessary, display the HOME tab.
4. Change the font size to 20.
5. Change the alignment to Align Right.
6. Change the font color to white.
7. Type `Tech Talk` and then press the ENTER key. Type `Campus Technology Club Newsletter` to finish the text (Figure 3–75).

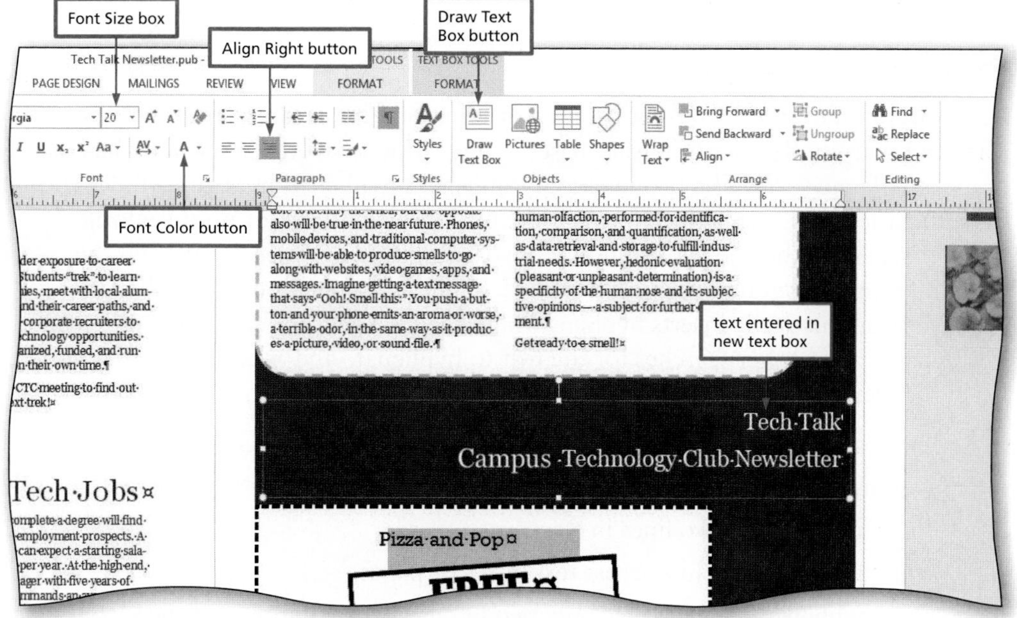

Figure 3 – 75

To Check the Spelling of the Entire Publication

The following steps check the entire publication for spelling errors.

1. Display the REVIEW tab.
2. Tap or click the Spelling button (REVIEW tab | Proofing group) to begin the spelling check in the current location, which in this case, is inside the caption text box.
3. If Publisher flags any words, choose the correct spelling in the Suggestions list, tap or click the Change button, and then continue the spelling check until the next error is identified or the end of the text box is reached.
4. Tap or click the Yes button (Microsoft Publisher dialog box) to tell Publisher to check the rest of the publication. If your publication displays a different error, correct or ignore it as necessary.
5. Tap or click the OK button (Microsoft Publisher dialog box) to close the dialog box.

To Run the Design Checker

The following steps run the Design Checker.

1. Tap or click FILE on the ribbon to open the Backstage view and, by default, select the Info tab.
2. Tap or click the Run Design Checker button in the Info gallery to display the Design Checker task pane.
3. If your publication has problems other than margin spacing, low resolution pictures, or objects near the margin, point to the problem in the 'Select an item to fix' box. When an arrow appears on the right side of the problem, tap or click the arrow and then tap or click the 'Go to this Item' command. Fix or ignore the flagged item as necessary.
4. Tap or click the Close button on the Design Checker task pane to close the Design Checker and return to the publication.

Hyphenation

Hyphenation refers to splitting a word that otherwise would extend beyond the right margin. Because Publisher bases hyphenation on words in its dictionary, it is a good idea to review the hyphenation. Publisher's hyphenation feature allows you to automatically or manually hyphenate the text, insert optional or **nonbreaking hyphens**, and set the maximum amount of space allowed between a word and the right margin without hyphenating the word. When you use automatic hyphenation, Publisher automatically inserts hyphens where they are needed. When you use manual hyphenation, Publisher searches for the text to hyphenate and asks you whether you want to insert the hyphens in the text. Some rules for hyphenation include:

- Hyphenate at standard syllable breaks.
- Do not change the hyphen location of words that already are hyphenated.
- Avoid hyphenating two lines in a row.
- Avoid hyphenating a line across text boxes or pages.
- Avoid hyphenations that leave only two letters at the beginning of the second line, when possible.
- Avoid hyphenating proper nouns.

To Check Hyphenation

1 EDIT OPTIONS | 2 IMPORT & CONNECT STORIES | 3 USE CONTINUED NOTICES | 4 CUSTOMIZE RIBBON
5 EDIT USING WORD | 6 CREATE MARGINAL ELEMENTS | 7 IMPORT GRAPHICS & REVISE | 8 CREATE TEMPLATE

The following steps hyphenate the stories. ***Why?*** *Hyphenating allows you to make decisions about where the hyphens will be placed.* You will choose to hyphenate manually, which means you can specify where the hyphen should occur, rather than have Publisher hyphenate the story automatically.

- Navigate to page 1 and tap or click in the first column of the lead story.
- Display the TEXT BOX TOOLS FORMAT tab.
- Tap or click the Hyphenation button (TEXT BOX TOOLS FORMAT tab | Text group) to display the Hyphenation dialog box (Figure 3–76).

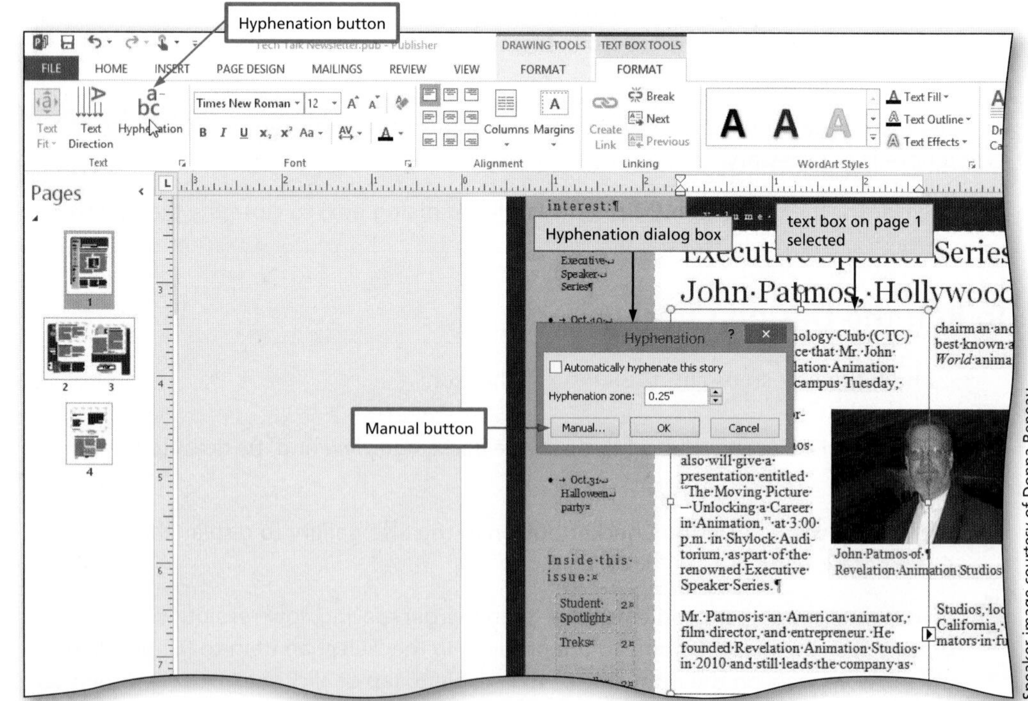

Figure 3–76

Q&A What is the hyphenation zone?
The **hyphenation zone** is the maximum amount of space Publisher allows between a word and the right margin without hyphenating the word. To reduce the number of hyphens, increase the hyphenation zone. To reduce the ragged edge of the right margin, decrease the hyphenation zone.

2

- If necessary, tap or click to remove the check mark in the 'Automatically hyphenate this story' check box.
- Tap or click the Manual button (Hyphenation dialog box) to hyphenate the story manually and to display the first hyphenation choice (Figure 3–77).

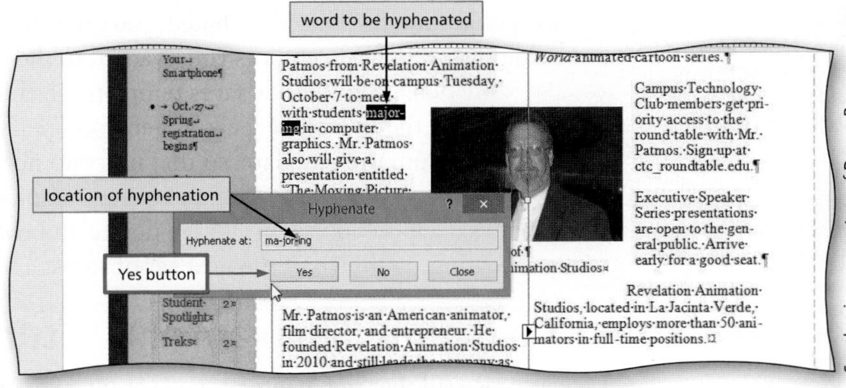

Figure 3–77

- Tap or click the Yes button to hyphenate the word, majoring, at the recommended place.
- Continue to tap or click the Yes button to accept Publisher's hyphenation until you get to the word, Series (Figure 3–78).

Q&A Why is the text already hyphenated?

The default value is automatic hyphenation. Publisher hyphenates after the standard syllables.

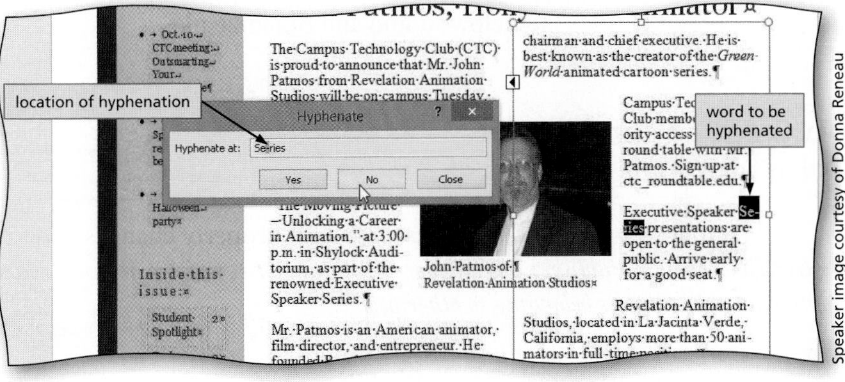

Figure 3–78

- Tap or click the No button so Publisher will not hyphenate the word, series, as proper nouns are not supposed to be hyphenated.
- Continue to tap or click the Yes or No button using the hyphenation rules listed previously.
- When Publisher finishes hyphenating the lead story, manually hyphenate the other stories in the newsletter.

Other Ways

1. Press CTRL+SHIFT+H, tap or click OK button (Hyphenation dialog box)

To Save the Revised Publication

The following step saves the publication again.

1 Tap or click the Save button on the Quick Access Toolbar to overwrite the previously saved file.

BTW

Quick Reference

For a table that lists how to complete the tasks covered in this book using touch gestures, the mouse, ribbon, shortcut menu, and keyboard, see the Quick Reference Summary at the back of this book, or visit the Quick Reference resource on the Student Companion Site located on www.cengagebrain.com. For detailed instructions about accessing available resources, visit www.cengage.com/ct/studentdownload or see the inside back cover of this book.

Creating a Template

Newsletters typically retain their masthead, color scheme, font scheme, and other graphics from issue to issue. In a first issue, you must make design choices and implement them to make sure the newsletter is displayed correctly — reviewing that takes time. You do not have to do all of that for subsequent issues. Once the decisions have been made and the publication has been distributed, you can reuse the same publication as a template. Additionally, Publisher allows you to add it to the templates on your computer.

By default, Publisher saves templates in the My Templates folder for easy access from the Backstage view. When you open a saved template, a new publication is created from the template, so that users do not overwrite the template file. In lab situations, you should not save a personal template in the My Templates folder. You should save it on your own storage device and change the system properties to prevent overwriting, as shown in the next set of steps.

BTW
Tags
Tags are one of many file properties to help you find and organize the files. In addition to tags, other properties include the Date Modified, Author, and Subject. They become the keywords in the Properties dialog box. Unlike some predefined properties, tags can be anything you choose, such as "Newsletters," "Vacation," or even "My Stuff."

Saving the Template and Setting File Properties

Recall that in Chapter 1, you set file properties using the Properties command from the File menu. Two specific properties can be set at the time you create a publication or template. The author and tag properties can be entered into any of the Save As dialog boxes, which can save you several steps. A **tag** is a custom property used to help you find and organize files.

To Create a Template with Property Changes

1 EDIT OPTIONS | 2 IMPORT & CONNECT STORIES | 3 USE CONTINUED NOTICES | 4 CUSTOMIZE RIBBON
5 EDIT USING WORD | 6 CREATE MARGINAL ELEMENTS | 7 IMPORT GRAPHICS & REVISE | **8 CREATE TEMPLATE**

The following steps create a template with property changes and save it on a personal storage device. ***Why?*** *Even though Publisher has a folder specifically for templates, it is not recommended to save templates on lab computers or computers belonging to other people.*

1

- Tap or click FILE on the ribbon to open the Backstage view.
- Tap or click the Save As command and then double-tap or double-click Computer or SkyDrive to display the Save As dialog box.
- Type `Newsletter Template` to change the name of the publication. Do not press the ENTER key.
- Tap or click the 'Save as type' button to display the list of file types (Figure 3–79).

Experiment

- Scroll through the many types of file formats available for publications.

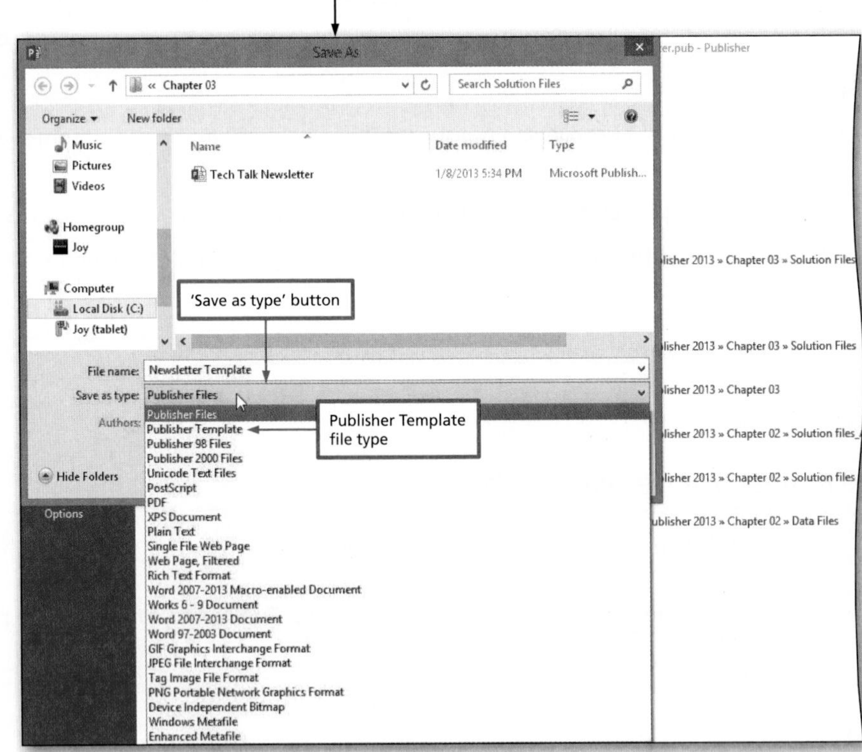

Figure 3–79

Q&A
Where should a company store its templates?
On a business computer, for an organization that routinely uses templates, you should save templates in the default location. Publisher stores templates within the program data in a folder named, Custom Office Templates. Templates stored in the default location are displayed in the catalog when you click the My Templates button. Templates, however, can be stored in several places: on a personal computer, on a web server, or on a common drive for use by multiple employees or students.

- Tap or click Publisher Template to choose to save the publication as a template.
- Navigate to your preferred storage location.

  If requested by your instructor, double-tap or double-click in the Authors text box in the lower portion of the dialog box, and then type your name to replace the text.
- Tap or click in the Tags text box, and then type **`monthly newsletter`** to add the tag words (Figure 3–80). The current text in the Tags text box will disappear as you start to type.

3

- Tap or click the Save button (Save As dialog box) to save the template.

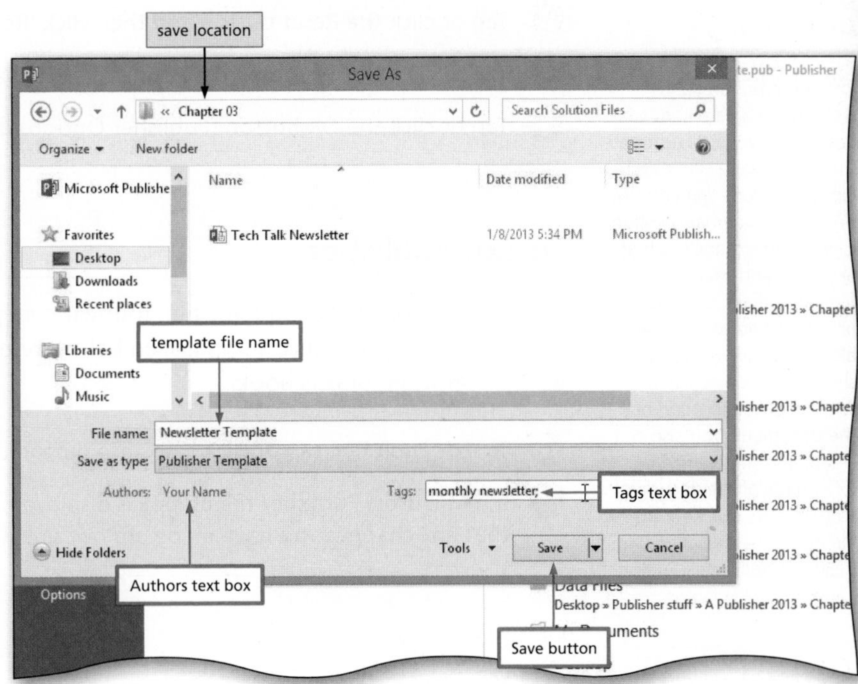

Figure 3–80

To Print the Newsletter

If you have access to a printer that can accept 17 × 11.5 inch paper, you can print double-sided and then fold the paper to create the newsletter. If you want to print double-sided on 8.5 × 11 inch paper, the newsletter will print on the back and front of two pages that you then can staple. For a detailed example of the procedure summarized below, refer to Chapter 2.

The following steps print the newsletter.

1. Ready the printer according to the printer instructions. Tap or click FILE on the ribbon to open the Backstage view.
2. Tap or click the Print tab in the Backstage view to display the Print gallery.
3. Tap or click the Print button in the Print gallery to print the document.
4. Make any necessary changes to the print settings for your paper size and duplex printing.
5. When the printer stops, retrieve the printed document.

BTW

Conserving Ink and Toner

If you want to conserve ink or toner, you can instruct Publisher to print draft quality documents by tapping or clicking FILE on the ribbon to open the Backstage view, and tapping or clicking Print in the Backstage view to display the Print gallery. Tap or click the Printer Properties link, and then, depending on your printer, click the Print Quality button and choose Draft in the list. Close the Printer Properties dialog box and then tap or click the Print button as usual.

To Remove All Ribbon Customization

When working in a lab environment, it is advisable to remove the ribbon customization. The following steps remove all ribbon customization.

1. Tap or click FILE on the ribbon to open the Backstage view, and then click Options to display the Publisher Options dialog box.
2. Tap or click Customize Ribbon in the left pane (Publisher Options dialog box) to display the options for customizing the ribbon.

BTW
Distributing a Document
Instead of printing and distributing a hard copy of a document, you can distribute the document electronically. Options include sending the document via email; posting it on cloud storage (such as SkyDrive) and sharing the file with others; posting it on a social networking site, blog, or other website; and sharing a link associated with an online location of the document. You also can create and share a PDF or XPS image of the document, so that users can view the file in Acrobat Reader or XPS Viewer instead of in Publisher.

3. Tap or click the Reset button and then click 'Reset all customizations' in the list.
4. Tap or click the Yes button (Microsoft Office dialog box).
5. Tap or click the OK button (Publisher Options dialog box) to close the dialog box.

To Exit Publisher

This project is complete. The following steps exit Publisher. For a detailed example of the procedure summarized below, refer to the Office and Windows chapter at the beginning of this book.

1. To exit Publisher, tap or click the Close button on the right side of the title bar.
2. If a Microsoft Publisher dialog box is displayed, tap or click the Don't Save button so that any changes you have made are not saved.

Chapter Summary

In this chapter, you learned how to select template options for a newsletter, edit the masthead and sidebars, import stories, insert continued notices across pages, and create original stories using the Edit Story in Microsoft Word command. You edited sidebars and inserted a coupon. In revising the newsletter, you used drag-and-drop editing techniques, hyphenated the stories, checked the spelling, and ran the Design Checker. The items listed below include all the new Publisher skills you have learned in this chapter.

Change Settings
Create a Template with Property Changes (PUB 182)
Customize the Publisher Ribbon (PUB 153)
Remove All Ribbon Customization (PUB 183)
Set Page Options (PUB 135)

Change the Layout
Add Pages to a Newsletter (PUB 138)
Delete Pages in a Newsletter (PUB 138)
Duplicate an Object (PUB 168)
Send an Object to the Back (PUB 168)

Edit Text
Drag-and-Drop Text (PUB 177)
Edit a Story Using Microsoft Word (PUB 156)
Edit Sidebars (PUB 161)
Edit the Masthead (PUB 139)

Format Text
Break a Text Box Link (PUB 147)
Check Hyphenation (PUB 180)
Continue a Story across Pages (PUB 144)
Format while Editing in Microsoft Word (PUB 158)
Format with Continued Notices (PUB 148)

Insert Objects
Insert a Coupon (PUB 169)
Insert a Pull Quote (PUB 164)
Replace a Graphic Using the Shortcut Menu (PUB 171)

Import Text
Import a Text File (PUB 142)

Navigate the Publication
Follow a Story across Pages (PUB 145)
Manually Continue the Story across Pages (PUB 147)
Exit Word and Return to Publisher (PUB 159)

What decisions will you need to make when creating your next newsletter?
Use these guidelines as you complete the assignments in this chapter and create your own publications outside of this class.

1. Decide on the layout.
   a) Select a template and options that matches your need.
   b) Set columns and options for each page purpose and audience.
2. Edit the masthead.

3. Gather the text content.
    a) Import stories when possible.
    b) Edit stories in Microsoft Word when necessary.
    c) Flow long stories to other text boxes.
    d) Format continued stories with jump lines.
4. Create and edit marginal elements.
5. Insert other elements such as advertisements.
6. Edit graphics and captions.
7. Revise as necessary.
    a) Proofread and check the publication.
    b) Run an hyphenation check.
8. Create a template for future use.

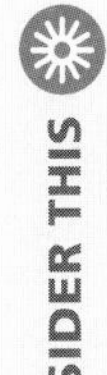

CONSIDER THIS

How should you submit solutions to questions in the assignments identified with a symbol?

Every assignment in this book contains one or more questions identified with a symbol. These questions require you to think beyond the assigned publication. Present your solutions to the questions in the format required by your instructor. Possible formats may include one or more of these options: write the answer; create a document that contains the answer; present your answer to the class; discuss your answer in a group; record the answer as audio or video using a webcam, smartphone, or portable media player; or post answers on a blog, wiki, or website.

Apply Your Knowledge

Reinforce the skills and apply the concepts you learned in this chapter.

Creating a Newsletter

Note: To complete this assignment, you will be required to use the Data Files for Students. Visit www.cengage.com/ct/studentdownload for detailed instructions or contact your instructor for information about accessing the required files.

Instructions: The local food pantry would like you to create a newsletter for them. They have provided some stories and will give you others at a later time. You produce the publication shown in Figure 3 – 81.

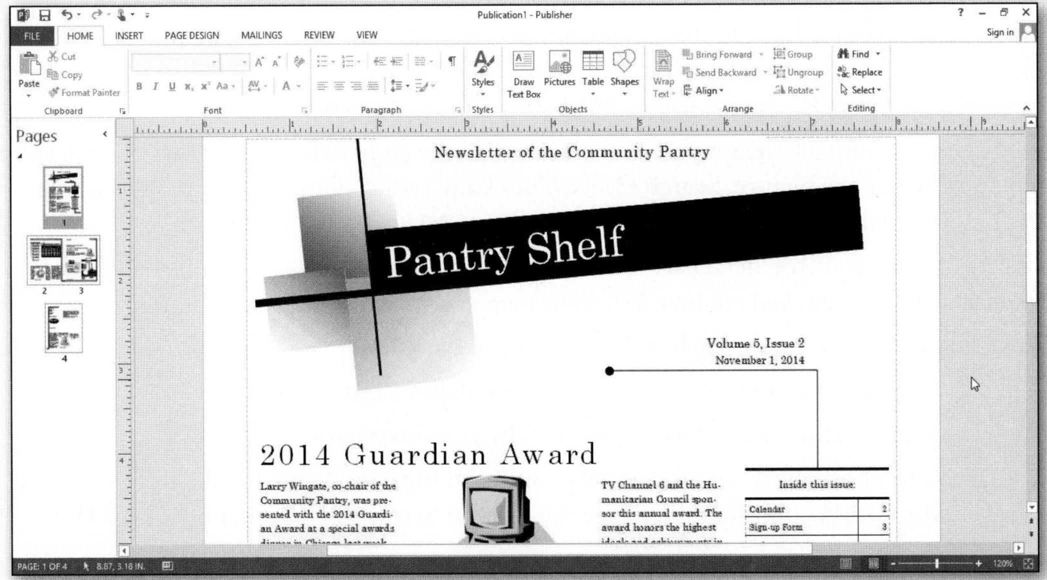

Figure 3 – 81

Continued >

Apply Your Knowledge *continued*

Perform the following tasks:

1. Run Publisher. Tap or click BUILT-IN, and then tap or click Newsletters.
2. Choose the Blends newsletter template, the Parrot color scheme, and the Oriel font scheme. Set the Page size to 'Two-page spread'.
3. Create the publication. Use the Options button (PAGE DESIGN tab | Template group) to choose a mixed format on pages 1 and 4. On page 2, include a calendar and a 3 column format. The date of your calendar may differ. On page 3, include a sign-up form and a 1 column format.
4. Edit the masthead as shown in Figure 3–81 on the previous page.
5. For the lead story, use the headline, **2014 Guardian Award**. Import the story, 2014 Guardian Award, from the Data Files for Students.
6. If necessary, customize the ribbon to display the 'Edit Story in Microsoft Word' button (REVIEW tab | New Group). See pages PUB 153 through 156 for instructions.
7. For the secondary story on page 1, press and hold or right-click the headline and then tap or click Best Fit on the shortcut menu. Type the headline **New Counseling Center to Open Soon.** Tap or click the placeholder text of the story. Tap or click the 'Edit Story in Microsoft Word' button (REVIEW tab | New Group). When Word is displayed, press CTRL+A to select all of the text. Type the following text, pressing the ENTER key at the end of each paragraph except the last:

   The Community Pantry will open a new counseling and referral center for its patrons on December 1. Counselors will be available to help with housing needs, utility assistance, transportation, and job placement, as well as our normal food services.

   Through gracious donations from the Community Foundation, the Pantry has expanded its physical space as well. Trained counselors are available during our normal Pantry hours. If you need assistance with any of these programs, please stop by the Community Pantry and talk to a counselor.

   The Pantry wants to be there when help is needed.

   Exit Word to return to Publisher.
8. Navigate to the bottom of page 2. Change the Inside Story Headline to **Thanksgiving Food Drive.** Import the story, Thanksgiving Food Drive, from the Data Files for Students.
9. On page 1, tap or click the graphic twice to select it. Use the shortcut menu to change the picture. Search Office.Com Clip Art for photos related to the search term, award. Change the caption to **Larry Wingate wins 2014 Guardian Award.**
10. On page 2, tap or click the graphic at the bottom of the page twice to select it. Use the shortcut menu to change the picture. Search Office.Com Clip Art for photos related to the search term, thanksgiving. Change the caption to **Share your blessings with others.**
11. If instructed by your teacher, change other text and graphics such as the table of contents sidebar, sign-up form, and coupon. Use your name and address at the top of page 4.
12. Save the file with the name Apply 3-1 Food Pantry Newsletter.
13. Remove the ribbon customization as described on pages PUB 183 and 184.
14. Submit the publication in the format specified by your instructor.
15. Do you think adding a calendar and sign-up form to pages 2 and 3 make them too busy? Why or why not? Would you rather type the story in Step 7 in Publisher or Word? Why?

Extend Your Knowledge

Extend the skills you learned in this chapter and experiment with new skills. You may need to use Help to complete the assignment.

Creating Page 1 of a Newsletter from Scratch

Instructions: Your school had a first-time callout for the Extreme Sports Club. You have been asked to create a layout for page 1 of a proposed newsletter. They need a newsletter to promote meetings and events. You decide to start from scratch to create the newsletter page shown in Figure 3–82.

September 15, 2014

CAMPUS EXTREME

Newsletter of the Extreme Sports Club

Volume 1 Issue 1

Lead Story Headline

Video provides a powerful way to help you prove your point. When you click Online Video, you can paste in the embed code for the video you want to add.

You can also type a keyword to search online for the video that best fits your document. To make your document look professionally produced, Word provides header, footer, cover page, and text box designs that complement each other.

TITLE TEXT

This is a good place to briefly, but effectively, describe your product or services.

TITLE

SIDEBAR

This is a good place to briefly, but effectively, describe your product or

Figure 3–82

Perform the following tasks:

1. Run Publisher. Tap or click BUILT-IN, and then tap or click Newsletters. Scroll to the Blank Sizes area, and then tap or click the 1/2 A4 Booklet 5.827 × 8.268 thumbnail to choose a paper size.
2. Choose the Clay color scheme and the Textbook font scheme. Tap or click the CREATE button to create the publication. When Publisher asks to insert pages automatically, click the Yes button.
3. Use Help to read about inserting Page Parts. Tap or click the Page Parts button (INSERT tab | Building Blocks group) to display the gallery, and then choose the Portal heading to use as a masthead. When Publisher inserts the heading, resize it to fit within the margins.
4. Press and hold or right-click the Title text, and choose Best Fit on the shortcut menu. Type `CAMPUS EXTREME` to change the title. Press and hold or right-click the subtitle text, and choose Best Fit on the shortcut menu. Change the subtitle to `Newsletter of the Extreme Sports Club`. Change the date to `September 15, 2014`. If requested to do so by your instructor, use the current date in the newsletter.
5. Use the Draw Text Box button (HOME tab | Objects group) to add a text box in the lower-right portion of the masthead. Insert the text, `Volume 1, Issue 1`, and then change the text color to white.
6. Again using the Page Parts button (INSERT tab | Building Blocks group), insert the Convention (Layout 3) sidebar. Resize the sidebar to fit the space below the masthead and at the left margin as shown in Figure 3–82. Your display may differ, depending on how you resize the sidebar.
7. Draw a text box below the masthead, approximately .5 inches tall and 3 inches wide. Insert the text, `Lead Story Headline`. Press and hold or right-click the text, and then click Best Fit on the shortcut menu.
8. Draw a text box below the lead story headline, approximately 1.5 inches wide and 2.5 inches tall. Position the text box in the upper-left corner of the blank area of the page. Create another text box, the same size and place it in the upper-right corner of the blank area. Tap or click the first text box, and then click the Create Link button (TEXT BOX TOOLS FORMAT tab | Linking group). Tap or click the second text box to link the two.

Continued >

Extend Your Knowledge *continued*

9. If necessary, customize the ribbon to display the 'Edit Story in Microsoft Word' button (REVIEW tab | New group). See pages PUB 153 through 156 for instructions.
10. Tap or click the first empty text box. Tap or click the 'Edit Story in Microsoft Word' button (REVIEW tab | New group). When Word is displayed, type `=rand(2,2)` and then press the ENTER key to generate random text. Delete any extra hard returns at the end of the text. Exit Word to return to Publisher.
11. Again using the Page Parts button (INSERT tab | Building Blocks group), insert the Convention (Layout 1) story. Resize the story to fit the empty space at the bottom of the page.
12. Tap or click one of the pictures in the side bar twice, to select only the picture. Replace the picture with a photo from Office.com Clip Art using the search term, extreme sports. Repeat the process for the other two pictures.
13. Save the file with the name Extend 3-1 Extreme Sports Newsletter.
14. Remove the ribbon customization as described on pages PUB 183 and 184.
15. Submit the file in the format specified by your instructor.
16. When would you use a template instead of creating a newsletter from scratch? What other page parts might you add to subsequent pages? Why?

Analyze, Correct, Improve

Analyze a publication, correct all errors, and improve the design.

Formatting Long Stories

Note: To complete this assignment, you will be required to use the Data Files for Students. Visit www.cengage.com/ct/studentdownload for detailed instructions or contact your instructor for information about accessing the required files.

Instructions: You have been given a newsletter for a local historical society. The newsletter is shown in Figure 3–83, but it has several issues. You decide to improve the newsletter. Run Publisher and open the file, Analyze 3-1 History Newsletter.

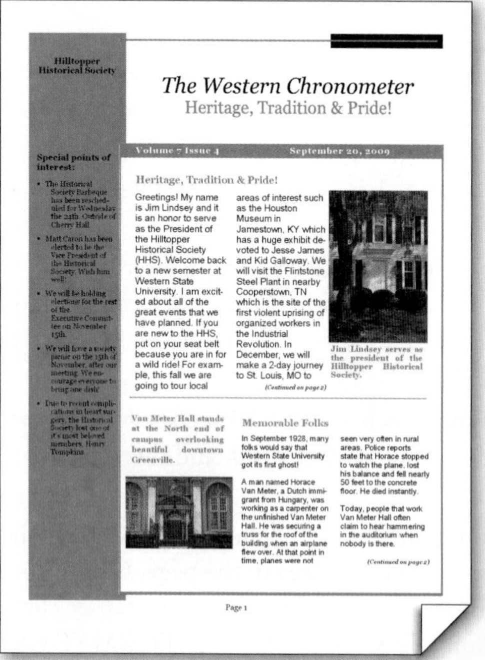

Hilltopper Historical Society

The Western Chronometer

Heritage, Tradition & Pride!

Volume 7 Issue 4 September 20, 2009

Special points of interest:

- The Historical Society Barbeque has been rescheduled for Wednesday the 24th. Outside of Cherry Hall
- Matt Caron has been elected to be the Vice President of the Historical Society. Wish him well!
- We will be holding elections for the rest of the Executive Committee on November 15th.
- We will have a society picnic on the 15th of November, after our meeting. We encourage everyone to bring one dish!
- Due to recent complications in heart surgery, the Historical Society lost one of it's most beloved members, Henry Tompkins

Heritage, Tradition & Pride!

Greetings! My name is Jim Lindsey and it is an honor to serve as the President of the Hilltopper Historical Society (HHS). Welcome back to a new semester at Western State University. I am excited about all of the great events that we have planned. If you are new to the HHS, put on your seat belt because you are in for a wild ride! For example, this fall we are going to tour local areas of interest such as the Houston Museum in Jamestown, KY which has a huge exhibit devoted to Jesse James and Kid Galloway. We will visit the Flintstone Steel Plant in nearby Cooperstown, TN which is the site of the first violent uprising of organized workers in the Industrial Revolution. In December, we will make a 2-day journey to St. Louis, MO to

(Continued on page 2)

Jim Lindsey serves as the president of the Hilltopper Historical Society.

Van Meter Hall stands at the North end of campus overlooking beautiful downtown Greenville.

Memorable Folks

In September 1928, many folks would say that Western State University got its first ghost!

A man named Horace Van Meter, a Dutch immigrant from Hungary, was working as a carpenter on the unfinished Van Meter Hall. He was securing a truss for the roof of the building when an airplane flew over. At that point in time, planes were not seen very often in rural areas. Police reports state that Horace stopped to watch the plane, lost his balance and fell nearly 50 feet to the concrete floor. He died instantly.

Today, people that work Van Meter Hall often claim to hear hammering in the auditorium when nobody is there.

(Continued on page 2)

Page 1

(a) Page 1

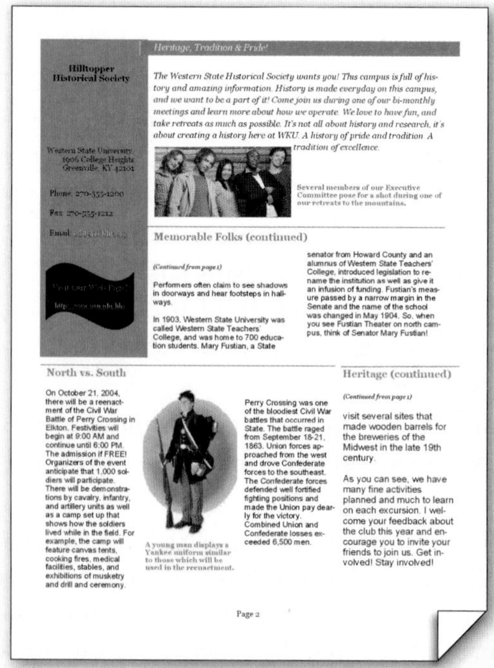

Heritage, Tradition & Pride!

Hilltopper Historical Society

The Western State Historical Society wants you! This campus is full of history and amazing information. History is made everyday on this campus, and we want to be a part of it! Come join us during one of our bi-monthly meetings and learn more about how we operate. We love to have fun, and take retreats as much as possible. It's not all about history and research, it's about creating a history here at WKU. A history of pride and tradition. A tradition of excellence.

Several members of our Executive Committee pose for a shot during one of our retreats to the mountains.

Western State University
1906 College Heights
Greenville, KY 42101

Phone: 270-555-1200

Fax: 270-555-1212

Memorable Folks (continued)

(Continued from page 1)

Performers often claim to see shadows in doorways and hear footsteps in hallways.

In 1903, Western State University was called Western State Teachers' College, and was home to 700 education students. Mary Fustian, a State senator from Howard County and an alumnus of Western State Teachers' College, introduced legislation to rename the institution as well as give it an infusion of funding. Fustian's measure passed by a narrow margin in the Senate and the name of the school was changed in May 1904. So, when you see Fustian Theater on north campus, think of Senator Mary Fustian!

North vs. South

On October 21, 2004, there will be a reenactment of the Civil War Battle of Perry Crossing in Elkton. Festivities will begin at 9:00 AM and continue until 6:00 PM. The admission if FREE! Organizers of the event anticipate that 1,000 soldiers will participate. There will be demonstrations by cavalry, infantry, and artillery units as well as a camp set up that shows how the soldiers lived while in the field. For example, the camp will feature canvas tents, cooking fires, medical facilities, stables, and exhibitions of musketry and drill and ceremony.

A young man displays a Yankee uniform similar to those which will be used in the reenactment.

Perry Crossing was one of the bloodiest Civil War battles that occurred in State. The battle raged from September 18-21, 1863. Union forces approached from the west and drove Confederate forces to the southeast. The Confederate forces defended well fortified fighting positions and made the Union pay dearly for the victory. Combined Union and Confederate losses exceeded 6,500 men.

Heritage (continued)

(Continued from page 1)

visit several sites that made wooden barrels for the breweries of the Midwest in the late 19th century.

As you can see, we have many fine activities planned and much to learn on each excursion. I welcome your feedback about the club this year and encourage you to invite your friends to join us. Get involved! Stay involved!

Page 2

(b) Page 2

Figure 3–83

1. Correct The publication has formatting errors related to text in overflow. Use Publisher tools to help you find those locations. Manually continue overflow stories to blank text boxes in the newsletter. Add headings to the continued stories. Use the format painter to match the headings to others in the newsletter.

2. Improve None of the continued stories has jump lines to guide the reader to the appropriate page. Use the Next and Previous buttons to find the rest of the story. Add jump lines to every continued story. Hyphenate all stories. Check the sidebars for hyphenation issues and use soft returns where necessary. Save the document using the file name, Analyze 3-1 History Newsletter Complete. Submit the revised document in the format specified by your instructor.

3. How did you make decisions about where to hyphenate? Which rules of hyphenation did you use? Was changing the hyphenated sidebar difficult? Why?

In the Labs

Design, create, or modify a publication using the guidelines, concepts, and skills presented in this chapter. Labs 1 and 2, which increase in difficulty, require you to create a solution based on what you learned in the chapter; Lab 3 requires you to create a solution, which uses cloud and web technologies, by learning and investigating on your own from general guidance.

Lab 1: Creating a Newsletter Template

Problem: The symphonic orchestra has asked you to create a newsletter they can distribute to their patrons. Currently, they have given you content for page 1 and page 4. You are to leave placeholder text and graphics on the inside pages. You create the newsletter shown in Figure 3–84.

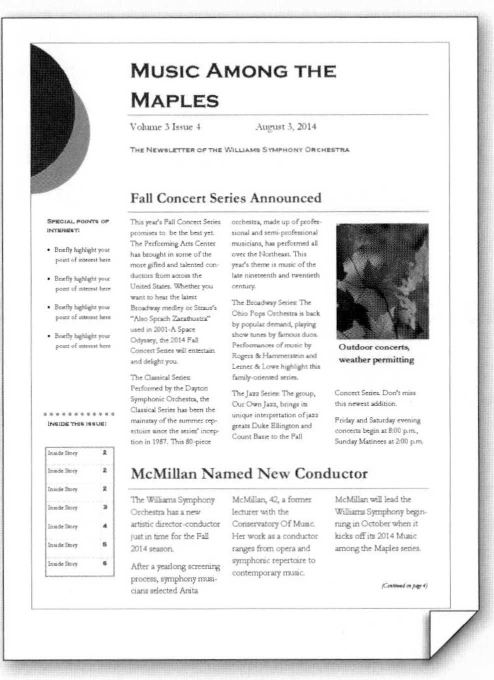

(a) Page 1

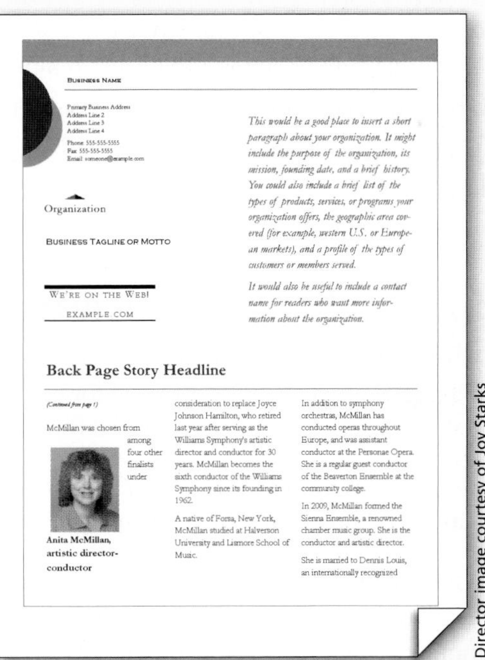

(b) Page 2

Director image courtesy of Joy Starks

Figure 3–84

1. Run Publisher. In the template gallery, tap or click BUILT-IN and then tap or click Newsletters.
2. In the More Installed Templates area, choose the Eclipse template.
3. Select the Aspect color scheme and the Etched font scheme. Choose to use a two-page spread. Create the publication.

Continued >

In the Labs *continued*

4. As you make changes to the newsletter, scroll and zoom as necessary. Turn on the display of formatting characters if desired.
5. Use the following text to edit the masthead on page 1.
   Newsletter Title: `Music Among the Maples`
   Volume and Issue: `Volume 3 Issue 4`
   Newsletter Date: `August 3, 2014`
   Business Name: `The Newsletter of the Williams Symphony Orchestra`
6. For the lead story, use the headline `Fall Concert Series Announced`. Import the lead story, Fall Concert Series, from the Data Files for Students.
7. Replace the graphic on page 1 using the shortcut menu. Search Office.com Clip Art for the term, maples. Edit the caption to read `Outdoor concerts, weather permitting`.
8. For the second story on page 1, use the headline, `McMillan Named New Conductor`. Import the story, McMillan Named New Conductor, from the Data Files for Students. When Publisher prompts you, flow the story to the last story on page 4. Use the same headline on page 4.
9. Add continued notices on page 1 and page 4 as appropriate.
10. At the bottom of page 4, tap or click the graphic twice to select it. Replace the graphic using the shortcut menu. Browse to the Data Files for Students and insert the Conductor graphic. Click the Fit button (PICTURE TOOLS FORMAT tab | Crop group) to make the graphic fit the area. If requested to do so by your instructor, use your picture instead of the one supplied in the Data Files for Students. Edit the caption to read `Anita McMillan, artistic director-conductor`.
11. Check your publication for spelling and design errors, and fix or ignore the flagged items as necessary. Hyphenate the stories according to the hyphenation rules on page PUB 180.
12. Save the newsletter on your storage device with the file name, Lab 3-1 Symphony Newsletter. Save the file again, this time as a Publisher template, named Lab 3-1 Symphony Newsletter Template.
13. Submit the file as directed by your instructor.
14. How do the font scheme and color scheme compliment the topic of the newsletter? How do you think page 1 would have looked if you had changed it to a mixed column format? Why might you want to change the format?

Lab 2: Publisher Newsletter Choices

Note: To complete this assignment, you will be required to use the Data Files for Students. Visit www.cengage.com/ct/studentdownload for detailed instructions or contact your instructor for information about accessing the required files.

Problem: Use a copy of a newsletter that you regularly receive, or obtain one from a friend, company, or school. Using the principles in this chapter, analyze the newsletter.

Run Publisher. Open the publication, Lab 3-2 Newsletter Analysis Table, from the Data Files for Students. Use the skills you learned in editing sidebars to fill in each of the empty cells in the table as it applies to your selected newsletter. The topics to look for are listed below:

- Purpose
- Audience
- Paper
- Distribution
- Font and color scheme
- Consistency
- Alignment
- Repeated elements
- Continued notices and ease of navigation
- Sidebars, pull quotes, patterns, etc.

Print the publication and attach a copy of the newsletter. Turn in both to your instructor.

Lab 3: Expand Your World: Cloud and Web Technologies

Converting Files

Problem: You would like to explore converting your newsletter to formats other than the .pub Publisher format. While Publisher has many formats in the Save As type list, a cloud tool may have even more choices.

Instructions:

1. Open a browser and go to zamzar.com (Figure 3–85).
2. In Step 1 of the Convert Files section, tap or click the Browse button, or the Choose Files button depending on your browser, and navigate to one of your completed newsletters.
3. In Step 2, tap or click the 'Convert files(s) to:' box and choose a conversion format such as html or an e-book format.
4. In Step 3, enter your email address.
5. In Step 4, tap or click the Convert button to send the converted file to your email. If you receive a message indicating the conversion is about to happen, tap or click the OK button.
6. When you receive the email from Zamzar, tap or click the link provided, and then tap or click the Download Now button. Your browser should direct you to save the download.
7. If your download is a compressed file, press and hold or right-click the zipped file to display a shortcut menu. Tap or click Extract or Extract All to extract the file.
8. Open the converted file.
9. Submit the assignment in the format specified by your instructor.
10. What format might you use to post your newsletter on the web? Would an HTML file be better than a download link? Why or why not? When might you convert to a PDF format?

© Zamzar 2006 – 2013

Figure 3–85

Consider This: Your Turn

Apply your creative thinking and problem solving skills to design and implement a solution.

1: Using Publisher vs. Word

Personal/Academic

Part 1: Using Publisher, create a blank print publication with a large text box that fills the page. Using the Edit Story in Microsoft Word feature, type an assignment, such as an essay or short report, for one of your classes.

Part 2: As you have worked in Publisher, make a list of things you found easier to do in Publisher and three things you found easier to do in Word.

2: Creating a Money Newsletter

Professional

Part 1: Use the Cascade newsletter template to create a newsletter template about the wise use of money and spending. Use the Green Color Scheme and the Trek font scheme. Use the title, You and Your Money. On page 1, change the lead story headline to The Road to Financial Freedom (you may use the default text in the story itself). Change the secondary story headline to You Take Over the Wheel (you may use the default text in the story itself). Link the story to one of the stories on page 2, and change the headline there as well. Replace the graphics with suitable pictures and caption. Submit your assignment in the format specified by your instructor.

Part 2: What other kinds of stories might you include in a money newsletter such as this one? Where might those stories come from? Who might be the author/organization for this newsletter? Who might be the audience?

3: Researching Templates

Research and Collaboration

Part 1: Many clubs and organizations publish their newsletters on the web. Browse the web and look for examples of newsletters. Choose a newsletter that you think displays good desktop publishing practices. Print the newsletter or copy its web address to distribute to each team member. Make a list of each object in the newsletter, such as the masthead, graphics, captions, stories, headlines, marginal elements, continued notices, etc. Discuss the newsletters and note which parts were most effective. List three things that stand out as good examples of newsletter content. List three things that need to be improved.

Part 2: How did you evaluate effectiveness? Did the marginal elements add value to the newsletter? How so? What elements caused you to read further into the newsletter and its stories? Why?

Learn Online

Reinforce what you learned in this chapter with games, exercises, training, and many other online activities and resources.

Student Companion Site Reinforce chapter terms and concepts using review questions, flash cards, practice tests, and interactive learning games, such as a crossword puzzle. These and other online activities and resources are available at no additional cost on www.cengagebrain.com. Visit www.cengage.com/ct/studentdownload for detailed instructions about accessing the resources available at the Student Companion Site.

Index

Quick Reference Summary

Microsoft Publisher 2013 Introductory Quick Reference

Task	Page Number	Ribbon	Other On-Screen Areas	Shortcut Menu	Keyboard Shortcut
Arrange Thumbnails	PUB 85	Arrange Thumbnails button (PICTURE TOOLS FORMAT tab | Arrange group)		Arrange Thumbnails	
Autofit Text	PUB 28	Text Fit button (TEXT BOX TOOLS FORMAT tab | Text group), Best Fit or Format Text Box Dialog Box Launcher (TEXT BOX TOOLS FORMAT tab | Text group), Text Box tab (Text Box dialog box), Best fit button		Best Fit	
Background	PUB 50	Background button (PAGE DESIGN tab | Page Background group)		'Apply to Background', Fill	
Bold	PUB 27	Bold button (HOME tab | Font group) or Font Dialog Box Launcher (HOME tab | Font group), Font style arrow (Font dialog box), Bold	Bold button on mini toolbar	Change Text, Font, Font style arrow (Font dialog box), Bold	CTRL+B
Boundaries	PUB 12	Boundaries check box (VIEW tab | Show group)			CTRL+SHIFT+O
Break Link	PUB 147	Break button (TEXT BOX TOOLS FORMAT tab | Linking group)			
Captions Gallery	PUB 107	Caption button (PICTURE TOOLS FORMAT tab | Picture Styles group)			
Check Spelling as You Type	PUB 21			Choose correct word	
Check Spelling of Entire Publication	PUB 109	Spelling button (REVIEW tab | Spelling group)			F7
Continue a Story across Pages	PUB 144		Yes or No button (Microsoft Publisher dialog box) until desired location is reached		

Microsoft Publisher 2013 Introductory Quick Reference *(continued)*					
Task	**Page Number**	**Ribbon**	**Other On-Screen Areas**	**Shortcut Menu**	**Keyboard Shortcut**
Continue a Story across Pages, Manually	PUB 147	Create Link button (TEXT BOX TOOLS FORMAT tab | Linking group), navigate to desired text box, tap or click text box	Text in Overflow button on selected text box	'Create Text Box Link'	
Continued Notice, Insert	PUB 148	Format Text Box Dialog Box Launcher (TEXT BOX TOOLS FORMAT tab | Text group), Text Box tab (Format Text Box dialog box), 'Include "Continued on page . . ."' check box		Format Text Box, Text Box tab (Format Text Box dialog box), 'Include "Continued on page . . ."' check box	
Copy Text	PUB 79	Copy button (HOME tab | Clipboard group)		Copy	CTRL+C
Coupon, Insert	PUB 169	Advertisements button (INSERT tab | Building Blocks group) or Show Building Blocks Library Dialog Box Launcher (INSERT tab | Building Blocks group), Advertisements folder (Building Block Library dialog box)			
Customize Ribbon	PUB 153	Customize Ribbon button (FILE tab | Options), Customize Ribbon		Customize the Ribbon	
Customize Ribbon, Remove	PUB 183	Customize Ribbon button (FILE tab | Options), Customize Ribbon, Reset button (Publisher Options dialog box)		Customize the Ribbon, Reset button (Publisher Options dialog box)	
Cut Text	PUB 78	Cut button (HOME tab | Clipboard group)		Cut	CTRL+X
Design Checker, Run	PUB 110	Run Design Checker button (FILE tab | Info tab)			
Drag-and-Drop Text	PUB 177		Drag selected text to new location, then lift finger or release mouse button		
Drop Cap	PUB 103	Drop Cap button (TEXT BOX TOOLS FORMAT tab | Typography group)			
Exit	PUB 47		Close button on title bar		ALT+F4
Font, Change	PUB 98	Font arrow (HOME tab | Font group)	Font arrow on mini toolbar	Change Text, Font, Font text box	CTRL+SHIFT+F
Font Size, Decrease	PUB 31	Font Size arrow (HOME tab | Font group) or Decrease Font Size button (HOME tab | Font group)	Font Size arrow on mini toolbar or Decrease Font Size button on mini toolbar	Change Text, Font, Font size arrow (Font dialog box)	CTRL+SHIFT+<
Font Size, Increase	PUB 31	Font Size arrow (HOME tab | Font group) or Increase Font Size button (HOME tab | Font group)	Font Size arrow on mini toolbar or Increase Font Size button on mini toolbar	Change Text, Font, Font size arrow (Font dialog box)	CTRL+SHIFT+>

Microsoft Publisher 2013 Introductory Quick Reference *(continued)*

Task	Page Number	Ribbon	Other On-Screen Areas	Shortcut Menu	Keyboard Shortcut
Format Painter	PUB 88	Format Painter button (HOME tab | Clipboard group)	Format Painter button on mini toolbar		CTRL+SHIFT+C, then CTRL+SHIFT+V
Formatting Marks, Display	PUB 77	Special Characters button (HOME tab | Paragraph group)			CTRL+SHIFT+Y
Hyphenation, Check	PUB 180	Hyphenation button (TEXT BOX TOOLS FORMAT tab | Text group), Manual button (Hyphenation dialog box)			CTRL+SHIFT+H
Hyperlink, Insert	PUB 48	Add a Hyperlink button (INSERT tab | Links group)		Hyperlink	CTRL+K
Import a File	PUB 142	Insert File button (INSERT tab | Text group)		Change Text, Text File	
Italicize	PUB 28	Italic button (HOME tab | Font group) or Font Dialog Box Launcher (HOME tab | Font group), Font style arrow (Font Dialog box), Italic	Italic button on mini toolbar	Change Text, Font, Font style arrow (Font dialog box), Italic	CTRL+I
Ligatures, Enable	PUB 100	Ligatures button (TEXT BOX TOOLS FORMAT tab | Typography group) or Symbol button (INSERT tab | Text group)			
Link Text Boxes	PUB 147	Create Link button (TEXT BOX TOOLS FORMAT tab | Linking group)	Text in Overflow button on selected text box	'Create Text Box Link'	
Maximize	PUB 4		Maximize button on Publisher title bar or double-tap or double-click title bar	Maximize button on Publisher title bar	
Object, Align	PUB 42	Align button (DRAWING TOOLS FORMAT tab | Arrange group) or Align button (PICTURE TOOLS FORMAT tab | Arrange group) or specific alignment button (TEXT BOX TOOLS tab | Alignment group)	Drag object until visual layout guides appear		
Object, Delete	PUB 24	Cut button (HOME tab | Clipboard group)		Delete Object	DELETE or BACKSPACE or CTRL+X
Object, Move	PUB 41		Drag boundary or Object Position button on status bar, x and y text boxes on Measurement toolbar		

Microsoft Publisher 2013 Introductory Quick Reference *(continued)*

Task	Page Number	Ribbon	Other On-Screen Areas	Shortcut Menu	Keyboard Shortcut
Object, Resize	PUB 42		Drag corner sizing handle or Object Size button on status bar, Width and Height text boxes on Measurement toolbar	Format Object, Size tab (Format Object dialog box), Size and rotate area or Format Picture, Size tab (Format Picture dialog box), Size and rotate area or Format Text Box, Size tab (Format Text Box dialog box), Size and rotate area	
Object, Bring to Front	PUB 168	Bring Forward arrow (DRAWING TOOLS FORMAT tab | Arrange group), 'Bring to Front' or Bring Forward arrow (PICTURE TOOLS FORMAT tab | Arrange group), Bring Forward	Bring Forward button on mini toolbar		
Object, Send to Back	PUB 168	Send Backward arrow (DRAWING TOOLS FORMAT tab | Arrange group), 'Send to Back' or Send Backward arrow (PICTURE TOOLS FORMAT tab | Arrange group), Send Backward	Send Backward button on mini toolbar		
Online Pictures, Insert	PUB 83	Online Pictures button (INSERT tab | Illustrations group)			
Pack and Go Wizard	PUB 116	'Save for a Commercial Printer' link (FILE tab | Export tab), Pack and Go Wizard button			
Page Navigation Pane, Collapse	PUB 14		'Collapse Page Navigation Pane' button in Page Navigation pane		
Page Navigation Pane, Expand	PUB 14		'Expand Page Navigation Pane' button in Page Navigation pane		
Page Navigation Pane, Hide	PUB 13	Page Navigation check box (VIEW tab | Show group)	'Current page in publication' button on status bar		
Page Navigation Pane, Open	PUB 11	Page Navigation check box (VIEW tab | Show group)	'Current page in publication' button on status bar		
Page Options, Set	PUB 135	Options button (PAGE DESIGN tab | Template group)			
Pages, Add	PUB 138	Insert Blank Page button (INSERT tab | Pages group)	Page thumbnail (Page Navigation pane), Insert Page		SHIFT+CTRL+N
Pages, Change	PUB 91		Page thumbnail (Page Navigation pane)		CTRL+PAGE DOWN or CTRL+PAGE DOWN or F12

Microsoft Publisher 2013 Introductory Quick Reference *(continued)*

Task	Page Number	Ribbon	Other On-Screen Areas	Shortcut Menu	Keyboard Shortcut
Pages, Delete	PUB 138		Page thumbnail (Page Navigation pane), Delete		
Paste Text	PUB 79	Paste button (HOME tab | Clipboard group)		Paste	CTRL+V
Picture Style, Apply	PUB 36	More button (PICTURE TOOLS FORMAT tab | Picture Styles group)			
Picture, Change Border Style	PUB 37	Picture Border button (PICTURE TOOLS FORMAT tab | Picture Styles group) or Format Shape Dialog Box Launcher (PICTURE TOOLS FORMAT tab | Picture Styles group), Colors and Lines tab (Format Picture dialog box)		Format Picture, Colors and Lines tab (Format Picture dialog box)	
Picture, Insert from a File	PUB 39	Pictures button (INSERT tab | Illustrations group)	Placeholder icon, Browse (Insert Pictures dialog box)		
Picture, Use as Background	PUB 87	Background button (PAGE DESIGN tab | Page Background group), More Backgrounds		Apply to Background, Fill	
Placeholder Text, Replace	PUB 17		Select text, type new text		
Preview Multiple Pages	PUB 112	'View Multiple Sheets' button (FILE tab | Print tab)			
Print	PUB 44	Print button (FILE tab | Print tab)			CTRL+P
Print, On Both Sides	PUB 114	'Print One Sided' button (FILE tab | Print tab) or Printer Properties link (FILE tab | Print tab), Page Setup tab			CTRL+P
Print, On Special Paper	PUB 113	Letter button (FILE tab | Print tab) or Printer Properties link (FILE tab | Print tab), Page Setup tab			CTRL+P
Publication Options, Choose	PUB 8	Template thumbnail (FILE tab | New tab), Color scheme or Font scheme button			
Publication Properties, Change	PUB 182	Publication Properties button (FILE tab | Info tab)			
Pull Quote, Insert	PUB 164	Page Parts button (INSERT tab | Building Blocks group) or Show Building Blocks Library Dialog Box Launcher (INSERT tab | Building Blocks group), Page Parts folder (Building Block Library dialog box)			

Microsoft Publisher 2013 Introductory Quick Reference *(continued)*					
Task	**Page Number**	**Ribbon**	**Other On-Screen Areas**	**Shortcut Menu**	**Keyboard Shortcut**
Run Publisher	PUB 4		Publisher 2013 tile on Windows 8 Start screen or Publisher 2013 in Charms bar search results		
Save as Web Publication	PUB 51	Publish HTML link (FILE tab | Export tab), Publish HTML button, 'Save as type' button (Publish to the Web dialog box) or Save As button (FILE tab), 'Save as type' button (Save As dialog box)			
Save New Publication	PUB 25	Save tab (FILE tab)	Save button (Quick Access Toolbar)		CTRL+S or F12 or CTRL+F12
Save Publication, New File Name	PUB 25	Save As tab (FILE tab)			F12 or CTRL+F12
Save Publication, Same File Name	PUB 33	Save tab (FILE tab)	Save button (Quick Access Toolbar)		CTRL+S
Select All Text	PUB 16		Drag through text		CTRL+A
Story, Follow Across Pages	PUB 145	Previous or Next button (TEXT BOX TOOLS FORMAT tab | Linking group)	Previous or Next button on selected text box		CTRL+TAB
Stylistic Set	PUB 100	Stylistic Sets button (TEXT BOX TOOLS FORMAT tab | Typography group)			
Swap Picture	PUB 82	Swap button (PICTURE TOOLS FORMAT tab | Swap group)	Swap icon, drag swap icon to new location	Swap button on mini toolbar	
Tear-Offs, Edit	PUB 23		Select tear-off text, type new text		
Template, Select	PUB 6	Template thumbnail (FILE tab | New tab)	Template thumbnail on Publisher start screen		
Template, Create	PUB 182	Save As tab (FILE tab), 'Save As type' button (Save As dialog box)			
Text Box, Draw	PUB 16	'Draw Text Box' button (INSERT tab | Text group) or Draw Text Box button (HOME tab | Objects group)			
Text Direction, Change	PUB 32	Text Direction button (TEXT BOX TOOLS FORMAT tab | Text group)			
Underline	PUB 31	Underline button (HOME tab | Font group) or Font Dialog Box Launcher (HOME tab | Font group), Font style arrow (Font Dialog box), Underline	Underline button on mini toolbar	Change Text, Font, Font style arrow (Font dialog box), Underline	CTRL+U
Undo	PUB 16		Undo button on Quick Access Toolbar	Undo	CTRL+Z

Microsoft Publisher 2013 Introductory Quick Reference *(continued)*

Task	Page Number	Ribbon	Other On-Screen Areas	Shortcut Menu	Keyboard Shortcut
Zoom	PUB 15	Zoom text box (VIEW tab | Zoom group) or Zoom arrow (VIEW tab | Zoom group)	Zoom slider or Zoom In or Zoom Out button on status bar or Touch Mode: Stretch or pinch as necessary	Zoom	F9
Zoom Objects	PUB 15	Selected Objects button (VIEW tab | Zoom group)	Touch Mode: Stretch or pinch as necessary	Zoom, Selected Objects	F9
Zoom Page Width	PUB 15	Page Width button (VIEW tab | Zoom group)	Touch Mode: Stretch or pinch as necessary	Zoom, Page Width	
Zoom Whole Page	PUB 15	Whole Page button (VIEW tab | Zoom group)	Show Whole Page button on status bar or Touch Mode: Stretch or pinch as necessary	Zoom, Whole Page	CTRL+SHIFT+L

Important Notes for Windows 7 Users

The screen shots in this book show Microsoft Office 2013 running in Windows 8. If you are using Microsoft Windows 7, however, you still can use this book because Office 2013 runs virtually the same way on both platforms. You will encounter only minor differences if you are using Windows 7. Read this section to understand the differences.

Dialog Boxes

If you are a Windows 7 user, the dialog boxes shown in this book will look slightly different than what you see on your screen. Dialog boxes for Windows 8 have a title bar with a solid color, and the dialog box name is centered on the title bar. Beyond these superficial differences in appearance, however, the options in the dialog boxes across both platforms are the same. For instance, Figures 1 and 2 show the Font dialog box in Windows 7 and the Font dialog box in Windows 8.

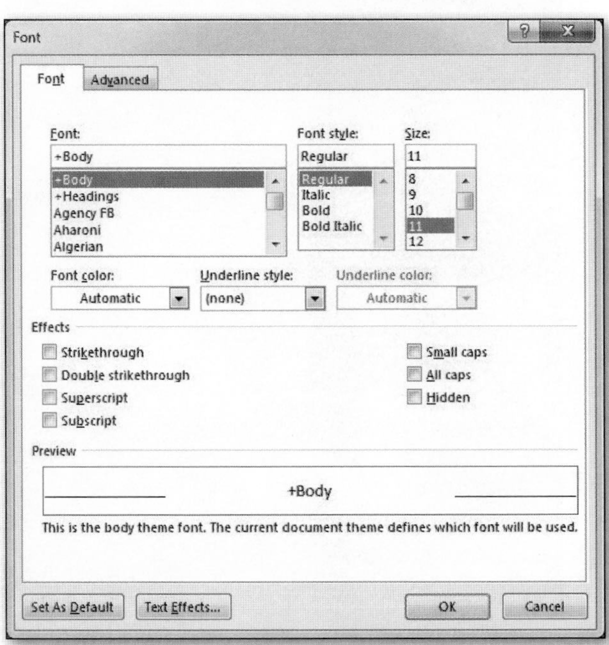

Figure 1 Font Dialog Box in Windows 7

Figure 2 Font Dialog Box in Windows 8

Alternate Steps for Running an App in Windows 7

Nearly all of the steps in this book work exactly the same way for Windows 7 users; however, running an app (or program/application) requires different steps for Windows 7. The following steps show how to run an app in Windows 7.

Running an App (or Program/Application) Using Windows 7

1. Click the Start button on the taskbar to display the Start menu.
2. Click All Programs and then click the Microsoft Office 2013 folder (Figure 3).
3. If necessary, click the name of the folder containing the app you want to run.
4. Click the name of the app you want to run (such as Excel 2013).

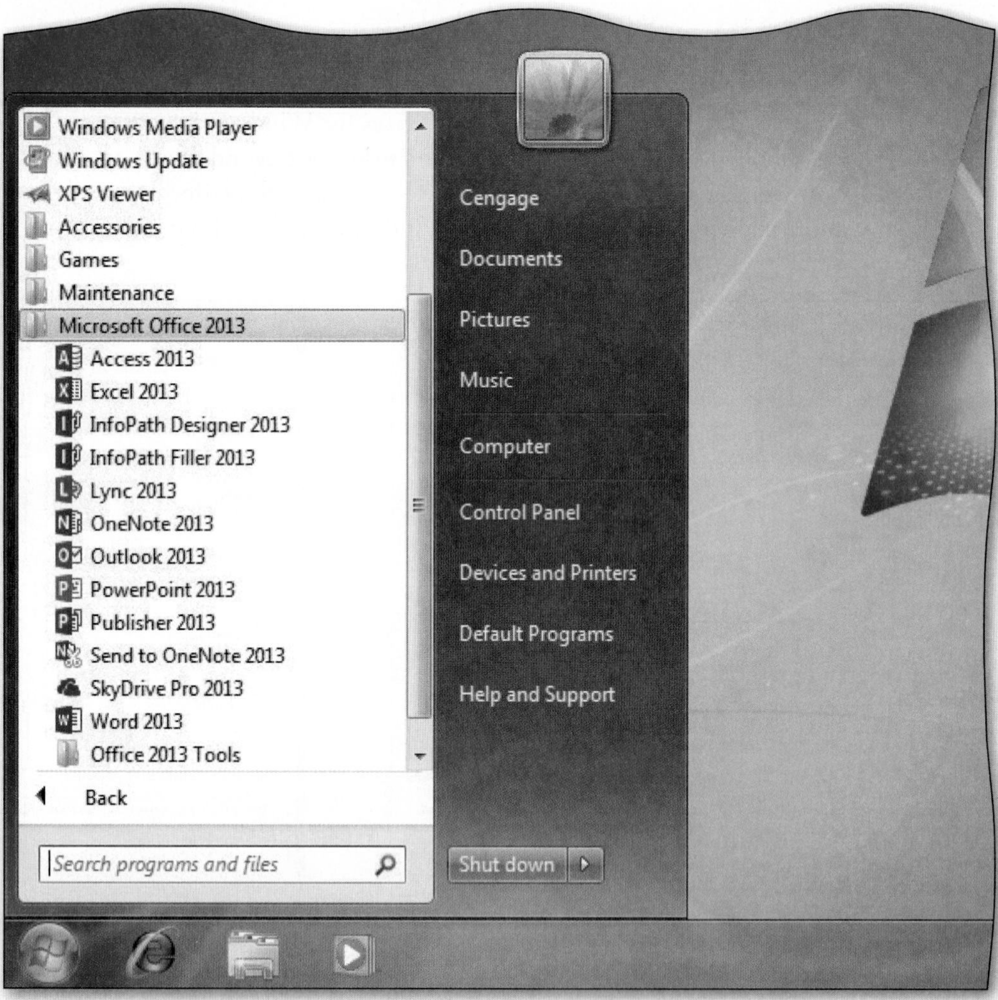

Figure 3 Running an App Using the Windows 7 Start Menu